HISTORIOGRAPHY
OF
IMPERIAL
RUSSIA

HISTORIOGRAPHY OF IMPERIAL RUSSIA

The Profession and Writing of History in a Multinational State

EDITED BY
THOMAS SANDERS

M.E.Sharpe
Armonk, New York
London, England

Publication histories for chapters 2, 4, 6, 7, 9, 11, 12, 13, 14, and 16
are supplied in source notes.

Library of Congress Cataloging-in-Publication Data

Historiography of Imperial Russia : the profession and writing of history in a multinational state / edited by Thomas Sanders.
p.   cm.
Includes bibliographical references (p.   ) and index.
ISBN 1-56324-684-8 (alk. paper)
1. Russia—Historiography. 2. Historians—Russia. I. Sanders, Thomas, 1951– .
DK38.H57   1999
947′007′2047—dc21   98-34921
CIP

Printed in the United States of America

The paper used in this publication meets the minimum requirements of
American National Standard for Information Sciences—
Permanence of Paper for Printed Library Materials,
ANSI Z 39.48-1984.

BM (c)   10   9   8   7   6   5   4   3   2   1

Contents

About the Editor and Contributors

Thomas Sanders is associate professor of history at the United States Naval Academy. Together with Ernest Tucker he is working on a book entitled *War in the Caucasus: Russian and Chechen Views.*

Boris Anan´ich is a member of the Russian Academy of Sciences and professor at St. Petersburg University. He is currently writing a biography of Sergei Witte.

Robert F. Byrnes, professor emeritus of history at Indiana University, died on June 19, 1997. He was the founder and longtime director of the Russian and East European Center at IU. Author and editor of many books and articles, he published two monographs in Russian history, most recently *V.O. Kliuchevsky: Historian of Russia* (Indiana University Press, 1995).

Terence Emmons is professor of history at Stanford University. His latest book is *Alleged Sex and Threatened Violence: Doctor Russel, Bishop Vladimir, and the Russians in San Francisco* (Stanford, 1997).

Gary M. Hamburg is professor of Russian history at the University of Notre Dame. He is the author of many books on the political and intellectual history of late imperial Russia. He has also edited and translated several works, including most recently *Liberty, Equality, and the Market: Essays by Boris Chicherin* (Yale, 1998).

Manfred Hildermeier is professor of East European history at the University of Göttingen, and his most recent work is *Geschichte der Sowjet Union, 1917–1991* (Munich, 1998).

Allison Y. Katsev is a lecturer in Stanford University's Introduction to the Humanities Program. She is currently revising her Ph.D. dissertation, *Social Identity and Russian Cultural Politics: Defining the Historian in the Pre-Reform Era*, for publication.

Adeeb Khalid teaches history at Carleton College. He is the author of *The Politics of Muslim Cultural Reform: Jadidism in Central Asia* (University of California Press, 1998) and is currently working on a book on Central Asia in the early Soviet period.

Bohdan Klid is co-director of the Canada-Ukraine Legislative Cooperation Project and assistant director of the Canadian Institute of Ukrainian Studies, University of Alberta. He has published numerous scholarly articles and is currently working on a biography of Volodymyr Antonovych.

Zenon E. Kohut is director of the Canadian Institute of Ukrainian Studies, University of Alberta. His many publications on Ukraine include *Russian Centralism and Ukrainian Autonomy: Imperial Absorption of the Hetmanate* (Cambridge, MA: Harvard University Press, 1988).

Benjamin Nathans is assistant professor of history at the University of Pennsylvania. His forthcoming book, *Beyond the Pale: The Jewish Encounter in Late Imperial Russia*, explores the dynamics of Jewish integration into Russian society.

Viktor Paneiakh is doctor of historical science and senior fellow at the St. Petersburg branch of the Institute of History of the Russian Academy of Sciences, and author of *Kholopstvo* (Leningrad, 1975).

Thomas Prymak is the author of numerous studies on Ukrainian historiography, including *Mykola Kostomarov: A Biography* (Toronto: University of Toronto Press, 1996).

Marc Raeff is emeritus Bakhmeteff Professor of Russian Studies at Columbia University and the author and editor of many books on Russian history, including most recently *The Romanovs: Their Empire, Their Books*, 1997.

Ana Siljak is managing editor of the *Journal of Cold War Studies*, a publication of the Harvard Project on Cold War Studies. She completed her dissertation, *Rival Visions of the Russian Nation: Teaching Russian History, 1890–1917*, at Harvard in 1997.

Melissa K. Stockdale is associate professor of history at the University of Oklahoma and author of *Paul Miliukov and the Quest for Liberal Russia* (Cornell University Press, 1996).

Frank E. Sysyn is director of the Peter Jacyk Centre for Ukrainian Historical Research at the Canadian Institute of Ukrainian Studies, University of Alberta. His publications include *Between Poland and Ukraine: The Dilemma of Adam Kysil, 1600–53* (1985).

Aleksei Nikolaevich Tsamutali is doctor of historical science and senior fellow at the St. Petersburg branch of the Institute of History and author of *Bor'ba napravlenii russkoi istoriografii* (Leningrad, 1986).

Margarita Georgievna Vandalkovskaia is doctor of historical science at the Moscow branch of the Institute of History, Russian Academy of Sciences, and author of *P.N. Miliukov, A.A. Kizevetter* (Moscow, 1992).

Cynthia Hyla Whittaker is professor of history at Baruch College and the Graduate Center of the City University of New York. Her book *The Origins of Modern Russian Education: An Intellectual Biography of Count Sergei Uvarov* will appear in Russian translation this summer.

Preface

This volume is designed for a diverse readership—advanced undergraduate and graduate students in Russian, Soviet, and post-Soviet studies, as well as mature scholars from those fields. In addition, it is hoped that its contents will be useful to scholars from other fields of history and other disciplines who have an interest in either the content or the culture of historical writing in the era of the Russian empire, across the divide of revolution into the early Soviet period, and—by extension—beyond. The goal was to provide a conceptually coherent collection that, while not aspiring to encyclopedic inclusivity, covered the main Russian—and significant non-Russian—historiographical traditions and established a point of first reference for those interested in the subject. The intent throughout has been to transmit information imbedded in an interpretive framework, both to render it meaningful and to avoid the soporific citation of authors and titles. If these articles heighten historical understanding, assist in the formulation of new interpretations, and promote interpretive cross-semination, the anthology will have succeeded.

The inspiration for the volume lies in my own graduate training in Russian history. Even then, the need for such a compendium was evident, since the main English sources, such as Mazour's *Modern Russian Historiography,* were so inadequate. While Rubinstein's *Russkaia istoriografiia* is a far more interesting and informative work than one would expect of a Stalin-era publication, heavy reliance on it in graduate training was a clear indication of the historiographical void that existed. Some works have appeared since then, usually as the introductory matter to translations of classic studies, but the need for cohesive volumes is still present. In fact, given the brave new historiographical world we are now entering, the need is greater than ever.

Doubtless, my own limitations have to be factored in, but discussions that dealt even tangentially with imperial Russian historiography were somewhat mystifying in those graduate student days of yore. The oblique references to all of those Solov'evs and Kizevetters, not to mention the Kostomarovs and Hrushevskys, were reminiscent of my parents' comments about rarely seen cross-country relatives—the names attached to some foggy memory that I felt vaguely and guiltily I ought to be able to remember and place better. Sadly, these historiographical "cousins" went unrecognized in any meaningful sense. They certainly did not inform and enhance my understanding of the historical experiences of the Russian empire in any active way that I was aware of.

It has seemed to me for some time that I was not unique in this and that the discipline as a whole has suffered as a result. The relative paucity of accessible and intellectually engaging historiographical studies reinforced the "historiographical backwardness" (to paraphrase Gerschenkron) caused in the first instance by extensive linguistic training. In short, the training needed to master one or more Eastern European languages reduces the amount of time students have to familiarize themselves with the historiographical traditions of their fields, and this cannot but contribute to a certain interpretive impoverishment. This is especially true relative to our colleagues in American history, for whom neither language requirements nor archival access are issues anywhere near the order of magnitude that they constitute in our field. The political and historiographical transformations of recent years only exacerbate the problem by adding long-neglected historical traditions to the mix. On the one hand, there are many more historical cultures to assimilate; on the other, the expanse and unboundedness of the historiographical horizon in the post-Soviet world makes all the more urgent the need for solid grounding in the main historical conceptions and interpretations of the past.

Hence, the idea for this volume is not new. What is new is the content to fill such a volume. A couple of years ago a critical threshold was passed. Some first-rate material was already in print but not readily accessible—such as Emmons's "Kliuchevskii's Pupils" and Raeff's writing on the historians in emigration. To that could be added the work of younger scholars, such as Stockdale and Katsev, with research currently underway or recently completed. This pool of scholarship made an anthology possible, but it achieved the dubious distinction of being both excessively and inadequately Russocentric. That is, it lacked both non-Russian "voices" and the perspective of native Russian historians. Those works had to be commissioned, as did many other individual pieces, such as Ana Siljak's article on Solov'ev. The final component to fall in place was the idea for senior scholars to think broadly about our collective enterprise and to—if not lay out an agenda for research—at least set out some markers in relation to which the coming generation of historians could orient itself as it set about producing new interpretations and agendas.

This volume is, then, as the current jargon has it, a "constructed" entity. As a result, it represents far more than a convenient compilation of already published pieces, and it required of its contributors much more than a quick signature of a "permission to republish" form. The appearance of new national republics and of new archival opportunities in the wake of the collapse of the Soviet empire makes this a particularly propitious time for a collective reconsideration of how our enterprise has functioned in past practice. The overwhelming majority of articles in this volume were commissioned specifically for this purpose. Writing for a volume on historical writing in the past, it is fair to say that the contributors to this anthology had their eyes very much on the future—like the young man in Repin's "Volga Boat-Haulers." This work is intended to serve not as a destination but as a point of embarkation.

"The appetite grows in the eating," the French say, and the same is true of this volume. As the volume expanded and the project grew more ambitious, the number of people who contributed to it directly or indirectly expanded. The first debt is to the contributors themselves, especially to those who undertook to write original pieces, often under significant time constraints. Anything substantive that this anthology adds to scholarship is primarily owing to them. Many other people gave of their time and counsel to assist in conceptualizing the enterprise. Boris Anan'ich, Aleksei Tsamutali, and Margarita Vandalkovskaia of the Institute of History of the Russian Academy of Sciences provided real impetus by embracing so eagerly my request for articles "in the Russian tradition." Mark von Hagen supported the idea from the outset and put me in touch with the Ukrainian studies community in Canada. The possibility of including a self-contained section on Ukrainian historiography as an exemplary non-Russian historical tradition emerged as a result of the responsiveness of Frank Sysyn, Zenon Kohut, and the Canadian Institute of Ukrainian Studies at the University of Alberta. Joerg Baberowksi has been his usual forthcoming self, providing advice about the German Slavic studies community. Professor Manfred Hildermeier has gone beyond the call of duty, finding time in an overwhelming schedule both to write and to help translate his article for the volume. Marc Raeff has been extremely gracious, both in adapting his thought piece to the overall structure of the volume and in reading and commenting on many of the articles. He has helped shape my thoughts and has saved me from some embarrassing gaffes. Special mention must be made of Professor Robert Byrnes, who was working on a special article for this anthology at the time of his death. We gratefully acknowledge Professor Byrnes's contribution reprinted from an earlier article in the *Review of Politics*. This dry listing does not do justice to the generosity of all contributors, many of whom, as Cynthia Whittaker did in going out of her way to get permission from the *Russian Review* to republish her article, took on extra responsibilities unbidden. Their spirit speaks volumes about our profession.

Many others deserve thanks as well. I am grateful to M.E. Sharpe for taking on the project. There is no telling where my stumbling efforts would have led without Patricia Kolb's constant and unstinting editorial direction. Her unflagging commitment to "the best volume possible" both inspired and sustained me through this long process. Elizabeth Granda has patiently answered all my queries about the intricacies of text preparation. "Brad" Bradley and *Russian Studies in History* are probably not aware of how much their openhanded assistance facilitated this publication.

Closer to home, I am indebted to the U.S. Naval Academy for research support. The staff of Nimitz Library has my deepest gratitude, especially Barbara Manvel and the Reference Department, who have answered more obscure inquiries than anyone should have to address; as does Ms. Florence Todd, for the yeoman service in interlibrary loan that enables us to pursue research without having a reference library at our disposal. Generous funding support from Dr. Reza Malek-Madani, director of research, and the Naval Academy Research Council was crucial to the completion of this project. Many of the preliminary discussions and follow-up visits were funded by Chairman Robert Artigiani and the History Department.

Closest of all, my wife Jolene (and Brookie and Joseph) has supported this effort with her patience, understanding, and unselfish sacrifices of time and energy. Without her help, this volume would not be in print.

Finally, I need to thank the person most responsible. It all begins with Terry Emmons. He was present, as it were, at the creation. My vision of Russian history and my understanding of Russian historiography come from him. More immediately, it was his imprimatur that convinced me that this project was worth pursuing. He has always been available for phone calls at 6:00 A.M. West Coast time, ready with his advice and suggestions, his insights and corrections. The volume owes him more than I can express. And so do I.

Annapolis, Maryland
April 1998

HISTORIOGRAPHY
OF
IMPERIAL
RUSSIA

1

Introduction:
"A Most Narrow Present"

Thomas Sanders

In its broadest outlines, the evolution of historical writing in pre-Stalinist Russia can be understood as the function of two parallel processes: maturation and alienation. Like so much else in the imperial Russian historical experience, the history of historical writing reveals a record of ever-expanding sophistication and approximation of European standards. At the same time, the academic historians found themselves continually more isolated from the other social and ethnic groups in the empire and alienated from the very government that supported them. Nonacademic historians dealt with themes and adopted political and social interpretations that more closely reflected the point of view of the empire's diverse population. Limitations imposed by tsarist censorship and academic politics kept these perspectives from finding institutional homes in which they could be nurtured and from which they could be propagated. These factors placed an enduring imprint on the historical profession and historical writing in imperial Russia, and subsequently influenced Soviet historical practice as well.[1]

Something identifiable as modern nonchronicle historical writing emerged in Russia in the eighteenth century. At first, this work was stilted, weighed down by excessively long citations from documents, dominated by foreigners, and triumphalist in relation to the state. Gradually, though, especially in the nineteenth century, state-generated demands for well-trained servitors led to the expansion of the university network in the empire and funding for students from Russia to study in European universities. In long developmental waves, historians in Russia acquired European approaches to historical study (e.g., French archival and source analysis, German-style seminars and graduate training, and the new, sociologically oriented historical analysis *à la* Guizot). Ultimately, it became necessary to write dissertations based on previously unutilized archival sources, and the level of analysis and interpretation was also continually enhanced.[2] By the end of the empire, the best historians in Russian universities—among them Vinogradov, Miliukov, Kareev, Vasil'ev—were at least on a par with their peers in European universities.

These changes in standards took root in three broad shifts. The first of these can be seen in the difference between Nikolai M. Karamzin (1766–1826) and Sergei M. Solov'ev (1820–1879). Eighteenth-century historical writing reached its apex—both in impact and in elegance—in Karamzin's *Istoriia gosudarstva rossiiskogo,* the first volume of which appeared in 1816.[3] The publication of this work might be taken as a last point of cultural consensus in Russian history. Karamzin was a member of the nobility at a time when that group viewed itself as the key support base of the autocracy and had only just begun to be seriously challenged in that role by outsiders armed with education, effort, and merit. Thus, while Karamzin could and did criticize the tsar (see, for example his *Memoir on Ancient and Modern Russia*), his approach to the autocrat and his practical definition of autocracy as the identifying characteristic of Russian history differed from later historiography. Karamzin's willingness to enter into a dialogue with the autocracy resembled the ancient Jewish relationship with Yahweh as presented in the Book of Job, in which the Covenant is treated as a mutual agreement, making it possible to take Yahweh to task or join with Him as an interlocutor, if He is thought to have violated the pact. In that regard, Karamzin's historiography is intimate and internal.[4] It also differed from much later historiography in the breadth and elegance of its exposition, so that in many cases later enhancement of professional standards was accompanied by dramatic reductions in the readership reached.

In the decades, remarkable and otherwise, between the publication of Karamzin's *Istoriia* and the notorious lecture series of Timofei Granovsky, the government lost the moral high ground as the main representative and interpreter of the unique historical experience of Russia.[5] From Pushkin to the Decembrists and on to Granovsky, a separation that would become an opposition had occurred; a crucial segment of the elite had begun to see progress as possible only against, in spite of, or once rid of the government. Certainly not with it. Only temporarily—in the first blush of the era of Great Reforms connected with the Peasant Emancipation of 1861 and in the euphoria inspired by the Revolution of 1905—would that conviction abate and the possibility of constructive work with the regime seem possible.

Tellingly, in both those situations the government appeared sufficiently weakened to make the kind of concessions the liberal elite deemed necessary and proper.

While Granovsky embodied the oppositional, Westernizer direction within historical writing, it was the patriotic, profoundly Orthodox, and state-oriented Solov'ev who was to serve as the paradigm of the new career historian and to produce an alternative to Karamzin's Romantic, literary, gentleman-of-leisure model. Solov'ev established historical writing as an academic specialization with strict standards. After him, writing history demanded extensive amounts of *Sitzfleisch* and archive time from those who would do it well and offered professional employment to those who did not violate the state's restrictions. These objective, professional criteria made possible a much more powerful critical and oppositional historical analysis. There would be other loyalist historians after Solov'ev—Platonov and Bogoslovskii, for example. But Solov'ev's career was an essential part of the process of disconnecting historical analysis from too close an identification with the state. By establishing independent, objective criteria for historical work, he pried the profession loose from the state as ultimate arbiter. It became possible to make of historical writing and teaching a profession in two senses: as career and as statement of oppositional principles (*profession de foi*). Once that had occurred, the further evolution of historical writing in a direction different from and critical of the policies of the imperial government was possible. Certainly, Solov'ev himself never wrote such history. In fact, his long, relatively undigested quotations from ancient sources and his mechanical volume-per-year publication schedule does not feel very modern.[6]

Nonetheless, his work constitutes a decided professional step forward compared to Karamzin. Continuing the biblical analogy begun above, the divide separating Karamzin and Solov'ev is the same as that separating Job from St. Paul. Like Paul, Solov'ev institutionalized the new faith. Institutionalization routinized the practice of history, but it also deprived it of some of its earlier emotional power.

The next evolutionary phase involved a synthesis of Karamzin's vision and artistry with Solov'ev's objectivity and scienticity. This phase was less the province of the profession as a whole than it was the achievement of a few exceptionally gifted individuals; Kliuchevskii, Platonov, and Miliukov were the most eminent among them. In this stage, historians of both insight and artistry were able to meld careful, detailed source mastery with a broadness of conception and style sufficient to attract and compel a wider reading audience. While Kliuchevskii and his school were Moscow-based and Platonov represented the self-consciously distinct Petersburg historiographical tradition, there was a great deal of cross-fertilization and mutual influence. The general distinction usually cited is that Kliuchevskii and the Moscow school tended toward greater abstraction and a broader theoretical perspective—often captured by the descriptor "sociological"—while the St. Petersburg tradition emphasized more narrowly defined topics and greater attention and closer adherence to the primary sources. Platonov was profoundly affected by Kliuchevskii's *Boiarskaia duma drevnei Rusi* and by his extraordinarily influential general survey of Russian history, *Kurs russkoi istorii,* which circulated in student-produced lithograph long before its publication, and Miliukov brought further Muscovite influence, by participating very actively in the historians' social and intellectual world, during his months of dissertation research in the St. Petersburg archives. Meanwhile, Petersburg historians—most notably Platonov, both in his historical works and as editor of the important *Zhurnal Ministerstva narodnogo prosveshcheniia,* but also, Lappo-Danilevskii, and later, Presniakov—would exercise a wide influence on historical practice. It is safe to say that Kliuchevskii and Platonov were the doyens of their particular schools, and what they accomplished was to move Russian historical science beyond mere biography and history of tsars' reigns to penetrating historical analysis, broadened in perspective to include the society as a whole, while avoiding stultifying tendencies of impersonal institutional and sociological treatments. Kliuchevskii accomplished the additional feat of writing approved history that was at once ardently in favor of the Russian people and mildly critical of the Russian political order, which had an additional appeal for the intelligentsia. In sum, a broadly diffused professional culture existed that in its highest practitioners combined a broadly understood structural analysis with a gripping depiction of Russian national evolution.

Echoing behind all this development and professional progress, like axes chopping offstage in a performance of "The Cherry Orchard," is the approaching footfall of the Revolution—heavy and ominous. Given the ultimate fate of tsarist Russia, a critical observer might ask how historians, a privileged group in a society awash with poverty and hardship, whose profession most generously defined involves nothing more nor less than the responsibility of composing a satisfactory national narrative, could be considered something other than a glorious failure.

In one of his aphorisms, the eminent Russian historian Vasilii O. Kliuchevskii maintained that "a professor before his students is a scholar; before the public—an artist." Unfortunately, far too few academic historians in imperial Russia managed this balancing act. As a consequence, clear gains in sophistication and professional standards did not result in a comprehensive, inclusive national narrative satisfying to the majority of the

empire's inhabitants. The positivist-inspired, Russocentric, vaguely oppositional nature of most academic historical writing failed to engage the imagination of most groups constituting imperial Russian society. Traced
along the academic track, historical writing went from being a well-inte-
grated source of legitimacy for the imperial government in the eighteenth
century to reflecting the ideals of a relatively isolated group of elite, politically alienated intellectuals in the twentieth.

Yet the fault here lay not so much with the historians as it did with the
"jagged" nature of Russian social evolution, the extremes of class and ethnic distinctiveness that had to be integrated in a single vision, and with the
dominant intellectual mode, that is to say, positivism. We shall look at each
in turn.

In a provocative and sadly neglected book, *Russia: Absent and Present*,
Wladimir Weidle characterized Russia as "a people, but no nation."[7] He is
referring, of course, to the absence of internal linkages, of a shared sense
of connectedness. Neither the Romanov dynasty nor the Russian intelligentsia could craft a unifying self-consciousness strong enough to sustain
the society through the chaos and crises of early twentieth-century Europe.
Nearly a century earlier, Petr Chaadaev had indicted Russia for having "no
charming recollections and no gracious images in our memory, no lasting
lessons in our national tradition[,] . . . not . . . a single fond memory, or one
venerable monument which forcefully speaks of bygone times. . . . We live
in a most narrow present, without a past."[8] Russian writers may indeed
have had "an obsession with history" precisely because they remained
incapable of generating a binding national vision that transcended class,
ethnicity, and locality.[9]

Weidle had an explanation for this failure. In his interpretation, Russian
civilization was

> always tending to return to its starting-point: to sink back, so to speak, to the
> level of the horizontal. The great creative works of ancient Russia are like the
> temples of Indo-China, swallowed up by the virgin forest that surrounds
> them. Only here it is not a question of the tropical forest, aggressive and
> poisonous; it is only a plain, extending far beyond the limits of the horizon,
> and a people of peasants. These can tell stories and sing beautiful songs; they
> can build white, pathetic churches, at the edge of a wood, among their fields,
> or beside rivers; they are a gifted people, skillful in all the manual arts, but
> completely indifferent to whatever may be done in Kiev, to the achievements
> of Moscow or Novgorod, content to adapt to their tastes what they appreciate
> and quietly leave all the rest alone.[10]

For Weidle, this repetitive return to the starting point occurred because of the failure to establish linkages between the "horizontal" popular culture of the masses and the "vertical" artistic culture of the elite. In a key passage, he asserts that

> Russia has had a popular culture, both rich and homogenous, a culture we here propose to describe as "horizontal." Their great difficulty has been to construct on this basis what may be called a high culture. Such a "vertical" culture—always complex and always more or less unstable—calls for continuous efforts of generations on end; it can be built only on foundations very carefully laid and capable of resisting the test of centuries. For these foundations to be sound, the first essential is that they should not be too vast.[11]

But Russia did not have the luxury of a finite, circumscribed zone in which to build the vertical–horizontal linkage.[12] "[T]he whole country" was, rather, "simply a gigantic plain, furrowed by great rivers that in their wide slow course encounter few if any obstacles: a gently undulating plain that extends for thousands of miles, with it uniform fields and forests and villages and nothing to break the majestic monotony. There is a beauty in this monotony, but it is a beauty different from that of the West, . . . jealous of its individual *otherness*."[13] Russia is a realm of *prostor,* or "free space"; as Kliuchevskii asserted in his second lecture of *Kurs russkoi istorii,* "The history of Russia is the history of a nation that is colonizing itself" (*kolonizuetsia*).[14] In more typical Kliuchevskii style, he states that the Russian people "migrated in short little bird flights from region to region, abandoning the places they had been and settling into new ones."[15] To people such an expanse and to wrest a living from it involved "long and patient endeavour and . . . an astonishing continuity of effort."[16] One might even say that the effort of developing the "horizontal" steppes did not leave time for the luxury of developing "vertical" steps up the ladder of elite culture.[17] The tragedy of Russian civilization can be seen precisely in this cultural rupture between the vertical and the horizontal.

But a broad cross section of elite academic historians—and it is even more true for nonacademic, populist historians—were far from indifferent to either the intellectual development of the people or to the chasm that separated elite and mass. If they did not establish meaningful connections, it was not for want of trying. The liberal academic in Russia was much more involved in educational outreach programs than the average American academic is today. They participated in public lecture series both in the capitals and out in the provincial centers, contributed articles to collections whose profits funded scholarships and other charitable undertakings, lectured in the Higher Women's Courses, assisted in the selection of works for Russian versions of the Everyman series, and so on. Unfortunately, these efforts only connected them to small minorities, and even with that there was a certain amount of "preaching to the choir." That is, those who came to the lectures or read the "classics" were already participants in the value system and adherents of the worldview of the academic elite. They connected, in Weidle's terms, not to representatives of the horizontal culture, but to the lower rungs of their own vertical culture.

Another hurdle they had to overcome was their inability to achieve conformity and agreement in historical discourse. In terms of Thomas Kuhn's analysis of scientific paradigms, they never arrived at a stage of "normal science," in which one historiographical interpretation is more or less uncontested and the practitioners of science merely go about filling in the tiles of a mosaic whose general outline has been sketched in. Their position was under assault from a watchful, suspicious government and an aggressive, dismissive Social Democracy. They were besieged from below by non-Russian nationalist historians and historical traditions that, while not free to formulate their ideas and interpretations fully because of tsarist censorship and educational restrictions on non-Russian cultures, nonetheless rejected the replacement of a Russian nationalist *russkaia istoriia* with a generic *rossiiskaia istoriia* not specifically linked to Russian nationalism.[18] In Weidle's terms, they were not only incapable of connecting Russian vertical and horizontal cultures, but they were also unable to establish linkages with the other vertical cultures of the Russian empire.

Weidle asserts the following: "A horizontal culture is something to admire, but the place it can claim in the hierarchy of values can never be that of true works of art. Its normal function is to feed a vertical culture, by which it submits in return to be directed and transformed. All the best it produces rises to the level of true culture and so forms part of it, while the values of the latter in due course descend and are eventually disseminated among the people as a whole."[19] This never happened in Russia in the sense of academic historians drawing from, reconstituting, and reimbuing the peoples of Russia with a uniform sense of national self-definition. "So what happened in the end in Russia was that the people kept what they had been able to assimilate, used it for the benefit of their own popular culture, and left to others the task of building a higher culture, a culture based on a foreign model."[20] That they imitated and even assimilated that culture is beyond dispute, but it remained a foreign model, an exotic import that could be dispensed with. It sank no roots in the loam of Russian horizontal culture.

For a variety of reasons, though, Russian historical culture ought not be dismissed so lightly. To be sure, the social gap separating the majority population from the elite would have to have been narrowed considerably for the Russian empire to have been a stable entity in the long term, but that task was not the responsibility of historians, was clearly beyond their power in political terms, and was one to which they directed considerable energies in cultural terms. While it is true that most historians—again, especially the dominant Russian academic historians—fell into the positivist, statist, political-history mode, this trap also ensnared the historians in Western Europe. In the West, the reaction against the intellectual constraints of positivist history was part of the general modernist reaction against mechanistic, Newtonian objectivism and generated such nonpositivist alternatives as Bloch's and Febvre's *Annales* school and Max Weber's "ideal type."

In Russia, too, there were interesting nonpositivist developments that might have proved productive in the long run had Solov′ev's Pauline historical order not given way to the Bolshevik Grand Inquisitor. The first of these was Kliuchevskii's fertile legacy. Kliuchevskii had many diverse aspects among his research interests—his careful perusal of the stories of saints' lives as historical sources, a study of the poll tax, and an examination of the history of the ruble, to cite a few examples—and historians studying the wide range of topics covered by the master could have found inspiration therein. Indeed, Kliuchevskii might be considered an *annaliste avant la lettre,* except that he lacked the unifying and invigorating theoretical vision that so inspired Bloch and Febvre. Just such a theoretical school was emerging in the 1920s—one can speculate that communist control of official state history and of the institutions of higher education might have finally freed Russian historians to pursue nonstatist, nonpolitical themes. However that may be, medievalists like Olga Dobiash-Rozhdestvenskaia (the first woman to receive the doctorate in history in Russia) and Lev Karsavin were working on topics like "social psychology, the 'history of everyday life,' the 'history of death,' the spatial–temporal orientations of medieval man, and religiosity among the people."[21]

Each of these developments—Kliuchevskii's in a typically Russocentric manner and the 1920s studies, with more hope of a multicultural orientation—would have gone some distance toward reinvigorating the historical profession in Russia. In addition, the paired cultural breaches between mass and elite and between Russia and the West served as a very powerful motive for Russian historians, in the same way that the relationship to Russia inspired historical problematics among non-Russian nationalities of the Empire. That is to say, their search for scientific certitude was wrapped around a political force field generated by the identity-peculiarity issue in regards to Europe. Powerfully motivated by political and social concerns, they were not at all dispassionate, disinterested, or completely objective. Yet they seem to have been invigorated by a sense of history as a "scientific" discipline, which may lack the mathematical formulae and predictive power of the natural sciences, yet was more than just an organized body of knowledge with a set methodology. In this regard, their "scientism" resembles the way that Marxism worked among European intellectuals as both "scientific socialism" and a belief system. Never quite the one or the other. Neither fish nor meat, as the Russian saying goes.

By moving the center of gravity of historical analysis away from the centrist, Russian-dominated, state-oriented focus that positivism favored, a Russian *annaliste* historiography would have at the very least pushed historical inquiry closer to the world inhabited by most Russians. It might have also led to problematics that bridged the Russian/non-Russian divide, moving Russians past the situation in which they, as Joan Neuberger has expressed it in another context, "did not yet have categories for thinking about difference that refused to be inferior."[22] This would not have solved all the social problems of the Russian empire, but it could hardly have helped but produce a more cohesive vision of their shared pasts. All this points to the conclusion that historical practice bode fair to experience another of its broad shifts forward had not Stalinist purges and Delo No. 1803, as the Platonov affair was officially known, not intervened.

Beyond all that, the main reason that the pre-revolutionary historiographical tradition deserves our attention is that its power to influence and inspire did not end with the fall of the tsar or the seizure of power by the Bolsheviks. Reference has already been made to the historical vitality of the 1920s, but in fact components of the pre-revolutionary historical legacy were incorporated into the teaching and writing of history even in the Stalinist era. In a way, this is not surprising, since the historical traditions established in the vertical, elite culture of the pre-1917 world were the only traditions to which the politically manipulated historians of Stalin's time could turn. Hence, in 1937, the worst year of the Stalinist purges as far as Russian popular memory is concerned, Platonov's study of the Time of Troubles was released in a new edition and his textbook on Russian history was reissued for use in the Higher Party School of the Communist Party of the Soviet Union. Tarle, who had been the most popular and inspiring teacher in St. Petersburg in the 1920s, returned from exile and imprisonment to serve for years in the Soviet historical community. Similarly, Got'e carried on the traditions of Kliuchevskii's Moscow school, a tradition more recently embodied in the work of Zaionchkovskii and through him to the current generation of scholars. The St. Petersburg tradition, if anything even more self-consciously preserved and handed down, ran from Platonov to Presniakov, and from him to Boris Romanov and Sigismund Valk (d. 1975), and on down to Boris Anan'ich and the present generation of Petersburg historians. The collapse of communism and of overt political controls has allowed this subterranean stream of influence and tradition to resurface, and it is the strongest historiographical force at work in Russia today.

Notes

1. I had no desire to write a "prequel" to the volume, replete with more or less easily recognizable references to the contents to follow. As a result, I have attempted to discuss in general terms the topography of historical writing and the profession, to provide a general lay of the land to the reader, who can then consult the individual articles for more precise bearings. My thoughts here, though, are broadly informed by the works of the contributors to this volume, and a failure to recognize their impact on my ideas would be both misleading and ungracious. In particular, the pieces by Professors Raeff, Emmons, Tsamutali, and Anan'ich and Paneiakh have affected the way that I interpret the historiographical moment of late imperial–early Soviet times, and their impact will undoubtedly be evident in my comments. In addition, Professors Raeff and Emmons read an earlier version of this chapter and made substantive comments that have greatly improved it. I am grateful to them for their insights and contributions.

2. On the general conditions in the universities, see James Flynn, *The University Reform of Tsar Alexander I, 1802–1835* (Washington, DC: Catholic University of America Press, 1988); Cynthia H. Whittaker, *The Origins of Modern Russian Education* (DeKalb, IL: Northern Illinois University Press, 1984); James C. McClelland, *Autocrats and Academics: Education, Culture, and Society in Tsarist Russia* (Chicago: University of Chicago Press, 1979); and Samuel D. Kassow, *Students, Professors, and the State in Tsarist Russia* (Berkeley, CA: University of California Press, 1989).

3. Nikolai M. Karamzin, *Istoriia gosudarstva rossiiskogo* (St. Petersburg, [1816]-1829).

4. This memoir was a private document, which has subsequently been published. For an English-language version and a discussion of the essay, see Richard Pipes, *Memoir on Ancient and Modern Russia* (New York: Atheneum, 1966).

5. On Granovsky see Priscilla R. Roosevelt, *Apostle of Liberalism: Timofei Granovsky* (Newtonville, MA: Oriental Research Partners, 1986).

6. Sergei M. Solov'ev, *Istoriia Rossii s drevneishikh vremen*, 29 vols. (St. Petersburg, 1897).

7. Wladimir Weidle, *Russia: Absent and Present* (New York: John Day Company, 1952), p. 30.

8. See "Letters on the Philosophy of History, 1829–31" in Thomas Riha, ed., *Readings in Russian Civilization,* vol. 2: *Imperial Russia, 1700–1917,* p. 304. Chaadaev says that some may see Russia as having a civilizing mission vis-à-vis Asia, but he asks: "What Asian peoples have we civilized? Apparently the mastodons and the other fossilized populations of Siberia. As far as I know, they are the only races we have pulled out of obscurity." See "Letters to A.I. Turgenev, 1833 and 1835," ibid., p. 308.

9. The phrase is taken from Andrew Baruch Wachtel, *An Obsession with History: Russian Writers Confront the Past* (Stanford, CA: Stanford University Press, 1994).

10. Weidle, *Russia: Absent and Present,* pp. 31–32.

11. Ibid., p. 19.

12. Perhaps the Russian historical tradition can be compared with that of the United States. Not only do we share the penchant for new beginnings. It has been said: "Breaking with the past is part of our past. Leaving tradition behind runs all the way through

our tradition" (Robert N. Bellah et al., *Habits of the Heart: Individualism and Commitment in American Life,* 1st paperback ed. [New York: Harper and Row, 1985]), p. 75.] But we too are a migratory people, whose energies went to expanding, rather than to deepening our culture. In this expanding, frontier-leaping America, "the ever-present task of shoring up the social framework inevitably exhausted energies that might otherwise have been devoted to filling the structure with finer things. . . . American popular culture in the nineteenth century created social institutions rather than art, literature, or science— in its context, a remarkable achievement indeed" (Rowland Berthoff, "The American Social Order: A Conservative Hypothesis," *American Historical Review,* vol. 65, no. 3 [April 1960]: 508). Perhaps for Russia, as for the United States, this was task enough.

13. Weidle, *Russia: Absent and Present,* p. 16.

14. Ibid., p. 17. Vasilii Osipovich Kliuchevskii, *Sochineniia v deviatikh tomakh,* vol. 1, *Kurs russkoi istorii,* p. 50.

15. Kliuchevskii, *Kurs russkoi istorii,* p. 50.

16. Weidle, *Russia: Absent and Present,* p. 17.

17. Nikolai Berdiaev also noted the impact of geography on the Russian national character: "In the soul of the Russian people there is much immensity, boundlessness, a tendency toward the infinite, as on the Russian plain." Quoted in Alexander A. Danilov et al., *The History of Russia: The Twentieth Century,* trans. Galina Ustinova (n.p.: The Heron Press, 1996), p. 360.

18. The distinction is difficult to make in English, where both *russkaia* and *rossiiskaia* are rendered by the common word "Russian." *Russkii* is an ethnic, linguistic, and cultural indicator: "Ia russkii" (I am a Russian), "russkii iazyk" (Russian language), "russkaia kultura" (Russian culture, as distinct from Ukrainian or Georgian). The empire was officially known, however, as "Rossiiskaia Imperiia." This was a significant distinction, because the autocrats did not view themselves as deriving their legitimacy from the Russian—or from any other—people. Even the Fundamental State Laws, set forth after the Revolution of 1905 had forced Nicholas II to concede a representative assembly (the State Council and Duma), contained a full title of the Imperial Majesty that indicated his sovereignty over specific territories, not peoples. Too long to quote here in full, it states in part: "With the help of God's grace, we, NN, emperor and autocrat of all Russia, of Moscow, Kiev, Vladimir, and Novgorod; tsar of Kazan´, tsar of Astrakhan´, tsar of Poland, tsar of Siberia, tsar of Chersonesus Taurica, tsar of Georgia; sovereign of Pskov and grand prince of Smolensk." See "The Fundamental State Laws of April 23, 1906," in George Vernadsky, ed., *A Source Book for Russian History from Early Times to 1917,* vol. 3; *Alexander II to the February Revolution* (New Haven: Yale University Press, 1972), pp. 772–73. By way of comparison, the Revolution of 1830 in France changed the designation of the French monarch, and Louis Philippe became the first who was crowned "King of the French" and not "King of France." Recently, Boris Yeltsin has taken to referring to himself as a "rossianin," a most interesting formulation that attempts to skirt the same issue in a Russia that is still multiethnic. Most non-Russian nationalist historians were not interested in membership in a kinder, gentler empire, whatever the designation.

19. Weidle, *Russia: Absent and Present,* p. 19.

20. Ibid., p. 20.

21. B.S. Kaganovich, *Peterburgskaia shkola medievistiki v kontse XIX–nachale XX v. Avtoreferat dissertatsii na soiskanie uchenoi stepeni kandidata istoricheskikh nauk* (Leningrad, 1986), pp. 13–14. Cited in B. Anan´ich and V. Paneiakh, "The St. Petersburg School of History and Its Fate," note 15 (chapter 7 in the current volume).

22. Joan Neuberger, *Hooliganism: Crime, Culture, and Power in St. Petersburg, 1900–1914* (Berkeley, CA: University of California Press, 1993), p. 69.

I

The Evolution of Historical Consciousness and Practice in Russia from the Eighteenth Century Through the 1920s

2

The Idea of Autocracy
Among Eighteenth-Century
Russian Historians

Cynthia Hyla Whittaker

The idea of autocracy changed profoundly in eighteenth-century Russia. Among the educated elite, secular justification for power replaced religious sanction. Dynamic change legitimized the office rather than maintenance of stability. Rationalist arguments superseded acceptance based on tradition. The figure of the Russian autocrat as the equivalent of other European absolutist monarchs supplanted the image of an isolated and unique Orthodox ruler. The vast majority of Russians clung to the older views, but the Petrine reforms and Enlightenment ideals propelled a general movement among the educated public toward greater participation in political culture and prompted an unprecedented reappraisal of its central feature, the autocracy. Diplomats, clergy, bureaucrats, journalists, scientists, professors, men and women of letters, army officers, court personnel, even autocrats themselves joined the public discussion, causing a political watershed: for the first time, Russians engaged in sustained and relatively widespread discourse about their form of government and thus transformed the political environment.[1]

The official documents, political treatises, histories, and various literary genres in which this discourse unfolded reveal attitudes that run contrary to current assumptions, since historians over the past century focused either on oppositional individuals and groups or on the alienation of society from government. A fresh reading of the materials indicates widespread support for autocracy and demonstrates its function as a source of integration and cohesion among the educated elite.[2] These Russians discussed autocracy's legitimacy, debated its feasibility, and elaborated sophisticated arguments drawn from the Enlightenment arsenal of ideas to arrive at a critical and rational endorsement. Furthermore, they perceived autocracy as a dynamic form of government, not as reactionary or even static, and therefore saw themselves as part of a progressive polity. The interpretation of autocracy itself became an ongoing enterprise that reflected shifts in domestic politics, changing Enlightenment criteria for good government, and varying public values, attitudes, and expectations.

Many groups participated in this new discourse, but among the most characteristic were eighteenth-century Russians who wrote histories of Russia. Leaving aside historiographical issues, this study will use these works as evidence for charting public attitudes toward autocracy over the course of the century. Histories constitute an illustrative set of sources for this purpose, since their authors include a cross section of politically attuned Russians and since the writing of history throughout Europe in the eighteenth century centered on interpretations of rulership.

Russian historians in this epoch were nearly all amateurs and thus more typical of the educated public than the monastic annalists who were their forebears or the trained academics who were their successors.[3] The historians under analysis—all those who wrote interpretations of large segments of Russia's past and perforce her rulers—came from a variety of political milieus, each affording a different perspective on autocracy. Their amateur status makes these authors doubly representative, because they mirror the intellectual world both of writers of history and of their actual professions. Aleksei Mankiev (d. 1723) was a diplomat who wrote *The Kernel of Russian History* while imprisoned during the Great Northern War.[4] Vasilii Tatishchev (1686–1750), an expert administrator in the areas of mining, manufacturing, and minting, spent thirty years writing his multivolume *Russian History* "at night" and between assignments.[5] Mikhail Lomonosov's (1711–1765) fame rests on his position as the father of modern Russian literature and of modern Russian science, but he also found time to author *Ancient Russian History.*[6] Mikhail Shcherbatov (1733–1790), the court historiographer, confessed that he wrote the many volumes of *Russian History from Ancient Times* "more for my own personal pleasure" and spent a lifetime in state service.[7] Ivan Boltin (1735–1792) published historical critiques while serving as an army officer and administrator.[8] Timofei Mal'gin (1752–1819) wrote *A Mirror for Russian Sovereigns,* alongside his duties as a translator with the civil service rank of collegiate assessor.[9] And Catherine the Great, while somewhat better known for her achievements as empress, published "Notes Concerning Russian History."[10] Six literary figures, who wrote less ambitious works about Russia's past, complete the list of fifteen published amateur historians.[11] The works of thirty-two anonymous writers remain unpublished (deservedly) in the archives.[12] Because only forty-seven authors were involved in writing histories of Russia, observations and conclusions about this body of evidence can be based upon complete coverage. Eighteenth-century historians thus constitute a useful historical source, since they include a wide but manageable sample of the Russian educated public.

Moreover, this group guarantees material for gauging attitudes toward autocracy since eighteenth-century Western and Central European histories centered around rulers, and Russians consciously copied Enlightenment genres.[13] As Lotman and Uspenskii have pointed out, the emergence of people who could "think historically . . . was one of the basic innovations of post-Petrine culture" and an example of "real, not mythological Europeanization."[14] Full-fledged participants in their century's trends, Russians wrote history *en philosophe,* which demanded the formulation of an idea of progress, the demonstration of secular causation, and the display of interpretive sweep and didactic intent. Enlightenment histories intertwined each of these features with monarchical activity—understandably, as nearly all European countries were monarchies—and hence insured Russian authors' placing their own rulers at center stage.

Yet another reason why European eighteenth-century histories were bound to center on monarchs was that the majority were written at their behest. Fedor Emin noted that "all over Europe, Christian monarchs are trying to assemble correct histories that document reigns, actions, bents, morals, various changes."[15] In Russia, this turned history into an exercise in national self-consciousness, since autocrats also wanted historians "to do battle" with foreign detractors of the country and its leaders.[16] Peter the Great appealed for a national history to counteract "Polish lies";[17] Empress Elizabeth summoned historians to refute German scholars who described the early Slavs as "barbarians, resembling beasts";[18] Catherine urged denunciation of the "falsehood . . . slander . . . and insolence" of the "frivolous Frenchmen" who wrote histories of Russia.[19]

Whatever the need to please a sponsor, philosophes genuinely regarded monarchs as high priests of the new secular morality. Eighteenth-century thinkers were not interested in stabilizing society but in improving it, and the linchpin in these plans for making progress toward secular salvation was the enlightened ruler.[20] Voltaire, who dominated historical thinking in the century, replaced providential with royal causality and claimed that it was "the great actions of kings that have changed the face of the earth." He enshrined monarchs as those rare examples of human genius who brighten a historical landscape otherwise filled with struggle, folly, and crime.[21]

For eighteenth-century Russian historians, the most vivid example of the necessary connection between progress and the royal person was close at hand. The full-scale reform program of Peter the Great made him the proto-type of enlightened monarchs in Europe and prompted Russian historians to advance a dynamic interpretation of autocracy that became a hallmark of the century. After Peter, rulers were expected to justify their enormous power by being "reforming tsars," activist agents of change and improvement.[22] Historians imposed this new validation on past sovereigns, and do-nothing tsars were given deprecating epithets such as Rostislav the Prayerful, Vsevelod I the Quiet, or Fedor III the Sickly when, in Mal'gin's words, "they made no important changes."[23]

The activity expected of a dynamic tsar went far beyond the centuries-old functions of warrior and judge and superseded the old primary role of defender of Orthodoxy. According to Lomonosov's typical list, the new duties included: increasing the population, eradicating idleness, fostering prosperity, raising the cultural level, battling superstition, encouraging geographical exploration, and, more traditionally, expanding borders.[24] Autocrats were to provide moral, if not necessarily spiritual, leadership: Catherine II claimed that a monarch was needed to save people "from envy," the vice most prominently mentioned by eighteenth-century Russian historians; Mankiev lauded autocrats who tried to eliminate drunkenness; Mal'gin looked to them to banish anti-Semitism from the realm.[25] Tatishchev portrayed Peter as an ideal monarch, since he enabled his country to thrive in everything from the tool industry to the administration of justice—despite a long and costly war.[26] As the century wore on, not only the traditional image of Orthodox Tsar but even that of Warrior-King receded in the wake of the perceived need for reform. Alexander Sumarokov deemed "domestic improvements . . . the greatest tasks of monarchs"; Mal'gin agreed that "domestic accomplishments are infinitely more precious than all victories and conquests."[27]

With monarchs considered the ultimate causal factor in the state, not only their personal virtues or triumphs but also their vices or failures ac-quired significance. Tatishchev concluded: "With the good judgment and proper behavior of a sovereign, a state is enhanced, enriched, and flourish-ing, but laziness, love of luxury, and cruelty [in a sovereign] are ruinous, and our history is filled enough with such examples."[28] Boltin and Abbé Raynal (1713–1796) likewise argued that "people do not have their destiny in their own hands but remain on their sovereign's [moral and cultural] level."[29] For this reason, Enlightenment historians felt duty-bound to in-struct monarchs on their tasks and to provide them with textbooks of politi-cal morality. The very first statement about writing secular history in Russia offered the hope that it would demonstrate to autocrats the "results of good and evil acts."[30] Lomonosov expected his history to "give sovereigns examples of governing,"[31] while Tatishchev claimed that history's "use" was providing rulers with "a knowledge of the past" so that they may "wisely discuss the present and future."[32] Nicholas Novikov suggested that a "Philosopher-King . . . could inculcate, spread, implant . . . support, encourage, and patronize knowledge"—using the entire litany of hortatory verbs typical of eighteenth-century writers in spurring or motivating their monarchs into enlightened action.[33]

The image of "reforming tsars" and the appearance of pragmatic didacticism announce the new secularism of Enlightenment history and its reaction against the providential or religious interpretations of monarchical rule that had reached their climax in France with the writings of Jacques Bossuet (1627–1704). Although a strict theory of divine right was never prominent in Russia, there did exist the tradition of ecclesiastical histories, really chronicles, that originated in medieval Kiev.[34] They stressed the autocracy's biblical origins and its ties with the House of Palaeologus, but especially its role in the expansion of the Orthodox Church.[35] About a dozen eighteenth-century historians continued the tradition, but only one was published.[36] However, the seventeenth-century *Synopsis* by Innokentii Gizel' retained an audience and became one of the most popular books in the eighteenth century.[37] This short work possessed an appealing triumphal quality with its emphasis on religious feats: the glorious conversion of the Russians to Orthodoxy under Vladimir I and the equally glorious victory of the Orthodox over the Tatar Horde under Ivan III. The rest of the book, though, consists of brief descriptions of princes and tsars whose quiescence was their paramount feature; they seemingly did little more than come to the throne, build a stone church or monastery, and then go to their heavenly reward. The abandonment of both this image of a passive ruler and a religious teleology marked the major innovation of eighteenth-century Russian historians.

Another similarity among these historians was their use of a common vocabulary but lack of precision in speaking about autocracy. They equated Russian autocracy (*samoderzhavie*) and European absolutism (*edinovlastie*) and used them interchangeably along with the generic monarchy (*monarkhiia*), and invested all the terms with the notion of the "independent and unrestricted power of one ruler, under God."[38] The historians also subscribed to the widely held opinion of the time that there existed three equally valid forms of government, each with its own corrupt form: monarchy (autocracy)/despotism; aristocracy/oligarchy; and democracy/anarchy.[39] Their discussions therefore centered on whether autocracy, despite the risk of despotism, might still be preferable in Russia to aristocracy or democracy, with their threat of becoming oligarchic or anarchic.

Despite these similarities among the historians, their differences in interpreting autocracy remain their single most prominent characteristic. These differences lend them what John B. Bury would call their "permanent interest," the fact that each arose "at a given epoch and is characteristic of the tendencies and ideas of that epoch" and especially, one may add, in an era when histories were unabashedly subjective.[40] While proclaiming the value of Baconian methodology in the search, compilation, analysis, and publication of major historical documents,[41] interpretive history was more prized in the eighteenth century and was still viewed throughout Europe as a branch of literature or as a practical extension of philosophy—philosophy teaching by example—and was expected to reflect the writer's own perceptions.[42] Thus, historians consciously and purposefully expressed the attitudes of their era, and, in Russia, the differences among them offer ideal gauges for charting the much broader discourse about the autocratic idea.

A close reading of the fifty-two extant histories reveals a discourse that falls into three distinct patterns of interpretation, which I am calling the dynastic, the empirical, and the nondespotic models; they are categorized according to what authors understood as the basis for the legitimacy and feasibility of autocracy in Russia. Each interpretation resulted in its own version of historical events, often contradicting the others, and each had its own candidate for the worst episode in Russian history, which I call the Antithetical Event. The first two models emerged in the Petrine and immediate post-Petrine eras, while the third was prevalent in Catherinian Russia. The interpretations neither replaced nor argued against each other but instead accumulated, overlapped, and offered complementary assessments of autocracy's legitimacy, feasibility, and preferability. By the end of the century, all three coexisted, producing a rich and nuanced understanding of the idea of autocracy that provided the intellectual context for political attitudes in modern Russia.

The Dynastic Interpretation

The early years of the eighteenth century marked the first break with the Orthodox approach of Gizel's *Synopsis*. Peter the Great's radical moves to modernize the country and secularize the state coincided with the early Enlightenment's movement away from medieval structures of knowledge and value systems based on tradition and religious authority. This atmosphere gave rise to a secular and dynamic interpretation of autocracy. It originated with Mankiev, who was motivated to write history precisely because he wanted to bear witness to the accomplishments of the Petrine era in which he lived and to place it in the context of Russia's past; in other words, he was writing history backward, influenced by a seminal epoch. Lomonosov, Vasilii Trediakovskii, Ivan Barkov, and a dozen unpublished historians repeated this approach, since they shared Mankiev's secular sensibility and the conviction that lay at the base of his work: namely, that Peter's reign represented the culmination of all Russian history. Given the lackluster character of post-Petrine rulers, that view remained strong until Catherine II ascended the throne.

The dynastic interpretation remained old-fashioned and wedded to the chronicle tradition in its premise that "the genealogy of monarchs forms the basis of Russian history"[43] and in the polite attitude that any legally born monarch "deserves praise," even an Ivan the Terrible.[44] Its novelty lay in its emphasis on secular events and material progress and its replacement of religious with dynastic sanction and causality. For example, Lomonosov's enormously popular *Short Russian Chronicle* devoted only six lines to the Christianization of Russia.[45] Previous works equated the history of Russia with the history of Orthodoxy in Russia, but the new histories equated it with the fortunes of Russia's two dynasties. The secular leadership of the Riurikids and the Romanovs was celebrated for causing the country's past strength and greatness and guiding it toward an even more glorious future.

Dynastic historians presented to the educated Russian public an autocracy the equal of any ruling house in the rest of Europe, an important desideratum when the country was just entering the Western family of nations. Legitimacy rested on resplendent lineage and constant efficacy, traits the historians accentuated even at the dawn of Russian history. The eighteenth-century public generally accepted the idea that "Russia" originated late in the ninth century when discordant Slavic tribes called Riurik and his kin from some distant land to rule over them. The dynasts, however, wanted to downplay the foreign origin of Russia's first dynasty and to heighten its grandeur. Embellishing a then-dubious and now-discredited chronicle, they upgraded Gostomysl'—the legendary last mayor of the Republic of Novgorod—into an internationally renowned prince whose advice was sought by rulers from "distant countries." They then claimed that his daughter, Queen Umila of Finland, was Riurik's mother; this genealogy resulted in a happy intersection (*peresechenie*) of bloodlines that connected the new dynasty with the family of the last Slavic "prince."[46] To further underscore that Riurik was "of the highest blood and lineage," these historians resurrected the old myth that he descended from a long imperial line that stretched from Assyrian and Egyptian monarchs to David and Solomon, Alexander the Great, Julius Caesar, Augustus and Prus.[47] For the dynastic school, the invitation to Riurik demonstrated that, like any proper people, the Russians recognized the need for an illustrious ruling clan, which, "by dint of a single blood and for the common good," could "unite the Slavic peoples into a single tribe under single rule." Once Riurik "established autocratic power," simultaneously Russia came into being and immediately "flourished," to use the most common verb (*tsvesti*) attributed to dynastic leadership.[48]

These authors, rooted in classical learning, depicted autocracy as preferable to the frequently idealized democratic republics. Having that form of government before Riurik, Russians were portrayed as living in an Hobbesian state of "envy, feuding, discord, and enmity."[49] Lomonosov rued that medieval Novgorod's "free charters resulted in a not small cause for the division of Russia"; he claimed delight when Ivan III finally "abolished the republic . . . and brought it under his own autocracy."[50] Since it was popular to recognize a similarity between Roman and Russian history,[51] Lomonosov felt forced to admit that Rome thrived when a republic, but concluded: "On the contrary, with difference of opinion and freedom Russia nearly fell into total ruin; autocracy from the beginning strengthened her and, after the unfortunate times, restored, fortified, and made her illustrious." Indeed, an anonymous historian elaborated, under autocratic leadership Russia's history had become "greater than even that of Greece or Rome." Thus, dynasts cast freedom and republicanism in a negative light, associating them historically in Russia with anarchy, civil war, and bloodletting. However, this did not imply that Russians had settled for slavery or despotism, since their autocrats were not tyrants but legitimate and dynamic rulers in whom breathed "the Spirit of Numa, the ancient Roman lawgiver."[52]

Peter the Great—despite his abrogating hereditary succession, something the dynasts chose to ignore—provided final proof of the benefits of hereditary autocracy for Russia. He was the "culmination" of the dynasty, indeed of all dynasties; one history allotted half of its nearly seven hundred pages to recounting Peter's day-to-day activities and recognized him as the best issue of an ancestral line traced back to Noah. Mankiev saw in Peter's reign a demonstration of the intimate connection between autocracy and progress: "He enlightened all Rus' . . . and it was as though reborn."[53] Lomonosov, likewise awed by Peter's dynamism, pioneered a progressive but cyclical view of Russian history, whose fortunes rose and fell depending on the strength of dynastic leadership. Each stage arose from the ashes of the previous, more glorious than before: "Farsighted sovereigns" ensured that "each misfortune was followed by a prosperity greater than before, each fall by a greater renewal."[54] Thus, the dynastic historians, inspired by Peter's achievements, celebrated his long line of Riurikid and Romanov ancestors. By no longer anchoring legitimacy in divine prescription or merely in bloodline, they announced a dynamic and secular definition of the autocracy, pronouncing it the one form of government with proven historical capacity to avoid anarchy and to bring Russia stability, grandeur, and progress.

The Empirical Interpretation

While the dynastic model became a standard way of viewing autocracy among the educated public, Tatishchev originated a second, more theoretical interpretation in the 1730s and 1740s, a view later repeated in the works of three unpublished historians and Emin.[55] Mankiev's formation as a historian resulted from Peter's Westernizing reign, but Tatishchev's arose from his participation in the "Events of 1730," when some members of the aristocracy and nobility had a passing flirtation with placing "conditions" or limitations on the monarch's power.[56] Tatishchev's *History* directly responded to the perceived threat of aristocratic government and to the succession of post-Petrine rulers whose weakness lessened their prestige and political control. Arguing within the intellectual context of the Enlightenment and focusing on the era's two most cherished traits, Tatishchev sought to demonstrate that, nevertheless, autocracy represented the most "rational" and therefore "natural" form of government for Russia—categories the dynasts had not employed, since they did not feel placed in a defensive posture.

In the empirical model, history became a laboratory for those abstract principles and natural laws of politics, "which we comprehend . . . through our senses and our reason," and which could be "scientifically" observed and tested.[57] Tatishchev especially valued the teachings of Christian Wolff and Christian Thomasius, two leaders of the German Enlightenment. Basing their observations on reason and experience, they concluded, like most European thinkers, that democracies are appropriate only in small states, aristocracies only where there are an educated population and protected borders, and limited monarchy of the British variety only where people are both enlightened and well acquainted with notions of individualism. None of these characteristics applied to Russia. Without such conditions, these thinkers supported a state headed by a willful ruler who would wield unlimited powers and work through a bureaucracy to effect the common good.[58] Logically, Tatishchev denied the feasibility of any form of government except autocracy in a country of Russia's size, location, and cultural level: "Large regions, open borders, in particular where the people are not enlightened by learning and reason and perform their duties from fear rather than an internalized sense of right and wrong, must be an [unlimited] monarchy." Anything less than absolute power would invite anarchy and invasion. Hence, Tatishchev reasoned, Peter's unlimited power gave him the right to choose his own successor without regard to bloodline; on this issue, the empiricists stood alone, since the other historians respected the overwhelming sentiment in favor of hereditary monarchy.[59]

Unlimited monarchy in Russia was not only the sole rational choice, Tatishchev asserted; experience further suggested that it was also the most natural or innately correct form of government, since it functioned like society's most natural and basic institution, the family. The source of autocratic power flowed from the proposition that "the monarch is like a father," with the state a family writ large; thus, the child's or subject's lack of freedom was natural and just, until the father or monarch could guide his charges to maturity. This paternal structure also implied an ethical foundation for autocracy, which had been missing with the retreat of the previously dominant religious sanction. Tatishchev believed that there existed natural prohibitions against arbitrary or despotic behavior since fathers and monarchs had no reason and "no power to harm or ruin" their children or subjects, only to promote their "welfare, happiness, [and] security"; at any rate, "natural law will always dictate what is useful or harmful." Thus, Tatishchev embraced the optimistic Enlightenment belief in the necessary functioning of laws that accorded with man's innate sense of morality and could conclude that unlimited power was not only necessary but by nature benevolent. This argument, of course, put a modern patina on the traditional paternal view of monarchical stewardship and gave it double resonance.

Switching similes, Tatishchev and Emin also based the legitimacy of autocracy upon its contractual origin, an argument that was considered empirical in the eighteenth century and that was made popular in Russia with the introduction of the writings of Samuel Pufendorf (1632–1694).[60] While the individual (*poddannyi*) is like a child of the ruler, the people as a whole (*narod*) is like a spouse. The contract between ruler and ruled was equated with a marriage contract: it is entered into "fully and rationally" and is "freely made."[61] The dynasts wrote simply that Riurik "established autocratic power" to bring order to the tribes, but Tatishchev and Emin emphasized that a contract had been forged between him and the people. It was the people who recognized the disaster of "freedom," of "each living according to his own will," and it was the people who concluded "that autocratic rule was preferable to anarchy."[62] Then, it was the people who besought "Riurik to take all the power alone" and "firmly establish absolutism"; they "deemed it best to submit to a single rule and, after unanimous agreement, they called Riurik."[63] Thereafter, his descendants signed themselves "tsar and grand prince and autocrat of Russia," again in keeping with popular consent since the people reasoned that without an unlimited monarch "there existed neither order nor justice."[64] Locke and his followers excepted, most thinkers in the first half of the eighteenth century, including Tatishchev, believed that such a contract "can be destroyed by no one."[65]

Tatishchev was so convinced of the continuing necessity for unlimited monarchy in Russia that, throughout his *History,* he judged tsars almost solely on their maintenance and increase of autocratic power. For instance, he had no trouble applauding Ivan IV's supposed strengthening of monarchical power, even through a policy of terror; he recognized that Boris Godunov was a "despoiler of the throne," but at least he ruled autocratically. Like the dynasts, the empirical school extolled Peter's reign, not as the culmination of dynastic glory but rather of unlimited power; by ending the patriarchate and denying the need for boyar assent in legislation, Peter finally established full autocracy.[66]

This school presented to the Russian educated public an autocracy whose unlimited power was empirically necessary by dint of physical and cultural circumstances, conformity to natural law, and force of contract. Nonetheless, while Tatishchev believed that autocracy alone was suitable in Russia for the foreseeable future, he also believed in progress. He defined it as the gradual accumulation of knowledge—under the leadership of a firm autocrat/father—with each generation building on the achievements of the previous one, until a fully enlightened population developed; then, and only then, could he envision a lessening of the autocracy's unlimited power and, presumably, only when both tsar and people agreed to renegotiate their contract.[67]

The Nondespotic Interpretation

The dynasts presumed unlimited power on the part of the autocrat and the empiricists regarded it as a necessity; indeed, throughout Europe, philosophes uncritically applauded absolutist monarchs for their capacity quickly to enact enlightened reforms. However, beginning in the 1770s, the focus shifted from the benefits of unlimited power to the danger of its becoming despotic, with power wielded in an oppressive, unjust, cruel, and arbitrary manner and with little concern for the common welfare. In Russia, the Bironovshchina during the reign of Anna Ioannovna, the alleged tyranny practiced by Peter III during his brief six months of rule in 1762, and Catherine II's assiduous contrast between her own "rule of law" and the "despotism" of her husband also encouraged discussion of the nature of autocratic power and preventing its dangers.[68] In this atmosphere, historians gave birth to a new model for interpreting autocracy; they include the remaining seven published authors and a half-dozen unpublished ones whose histories were written in roughly the last third of the century. Theirs can be called the nondespotic school, since its members strove to validate Russia's form of government as a monarchy and to fight its equation with despotism. These historians absorbed the previous patterns' image of a dynamic and secular tsar of glorious lineage, proven competence, and empirical necessity. However, the dynasts and empiricists applauded unlimited power. The nondespotic group denied its existence and based the legitimacy and feasibility of autocracy on the grounds that its power had always been de facto limited and on the assumption that de jure limitations were close at hand.[69]

This school of historians took a defensive posture vis-à-vis Europe in describing autocracy. Probably, this stemmed in part from their feeling that they were full-fledged, not just fledgling, participants in the Enlightenment, but that Russia was not yet recognized as having come of age. Certainly, they were aggravated that some Europeans regarded autocracy not as the Russian variant of absolutism but as a separate form of "primitive despotism." Boltin, for instance, was incensed by the statement of a French historian that "from ancient times they [the Russians] lived in slavery and always recognized bondage as their natural condition"; Boltin penned two volumes of uninterrupted spleen trying to refute such conceptions.[70] But it was Catherine II who led the attack by beginning her famous *Instruction* to the Legislative Assembly of 1767 with the dictum, "Russia is a European state"; also, in her "History," she reminded Enlightenment thinkers of their precept that "humankind everywhere and forever has the same passions, desires, and inclinations, and for achieving them not rarely uses the same means."[71] In this spirit, Boltin was willing to admit that Ivan IV was a tyrant, but only while insisting that he was little different from other rulers of the era, such as Louis XI (1461–1483) of France.[72] In other words, the nondespotic school was intent on defining autocracy as limited in nature, in the same way, mutatis mutandis, that other European monarchies were limited by customs, intermediary bodies, or fundamental laws, and thus precluding any equation with despotism. Most went further and postulated a firm connection between autocratic government and security of person and property, a commonly held definition of "freedom" in the late eighteenth century, hence bringing the idea of autocracy—sincerely "reinvented"—even more into step with Enlightenment ideals and Russian aspirations.

Prince Shcherbatov, himself a member of one of Russia's oldest aristocratic families, was unique among this group in propounding an aristocratic limitation. His depiction of autocracy centered on its necessity in Russia and on its need to cooperate with the aristocracy; both aspects resulted from the weakness of human nature. Shcherbatov greatly admired David Hume, especially his emphasis on the psychology of both rulers and ruled as causal factors in history. Shcherbatov believed that people in general lack moderation; they act either like "wild beasts after blood" or "like lambs" and eternally engage in a contest between passion and reason, and virtue and vice. While Tatishchev marshaled cool abstractions to prove a natural need for autocracy, Shcherbatov stressed that mankind's natural bestiality required the guidance of an authoritarian ruler. He believed, like most Enlightenment thinkers, that monarchs were the primary causal factors in state and society, but he deviated in viewing the people as inert or passive under their dominance. A more enlightened population would make more freedom possible, he agreed, but until then the people were tabulae rasae upon whom the monarch impressed his mark. The ruler's psychological makeup, intelligence, and character informed the level of laws and these in turn informed the level of morals and manners among the people. In Russia, Shcherbatov warned, whenever the people prematurely tried to control the government, for instance in the Republic of Novgorod, freedom "turned into an evil and one of the causes for Russia's ruin."[73]

While arguing the necessity of autocracy in Russia, Shcherbatov recognized that monarchy, too, had an inherent weakness: rulers themselves were human and hence tempted by such vices as "ambition and despotism." In a theory reminiscent both of premodern Russian conceptions of a "good tsar" and of Montesquieu's *thèse nobiliaire,* he averred that Russian autocrats had avoided these weaknesses by acting in harmony with a council of wise aristocratic elders or boyars;[74] from the time of Riurik, only this "holy union" had provided Russia's defense against despotism. In other words, for Shcherbatov there were two collective actors on the historical stage, rulers and aristocrats. He alone of all the historians made the causal connection that "the state flourishes and its prosperity increases where there is fidelity, honor, unity, and strength in the hearts of the aristocracy," not just of the monarchs. For instance, Shcherbatov directly blamed the dim and childless Tsar Fedor for the rise of despotism during the Time of Troubles since he relied on the upstart Boris Godunov for advice rather than on "the most worthy, most farsighted true servants of the fatherland," the old boyars. The problem was compounded by Boris's psychological makeup; he demonstrated a capability for ruling, but his fatal vice, "lust for the throne," led to his hostility to the boyars and thus to his "becoming despotic." The causal flow led, in turn, to the collapse of the economy and autocracy and near-extinction at the hands of Sweden and Poland.[75]

Shcherbatov's treatment of Peter the Great was more equivocal. The emperor committed the prince's trio of mortal sins: he was a man of passion; he failed to consult with his boyars; he used despotic measures. However, Shcherbatov forthrightly admired Peter and forgave his sins as normal in the era and because backward Russia needed a forcible thrust into the modern age. While Shcherbatov agreed that Peter "raised despotism to a new extreme," Peter also brought "Russia out of weakness into strength, out of disorder into order, and out of ignorance into enlightenment." In the end, "from his despotism, we received enough enlightenment to criticize that despotism"—a theme that lay at the heart of political discourse in post-Petrine Russia.[76]

Shcherbatov's sponsorship of his own small group's ability to curb despotism had limited appeal among the educated public. In addition, the fact that the boyars were powerless to prevent Ivan IV's tyranny weakened Shcherbatov's own confidence in the aristocratic limitation. By the last volume of his *History,* which extends to the year 1610, he seemed to concede that formal guarantees offered more certainty, a solution that grew ever more popular as the century wore on. Vasilii Shuiskii, the "unlucky" Boyar-Tsar who ruled during the Time of Troubles, was adjudged "glorious among all earthly rulers," since he wanted to take an oath "in keeping with the institution of monarchical power" but with guaranteed legal protection at least of boyar life and property. Shcherbatov, in the dedication of his *History* to Catherine, prodded her to follow suit: "Since the people have been oppressed for so many centuries already they await from Your hand their happiness and freedom . . . the most precious gift of mankind."[77]

Other writers reexamined the historical evidence for curbs on despotism and discovered a Russian political tradition rooted in an ongoing elective principle, thus completely contradicting the dynasts' picture in which Riurik imposed autocracy or Tatishchev's concept of a contract in which the people once and forever gave Riurik and his descendants unlimited power. Ivan Elagin emphasized that among the early Russians, "we do not find the slightest sign of autocracy, and even less of despotism, and neither a hereditary throne," but rather "examples of the free election of Leaders or Princes." Other historians of this epoch claimed that Riurik was "never given unlimited power," and that is why his descendants never took a kingly title or crown.[78]

Russian rulers, they contended, were never "considered the image of God or earthly gods," and hence "princes, boyars and the people took part in government, and the power of the grand princes was not autocratic"; in fact, from the beginning, "the Russian people were free." Boltin cited the people of the city of Vladimir saying: "We are a free people. We chose the princes ourselves, and they kissed the cross to us." Professor Chebotarev of Moscow University, Catherine's mentor on history, confirmed that "autocratic government in Russia . . . was founded on free and voluntary election" but added that over the centuries people had constantly renewed the election since autocratic rule was consonant with the common good.[79] The motif of autocracy being "chosen" time and again dominated histories in the last third of the century.

The nondespotic school was also anxious to prove that, throughout Russian history, autocracy better guarded freedom, or security of person and property, than the other two forms of government. Medieval Novgorod, according to Chebotarev, demonstrated "the natural and ruinous results of a democracy": "It is not strong enough to uphold and defend the freedom and rights of its citizens." Boltin agreed: "Experience demonstrates that a democratic government cannot preserve the security and tranquillity of individual people" as "freedom turns into wilfulness or lack of restraint." For this reason, he explained, Russians long ago understood that "the rule of a single person is incomparably better, more profitable, and more utile both for society and especially for the individual than the rule of many," where "envy, squabbling and hatred reign." In addition, "monarchy in a large state is preferable to aristocracy, which normally wastes time in argumentation and is not given to daring views; only a Monarch can launch and carry through actions of great purport." Boltin concluded: "Monarchical government occupies the middle ground between despotism and republics and is the most reliable safeguard of freedom."[80]

In their association of freedom and autocracy, the nondespots tended to be critical of Peter the Great for his use of force in promulgating legislation. Boltin, unlike Shcherbatov, believed that the people, not the tsars, should ultimately make the laws because "laws conform to behavior rather than behavior to laws." He thus preferred Catherine the Great as a "model of wise and great sovereigns," since, in her "golden age," Peter's use of force was no longer employed. But serfdom remained a problem. After agreeing with Rousseau that slavery is "the primary sin against nature," Boltin temporized and took the position that became standard among moderate and enlightened Russians until the eve of Emancipation: only after the soul is freed through education can the body be freed, and then only "by degrees and gradually." He depicted Catherine the Great as pushing the process forward, since she understood how "to teach each subject how to use freedom for the benefit of himself as well as of his neighbor and the fatherland." Himself the owner of nine hundred male "souls," Boltin hoped that soon legislation would be passed "to limit the powers of landowners over their serfs" and trusted that full freedom, even for the serfs, would be harvested as the "fruit of Catherine's labors."[81] Elagin was equally optimistic. While he was nearly alone among the Russian historians in ruing the "beating down of Novgorod's freedom," that "indubitable beginning of Russian history," he was confident that under Catherine, Novgorod's form of government would be resumed in Russia.[82] Another instance of history being written backward, Elagin's ideal government not so mysteriously resembled the balance of power and rule of law attained by the eighteenth-century British monarchy.

Thus, this pattern defined autocracy as inherently nondespotic, since its power had always been limited de facto by aristocratic counsel, fundamental laws, and an elective principle that offered continuous validation. Furthermore, while always protecting freedom, autocracy offered the best hope for evolving de jure limitations and guarantees of freedom in the future—especially under the guidance of the "ever-wise legislator," as Catherine the Great liked to be called.[83]

The Antithetical Event

Underscoring their differences, stylistic analysis of the historians' texts discloses their unconscious fixation on what can be called the Antithetical Event: that moment in history when the autocracy as interpreted, legitimized, justified, or defined by a given group was undermined or confronted with its negation. In describing this occurrence, the historians wrote at greater length and used emotional and hyperbolic language in contrast to their usual dry and factual presentations, which more often than not consisted of a ponderous rephrasing of old chronicles. In effect, during narrations of the Antithetical Event, history was transformed into a morality play or cautionary tale. Since this appears to be an unconscious process, it attests to the sincerity of the authors' professed interpretation of the autocracy. In addition, the negative portrayal of certain tsars implied the opposite positive characteristics and confirmed the didactic purpose of Enlightenment history.

Mankiev's *History* is a calm, rather dull, dynastic tale. The author treated the legitimate Ivan the Terrible with gentle courtesy. He even recognized Shuiskii as a legal monarch since he could trace his lineage back to Riurikid grand princes; the Boyar-Tsar's problems were attributed to "the envy and lack of unity among Russians themselves." The tone dramatically altered when the "illegitimate" Boris Godunov ascended the throne. The dynasts maintained that Fedor, the last of the Riurikid rulers, wanted the throne to go to his cousin, a Romanov; there would then have been yet another "intersection with Riurikid blood" since Anastasia Romanovna had been married to Ivan IV during the "good" part of his reign.[84] Instead Boris, Fedor's brother-in-law, conspired to seize the throne, and the illegitimacy of his reign caused the Time of Troubles—not the failure to consult with boyars as Shcherbatov insisted. Mankiev described Boris as odious and personally responsible for flood, famine, inflation, widespread crime, smoking, and drunkenness; in addition, he stood accused of arresting and robbing boyar clans; supposedly, his policies in Astrakhan' resulted in such poverty that parents were forced to sell their children into slavery; of course, he had Dmitri of Uglich, the last of the Riurikids, killed. With a sigh of relief, Mankiev welcomed the return of legitimacy: "And thus, although Boris Godunov, having wanted to rule himself, killed the Tsarevich Dmitri and sought to kill others, nonetheless, he could not kill the legitimate successor to the Muscovite throne," Mikhail Romanov. Because he was legitimate, the first Romanov was able to undo Boris's damage and "save Russia from the Swedish and Polish wolves." For dynasts, tirades against Godunov for "alienating the whole people," as Barkov put it, often filled more pages than the deeds of good rulers and occupied as much as one-third of the narrative.[85]

Other dynastic historians indicted Sophia Alekseevna for trying to interrupt normal laws of succession. Relying on the support of *streltsy,* or guards' regiments, her regency—an attempt to keep her half brother Peter I and her brother Ivan V from the throne—lasted from 1682 until 1689, when she finally "lost her lust for the autocracy," as Lomonosov heatedly put it. Lacking an Antithetical Event, his *Chronicle,* while popular, could not be duller in presentation; it consisted of columned tables with the names and dates of rulers, their degrees of removal from Riurik, and pithy descriptions of their years in power. But when confronting the usurper Sophia, Lomonosov wrote a separate essay that depicted the confiscation, terror, pillage, heresy, and ill-gotten gains that resulted from this illegitimate rule. While "the boyars, the nobility, and the people loved their sovereigns and ardently desired that they take the reins of government into their own hands," they were filled with "fear." Lomonosov even condoned Peter's personally taking on the role of executioner to finally undo the power of the streltsy: "He made silent his mercy in order to render the justice due."[86]

In a revealing contrast, Alexander Sumarokov, who anchored the true legitimacy of an autocrat in both "inheritance and laws," likewise found his Antithetical Event in Sophia's regency but for reasons stemming from the nondespotic interpretation. He considered Sophia a usurper not because of bloodline (she herself was a Romanov) but because "the public had elected" Peter tsar. With the support she received from those "most vile and venomous" armed guards, the government became the tyranny that the nondespotic school feared. Indeed, Sumarokov rendered an exceptional portrait of a good monarchy's antithesis, one similar to the rule of a Caligula or Nero: "the love and warm feeling between monarchs and subjects" disappeared; subjects were turned into "slaves who trembled day and night"; "weapons and wilfulness" replaced regularity of rule; there was a disregard of law, "the foundation on which the prosperity of all the Russian people is based." Sumarokov ended with the didactic peroration that the streltsy episode was "our disgrace!" and Russians should "know the truth and learn."[87]

For Tatishchev and Emin of the empirical school, the Antithetical Event occurred not once but whenever unlimited autocracy was replaced by aristocracy. Darkness and disgust clouded their otherwise arid prose until joy emerged at the return of autocracy. For instance, monarchical power disintegrated in the eleventh and twelfth centuries and in part paved the way for the Mongol Yoke of the thirteenth and fourteenth centuries. Tatishchev sorrowed:

> Thus arose aristocracy, but it was without decency . . . and there was a great bloodletting; and all this gave free rein to the Tatar invader to destroy everything and subjugate everyone to its power and, because of this, autocracy, the strength and honor of Russian sovereigns, was extinguished . . . as was church learning, and the people were plunged into superstition. . . . And thus it continued for 130 years . . . until the restoration of the ancient monarchy.[88]

Concerning the Time of Troubles, Boris did not trouble the empiricists, since he ruled autocratically, but Shuiskii, Shcherbatov's hero, was accused of overseeing "a pure aristocracy" of seven families, and "because of this wayward government, soon the state fell into such extreme ruin and collapse that it barely escaped partition or Polish overlordship." The same seven families attempted to substitute aristocratic rule in 1730, and in Tatishchev's circles open comparisons were made between the two episodes. "A great many" of these "vindictive grandees . . . were power-hungry, others money-hungry, and others filled with uncontrollable spite against their opponents," and none had any concept of working for the common good or the enlightenment of the people, "the true aims of government," according to Tatishchev.[89] Indeed, a motivation for Tatishchev's writing his history was to discredit forever the proponents of aristocracy in Russia by propounding a convincing denunciation drawn from these two historical events.

Shcherbatov defined a good autocrat as one who took boyar advice, and thus his Antithetical Event was the reign of Ivan IV, against whom he directed over twelve hundred pages of diatribe. When Ivan first began to reign, Shcherbatov asserted, "the conduct of the ruler was completely praiseworthy, as he did nothing of importance without the advice of his relatives and boyars";[90] it should be noted that most other historians, regardless of "school," attributed Ivan's problems to the "envy, bribery, and hypocrisy" he witnessed while under boyar care as a youth.[91] At any rate, for Shcherbatov, when the union between tsar and boyar was broken, "good spirit, love for the fatherland, and fidelity to the ruler were extinguished with fire and sword and in their places were put fear and trembling"; this resulted in the "unbridled power," or despotism, "which autocrats so desire" and can obtain unless restrained by their best and brightest boyars.[92]

In the nondespotic school, Boltin and Mal'gin considered Ivan a unique aberration and recognized that Boris Godunov had been elected to the throne by a legal assembly. Their Antithetical Event occurred during the reign of Anna Ioannovna, who was herself not a despot—leaving Ivan IV as "the only one" in Russian history—but was dominated by her German favorite, Biron, "an ignoble tyrant" who "robbed the people blind." To heighten their accusation, they contrasted the era of Biron with the golden age of Catherine, when "everyone expresses his opinion freely." But in the 1730s, "a wife was afraid to speak with her husband, a father with his son, a mother with her daughter about their disastrous condition for fear they would be overheard by servants and denounced." Boltin treated Biron's control of the government and subsequent weakening of monarchical power as a de facto aristocracy: "There you have the fruits of aristocratic power. . . . The evil will incessantly multiply and its politics will turn into intrigues, into conspiracies, into confrontations, into discord . . . while ambition and cupidity profit from its disorder."[93]

Inflation of prose, character, and incident occurred whenever the historians' arguments in favor of the legitimacy and feasibility of autocracy were refuted by an actual event that betrayed its weaknesses as a form of government: rule by favorites; the chaos that ensued when the line died out; the incapacity or youth of a monarch that left open an opportunity for a usurper; the tragic results when a monarch wielded power despotically. Nonetheless, the historians rejected the alternatives. After all, aristocracies and democratic republics were held in low repute or deemed unworkable throughout most of Europe, especially in a large state, and it would seem wisest to take a chance with autocracy. As a dynast, Lomonosov feebly claimed that "the insolence" of a tyrant would be "cut short by death." Tatishchev, the empiricist, considered Ivan IV the single despot and judged that "it would not be sensible to change the former order for such an extraordinary situation." After intense analysis, Boltin concluded: "The ills of a monarchy are ephemeral and light" but "weaknesses in republics are never rectified and remain heavy and lasting"; indeed, "all things considered, it is better to leave things the way they are."[94] Such conclusions were neither reactionary nor even defensive of the status quo. The hope!gleamed among these historians that once Russia had achieved an enlightened population, an enlightened autocrat would establish institutionalized limits on absolute power so that, in the words of an often-quoted political aphorism, the ruler would "have all the power to do good and none to do evil." Such a government was the "last, best hope" of most eighteenth-century Europeans, not just Russians, as they moved from adulation of absolutism to a desire for its constitutional limitation.

Overall, the more the critical spirit of the Enlightenment induced eighteenth-century Russian historians to analyze autocracy, the more they became persuaded that it best suited the country's interests. Their message reached a small but influential audience among the educated elite, who all breathed the same rarefied intellectual air and spoke the same "language."[95] The rulers also shared this climate, and this resulted in a dialogue between autocrat and historian never equalled in Russian history. Peter inspired Lomonosov and Tatishchev with his modernizing, Westernizing vision, and they, both as historians and in their other positions, in turn tried to communicate it to his successors. Historians writing during Catherine's era were all as anxious as she to cooperate in making Russia as "civilized" and up-to-date as the rest of Europe. Throughout the century, the historians' negative pictures of antithetical tsars and positive pictures of ideal rulers fulfilled the didactic purpose of Enlightenment history and invited autocrats to apply current Enlightenment standards to their own reigns.

In the next century, historians no longer enunciated a coherent message concerning autocracy. Nicholas Karamzin urged rulers to stand fast and not to follow the path of constitutional monarchy. Sergei Solov'iev's "state school" of historiography, on the contrary, inherited the eighteenth century's emphasis on evolutionary change from above. Vasilii Kliuchevskii shifted the focus of history almost entirely away from autocrats to socioeconomic issues. The often reactionary nature of late imperial politics led to the negative portrayals of autocracy that have dominated the twentieth century and once again resulted in its equation with despotism.

In contrast, eighteenth-century histories provide evidence that a representative sample of the educated public engaged in a political discourse that reflected a broad consensus. The idea of autocracy, of course, had long been central to Russian political culture and maintained by silent and iconic support based on tradition and religion. But the more modern and secular political context of the eighteenth century fostered a rush to redefine the bases of support. Russians, autocrats included, transformed the idea of autocracy from a static concept into a vital force that could absorb waves of Enlightenment thinking and project a dynamic, rational, Western image. This constant redefining, reinterpreting, perhaps even reinventing of the idea of autocracy was not necessarily cynical or opportunistic; the scope and quality of discourse suggest sincere belief and serious conviction. Moreover, in this process, autocracy served as a centripetal force in society and was seen to embody its ideals and aspirations, in effect taking the place usually assigned to "civil society."

Revolutionary doctrine remained aberrant in the eighteenth century since the educated public, like the historians, believed that fundamental reforms—emancipation and a limited monarchy—were still premature. An activist and enlightened autocrat engineering gradual change seemed to provide a lucid and pragmatic plan for the present and the future. This program was also consonant with the highest political expectations since, translated to Central and Eastern Europe, the French Enlightenment offered a prescription for modernizing and centralizing a state, not liberating mankind. But by the end of the eighteenth century, autocrats began to show signs of falling behind the times and failing to satisfy newer values and visions, and the educated public itself developed into a more disparate and less accommodating group. While these eighteenth-century thinkers may seem naively optimistic, their identification of autocracy with progress and enlightenment became the fundamental problematic of future political thought—the hope of some, the despair of others.

Notes

1. The attitudes of all these groups will be analyzed in my forthcoming book, *The Idea of Autocracy in Eighteenth-Century Russia: Political Discourse and the Rise of Reform Conservatism.* This article, like its companion piece, will focus on the autocrat as a domestic ruler, not as an emperor. See Cynthia H. Whittaker, "The Reforming Tsar: The Redefinition of Autocratic Duty in Eighteenth-Century Russia," *Slavic Review* 51 (Spring 1992): 77–98.

2. The studied manner in which the Russian monarchy worked to elicit such support is a theme in Richard S. Wortman, *Scenarios of Power: Myth and Ceremony in Russian Monarchy,* vol. 1, *From Peter the Great to the Death of Nicholas I* (Princeton, 1995).

3. The three professional historians who were at work in Russia in the century—Gottlieb Baier, Gerhard Müller, and August-Ludwig Shlözer—are not included in this study since they were imported German academicians, and therefore their works would not necessarily reflect Russian perspectives on the autocracy. See, however, A.B. Kamenskii, "Akademik G.F. Miller i russkaia istoricheskaia nauka XVIII veka," *Istoriia SSSR,* 1989, no. 1: 144–59. Also consult S.M. Solov'ev, "Pisateli russkoi istorii XVIII veka," *Arkhiv istoriko-iuridicheskikh svedenii,* 1855, no. 2: 3–82; P.N. Miliukov, *Glavnye techeniia russkoi istoricheskoi mysli* (Moscow, 1897), 17–19, 70–146; and S.A. Peshtich, *Russkaia istoriografiia XVIII veka,* vol. 1 (Leningrad, 1961), 194, 222–62.

4. A.I. Mankiev, *Iadro rossiiskoi istorii* (St. Petersburg, 1770, 1784, 1791, 1799).

5. V.N. Tatishchev, *Istoriia rossiiskaia,* 6 vols. (Moscow, 1768–84), and *Istoriia rossiiskaia,* 7 vols. (Moscow, 1962–68).

6. M.V. Lomonosov, *Kratkii rossiiskii letopisets s rodosloviem* (St. Petersburg, 1759); idem, *Drevniaia rossiiskaia istoriia ot nachala rossiiskago naroda do konchiny velikago kniazia Iaroslava Pervago ili do l054 goda* (St. Petersburg, 1766), written from 1754 to 1758.

7. M.M. Shcherbatov, *Istoriia rossiiskaia ot drevneishikh vremen,* 7 vols. (St. Peters-

burg, 1774–91). The quotation is located in Shcherbatov, *Pis 'mo kniazia Shcherbatova k priiateliu* (Moscow, 1788), 140.

8. I.N. Boltin, *Primechaniia na istoriiu drevniia i nyneshniia Rossii Leklerka,* 2 vols. (St. Petersburg, 1788); idem, *Kriticheskiia primechaniia na istoriu Kn. Shcherbatova,* 2 vols. (St. Petersburg, 1793–94).

9. T.S. Mal'gin, *Zertsalo rossiiskikh gosudarei ot rozhdestva Khristova s 862 po 1791 god* (St. Petersburg, 1791).

10. Catherine II is the only writer of history in this group who is not Russian-born. Ekaterina II, "Zapiski kasatel'no rossiiskoi istorii," *Sobesednik liubitelei rossiiskago slova* 1–11 (1783), and 12–15 (1784). Published anonymously, the "Zapiski" take up roughly seventy pages of each issue of the journal. Catherine followed an outline prepared for her by Professor Kh.A. Chebotarev (1746–1815) of Moscow University, *Vstuplenie v nastoiashchuiu istoriiu o Rossii* (Moscow, 1847). Also consult A.N. Pypin, "Istoricheskie trudy Ekateriny II," *Vestnik Evropy* 5 (September 1901): 170–202, and 6 (December 1901): 760–803.

11. In order of date of birth, they include: V.K. Tred'iakovskii (1703–1769), *Tri razsuzhdeniia o trekh glavneishikh drevnostiakh rossiiskikh* (St. Petersburg, 1773); A.P. Sumarokov (1718–1777), "Kratkaia moskovskaia letopis' (1774)," "Kratkaia istoriia Petra Velikago (n.d.)" and "Streletskii bunt (1768)," *Polnoe sobranie sochinenii* (Moscow, 1781), 6: 161–79, 234–42 and 185–228; I.P. Elagin (1725–1794), *Opyt povestvovaniia o Rossii* (St. Petersburg, 1803); I.S. Barkov (1732–1768), "Sokrashennaia rossiiskaia istoriia," in Gilmar Kuras, *Sokrashennaia universal'naia istoriia* (St. Petersburg, 1762), 357–90; F.A. Emin (1735–70), *Rossiiskaia istoriia* (St. Petersburg, 1767–69); and N.I. Novikov (1744–1818), *Opyt istoricheskago slovaria o rossiiskikh pisateliakh* (St. Petersburg, 1772).

12. I have read, as far as I can judge, all the extant histories. The manuscripts are located in the Archive of the St. Petersburg Institute of History of the Russian Academy of Sciences (SOII), the Library of the Russian Academy of Sciences, St. Petersburg (BRAN), the Manuscript Division of the Russian National Library, Moscow (RO), and the Russian State Archive of Ancient Acts, Moscow (RGADA). I have not included the hundreds of chronologies and genealogies, since they offer little interpretation. I am grateful to Dr. E.B. Beshenkovskii, the Slavic bibliographer of Columbia University, for sharing with me his deep knowledge of these manuscript collections.

13. In the tradition of Pierre Bayle's *Dictionnaire historique et critique* (1697) and J.G. Walch's *Philosophisches Lexicon* (1726), Tatishchev attempted a compendium of knowledge but only reached the entry "kliuchnik." See his *Leksikon rossiiskoi: Istoricheskoi, geograficheskoi, politicheskoi i grazhdanskoi,* 3 vols. (St. Petersburg, 1793). Shcherbatov translated works on legal, ethical and philosophical themes (M. D'iakonov, "Vydaiushchiisia russkii publitsist XVIII veka," *Vestnik prava* 7 [1904]: 1–27). Boltin had a superb library of Enlightenment books and translated the *Encyclopédie* to the letter "k" (V. Iushkov, *Ocherk iz istorii russkago samosoznaniia XVIII-go veka: Obshchie istoricheskie vzgliady I.N. Boltina* [Kiev, 1912]). Elagin was typical in the sources he used and cited: Mably, Rousseau, Robertson, Hume, d'Alembert, Voltaire and Pufendorf (*Opyt,* passim). Edward L. Keenan agrees that Western culture was rapidly assimilated in this century, while Stephen L. Baehr disagrees. See Keenan, "The Trouble with Muscovy: Some Observations upon Problems of the Comparative Study of Form and Genre in Historical Writing," *Medievalia et Humanistica* 5 (1974): 104; and Baehr, *The Paradise Myth in Eighteenth-Century Russia* (Stanford, 1991), xi.

14. Iu.M. Lotman and B.A. Uspenskii, "The Role of Dual Models in the Dynamics of Russian Culture," in *The Semiotics of Russian Culture,* ed. A. Shukman (Ann Arbor, 1984), 35.

15. Emin, *Rossiiskaia istoriia* 1: 1–2.

16. The quotation is found in *Russkaia istoriografiia* (Moscow, 1941): 138. On the broader implications of this topic consult Hans Rogger, *National Consciousness in Eighteenth-Century Russia* (Cambridge, MA, 1960).

17. As quoted in Mankiev, *Iadro, i.* For similar injunctions see "Istoriia rossiiskaia s 1450 po 1617 (c. 1711)," SOII, f. 115, n. 543: 45; and Tatishchev, *Istoriia rossiiskaia* (1962), 1: 81.

18. Lomonosov, "Report (21 June 1750)," *Polnoe sobranie sochinenii* (Moscow, 1952), 6: 79–80; idem, "Zamechaniia na dissertatsiiu G.F. Millera 'Proiskhozhdenie imeni i naroda rossiiskogo'," *PSS* 6: 17–79; idem, *Istoriia,* 173–216. See also Walter Gleason, "The Course of Russian History According to an Eighteenth-Century Layman," *Laurentian University Review* 10 (1977): 17–29. This sensitivity was not confined to Russians; at this time a historian, Fréret, was sent to the Bastille for maintaining that the Franks were not of the Gallic race. See G.P. Gooch, *History and Historians in the Nineteenth Century* (Boston, 1959), 13.

19. Boltin, *Leklerk* 1: 1. See also V.O. Kliuchevskii, "Lektsii po russkoi istoriografii," *Sochineniia* (Moscow, 1959), 426.

20. On this issue, consult Franco Venturi, "History and Reform in the Middle of the Eighteenth Century," in *The Diversity of History,* eds. J.H. Elliott and H.G. Koenigsberger (Ithaca, 1970), 225–44.

21. Voltaire, *Collection complète des oeuvres* (Geneva, 1768–77), 12: 52 ("L'Esprit des Lois de M. Montesquieu"), and 30: 455 ("Sommaire de l'Histoire"). When, in 1756, his *Essai sur les Moeurs et l'Esprit des Nations* went on sale in St. Petersburg, it sold an unprecedented three thousand copies on the first day. See Emile Haumant, *La Culture française en Russie* (Paris, 1910), 110.

22. Whittaker, "The Reforming Tsar," passim.

23. Mal'gin, *Zertsalo,* 3.

24. G. Vasnetskii, *M.V. Lomonosov: Ego filosofskie i sotsial'no-politicheskie vzgliady* (Moscow, 1954), 14–18.

25. Ekaterina II, "Istoricheskoe predstavlenie iz zhizni Riurika: Podrazhenie Shekspiru," *PSS* (St. Petersburg, 1893), 1: 133; Mankiev, *Iadro,* 180–81; Mal'gin, *Zertsalo,* 28

26. Tatishchev, "Kratko iz''atie iz velikikh del Petra Velikogo, Imperatora vserossiiskogo," in P. Pekarskii, "Novye izvestiia o V.N. Tatishcheve," *Zapiski Imperatorskoi Akademii nauk* 4 (1864): 1–19; idem, *Istoriia rossiiskaia* (1962), 1: 87. Also consult A.I. Iukht, "V.N. Tatishchev o reformakh Petra I," *Obshchestvo i gosudarstvo feodal'noi Rossii,* ed. V.T. Pashuto (Moscow, 1975), 209–18. In a similar vein, see Feofan Prokopovich, *Istoriia imperatora Petra Velikago, ot rozhdeniia ego do Poltavskoi batalii* (Moscow, 1788), written at the beginning of the century and not a history but a chronology.

27. Sumarokov, "Streletskii bunt," 179; Mal'gin, *Zertsalo,* 141–43. Mal'gin's entry for Peter the Great, for instance, devoted 95 percent to his domestic deeds, while Lomonosov devoted 95 percent to his military exploits; 95 percent of Mal'gin's entry on Catherine relates to domestic events, and Peter III is condemned for being an "enthusiast for military affairs."

28. Tatishchev, *Istoriia rossiiskaia* (1773), 2: 460.

29. V. Ikonnikov, "Boltin," *Russkii biograficheskii slovar'* (New York: Kraus Reprint, 1962), 3: 188.

30. "Predislovie k istoricheskoi knige, sostavlennoi po poveleniiu Tsaria Fedora Alekseevicha," in E. Zamyslovskii, *Tsarstvovanie Fedora Alekseevicha* (St. Petersburg, 1871), appendix 4: xxxix. See also David Das, "History Writing and the Quest for Fame

in Late Muscovy: Andrei Lyzlov's *History of the Scythians*," *Russian Review* 51 (October 1992): 502–9.

31. Lomonosov, *Istoriia*, 171; idem, "Posviashchenie k pervomu tomu 'Istorii rossiiskoi' V.N. Tatishcheva," *PSS* 6: 15–16. See also P. Hoffmann, "Lomonosov als Historiker," *Jahrbuch für Geschichte der UdSSR und Volksdemokratischen Länden Europas* 5 (1961): 361–73.

32. Tatishchev, *Istoriia rossiiskaia* (1768), 1: i-iv; idem, *Razgovor o pol'ze nauk i uchilishch* (Moscow, 1887), 65 (written in 1733). Also consult Miliukov, *Glavnye techeniia*, 21–30, 122–33.

33. Novikov, *Opyt*, 1–3.

34. See, for instance, Ellen Hurwitz, "Metropolitan Hilarion's Sermon on Law and Grace: Historical Consciousness in Kievan Rus'," *Russian History* 7 (1980): 322–33; and M.N. Tikhomirov, "Razvitie istoricheskikh znanii v Kievskoi Rusi ... X–XVII vv.," in *Ocherki istorii istoricheskoi nauki v SSSR*, ed. M.N. Tikhomirov (Moscow, 1955), 89–105.

35. "Istoriia o nachale russkoi zemle (1760–1761)," RO, f. 735, n. 178: 41–46; "Nashestvie tatar' v Rossiiu i rodoslovie velikikh kniazei rossiiskikh," SOII, f. 36, op. 1: 451–61; "Letopisets, 1222–1555," SOII, f. 36, op 1: 129–440; "Letopisets kratkii do 1659 goda: Sbornik 1754 g.," RO, Rumiantsev, f. 256, n. 374: 252–57; "Kratkii letopisets: Khronograf Dorofeia Monemvasiiskogo (1731)," RO, f. 178, n. 1256: 334–56; "Vypiski iz letopistsa za 1154–1571 gg. (1784–1791)," RO, f. 151: 40–42.

36. The exception was P.A. Zakhar'in (1750–1800), *Novyi sinopsis* (Nikolaev, 1798). But most, often lengthy and laboriously copied, remained in the archives; for instance, "Russkaia istoriia (1758)," SOII, Likhachev, f. 238, n. 1; and "Letopisets rossiiskii (1756)," BRAN, 16.4.1: 1 660.

37. Innokentii Gizel', *Sinopsis* (published in Kiev in 1674, 1678, 1680, and 1683; in St. Petersburg, published twenty-eight times in the eighteenth century and in 1823, 1836, and 1861).

38. On the problems of translating these terms, consult Isabel de Madariaga, "Autocracy and Sovereignty," *Canadian-American Slavic Studies* 16 (Fall–Winter 1982): 369–87, definition on p. 374.

39. However, Montesquieu, in Book 2 of *The Spirit of the Laws*, defines the "three species of government" as republican (under which he subsumes aristocracy and democracy), monarchical, and despotic.

40. John B. Bury, *The Ancient Greek Historians* (New York, 1909), 252.

41. On Tatishchev's contributions, consult S.N. Valk, "V.N. Tatishchev i nachalo novoi russkoi istoricheskoi literatury," *XVIII vek* 7 (1966): 71–72. Boltin, as another example, edited a model edition of *Pravda russkaia* (St. Petersburg, 1792).

42. See, for instance, J.B. Black, *The Art of History: A Study of Four Great Historians of the Eighteenth Century* (New York, 1965); and Preserved Smith, *The Enlightenment, 1687–1776* (New York, 1962), 202–30.

43. "Rodoslovie gosudarei rossiiskikh ot pervoi Riurika do tsaria Feodorova Ivanovicha (c. 1750)," RGADA, f. 187, op. 2, ed. khr. 115: 2. In the archives, there are dozens of lengthy genealogical studies that examine every rivulet of the Riurikid clan. See, for example, "Sbornik: Otryvok iz rodoslovnoi velikikh kniazei i gosudarei do Ekateriny (1776)," RO, f. 218, n.695: 1–114; "Kniga rodoslovnaia (1765)," 4.1.36: 182 pages of graphs; and "Nachalo kniazheniia rossiiskikh kniazei do Elizavetoi Petrovnoi," RO, f. 218, n. 676: 26–52.

44. Mankiev, *Iadro*, 181.

45. D.D. Shampai, "O tirazhakh 'Kratkogo rossiiskogo letopistsa s rodosloviem'," *Literaturnoe tvorchestvo M.V. Lomonosova*, eds. P.N. Berkov and I. Serman (Moscow,

1966), 282–85 (it was published in a run of twenty-four hundred, the largest in the century); J.L. Black, "L'Histoire au service de l'état: Le Synopsis du XVIIe siècle et son héritage historiographique," *Laurentian University Review* 10 (1977): 7–15. While dynastic histories concentrated on the political struggle between autocracy and republicanism in fifteenth-century Novgorod, the ecclesiastical histories were concerned with its flirting with foreign faiths. See "Gistoriia drevniaia rossiiskaia o kniazhei (1756)," BRAN, 16.4.1: 4.

46. Catherine includes all these emendations to Russian history in her "Zapiski," 2: 75, 78–79, 87–89, and in her play, "Istoricheskoe predstavlenie," 120–21. Riurik also began to "speak Slavic" by the end of the century (Zakhar'in, *Novyi sinopsis,* 26; Mal'gin, *Zertsalo,* 2). See also A.S.C. Ross, "Tatishchev's 'Joachim Chronicle'," University of Birmingham Historical Journal 3 (1951): 53–54.

47. "O tsariakh." SOII, f. 36, op. 1, n. 644: 5–31; "Letopisets ot nachala russkoi zemli do tsaria Alekseia Mikhailovicha," RO, f. 310, n. 1283: 5; "Rodoslovnaia kniga velikikh i udel'nykh kniazei: 81 glava s tablitsami (1768)," RGADA, f. 181, op. 1, ed. khr. 176: 1–7.

48. Lomonosov, *Letopisets,* 291–96; idem, *Istoriia,* 214–16. An anonymous historian claimed that Riurik built "over 100 cities." See "O prishestvii velikago kniazia Riurika na veliko novogorodskoe kniazhenie i o velikikh kniazekh i tsarei prezhde byvshikh v Rossii (1768)," BRAN, 31.4.16: 23. See also the classic by I.K. Kirilov, *Tsvetushchee sostoianie vserossiiskogo gosudarstva,* ed. V.A. Rybakov (Moscow, 1977), reprint of version published in 1727–30.

49. Mankiev, *Iadro,* xi-xii.

50. Lomonosov, *Letopisets,* 300, 319. Alexander Radishchev's preoccupation with Novgorod is evident in his historical jottings ("K rossiiskoi istorii," *Polnoe sobranie sochinenii* [Moscow, 1952], 3:31–40).

51. "Razsuzhdenie o rossiiskoi i rimskoi pravitel'stvakh," SOII, f. 17, n. 343; E.K. Putnyn', *Istoki russkoi istoriografii antichnosti: M.V. Lomonosov, A.N. Radishchev* (Saratov, 1968); Allen McConnell, "Radishchev and Classical Antiquity," *Canadian-American Slavic Studies* 16 (Fall–Winter 1982): 469–90; Stephen L. Baehr, "From History to National Myth: *Translatio imperii* in Eighteenth-Century Russia," *Russian Review* 27 (January 1978): 1–14.

52. Lomonosov, *Istoriia,* 171, 214–16, 220.

53. "Istoriia russkaia (c. 1750)," BRAN, 32.13.1: 372–671. Another allots 138 of its 213 pages to Peter. See "Drevniaia rossiiskaia istoriia do 1710 goda (1786)," SOII, f. 11, ed. khr. 19. One anonymous author began in the style of an ecclesiastical history but then, as if unable to suppress himself, spent the rest of the manuscript recounting Peter's deeds ("Russkaia istoriia svodnaia [c. 1750]," BRAN, 25.1.3: 42–179). See also Mankiev, *Iadro,* 383–84.

54. Lomonosov is quoted in F.Ia. Priima, "Lomonosov i 'Istoriia rossiiskoi imperii pri Petre Velikom Voltera," *XVII vek* 3 (1958): 183. On Lomonosov's political views, which were quite unsophisticated despite his being tutored by Christian Wolff, consult A.A. Morozov, "M.V. Lomonosov i teleologiia Kristiana Vol'fa," *Literaturnoe tvorchestvo M.V. Lomonosova,* 163–96; M.I. Sukhomlinov, "Lomonosov—student Marburgskogo universiteta," *Russkii vestnik* 31 (1861): 127–65; and Walter Gleason, "The Two Faces of the Monarch: Legal and Mythical Fictions in Lomonosov's Ruler Imagery," *Canadian-American Slavic Studies* 16 (1982): 399–409.

55. On Emin's strange career, consult E.B. Beshenkovskii, "Zhizn' Fedora Emina," *XVIII vek* 11 (1976): 186–203; and idem, "Istoriograficheskaia sud'ba 'Rossiiskoi istorii' F.A. Emina," *Istoriia i istoriki* (Moscow, 1973).

56. Peter the Great, though, was Tatishchev's original inspiration for writing history

as well. See P. Znamenskii, "Tatishchev i ego istoriia," *Trudy Kievskoi dukhovnoi akademii* 1 (1862): 197–228. These "Events" have received varied interpretations over the past 270 years. Consult the bibliographical essay by David Ransel, "Political Perceptions of the Russian Nobility: The Constitutional Crisis of 1730," *Laurentian University Review* 3 (1972): 20–38.

57. Tatishchev, *Istoriia rossiiskaia* (1962), 1: 359.

58. S.C. Feinstein, "V.N. Tatishchev and the Development of the Concept of State Service in Petrine and Post-Petrine Russia" (Ph.D. diss., New York University, 1971). Tatishchev acknowledged his debt to the pioneers of "scientific" methods, such as Bacon, Descartes, Newton, Locke, and Fontenelle, plus Grotius and Pufendorf.

59. Tatishchev, *Razgovor,* 136–37; idem, *Istoriia rossiiskaia* (1962), 1: 362, 371. In *Russia Under Catherine the Great,* vol. 2 (Newtonville, 1978), 18–19, the editor, Paul Dukes, claims that Tatishchev influenced Montesquieu in this view.

60. S. Pufendorf, *L'Introduction á l'histoire générale . . . oùl'on voit . . . les interêts des souverains* (Amsterdam, 1743), translated into Russian and published in 1718, 1723, 1767, and 1777.

61. Tatishchev, *Istoriia rossiiskaia* (1962), 1: 359–61; idem, *Razgovor,* 135–40; idem, "Proizvol'noe i soglasnoe razsuzhdenie i mnenie sobravshegosia shliakhetstva russkogo o pravlenii gosudarstvennom," *Utro* (1859): 371. See also Emin, *Istoriia* 1: x. For a negative interpretation of "paternalism" in Russian thinking consult E.V. Anisimov, *The Reforms of Peter the Great: Progress through Coercion in Russia* (Armonk, 1993), 32–36.

62. Mankiev, *Iadro,* 18–27; Tatishchev, *Istoriia rossiiskaia* (1963), 2: 33–34; Emin, *Istoriia* 1: 38–39.

63. "Drevniaia rossiiskaia istoriia do 1710 goda (1786)," SOII, f. 11, ed. khr. 19: 35.

64. "Russkaia letopis' s drevneishikh vremen do 1700 g. (1741)," RGADA, f. 181, op. 1, ed. khr. 358: 707.

65. Tatishchev, *Istoriia rossiiskaia* (1963), 2: 33–34; Emin, *Istoriia* 1: 38–39; "Russkaia istoriia ot Riurika do Ekateriny (c. 1735)," BRAN, 32.6.1: 1–16.

66. Tatishchev, "Razsuzhdenie," 369–79; idem, *Istoriia rossiiskaia* (1962), 1: 87; idem, "Kratkoe iz''iatie," 18–19; Emin, *Istoriia* 1: 27.

67. Tatishchev, *Istoriia rossiiskaia* (1768), 1: 18, and (1963), 2: 137–43.

68. The latest assessment of Peter III's reign is Carol S. Leonard, *Reform and Regicide* (Bloomington, IN, 1993).

69. The question of whether there were limitations on the tsar's power has its own long history. See, for instance, Daniel Rowland, "Did Muscovite Literary Ideology Place Limits on the Power of the Tsar (1540s–1660s)?" *Russian Review* 49 (April 1990): 125–55.

70. Boltin, *Leklerk* 2: 471. See also V.S. Ikonnikov, *Istoricheskie trudy Boltina* (St. Petersburg, 1902), 18–20. He attacked Nicholas LeClerc, *Histoire physique, morale, civile, et politique de la Russie ancienne et moderne,* 6 vols. (Paris, 1783–94), which was based on P.S. Levecque, *Histoire de Russie,* 5 vols. (Paris, 1782–83).

71. Ekaterina II, "Zapiski," 1: 105; idem, "Mnenie Gosudaryni Ekateriny II o tom, kak dolzhno pisat' russkuiu istoriiu," *Russkii vestnik* 5 (1816): 3–11. Boltin agreed: "Read through the past centuries of all kingdoms and of all republics and you will find the same behavior, conduct, and actions. . . . Virtue and vice belong to all ages and to all nations," and to both sexes, he added, when someone tried to claim that female monarchs are more kindly and moderate than male ones: "Women are simply people and have the same virtues and the same vices" (Boltin, *Leklerk* 2: 1, 82–87, 172–73, 423–24).

72. Boltin, *Leklerk* 1: 306–10, and 2: 17. Michael Cherniavsky makes much the same argument in "Ivan the Terrible as Renaissance Prince," *Slavic Review* 27 (1968): 195–211.

73. Shcherbatov, *Istoriia* (1794), 1: xv, 280–81, and (1805), 2: 257. Please see

Anthony Lentin, "Introduction," *Prince M.M. Shcherbatov: On the Corruption of Morals in Russia* (Cambridge, Eng., 1969), 1–102; and Joan M. Afferica, "The Political and Social Thought of Prince M.M. Shcherbatov" (Ph.D. diss, Harvard University, 1966), 144–212.

74. Paul Bushkovitch, "The Formation of a National Consciousness in Early Modern Russia," *Harvard Ukrainian Studies* 10 (December 1986): 363–74.

75. Shcherbatov, *Istoriia* (1783), 2: 541–42;(1786), 5, pt. 2: 111; (1790) 6: 50–53; and (1790) 7, pt. 1: 262–64; idem, *Istoriia rossiiskaia* (1766), BRAN, 45.8.268: 9. On Shcherbatov's aristocratic bias, consult A. Fedosov, *Iz istorii russkoi obshchestvennoi mysli XVIII stoletiia: M.M. Shcherbatov* (Moscow, 1967), 44–68; and L.V. Cherepnin, *Russkaia istoriografiia do XIX veka* (Moscow, 1957), 218–35.

76. Shcherbatov, "Razsmotrenie o porokakh i samovlastii Petra Velikago," *Chteniia v Imperatorskom Obshchestve istorii i drevnostei rossiiskikh* (1860): 8–9, 14, 19.

77. Shcherbatov, *Istoriia* (1790), 7: 131, and (1794), 1: n.p.

78. The quotations are Elagin's, *Opyt* 1:81, 166–67. Similar sentiments are expressed in "Istoriia rossiiskaia ot Ivana Groznogo do kontsa XVII veka," SOII, f. 115, ed. khr. 91: 80; "Ob izbranie na tsarskii prestol Mikhaila Feodorovicha," SOII, f. 36, op. 1, n. 645: 107–9; Boltin, *Shcherbatov* 1: 230–31; and idem, *Leklerk* 1: 250–51, and 2: 289–90, 464, 471–75.

79. Shcherbatov, *Istoriia* (1794), 1: 191–92, 225, and (1805), 2: 5; Boltin, *Shcherbatov* 1: 176–78. For Boltin's views on Vladimir see *Otvet general maiora Boltina na pis'mo kniazia Shcherbatova* (St. Petersburg, 1789), 129–30; E.A. Bolkhovitinov (Mitropolit Evgenii, 1767–1837), *Istoricheskoe obozrenie rossiiskago zakonopolozheniia* (St. Petersburg, 1826); v (orig. ed. 1797); and Chebotarev, *Vstuplenie,* 19.

80. Chebotarev, *Vstuplenie,* 4; Boltin, *Leklerk* 2: 476–78.

81. Boltin, *Leklerk* 1: 316–18, and 2: 22–23, 104, 172, 206–9, 233–37, 251, 254–55, 330, 360–62. Cherepnin, for instance, had difficulties fitting Boltin into Marxist categories because of this large landowner's sympathetic views on the serf question (*Istoriografiia,* 237–46).

82. Elagin, "Opyt povestvovaniia o Rossii (1790)," RGADA, f. 181, ed. khr. 34, pt. 1: 1–28.

83. Zakhar'in, *Novyi sinopsis,* v.

84. This handing over of the sceptre, with "Godunov looking on with envious eyes," is one of the great "moments of Russian history" that Lomonosov thought should be depicted in painting ("Idei dlia zhivopisnykh kartin iz rossiiskoi istorii," *PSS* 6: 371).

85. "Rodoslovie gosudarei rossiiskikh ot pervoi Riurika do tsaria Feodorova Ivanovicha (c. 1750)," RGADA, f. 187, op. 2, ed. khr. 115: 4; Mankiev, *Iadro,* 210–31, 264, 271, 236, 328; "Russkaia letopis' s drevneishikh vremen do 1700 g. (1741)," RGADA, f. 181, op. 1, ed. khr. 358: 1117; "Kratkoe ob''iavlenie o samoderzhavtsakh rossiiskikh (1759)," RGADA, f. 1274, op. 1, n. 3016: 20–30; Barkov, *Istoriia,* 372–75.

86. "Russkaia letopis' s drevneishikh vremen do 1700 g. (1741), RGADA, f. 181, op. 1, ed. khr. 358: 1176–1255; Lomonosov, "Opisanie streletskikh buntov i pravleniia tsarevny Sof'i," *PSS* 6: 100–131. On Sophia's reign consult Lindsey Hughes, *Sophia: Regent of Russia, 1657–1704* (New Haven, 1990).

87. Sumarokov, "Bunt," 192–97, 205, 218–19.

88. Tatishchev, *Istoriia rossiiskaia* (1962), 1: 366–67. See also Emin, *Istoriia* 2: 522.

89. D.A. Korsakov, "Artemii Petrovich Volynskii i ego 'konfidenty," *Russkaia starina* 10 (1885): 28. Tatishchev made his argument in four places: *Istoriia rossiiskaia* (1962), 1: 366–68 and (1964), 4: passim; *Razgovor,* 138–39; and "Razsuzhdenie," 370–73. On his commitment to enlightenment, see *Istoriia rossiiskaia* (1963), 2: 78–81; and

the thorough discussion in Feinstein, "Tatishchev," 77–132. In contrast, the older ecclesiastical histories were more concerned about the threat of Roman Catholicism replacing Russian Orthodoxy if Poland had succeeded in conquering Russia. See "Istoriia rossiiskaia (1740)," BRAN, 16.13.6: 396–419; "Gistoriia drevnyia rossiiskaia o kniazhei (1756)," BRAN, 16.4.1: 81–96; and "Istoriia rossiiskaia (1715)," RO, n. 4698: 106 245.

90. Shcherbatov, *Istoriia* (1786), 5, pt. 3: 217. Another historian who shared Shcherbatov's views devoted 312 pages of a 675–page narrative to the "Tsar-Tormentor" ("O samoderzhavstve gosudarei tsarei vseia Rossii (1768)," BRAN, 31.4.16, II: 45–367.

91. Mankiev, *Iadro,* 190; "Istoriia rossiiskaia (1740)," BRAN, 16.13.6: 386.

92. Shcherbatov, *Istoriia* (1786), 5, pt. 2: 91, 287–89, and pt. 3: 222–23.

93. Boltin, *Leklerk* 2: 467–71, 476–78, 522–23. Mal'gin quotes Boltin's condemnation word for word but adds that he was just as bad as Ivan the Terrible (*Zertsalo,* 117).

94. Lomonosov, *Istoriia,* 233; Tatishchev, "Razsuzhdenie," 373; Boltin, *Leklerk* 2: 476–78, 355.

95. Their works began appearing in 1755 during the publication explosion of the last half of the century and were usually published in runs of 600, 1,200, or 2,400. Readership figures are not available, but they are probably small. See Gary Marker, *Publishing, Printing, and the Origins of Intellectual Life in Russia, 1700–1800* (Princeton, 1985); and Frederick Starr, "The Russian Empire and the Printed Word" (paper delivered at the University Seminar on Slavic History and Culture, Columbia University, NY, 19 October 1973). For a definition of "language" in semiotic terms, see B.A. Uspenskii, "Historia sub specie semioticae," in *Soviet Semiotics,* ed. Daniel P. Lucid (Baltimore, 1977), 107–8.

3

In the Forge of Criticism
M.T. Kachenovskii and Professional Autonomy in Pre-Reform Russia

Allison Y. Katsev

Professionalization has served as a prism through which historians of imperial Russia in recent years have examined one of the central problems of prerevolutionary history: the relations of autonomy and dependence between an emerging civil society and the state. Professions are defined by sociologists as self-governing entities, controlling access into their fields and the standards of behavior of their members. In theory, then, professionals, like civil society, create new spheres of activity outside state control. Yet historians have found that the historical relationship between professionals and autonomy is far more complex than that predicted by sociological models. Even in the paradigmatic Anglo-American case, professionals looked to the state to bolster their authority. In Europe, including Russia, the state often played a fundamental role in the creation of professions, establishing the institutions that educated would-be professionals and providing them with employment within the bureaucracy. In such circumstances, the state might be seen by professionals at least as much as a force for liberalization and modernization as a source of interference in the development of professional autonomy.[1]

Although Russia's particular experience of professional autonomy is most often analyzed for possible connections to the Revolution of 1917, the process of professionalization can reveal as much about how Russia worked as it can about why it ultimately fractured. Historians have asked why, unlike in America and England, professionals in late imperial Russia did not become potent political forces influential enough to extract democratic political reform from the autocracy and avert the descent into revolution.[2] From this perspective, the subtleties of the relationship between autonomy and dependence are much less important than the fact that more of the latter meant less of the former. However, many studies of the professions in the late imperial era, including those by historians who insist that such anomalies contributed to Russia's failure to reform peacefully, have indicated that for professionals the lines between state and professional interests were often blurred. Members of the professions themselves were a heterogeneous group, with some supporting the autocracy, many working for the state, many finding local organs of self-government no more democratic than the centralized bureaucracy, and at least a few hoping to gain through the civil service the status denied to them by the leading professionals of their own fields.[3] As the last example suggests, the striving for professional autonomy itself involved complex motivations. Support for professional autonomy did not necessarily translate into a recognition of every individual's right to personal autonomy. In fact, despite their often liberal point of view concerning the ideal relationship between profession and state, many professionals shared with the state a paternalistic understanding of their relationship to the people, whom they saw as innocents, unable to act as autonomous agents, upon whom projects for social improvement could be enacted.[4] Perhaps this shared frame of reference enabled professionals to develop an identity based on service, one that historians have argued combined new ideals of service to the people with the traditional values of service to the state.[5] These diverse career paths, ideologies, and worldviews, all potentially encompassed under the rubric of "service," suggest that the historical actors' experiences and understandings of professional autonomy and state dependence are not reducible to a zero-sum game.

In this article, I argue that in pre-reform Russia dependence on the state and a desire for professional autonomy were experienced as complementary—not contradictory—forces.[6] I will explore how, at a time when professional identities were only beginning to take shape, one educated Russian experienced and manipulated the possibilities for autonomy and dependence in his attempts to create a space for himself as a historian. As editor of a leading journal of his time and professor of Russian history at Moscow University from 1821 to 1835, M.T. Kachenovskii was positioned at the crossroads of many possible identities as a historian. Although the phenomenon of the professionalization of Russian historians as a group has not been studied, research on the related issue of the development of historical thought indicates that this period was one in which historians were just beginning to define their field.[7] At the same time, the country had yet to undergo peasant emancipation and the legal and administrative reforms that in the 1860s were to promise new possibilities for organized professional activity outside state institutions and control. Russia in this period would thus seem to offer limited opportunities for politically acceptable social roles not bound by traditional ties of service to the state.[8] In these circumstances, what role did Kachenovskii find it possible to demarcate for the historian, and what forces led him to do so?

I answer these questions by closely analyzing two contentious episodes during which Kachenovskii felt compelled to stake his claim to the authority to practice history. My interest in periods of conflict is twofold. At these moments Kachenovskii provided his clearest definitions of the historian. At the same time, his statements emerged in the course of cultural debates and against the backdrop of major political events. An analysis of the contexts in which Kachenovskii refined his representations of the historian reveals a great deal about the process of professionalization in Russia. First of all, I determine what tensions provoked in Kachenovskii the desire to bolster his legitimacy. In response to whose encroachments did he seek autonomy? Second, I uncover the ways in which the process itself influenced his conceptions. The sociologist Pierre Bourdieu has argued that the polemical moment does more than provide the forum and the necessity for expressing one's previously unstated beliefs. The polemic itself establishes categories and principles in relation to which all participants now define themselves.[9] Kachenovskii's struggles in the heat of battle to delineate authoritative boundaries for his field shed light not only on the resulting definition of the historian but also on the battle itself. His steps toward articulating a professional identity not only expand our understanding of the evolution of the historical profession but also reveal effective constraints and opportunities that linked members of professions with state and society in pre-reform Russia.

Opportunities for Autonomy and Dependence in Pre-Reform Russia

The ambiguous status of the historian in the institutions in which Kachenovskii worked and the controversial content of his writings provided him with ample opportunities and motives for articulating the sources of his legitimacy. As a champion of a radical revision of Russia's understanding of its past, Kachenovskii was forced to define and defend his credentials. In his most well-known historical writing, published in 1829, he called into question the authenticity of one of the most fundamental manuscripts from Russia's ancient past. Rejecting a patriotism that demanded the sacrifice of historical truth, Kachenovskii asked that Russians follow the example of "our enlightened Europe" and subject *Russkaia pravda,* Russia's oldest code of laws, to the "crucible of criticism." This process, he insisted, would clearly reveal as myth the purported origins and author of *Russkaia pravda.*[10] For almost a decade, he and his students expanded on this claim, asserting that in its childhood Russia lacked the level of culture necessary to produce accurate historical documents. Kachenovskii came to be considered the father of what was dubbed by others the "Skeptical School."

On whose authority did Kachenovskii rely to make such controversial, and as it turned out historically incorrect, statements? Historiographers offer conflicting answers, which in large part reflect their own understandings of the relationship between scientific and social progress. Although Cynthia Whittaker has demonstrated that in the eighteenth century an embrace of "the critical spirit of the Enlightenment" only strengthened historians' conviction of the necessity of the autocracy,[11] most historiographers equate Kachenovskii's use of criticism with an assault on state authority. They assert that he made a significant contribution to the progress of the historical sciences through his advocacy of the principle of criticism. Prerevolutionary writers interpreted this methodological stance in terms of a battle between patriotic and scientific history; Soviet authors contrasted "official-monarchist" and "bourgeois" history.[12] However, the pre-revolutionary historian S.M. Solov'ev insisted that Kachenovskii's critical attitude had no political content, stressing instead his moderate qualities as a scholar and his conservativeness as a subject of the Russian Empire and a Christian. The Soviet scholar A.G. Kuz'min highlighted the evidence of Kachenovskii's subservience to his superiors at Moscow University, concluding that the autocracy's loyal subject played no role in furthering criticism, historical or otherwise.[13] In Kachenovskii, historiographers have found evidence of both the proto-professional historian and the dutiful state servant.

These opposing interpretations reflect not only the conflicting agendas of the writers but also the myriad uncertainties inherent in the settings in which Kachenovskii wrote history and described his work as a historian. Born in 1775, the son of a wine trader, and having served in the army for a decade, in 1805 Kachenovskii began his affiliation with the two institutions that were to dominate his intellectual life. In that year, he began working at Moscow University. After receiving master's and doctoral degrees, he remained at the university, first teaching fine arts and archeology. In 1821 he received the chair in Russian history, statistics, and geography, where he remained until he was transferred to the newly established chair in the history of Slavic languages and literature in 1835. He also filled various administrative posts, including rector, the position he held in the years before his death in 1842.[14] In 1805 Kachenovskii also became the editor of *Vestnik Evropy,* the journal founded by the writer and historian N.M. Karamzin. For twenty-five years, Kachenovskii's views reached the general public through this forum. Here he participated in polemics both historical and literary.[15]

The pages of Russian journals capture contemporary ambivalence concerning the legitimate activities of the historian. Historiographers generally depict the 1820s as representing the very beginning of a shift toward a narrower definition of history as science. The great literary figure Karamzin was finishing his immensely influential magnum opus, *The History of the Russian State,* and a new crop of historical researchers was to demand that historical works adhere to rigorous, scientific criteria.[16] At the same time, the very definitions of "science" and "scientific history" were also in flux. Historians of Russia commonly trace the origins of a "modern" conception of science in general and of the historical sciences in particular to the first half of the nineteenth century, with its triumph coming only after the 1850s.[17] Was the historian to be a collector or a theoretician? Should his work serve a moral function, or did he pursue truth for its own sake?[18] This lack of a precise definition and boundaries for the study of history created the space for a boom in "historical" works representing a multitude of genres, methodologies, and agendas. Journals, including Kachenovskii's, were the main vehicle for evaluating and presenting to the public these diverse and often competing narratives.

The university epitomizes a different set of ambiguities—not over who had the right to call himself a historian, but rather over who gave him that right. The professor of history had clear grounds for considering himself a historian. But who made him professor? The university could be seen as symbolizing the sanction of either the state or the scholarly community, for in this institution the two were intertwined. For almost the entirety of Kachenovskii's career the university enjoyed a degree of independence that distinguished it not only from other state institutions of the pre-reform era but also from the university itself during most of the post-reform era.[19] From 1804 through 1835 Moscow University, though formally under the control of the Ministry of Education, was almost entirely autonomous. The faculty chose new professors and elected from among its ranks the departmental deans and the rector, the highest official on the school grounds. The rector, the deans, and other professors were in charge of educational, administrative, and internal judicial matters. In addition, the university administered the local school districts. However, autonomy in practice did not equal formal independence. A ministerially appointed and imperially approved superintendent was assigned to each university. Although the superintendent lived in St. Petersburg and exercised little day-to-day control over his district, all appointments, from school director to professor to rector, had to gain his official approval. In addition, Moscow University owed both its existence, since 1755, and its unusual privileges, as presented in the University Charter of 1804, to the benevolence of the autocrat. And, most significantly, professors were members of the state civil service, awarded rank and title in the manner of other bureaucrats.[20] Kachenovskii's long career at this academic institution can be interpreted as reflecting either his acceptance of the authority of the state or his desire for autonomy as a scholar.

Kachenovskii's navigation of these intersections of possible professional identities illuminates the ways that conceptions of autonomy and dependence shaped the process of professionalization in pre-reform Russia. Uncertainty can be a source of opportunity or anxiety. Although the lack of clarity concerning the historian's work and credentials created the space for a range of "historians," it also engendered the countervailing desire to silence opposing voices and establish one kind of history as authentic. As Kachenovskii sought to legitimize his own work, which voices and which ambiguities did he perceive as threats? Whose authority did he seek to marginalize, and whose sanction did he embrace?

The Historian's Sphere of Competence

Kachenovskii's first steps toward claiming for the historian a privileged status, free from at least some types of interference, took the form of critiques of Russia's most venerated writer of history of the time, Nikolai Karamzin (1766–1826). Karamzin was one of the leading Russian cultural figures of his day. In addition to sentimentalist poetry and prose, Karamzin also wrote penetrating analyses of Russia's past and present. In letters and essays, he asserted that his country's strengths lay in political autocracy and cultural enlightenment. Profoundly affected by the French Revolution and the ensuing terror, he insisted that Russia remain faithful to its traditional form of government. He did not, however, advocate the arbitrary use of power. Russia's rulers were morally obligated to insure both the security and the spiritual and intellectual development of their subjects.[21] In 1803 these views conformed to the goals of the young emperor, Alexander I, and Karamzin was made the state's historiographer. His mission was to write his country's history. The first eight volumes of his *History of the Russian State* were published in 1816, with another four volumes released before his death in 1826.[22] The debates that followed the publication of this work were some of the most heated of the era.

Why did Karamzin's *History* provoke Kachenovskii to articulate his vision of the legitimate historical enterprise? The task of sorting out Kachenovskii's motives, or those of any of Karamzin's critics, is complicated both by the diversity of issues that converged in this debate and by the tendency among contemporaries and later historians to conflate often distinctly different concerns.[23] Politically, Karamzin was a hero to conservatives who appreciated his status as official state "historiographer," as well as his historical narrative's underlying message that autocracy was a definitive feature of Russia. At the same time, for many of his literary defenders Karamzin personified enlightenment. He had waged the battle for the modernization of the Russian language, and now he had discovered Russia's past both for the Russian public and for Western Europeans. More fundamentally, he embodied the qualities of the ideal Russian, "honestly fulfilling his civil obligations."[24] In addition, discussion of Russian enlightenment was itself highly politicized during the late 1810s and early 1820s. At that time, Alexander I became enthralled with the mystic and increasingly obscurantist Russian Bible Society.[25] Karamzin's condemnation of despotic tsars, especially in later volumes, was read by some as an implicit criticism of the official attack on enlightenment. Therefore, both contemporaries and later historians have speculated that attacks on Karamzin during those years carried official sanction, despite his status as state "historiographer."[26]

For researchers of Russia's past both Karamzin's methodology and his depiction of ancient Russia posed threats to an emerging consensus among some concerning the best way to write history. Taking advantage of his exceptional access to archives as state historiographer, Karamzin wanted to give Russians a history that would be fascinating.[27] He believed that, although the historian should not lie, he should emphasize those parts of the past that are interesting and spend little time on the boring. And where sources were scarce, he was not above embellishing a bit in order to inspire his readers and give them some food for thought. In addition, Karamzin readily attributed to Russia's ancient princes the concerns and consciousness of modern emperors. He thereby rejected what had become a fundamental tenet among many who studied Russia's past: Russia had undergone historical development and therefore its level of culture in its infancy could not be equal to that of the present.[28] Researchers criticized the work for being too literary, for departing from the sources, and for following the sources too faithfully without using critical methods.[29] As conceptions of scientific history changed, so did the charges against Karamzin. By the mid-1820s, with the rise of Romanticism, he was faulted for failing to appreciate the unique forces originating in Russian *narodnost'* (nationality).[30] With all three thousand copies of the first edition of Karamzin's

History selling out within a month, those who did not approve of his work had good reason to fear its influence. Even Russians who did not actually read his *History* would have encountered this version of Russia's past in books, in plays, and in school. According to Joseph Black, Karamzin became "the standard authority of Russian history until the 1850s."[31]

The contentiousness of criticism itself at this time added another layer of meaning to the polemics surrounding *The History of the Russian State.* At issue were the definition and function of criticism in Russian literary life. Although criticism was clearly a central feature of the Enlightenment, some proponents of Russian enlightenment were wary. As Kachenovskii's predecessor at *Vestnik Evropy,* Karamzin set an oft-cited example when he insisted that criticism was a luxury that Russian literature could not yet afford and that would have no place in his journal. While criticism might help to educate the readers, to Karamzin and others Russia's forays into the world of art and literature remained too fragile to withstand attack.[32] Clearly, debates over criticism concerned what path to take to reach a common goal, that of an enlightened society. But the polemics also touched on a more fundamental issue. As William Todd suggests, as they argued about the role of criticism, Russians were struggling over how their society would look once it reached its goal. Would it reflect the manners, the style, and the language of the literary salon, a setting that admitted only polite talk among friends? Or would it accept a different standard of behavior, signaling the growing dominance of new, nonaristocratic values among educated Russians?[33]

In this volatile confluence of issues, Kachenovskii became something of a lightning rod when he published in 1818 one of the first critiques of Karamzin's *History.* Karamzin's defenders responded by assailing his right to criticize.[34] Although Kachenovskii was by no means the only critic of the *History of the Russian State,* Karamzin's most ardent supporters reserved some of their most virulent assaults for him.[35] The poet and literary critic P.A. Viazemskii charged that Kachenovskii was a "zoilus" (envious, spiteful critic). He satirized Kachenovskii in a biting six-page poem, which included the following:

> Let the Zoilus trade in tedium and lies,
> Powerless to defeat the mature fruit of mature abilities, . . .
> Let this appraiser of words and expert on the alphabet,
> From the professor's podium pick at a labor of the intellect,
> Like a mouse who has turned grey in the corner of a dusty archive,
> Now gnawing on charters with an over-scrupulous fury.[36]

The war of epigrams and poems waged against him was so effective that some Russians avoided criticizing Karamzin solely out of fear that they would be associated with Kachenovskii.[37]

Although contemporaries and later historians have attributed a variety of meanings to the Karamzin polemics and to Kachenovskii's participation in them, the evidence does not suggest that Kachenovskii's critiques represented a sally for political or cultural conservatism. While officials in the newly created Ministry of Education and Religious Affairs may have approved of attacks on Karamzin's work, assertions that Kachenovskii published his reviews of the Historiographer in order to ingratiate himself with the authorities are unjustified.[38] Proof of this is his response to a request in 1817 by the university's superintendent that he tailor his journal to the teachings of the Bible Society's ideologues. He recounted in a letter to a friend his response to his superior: "[If I were to do so,] then I would be outside of my own field of competence (*vzialsia by ne za svoe delo*), and theological scholars would laugh at me as an ignoramus."[39] In the early 1820s, when some of the Bible Society's most ardent proponents began attacking both learning and mysticism as threats to the state and the Orthodox Church, Kachenovskii implicitly challenged in print this revised version of quasi-official obscurantism. In response to an unnamed critic who accused a scholar of spreading heretical ideas, Kachenovskii insisted that the critic had overstepped his bounds by presuming to comment on questions of morality.[40] Kachenovskii nowhere indicated any sympathy with the antienlightenment policies of the regime.

In fact, as an editor Kachenovskii, like Karamzin, consistently championed enlightenment, although unlike his predecessor at *Vestnik Evropy,* he almost immediately embraced the principle of criticism as well. From the moment he began writing for the public, Kachenovskii proclaimed himself a defender of enlightenment. In 1804 he described what he saw as the challenge facing his country: "The wholesome tree of enlightenment, transplanted from foreign climates to our beloved fatherland, has already sprouted deep roots; ... and we will see young branches covered with flowers—but fruit? ... Let's hope so."[41] Constantly confronted with criticism as an editor, Kachenovskii was forced to take a position on the critic's role in furthering Russia's enlightenment.[42] Although at first ambivalent about the value of criticism, beginning in the late 1810s he began touting "scholarly criticism" as distinguished from uninformed and ill-intentioned polemics.[43] Rejecting Karamzin's argument that criticism endangered Russia's progress, Kachenovskii institutionalized a section on *Kritika* in the journal that Karamzin had founded.[44] By the time of the Karamzin debates, Kachenovskii had long defended the principle of "criticism" by aligning it with "scholarliness" and "enlightenment."

When Kachenovskii waged his battle with Karamzin in the late 1810s, he did not invoke the authority of politics or tradition, but rather the principles of modern scholarship.[45] Certainly, this stance itself might imply a political agenda, with a critique of Karamzin's obsolete historywriting standing in for a critique of the autocracy that Karamzin supported.[46] The next section will deal with Kachenovskii's abiding attitudes toward the state, as articulated in other debates. In his discussions of the *History of the Russian State,* however, he employed only the weapons of the researcher. Faced with the dual threat of Karamzin and his defenders, Kachenovskii fortified his right to criticize both the documents and the Historiographer. He did so by defining what he called the historian's *delo* (mission, sphere of competence) so that it excluded the work of Karamzin. When he first challenged Karamzin's *History* in 1817–19, he indicated that recounting Russia's past was not the only requirement for the historian. In an essay that he had written as an outline for a textbook he never published, he spoke of a different kind of narrator, the "annalist" (*deepisatel'*).[47] Russia's first chroniclers were such annalists, resorting to their imaginations when they lacked reliable information. "[G]iven the present state of historical sciences, such a method of satisfying curiosity is justly considered unworthy of well-intentioned readers and disgraceful for the historian."[48] Although Kachenovskii did not mention Karamzin, the knowing readers of the day would have inferred to whom that comment was addressed. Kachenovskii made this connection somewhat more explicit in 1818. Taking issue with Karamzin on his description of a building, he insisted that citing Russia's ancient and sainted chronicler, Nestor, did not constitute proof. Even if historians could be sure that they possessed an exact copy of the original manuscript, even if they could be certain that they were quoting Nestor himself, the document would need to be subjected to "the purgatory of higher historical criticism." Nestor, after all, influenced by "the spirit of his times, could err. We, people of the nineteenth century, should know many things better than literate Kievans, who knew only what they could learn from the Byzantines."[49] According to Kachenovskii, contemporary theories of criticism demanded that even the word of Russia's most sacred chronicler be questioned. This in turn required that historians rely on the modern tool of their trade, that is, criticism.

Kachenovskii elucidated the relationship between the historian's *delo* and criticism later that year in his review of Karamzin's *History.* Before any histories could be written, he asserted, the sources must be "cleaned" by criticism. Although the historian might not perform this task himself, Kachenovskii implied that a scholarly historian would recognize his dependence on the critic. Kachenovskii remarked, it seems with tongue in cheek, that work that was "tedious to the historian" might be fascinating to the "restorer of texts, the critic, in that it will not only bring him pleasure but *glory*; it will make him famous if not to the entire public, then at least to the scholarly world, and some people treasure such glory more than the praises of . . . brilliant wags and semi-literate people." It was the historian's obligation to enlighten the public by bringing to their attention only "cleaned sources."[50] Not every historian had to be an expert in source criticism, but without criticism there could be no historians.

Even if he began with cleaned texts, the historian would still need to employ his critical faculties to elicit from the documents an authentic history. The historian, Kachenovskii claimed, was "neither novelist nor epic poet." The historian entertained his readers not through invention and exaggeration, but through the truth. This truth did not consist of "a chronicle or a journal of daily events, in which one puts all kinds of things." History must have "unity," "a plan," "completeness, a systematic arrangement of its parts." History would be true, and thus fascinating, when it included only "what was relevant to the *delo*, . . . only what was essentially necessary." When Kachenovskii then took issue with Karamzin's periodization of Russian history, he suggested that Karamzin was unable to recognize the *delo*, the essential.[51]

In his discussions of Karamzin, Kachenovskii for the first time presented the public with an exclusive definition of the historian. He had for many years called for "higher" as well as "lower criticism." By this, he meant that even after the original text had been restored, critical methods should be applied in order to evaluate the content of the source.[52] Beginning in 1817, he used this definition of criticism in a way not seen in his earlier writings. It now became the shibboleth that determined who could enter into the ranks of the historians. In 1809 Kachenovskii had fervently insisted that researchers employ critical methods in order to cleanse Nestor's chronicle. Yet, although Nestor knew no such techniques, Kachenovskii had praised him as "always truthful, a lover of simplicity and order," qualities that now led "foreign scholars to pronounce [his] name with awe" and that should serve as "an example to inspire Russians."[53] But by the late 1810s he chose to emphasize modern methods, rather than eternal values. His conceptualization of the historian, originally accommodating in its vagueness, now had no room for Karamzin.

Kachenovskii's maneuvers firmly situate him within broader sociological and historical paradigms of professionalization. Like all professionals, Kachenovskii was beginning to erect orderly, objective guidelines for his sphere of competence. More specifically, many of his actions parallel those of professionalizing historians in other countries. He not only publicly challenged Karamzin's methods, but also clarified for the readers the criteria that he would expect all historians to meet. Kachenovskii, like French historians of a later generation, insisted that history writing employ the modern tools of the scientist, thus distinguishing the "true" historian from the writer or the dilettante.[54] A critical method, as articulated and refined by Leopold Ranke from the 1820s through the 1870s, would also become central to the identity of professional historians in Germany and England.[55] At the same time, by claiming specialized standards of evaluation, Kachenovskii seemed to be anticipating the strategy of American historians at the end of the century, who attempted to sidestep morally charged issues by removing history from "general intellectual discourse."[56] By no means did Kachenovskii "professionalize" his field. As Leonard Krieger points out about the emergence of the professional historian in Germany, what gave Ranke's methods resonance beyond the individual historian was his ability to create and disseminate a memorable paradigm through his writing and through institutional innovations, such as the seminar. He thus was able to pass on his approach to disciples and create a school.[57] Intellectually and institutionally, Kachenovskii's was an individual enterprise. However, as he articulated in print an exclusive definition of the historian, as he inspired his readers and his students with his talk of a scientific method of criticism that would discern the system underlying the chaos of past events, he provided other historians with terms and tools for defining the boundaries of their field.[58]

Although Kachenovskii's steps toward delineating the historian's domain coincide with models of comparative professionalization, they are revelatory of the local forces to which they were in large part a response. Kachenovskii was confronted with the concrete threat of a historical narrative that he considered unscholarly, yet which carried the double sanction of both official—if equivocal—support and overwhelming public popularity. Any response entailed a defense of his authority to criticize. If, as William Todd argues, the polemics over criticism served as a forum for articulating opposing visions of an ideal Russian society, then Kachenovskii, by promoting "scholarly criticism," was asserting the superiority of skills over aristocratic manners. At the same time, the forum itself left its mark on his ideal. Kachenovskii's definition of the historian shows signs of the reductionism that Bourdieu attributes to polemics, during which participants are forced to define themselves "on the basis of a single principle."[59] Perhaps the hopelessly blurred lines between various kinds of criticism—political, personal, intellectual—induced Kachenovskii to demarcate the historian, and defend himself, precisely through the principle of "criticism." As he described the historian's uses of modern scientific criticism, he also indicated to his attackers and his readers the restricted nature of his own criticism of Karamzin and the appropriate boundaries for those who wished to respond. From words expressed in self-defense, the outlines emerged of a historian who was both distinguished and protected by his expertise at using the most up-to-date methods of scholarship.

The Historian's Credentials

Did Kachenovskii believe that the legitimacy of the historical field should come exclusively from its members and their work, or did he seek validation elsewhere?[60] His most explicit statements on the source of his authority as a historian can be interpreted as invoking either scholarly autonomy or state dependence. In 1826, in his call for subscriptions to his journal, he for the first time identified himself as a historian by trade and clearly traced his legitimacy in that activity to one institution—the university. He no longer simply said, "The editor's attention will be directed at subjects," among which he listed Russian history.[61] Although he had held the chair in Russian history and statistics for five years, he only now told the reader: "*Vestnik Evropy* henceforth will primarily contain the history and statistics of the Russian Empire, the Polish Kingdom, and Grand Duchy of Finland, being subjects to which the Editor dedicates his labors in the course of the duties of his place of service" (*sluzhba*).[62] He underlined this institutional basis of his area of expertise in his list of credentials. Whereas before, along with his other affiliations, he had been merely a "professor," he now referred to himself as "Professor of History, Statistics, and Geography of the Russian State."[63]

Kachenovskii's embrace of his affiliation with the university is particularly intriguing because it coincides with two events—political and intellectual—whose effects on issues of autonomy and dependence are themselves open to interpretation. Given the political climate in its wake, it is not surprising that Kachenovskii did not refer in his articles or his known letters to the Decembrist uprising in 1825. On 14 December 1825, taking advantage of the confusion caused by the unexpected death of Alexander I, a group of officers led a rebellion in order to force upon Russia a constitutional regime. While the uprising in St. Petersburg was quashed in a day, the new tsar, Nicholas I, responded with arrests, police surveillance, and the public abandonment of fundamental reform.[64] The dominant theme of Nicholas I's reign was paternalism. Ideally, the emperor and his most trustworthy servitors would perfect Russia through secret committees and would attend to his subjects' needs through the political police.[65] Could this system, which clearly would not allow any group complete autonomy, accommodate a professional sphere? Historians have debated whether Nicholas's paternalistic ideology was a cynical attempt to stymie all individual initiative and free thought, or whether, in fact, he hoped to create an alliance with society, albeit one in which he held all the power.[66] This question had particular import for Kachenovskii, who in the latter half of the 1820s began publishing his controversial theories questioning the authenticity of Russia's most ancient and treasured documents. In the aftermath of the Decembrist uprising, when Kachenovskii claimed the university's sanction, was he reminding the public and the censors of the professor's right to establish and pursue scholarly standards, or was he abandoning his insistence on the primacy of criticism in order to cloak his possibly politically suspect historical narrative in the mantle of state service?

In the introduction to "My View of *Russkaia Pravda,*" Kachenovskii left no room for doubt: his invocation of the university was meant not to replace his long-held intellectual standards, but rather to reinforce his right to proclaim them. He claimed that, after diligently gathering "corroborating evidence according to the rules of Criticism," he had decided to publish his thoughts on the ancient law codes, so that he could expose them to "the open forum of the judgment of scholarly, unbiased experts," without whose advice "I cannot start publishing several works, which will mark my existence in this world as *Professor of the History and Statistics of the Russian State.*"[67] Perhaps Kachenovskii highlighted his institutional credentials in anticipation of any attempts to brand his views politically subversive. Or perhaps he was responding to a perceived threat from another corner. Beginning in 1827, when Kachenovskii began publicizing his doubts about Russia's past, he shifted from advocate of the ideas and values of the world of scholars to challenger of facts long accepted in that world.[68] The sanction of the scholarly community would need to be replaced, or at least supplemented, by a different source of validation. That he turned to the university suggests an expectation that it would not be inimical to his intellectual pursuits.

However, another conflict over the role of criticism, contemporaneous with Kachenovskii's "skeptical" articles, makes clear that the academic autonomy that Kachenovskii sought through the university cannot be equated with a modern vision of the relationship between the historian and the state. We have already seen that he called the university his place of service. As a professor he was a "scholarly *chinovnik* [state servitor]," and throughout his career referred to himself as such in documents generated within the university.[69] Employing Weberian ideal types, we might ask which kind of relations—traditional or modern—better describe the type of servitor Kachenovskii intended to be? The modern servitor shares many traits of the autonomous professional, including obedience to the *impersonal* standards of his occupation and a clear sense of his sphere of competence. Along with these should come the expectation of a boundary between the obligations and the privileges of his office and those of his private life.[70] At the end of the 1820s, again in the heat of battle, Kachenovskii defended his authority as professor, thereby providing his clearest articulation of his understanding of the nature of his service.

This time the threat was not to Kachenovskii's identity as a historian but rather to his success as a journalist. In 1825 Nikolai Polevoi, once a contributor to *Vestnik Evropy,* had started his own journal, *Moskovskii telegraf.*[71] To some historians, Polevoi represents the rise of professional journalism in Russia. The son of a merchant, Polevoi wooed a growing reading public by adopting an encyclopedic format and stricter editorial standards. In addition, he attempted to include material that would appeal to a broad audience. Polemical attacks—ostensibly literary, but in fact often personal—were a sure draw. *Telegraf* was hugely successful from the moment it opened. Whereas *Vestnik Evropy* had been one of the most popular journals in the early 1820s, with about 1,200 subscribers, *Telegraf* could boast over 1,500 subscribers by the end of its first year.[72]

Kachenovskii responded by seeking reinforcements from both the educated public and the university. While promising the public that he would satisfy a broad range of interests, he implored them to rally behind his high standards of scholarship. Beginning in 1827, without abandoning his own pledge to devote himself to the topics dictated by his job at Moscow University, he also assured his readers he would include works on the theory of fine arts, general history, and scholarly criticism.[73] At the same time, he sought to educate his readers so that they could appreciate the quality of the material he presented to them. In 1829 he devoted an entire letter to his readers to explaining the difference between a good "scholarly" polemic (although "the interest of the readers does not weaken, ... the subject becomes clearer and clearer") and a bad polemic ("filled with only personal remarks and impudence ... inspired by all sorts of shameful cupidity"). Kachenovskii admitted that the "crowd" (*tolpa*) might be drawn to the latter. But he appealed to his readers, reminding them that his own efforts "depend on the gracious assistance of the Public."[74] *Vestnik Evropy* closed in 1830 for lack of subscriptions.[75] Educated Russians failed to heed Kachenovskii's call to defend those endeavors that he considered scholarly.

In the midst of his battle to win readers, Kachenovskii also unsheathed a weapon that Polevoi did not possess—his position at Moscow University. In 1828, offended by comments in Polevoi's journal, Kachenovskii filed a complaint with the Moscow Censorship Committee against *Telegraf*'s censor, Sergei Glinka. Kachenovskii claimed that Glinka had violated the censorship code by allowing to appear in print "expressions reproachful of my person and no less harmful to the place where I have the happiness of serving with honor, with academic degrees and the title of full professor."[76] He also publicized his grievances on the pages of his journal. In another author's polemical piece against *Telegraf,* Kachenovskii appended his own comment. He would not engage in "fruitless polemic," he informed his readers, having taken "other measures to protect my person (*lichnost'*)." He only read *Telegraf* at all in order to keep apace of the results of its "disloyalty, concerning the honor of my service and the dignity of the position where I have the happiness of continuing to serve."[77] When Kachenovskii was asked by the Censorship Committee to list the specific passages to which he objected, he complained that *Telegraf* had stated: (1) "*Vestnik Evropy* under its present publisher is dry and heavy"; (2) "In *Vestnik Evropy* . . . one encounters on every page half a dozen barbarisms"; and (3) that *Vestnik Evropy* had not published the types of works promised.[78] Although he claimed to be defending his honor as a professor and as a person, every example he mentioned referred only to his journal and his role as editor.

Kachenovskii's self-representation does not conform to key features of the "modern" autonomous individual. He recognized no boundaries between his rights and obligations as an individual, a servitor, and a professor of history. Not only did he fail to distinguish between the literary and the personal, but he also implied that the honor and respect he deserved— personally and professionally—emanated first and foremost from his title and place of service. Did Kachenovskii believe that in all his activities he represented his university, or did he simply emphasize what he believed to be his strongest argument?[79] Stressing those sources of his own authority that Polevoi lacked, Kachenovskii reminded both reader and censor that he bore the imprimatur of the university, of the authorities. Kachenovskii probably expected his title to instill respect in potential readers, as well as caution in possible critics. While he may have been motivated by considerations of strategy, his choice of maneuvers indicates that Kachenovskii did not conceive of a need to limit the university's claims on him to a purely professional arena.

The Structure of Professional Autonomy in Pre-Reform Russia

Kachenovskii's struggles to define and defend his field suggest a historical experience in pre-reform Russia that engendered in emerging professional groups a strong desire for autonomy, but a type of autonomy unlike that predicted by Western models. In the first decades of the nineteenth century, Kachenovskii clearly perceived both the necessity and possibility of delineating a sphere of activity in which he could pursue his work unimpeded.

However, the impediments he sought to overcome originated not in high politics or in local state institutions but rather in the cultural dynamics of educated society. Although the Decembrist uprising and its aftermath might have encouraged him to highlight his position as a civil servant at the university, Kachenovskii's clearest articulations of the qualifications and credentials of the historian were forged in heated battles over the uses and limits of criticism—literary and historical, not political. The boundaries of his field were largely determined by the enemy he sought to marginalize. Unlike Karamzin, Kachenovskii appreciated the importance of criticism. Unlike Polevoi, Kachenovskii's brand of criticism carried the sanction reserved by the state for its loyal servitors. The historian's right to practice was imbedded in both his qualifications and his rank.

Although from the perspective of 1917 Kachenovskii's experiences confirm the weaknesses of Russian professionalization, when judged within the context of their times, they suggest that Russia's uniqueness in this arena is directly related to its participation in wider European cultural trends. The peculiar configuration of professional autonomy and state dependence articulated by Kachenovskii did not augur well for imperial Russia's ability to conform to a paradigm that linked professional autonomy to political power and democratization. For Kachenovskii, an influential historian working at a pivotal time for the profession, the authority of the state played no small role in the legitimization of his professional activities. State support was not merely a necessary evil, reflecting Russia's political realities. Rather, Kachenovskii welcomed the autocracy's role as a cornerstone of the historian's work, protecting the scholar from the unenlightened and ill-intentioned. Even in the greatly altered circumstances of post-reform Russia, it would be difficult to abandon completely the institution that had not only sanctioned historical study, but had also at times seemed to be the only guarantor of its progress. At the same time, Kachenovskii's definition of progress—enlightenment, scientific truth, critical methods—firmly situate him within a Western context. Just as paternalism persisted among liberal professionals in the post-reform era, in an earlier era paternalistic protoprofessionals found it possible to adhere to values associated with a new age. In pre-reform Russia, one could believe in and in fact practice the pursuit of "modern" standards of scholarship through reliance on traditional bonds to the state.

Notes

The research and writing of this chapter have been funded in part by the Center for Russian and East European Studies at Stanford University, a Mazour Award, and a

Whiting Fellowship in the Humanities. I would like to thank Terence Emmons, Vladimir Golstein, Katherine Jolluck, and Thomas Sanders for suggestions on earlier drafts.
1. For a synthesis of sociological definitions of professions, as well as a discussion of the weaknesses of these models generally and specifically in their applicability to the Russian experience, see Harley Balzer's introduction to *Russia's Missing Middle Class: The Professions in Russian History,* ed. Harley D. Balzer (Armonk, NY: M.E. Sharpe, 1996), 4–8. In addition to autonomy, Balzer lists other essential characteristics of professions: a shared knowledge arising from formal training; shared standards of behavior emphasizing service; and socialization of standards through formal institutions such as journals, organizations, and universities.

2. Studies that argue that a key feature of professionalization in Russia was the failure to wrest meaningful autonomy from the autocratic state include: Nancy Mandel-ker Frieden, *Russian Physicians in an Era of Reform and Revolution, 1856–1905* (Princeton, NJ: Princeton University Press, 1981); Scott J. Seregny, *Russian Teachers and Peasant Revolution: The Politics of Education in 1905* (Bloomington, IN: Indiana University Press, 1989); Samuel D. Kassow, *Students, Professors, and the State in Tsarist Russia* (Berkeley, CA: University of California Press, 1989) and his essay "Professionalism Among University Professors," in *Russia's Missing Middle Class,* 197–221; Harley D. Balzer, "The Problem of Professions in Imperial Russia," in *Between Tsar and People: Educated Society and the Quest for Public Identity in Late Imperial Russia,* eds. Edith W. Clowes, Samuel D. Kassow, and James L. West (Princeton, NJ: Princeton University Press, 1991), 183–98; and his introduction to *Russia's Missing Middle Class,* esp. 5, 8.

3. William Wagner, *Marriage, Property, and Law in Late Imperial Russia* (Oxford: Clarendon Press, 1994); Kassow, *Students, Professors, and State,* 388–89; Scott J. Seregny, "Professional Activism and Association Among Russian Teachers, 1864–1905," in *Russia's Missing Middle Class,* 184–89; Christine Ruane and Ben Eklof, "Cultural Pioneers and Professionals: The Teacher in Society," in *Between Tsar and People,* 210.

4. Wagner, *Marriage, Property and Law;* Laura Engelstein, *The Keys to Happiness: Sex and the Search for Modernity in Fin-de-Siècle Russia* (Ithaca, NY: Cornell University Press, 1992), esp. ch. 5.

5. While Kassow refers to the tension between these two types of service (Kassow, *Students, Professors, and State,* 388) and Frieden describes among physicians "a service ethos joined to public employment" (Frieden, *Russian Physicians,* 322), Christine Ruane analyzes in depth the "public service" identity that emerges from this combination of dedication to government and people (Christine Ruane, *Gender, Class, and the Professionalization of Russian City Teachers, 1860–1914* [Pittsburgh, PA: University of Pittsburgh Press, 1994]).

6. This article is based on and incorporates parts of chapters 1 and 2 of my dissertation, "Social Identity and Russian Cultural Politics: Defining the Historian in the Pre-Reform Era" (Ph.D. diss., Stanford University, 1997).

7. Although Samuel Kassow has examined the professionalization of the university professors, he focuses on professional identity across the disciplines (i.e., as a professoriate), rather than within disciplines (e.g., as historians) and he concentrates on the late imperial period (Kassow, *Students, Professors, and State;* and Kassow, "Professionalism Among University Professors").

8. Richard Wortman's study of the early history of the legal profession indicates that the young jurists who were devoted to the new "legal ethos" that emerged toward the end of the pre-reform period had difficulty conforming to the traditional standards of civil service. However, Wortman does not say if these jurists, in addition to chafing at

the inefficiencies of the tsarist bureaucracy, also disdained the very idea of serving the autocracy (see Richard S. Wortman, *The Development of a Russian Legal Consciousness* [Chicago, IL: The University of Chicago Press, 1976]).

9. Pierre Bourdieu, *Homo Academicus,* trans. Peter Collier (Stanford, CA: Stanford University Press, 1988), 81.

10. K-ii [M.T. Kachenovskii], "Moi vzgliad na Russkuiu pravdu," *Vestnik Evropy* (henceforth *VE*), 1829, no. 13:26–28.

11. Cynthia Hyla Whittaker, "The Idea of the Autocracy Among Eighteenth-Century Russian Historians," *Russian Review,* vol. 55, no. 2 (April 1996):170.

12. Among prerevolutionary historians who make this argument, an in-depth analysis of the Skeptical School is provided by V.S. Ikonnikov, in "Skepticheskaia shkola v russkoi istoriografii i ee protivniki," *Universitetskie izvestiia* (Kiev), 1871, no. 9: 1–38; no. 10: 1–40; no. 11: 1–30. For representative Soviet treatments, see A.M. Sakharov, "Skepticheskaia shkola," in *Sovetskaia istoricheskaia entsiklopedia,* vol. 12 (Moscow, 1969), 952–53; V.I. Shevtsov, "Voprosy russkoi istorii v osveshchenii maloizvestnykh predstavitelei 'skepticheskoi shkoly,' " in *Voprosy otechestvennoi i vseobshchei istorii v trudakh russkikh istorikov XIX–nachala XX veka* (Voronezh, 1983), 54–65; and R.A. Kireeva, " 'Skepticheskaia shkola' v russkoi istoriograficheskoi literatury dooktiabr'skogo perioda," in *Problemy istorii russkogo obshchestvennogo dvizheniia i istoricheskoi nauki,* eds. E.M. Zhukov et al. (Moscow, 1981), 241–51. Shevtsov and Kireeva vary in emphasis, with the former stressing the scientific content of the Marxist categories, and the latter stressing their political content.

13. S.M. Solov'ev, "M.T. Kachenovskii," in *Biograficheskii slovar' professorov i prepodavatelei Imperatorskogo moskovskogo universiteta,* vol. 1 (Moscow, 1855), 388; and by the same author, "Moi zapiski dlia detei moikh a, esli mozhno, i dlia drugikh," *Izbrannye trudy: Zapiski,* eds. A.A. Levandovskii and N.I. Tsimbaev (Moscow, 1983), 256; A.G. Kuz'min, "Skepticheskaia shkola v russkoi istoriografii," in *Uchenye zapiski Riazanskogo pedagogicheskogo instituta,* vol. 62 (Riazan, 1969), 329. Solov'ev is primarily interested in creating through Kachenovskii a model for negotiating the Westernizer/Slavophile debates (see Katsev, "Social Identity and Cultural Politics"), while Kuz'min analyzes Kachenovskii from a nationalistic perspective, criticizing him for his "national nihilism," which led him to an unscientific rejection of Russia's great past. Two other interpretations of Kachenovskii's work are notable. His rival at Moscow University, M.P. Pogodin, published a detailed refutation of his suppositions, explaining them as a product of Kachenovskii's susceptibility to ideas in vogue in the West (M.P. Pogodin, "O skepticheskom povetrii," in Pogodin's *Issledovaniia, zamechaniia, i lektsii o russkoi istorii,* vol. 1 [Moscow, 1846; reprint, The Hague: Mouton, 1970], 325–29). P.N. Miliukov portrays Kachenovskii as an amateur who served as a conduit for new ideas and methods—including a critical awareness of the ways that documents are shaped by their times—but lacked the rigorous training to understand and implement them himself (P.N. Miliukov, "Skepticheskaia shkola," in *Entsiklopedicheskii slovar',* vol. 30 [St. Petersburg: Brokgauz & Efron, 1900], 195–96; and by the same author, *Glavnye techeniia russkoi istoricheskoi mysli,* 3d ed. [St. Petersburg, 1913], 225–53). No Western work has been devoted to his life or thought.

14. For the first and most extensive biography of Kachenovskii, see Solov'ev, "Kachenovskii," 383–403. Additional biographical material can be found in the following articles: "Mikhail Trofimovich Kachenovskii," in *Russkii biograficheskii slovar',* vol. 8 (St. Petersburg, 1897), 577–80; "M.T. Kachenovskii," in *Slovar' chlenov Obshchestva liubitelei rossiiskoi slovesnosti pri Moskovskom universitete (1811–1911)* (Moscow, n.d.), 136–37; N.P. Barsukov, "M.T. Kachenovskii, professor Moskovskogo universiteta," *Russkaia starina,* 1889, no. 10: 199–202; and G.V. Makarova, "M.T.

Kachenovskii i stanovlenie slavianovedeniia v Rossii," in *Istoriograficheskie issledovaniia po slavianovedeniiu i balkanistike,* ed. V.A. D'iakov (Moscow, 1984), 63–96. A more personal, if less objective, portrait is provided by Kachenovskii's son Vladimir in his article "M.T. Kachenovskii: K ocherku N.P. Barsukova v 10-i knige 'Russkoi stariny,' 1889 g.," *Russkaia starina,* 1890, no. 6: 685–94.

15. On Kachenovskii's not-uninterrupted tenure as editor, and on the content of the journal, including Kachenovskii's contributions, see M. Poludenskii, *Ukazatel' k Vestniku Evropy* (Moscow, 1861), viii–xi.

16. Miliukov, *Glavnye techeniia,* 178–79.

17. Alexander Vucinich, *Science in Russian Culture,* vol. 1: *A History to 1860* (Stanford, CA: Stanford University Press, 1963), 365; S.R. Mikulinskii,"Istoricheskie usloviia i osobennosti razvitiia estestvoznaniia v Rossii v XIX veke," in *Razvitie estestvoznanie v Rossii (XVIII–nachalo XX veka),* eds. S.R. Mikulinskii and A.P. Iushkevich (Moscow, 1977), 136. For representative discussions of the development of the historical sciences, see Anatole G. Mazour, *Modern Russian Historiography: A Revised Edition* (Westport, CT: Greenwood Press, 1975), 112; A.M. Sakharov, *Istoriografiia istorii SSSR: Dosovetskii period* (Moscow, 1978), 112–16, and Miliukov, *Glavnye techeniia,* 224–27. Despite differences in terminology (Sakharov is concerned with the emergence of "bourgeois" historiography, while Miliukov focuses on the new appreciation of a philosophy of history, particularly after Karamzin's death), all see the first decades of the century as transitional.

18. Vucinich, *Science in Russia,* 182; Miliukov, *Glavnye techeniia,* 107–09.

19. On the structure of the university after 1835, see Steven H. Allister, "The Reform of Higher Education in Russia during the Reign of Nicholas I, 1825–1855" (Ph.D. diss., Princeton University, 1974); and Kassow, *Students, Professors, and State.*

20. *Polnoe sobranie zakonov Rossiiskoi imperii,* 1st ser., vol. 28, no. 21,498, 5 November 1804. For an analysis of university policy during this period, see James Flynn, *The University Reform of Tsar Alexander I, 1802–1835* (Washington, DC: The Catholic University of America Press, 1988).

21. On the development of Karamzin's understanding of Russian history and politics, see Richard Pipes's introduction to N.M. Karamzin, *Memoir on Ancient and Modern Russia,* ed. and trans. Richard Pipes (Cambridge, MA: Harvard University Press, 1959), esp. 43–63; and Andrzej Walicki, *The Slavophile Controversy* (Oxford: Clarendon Press, 1975), 32–45.

22. Mazour, *Russian Historiography,* 80.

23. On the following discussion of the nonhistorical, as well as historical, issues involved in the Karamzin debate, see V.P. Kozlov, "Polemika vokrug 'Istorii gosudarstva Rossiiskogo' N.M. Karamzina v otechestvennoi periodike (1818–1830 gg.)," *Istoriia SSSR,* 1984, no. 5: 88–102; and by the same author, *"Istoriia gosudarstva Rossiiskogo" N.M. Karamzina v otsenkakh sovremennikov* (Moscow, 1989); Joseph L. Black, *Nicholas Karamzin and Russian Society in the Nineteenth Century: A Study in Russian Political and Historical Thought* (Toronto: University of Toronto Press, 1975), 135–45; and Miliukov, *Glavnye techeniia,* 215–16.

24. Kozlov, "Polemika vokrug 'Istorii,' " 89.

25. For a detailed account of the Russian Bible Society Era, see Aleksandr Pypin, *Religioznye dvizheniia pri Aleksandre I,* vol. 1 of *Issledovaniia i stat'i po epokhe Aleksandra I* (Petrograd, 1916).

26. See Pypin, *Religioznye dvizheniia pri Aleksandre I,* 158; and Kozlov, "Polemika vokrug 'Istorii,' " 94–95.

27. Mazour, *Russian Historiography,* 83; Miliukov, *Glavnye techeniia,* 211–12. Karamzin's access to archives in the end benefited all historians. After the Moscow

fire of 1812, Karamzin's notes were all that remained of many important documents (Mazour, *Russian Historiography*, 80–81).

28. Miliukov, *Glavnye techeniia*, esp. 118–21, 145–46, 167, 223–28.

29. Ibid., 217–19.

30. B.I. Syromiatnikov, "Proiskhozhdenie feodal'nykh otnoshenii v drevnei Rusi: Vvedenie. Traditsionnaia teoriia russkogo istoricheskogo razvitiia. (Istoriograficheskii ocherk)" (Moscow, 1911, Printed but unpublished), 280–90. Terence Emmons brought this work to my attention and provided me with a copy of it. For an abridged version of Syromiatnikov's views on the development of Russian historiography, see B.I. Syromiatnikov, "Osnovnye momenty v razvitii istoricheskoi mysli," *Russkaia mysl'*, 1906, no. 12: 71–97.

31. Black, *Karamzin and Society*, 129–33, 138. In Kachenovskii's review of Karamzin's *History*, he betrayed this worry when he spoke of Karamzin's access to the archives, his great talents, his certain popularity, and the influence his work would have (F., [M.T. Kachenovskii], "Ot kievskogo zhitelia," *VE*, 1818, no. 18: 124).

32. Poludenskii, *Ukazatel' k VE*, ix; William Mills Todd III, *Fiction and Society in the Age of Pushkin* (Cambridge, MA: Harvard University Press, 1986), 89.

33. Todd, *Fiction and Society*, 89–90.

34. According to Kozlov, the argument over what constituted "true criticism" was a central feature of the Karamzin polemic (Kozlov, "Polemika vokrug 'Istorii,'" 98). Karamzin himself not only refused to respond to critics, but told one of his defenders, I.I. Dmitriev, that Kachenovskii's criticism "is very instructive and conscientious." Karamzin added that he had cast his vote, as well as Dmitriev's and V.A. Zhukovskii's, in favor of Kachenovskii's acceptance into the Russian Academy (N.M. Karamzin to I.I. Dmitriev, 21 April 1819, as quoted in Ikonnikov, "Skepticheskaia shkola," no. 10: 12n).

35. Black, *Karamzin and Society*, 139; Kozlov, "Polemika vokrug 'Istorii,' " 93–94.

36. P.A. Viazemskii, "Poslanie k M.T. Kachenovskomu," *Syn otechestva*, 1821, no. 2: 78–79.

37. Kozlov, "Polemika vokrug 'Istorii,' " 95.

38. Kozlov cites a letter by I.I. Dmitriev from 17 October 1818, in which he stated concerning Kachenovskii's intention to criticize Karamzin's *History*: "Many are claiming that the journalist is doing this to please the minister of education" (Kozlov, *"Istoriia" Karamzina*, 56).

39. M.T. Kachenovskii to V.M. Perevoshchikov, 11 July 1817, Rossiiskii gosudarstvennyi arkhiv literatury i iskusstva (RGALI) (formerly TsGALI), f. 46, op. 4, d. 6l, 7v.–8.

40. K. [M.T. Kachenovskii], "Primechaniia na stat'iu o Filosofii," *VE*, 1820, no. 1:34. In a more explicit statement of his sentiments, in a personal letter in 1820, Kachenovskii wrote to V.M. Perevoshchikov, a professor at Kazan University, that he feared to send him a copy of *Vestnik Evropy* in light of the fact that the superintendent of that university—a leading proponent of obscurant policies—"famous for his scholarship and love for his neighbor, wishing to caution teachers and students against the Devil's traps, has forbidden them to read the impious journals published here and in St. Petersburg" (Kachenovskii to Perevoshchikov, 13 July 1820, RGALI, f. 46, op. 4, d. 6, l. 13).

41. Second ellipses are Kachenovskii's. M. Kachenovskii, "Vzgliad na Blagorodnyi pansion pri imperatorskom Moskovskom Universitete," *VE*, 1804, no. 19: 223.

42. For a detailed description of the major literary polemics of the first quarter of the nineteenth century and Kachenovskii's participation in them, see N.I. Mordovchenko, *Russkaia kritika pervoi chetverti XIX veka* (Moscow-Leningrad, 1959), esp. 70–72, 80, 89–91, 96–97, 292–95. For the most thorough analysis of

Kachenovskii's positions in historical debates, see Ikonnikov, "Skepticheskaia Shkola," no. 9: 1–38; no. 10: 1–12; and Solov'ev, "Kachenovskii," 391–403.

43. See for example, Publisher [M.T. Kachenovskii], "O poslanii k Privete," *VE,* 1807, no. 19: 213; K. [M.T. Kachenovskii], "Parallel'nye mesta v russkikh letopisiakh," *VE,* 1809, no. 18: 140; K-ii [M.T. Kachenovskii], "Razyskaniia po povodu starinnoi zolotoi medali, nedavno otkrytoi," *VE,* 1822, no. 15: 189; K-ii [M.T. Kachenovskii], "Eshche razyskaniia o chernigovskoi zolotoi medali," *VE,* 1829, no. 12: 288. For an in-depth discussion of Kachenovskii's changing representations of "criticism" and "scholarship," see Katsev, "Social Identity and Cultural Politics," chapter 1.

44. V.V. Gippius, "Vestnik Evropy," in *Ocherki po istorii russkoi zhurnalistiki i kritiki,* ed. V.E. Evgen'ev-Maksimov, et al., vol. I (Leningrad, 1950), 181, 183–84; Poludenskii, *Ukazatel' k VE,* ix–x.

45. Among those historians who attribute to Kachenovskii scholarly motives are Solov'ev, "Kachenovskii," 395–96; Black, *Karamzin and Society,* 138; Natan Eidelman, *Poslednii letopisets* (Moscow, 1983), 101; and Kozlov, *"Istoriia" Karamzina,* 58, although he also imputes to Kachenovskii political motivations, as discussed above.

46. A.M. Sakharov, for example, makes this argument in his entry on "Kachenovskii, M.T.," in the *Modern Encyclopedia of Russian and Soviet History,* ed. Joseph L. Wieczynski, vol. 15 (Gulf Breeze, FL: Academic International Press, 1980), 163.

47. K. [M.T. Kachenovskii], "Probnye listki iz rukovodstva k poznaniiu istorii i drevnostei rossiiskogo gosudarstva," *VE,* 1817, no. 3: 204, 205. See also, K-ii [M.T. Kachenovskii], "Istoriia gosudarstva rossiiskogo t. XII," *VE,* 1829, no. 17: 6, where he referred to Karamzin with the similar term *bytopisatel'.*

48. K. [Kachenovskii], "Probnye listki iz rukovodstva," 205.

49. K. [M.T. Kachenovskii], trans., "O mednykh dveriakh Sofiiskogo sobora v Novgorode," *VE,* 1818, no. 8: 293–95.

50. Italics are Kachenovskii's. F. [Kachenovskii], "Ot kievskogo zhitelia," 1819, no. 6: 125, 126.

51. F. [Kachenovskii], "Ot kievskogo zhitelia," 1819, no. 3: 198–99; no. 4: 295–97; no. 6: 128–38.

52. Kachenovskii's methodology was greatly influenced by the German historian August Schlözer. On Kachenovskii's understanding of historical criticism, see A.M. Sakharov, "Skepticheskaia shkola," 952; Ikonnikov, "Skepticheskaia shkola," no. 9: 6.

53. K. [M.T. Kachenovskii], "Ob istochnikakh dlia russkoi istorii," *VE,* 1809, no. 5: 9; no. 3: 198.

54. William R. Keylor, *Academy and Community: The Foundation of the French Historical Profession* (Cambridge, MA: Harvard University Press, 1975), 30, 57.

55. Doris S. Goldstein, "The Professionalization of History in Britain in the Late Nineteenth and Early Twentieth Centuries," *Storia della Storiografia,* 1983, no. 3: 7–11; and Leonard Krieger, *Ranke: The Meaning of History* (Chicago, IL: Chicago University Press, 1977).

56. This approach is described by Peter Novick, *That Noble Dream: The Objectivity Question and the American Historical Profession* (Cambridge: Cambridge University Press, 1988), 51–53.

57. Krieger, *Ranke,* 2–4.

58. Although Kachenovskii's lectures were apparently generally quite dull, his former students, including some of the next generation's cultural leaders, remembered his thrilling statements at the lectern rejecting as myth much of what they had been taught in school (see, for example, I.A. Goncharov, *Ocherki. Stat'i. Pis'ma. Vospominaniia sovremennikov* [Moscow, 1986], 108).

59. Bourdieu, *Homo Academicus,* 81.

60. One cannot infer an answer from Kachenovskii's comments on Karamzin's *History*. Since that work boasted both official state sanction and scholarly condemnation, Kachenovskii's criticism could signal his disdain for government sponsorship or his solidarity with fellow researchers or both.

61. [M.T. Kachenovskii], "Ob''iavlenie," *VE*, 1826, no. 1: 77.

62. [M.T. Kachenovskii], "Ob''iavleniia," *VE*, 1826, no. 18: 157.

63. Ibid., 156.

64. For a detailed description of the uprising, its causes, and its aftermath for the participants, see Anatole G. Mazour, *The First Russian Revolution, 1825* (Stanford, CA: Stanford University Press, 1964).

65. For classic analyses of Nicholas I's reign and policies, see M.A. Poliektov, *Nikolai I: Biografiia i obzor tsarstvovaniia* (Moscow, 1918); A.E. Presniakov, *Apogei samoderzhavie: Nikolai I* (Leningrad, 1925); Nicholas Riasanovsky, *Nicholas I and Official Nationality in Russia, 1825–1855* (Berkeley, CA: University of California Press, 1959); and W. Bruce Lincoln, *Nicholas I, Emperor and Autocrat of All the Russias* (Bloomington, IN: Indiana University Press, 1978).

66. Compare, for example, histories of the Third Section (the political police) in Mikhail Lemke's *Nikolaevskie zhandarmy i literatura 1826–1855 gg.*, 2d ed. (St. Petersburg, 1909); and Sidney Monas's *The Third Section: Police and Society in Russia Under Nicholas I* (Cambridge, MA: Harvard University Press, 1961).

67. Italics are Kachenovskii's. Kachenovskii, "Moi vzgliad na Russkuiu pravdu," no. 13: 24.

68. In 1827 Kachenovskii wrote a series of articles in which he alleged that contemporary theories concerning ancient Russia's system of currency must be incorrect because they overestimated the country's level of cultural development in its infancy (K-ii [M.T. Kachenovskii], "O starinnykh nazyvaniiakh v Rossii deneg metallicheskikh v smysle khodiachei monety," *VE*, 1827, no. 14: 122–25, and in following issues). Kachenovskii's theory did have some precedents, though not among researchers of Russian history. Kachenovskii was strongly influenced by Barthold Niebuhr, who applied a similar skeptical method to his study of ancient Rome. His fate in the historiography also parallels Kachenovskii's: Lord Acton concludes that although his history was repudiated, he furthered the use of criticism in his field (Herbert Butterfield, *Man on His Past* [Cambridge University Press, 1955], 75–77).

69. In a report on the conditions of schools in 1819, Kachenovskii explained that according to law and practice, "The rank levels for scholarly *chinovniki* at either a university or an institution under the jurisdiction of the university are assigned in the exact same manner as they are assigned in the Table of Ranks of 1722 for *chinovniki* of the Army, the Guards, the Civil Service, and so on" (M.T. Kachenovskii's report to School Committee, 4 February 1819, Tsentral'nyi gosudarstvennyi istoricheskii arkhiv g. Moskvy [TsGIA g. Moskvy], f. 418 [archive of Moscow University], op. 74, d. 34, ll. 49v., 50). For a later reference to "scholarly *chinovniki*," see report from M.T. Kachenovskii to University Board, 4 August 1826, TsGIA g. Moskvy, f. 459 (archive of superintendent of Moscow University), op. 1, d. 3090, l. 4v.

70. Max Weber, *Economy and Society,* ed. Guenther Roth and Claus Wittich, (Berkeley: University of California Press, 1978) vol. 1: 218, 220; vol. 2: 1028–31.

71. Chester M. Rzadkiewicz, "Russian Journalism During the Romantic Era: A Study of N.A. Polevoi and Moscow Telegraf, 1825–1834," (Ph.D. diss., SUNY, Buffalo, 1987), 50–51; Makarova, "Kachenovskii i slavianovedenie," 84.

72. V. Orlov, *Nikolai Polevoi: Materialy po istorii russkoi literatury i zhurnalistiki tridtsatykh godov* (Leningrad, 1934), 37–43; Rzadkiewicz, "Polevoi," 11, 20–23, 87, 342–43n. *Telegraf* eventually maintained from two to three thousand annual subscriptions.

73. [M.T. Kachenovskii], "Ob''iavlenie," *VE,* 1827, no. 20: 309–310; [M.T. Kachenovskii], "Ob''iavlenie o podpiske na Vestnik Evropy," *VE,* 1828, no. 18: 155–56.

74. Publisher [M.T. Kachenovskii], "K chitateliam," *VE,* 1829, no. 18: 141–45.

75. Makarova, "Kachenovskii i slavianovedenie," 84.

76. N.P. Barsukov, *Zhizn' i trudy M.P. Pogodina,* vol. 2 (St. Petersburg, 1889), 265.

77. Nikodim Nadoumko [N.I. Nadezhdin], [M.T. Kachenovskii's comments], "Otklik c patriarshikh prudov," *VE,* 1828, no. 24: 304.

78. Barsukov, *Pogodin,* vol. 2: 268–269.

79. Reception of Kachenovskii's argument suggests that not only within Kachenovskii, but also among members of Russian society, "traditional" and "modern" conceptions of individual and state intermingled. While the Moscow Censorship Committee supported Kachenovskii, the Minister of Education, Karl Liven, reversed the decision, explaining that the statements in *Telegraf* were not offensive to Kachenovskii's person and adding, "One should not interject into a purely literary argument the dignity of government service and of the highest academic estate," [*uchebnoe soslovie*] (Barsukov, *Pogodin,* vol. 2: 274).

4

The Third Opponent

Dissertation Defenses and the Public Profile of Academic History in Late Imperial Russia

Thomas Sanders

> A dissertation is a work with two opponents and no readers.
> —*Vasilii O. Kliuchevskii*

In late October 1917 George Vernadsky[1] journeyed from Perm, where he had taken a teaching position in September, to Petrograd in order to defend his dissertation on freemasonry in eighteenth-century Russia.[2] He found Petrograd a "gloomy" city, living "in anticipation of the approaching tragedy." Despite the circumstances, his greatest concern was that he was distracted from his preparations for the defense by a futile search for the proper attire: his frock coat violated the tradition of wearing dress tails to a defense. With the days growing short in the northern capital, and people "afraid to walk the streets, especially at night, when all sorts of bandits" were active, Vernadsky was pleasantly surprised that a respectable crowd turned out to witness his defense.3 In addition to the official participants, a certain N.P. Kiselev made "several interesting observations" about Masonic mysticism, and there were brief remarks by two or three other people in the audience. After the history faculty had unanimously confirmed Vernadsky's degree, the official party repaired to the apartment of

Vernadsky's parents for a celebration.[4] The supply situation in the capital was such that any food around "quickly disappeared" from the shelves. Nevertheless, his mother managed to provide all the essentials—"tea, sandwiches, sweets and wine. There was even champagne." Joined by Aleksandr Presniakov and the entire complement of his former "circle of young historians," Vernadsky and his family basked in the "warm and friendly" atmosphere which reigned in the wake of his successful dissertation defense.

On the one hand, Vernadsky's dissertation defense appears a trivial, if very human, scene played out against the backdrop of the looming national tragedy. On the other hand, it is a rather astonishing occurrence, a remarkable example of the fidelity with which a certain select section of educated society continued to observe the niceties of a cultural institution of their own crafting. The country was sliding at an accelerating rate into the "abyss" of civil chaos and war, yet the Vernadsky family fretted over frocktails and petits fours, faculty votes and the Enlightenment-era Masonic movement. How had it come to pass that the academic ritual of "defending" one's dissertation had become so well-established a component of the cultural life of the educated elite that they performed its rites on the very eve of destruction?

This chapter examines the origins, the evolution, the workings, and the social function of this cultural institution: the dissertation defense. For all its evocation of images of dry-as-dust academic obscurity, the history of the defense provides unexpected insights. For one thing, by refracting historians' experience through the prism of the defense, we can derive a very clear picture of the maturation of the history professoriate both as representatives of a discipline and as members of a distinct subculture in an increasingly complex and politicized tsarist society. At its origins the dissertation defense as a public affair actually represents an instance of implicit agreement between the tsarist government and educated noble society. Of perhaps greater significance is the fact that the defense also presents us with an example of the manner in which such governmentally mandated practices could be transformed by an emerging social group to meet the group's own evolving standards and could ultimately be coopted by that social formation as an agency for status affirmation and self-representation in ways quite antithetical to the government's purposes. Furthermore, the different phases of the evolution of the defense reflect the elaboration and articulation of a highly educated cultural elite within the Russian social system, a case study of the phenomenon described by Abbott Gleason as the transition from society to public, from *obshchestvo* to *obshchestvennost'*.[5]

It might seem a bit odd that in an authoritarian, closed system like that of eighteenth-century Russia public intellectual discourse should have been adapted so readily. Nonetheless, it is a fact that disputes, lectures, and disputes about disputes and lectures were a part of the academic culture in Russia from the foundation of the first university in 1755.[6] The Petrine reforming impulse had led to the elimination of the illiterate nobleman as a dominant social type. In the higher ranks of Russian society (*obshchestvo*) there developed in the eighteenth century the reading habits and the publishing infrastructure that would ultimately transform Russian intellectual culture from the 1840s on.[7] In the still-nascent state of Russian literary culture and the confined conditions of Russian intellectual life of the Catherinian age, however, public presentations and disputations represented an important complement to private reading.[8] They were a prominent part of the intellectual intercourse of the day, and "public lectures and disputes at the university nourished and maintained the constant attention of the Moscow public of all social categories."[9] "Already in that [initial] period," Kizevetter wrote, "one feature of life at Moscow University grabs one's attention: the link between the university and society."[10] The university issued a "cordial" invitation to society, which "eagerly responded" by "fill[ing] the university halls on the days of public gatherings, speeches, [and] disputes."[11]

Shevyrev in his centennial history of Moscow University transmits a strong sense of the importance of the public occasions. "Speech-days at the University," he writes, "were carried out with a habitual solemnity consistent with the spirit and customs of the time." The most important days were April 25 and September 5, the coronation day and name day, respectively, of Empress Elizabeth, and April 26, since Moscow University had been opened in connection with Elizabeth's coronation day. In addition, the completion of examinations in July and December "was accompanied by speeches and public disputes between university students, and speeches by *gimnaziia* students in ancient and modern languages."[12] All this was wrapped about with pomp and ceremony. Students giving speeches who did not already possess the right were "ceremonially invested with swords." Not only were gold and silver medals dispensed "in great number," but books were also awarded. Special large placards announcing these events in ornate prose and printed in both Russian and Latin were posted, inviting "all lovers of science."[13] They were true social events with "the higher clergy, distinguished personages of Moscow, foreigners, and all of educated society continually [taking] part in these solemn occasions."[14]

The activities of the leading intellectual figure at the University of Moscow in the second half of the century, Anton Alekseevich Barsov, exemplify this aspect of eighteenth-century intellectual life. In the nineteenth century, Barsov's discipline would be called philology (*slovesnost*´), but in his own day he was a professor of eloquence (*krasnorechie*). That is fitting enough; Kizevetter calls him "the first orator at university celebrations."[15] Barsov's speeches comprised "an essential part of [his] literary activity"; highly valued in their own day as "superlative" examples of the genre, as late as 1819 a collection of them was published by the *Obshchestvo liubitelei rossiiskoi slovesnosti* as models.[16] The now-obsolete word used to describe the speeches and speech days, *akty,* conveys wonderfully the sense of public display and spectacle inherent in these occasions. The Russian phrase *aktovyi zal,* meaning assembly hall, preserves the same semantic sense: the reason they assembled was to hear a public presentation or see a public dispute.

Of course, as was true in the West, programs that attracted "all lovers of science" were bound to present challenges for the guardians of religious orthodoxy. Shevyrev cites the participation and approval of the higher clergy in these public affairs, but they were not enthralled with all aspects of this new dissemination of knowledge. The first controversy over the public discussion of secular knowledge involved the defense of Dmitrii Anichkov's dissertation on natural theology entitled *Concerning the Origin and Occurrence of the Natural Worship of God* [O nachale i proisshestvii natural'nogo bogopochitaniia].[17] Archbishop Ambrose of Moscow complained to the Holy Synod about the defense of this dissertation at Moscow University in August 1769. The "seductive and harmful" speech about this "atheistic essay" contained "superstition," and even other faculty members attacked its contents.[18] Anichkov made the suggested changes and the work was reprinted. Although Anichkov paid for his indiscretion by being denied a promotion until 1771, the Synod was stymied in its attempt to gain the right to censor all publications dealing with religion.[19] The state would not accept constraints and restrictions on dissertation defenses unless its own interests were threatened.

One can speculate that the naturalness with which both government and society took to public intellectual discourse derived from a shared perception that knowledge had importance as a social fact, and not as something acquired by and transformative for the individual.[20] This may be just another way of saying that for both the leadership of the state and for members of society knowledge had instrumental value. It also bears noting that there was an element of superficiality to public culture in Moscow in the eighteenth century, indicating the absence of real intellectual seriousness. Kizevetter remarks that in the first years the professors were correct in perceiving that "their main task consisted of the propagation of general interest in science and of the explanation of its significance."[21] Nonetheless, whatever the public's motivation or level of involvement, the practice of the public presentation and discussion of serious intellectual issues took root. By the time that an autonomous and truly sophisticated culture developed among a significant segment of the elite in the second half of the nineteenth century, the tradition of the public presentation of knowledge and ideas via lectures and disputes was already well developed.

Before the public and professors could come together to create the social institution of the dissertation defense, however, university culture had to win noble acceptance, and it had to be established on a broader, more stable, and more mature foundation. The interaction between university and noble culture discussed so far was based on the dilettantish taste of a nobility educated by private tutors and in special noble schools. Noble participation in university culture was the strictly passive one of spectator, was at any rate an exclusively Muscovite phenomenon, and did not imply nobles' acceptance of university education for themselves. Even had such acceptance been forthcoming, however, a functioning university system was not yet in place to accommodate them. Recent historiography has demonstrated that the first few decades following the establishment of the new university system in 1804 were a trying time.[22] Ill-considered administrative decisions proved overly burdensome to a university faculty that had enough difficulties teaching its own students, especially since many professors could not lecture in Russian.[23] In addition, the French invasion, Alexander I's drift into mysticism, the insufficiency of properly trained professors, the low status of the universities, and the climate of the times presented significant hurdles to the progress of the new structure of higher education. Incredibly, by the mid-1830s, having survived what James T. Flynn calls the "Bible Society decade,"[24] the university system had managed to address all these problems and had entered a brief period of relative stability prior to the harsh conditions of the last years of Nicholas's reign.

By the mid-1840s, the dispute would threaten to break out of this selective isolation and establish closer contact with a broader society, but the retrenchment and repression of the late Nikolaevan era smothered this movement. As a result, the professoriate and the public reconnected only in the reformed Russia, the elaboration of which began in 1855. In the meantime, the dispute was more of an intra-university affair.[25] That does not mean that there was no public participation or that the dispute lost all significance. On the contrary, owing to the relative isolation of the universities and to the somewhat circumscribed nature of public participation in disputes during the first half of the nineteenth century, it was precisely in these years that the dissertation defense was most fully integrated into the intellectual life of the university.

The historian Mikhail Pogodin was a self-avowed champion of the dissertation defense, as an "institution that occupied an important place in the whole of university life."[26] The most important distinction between defenses in the first half of the century and those conducted in the mid-1850s was the prominent place previously occupied by students. Students had, he writes:

> played the main role. They started disputes, and they sometimes even concluded them. It was a completely open arena, where they could prove their worth and attract the attention of professors. On examinations they were required to give an account of what they had heard, . . . but at the disputes they presented their own ideas, revealed the workings of their own minds.[27]

Pogodin highly recommended this as a pedagogical device, emphasizing both the independence of the intellectual activity, its motivational power, and the amount of time devoted to preparation. Students looked forward to these defenses as "special holidays," kicking them about among themselves well in advance of the actual event and continuing to discuss them in the auditoriums and dormitories for some time after the fact.[28] So enamored was Pogodin of the old-style dissertation defense that he recommended defenses be scheduled at times that allowed any student to raise all questions and issues on his mind. He even urged the construction of a special hall for their staging, similar to the one he had seen at Leiden University, so that the disputants would be visible to all present.[29]

In this era, when the subject matter of the dissertations was not yet overly specialized and was therefore more directly accessible to the average student (at least as far as history and philology were concerned), the defense was clearly a more intimate component of the curricular and pedagogical life of the university. Fedor Buslaev relates in his memoirs an instance when one of his professors, Ivan Ivanovich Davydov, distributed to his class several copies of Aleksandr V. Nikitenko's dissertation.[30] Having given the students time to familiarize themselves with the dissertation, Davydov staged a mock or model (Buslaev uses the word *primernyi* in quotation marks) dispute. While Davydov staunchly defended the dissertation's position, "we helter-skelter thundered against the fortress from all sides and smashed it to smithereens (*raznesli ee v pukh i prakh*).[31] Even the order followed in the disputes indicates that they were student-oriented teaching experiences rather than carefully stylized and extremely erudite clashes of academic titans. Students initiated the questioning at the defense, followed by holders of the *kandidat* degree, or the *magister* ("who at disputes usually gave the faculty a chance to get to know them"). After them came the public, and only at the very end the faculty, "to whom ordinarily it remained merely to say a few words providing a definitive judgment."[32] There was even at this time a special participant, called a *zashchitnik* (defender, protector, or in legal usage, counsel for the defense), whose job it was to make sure that the discussion stayed on track and that no unfair questions were asked.[33] Most likely, the *zashchitnik* was necessary because of the relatively chaotic and democratic procedures of the dissertation defense before mid-century. As the order became more structured and professorial, this protector was deemed (rightly or wrongly) unnecessary.

As time went by, such informally conducted defenses were no longer feasible. By mid-century, the Russian university had become "a real scientific center of the European type."[34] Russian university culture had matured.[35] Although this maturation was a continuous, incremental process, the pivotal era was clearly the 1830s. One reason for this was the significant step forward represented by the university statute of 1835, which relieved the universities of their responsibilities for the lower educational organs, while simultaneously improving the quality and the socioeconomic status of the professoriate.[36] The new statute required professors to have the doctorate, and a number of the earlier faculty, including Shevyrev, scrambled to complete and defend a dissertation within the year allotted, while others simply lost their positions.[37] Whether because of these reforms or because of Nicholas's insistence on university education for the service nobility and his carrot-and-stick policies to achieve that goal, the universities lost the stigma attached to them in the early decades and moved into a new era.

Far and away the most significant factor elevating the scholarship, erudition, and sophistication of university culture was the quantum improvement in the faculty, beginning with the brilliantly successful experiment with the so-called Professors' Institute at Dorpat University.[38] Observers are unanimous on the importance of this influx of new, better trained, and more vital professors. Buslaev recalls that the new professors who returned to take up teaching posts beginning in 1835 provided "the first decisive impetus towards a more detailed definition of the scholarly specialization of each department."[39] Cynthia Whittaker called the Professors' Institute "the single most important action taken to prepare the renaissance of Russia's universities."[40] Grigor'ev indicates that the period up to 1831 was "far from brilliant," but that with the return of these young scholars, along with the continued steady influx of *komandirovka*-trained professors, "there began for our, as well as for other Russian universities, another period, a better life."[41] Kornilov assesses the results of the program to train young scholars abroad as: "splendid. During the Forties a whole pleiad of young Russian scholars who had been abroad appeared, and they contributed greatly to the education of the following generation of the *intelligentsia*. To mention a few names: Granovsky, Riedkin, Kriukov, Buslaev (in Moscow), Meyer (Kazan), Nievolin, Kutorga (Petrograd)."[42] The process by which the Russian professoriate achieved European standards of scientific training, scholarship, and intellectual rigor—a process that until the very end of the empire would continue to produce an ever more sophisticated professoriate—began in the 1830s. It was the *sine qua non* of the new university culture.

This change to a new type of professor constituted a qualitative difference, because the new professoriate came back from their research trips with more than a novel methodology: they came armed with the Western secular-scientific worldview. Kizevetter's words on this bear quoting at length. The 1830s marked "the beginning of a new epoch in the development of Moscow University," he writes, because

> the pleiad of young professors that appeared in Moscow in the 30s and 40s was with only individual exceptions imbued with an exalted conception of the purpose of a professor. In this conception service to science was indissolubly linked with the appearance in the consciousness of society of the ideals of humanitarian progress.
>
> The young professors of the 30s, in Herzen's words, "brought with them passionate faith in science and in people. They retained all the ardor of youth and the [university] rostrum was for them a pulpit from which they had been called to spread the truth [*blagovestit'*—also means to ring the bells as a summons for church]. They appeared in the auditoriums not as parochial [*tsekhovye*] scholars, but as missionaries of the human religion."[43]

Seen from this perspective, the dissertation defense was the ceremonial ordination of a new priest.

Of course, the universities did not exist in a vacuum. They developed in an environment of upper-class culture characterized by better education, more cosmopolitan worldviews, and greater sophistication both among the public in general and within the student body as well.[44] It was in the 1830s that groups such as the Stankevich circle, "founded in the shadow of Moscow University," came into existence.[45] By the late 1830s and 1840s, the "ranks and interests of the educated public, while still limited, expanded to support a growing number of learned societies, theaters, public lectures, publishing ventures and schools at all levels."[46] The incipient appearance of a new type of educated public on the Russian scene was spectacularly demonstrated by the enormous popularity of the lecture series given by Granovsky, so dramatically recaptured by Priscilla Roosevelt. Annenkov relates that on his arrival in Moscow in the autumn of 1843 he "found a scholarly and, so to speak, joint-class elation going on in Moscow on the occasion of the first public lectures of Granovsky, who had gathered around himself not only the scholars, the literary parties, and his usual ecstatic auditors—the young people of the University—but also the whole *educated* class of the city."[47] This was an unprecedented occurrence, inconceivable and impossible until "objects of respect for the mass of the public, aside from the ones long since sanctioned officially and by general consensus"[48] had appeared, objects of respect forged in the fires of the new university culture.

The tsarist government was not yet reconciled to the appearance of an overtly oppositionist intellectual culture, and a period of reaction soon followed. As part of the reaction to 1848, the student body was reduced, *komandirovki* abroad were prohibited, and even the practice of making lithographs of courses available at the Public Library was stopped. After the scandal generated by Granovsky's *magister* defense in 1845, new rules were issued restricting access to public defenses and establishing a ticketing system.[49] According to the system set up "for the prevention of disorders at public defenses of scholarly dissertations," tickets for redistribution were allotted to the faculty according to rank, with the rector free to invite as many as he wanted. Furthermore, the administrator of the educational district could issue additional tickets "to make scholarly disputes accessible to supporters of education," but obviously under very controlled conditions.[50] If this was not enough, the next month a circular laid down strictures calling for supervision not only of the dissertations themselves but also of the theses drawn from them as the basis of the dispute, rendering it impossible "to understand in various ways one and the same proposition." Administrators were also to insure that there was no discussion "in an approving sense of principles opposed to our governmental structure" at defenses.[51] It was this atmosphere that could produce a dissertation defense in embryology at which the candidate was accused of disloyalty to Russia because he employed Latin, French, and German scientific terminology, a defense that was more like "a police denunciation instead of a scholarly examination."[52] It was only with the relenting of this oppressive atmosphere after the Crimean defeat and the death of "Impernikel" (Nicholas I, in Herzen's disrespectful phrasing) that the educated public, together with the academic community, both of which continued to expand and develop the while, could fashion out of dissertation defenses a public means of intercommunication and social affirmation.

As the brief description of Vernadsky's 1917 defense indicated, a combination of formal process and elaborate ritual evolved over time. In practice, for the entire period for which a formal university degree-granting system existed, 1804–1917, progress up the ladder proceeded roughly as follows.[53] A student successfully completing the university course earned a *diplom*.[54]

If he had done well enough and impressed a faculty member by winning the gold or silver medal in an essay competition, he would be "retained at the department" for "preparation for the professorial calling."[55] After further study, the student took both oral and written examinations in a variety of fields. For a candidate in Russian history, this involved, in its least complicated variant, examinations in Russian history, universal history, and political economy. The oral examinations were attended by all members of the department, and other degree holders and people with established scholarly credentials could also be present. Successful completion of these, which was by no means a given,[56] allowed the student to go on to the research and writing of the dissertation. To support themselves while investigating and writing the dissertation, many found it necessary to teach in a *gimnazium,* at the Higher Women's Courses, as a *privat-dotsent* at the University, or in some other institution. It was the norm from around mid-century for the person preparing a dissertation to take at least one *komandirovka* for research purposes; some went abroad for two years or more, although not all research trips involved foreign travel.

Once a candidate had finished writing the dissertation, he submitted it to the department for approval. The department assigned one or more faculty members to review the work, although in theory all were supposed to read it. On the basis of that review, or *otzyv,* the department decided whether to allow a defense. If the decision was negative, changes could be suggested or the dissertation could be rejected outright. At that point, the candidate could seek out another university and attempt to have the dissertation accepted and defended there. Assuming a positive review, however, it was now the candidate's responsibility to have the work published.[57] Sometimes, a dissertation would be serialized in a thick journal, such as *Russkaia mysl'* or the journal of the Ministry of Education, in addition to its publication in book form. Frequently, reviews of the work would appear before the defense; in fact, one reason for this procedure was to allow wide familiarity with the work before the dispute. In addition, the defense had to be announced three times in the local press. These steps assured a certain degree of public awareness among those interested. Some defenses attracted packed houses, but the author of even the driest and most obscure dissertation could count on the attendance of his friends, family, and students. Furthermore, there was a much greater awareness of serious historical study among the better-educated elements of the population in the nineteenth century, as is indicated by the fact that the major newspapers commonly included information about new historical publications and reports about dissertation defenses. Since many of these candidates had been active researchers and teachers for a number of years, they had a certain profile among the interested public and most disputes attracted a respectable crowd.[58] In addition to the merits of the candidate or his thesis, the regular participation of the luminaries of the academic world in these disputes attracted the public.

Whoever was in charge of the defense would convene it with a descriptive reading of the candidate's *curriculum vitae,* followed by a presentation by the candidate himself.[59] In some cases, for example that of Aleksandr S. Lappo-Danilevskii in 1890 and of Aleksandr E. Presniakov in 1918, this part of the defense—the aptly named *rech' pered zashchitoi*—resulted in a theoretically sophisticated, sometimes elegant speech.[60] The appreciative audience generally greeted the conclusion of this speech with "thunderous" applause, after which the official opponents proceeded with their remarks.[61] It was customary for them to praise certain aspects of the work before bringing up any criticisms. After each opponent completed his remarks, the candidate had an opportunity to respond, and following the final exchange between an official opponent and the candidate, the chairman turned to the audience and asked if anyone else had something to bring up (*Ne ugodno li eshche komu-nibud' vozrazit'?*).[62] It seems that "unofficial opponents" were given wide latitude to engage the candidate in prolonged debate so long as they were considered somehow respectable interlocutors. As a result, a dispute could go on for some time. Ultimately, though, questions would run out and the faculty would vote on the acceptance of the dissertation. This had been reduced to merely formal significance. If a candidate was allowed to, so to speak, go public, his confirmation in the degree (subject to confirmation by the Ministry) was a foregone conclusion. Usually the faculty did not quit the room to take the vote, and it was even fairly common for the chairman to announce the confirmation (the candidate is "fully worthy of the degree sought") without any formal consultation with the faculty members present. At this point, the new degree holder was treated to rousing applause and to congratulatory embraces and exchange of kisses from the faculty. Sometime during the next few days, the successful candidate would put on a celebration dinner or party for his inner circle and for the official participants.[63]

Krichevskii provides some interesting statistical information concerning the results of this arduous process. Excluding medical degrees, there were 625 advanced degrees earned through 1863, of which 160 were doctorates. Almost half were earned at Moscow (153) and St. Petersburg (152), despite the fact that St. Petersburg University only opened in 1819 and witnessed its first defense only in the 1830s. Of the total, the share of the historical–philological faculty was 30 percent.[64] After 1863 the number of degrees granted more than tripled, but the general pattern was remarkably similar.

St. Petersburg (760) and Moscow (538) accounted for a bit over half of the 2,266 advanced degrees granted (880 doctorates). The percentage awarded by historical–philological faculties was unchanged, but St. Petersburg emerged from under the shadow of Moscow University, claiming pride of place at the expense of its older rival.[65] Of course, not everyone who earned a *magister* went on to do a doctorate, but for those who did, the average amount of time between the completion of the two degrees was five and a half years. For the most part, they truly did "earn" their degrees.[66]

The half century from the accession of Alexander II in 1855 to the outbreak of revolution in 1905 can be considered the golden age of the dissertation defense. It was in that period (especially the second half of it) that scholars observing the strictest world standards in their fields met before an appreciative and attuned public to discuss and dispute the issues raised in their dissertation research. As we have seen, defenses continued to take place up to the very end of the empire and even beyond. It is incontrovertible, however, that the institution of the defense was more important in some periods than in others. For example, any public gathering assumed more significance in the doldrums of the 1880s following the assassination of Alexander II.[67] Eventually, the creation of a national representative body and of legal politics after 1905 served to eliminate the more overt political aspects from most disputes. By 1906, because of their faith "in the stability of the new constitutional structure, most professors now hoped that the university question would simply fade away. The Duma would replace university auditoriums as the nation's political forum."[68] Picheta, who comments on this phenomenon more directly than any other observer, thought that after the 1905 Revolution few outsiders attended defenses, leaving them exclusively to the hard core of professors, students, and acquaintances of the candidate.[69] Nonetheless, the dispute retained a social, intellectual, and political importance for the life of the system.

What made this fifty-year span *l'âge d'or* of the dispute was what might with intentional ambiguity be called cultural politics. The dispute became an arena in which the oppositional politics characteristic of the secular, progressive, liberal *Weltanschauung* of many professors could be more or less safely displayed and could receive reciprocal support from the public. It is "unequivocal" that disputes possessed "a public character, extremely important in the era of that reaction with which aristocratic [*fin de siècle*] Russia was burdened."[70] In addition, both the professoriate and the public utilized the dispute as a means of social interaction, bonding, and support, where they could find "the living word, the living thought . . . [that] could be expressed nowhere else."[71] In part, this communion served to counteract the isolation, guilt, and self-doubt that assailed them as members of a very exclusive elite wedged between an antithetically oriented government and a popular mass either indifferent or hostile.[72] For the educated elite, *nauka* (science) was a cardinal element of their progressive faith and their self-justification. Finally, in certain instances the dissertation defense became the battleground on which more conservative, chauvinistic, or statist professors confronted the challenges to their understanding of orthodoxy.

Certain defenses were less disputes than "celebrations of scholarship" (*torzhestvo nauki*). At the 1886 doctoral defense of Pavel G. Vinogradov, for example, the discussion was conducted "in very amicable tones." M.M. Kovalevskii's remarks in particular were expressed "in a tone of exceptionally friendly closeness," and he left out of his discussion with Vinogradov several minor points, saying, "Well, I'll have the opportunity to talk to you about this some more in our private conversations."[73] At Aleksandr Kizevetter's master's defense, Kliuchevskii "conducted the dispute in a tone that allowed all present to clearly understand that he recognized his student as a colleague."[74] Kizevetter and Liubavskii served as official opponents for the master's dispute of M.M. Bogoslovskii, and they "all conducted themselves in the most gentlemanly (*dzhentel'menskii*) tone of comrades in science."[75] At the doctoral defense in philosophy of Prince S.N. Trubetskoi, the hall was "full of representatives of the Moscow nobility," and French was the dominant language.[76] The atmosphere of another dispute was described as "cozy, endearing, and benevolent."[77]

A model of this sort of defense was that of V.O. Kliuchevskii. Kliuchevskii had been delivering his lectures—one is tempted to say performances—on Russian history to jammed auditoriums at Moscow University for three years, had taught at other Muscovite educational institutions for many more years, and was well known in educated circles of the city (and beyond) by the time "his long-awaited doctoral dispute"[78] of *Boiarskaia duma drevnei Rusi*—"the real 'event of the day' this past week"[79]—took place "under extraordinarily festive and triumphant circumstances" in September 1882. According to the account in *Russkie vedomosti,* the large lecture auditorium was set aside for the occasion and arranged with long lines of chairs. A balustrade section was reserved for the "members of the university corporation and for honored guests." The preparations were clearly necessary, because an hour before the defense was to start, the auditorium was already so packed with people that "as they say, there was not room for an apple to fall."[80] The "noisy and unanimous rapture" that Kliuchevskii encountered when he entered was such as "the ancient walls of the local alma mater had not witnessed for a long time," "perhaps never."[81] In an atmosphere of "reverent silence," the "talented toiler" discussed his "microscopic investigation" in a speech as impressive for "the profundity of its content as for the elegance of its form."[82] The dispute lasted four hours, at the end of which the audience roared its approval with shouts of "Bravo!" a ten-minute standing ovation, and applause that accompanied Kliuchevskii "to the very doors of the university."[83] A scholar of the erudition and reputation of Kliuchevskii could literally fill the house.

Other disputes were compelling because of their notoriety, since "official opponents did not always simply pay court to the candidate and pay him various compliments."[84] Owing to the advance publication and review of the works in question and to the workings of a grapevine among the elite, instances of such "disputed" dissertations were known in advance and attracted an audience. They could get nasty within the bounds of their "gentlemanly" limits. Nikolai A. Rozhkov was subjected to a "thorough dressing down" by Kliuchevskii who "mercilessly went through the methodological imperfections of [Rozhkov's] work with a fine-toothed comb."[85] V.E. Iakushkin was so disturbed by the rough handling he received at his master's dispute that he quit his teaching job.[86]

A dramatic instance of this type of controversy was the master's defense by A.N. Giliarov of his work "O sofistakh". Giliarov was greatly agitated in anticipation of his defense, because, as he told some of his *gimnaziia* students, "they say the historian [Pavel G. Vinogradov, the second official opponent] is going to devour me."[87] Because of "unflattering" and "sensational" rumors flying about beforehand, the assembly hall was filled.[88] The first opponent, the Slavist N.Ia. Grot, also had some harsh criticisms, and the dispute "soon turned into a heated, venomous, and unpleasant exchange of fire. Both revealed personal irritation. Grot seemed biased; Giliarov in turn was sharp and rude. The atmosphere grew heated, the public got nervous and with their applause poured oil on the fire."[89]

In this volatile situation, Giliarov launched a preemptive strike, suddenly pulling a letter from his pocket and asking in a loud voice "And who wrote me that this is a brilliant dissertation?"[90] Before finding out about Vinogradov's highly condemnatory review, Grot had written the candidate reassuring words, the revelation of which produced "the effect of a scandal."[91] Giliarov's backers among the audience responded to this bombshell by breaking into "furious" applause, which so stunned Grot that all he could do was to exclaim weakly "What means you will resort to!"[92] In short, Maklakov concluded indignantly, "the dispute was conducted not in circumstances of academic seriousness, but as if it were a mass political meeting" (*miting*).[93]

The political dimensions of many of the most celebrated defenses are not hard to discover. In the case of Timofei Granovsky's *magister* defense in 1845, Granovsky himself had become a political issue, owing primarily to the notoriety and adulation he had earned as a result of his public lectures.

That explains why at his dispute some seven hundred students jammed in the choir and even perched on the school benches and tables, punctuated the proceedings with prolonged outbursts of applause, booing, and hissing, and transformed his departure into a victorious procession. Despite the protestation of one of Granovsky's opponents that "this is not a theater!" it was tremendous political melodrama.[94]

Certain dissertations were hedged about with all sorts of political considerations, with career costs for the authors. Nikolai Kareev produced a left-oriented analysis of the French peasantry in the last quarter of the eighteenth century.[95] Kliuchevskii wondered whether he feared it would brand him a socialist; Petr Lavrov convinced him to soften it by dropping the word "revolution" from the title.[96] At the defense, Ger'e was already very upset, a condition only aggravated by the repeated applause of the audience, first for Kareev himself, and then for Maksim Kovalevskii, who "showered excessive praise on the dissertation with the precise intention of causing Ger'e pique."[97] Kareev paid for that pique. He was not kept on permanently at Moscow University. Furthermore, rather than receiving a post at another Russian university of a status commensurate with his scholarship, he was shipped off to the relative intellectual exile of the University of Warsaw. Later, progress in the processing of his doctoral dissertation was greatly retarded by the lingering effects of this earlier argument. It was risky to be too controversial in a state-run system of education.[98]

Like Kareev's, Vasilii I. Semevskii's *magister* dispute in February 1882 combined political notoriety and scholarly appeal. The dissertation had encountered innumerable obstacles at St. Petersburg University, where Konstantin N. Bestuzhev-Riumin was shocked by the political implications of Semevskii's subject, his treatment of it, and its "dangerous thoughts," and ultimately refused to accept it.[99] Forced to submit the work to another university, Semevskii won the right to present it at Moscow, despite the "cool" (Kliuchevskii) and "hostile" (N.A. Popov) reception accorded it.[100] This "previous fate of the work and the oddity of presenting a *Petersburg* dissertation in Moscow," in addition to the importance of the subject matter, awakened "a lively interest" in the public.[101] For these reasons,

> the dispute had unusual significance and attracted many members of the public [*massa publiki*], filling the large auditorium, which in recent times is very rarely set aside for disputes. Everyone wanted to get more closely acquainted with the contents of the book and to judge on the basis of the evidence of the author himself the truth of the stupid rumors that have been so zealously set in circulation.[102]

Semevskii returned to Petersburg University to teach as a *privat-dotsent* despite Bestuzhev-Riumin's "him or me" ultimatum, but was released four years later owing to Bestuzhev's inveterate backdoor politicking.[103] The public had a keen nose for any whiff of scandal.[104]

All this indicates that the public was not a mere passive backdrop to disputes. As we have seen, at controversial disputes the public came to the arena having independently arrived at an idea of which side was right, and then injected themselves into the debate by means of their applause, with both their moral and their oral support. Moreover, the public did not show up for just any defense or public lecture; our review indicates that the educated public preferred to pick and choose the defenses they attended.[105] There were clearly defined "consumer" tastes concerning both the subject matter and the personalities involved in disputes. Finally, over the years the public worked out, in conjunction with the professoriate, an elaborate body of etiquette and expectations concerning disputes.

The workings of this code can be seen in the star system that developed. By all accounts, the most popular public lecturer was Kliuchevskii. According to Maklakov, this "god" of the Moscow historians (Picheta) could not really "play" during his public lectures, because he was too thoroughly prepared for them. There were times, however, when he stood before the public without a script, "and then his dialectical talent showed forth in all its brilliance. That was on the occasion of scholarly disputes."[106] According to Kizevetter's self-evaluation, he had a certain reputation among the public and his dissertation topic enjoyed a certain interest there, too, which partially explained the large showing for his master's defense. Still, "the main enticement was the fact that Kliuchevskii was to appear as official opponent, and, you know, to hear Kliuchevskii conduct a dispute was the supreme delight for connoisseurs [*tonkie tseniteli*] of scholarly debates."[107] On these occasions, he combined "a game of cat and mouse with a gentle examination of the candidate,"[108] during which he revealed his true "dialectical artistry and manner."[109] So popular was Kliuchevskii that people would come just to hear him. At M.K. Liubavskii's dispute, part of the audience left after Kliuchevskii's comments, apparently indifferent to what the next official opponent, Mitrofan V. Dovnar-Zapol'skii, either thought or felt. Indeed, Liubavskii himself, who was "servile" in his answers to Kliuchevskii, without provocation turned "persistent and sharp to the point of rudeness" and "rather coarsely sarcastic" in responding to Dovnar-Zapol'skii.[110] These different, but equally rude, responses demonstrate the workings of the star system, and they also indicate that the public and the professors shared a common set of values and rules concerning the acceptable and expected at disputes.

Another titan of the public lecture halls was Maksim Kovalevskii. Appearing as second opponent at the doctoral dispute of Pavel Vinogradov, and speaking after the "prolix, fairly boring" V.I. Ger′e, Kovalevskii "riveted the attention and forced the entire enormous hall to prick up its ears." Everyone was impressed by his "colossal scholarly erudition." A young barrister's assistant was beside himself. After the dispute, he "couldn't quiet down for a long time and kept exclaiming 'Wow! What a memory Kovalevskii's got! What power! Ah, damn him! That's not a human being! That's some sort of supernatural phenomenon!'"[111] Kovalevskii's performance at the dissertation defense of A.S. Alekseev on Jean-Jacques Rousseau's political thought displays another facet of the interaction at disputes. An extant description of the dispute reveals a now-familiar scene:

> The whole circumstance of the dispute had an extraordinarily celebratory character. The assembly hall of the university was overflowing with the public. In the front row sat several "star-bearers" [high-ranking and highly decorated civil servants], among whom was the congenial old codger K.I. Sadikov, ... who was evidently there for purely decorative purposes, since the whole time he dozed lightly in his chair, waking up now and again and smacking his lips. But even he, I remember, woke up a bit when, after the opening speech by Alekseev, Kovalevskii suddenly began to talk.[112]

Why did Sadikov awaken from his pleasant slumber? What had the public come to witness? It was to hear a "steady stream of eloquent, glittering witticisms." To witness as "murderous sarcasm uninterruptedly flew from his lips, and he poured it on the poor candidate like shrapnel." The public was rewarded for its presence by seeing Kovalevskii in such "rare form."[113]

This was not a jaded Roman public delighting in the spectacle of the slaughter of the candidate-Christians by the lions of the Russian academic world. What the public wanted was the flash and fire of wit and culture. That is why they so enjoyed Kliuchevskii's game of cat and mouse. Similarly, they liked the "lively and witty" performance of Vladimir I. Lamanskii at the doctoral dispute of Nikolai D. Chechulin, in which he managed to include allusions to Tolstoi's *Anna Karenina,* Denis Fonvizin's *The Minor,* the romantic historical novelist Marlinskii, and the comic characters Dobchinskii and Bobchinskii from Gogol's *The Inspector General.* His talk "consisted of a series of witty and apt separate observations that put the public in a good mood."[114] At Kizevetter's doctoral dispute, he and his opponents Liubavskii and Bogoslovskii "argued in a very lively fashion, not without joking sarcasm from all sides, and the public cheerfully applauded each of us several times."[115] Until the very end of the old order, the public would continue to revel in the erudition and wit of the academic elite by means of a social mechanism that they themselves had helped to shape and direct.

This chapter began with a description of the circumstances surrounding George Vernadsky's dissertation defense. Despite their joy at the successful outcome of the defense and the "warm and friendly" feeling of their fête, the assembled company was aware that something momentous in Russian history was in the offing. Despite themselves, they could not shake the gnawing awareness they "and all of Russia were on the very edge of the abyss." George Vernadsky left Petrograd on 25 October. He was to find out later that a Red Guard unit had "requisitioned" his parents' car as they returned from the railroad station. He himself rode to Perm, perched on the top berth in a cabin packed with deserting soldiers, and arrived to learn from his wife of the revolution that had occurred in the city he had just quit. They stood at the end of an age. Yet, although Vernadsky said that it "was already that time when people began to forget about traditions," Vernadsky and his segment of society stuck doggedly to their ways amidst the rising ruin of Russia. They would have been saddened to know that the dissertation defense as they knew it could not survive the demise of their class, but they could have comforted themselves with the thought that they had been faithful to their own self-constructed traditions to the bitter end.[116]

Conclusion

The public dissertation defense or dispute arose as part of elite culture in the eighteenth century. Once the government had committed itself to creating an educated corps from which to recruit the bureaucracy, it also moved greatly to expand the university system. In order to staff those universities with reliable, Russian professors, the government established extremely demanding requirements for advanced degrees, sought out promising candidates, and shepherded them through graduate programs. Eventually, the professoriate thus created moved toward a situation of moderate self-assurance, limited autonomy, and professional self-definition. The universities and the professoriate matured in tandem with educated society, a portion of which became the social milieu supporting and sustaining the professoriate. Together, the professoriate and the public fashioned a social mechanism with its own rituals, practitioners, and constituency. Numerous participants and observers remembered fondly and in detail the passage "through fire and water" of publishing and defending a dissertation.[117] Thus, the government, in establishing defenses as public affairs in a manner consistent with contemporary elite social practices but for its own state-directed purposes gave rise to both a new social grouping and a new social forum. That social forum assumed an important function, allowing the professoriate to demonstrate its skill, expertise and erudition, to draw support from the assembled public, and to share with them a sense of their common devotion to and familiarity with *kultura* and *nauka*. This development represents a significant example of the shaping of an autonomous area of social behavior outside of government.

We have seen that public disputes were a part of scholarly culture from the beginnings of university life in Russia. This is thoroughly consistent with the didactic disposition of the tsarist government, the sponsor of the institutions of higher education. Of course, the government was primarily interested in producing a pool of well-trained servitors on which it could draw. But the leadership (in the person not only of the emperors and empresses, but also of figures such as Speransky, Uvarov, Miliutin, and so on) also attempted to inculcate in the higher ranks of society cultural habits consistent with its image as a European power and conducive to the proper acceptance by the elite of the government's educational requirements. Thus, the public display of knowledge via disputes—as was true of education in general—was not an end in itself, but was viewed instrumentally by the tsarist government.

This explains why the government continued to tolerate public disputes and only rimmed them about with restrictions even in the darkest days of Nikolaevan reaction. It also helps to explain why Granovsky's lectures and his defense were such controversial affairs. They did not occur in a neutral environment; rather they represented the first incursion of Westernized intellectuals into an arena the government had reserved for its own purposes. Moreover, Granovsky's public presentations were the first instance of the implement of education slipping out of the government's control, exactly as earlier the instrument of culture had been turned to other purposes by Novikov, Radishchev, and others. Yet the public lecture or dispute was a natural one for the educated elite, embodied in the professoriate, to take over. After all, this was their *métier*. Furthermore, the public nature of the event imparted to it an important affirmative, societal function. Much as did the salons in the eighteenth century and the *kruzhki* in the first half of the nineteenth, disputes marked both participants and audience as members of a certain group, reinforcing their sense of belonging, reaffirming their belief in an unspoken credo of common values. Educated society had as great a need for such social mechanisms as did the general populace for their artels and their *zemliachestva*.

The way in which the Russian scholarly community with the active participation of the educated public took the government-imposed public defense and transformed it into a legitimate social ritual is an impressive example of independent activity in the social realm. The close examination of discrete components of Russian prerevolutionary society and of thick descriptions of various aspects of their existence holds out promise as a very fruitful methodological device through which to achieve a better understanding of Russia of the late imperial period. The examination of particular microcommunities or subcultures will assist in the process of conceptual refinement, providing empirical foundation for productive theoretical concepts, such as Gleason's idea of the transition from *obshchestvo* to *obshchestvennost'*. Alfred J. Rieber recently exhorted students of Russian social history to be "bold enough to cross boundaries into institutional and legal history, . . . [and to] march in the opposite direction toward culture defined in its broadest anthropological sense to include institutional norms and material artifacts as well as values, belief systems, and attitudes."[118] This study has attempted to draw conclusions of general relevance from an analysis of dissertation defenses, but much work remains to be done in the area of a more broadly defined, more generously understood social history of tsarist Russia.

Notes

The author gratefully acknowledges support in preparing this article from the Naval Academy Research Council. Reprinted from *Jahrbücher für Geschichte Osteuropas* 41, no. 2, pp. 242–65, by permission of the journal.

1. George V. Vernadsky (1887–1973), the eminent Yale professor and one of the founders of Russian studies in the United States, was the son of Vladimir I. Vernadsky, the brilliant Russian and Soviet academician and creator of the idea of the biosphere. On Vernadsky *père*, see Kendall E. Bailes, *Science and Russian Culture in an Age of Revolutions: V.I. Vernadsky and His Scientific School, 1863–1945* (Bloomington, IN: Indiana University Press, 1990).

2. This was Vernadsky's *magister* dissertation, *Russkoe masonstvo v tsarstvovanie Ekateriny II*, ch. 137 *Zapiski Istoriko-Filologicheskogo Fakul'teta Petrogradskogo Universiteta* (Petrograd, 1917). My recounting is based on G. Vernadsky, "Iz vospominanii (gody ucheniia S.F. Platonova)," *Novyi zhurnal*, no. 100 (New York, 1970): 219–21. I have changed the order of some of the quotations and details, while preserving the original sense.

3. The official opponents were Sergei F. Platonov (1860–1933), the leading historian of Russia after Kliuchevskii's death; Sergei V. Rozhdestvenskii (1868–1934), best known for his histories of education in Russia; and Il'ia A. Shliapkin (1858–1918), professor of Russian literature at St. Petersburg University and editor of Griboedov's collected works.

4. Shliapkin excused himself.

. 5. Abbott Gleason, "The Terms of Russian Social History," pp. 15–27, in Edith W. Clowes, Samuel D. Kassow, and James L. West, eds., *Between Tsar and People: Educated Society and the Quest for Public Identity in Late Imperial Russia* (Princeton, NJ: Princeton University Press, 1991), esp. pp. 21–22. He treats the same subject at the beginning of his study *Young Russia: The Genesis of Russian Radicalism in the 1860s* (New York: Viking Press, 1980): 2.

6. It is common practice to refer to Moscow University as Russia's first university,

but the institute of the Academy of Sciences qualified as a type of university. In eighteenth-century Europe it was not immediately evident that the newer and more innovative national academies established in various countries would not serve as the institutional bases for the type of research and teaching centers that ultimately came to be housed in reformed and rejuvenated universities. The German university would acquire the status of a worldwide model by the end of the nineteenth century, but, according to Daniel Fallon, "At the end of the eighteenth century most universities in German-speaking Europe could be characterized as sites of rote disputation inhabited largely by pedants." Daniel Fallon, *The German University: A Heroic Ideal in Conflict with the Modern World* (Boulder, CO: Colorado Associated University Press, 1980): 5.

7. See Gary Marker, *Publishing, Printing, and the Origins of Intellectual Life in Russia, 1700–1800* (Princeton, NJ: Princeton University Press, 1985). For another side of the emergence of public intellectual life, the public library, see Mary Stuart, *Aristocrat-Librarian in Service to the Tsar: Aleksei Nikolaevich Olenin and the Imperial Public Library,* Boulder, CO: East European Monographs, no. 221 (New York: Columbia University Press, 1986).

8. I am concentrating on Moscow University to establish that public, oral disputations were an accepted part of university culture by the time a real university system on German lines appeared in the first half of the nineteenth century. Our discussion of disputes and defenses from 1804 on refers specifically to the *magister* and *doktorat* defense, whereas the discussion of disputes before 1804 involves any public disputation of a "learned" question. In fact, such practices seem to have been common in elite intellectual life in the eighteenth century. Freeze relates the example that: "Provincial bishops even tried to make the annual (or biannual) theological debate (*disput*) into a public event. The debates were ostensibly designed to display the seminarians' knowledge of philosophy and theology; ... But in fact the debate became a great social occasion. The bishop invited local nobles to attend the festivities, which included not only theological debates but also recitations of poetry, music, and refreshments. Seminarians were also called upon to perform a similar role in various public ceremonies; the opening of the new guberniias in 1778, for example, was celebrated by public assemblies, where seminarians recited adulatory verse about the empress and local dignitaries." Gregory L. Freeze, *The Russian Levites: Parish Clergy in the Eighteenth Century* (Cambridge, MA: Harvard University Press, 1977): 102.

9. S.P. Shevyrev, *Istoriia imperatorskogo Moskovskogo universiteta napisannaia k stoletnemu ego iubileiu ordinarnym professorom russkoi slovesnosti i pedagogii Stepanom Shevyrevym, 1755–1855* (Moscow, 1855): 568–69.

10. Aleksandr A. Kizevetter, "Moskovskii universitet," p. 43, in Parizhskii komitet po oznamenovaniiu 175-letiia Moskovskogo universiteta, *Moskovskii Universitet 1755–1930: Iubileinyi sbornik,* eds. V.B. El'iashevich, A.A. Kizevetter, and M.M. Novikov (Paris, 1930).

11. Ibid.

12. Ibid., p. 66. In later years, January 12 would be the day on which the celebration of the founding of the university was commemorated. *Tat'ianin den'* was the day the *ukaz* ordering the establishment of the university was signed. Judging from what Shevyrev says, it was not celebrated at this time.

13. See ibid. for the text of one of those announcements.

14. Ibid.

15. Kizevetter, "Moskovskii universitet," p. 25.

16. S.A. Vengerov, *Kritiko-biograficheskii slovar' russkikh pisatelei i uchenykh (ot nachala russkoi obrazovannosti do nashikh dnei),* 6 vols. (St. Petersburg, 1886–1904), vol. 2 (1891): 159.

17. Kizevetter writes of Anichkov that he was "apparently the first serious and eminent scientist" from the ranks of Moscow University alumni. Kizevetter, "Moskovskii universitet," p. 34. For his discussion of Anichkov's dissertation difficulties, see pp. 60–61.

18. "Disput v Moskovskom Universitete 25 Avgusta 1769," reported by S.M. Solov'ev, *Russkii arkhiv* 1875, no. 11, p. 313; and Shevyrev, *Istoriia imperatorskogo Moskovskogo universiteta,* p. 142, where the public discussion is given as 24 August.

19. Shevyrev, *Istoriia imperatorskogo Moskovskogo universiteta,* p. 142; and "Disput v Moskovskom Universitete," p. 313.

20. It is artificial to divide the educated elite in the eighteenth century into "state" and "society," since they had not yet reached their "parting of the ways." Also, please excuse the use of the impersonal terms state and *obshchestvo.* Unqualified use of such terms tends to reify the ideas they represent divorced from the actions of flesh-and-blood individuals. One point of this paper is that we need to look behind some of the forms of tsarist society to see what was actually there.

21. Kizevetter, "Moskovskii universitet," p. 43.

22. The foundation legislation of the modern university system in Russia was the statutes of 1804 (the main revisions of the statutes were issued in 1835, 1863, and 1884). As far as the requirements for advanced degrees, however, some legislation preceded the 1804 foundation legislation and subsequent reforms proceeded independently from the main "university question." The *ukaz* of 24 January 1803 established three academic degrees: *kandidat* (essentially a bachelor's degree), *magister,* and *doktorat.* Meanwhile, the *magister* and *doktorat,* for which there were both oral and written examinations as well as the public defenses, were truly advanced degrees. Following the so-called "Derpt affair," in which some degrees were sold, a reform established gradations of the bachelor's degree. All finishing the full university course of study now earned the title of *deistvitel'nyi student.* By successfully taking examinations after at least a year had passed, a *deistvitel'nyi student* acquired the additional degree designation *kandidat.* From there one could proceed to earn the other advanced degrees with at least a year intervening between each degree. Subsequent legislation did not fundamentally alter this system, with changes affecting only such things as the language of the dissertation (i.e., Russian, Latin, or German), the structure of the faculties and of the examinations, the categories in which one could earn a degree, and eventually in 1863 the elimination of the examinations for the doctoral degree.

23. Drawing on French models dating from Condorcet's proposal to the revolutionary Assembly, the Russians initially had attempted to integrate the school system in a vertical manner, with each of the six universities overseeing the primary and secondary schools in its district. The six universities were Moscow, Derpt (Dorpat), Kazan, Kharkov, Vilnius, and from 1819, St. Petersburg. In the wake of the Polish uprising of 1830, Vilnius was closed in 1832 and the new St. Vladimir University opened in Kiev (1832–33). See Constantin Galskoy, "The Ministry of Education Under Nicholas I (1826–1836)," (unpub. Ph.D. diss., Stanford University, 1977), pp. 199–208.

24. See James T. Flynn, *The University Reform of Tsar Alexander I, 1802–1835* (Washington, DC: Catholic University of America Press, 1988), ch. 4, "Universities in the Bible Society Decade."

25. Interestingly enough, I have come across no indication that there was ever any consideration of dropping the public defense. The implicit acceptance of this ritual may have stemmed from the common acceptance of the public nature of knowledge and the state-oriented goals of education. Another important influence may have been foreign models. The drafters of the university statutes of 1804 took into account Condorcet's

writings on universities, the recently established (1783) Polish system, and Christoph Meiners's study of German universities, *Über die Verfassung und Verwaltung deutscher Universitäten,* 2 vols. (Göttingen, 1801–1802), as well as direct communication with Meiners. See Kizevetter, "Moskovskii universitet," p. 64. Meiners discusses examinations and disputes, see Band 1: 345–65 in the reprint edition (Darmstadt, Germany: Scientia Verlag Aalen, 1970). Marc Raeff stresses the significance of Germany as a transmitter of Western forms and ideas to Russia, and the Russian university system most closely resembled the German.

26. Mikhail Pogodin, "Disput g. Gladkova," *Zhurnal Ministerstva Narodnogo Prosveshcheniia* (February 1856): 37–46. He felt compelled in 1856 to write about the earlier history of the dissertation defense because of the skimpy treatment accorded disputes in Shevyrev's centennial history, which had just appeared. See p. 37.

27. Ibid., p. 38.

28. Ibid., pp. 28–29.

29. Ibid., p. 40.

30. This is the famous censor, literary critic, and diarist A.V. Nikitenko (1804–1877) and his dissertation, *O tvorcheskoi sile poezii, ili poeticheskom genii* (St. Petersburg, 1837). This is one of those hastily prepared dissertations whose sole function was to allow its author to keep teaching, and Buslaev's description of it indicates the distance between his type of rigorous scholarship and this sort of work: "At present, I can remember neither its title nor its contents. I do remember well, though, that in general it discussed the elegance of art, the beautiful, and poetry in the complete absence of any concrete facts." Fedor I. Buslaev, *Moi vospominanii* (Moscow, 1897): 122.

31. Ibid.

32. Pogodin, "Disput g. Gladkova," pp. 38–39.

33. Ibid., pp. 37–38.

34. Kizevetter, "Moskovskii universitet," p. 122. Kizevetter is speaking only of his alma mater, but it applies to the entire university system.

35. This was an ongoing, evolutionary movement; Kizevetter, for example, notes significant instances of faculty renewal, 1780–1800, 1832–1848, 1855–1863, as well as the contributions of outstanding new faculty members in individual areas, such as Vasilii O. Kliuchevskii and Pavel G. Vinogradov in history. See Kizevetter, "Moskovskii universitet," pp. 54, 101, 120, 123–24.

36. The government recognized that it was redirecting the professors' attention away from administration to science. See Shevyrev, *Istoriia imperatorskogo Moskovskogo universiteta,* p. 487. Galskoy, "Ministry of Education," p. 238, indicates that the 1835 statute roughly tripled the salaries of the professors.

37. Cynthia H. Whittaker, *The Origins of Modern Russian Education: An Intellectual Biography of Count Sergei Uvarov, 1786–1855* (DeKalb, IL: Northern Illinois University Press, 1984): 161. She cites information from Nikitenko that thirteen professors from St. Petersburg University were phased out, owing to the new requirements. See also Galskoy, "Ministry of Education," pp. 237–38.

38. In the 1820s two groups of students had been sent to study at Dorpat for a period of time and then abroad to Paris or Berlin for two more years. On the Professors' Institute, see also Shevyrev, *Istoriia imperatorskogo Moskovskogo Universiteta,* pp. 485–87, Flynn, *University Reform,* pp. 181–85, and Galskoy, "Ministry of Education," pp. 239–40.

39. Buslaev thought this a natural outgrowth of the specialization of knowledge and of teaching, both in Russia and in the West. "The further one goes into the past, the more often one encounters encyclopedic professors [*professory-entsiklopedisty*]," who are "unsatisfactory for the serious demands of university science." Incidentally, he consid-

ered Davydov the model of the encyclopedic professor. F.I. Buslaev, *M.P. Pogodin, kak professor* (Moscow, 1876): 9.

40. Whittaker, *Uvarov,* pp. 161–62 (quotation, p. 161).

41. V.V. Grigor'ev, *Imperatorskii Sankt-Peterburgskii universitet v techenie pervykh piatidesiati let ego sushchestvovaniia: Istoricheskaia zapiska* (St. Petersburg, 1870): 83, 87.

42. Alexander Kornilov, *Modern Russian History* (New York: Alfred A. Knopf, 1943): 282. See also, Galskoy, "Ministry of Education," pp. 239–240.

43. Kizevetter, "Moskovskii universitet," p. 115.

44. Kizevetter remarks that the students were a far cry from the "juveniles" who in the 1820s "cavorted" at the lectures of "boring professors." In the 1830s and 1840s the students were "much more mature and much more strongly carried away by serious interests." They were up on the latest literature, attended literary, philosophical, and political debates, and formed serious *kruzhki*. Kizevetter, "Moskovskii universitet," p. 116.

45. P.V. Annenkov, *The Extraordinary Decade: Literary Memoirs,* ed. Arthur P. Mendel, trans. Irwin R. Titunik (Ann Arbor, MI: University of Michigan Press, 1968): 2.

46. Whittaker, *Uvarov,* p. 153. For some detail on the emerging intellectual press, see p. 116.

47. Annenkov, *The Extraordinary Decade,* p. 81. Emphasis in the original.

48. Ibid.

49. Priscilla Reynolds Roosevelt, *Apostle of Russian Liberalism: Timofei Granovsky* (Newtonville, MA: Oriental Research Partners, 1986): 106.

50. Delo Soveta Imperatorskogo S. Peterburgskogo Universiteta, O priglashenii lits k prisutstviiu na publichnykh zashchishchenii uchenykh dissertatsii, 20 December 1850, Leningradskii Gosudarstvennyi Istoricheskii Arkhiv, f. 14, op. 1, d. 4965, l. 1.

51. S.V. Rozhdestvenskii, *Istoricheskii obzor deiatel'nosti ministerstva narodnogo prosveshcheniia, 1802–1902* (St. Petersburg, 1902): 264.

52. Quotation cited by Roosevelt, *Granovsky,* p. 142 from Nikitenko, *Dnevnik,* 6 December 1848, vol. 1, p. 316. See also Roosevelt, n. 61, p. 210.

53. For the purposes of this general discussion, I am assuming that there is no special *kandidat* degree (as per 1884 legislation) and that doctoral candidates did not take examinations (1863 reform).

54. Each of the university degrees carried with it rank, or *chin*, in the tsarist Table of Ranks. What rank came with what degree varied over the course of the century or so that the system was in place. Also, the connection between the university degree as *nauka* and *chin* as bureaucratic ranking disturbed some members of the academic community. We will leave these issues alone, since our concern is with the defenses and their role.

55. As far as I can ascertain, only two women earned advanced degrees in history at Moscow and St. Petersburg Universities under the old regime, Maria A. Ostrovskaia and Ol'ga A. Dobiash-Rozhdestvenskaia. Ostrovskaia defended her *magister, Zemel'nyi byt sel'skogo naseleniia russkogo severa v XVI–XVIII vekakh* (St. Petersburg, 1913) in March 1914. Unless a woman earned an advanced degree at one of the other Russian universities, Ostrovskaia's would be the first in the discipline of history. Dobiash-Rozhdestvenskaia became the first woman to earn a *magister* in universal history with her defense in May 1915 of the work *Tserkovnoe obshchestvo Frantsii v XIII veke* (St. Petersburg, 1914) and the first woman to earn a doctorate in universal history with the defense in April 1918 of her dissertation *Kult' sv. Mikhaila v latinskom srednevekov'e* (produced only in a lithograph of a typewritten copy because of the conditions in the country at the time). On Ostrovskaia, see V. Semevskii, "M.A. Ostrovskoi," *Golos minuvshego,* 1914, no. 4, pp. 292–97; for Dobiash-Rozhdestvenskaia see V.M. Ershova, *O.A. Dobiash-Rozhdestvenskaia* (Leningrad, 1988): 47–50, 60–61. I am grateful to Aleksei N. Tsamutali for pointing out this work to me. The entry for Dobiash-Rozhdestvenskaia by A.D. Liublinskaia in *Modern Encyclopedia of*

Russian and Soviet History, ed. Joseph L. Wieczynski, v. 9 (Gulf Breeze, FL: Academic International Press, 1978): 184 is phrased in a slightly ambiguous way, asserting that she was "the first woman in the Russian Empire to receive the masters degree (in 1915) and the doctorate (1918)." Of course, the empire did not exist in 1918, and she was the first to receive both the *magister* and the doctorate, but she was not the first to earn a *magister* in history, even at St. Petersburg University, not to speak of the empire. See "Magisterskii disput M.A. Ostrovskoi v Peterburgskom universitete," *Nauchnyi istoricheskii zhurnal,* 1914, no. 5, p. 143, where it is described as "the first woman's dispute at Petersburg University."

56. Nikolai P. Pavlov-Sil'vanskii, who went on to achieve a certain eminence, in particular for his work on Russian feudalism, failed his master's examinations (apparently because of the objections of Nikolai Kareev) and abandoned his attempt to earn a higher degree. See Aleksei N. Tsamutali, *Bor'ba napravlenii v russkoi istoriografii v period imperializma: Istoriograficheskie ocherki* (Leningrad, 1986): 212. If a student failed, he could take the examinations again, but no sooner than one year later.

57. An indication of how seriously this ritual was taken is Platonov's angry reaction when he found out that Vernadsky had had his dissertation published in 1917 before approval had been granted by the dean of the department. Despite the fact that the department had already arranged to publish the dissertation in its *Zapiski,* indicating a high level of approbation, Platonov was quite upset. This "blunder, which almost spoiled my relations with Platonov" had to be smoothed over. See Vernadsky, "Iz vospominanii," pp. 218–19.

58. Remember, a doctoral candidate would already have published his *magister* dissertation. Even candidates for the *magister* frequently had publications and reviews under their belts.

59. I am concentrating on defenses in history for the *magister* and the doctorate at St. Petersburg and Moscow Universities. Rules and practices differed from university to university and from *kafedra* to *kafedra.* History, as a more public and more accessible discipline, undoubtedly attracted more attention from the general educated public than did chemistry or comparative anatomy, but the overall pattern of public controversy surrounding degrees holds for the tsarist university system taken as a whole. See the "police denunciation" over the embryology degree discussed above. There is also a famous incident involving V.O. Kovalevskii. A person with a doctorate from a foreign university could submit that dissertation as fulfillment of the *magister* requirement after having passed the requisite examination. (See *Sbornik postanovlenii po Ministerstvu Narodnogo Prosveshcheniia,* t. 3: *Tsarstvovanie Imperatora Aleksandra II, 1855–1864* [St. Petersburg, 1865]: No. 472, 18 Iunia 1863, "Obshchii Ustav Imperatorskikh Rossiiskikh Universitetov," Glava IX, Primechanie to Item 113, p. 952.) Kovalevskii, whose dissertation at the University of Jena was considered the best in paleontology for the preceding twenty-five years and who is today counted as one of the founders of comparative paleontology, was forced to take his *magister* examinations twice, owing to professional jealousy. See E.V. Soboleva, *Organizatsiia nauki v poreformennoi Rossii* (Leningrad, 1983): 209. I am grateful to Alexander Vucinich for bringing this controversy to my attention.

60. See the reproduction of Lappo-Danilevskii's speech before the defense of his *magister* dissertation, *Organizatsiia priamogo oblozheniia v moskovskom gosudarstve so vremen smuty do epokhi preobrazovanii,* in "Istoricheskie disputy v 1890 g." *Istoricheskoe obozrenie,* v. 1 (St. Petersburg, 1890): 283–94, and for his doctorate A.E. Presniakov's *Rech' pered zashchitoi dissertatsii pod zaglaviem "Obrazovanie Velikorusskogo Gosudarstva"* (Petrograd, 1920).

61. It is not clear what regulations governed the selection of official opponents other

than the stipulation that there be at least two of them. See Ministerstvo narodnogo prosveshcheniia, *Sbornik postanovlenii po Ministerstvu narodnogo prosveshcheniia,* t. 2: *Tsarstvovanie imperatora Nikolaia 1825–1855,* otdelenie vtoroe, 1840–1855 (St. Petersburg, 1864): 364, art. 47 (1844), which stipulates that there be not less than two "respondents to the theses" [*vozrazhateli na tezisy*], as official opponents were then called. With Kareev, for example, Ger'e was his *Doktorvater* and served as an official opponent at both of his defenses. On the other hand, at the defense of M.M. Bogoslovskii, a student of Kliuchevskii's, the official opponents were M.K. Liubavskii and Kizevetter, the latter of whom had yet to defend his own master's dissertation. Aleksandr A. Kizevetter, *Na rubezhe dvukh stoletii (Vospominaniia 1881–1914)* (Prague, 1929): 24–25, where he discusses the absence or scarcity of public arenas. He does not discuss defenses in this context.

62. N.N., "Po povodu odnogo disputa," *Istoricheskii vestnik* (October 1888): 263.

63. This generalized model is based on wide reading on the subject. The most thorough general survey of the degree-granting process for all fields is G.G. Krichevskii, "Uchenye stepeni v universitetakh dorevoliutsionnoi Rossii," *Istoriia SSSR,* 1985, no. 2: 141–53. Some parts of the preceding paragraph rely on his discussion, pp. 145–50. Another interesting related work is Soboleva, *Organizatsiia nauki v poreformennoi Rossii.* See chap. 3, "Podgotovka nauchnykh kadrov," pp. 170–242.

64. Krichevskii, "Uchenye stepenyi," p. 143. Figures for the other universities were as follows: Derpt, 135; Kharkov, 80; Kazan, 45; and Kiev (also a late starter), 60.

65. Ibid., p. 150. Figures for the rest of the expanded university system: Kiev, 218; Derpt, 214; Kharkov, 184; Kazan, 179; Novorossiisk, 125; Warsaw, 42; Tomsk, 6. Krichevskii notes, but does not explain, "a sharp decrease in their number [i.e., defenses]" in Moscow from 1880 to the beginning of the twentieth century and in Petersburg in the 1890s. The explanation for this drop is most likely the 1884 educational reform with its much stricter classical requirements. Soboleva certainly attributes the drop directly to that reform. She calculates that, excluding medical doctors, in the decade 1863–74 twenty-six men earned doctorates, and twenty-four, *magister* degrees, per annum. For the ten-year period 1886–96 the corresponding figures are twelve and fifteen. Soboleva, *Organizatsiia nauki,* p. 207.

66. This was constant for the entire period from 1860 to the end of the empire. In the physics–mathematics and juridical faculties, meanwhile, the average time went from 3.5 years between *magister* and doctorate in physics–mathematics in the 1860s to 6.7 years in the decade 1900–1909 and from 4.7 years for the juridical faculty in the 1860s to 6.4 years in the first decade of this century. Ibid., p. 149.

67. See Kizevetter, *Na rubezhe dvukh stoletii,* p. 280.

68. Samuel D. Kassow, *Students, Professors and the State in Tsarist Russia* (Berkeley, CA: University of California Press, 1989): 296. This recent work is the best single treatment of the tangle of professional, pedagogical and political issues involving the professoriate as a whole.

69. Picheta was trained under the old regime and had a distinguished career as a historian and Slavist under the Soviets; see V.D. Koroliuk, "Vladimir Ivanovich Picheta," in *Slaviane v epokhu feodalizma: k stoletiiu akademika V.I. Picheta* (Moscow, 1978): 5–25. This quotation comes from his "Vospominanii o Moskovskom universitete (1897–1901 gg.)," in *Slaviane v epokhu feodalizma,* p. 61. This memoir, which actually covers later years as well, was written in 1931 at what may have been the darkest time for historians in the Stalin era, and its assessments in various places appear suspiciously politically correct. This relates more to specific historians and their interpretations, however, than it does to his evaluation of the role of disputes in society—for example, when he writes about the doctoral dissertation (*Litovsko-russkii seim: Opyt po istorii*

uchrezhdenii v sviazi s vnutrennim stroem i vneshneiu zhizn'iu gosudarstva [Moscow, 1901]) of the politically and methodologically conservative M.K. Liubavskii: "The shortcomings of this work, despite its enormous value, are clear to me now, but in my student days it seemed exemplary to me" (p. 64). On Picheta, see also note 115.

70. Picheta, "Vospominanii o Moskovskom universitete (1897–1901 gg.)," in *Slaviane v epokhu feodalizma*, p. 61.

71. Ibid. I can only echo Picheta's regret that "no one prepared a stenograph of the disputes."

72. An idea of how small a slice of imperial society constituted the educated elite comes across anecdotally in Jeffrey Brooks's presentation of A.A. Kaspari's (one of the founders of the weekly *Rodina*) understanding of the reading public. According to Brooks, who quotes Kaspari, "No publication was intended exclusively for those with a university education because 'it is impossible to publish a magazine for a handful of people.' " Jeffrey Brooks, *When Russia Learned to Read* (Princeton: Princeton University Press, 1985): 114.

73. Akademiia nauk SSSR, Arkhiv AN SSSR, *M.M. Bogoslovskii:Istoriografiia, memuaristika, epistoliariia (Nauchnoe nasledie)*, ed. A.I. Klibanov (Moscow, 1987): 75.

74. Kizevetter, *Na rubezhe dvukh stoletii*, p. 278.

75. Ibid., p. 280.

76. Picheta, "Vospominanii o Moskovskom universitete," p. 63.

77. Ibid., pp. 62–63.

78. G.D., "Doktorskii disput V.O. Kliuchevskogo," *Russkie vedomosti*, 10 October 1882, no. 268, p. 3.

79. Report in *Golos*, 4 October 1882, no. 269, p. 2.

80. G.D., "Doktorskii disput V.O. Kliuchevskogo," p. 3.

81. *Golos*, 4 October 1882, no. 269, p. 2.

82. Ibid.

83. G.D., "Doktorskii disput V.O. Kliuchevskogo," p. 3.

84. Picheta, "Vospominanii o Moskovskom universitete," pp. 61–62.

85. Kizevetter, *Na rubezhe dvukh stoletii*, p. 262.

86. Iu. V. Got'e, "Universitet," p. 558, in *Moskovskii universitet v vospominaniiakh sovremennikov: Sbornik*, comp. Iu.N. Emel'ianov (Moscow, 1989). His dissertation, *Ocherki po istorii russkoi pozemel'noi politiki v XVIII i XIX vv.*, also was worked over in the press by P.N. Miliukov, V.A. Miakotin, and others. See ibid., n. 2, p. 673.

87. *Bogoslovskii: Istoriografiia, memuaristika, epistoliariia*, p. 83.

88. Maklakov, "Otryvki iz vospominanii," in Parizhskii komitet po oznamenovaniiu 175–letiia Moskovskogo universiteta, *Moskovskii Universitet 1755–1930. Iubileinyi sbornik*, ed. V.B. El'iashevich, A.A. Kizevetter, and M.M. Novikov (Paris, 1930): 314.

89. Maklakov, "Otryvki iz vospominanii," p. 314.

90. *Bogoslovskii: Istoriografiia, memuaristika, epistoliariia*, p. 83. Maklakov relates the same incident, remembering Giliarov's words as, "And how is it that in this letter you wrote me that my dissertation is brilliant?" Maklakov, "Otryvki iz vospominanii," p. 314.

91. *Bogoslovskii: Istoriografiia, memuaristika, epistoliariia*, p. 83.

92. Maklakov, "Otryvki iz vospominanii," pp. 314–15.

93. Ibid., p. 315.

94. Roosevelt, *Granovsky*, p. 106. See also, A.N. Afanas'ev, "Moskovskii universitet (1844–1848 gg.)," in *Moskovskii universitet v vospominaniiakh sovremennikov*, comp. Iu.N. Emil'ianov (Moscow, 1989): 268–71. His thesis was entitled *Volyn, Iamsburg, i Vineta*. Roosevelt, perhaps with the natural sympathy of a biographer, rates Granovsky's scholarship very highly, and she argues that Granovsky's use of Western

science versus the Slavic myths surrounding these settlements was a basis for the attacks on him. I have a sense that it relates more directly to Granovsky as *the* symbol, and the dissertation fracas was a convenient pretext. I.P. Kochergin found Granovsky to be more "a social actor than a *kabinetnyi uchenyi,* and one can evaluate him only in connection with the life of society" (editor's note 19, p. 641). Afanas'ev had a very low opinion of Granovsky as a scholar, considering him lazy, more in love with playing cards than with note cards, and dealing with problems "already elaborated in an excellent fashion by foreign scholars" (p. 268). Everyone is agreed, however, on Granovsky's fantastic popularity in his own day, and his influence is cited by many eminent scholars of later years.

95. Kareev went against the advice of his adviser, Vladimir Ger'e, in writing *Krest'iane i krest'ianskii vopros vo Frantsii v poslednei chetverti XVIII v.* (Moscow, 1879). It was a ground-breaking, highly regarded work, but it found feudal dues rising in the years before 1789, carrying the implication that the Revolution was necessary.

96. Having read the work, Kliuchevskii later asked Kareev, "And you're not afraid they will accuse you of being a socialist?" Nikolai I. Kareev, *Prozhitoe i perezhitoe* (Leningrad, 1990): 140. For more on the dispute, see *Kriticheskoe obozrenie,* 1879, 9, pp. 17–36, and 10, pp. 45–48.

97. Kareev, *Prozhitoe i perezhitoe,* pp. 139–40. According to Kareev, Ger'e behaved "ungraciously." Kovalevskii, who spoke as an unofficial opponent and who liked the work so much that he would send a copy to Marx, was put off by Ger'e. This aggravated already uneasy relations between Ger'e and Kovalevskii. See Kovalevskii, "Otryvki iz vospominanii," p. 281.

98. See Kareev, *Prozhitoe i perezhitoe,* editor's note 20, p. 329. Restrictions on the professoriate were somewhat softened by the fact that those who ran afoul of the Ministry of Public Education could teach in higher educational institutions run by other departments of the government.

99. The work, *Krest'iane v tsarstvovanie Imperatritsy Ekateriny II,* had been serialized in the *Zapiski* of the historical–philological faculty (*Istoriko-Filologicheskii fakul'tet*). It was only when the completed work was presented to Bestuzhev-Riumin that he balked. See Z., "Disput g. V.I. Semevskogo v Moskve," *Vestnik Evropy* (May 1882): 442–44, and A.M. Stanislavskaia, "Narodnicheskaia istoriografiia 70–90kh godov," chap. 3 in Akademiia nauk SSSR, Institut istorii, *Ocherki istorii istoricheskoi nauki v SSSR,* v. 2 (Moscow, 1960): 207–8. In the immediate wake of the assassination of Alexander II, in fact on March 9, Bestuzhev, who was the doyen of Russian historians at Petersburg, rejected the dissertation outright. See Michael B. Petrovich, "V.I. Semevskii (1848–1916): Russian Social Historian," in John Shelton Curtiss, ed., *Essays in Russian and Soviet History in Honor of Geroid Tanquary Robinson* (New York: Columbia University Press, 1963): 67.

100. Petrovich, "V.I. Semevskii," p. 68.

101. Z., "Disput Semevskogo," pp. 442–43, emphasis in the original; and James A. Malloy, Jr., "Vasilii Ivanovich Semevskii," *The Modern Encyclopedia of Russian and Soviet History,* ed. Joseph L. Wieczynski, v. 33 (Gulf Breeze, FL: Academic International Press, 1983): 239–243.

102. Z., "Disput Semevskogo," pp. 442–43.

103. V.S. Svidenko, "Konflikt mezhdu V.I. Semevskim i K.N. Bestuzhev-Riuminym," *Voprosy istorii* (August 1988): 137–38. The Minister of Public Education, T.D. Delianov, opined that Semevskii's teaching "could only incite in young minds a basic feeling of indignation against the past without enriching their basic conceptions." Cited in Petrovich, "V.I. Semevskii," p. 70.

104. Another instance of personal and political intrigue was the *magister* defense of Miliukov in 1892. His personal relations with Kliuchevskii were cool; an additional

complication was his expectation of getting the doctorate in recognition of the erudition of his dissertation. Rumors of conflict with so noteworthy a figure as Kliuchevskii, combined with the interest inspired by his revisionist study of the reforms of Peter the Great, drew a packed house. In this case, however, there was not a major argument concerning national politics between professor and candidate. P. Miliukov, *Gosudarstvennoe khoziaistvo Rossii v pervoi chetverti XVIII stoletiia i reforma Petra Velikogo* (St. Petersburg, 1892). See Pavel N. Miliukov, *Vospominaniia*, v. 1 (Moscow, 1990): 157–61; and Thomas Riha, *A Russian European: Paul Miliukov in Russian Politics* (Notre Dame, IN: University of Notre Dame Press, 1969): 18–20.

105. For example, V.I. Picheta noticed that the hall was a lot more crowded when Kliuchevskii's lectures involved the personalities of the Russian tsars. Picheta, "Vospominanii o Moskovskom universitete," p. 53.

106. Maklakov, "Otryvki iz vospominanii," p. 302.

107. Kizevetter, *Na rubezhe dvukh stoletii*, p. 278.

108. Ibid.

109. Maklakov, "Otryvki iz vospominanii," p. 304.

110. Picheta, "Vospominanii o Moskovskom universitete," pp. 64–65.

111. Prince B.A. Shchetinin, "M.M. Kovalevskii i Moskovskii Universitet 80–kh godov (Stranichka iz vospominanii)," *Istoricheskii vestnik* (May 1916): 487.

112. Shchetinin, "Kovalevskii i Moskovskii Universitet," pp. 486–87.

113. Ibid., pp. 486–87.

114. On this dispute, see "Disput g. Chechulina," *Istoricheskii vestnik* (January 1897): 373–74; "Neskol'ko slov o dispute g. Chechulina," *Sanktpeterburgskie vedomosti*, 1896, no. 344, p. 2; and "Doktorskii disput v universitete," *Novosti i birzhevaia gazeta*, 9 December 1896, no. 340, p. 2, from which the quotation is taken.

115. Kizevetter, *Na rubezhe dvukh stoletii*, p. 281.

116. The traditions lingered on for at least a bit. The recently discovered diary of Iurii V. Got'e includes two mentions of the dissertation dispute of V.I. Picheta involving his doctoral work *Agrarnaia reforma Sigizmunda-Avgusta v Litovsko-russkom gosudarstve*. On 3 March 1918 he noted, "We celebrated our academic holiday today—V.I. Picheta's dissertation defense. Liubavskii and I were the opponents. As far as I am concerned, the defense was a success in terms of both the general mood and the character of the criticisms. Afterward there were refreshments at Picheta's house; tongues were loosened, it was cozy, but it was impossible to forget the general horror." Iurii Vladimirovich Got'e, *Time of Troubles, The Diary of Iurii Vladimirovich Got'e: Moscow July 8, 1917 to July 23, 1922*, trans. and ed. Terence Emmons (Princeton, NJ: Princeton University Press, 1988): 113. Later, he recorded, "Today we had Picheta's second [?] dissertation defense; . . . It would be interesting to know if that is our last defense or not. Will this custom drown in the garbage heap or will Herostratus-futurist Lunacharskii not defile our sanctuary?" (p. 124). Emmons notes, "Herastratos was a Greek from Ephesus who in 356 b.c. burned the temple of Artemis in Ephesus (one of the seven wonders of the world) to make his name immortal" (n. 47, p. 115). Lunacharskii was the commissar of enlightenment. I am grateful to Professor Emmons for this reference.

117. The phrase is Buslaev's; see *Moi vospominanii*, p. 309.

118. Alfred J. Rieber, "The Sedimentary Society," p. 346, in Clowes et al., eds., *Between Tsar and People*.

5

Inventing the "State School" of Historians, 1840–1995

Gary M. Hamburg

Not long ago V.A. Kitaev, a well-known historian of Russian social thought, claimed that in light of the state's indisputably "leading role" in modern Russian history, post-Soviet scholars should reevaluate the contributions of the "state school" (*gosudarstvennaia shkola*) of historiography to Russian national self-understanding. Until the late 1980s, he wrote, Soviet specialists on historiography had viewed the state school from the jaundiced perspective of Marxism, which demanded the "decisive rejection of the methodological and conceptual baggage of Russian historical scholarship of the second half of the nineteenth century." However, the dramatic events of M.S. Gorbachev's perestroika occasioned the rejection of Marxism for the sake of a "new synthesis" of Russian history. Contemporary historians now found themselves "overtly returning to the ideas of the state school or spontaneously gravitating toward them."[1] Under the circumstances, Kitaev concluded, the time was ripe for a new, positive evaluation of the state school.

Kitaev's sympathy for the state school of historians is a part of a broader pattern of ongoing national reorientation in which post-Soviet Russians are "rehabilitating" the imperial past and rediscovering their heretofore hidden cultural links and affinities with the empire.[2] Such a phenomenon may be heartening insofar as it promotes self-critical historical awareness, but it is not without danger. The search for a "usable" past, as Bernard Lewis has warned in another context, can easily lead from salvaging memory to improving memory, from recovering the past to inventing it.[3]

This chapter begins by surveying recent uses of the term "state school" as an analytical device in Soviet, post-Soviet, and Western scholarship. It then argues that the moniker "state school" of historiography, like its variant name "juridical school" (*iuridicheskaia shkola*), was invented by opponents of the school's alleged members in order to discredit them; that the state school never existed in the sense that other historians have commonly described it; and that therefore the term "state school" should be discarded in favor of more appropriate conceptions. In short, the chapter demonstrates that we do not need a new, positive reevaluation of the state school but a skeptical reappraisal and rejection of the very term.

I

During the post-Stalin Soviet period the term "state school" was employed to categorize five scholars active from the early 1840s to the late 1870s/early 1880s. Three of these scholars—K.D. Kavelin, S.M. Solov'ev, and B.N. Chicherin—were regarded as the school's founders. A "second generation" of so-called statists—V.I. Sergeevich and A.D. Gradovskii—came to maturity in the 1860s and was credited with extending the founders' research agenda to include the history of local self-government and problems of comparative political and legal history.

According to V.E. Illeritskii, the Soviet historiographer who provided the "canonic" summary of the state school's intellectual achievements, all adherents of the school recognized the state as "the fundamental creative element of history and its motive force." The people or nation (*narod*) was significant only insofar as the state emerged organically from the popular/national milieu; taken in isolation from the state, the *narod* was an amorphous, largely undifferentiated mass, "inert" as a historical force.[4] The most extreme version of this formula allegedly belonged to Chicherin, whom Illeritskii accused of viewing the *narod* as the state's creation.[5]

From the bedrock assumption of the state's creative role in history, the state school supposedly deduced two methodological corollaries: namely, that the state's appearance and development should constitute the chief subject of Russian historical scholarship; and that historians seeking to understand the evolution of the state should study systematically the development of private, civil, and public law.

Even more significant was the political corollary of the statists' initial hypothesis. According to Illeritskii, emphasis on the state's creative force inevitably led members of the state school to support the Russian monarchy, for they saw in the Romanovs a formidable bulwark against revolutionary challenges to Russia's propertied interests. By Illeritskii's reckoning, the state school was not a mere stage in the progress of Russian historiography but part of an ideologically pernicious movement allied with the hated monarchy—a movement that had to be unmasked and destroyed.

The danger inherent in apotheosizing the state, Illeritskii contended, was palpable in the state school's attitude toward serfdom in Russia. To explain the state's role in the creation and abolition of serfdom, members of the state school elaborated a peculiar, but subsequently very influential theory of the "binding and unbinding" of society (*kreposhchenie i raskreposhchenie obshchestva*). According to them, Russian serfdom was a terrible but logical consequence of the modern state's development. To protect Russia from foreign invasion, the Russian state bound the landed nobility to government service and the Russian peasantry to the land; by these means, the state created a military and bureaucratic apparatus strong enough to defend the nation against external enemies. Without serfdom, neither the Russian state nor the Russian people could have survived. Thus, membership in the state school implied not only a scholarly interest in the state's creation of the serf order, but an insistence that serfdom in its day was a historically "lawful," even progressive institution. Of course, members of the state school also insisted on the abolition of serfdom, for they saw eventual emancipation of the nobility and the peasantry as logical, lawful, and progressive consequences of the state's passage into modernity. Once the state had achieved the security it sought, it had to release nobles from their service obligations and the peasants from their ties to the land. Since the abolition of serfdom came from above by legal means, rather than from below by revolutionary means, the main consequences of the 1861 emancipation were the preservation of inequitable property relations and the strengthening of the monarchy. Therefore, according to Illeritskii, the state school's theory of the "binding and unbinding of society" was merely a vehicle to defend class privilege and the existing political order.

This ideologically tendentious, reductive portrait of the state school colored Soviet accounts of historiography through the late 1980s.[6] Even as late as 1988, the long and otherwise respectful introduction to S.M. Solov'ev's *History of Russia from Ancient Times* [Istoriia Rossii s drevneishikh vremen] by S.S. Dmitriev and I.D. Koval'chenko observed that "the general notion that the development and subsequent perfection of the social organism occurred under the state's tutelage is obviously inadequate to depict the internally contingent course of historical development. Solov'ev did not see the real economic, social, and other contradictions connected with the genesis and development of capitalism in the context of the retention of feudal–serfowning relations."[7] After the fall of Soviet power in late 1991, Russian historians dropped their (by now formulaic) ideological objections to the state school but generally retained the inherited view of the school's operative assumptions. Both Kitaev's "re-evaluation" of the state school and the Petersburg historian A.L. Shapiro's impressive survey of Russian historical science accepted without demur Illeritskii's interpretation of the school's methods and its chief insights.[8] Only A.N. Medushevskii and A.M. Dubrovskii have raised questions about past characterizations of the school's work, but both scholars have continued to employ the term.[9]

From Soviet historiography the term "state school" (or the variant "juridical school") passed into common usage in Western scholarship. Anatole Mazour's *Modern Russian Historiography* asserted that Kavelin and Chicherin believed in the state's creative force and the common people's marginal role in history; Mazour attributed to Solov'ev the conviction that "the history of Russia is the history of its government."[10] J.L. Black has provided a more nuanced picture of the state school, stressing its debts to M.N. Karamzin and the school's amorphousness but not challenging its existence.[11] With the important exception of Klaus-Detlev Grothusen, German scholars have followed Soviet characterizations of the state school.[12]

Thus the notion that the state or juridical school of historiography dominated Russian historical scholarship between 1840 and 1880 and that its chief conviction was the supremacy of the Russian state over the inert *narod* became firmly established in recent Soviet, post-Soviet, and Western scholarship. In spite of Kitaev's call for re-evaluating the achievements of the state school, Illeritskii's identification of the school's membership and intellectual assumptions remains intact.

Is this picture of nineteenth-century Russian historiography justified? To answer the question, let us turn to the more distant history of the terms "state school" and "juridical school."

II

The very term "state school" of historiography is controversial. The school's presumed members did not describe themselves as members of a "state school," or any other school for that matter. Of course, the "first generation" of statists did have certain experiences and attitudes in common: their academic connection with Moscow University;[13] their participation in the Westernizer–Slavophile debate and their generally pro-Westernizer orientation;[14] their hostility toward serfdom; and their basically pro-monarchist sentiments. In historical work their interests occasionally overlapped, especially in the mid-1840s.[15] Despite their common experiences and their mutual respect, their readings of Russian historical development were by no means identical and sometimes led to sharp clashes of opinion, as we shall see below.[16] Moreover, Chicherin and Kavelin differed passionately on important political questions, such as their attitude toward Herzen, their reaction to the student movement of 1861 and—most importantly for the present theme—in their attitude toward the centralized state. These differences were so profound that in 1861 Kavelin broke all personal relations with Chicherin and never restored them. Given the range and depth of issues dividing Kavelin and Chicherin, Illeritskii's argument about Chicherin "influencing" his former teacher Kavelin seems implausible on its face.

If the so-called "first generation" statists did not consider themselves a school, neither did the second generation. Indeed, Sergeevich's first major book attacked Solov'ev's theory of princely succession and rejected Chicherin's scheme of Russian historical development as well.[17] Gradovskii's first serious article was a long, quite negative review of Chicherin's book *O narodnom predstavitel'stve* [On Popular Representation, 1866], a book usually cited as one of the capital works of the state school.[18] Thus, neither the first nor the second generation of scholars said to comprise the membership of the state school was aware of the school's existence. If the concept did not originate with the school's members, what was its origin?

The concept of the state school apparently evolved in three stages. First, radical critics of Solov'ev, Kavelin, and Chicherin identified the three scholars as proponents of a "new historical school" concerned with the development of the Russian state.[19] The critics' assessment that the "new school" was interested in explaining the evolution of Russian political institutions was sometimes accompanied by accusations that members of the new school were proponents of centralization.[20] After his controversial attack on Tocqueville's *L'Ancien Régime et la Révolution* in 1858, Chicherin became a magnet for such criticism. Herzen called him a "governmentalist," a "theosophist of bureaucracy."[21] Bestuzhev-Riumin called Chicherin a statist and doctrinaire.[22] Even Kavelin accused Chicherin of making obeisance to the "New Baal"—the modern state.[23] Generally speaking, the critics were less concerned about the assumptions guiding the historical writing of Solov'ev, Kavelin, and Chicherin than about the political stance adopted by these figures.

The second stage in the evolution of the concept began with the publication in 1886 of P.N. Miliukov's article "The Juridical School in Russian Historiography."[24] According to Miliukov, the juridical school (Solov'ev, Kavelin, Chicherin, and Sergeevich) understood history as a developing process, analyzed this process by studying the evolution of political–juridical forms, and constructed "schemes explaining the evolution of these forms that was, in essence, the same scheme." In Miliukov's opinion, the basic proposition from which the juridical school proceeded was "the idea of the descent of statist and private legal forms from patriarchal-clan relations."[25] However, Miliukov admitted that there were sharp differences distinguishing Chicherin and Sergeevich, on one hand, from Kavelin and Solov'ev, on the other.[26] Indeed, Miliukov's main purpose was less to persuade the reader that the members of the juridical school had adopted a common interpretation of Russian history—a task in which he failed—than to prepare the ground for a new historical methodology that would incorporate more fully the history of society, including the common people. Therefore, he agreed with the Slavophile complaint that Solov'ev and Chicherin had confined their histories to "forms alone" (that is, to institutions and legal monuments) while ignoring the constituent elements of society.[27] It is worth noting that Miliukov did not use the label "state school," because he was aware that such a label could not easily accommodate the contention of Chicherin and Sergeevich that there was no state proper in Old Russia.

The third stage in the evolution of the concept began with the search of early twentieth-century historians to discover a way of explaining nineteenth-century historiography via Marxian notions of class interest. In 1906 the young Marxist B.I. Syromiatnikov argued that in both Europe and Russia, the formation of nation-states had led to the "apotheosis of absolutism, of state power . . . as the 'creator' of history and the greatness of peoples." In his opinion, Russia's "state school" was merely a local instance of a general phenomenon. Syromiatnikov warned that the "cult of nation and state" built by previous historians was on its way out, because "in the life of peoples the importance of politics has diminished compared to issues of a sociopolitical character. The national-statist historical theory with its exaggerated deference to nationalism, with its faith in the peculiar character of a national soul and its exclusive interest in political history, must gradually leave the scene."[28] In his footnotes, Syromiatnikov made clear that his ire was directed chiefly against Solov'ev, Gradovskii, and Sergeevich.

After the Bolshevik Revolution, in articles and lectures written between 1923 and 1928, M.N. Pokrovskii discussed the contributions of Chicherin, Solov'ev, and Sergeevich to historiography. However, for various reasons he did not treat Chicherin and Solov'ev as members of the same school,[29] and he stressed that Sergeevich, a mere jurist, was no historian at all.[30] Alone among Soviet historians before Illeritskii, N.L. Rubinshtein argued for the existence of the "state school," in which he included Kavelin and Chicherin. However, Rubinshtein placed Solov'ev in a separate category. He argued that, while Solov'ev's idealistic worldview and formal scheme of historical development were similar to those of Chicherin and Kavelin,

Solov'ev's theory of organic change, his historicism, distinguished him from the so-called "statists."[31]

As the history of the concept "state school" suggests, the term was not employed as a descriptive label by alleged members of the school, but was imposed upon them by others. At first the term was intended mainly as a pejorative label. With Miliukov's notion of "juridical school" we see the first attempt by a professional historian to fashion a heuristic category for understanding the scholarship of the principal figures in question. In the Soviet period "state school" was adopted both as heuristic category and as pejorative label describing those major historians who preceded Kliuchevskii. Yet until Illeritskii's 1959 article, Soviet historians could not agree among themselves who belonged to the state school and who did not.

III

Kavelin, Solov'ev, Chicherin, Sergeevich, and Gradovskii agreed that the appearance of the state was an important moment in Russian history. However, they disagreed on three substantive issues crucial to the interpretation of this phenomenon: (1) when in fact the state had made its appearance on the historical scene; (2) whether the appearance of the state in Russia followed the same pattern and laws of development as did Western European states; and (3) the relationship between society and state in Russia.

According to Kavelin, who was the first to elaborate a general theory of Russian historical development, the Russian state appeared as a result of a three-stage process. First, early Rus' was divided into clans, and blood relations were the organizing principle of social life. The Varangian princes exercised authority according to the seniority system. Second, after the death of Yaroslav the Wise the clan system broke down, giving way to a territorial system organized around princely control of *votchina* estates. This system persisted until the middle of the sixteenth century, when Ivan IV succeeded in asserting the dominance of Muscovy over other principalities and over the boyar class. Ivan's triumph was the first victory of the unitary state over centrifugal forces. The third phase of historical development consisted of a transitional period lasting from the reign of Ivan IV to Peter the Great. During this transition Ivan's state system confronted challenges by the boyars, by foreign states, and by the peasantry. It was not until Peter's reign that the unitary state was secure. Thus, in Kavelin's view, the modern Russian state system was a recent development, appearing eight centuries after the Varangians.[32]

While Kavelin's intention to relegate the state to a late stage in Russian history was clear enough, his actual use of the term "statehood" was not at all consistent. For example, he wrote that the Varangians introduced the "seeds (*zachatki*) of statehood and of the political, governmental unity of all Russian lands." He described Yaroslav as the first prince who "thought about how to lay the foundation of statehood in Rus', to build its political unity on the clan principle."[33] At times, as Rubinshtein has observed, Kavelin seemed even to treat the *votchina* system as a phase of state development, as its embryonic form; Kavelin remarked that "from behind the grand duke's *votchina* the state shows its face."[34] Thus, Kavelin's analysis of the genesis of the state was murkier than first appearances might suggest.

Solov'ev never tired of emphasizing the organic nature of Russian development and for this reason was quite reluctant to speak of definite periods in Russian history.[35] As a historical artist, Solov'ev paid less attention to the broad strokes needed to delineate one period from another than to the fine blending of coloration needed to show the languid continuities of a single form. Therefore, Solov'ev wrote of the clan system as extending well into the sixteenth century and of the state system as having its roots in the eleventh and twelfth centuries. On these grounds some historians have construed Solov'ev's periodization of Russian history as follows: the clan phase, succeeded by a transitional phase of struggle between the statist and clan principles, and finally the triumph of the state system under Ivan IV. Like Kavelin, Solov'ev was prone to inconsistency in his use of labels: in his 1851 public lectures on pre-Petrine history Solov'ev referred to the early Riurikovids as representatives of the "governmental principle" (*pravitel'stvennoe nachalo*).[36]

Chicherin took his philosophy of history not from Kavelin and Solov'ev, as is often suggested, but from his teacher T.N. Granovskii. Following Granovskii, Chicherin argued that all historical societies have gone through three stages of development: a period of small-scale social organization in tribes, clans, and families; a period of individualism when the ties binding society consisted of private contracts; and a period of statehood, characterized by large-scale social organization, public institutions, and public law. In Russia, Chicherin contended, clan organization disintegrated almost immediately after the arrival of the Varangians. Early Russian history, therefore, witnessed the domination of individualism based on the creation of private property and private contract law. No state stood above contending individuals to mediate private disputes. Administration was the private affair of this or that prince, was supported by private revenues, and aimed to enhance the individual prince's welfare—not the common good. As in every European society, individualism eventually proved unable to sustain itself. In Russia between the end of the fifteenth and the end of the seventeenth centuries a state apparatus took shape on the tabula rasa of Russian life. Peter the Great simply made this already extant state system more efficient.[37] Unlike Kavelin and Solov'ev, Chicherin was quite consistent in his use of terms: no state existed before the late fifteenth century; what came before was literally anarchy.

Thus, the three principal historians in the so-called "first generation" of the state school disagreed over when elements of statehood first appeared in Russia, a disagreement that was particularly sharp in the thinking of the organicist Solov'ev and the philosophically precise Chicherin. In the "second generation" of the state school comparatively little attention was paid to the question of periodization or to the larger scheme of Russian historical development, perhaps because Gradovskii and Sergeevich were professional jurists more than historians. What concerned Sergeevich, for example, was how to define the form of Russian governmental authority according to the classical scheme of Aristotle. Sergeevich contended that after the Varangians authority in Russia was a combination of monarchical (princely) and democratic (*veche*) power. In Muscovy until the seventeenth century the government continued to be a combination of monarchical and democratic authority, the only difference being that the monarchical element was stronger than before and the representative-democratic element (the *zemskii sobor*) weaker.[38] Sergeevich's lack of historical sophistication so irritated Miliukov that the latter complained that in the 1860s the idea of periodization had vanished altogether from Sergeevich's work.[39]

During the 1840s and 1850s, as Westernizers and Slavophiles struggled to define Russia's identity vis-à-vis Western European nations, Kavelin, Solov'ev, and Chicherin weighed the question of Russia's historical uniqueness. Kavelin and Solov'ev argued that before the reign of Ivan IV—indeed, in some respects before the Petrine reforms—Russia followed a different course of development than did the West. Kavelin flatly declared: between early Russia and Western Europe "there is no common trait and there are many contradictory ones."[40] Having taken this extreme position, Kavelin immediately noted that Russia was a European nation in the sense that it too was capable of historical change. He added that with the Petrine reforms Russia discovered much common ground with the West. In his review of D.A. Valuev's 1845 Slavophilic *Sbornik,* Kavelin asserted: "With Peter the Great's reforms everything we have is common with Europe, and each day more and more so; its syllogisms, its ambitions have become our ambitions; its business—our business, its science—our science."[41]

Like Kavelin, Solov'ev noted the divergence of early Russian history from the Western European pattern—a divergence Solov'ev traced not to the superiority of one or another people but to geographical circumstances.[42] Like Kavelin, Solov'ev regarded the Petrine reforms as the culmination of a process by which Russia entered the family of European nations. It is fair to conclude that Kavelin and Solov'ev regarded Russia's modern destiny as interwoven with that of Europe; hence, they may legitimately be called Westernizers. Nevertheless, their treatment of early Russian history with its emphasis on Russian uniqueness was strongly influenced by Slavophilism.[43]

Chicherin was a rigorous opponent of Slavophilism, a doctrine that he believed to be unscientific, even mystical in nature.[44] Hence, Chicherin insisted that Russia followed the same laws of history as Western European nations. Of course, Chicherin was too shrewd a historian not to notice that Russian institutions and mores had certain peculiarities. For example, in early Russia scarcity of population led to fewer strong local associations among the people than in the West. In the statist period of Russian history the government acquired concentrated authority unparalleled in the rest of Europe. Nevertheless, Russia remained a European nation, even if in certain spheres it occupied an extreme position on the European spectrum.[45]

Thus, the "first generation" of the state school did not appraise the modern Russian state from an identical perspective. For Kavelin and Solov'ev the Petrine state was happy proof that Russia had finally overcome its peculiarities and merged with the European comity. For Chicherin the Petrine state was simply another step along a path Russia had always shared with the West.

Gradovskii and Sergeevich did not come of intellectual age until the mid-1860s—a full generation after the initial Westernizer–Slavophile controversy. As one might expect, their work did not betray the single-minded determination to define Russia's identity vis-à-vis Europe that characterized the previous generation. As founders of the discipline of Russian public law, Sergeevich and Gradovskii took for granted both Russian membership in the European community and the unique elements of Russian law. In spite of their distance from the ideological disputes of the 1840s, however, both scholars can be classified as Westernizers. For example, Sergeevich's analysis of Russian assemblies of the land treated the assemblies as almost exact analogues to European estate assemblies; by denying that the Russian assemblies differed from their European counterparts, Sergeevich suggested an almost uncanny resemblance between the Russian and European state systems. In this respect, he was an even more extreme Westernizer than Chicherin.[46]

Perhaps the most controversial issue confronting scholars between the 1840s and the Bolshevik Revolution was the relationship between the state and society in Russia. As we noted above, the earmark of the state school was supposedly its contention that the state was the sole creative element of

Russian history, while the common people were an "inert" mass shaped by the state.

This hypothesis surely cannot fairly be applied to Solov'ev's analysis of Russian history. In his multivolume history of Russia Solov'ev treated the contributions of all layers of society—the church, from metropolitans to common priests; the boyars and service gentry; the peasantry and merchants—to Russian history. When the Russian state was virtually destroyed during the Time of Troubles, did not society recreate it from below? Solov'ev's depiction of society emphasized not its lack of will or creativity, not its "inertness," but its lack of enlightenment, its violence, and its corruption. Society's realization of the need for improvement led to the appearance of reformers in the seventeenth century and eventually to the Petrine reforms. Solov'ev regarded state and society as complementary, closely linked categories—not as self-enclosed, mutually exclusive entities, the one active and the other passive.

Still less can this hypothesis be applied to the "second generation" statists. On the first page of his book *Veche i kniaz'* (1867) Sergeevich suggested that old Russia's public life consisted of a princely and democratic element; without popular participation in the *veche* the system would have collapsed.[47] In his monograph on assemblies of the land Sergeevich wrote: "The sovereigns [of England, France, and Muscovy] did not look upon the people that they had united as a passive mass; in all difficult circumstances they appealed to this people as a genuine force, and they sought in unity with the people to find support for their actions."[48] For his part Gradovskii treated government as a "true reflection of popular life."[49] As soon as an element of society achieves education and self-consciousness, it must be integrated into the administrative sphere, Gradovskii thought; otherwise, the government would soon face revolution.[50] Gradovskii's analysis of the modern state suggested that the state cannot be conceived apart from society, and that the state is merely "the sum of organizations, the totality of authorities of different kinds that existed before it in society."[51] In this reading, the strength of the state depends on the creativity of society. In a society where the people is "inert," no modern state could exist.

Indeed, the hypothesis that the state school regarded the state as "creative" and the people as "inert" can plausibly be applied only to Chicherin. Even so, Illeritskii's manner of phrasing the hypothesis misrepresents Chicherin's actual position. Illeritskii implies that Chicherin reduced all Russian history to the state's activity. As we have seen, Chicherin refused even to speak of the state's existence until late in the fifteenth century. Illeritskii also argues that Chicherin believed that the state "created" the people—a *reductio ad absurdam*. What Chicherin actually wrote was that the Russian state had created the *soslovie* system, a situation he contrasted with Western Europe, where estates were the product of society's initiative. Moreover, Chicherin contended that in the nineteenth century Russian society was slowly coming of age and learning to exert itself as an independent force. He looked forward to an "equilibrium" between Russian government and society to replace the imbalance that had existed from the fifteenth to eighteenth centuries.[52] Thus, if the Russian people had at one point lacked initiative, this was the result, Chicherin thought, of a determinant historical process; Chicherin did not apply to the Russian people an aprioristic disdain because they stood outside the "creative" governmental machinery. It is worth mentioning in this connection that Chicherin had more confidence in the political judgment of the common people than he did in the titled nobility. Thus, his position was not the result of narrow class prejudice.

In summary, on three substantive issues central to interpretation of the state's role in Russian history—the timing of the state's appearance, the regularity of this appearance according to comparative historical law, and the relationship between state and society—the state school of historians was no school at all.

IV

What bound together Kavelin, Solov'ev, Chicherin, Sergeevich, and Gradovskii was not the conviction that the state was the "fundamental creative element of history and its motive force," but a scholarly interest in certain questions about Russian development. First, all five scholars studied the historical past of Russian political institutions. Naturally enough, they were curious about the origins of the centralized autocracy, but their curiosity extended to other agencies that claimed or actually wielded political power. Thus, Solov'ev's magisterial history of Russia commented on the role of the Orthodox Church in political life. Sergeevich wrote a monograph about the relationship between the *veche* assemblies and princely government, a monograph describing the countless local variations of this relationship. Chicherin and Gradovskii analyzed the appearance of the land assemblies and assessed the political impact of these assemblies before their disappearance in the seventeenth century. Chicherin was also the first serious historian of Russian provincial government. His analysis of seventeenth-century Russian administration demonstrated not only the effect of Muscovite authority in the provinces but also the limits of that authority— the degree to which Russian provincial life had an autonomy not easily destroyed by the state. Perhaps a fascination with political institutions that could coexist in or even compete with autocracy led Chicherin to participate for thirty years in the local zemstvo and to become one of the zemstvos' first historians.[53]

Second, all five scholars tried to account for the historical relationship between the autocracy and Russian society. For Kavelin, Solov'ev, and Chicherin this question was especially pressing, for they had endured seven distressing years of "censorship terror" at the end of Nicholas I's reign. If Chicherin wrote caustically about the "passivity" and lack of creativity of the Russian masses, his remarks were as much expressions of frustration over Nikolaevan tyranny as they were considered judgments about the more distant past. For Sergeevich and Gradovskii, whose political environs in the 1860s and 1870s were marked by struggle between society and autocracy, the natural temptation was to locate in history the distant roots of that struggle. Thus, a single question asked by all five historians almost inevitably yielded different answers.

Third, all five scholars thought it essential to place the development of Russia in comparative perspective. Again, for Chicherin, Kavelin, and Solov'ev the question of Russian identity was more acute than for their successors. Even Solov'ev, whom Chicherin regarded as unconversant with European history, felt compelled to compare Russia to Western Europe. If Gradovskii and Sergeevich can be classified as second-generation Westernizers, they did not approach the national identity question with the same seriousness as the older generation. Gradovskii and Sergeevich thought it sufficient to apply to Russian national law methodological strategies that were acceptable in Western European scholarship as well; their treatments of Russian law frequently contained implied comparisons that they did not raise to the level of explicit commentary.

Fourth, these scholars showed an interest in the question of historical progress, especially progress through reform. Chicherin's theory of the "binding" and "unbinding" of society was simply one of several ideas expressed by these scholars about how historical progress occurred in Russia. Solov'ev's and Kavelin's fascination with the Petrine reforms and their ideological support for progressive monarchy were also responses to the same question. Gradovskii was convinced that historical progress was inevitable, whether by reform or by revolution. He was particularly interested in the place of education in nurturing social change: hence, his stress on the need for government to respond to public opinion.[54] Sergeevich was perhaps the least interested of the five in the problem of progress and reform; there is considerable justice in Miliukov's complaint that Sergeevich was not a historian at all, but a pure jurist. Yet Sergeevich's monograph on the assemblies of the land revealed a keen awareness of the importance of progressive monarchical ideology in recognizing the value of democratic assemblies.

This intellectual agenda—interest in the history of political institutions, in the relationship between the autocracy and society, in Russian national identity, in the motors of peaceful historical progress—was fully compatible with liberal politics and values. In 1856 Chicherin's essay "Contemporary Tasks of Russian Life" described the dawn of a new period in Russian history in which state power would be balanced by an autonomous, well-educated society. The goal could be achieved, Chicherin argued, by the granting of seven freedoms: freedom of conscience; freedom from serfdom; freedom of public opinion; freedom of the press; academic freedom; freedom to publicize all governmental activity whose exposure would not harm the state; and public conduct of legal procedures.[55] Chicherin warned against the danger of securing these freedoms by revolutionary means, and he urged the regime to promulgate them from above. These goals were explicitly endorsed by Kavelin, who helped Chicherin arrange publication of the essay in London, and were implicitly defended by Solov'ev and Gradovskii in various forums.[56]

Despite its undeniable compatibility with liberal politics, this intellectual agenda did not derive its power from liberal principles. Indeed, the historical research of Chicherin, Kavelin, and Solov'ev was influential in the second half of the nineteenth century not chiefly because of its liberal tone, but because other historians and nonhistorians recognized that these three great figures had asked important questions. It was only when a new generation of historians demanded attention to problems of social and economic history and when they criticized their predecessors' poor understanding of these matters that the intellectual agenda set in the 1840s and 1850s began to diminish in appeal. The process by which the new agenda of social and economic history displaced the "classical" political historiography is the central phenomenon in the so-called "crisis of bourgeois historiography" at the turn of the century.[57]

V

As this article has demonstrated, the concept of the state school of historiography was a by-product of partisan political struggle in Russia and of a paradigm shift in historiography. Since the concept was not the creation of the school's alleged membership, it can be defended only as a heuristic category. Yet analysis shows that on the central issues of the state's role in Russian history—the timing of the state's appearance, the regularity of this appearance according to comparative historical law, and the relationship between state and society—the concept of the state school is unhelpful, for it masks serious disagreements among alleged members while implying that, by definition, they must have a common outlook on these issues. Thus, we are left with the choice of using the term "state school" while acknowledging its inherent limitations as a category of analysis or of discarding it in favor of some alternative.

Two possibilities suggest themselves. The first is to refer to the dominance of political history in mid-nineteenth-century Russian historiography. "Political history," in the sense it was understood by Chicherin, Kavelin, and Solov'ev, contrasted sharply with its predecessor, the more narrowly dynastic history of Karamzin, and with its successor, the socioeconomic history written in the late nineteenth and early twentieth centuries. The second possibility is to speak of the liberal current in Russian historiography. This latter term might encompass Granovskii at one chronological extreme and the Kliuchevskii school at the other extreme.[58] The term would connote not party affiliations or oppositional politics of the reformist variety but broad acceptance of the intellectual values and research agenda articulated by liberal historians in the 1840s and 1850s. Neither of these alternative possibilities is without difficulties, but both are preferable to an argumentative construct that obfuscates more than it clarifies the scholarly intentions of nineteenth-century Russia's most fertile historical minds.

Notes

1. Vladimir Anatol'evich Kitaev, "Gosudarstvennaia shkola v russkoi istoriografii: vremia pereotsenki?" *Voprosy istorii,* 1995, no. 3, pp. 161–64, here p. 164.

2. For an overview of the process of reorientation in philosophy, see James Scanlan, ed., *Russian Thought After Communism: The Recovery of a Philosophical Heritage* (Armonk, NY: M.E. Sharpe, 1994). In historical writing the most obvious sign of a sympathetic return to the past is the rehabilitation of Nicholas II. See, for instance, A.N. Bokhanov's treatise on Nicholas as Christian ruler in A.P. Korelin, ed., *Rossiiskie samoderzhtsy 1801–1917* (Moscow, 1994). The deep cultural significance of the Nicholas revival is indicated by the 1996 decision of the Russian Orthodox church to canonize Nicholas and his family as martyrs of the faith.

3. See the provocative and intelligent remarks of Bernard Lewis on historical invention in *History: Remembered, Recovered, Invented* (Princeton, 1975), pp. 55–69. Lewis distinguishes collective memory (operating through heroic narratives, religious and secular festivals of commemoration, and customary law), the recovery of the past (by scholars who fill the gaps of collective memory and correct it in the interest of accuracy), and the invention of the past. This last process may amend memory "to achieve a new vision of the past better suited to needs in the present and aspirations for the future." It may also seek to predict or control the future. For Lewis, the invention of the past is a deviation from scholarly objectivity. I have used the term in Lewis's sense.

Please note that other historians have used the term "historical invention" in a positive sense. For example, in a famous essay Lucien Febvre applauded Jules Michelet's "invention" of the Renaissance. See Lucien Febvre, "How Jules Michelet Invented the Renaissance," in Peter Burke, ed., *A New Kind of History: From the Writings of Febvre* (New York, 1973), pp. 258–67.

4. See V.E. Illeritskii, "O gosudarstvennoi shkole v russkoi istoriografii," *Voprosy*

istorii, 1959, no. 5, pp. 141–59, here p. 143. This essay found its way, in slightly altered form, into the Academy of Science handbook on historiography: AN SSSR, Institut istorii, *Ocherki istorii istoricheskoi nauki v SSSR* 2 (Moscow, 1960) pp. 103–28.

5. Illeritskii, "O gosudarstvennoi shkole," pp. 143–46.

6. Illeritskii's theory is the organizing principle behind A.N. Tsamutali, *Bor'ba techenii v russkoi istoriografii vo vtoroi polovine XIX veka* (Moscow, 1977), which is the most comprehensive treatment of the state school. On Solov'ev, see V.E. Illeritskii, *Sergei Mikhailovich Solov'ev* (Moscow, 1980); L.V. Cherepnin, "S.M. Solov'ev kak istorik," in S.M. Solov'ev, *Istorii Rossii s drevneishikh vremen* 1 (Moscow, 1959), pp. 5–51; and most recently Nikolai Tsimbaev, *Sergei Solov'ev* (Moscow, 1990). On Chicherin, see G.B. Kizel'shtein, "K evoliutsii istoriko-politicheskikh vzgliadov B.N. Chicherina," *Istoriia i istoriki: Istoriografiia istorii SSSR* (Moscow, 1965), pp. 429–39; V.A. Kitaev, *Ot frondy k okhranitel'stvu: Iz istorii russkoi liberal'noi mysli 50–60-kh godov XIX veka* (Moscow, 1972), especially pp. 86–136. M.V. Nechkina, *Vasilii Osipovich Kliuchevskii* (Moscow, 1974).

7. I.D. Koval'chenko and S.S. Dmitriev, "Istorik Sergei Mikhailovich Solov'ev: Ego zhizn', trudy, nauchnoe nasledstvo," in S.M. Solov'ev, *Sochineniia v 18-i tomakh* (Moscow, 1988) 1, pp. 6–48; here p. 40.

8. Kitaev, "Gosudarstvennaia shkola v russkoi istoriografii," p. 163; A.L. Shapiro, *Istoriografiia s drevneishikh vremen do 1917 goda,* 2d ed. (St. Petersburg, 1993), p. 430.

9. Medushevskii has tried to redirect attention from the political dimension of the school to its philosophical orientation, particularly its indebtedness to Hegelianism. See A.N. Medushevskii, "Gegel' i gosudarstvennaia shkola russkoi istoriografii," *Voprosy filosofii,* 1988, no. 3, pp. 103–15. Dubrovskii has noted that the state school did not limit itself to the exclusively political history practiced by M.N. Karamzin, but "engaged in a deeper analysis of the historical process, studying the evolution of political relationships [between classes], of political institutions and the like." He added that historians of the state school devoted "substantial attention to sociopolitical history, to problems connected with the activities of the state and to uncovering the social content of the historical process." See A.M. Dubrovskii, "Gosudarstvennoe napravlenie," *Otechestvennaia istoriia. Istoriia Rossii s drevneishikh vremen do 1917 goda. Entsiklopediia* (Moscow, 1994), pp. 614–15.

10. Anatole Mazour, *Modern Russian Historiography: A Revised Edition* (Westport, CT, and London, 1975), pp. 113–27.

11. See J.L. Black, "The 'State School' Interpretation of Russian History: A Re-Appraisal of Its Genetic Origins," *Jahrbücher für Geschichte Osteuropas* 21, no. 4 (1973), pp. 509–30; idem, "The 'State School' of Russian Historians," in *Modern Encyclopedia of Russian and Soviet History* (Gulf Breeze, 1984) 37, pp. 118–25.

12. Grothusen's monograph, *Die Historische Rechtsschule Russlands* (Giessen, 1962), accepted Illeritskii's notion that the state school encompassed two generations, but Grothusen added to the supposed members of the "second generation" several scholars not mentioned by Illeritskii. Among them were: F.M. Dmitriev, N.V. Kalachov, N.I. Khlebnikov, F.I. Leontovich, A.I. Nikitskii, P.V. Polezhaev, A.F. Turin, I.E. Zabelin, and N.P. Zagoskin. Grothusen explored the philosophical allegiances of the school in considerable detail. More typical is Klaus Zernach's 1985 discussion of the state school in Hans-Joachim Torke, ed., *Lexicon der Geschichte Russlands: Von den Anfängen bis zur Oktober-revolution* (Munich, 1985), pp. 152–55. Zernach followed Illeritskii both in identifying members of the school and in describing its main principle of state primacy in the historical process.

13. Kavelin left Moscow in 1848 for St. Petersburg, where he worked in the Minis-

try of Internal Affairs; thus, his tenure at Moscow University overlapped with Chicherin's early student years.

14. Chicherin was the most consistent or extreme anti-Slavophile. Early in the 1840s Kavelin was deeply influenced by the Slavophiles and even described himself as "half Slavophile." Tsamutali, *Bor'ba techenii,* pp. 16–17. Solov'ev admitted that he had learned much from the Slavophiles and did not regard himself as a radical opponent of their views.

15. Solov'ev's theses, *Ob otnoshenii Novgoroda k velikim kniaz'iam* (Moscow, 1845) and *Istoriia otnoshenii mezhdu russkimi kniaz'iami Riurikova doma* (Moscow, 1847), both touched on the "clan theory" of early Russian history first suggested by Evers. Kavelin's article "Vzgliad na iuridicheskii byt drevnei Rusi," *Sobranie sochinenii K.D. Kavelina,* 4 vols. (St. Petersburg, 1899–1904) 1, pp. 6–66, also developed this theme.

16. See, for example, Kavelin's review of Chicherin's master's thesis, "O knige g. Chicherina," *Sobranie sochinenii K.D. Kavelina,* pp. 508–70. For Kavelin's break with Chicherin, see *Vospominaniia Borisa Nikolaevich Chicherina: Puteshestvie za granitsu* (Moscow, 1932), pp. 57–62, and the sequel volume of the same memoirs, *Moskovskii universitet* (Moscow, 1929), pp. 59–66.

17. See V.I. Sergeevich, *Veche i kniaz'* (Moscow, 1867).

18. A.D. Gradovskii, "Russkaia uchenaia literatura," *Russkii vestnik* 70 (1867), pp. 717–48; and *Russkii vestnik* 71 (1867), pp. 287–31. In his biting conclusion Gradovskii wrote that Chicherin's book "could have been written by any bureaucrat given to journalism" (p. 314).

19. See, for example, N.G. Chernyshevskii, "Ocherki Gogolevskogo perioda russkoi literatury" (St. Petersburg, 1893), pp. 224–25. "Around 1835, after the unconditional adulation of Karamzin, we see, on the one hand, the skeptical school, which deserves great respect because it was the first to call for analysis of problems of domestic life, although it did not analyze them convincingly; on the other hand, Polevoi's 'higher vision' of Russian history. Ten years later there was nothing left of this higher vision, of skepticism: instead of these weak, superficial modes of analysis, we encounter the severely scholarly vision of a new historical school, the main representatives of which were Solov'ev and Kavelin: here for the first time is explained to us the logic of events and development of our political life." Quoted in N.L. Rubinshtein, *Russkaia istoriografiia* (Moscow, 1941), p. 290.

20. Chernyshevskii called Solov'ev and Chicherin "adherents of bureaucratic centralization." N.G. Chernyshevski, *Polnoe sobranie sochinenii* 7, p. 796.

21. See A.I. Gertsen, *Sobranie sochinenii v 30-ti tomakh* (Moscow, 1956) 9, pp. 250–53.

22. K. Bestuzhev-Riumin, "Istoricheskoe i politicheskoe doktrinerstvo v ego prakticheskom otnoshenii," *Otechestvennye zapiski,* 1861 (139), no. 1, pp. 1–10.

23. See Kavelin's letter to Katkov, dated 7 June 1857: "Chicherin's view of the state is not only a mistake and an error (*lozh'*) in the theoretical sense, but especially at the present juncture it is a dangerous and untimely delusion. One must rise up with all one's strength against the banner of centralization he has lifted, against the New Baal, the idea of the state to which he offers bloody sacrifices" (RORGB, fond 120 [fond M.N. Katkova] op. 4, ed. khr. 4, 11.5 verso–6). Quoted in V.A. Kitaev, "Slavianofily i zapadniki na rubezhe 1850–1860-kh godov (k kharakteristike liberalizma epokhi pervoi revoliutsionnoi situatsii v Rossii)," unpublished doctoral dissertation (Gor'kii, 1980), p. 258.

24. "Iuridicheskaia shkola v russkoi istoriografii (Solov'ev, Kavelin, Chicherin, Sergeevich)," *Russkaia mysl',* 1886, no. 6, pp. 80–92.

25. Miliukov, "Iuridicheskaia shkola," p. 83.

26. Neither Kavelin nor Solov'ev was concerned with the philosophical coherence of his system, whereas philosophical coherence was essential to Chicherin. Chicherin was searching not for a convincing explanation of Russian national development in the abstract, but for a general "law" of development that would demonstrate where Russia fit in the European pattern. Miliukov, "Iuridicheskaia shkola," p. 85. Miliukov admits that whereas Kavelin and Solov'ev saw early Russia as generating elements of state authority, Chicherin asserted that "Old Rus' had no concept of the state" at all. Ibid., p. 87. Sergeevich broke so sharply with Solov'ev that Miliukov was constrained to admit that "indeed, the final form of the juridical scheme preserved little of the first." Ibid., p. 88.

27. Miliukov, "Iuridicheskaia shkola," pp. 91–92.

28. B.I. Syromiatnikov, "Osnovnye momenty v razvitii istoricheskoi nauki," *Russkaia mysl'*, 1906, no. 12, pp. 71–97. One might add to the list of prerevolutionary critiques of the state school Iu.V. Plekhanov, *Istoriia russkoi obshchestvennoi mysli v trekh tomakh* (Moscow, 1914–15) which criticized the tendency in Solov'ev and Kliuchevskii to stress the primacy of politics over economics.

29. For Pokrovskii Chicherin was a *gosudarstvennik* to be sure, but Pokrovskii had difficulty categorizing Chicherin's class origins. At one point he said Chicherin's philosophy of history was that of a Tambov "semi-seigneur" (*tambovskii polukrepostnik*). At another point he wrote: "It is no accident that the seigneur Chicherin created a seigneurial theory [*barskuiu teoriiu*] of history." At still another point he treated Chicherin as the "first (sic) Russian Hegelian," and wrote that Hegelianism was a "bourgeois theory" that could only have been generated and spread where industrial capitalism operated. "And so you understand that from the Hegelian formula, which essentially is tantamount to a 'bourgeois revolution,' Chicherin could accept only the first part—'bourgeoisie'—but the second part—'revolution'—he could not accept." See M.N. Pokrovskii, "Bor'ba klassov i russkaia istoricheskaia teoriia razvitiia russkogo samoderzhaviia," in *Istoricheskaia nauka i bor'ba klassov* (Moscow–Leningrad, 1933), here pp. 31–38; 45; 173; 179. Solov'ev was not of seigneurial stock, but an "urban dweller" (*gorodskoi zhitel'*) whose conception of life was therefore (?) "profoundly bourgeois, not only in the field of history, in the sphere of books, but also in everyday affairs" (*v oblasti bytovoi*). Ibid., p. 53. Pokrovskii's crude sociologizing reflects badly on the level of historiographical discourse in the early Soviet period.

30. "This juridical school," by which Pokrovskii meant Nevolin, Sergeevich and D'iakonov, "is easiest of all to decode because it has no historical conception at all, and indeed cannot have one. All these jurists . . . think that juridical norms—legal categories—are something eternal, something unchanging, and when a jurist turns to history, his purpose is to study the application of these norms." Pokrovskii, *Istoricheskaia nauka i bor'ba klassov*, p. 75. Pokrovskii says that Sergeevich accepts a "piece of an alien conception"—Chicherin's theory of enserfment by state decree—but otherwise does not share Chicherin's views.

31. N.L. Rubinshtein, *Russkaia istoriografiia*, pp. 289–342. "Of course, in certain respects Solov'ev actually was close to Chicherin. This proximity (*sblizhenie*) on the ground of the state theory was the result of the bourgeois-idealistic nature of his philosophical-historical positions. . . . But this far from exhausts the content of his historical views. A correct assessment of the historical significance of Solov'ev's work demands precisely an analysis of the peculiarities of Solov'ev's views, which distinguished him from the state school. Identification with the latter has only obscured for previous historians his more progressive and valuable sides." Ibid., p. 314.

32. See "Vzgliad na iuridicheskii byt drevnei Rusi," in *Sobranie sochinenii K.D. Kavelina* 1, pp. 6–66. The fullest discussion of Kavelin's scheme is A.N. Tsamutali, *Bor'ba techenii v russkoi istoriografii*, pp. 41–61.

33. "Vzgliad na iuridicheskii byt," p. 26.

34. Ibid., p. 46; see Rubinshtein, *Russkaia istoriografiia,* pp. 296–97.

35. See S.M. Solov'ev's preface to the first volume of his history of Russia, where he writes: "Not to divide, not to split Russian history into separate parts, periods, but to unite them, to concentrate mainly on the connection between phenomena, the direct succession of forms, . . . this is the historian's responsibility at present as the author of this book understands it." S.M. Solov'ev, *Istoriia Rossii s drevneishikh vremen, Tom 1,* in *Sochineniia* 1, p. 51.

36. "Vzgliad na istoriiu ustanovleniia gosudarstvennogo poriadka v Rossii," in S.M. Solov'ev, *Izbrannye trudy: Zapiski* (Moscow, 1983), p. 27.

37. See B.N. Chicherin, *Oblastnye uchrezhdeniia Rossii v XVII-m veke* (Moscow, 1856), especially pp. 1–56; 574–91; idem, *O narodnom predstavitel'stve* (Moscow, 1866), book 3, especially pp. 197–220.

38. See V.I. Sergeevich, *Lektsii i issledovaniia po drevnei istorii russkogo prava,* 4th ed. (St. Petersburg, 1910), pp. 140–245; idem, *Veche i kniaz'.*

39. Miliukov, "Iuridicheskaia shkola," pp. 88–89.

40. See "Vzgliad na iuridicheskii byt," p. 5.

41. *Sobranie sochinenii K.D. Kavelina* 1, p. 718; quoted in Tsamutali, *Bor'ba techenii v russkoi istoriografii,* p. 38.

42. See S.M. Solov'ev, *Istoriia Rossii s drevneishikh vremen* 7, chapter 1.

43. See Solov'ev's remarks on his relations with the Slavophiles in *Izbrannye trudy: Zapiski,* pp. 299–306. Solov'ev admitted that in his student days he was a "fervent Slavophile" and that, despite his latter recognition of the need for the Petrine reforms, "I preserved from my previous studies, from my previous Slavophilism, all the warm sympathy toward ancient Russia and its people" (p. 299).

44. See, for example, the polemical articles by Chicherin, "O narodnosti v nauke," *Russkii vestnik,* 1856, no. 5, pp. 62–71; *Russkii vestnik,* 1856, no. 9, pp. 8–27; the Slavophile position was defended by Iu.F. Samarin, "Dva slova o narodnosti v nauke," *Russkaia beseda,* 1856, no. 1, pp. 35–47.

45. Chicherin argued this position in many articles and books. See, for example, the introductory comments to his treatment of *zemskie sobory* in *O narodnom predstavitel'stve,* pp. 355–56.

46. See V.I. Sergeevich, "Zemskie sobory," in *Lektsii i issledovaniia po drevnei istorii russkogo prava,* pp. 172–240. "The institutions of European states in the Middle Ages present many analogous features, despite the profound difference of political life of those peoples where such analogies are observed. We will compare the peculiar features of land assemblies in Muscovy with what we know about the French Estates General and about the original character of English representation in the first hundred years of its existence. The resemblances between these institutions are so multidimensional that they cannot be attributed to chances but must be explained as the consequence of identical causes" (pp. 172–73). This position is elaborated at great length elsewhere in the discussion.

47. Sergeevich, *Veche i kniaz',* p. 1.

48. Sergeevich, "Zemskie sobory," p. 180.

49. Gradovskaia uchenaia literatura," *Russkii vestnik* 70, p. 726.

50. Ibid., p. 746.

51. A.D. Gradovskii, "Vstupitel'naia lektsiia po gosudarstvennomu pravu, chitannaia v St. Peterburgskom universitete A. Gradovskim 10 oktiabria 1866 goda," *Sobranie sochinenii* 1 (St. Petersburg, 1895), pp. 1–20; here pp. 12–14.

52. B.N. Chicherin, "Sovremennye zadachi russkoi zhizni," *Golosa iz Rossii* 4 (London, 1856), pp. 67–73.

53. See especially *Vospominaniia Borisa Nikolaevicha Chicherina: Zemstvo i Moskovskaia Duma* (Moscow, 1934), pp. 19–164; 261–317 passim; idem, *Voprosy politiki* (Moscow, 1904) is largely devoted to zemstvo politics in the 1890s.

54. Gradovskii, "Russkaia uchenaia literatura," *Russkii vestnik* 70, p. 746.

55. "Sovremennye zadachi russkoi zhizni," pp. 110–13.

56. On Kavelin's role in the publication of this essay, see *Vospominaniia Borisa Nikolaevicha Chicherina: Moskva sorokovykh godov* (Moscow, 1929), pp. 153–72.

57. On the crisis of historiography, see I.D. Koval'chenko and A.E. Shiklo, "Krizis russkoi burzhuaznoi istoricheskoi nauki v kontse XIX–nachale XX veka," *Voprosy istorii,* 1982, no. 1, pp. 18–35; A.N. Tsamutali, *Bor'ba napravlenii v russkoi istoriografii v period imperializma: Istoricheskie ocherki* (Leningrad, 1986), pp. 3–24; 66–277 passim.

58. On the Kliuchevskii school, see Terence Emmons, "Kliuchevskii's Pupils," in this volume.

6

Kliuchevskii's Pupils

Terence Emmons

The idea of looking into the relations between the great Russian historian
V.O. Kliuchevskii (1841–1911) and his pupils came to me while reading a
remark by Hayden White, the man who would make formalists of us all:

> What is usually called the "training" of the historian consists for the most
> part of study in a few languages, journeyman work in the archives, and the
> performance of a few set exercises to acquaint him with standard reference
> works and journals in his field. For the rest, a general experience of human
> affairs, reading in peripheral fields, self-discipline, and *Sitzfleisch* are all that
> are necessary. Anyone can master the requirements fairly easily.[1]

This view resonates with Paul Veyne's observation, in his very stimulating
book *Comment on écrit l'histoire,* that "history has no method" of its own;
it shares a common critical method with any number of other disciplines.[2]

If there is no historical method, what do we teach our students? Narrative
techniques? But Jack Hexter was right to say there are no handbooks on
how to write history; that is, how to get from our note cards or data bases to
the proverbial "write-up."[3] Is history a science or an art?

It seemed to me that some scrutiny of the relations between Kliuchevskii
and his pupils ought to be interesting in the context of this perennial question. In Russian historiography, Kliuchevskii is, of course, the preeminent
challenge for those who would take sides in the debate about history as
science or art: a scholar who subscribed throughout his life to the idea of
scientific history of the mid-nineteenth-century sociological positivist variety, and was at the same time an artist whose lectures were major cultural
events, described in the memoirs of many auditors as unforgettable esthetic

experiences, and whose *Course of Russian History* instantly became one of the great monuments of modern Russian literature when it was published at the beginning of this century.[4]

What did Kliuchevskii give to his pupils—science or art, method or inspiration, an agenda or a coherent view of Russian historical development, all of the above or some part of it? It was with these rather obvious questions that I decided to poll Kliuchevskii's pupils.[5]

Two caveats at the outset: The first is that I did not set myself the task of tracing the filiation of concepts or interpretations about specific issues—the four phases of Russian history elaborated by Kliuchevskii; his well-known views on the socioeconomic structure of Kiev Rus', the origins of serfdom, the national assemblies *(zemskie sobory)* of the sixteenth and seventeenth centuries, the enserfment–disenserfment *(zakreposhchenie–raskreposhchenie)* cycle, and so on. Kliuchevskii's interpretations, especially his overall periodization scheme, have of course been enormously influential, on his immediate pupils to varying degrees and on much broader circles and succeeding generations of historians: one has only to look at the table of contents of Professor Riasanovsky's popular textbook to see that influence.[6] But that is a vast subject I deliberately eschew, although some very general comments about it appear here and there. All I have done is look at what Kliuchevskii's pupils themselves have to say about their relations with their teacher—primarily in their memoirs and the introductions to their principal scholarly works; from time to time, a glance at the works themselves has seemed in order as well.

The second caveat is that by "pupils" I mean not the tens of thousands of students who sat in on Kliuchevskii's lectures over the long course of his career in several institutions, or even the hundreds, perhaps thousands, of students over more than thirty years who "took" his course while formally enrolled in the historico–philological faculty of Moscow University. I refer, somewhat arbitrarily, to the graduates who were *ostavleny pri kafedre,* kept on to write dissertations and prepare for teaching at the university, and who actually defended their dissertations before Kliuchevskii. Of these there were only six:

P.N. Miliukov	(May 17, 1892)
M.K. Liubavskii	(May 22, 1894)
N.A. Rozhkov	(May 19, 1900)
M.M. Bogoslovskii	(November 2, 1902)
A.A. Kizevetter	(December 19, 1903)
Iu.V. Got'e	(December 3, 1906)

The dates are the dates of their *magistr* (magister) dissertation defenses. Although several of them went on to write doctoral dissertations, only one of these, Liubavskii's, was defended before Kliuchevskii (May 28, 1901). A number of others who went on to make names for themselves as historians, including M.N. Pokrovskii, A.I. Iakovlev, V.I. Picheta, S.V. Bakhrushin, S.K. Bogoiavlenskii, V.A. Riasanovsky, M.M. Karpovich, and G.V. Vernadsky, quite rightly considered themselves Kliuchevskii's students—there was a curriculum only at the undergraduate level. But they either did not take higher history degrees at the university or did so after Kliuchevskii's retirement (in fact, Bogoslovskii, Kizevetter, and Got'e from the above list also defended their dissertations after Kliuchevskii's formal retirement from the *kafedra* in 1901; but he continued to participate in dissertation defenses for several years, and, indeed, he continued to lecture until shortly before his death in 1911).

First, I will consider the testimony of Kliuchevskii's pupils identified above. Then I will proceed to a few observations that seem warranted, or are at least suggested, by this evidence. In doing all this, I do not in any way want to suggest that Kliuchevskii exercised an exclusive or even dominant influence on these historians, whose professional–intellectual formation, like that of Kliuchevskii himself, involved exposure to a large and cosmopolitan body of historical, sociological, and philosophical literature.

* * *

The view is widespread that Kliuchevskii inspired but did not teach: he inspired with the art of his lecturing and the original and penetrating insights about the Russian past that he presented in his lectures, but his *modus operandi* was not accessible to students; even his seminars were lectures; he presented his students with an unapproachable *fait accompli*. In all this Kliuchevskii stood in particular contrast to P.G. Vinogradov (later Sir Paul Vinogradoff), who drew the students in his seminars on ancient and medieval European history into "hands-on" work with sources, showing them how to criticize and interrogate them and involving the students in active discussion of the historian's craft. This view derives in large part, one suspects, from the well-known memoirs of P.N. Miliukov (1859–1943), who was Kliuchevskii's first "graduate student" and was already pursuing his undergraduate studies at Moscow University when Kliuchevskii succeeded to the chair of Russian history following the death of S.M. Solov'ev in 1879: "His insight was amazing, but its source was not accessible to all of us. Kliuchevskii read the meaning of Russian history, so to speak, with an inner eye. . . . This kind of 'intuition' was beyond us and we could not follow in our teacher's footsteps." And a little further:

> The professor imposed his elegant finished structure on our *tabula rasa*. We saw by his example that Russian history could also be a subject of scholarly study; but the door to this structure remained closed to us.

As is evident from the above, I worked mostly with P.G. Vinogradov; it was impossible to work with V.O. Kliuchevskii.

At this point, of course, Miliukov has to explain why he nevertheless chose Russian history as his field of specialization, and he gives a rational explanation that has nothing to do with Kliuchevskii: "My main motive in this choice was that working in Russia on the history of foreign states would be "carrying coals to Newcastle," the more so that degree dissertations were written in Russian and did not reach foreigners; and further work after receiving the degree would necessarily be hampered by lack of material and the difficulty of communicating abroad."[7] Miliukov's memoirs need to be supplemented by his reminiscence about his first encounter with Kliuchevskii, which he gave in a memorial lecture in 1912. It throws a rather different light on the matter of Kliuchevskii's influence on him:

> I have mentioned that I first met Kliuchevskii as a professor in 1879. . . . We didn't know Russian history then and felt no need to know it. But we had already learned the latest words of European scholarship, and we made certain demands of any teacher before submitting to his influence. If Kliuchevskii conquered us immediately, it was of course not only because he told historical anecdotes in a charming and effective way. We sought and found in him primarily a thinker and a researcher whose views and methods corresponded to our requirements [*zaprosy*].
>
> What were these requirements? The answer even now, after thirty-odd years, is given by the first two lectures of V.O. Kliuchevskii's *Course of Russian History*. Despite certain later accretions of phraseology and thought, the essential content of Kliuchevskii's methodological views on the study of Russian history remains the same there as we knew it then and as it had taken shape under the direct influence of the contemporary needs of our generation in matters of methodology and philosophy of history.

These "needs" or "requirements," Miliukov goes on, included the eschewing of externally imposed schemes or goals, whether Westernizer or Slavophile, and the study of Russian history

> like any other, from the point of view of the general scientific problem of the internal organic evolution of human society. We did not yet call this problem a *sociological* problem. . . . We only wanted to ascertain manifestations of regularity [*zakonomernost'*]. We sought "laws" in history.
>
> To these demands of ours V.O. Kliuchevskii responded not with discourses and theories but with the very fact of his relation as a researcher to Russian history as a subject of study. We read his discourses on this matter later in the first lectures of volume 1, and found their deductions to be corresponding to our own.[8]

Miliukov summed up the significance of Kliuchevskii for his generation of students in a memoir about A.A. Kizevetter, who was one of Miliukov's first pupils as well as a pupil of Kliuchevskii:

> We were united above all by our common deference to our teacher, V.O. Kliuchevskii, whose talent and erudition seemed to us unattainable heights. His construction of Russian history immediately became our guideline in the labyrinth which that same Russian history had seemed to us in the treatment of Kliuchevskii's predecessors. For us, Kliuchevskii was a genuine Columbus, who had opened the way to unexplored lands. . . .
>
> In the friendly exchange of our circle, which was held together by our acceptance of the new tasks and methods recommended by our university teachers (in addition to Kliuchevskii, P.G. Vinogradov should also be mentioned here), we elaborated common views of history as a science and identified suitable timely themes for scholarly studies. All this taken together also later gave a common character to the Moscow historical school.[9]

And indeed, in his first major work, his *magistr* dissertation on state finances and administration under Peter the Great, Miliukov acknowledged his intellectual debt to Kliuchevskii, "whose university lectures have determined to a very great degree the substance of my views on the question at hand."[10] He was referring here undoubtedly to Kliuchevskii's critical judgment of Peter's reforms and the emphasis on their reactive character and heavy costs, themes that Kliuchevskii had raised in his lectures on Peter in a much more incisive way than had Solov'ev.[11] In the same introduction, Miliukov seems to acknowledge a debt to Kliuchevskii that goes beyond interpretation of the reign of Peter to the historiographical agenda as a whole: "[Historical] science, in our understanding of its contemporary tasks, has put on the agenda the study of the material side of the historical process, the study of economic and financial history, of social history and the history of institutions: these are all branches in relation to Russian history that still await their foundation through the mutual efforts of many scholars."[12] This declaration bears a marked resemblance to the manifesto of the "new history" with which Kliuchevskii began his doctoral dissertation on the Boyar Duma (*Boiarskaia duma*), first published in 1880–81 in the journal *Russkaia mysl'*:

> Thus in the history of our ancient institutions the social classes and interests concealed behind them and through which they operated remain in darkness. Having examined attentively the exterior of the old state edifice and cast a quick glance at its internal structure, we have not studied adequately either its foundations or its structural material, or the concealed internal relations that held its parts together; and when we have studied all this, then perhaps the formative process of our state order and the historical significance of the governmental institutions supporting it will appear to us in a rather different light from that in which they appear to us now.[13]

As several commentators on Kliuchevskii's work have pointed out, this was in its day an unprecedented "new history" manifesto. The sociological bent of Kliuchevskii's approach was pointed up in the two-line summary following the title, which did not survive into the book edition: "In the present inquiry the boyar duma is examined in connection with the classes and interests that dominated in old-Russian society."[14]

It is noteworthy in this regard that Kliuchevskii's name does not figure in the theoretical, sociologizing introduction to the early editions of Miliukov's great synthesis, *Ocherki po istorii russkoi kul'tury* [Essays on the History of Russian Culture], which began to appear in 1896. But this is hardly surprising, considering that Miliukov's theoretical stance was already well developed before Kliuchevskii's appearance at the university; that Kliuchevskii's sociology was derivative from well-known sources; and that, in any case, his theoretical "discourses" were not in print, and Miliukov was no longer a student in the one year of 1884/85 when Kliuchevskii gave an entire course on "methodology."[15] The fact remains that Miliukov's discourse in his theoretical introduction to the *Ocherki* on how the peculiarities of Russian historical development reflected universal sociological laws bears a striking resemblance to Kliuchevskii's remarks about the theoretical value of studying local (that is, national) history in the opening lecture of his *Course* first published in 1904.[16]

Miliukov does refer to Kliuchevskii in the introduction to the first volume of the "jubilee edition" of *Ocherki,* published in 1937, where, after an extensive exposition of his updated sociology, he attributes the tendency in his *Ocherki* to emphasize the peculiarities of the Russian historical process more than its similarities to the general-European to the probable influence of Kliuchevskii: "[The author] has built the Russian historical process on a synthesis of both features—similarity and peculiarity [*skhodstvo i svoeobrazie*]. Withal, however, features of peculiarity are emphasized rather more sharply than features of similarity. In this is reflected, most likely, the influence of my university teacher, V.O. Kliuchevskii—the most original [*svoeobraznyi*] of Russian historians."[17]

Miliukov's *chef d'oeuvre* as a whole constitutes a complement to Kliuchevskii's *Course,* supplying the discussion of cultural and intellectual developments (only from the Muscovite period forward, of course) that the latter largely lacks.[18]

The published remarks of M.K. Liubavskii (1860–1936), Kliuchevskii's second "graduate student," about his teacher are much less extensive than Miliukov's, and are mostly of a celebratory kind—speeches on the occasions of Kliuchevskii's nomination as an honorary member of Moscow University and of his death (both in 1911). Although the occasions may have been conducive to exaggeration in regard to continuity, there seems little reason to doubt that Liubavskii saw his own work as a direct-line continuation of Kliuchevskii's, or more precisely as work on an agenda established by Kliuchevskii. He quotes approvingly the preface to the *Festschrift* prepared for Kliuchevskii in 1909 (it seems not unlikely that he wrote it himself):

> We went further into specific questions, studying the Time of Troubles, the reforms of Peter, Lithuanian Rus', the history of the Russian monarchy and of state obligations, the fate of the Russian village, the past of the Russian town; from the southern borders of the Muscovite state we proceeded through the Moscow region to the far Maritime North with its peasant communities—whatever we worked on, we have always proceeded from your *Course* and returned to it as the matrix whose individual parts we studied.[19]

Liubavskii's article on Solov'ev and Kliuchevskii, in which he emphasized the continuity between the two great historians, with Kliuchevskii essentially "extending the agenda" of his teacher from the history of legal forms and state institutions to their social and economic content, can probably be read as a paraphrase of his own perceived relation to his teacher, Kliuchevskii.[20]

In his monographic work on the history of the Lithuanian-Russian state (based, as was much of Kliuchevskii's work, on the Moscow archives of the Ministry of Justice, in Liubavskii's case specifically on the Lithuanian *metrika*) and historical geography (or the role of geographical factors in Russian historical development), Liubavskii clearly saw himself proceeding from Kliuchevskii's work.

Liubavskii's work on the history of Lithuanian Rus (*Litovskaia Rus'*) has been seen as a partial reversion to the more legalistic and political-institutional approach characteristic of the state school,[21] but overall the work bears a striking resemblance to Kliuchevskii's in *Boiarskaia duma:* there is the same kind of attention to the social content of institutions; or, perhaps more precisely, the same kind of approach to sociopolitical "realities" through the study of institutions. Even the title of his doctoral dissertation bears a close resemblance to Kliuchevskii's doctoral work: *The Lithuanian-Russian Seim: An Inquiry into the History of the Institution in Relation with the Internal Order and Public Life of the State.* The first sentence in the introduction to that work states: "One can say that in [the laws of the 1566 statute relating to the "Great Free Seim"] is expressed the most general summation of the sociopolitical history of that state over the period of its iodependent eyistence."[22]

Liubavskii's rationale for his inquiries is rather narrowly academic, but his focus on the history of political decentralization and "estate-representation" in the west-Russian past harks back to Kliuchevskii's remarkably present-minded rationale in the introduction to the first printed version of *Boiarskaia duma,* which included providing an answer to the question: "Have there been in our past social relations that could still be revived and made to serve the interests of the present; and are there in society of today forces and elements capable of bearing the burden of public initiative, which would not complicate but rather facilitate the government's activity in the interests of the national welfare?"[23] For Kliuchevskii, this question—that is, the question of the future political evolution of the country—had been put on the agenda by the emancipation and the other "great reforms" of the 1860s; it was hardly less pertinent at the turn of the century when Liubavskii was writing, and the "actuality" (*aktual'nost'*) of Liubavskii's inquiries into the causes of political decentralization and institutionalized limitations on the power of the crown in a part of modern Russia's historical patrimony does not seem fortuitous.

When Liubavskii got around to publishing his own general course on Russian history in 1915 (*Lektsii po drevnei russkoi istorii do kontsa XVI veka*), he intended it to complement Kliuchevskii's work:

> By way of explanation for the sketchy and uneven presentation [here], I must say that this presentation was prepared with the intention that V.O. Kliuchevskii's classic *A Course in Russian History* be studied obligatorily by the students. My own course was in certain cases an expansion and supplement of that course, and on the other hand it dealt summarily with matters treated particularly fully and thoroughly by Kliuchevskii. It goes without saying that in addition to these differences, the arrangement and content of my course was also determined by differing views on certain aspects of the Russian historical process.[24]

Kliuchevskii's third "graduate student," N.A. Rozhkov (1868–1927) had very little to say explicitly about his relations with his teacher. He made no contribution to the 1909 *Festschrift,* nor to the memorial literature that appeared shortly after Kliuchevskii's death in 1911.

Kliuchevskii's contribution to Rozhkov's passionate search for a science of society, which dominated his historical writing subsequent to his *magistr* dissertation on sixteenth-century agriculture (that is, after circa 1900), appears to have been considerable: Kliuchevskii's teaching, along with the writings of Comte, introduced him to the sociological perspective on history.[25] In a way, Rozhkov's "economic materialism," his idiosyncratic but consistent monism based on a combination of Comtian positivism and Marxism, was the playing out, into the second generation, of Kliuchevskii's commitment to the search for "historical laws," which the master's turn of mind and addiction to applied research had prevented him from pursuing.[26]

In contrast to his later work, Rozhkov's dissertation, an inquiry into the state of agriculture and the economic crisis of the late sixteenth century, was the kind of broadly conceived "economic history" that fit very well into the Kliuchevskii-inspired corpus: it deals with climatic and soil conditions, demographics, trade, and property relations as well as agriculture *in sensu stricto.* It was based, also typically, on a vast amount of archival research, and in its elucidation of the material conditions underlying the process of enserfment it has been read as a confirmation of Kliuchevskii's theory on the genesis of serfdom.[27]

Rozhkov's subsequent work took leave of the conventional historical framework, but in *Gorod i derevnia v russkoi istorii* [Town and Country in Russian History], his eighty-four-page sketch of Russian economic history first published in 1902—despite its novel, consistently materialist or economic-determinist viewpoint—the essentially Kliuchevskian four-phase periodization was still preserved: Kievan, appanage, Muscovite, and pre-reform imperial (Rozhkov only added a fifth period, the post-reform era).[28] The fundamental place of demographic change in Rozhkov's economic-determinist version of Russian history may also owe more than a little to Kliuchevskii.

If Rozhkov was the most theoretically oriented of Kliuchevskii's pupils, his near-coeval and Kliuchevskii's fourth dissertation student, M.M. Bogoslovskii (1867–1929), was probably the least so. In his article for the 1912 Kliuchevskii memorial volume, Bogoslovskii, like Liubavskii, emphasized the continuity between Kliuchevskii and his teacher, Solov'ev. He quotes approvingly from memory Kliuchevskii's remark, "I am Solov'ev's pupil—that is all I have to be proud of as a scholar."[29]

Bogoslovskii rather obviously saw himself standing in the same relation to Kliuchevskii as he saw Kliuchevskii vis-à-vis Solov'ev. In 1911, following Kizevetter's resignation in the Kasso affair along with many other faculty members, Bogoslovskii was appointed to the chair of Russian history. He wrote about that occasion the following comment in his unpublished memoirs:

> Having stayed, I was quite right to take the chair left empty after Kizevetter's departure, and it was a good thing I did. If I hadn't taken it, Dovnar-Zapol'skii or someone worse would have been put in it and would have propagated his own school. But I preserved for the Moscow chair the traditions of the head of our school, V.O. Kliuchevskii, I preserved them in their purity, and have the right to be proud of that.[30]

Bogoslovskii also insists on Kliuchevskii's aversion to abstract thought ("His mind always needed concrete, real factual material, like fuel for a fire.

For him, facts seemed to take the place of logical constructs"), the strictly inductive character of his historical reasoning, and his heroic capacity for sifting documents in the archives ("a truly Solov'evian capacity for work"). He concludes, with an obvious dig at Marxism: "That is why he was organically incapable of setting himself the task of extrapolating the entire course of Russian history from any kind of abstract principle."[31]

Bogoslovskii nevertheless allows that Kliuchevskii had a predilection for certain groups of facts—political, social, and economic facts, particularly social. Within these groups his interest lay especially with the history of "social classes": "If it were necessary to define Kliuchevskii's main, dominant inclination as a historian, I would call him a historian of social classes." Moreover, it was particularly the history of the political elite that held his interest:

> In both *Boiarskaia duma* and his course he studies in detail the evolution of the elite ruling strata: the commercial aristocracy of Dnieper Rus', the land-owning retinue [*druzhina*] and monastery society of Upper Volga [Rus'], the titled Moscow boyardom [*boiarstvo*] of the fifteenth and sixteenth centuries, and its successor, the variegated small landowning gentry [*melkopomestnoe dvorianstvo*] of the eighteenth and nineteenth centuries, which carried out palace coups through the guards regiments.[32]

In his unpublished memoirs, Bogoslovskii makes the comparison, familiar from Miliukov's memoirs and echoed by several other students, between Kliuchevskii and Vinogradov as teachers. Unlike Vinogradov's, Kliuchevskii's strength was not in the seminars, where he was a "dogmatic," laying out his prepared conclusions and never ending his critical comments with a question mark. Bogoslovskii came to the conclusion as a student that Kliuchevskii was at home in the lecture hall, where the student would passively listen to his conclusions, but not in a laboratory where the student would learn methods through independent work under the guidance of the instructor. It was Kliuchevskii, nevertheless, who suggested the theme of his undergraduate thesis: "The origin, content, and significance of the census books [*pistsovye knigi*] as sources for the history of the Muscovite state in the fifteenth, sixteenth, and seventeenth centuries."[33]

It is interesting to look at Bogoslovskii's own work in the light of these remarks. From his first undergraduate dissertation on tie *pistsovye knigi,* through his massive *magistr* and doctoral dissertations, *Peter the Great's Local Reform* [Oblastnaia reforma Petra Velikogo] (1902), and *Local Self-Government in the Russian North in the Seventeenth Century* [Zemskoe samoupravlenie na russkom severe v XVII veke] (1909–12), to his final unfinished *opus magnum,* the biography of Peter the Great, that work is characterized by a strong penchant for massive, detailed work in previously unused and ill-organized archives.[34] His undergraduate paper, which comprises five thick bound notebooks in his archive, carried the epigraph: *V nauke priatno byt' i prostym chernorabochim* (In scholarship, it is good to be a simple toiler).[35]

Bogoslovskii's *magistr* thesis seems to continue the line of confronting the theory of the Petrine reforms with their reality that is characteristic of late-nineteenth-century scholarship and can be traced back, through Miliukov, to Kliuchevskii. His doctoral dissertation, like Liubavskii's work on the Lithuanian-Russian state, pursues the line issuing from Kliuchevskii's agenda in the introduction to *Boiarskaia duma:* precedents and alternatives to autocracy, or more precisely, to bureaucratic absolutism, in the pre-Petrine Russian past. In Bogoslovskii's study of the institutions of self-government in the Russian north, where he found them to be surviving intact into the mid-seventeenth century, the task is set in the terms established by the master in his introduction to *Boiarskaia duma* (and pursued in Bogoslovskii's first dissertation, of course): to get from the legislation on the self-government [*zemskie*] institutions of Muscovy to the reality behind it, "how [it] was in fact carried out and to what extent it became reality." The element of present-mindedness in his inquiry is clearly betrayed in his conclusion:

> In developing an absolutist central power and emerging under its aegis from the feudal order, the Muscovite State passes through two successive stages in the development of its form of government, distinguished by the instruments utilized by the autocracy. In the period [from the mid-sixteenth to the mid-seventeenth century] the Moscow State may be called an *autocracy of the land* [*samoderzhavno-zemskoe*]. From the middle of the seventeenth century it becomes a *bureaucratic autocracy* [*samoderzhavno-biurokraticheskoe*].

In the first of these periods

> The entire state structure, with the national assembly [*zemskii sobor*] at the top and the self-governing counuies and townships [*samoupravliaiushchiesia uezdy i volosti*] at the bottom, is imbued with the principle of popular self-governance [*zemskoe samoupravlenie*]; it is entirely bound up with this principle, and the *zemskii sobor* at the top rests on the district and township self-governments as on a necessary foundation. Popular representation at the center was the inevitable crowning [*zavershenie*] of local, county, and township autonomy.[36]

If a penchant for pathbreaking archival research and a present-minded interest in old-Russian political institutions linked Bogoslovskii to his teacher, so too did his abiding interest in the history of the political elite, which he carried over into the study of the eighteenth-century nobility.[37]

Among Kliuchevskii's pupils, his most pious admirer, and apparently his favorite student as well, was A.A. Kizevetter (1866–1933).[38] "It would be inadequate to say," Kizevetter wrote in an obituary article about Kliuchevskii, "that Kliuchevskii advanced or reformed the science of Russian history. We will be much closer to the truth in saying that he founded that science."[39] For Kizevetter, Kliuchevskii represented the unique combination of scholar and poet that it takes to make a truly great historian: "Scholar and poet, a great systemist-schematist and a sensitive portrayer of the concrete phenomena of life, a first-class master of broad generalizations and an incomparable analyst who valued and loved detailed, microscopic observations—such was Kliuchevskii as historian."[40]

There is little reason to doubt that Kizevetter aspired to be a "most remarkable scholarly researcher and brilliant teacher of his science"[41] himself. Kizevetter was in fact generally considered to be the best literary stylist and lecturer among Kliuchevskii's students. Even the sober Miliukov was willing to allow that he fulfilled this aspiration to a considerable degree: "We all tried in those days more or less to imitate Kliuchevskii. But Kizevetter had special talents for that. . . . The ability to paint vivid word pictures, to find the right colors and to make unexpected connections that penetrated to the essence of a subject, distinguished Kizevetter as a lecturer and a teacher to the end of his days."[42] It was Kliuchevskii's talent as a teacher, that is, primarily as a lecturer, that Kizevetter chose to write about in his contribution to the 1912 memorial volume; he describes there in great detail the nature of Kliuchevskii's art as a lecturer, by which "imperceptibly but with unusual force the underlying concrete basis of his complex and subtle scholarly generalizations was made clear."[43] There is some reason to believe that Kizevetter's attention to Kliuchevskii's art as a lecturer went as far as imitating some of his unusual speech patterns.[44]

In any case, this talent, Miliukov goes on, was indeed combined with a real love for detailed historical analysis and rooting in the archives, and he approvingly refers the reader to Kizevetter's memoirs on that score.[45] Kizevetter's monographic work on the Russian town in the eighteenth century, especially his monumental dissertation, *The Urban Estate in Eighteenth-Century Russia* [Posadskaia obshchina v Rossii XVIII st.] (1903), certainly qualified him as a follower of Kliuchevskii on this side of the ledger as well: it was the plowing of new ground based on massive archival research (typically, the Moscow archives of the Ministry of Justice for the most part), and it aimed at illuminating the socioeconomic and political realities behind the institution (the *posadskaia obshchina*) that served, again typically, as the focal point of the inquiry.[46] Kizevetter's study has properly been considered the pioneering study of Russia's "third estate" in the eighteenth century.

Like his colleagues Miliukov and Bogoslovskii, Kizevetter emphasized the tragic gap that separated the schemes of the eighteenth-century absolutist state from the "Muscovite" reality that lay behind them, and the judgment was negative:

> The entire government policy of the eighteenth century toward urban self-government can be characterized as an attempt to reach a completely unreachable goal: realization of the elevated cultural tasks of internal policy on the old foundation of servitude [*tiaglo*]. As a result, the elevated cultural goals were not achieved, and the urban obligations became heavier than before; and only one conclusion was forthcoming in the consciousness of the urban population: that the paternalistic attentions of the government cost very dearly, that life had become harder, not better.[47]

One is instantly reminded of the memorable phrase with which Kliuchevskii characterized the "modern period" in Russian history: "*Gosudarstvo pukhlo, a narod khirel* [The state grew fat, but the people wasted away]."[48]

The conclusion Kizevetter drew from this observation in his dissertation-defense speech points up how much his work was also true to type as a present-minded inquiry into the historical roots of self-government in Russia: "Historical study of past epochs in the development of our self-government leads ... to the same conclusion as observation of our present situation: one thing above all else is desirable for the satisfaction of the most urgent needs and requirements of our motherland—that all the doors and windows of Russia's state edifice be opened wide to the principles of genuine public initiative."[49]

Iurii Vladimirovich Got'e (1873–1943), the last of Kliuchevskii's pupils to defend his dissertation before his teacher, has left two reminiscences about his relations with Kliuchevskii during his student years between 1891 and 1895.[50] On the whole, Got'e confirms the familiar impression of Kliuchevskii as a rather distant and magisterial teacher, whose seminars were more like lectures and whose general course, which he informs us was read virtually unchanged from year to year, inspired his students, above all "to love the history of their native land."[51]

Like the others, too, Got'e compares Kliuchevskii in this respect to Vinogradov, whose seminars "taught [him] how to work. ... He was precisely what a professor ought to be in relation to his students: unceremonious and accessible within the limits that separate a genuine major scholar from beginning students." Moreover he attributes the greatest influence on his formation as a historian of Russia to the seminar of P.N. Miliukov, which was conducted, he writes, "fully in the Vinogradov style": "The same attentiveness, both pedagogical and scholarly, in the selection of topics, the same attentive relations with the students, the same restrained strictness and attention to the analysis of the topics." And it was in fact for Miliukov that Got'e prepared his undergraduate thesis on the defense of the southern borders of the Muscovite state in the sixteenth century, in the preparation of which he met frequently with Miliukov at the university and at Miliukov's home to discuss details, get bibliographical and source references and the like: "Work in Miliukov's seminar and, perhaps, even more so the work on the undergraduate thesis under P.N.'s direct supervision deepened and defined my scholarly interests. I decided definitely to become a Russian historian. And for this supervision I will always be grateful to P.N. Miliukov, whom I consider to be my teacher just as much as V.O. Kliuchevskii."

Got'e summed up the influence of his two teachers as follows: "[Kliuchevskii] lit a special interest for Russian history in me, and in Miliukov's seminar I completed my first scholarly work."[52]

According to Got'e, however, Kliuchevskii's influence on him went considerably deeper than a matter of general inspiration, and he rejects the common view that Kliuchevskii was "a great man, but not a pedagogue." He recounts the story of how he tried to get some detailed advice about the literature on the questions that had been selected for his *magistr* exams, and was finally told by his irritated teacher to "get it for himself," to "look it up in Mezhov" (that is, the works of Russia's greatest bibliographer, V.I. Mezhov, 1830–94). He understood later, he writes, that this was not indifference on Kliuchevskii's part, but part of a deliberate pedagogical strategy to make aspiring professionals aware of their own responsibility in "getting it for themselves" and of the primary importance of sources, rather than secondary literature:

> In his refusal to lift the curtain of scholarship for the uninitiated; in a certain skepticism toward those who had not succeeded in demonstrating their love and devotion to their chosen activity; in his demand that such a person "get it for himself," deepen his own knowledge, and grow accustomed to independent scholarly work; and finally, in his warm involvement with and generous help to those who in his opinion had demonstrated or were demonstrating their sincere love for their chosen subject and were showing some talent for finding their own way and working independently—in all this one cannot fail to see the conscious devices of an original scholarly pedagogy that had been worked out through long years of practice and the lengthy meditations of a powerful and original mind.[53]

Got'e's major works, his *magistr* and doctoral dissertations, fit squarely into the Kliuchevskian pattern familiar from the work of Kliuchevskii's earlier pupils. *Zamoskovnyi krai v XVII veke: Opyt issledovaniia po istorii ekonomicheskogo byta moskovskoi Rusi* [The Moscow Region in the Seventeenth Century: An Attempted Investigation into the History of Economic Conditions in Muscovy], first published in 1906, is based in large part on the study of the *pistsovye knigi,* like Rozhkov's first thesis and Bogoslovskii's second, and is the kind of economic history or "history of economic conditions" that one would expect from the Kliuchevskii school: it includes the study of administrative structures ("regional divisions," as per Liubavskii), population geography, and landholding relationships, in addition to the strictly "economic" matter of agricultural production. Rozhkov investigated the socioeconomic background of the Time of Troubles; Got´e studied its socioeconomic aftermath.[54]

Got´e's monumental history of regional administration in Russia from Peter I to Catherine II, of which the first volume was published in 1913 as his doctoral dissertation, in characteristic fashion attempts to go beyond the administrative statutes and structures to the operational and social realities. In a manner analogous to Kizevetter's work on the *posadskaia obshchina,* Got´e's looks at the entire post-Petrine eighteenth-century experience of regional administration from the perspective of the origins of the corresponding Catherinian reforms. (The second volume, completed in 1922 but published only in 1941, is largely devoted to the immediate background and results of the 1775 reform.[55]

As the youngest of this group of Kliuchevskii's pupils, Got´e conceived of his own work as a continuation not only of the master's work but of that of his older fellows. And indeed, according to his own testimony, he got the idea of his first dissertation from Rozhkov's work on the sixteenth-century economy, and the second was conceived as a continuation of Bogoslovskii's thesis on the regional reforms of Peter.[56]

Another characteristic of Got´e's work, again according to his own testimony, was its central concern with the history of the political elite, the *dvorianstvo.* In the diary he kept during the revolution and civil war, he describes *Zamoskovnyi krai* as "in essence the history of the nobility in the seventeenth century in its main features," and the history of the eighteenth century regional administration as "nothing other than the *everyday* history of the nobility from Peter to Catherine II, when they essentially conquered everything."[57] In the fall of 1919 he set down a sketch of his life's work, both those parts completed and those left to be done, a "series of monographs in which all my views on the entirety of Russian history would be developed." The result, he wrote, "would be an integrated cycle on the history of gentry Russia [*dvorianskaia Rossiia*], which arose in the fifteenth–sixteenth centuries and fell in the twentieth."[58]

In this way, the youngest of the first generation of Kliuchevskii's pupils aspired to complete an agenda that had been Kliuchevskii's own.[59] Got′e's fascination with the role of the nobility in modern Russian history seems akin to that of his teacher: the fascination of a plebeian who through education shared the European culture which had been historically, in Kliuchevskii's words, "the caste monopoly of the masters"; it was a role *manqué:* having been exposed to enlightenment and attained the status of a privileged estate by the late eighteenth century, the nobility, content with its privileges, failed to develop into a true first estate, thereby retarding Russia's development into a modern European nation.[60]

This remark raises the interesting question of the social background of Kliuchevskii's pupils, which may serve as a kind of capstone to this little survey. It would be somehow satisfying to learn that they all, like Kliuchevskii himself, were of plebeian origins. Four of the six in fact were: Liubavskii had been a seminarian like Kliuchevskii (that is, he was born into the clerical estate, the *dukhovenstvo*), and Bogoslovskii's father had been a seminarian; Rozhkov was the son of a "third-element" provincial school teacher, that is, he was from the petty or "democratic" intelligentsia; and Got′e was from a merchant family of booksellers (his great-great-grandfather was a French bourgeois named Gautier who immigrated to Russia during the reign of Catherine). Miliukov, however, was from a modest serving-noble (*chinovnik*) family on his father's side (his mother was from a more elevated gentry family), and Kliuchevskii's favorite pupil, Kizevetter, was the son of a privy councillor (*tainyi sovetnik);* that is, he was from the upper stratum of the serving nobility.

Statistically, their collective social background was, at any rate, more plebeian than that of the Moscow university faculty taken as a whole, or of the historico-philological faculty in particular. Especially noticeable is the absence of individuals of landed-gentry background among Kliuchevskii's pupils.[61] Nor did they include anyone in their number who could be considered an apologist for noble interests.

Kliuchevskii's pupils were otherwise a diverse lot politically and ideologically, ranging (in terms of a simple indicator) from the sometime Bolshevik Rozhkov on the left to the very moderate constitutional monarchist Liubavskii on the right. In between were the probably equally moderate constitutional monarchist and sometime Octobrist Bogoslovskii, the slightly more left-oriented and sometime Constitutional-Democrat (Kadet) Got′e (whose political views were very close to those of Petr Struve),[62] the radical democrat and leader of the Kadet party Miliukov, and his close party associate Kizevetter. The *popovichi* (priests' sons) were the most conservative, and the "third elementer" was, not surprisingly, the most radical, followed by the scions of the service nobility. The most European or ecumenical in outlook were probably Miliukov[63] and Rozhkov, in their different ways, followed by Kizevetter, while the others were more nationalist in outlook. None of them, however, could be called Slavophile or populist, at least not in the sense of idealizing Russian ways or the peasantry.

* * * *

This review of Kliuchevskii's pupils leads to several observations, following more or less directly from the evidence presented. According to a number of influential Soviet historiographers, there was no "Kliuchevskii school" of historians, and this for the simple reason that Kliuchevskii lacked a coherent theory of history. Not only did he have a wrong idea of what a social class is and fail to grasp the ultimate historical motor force, the class struggle—he did not have any monist conception of history at all: despite his inclination toward "economic materialism" (read: primacy of the economic factor without the dialectic), he was in the end an eclectic. No theory = no method = no school. It was stated most colorfully, if not most respectfully, by Pokrovskii, the leading figure in the first generation of Soviet Marxist historians, who apparently never got over having been flunked on his *magistr* examination by Kliuchevskii:

> One is accustomed to speak of the "school" of Kliuchevskii. If there ever was a scholar organically incapable of having a school, it was precisely the author of *Boiarskaia duma,* whose only method consists of what used to be called in the old days "divination." Thanks to his artistic fantasy, Kliuchevskii was able to resurrect an entire picture of everyday life from several lines of an old charter, to reconstruct an entire system of relations from one sample. But he couldn't any more teach someone how to do this than Chaliapin could teach someone to sing as he does. For the one you need the voice of a Chaliapin, and for the other you need the artistic imagination of a Kliuchevskii.[64]

The same essential argument has been used by Kliuchevskii's biographer, and Pokrovskii's student, M.V. Nechkina. It was Kliuchevskii's "tragedy," Nechkina wrote in her 1930 essay on the historian, that he didn't make it to Marxism,[65] and she held to that view in all her later writing about Kliuchevskii.

If, however, we can accept the idea that history is a sublunary enterprise (I borrow the phrase from Paul Veyne) that really has nothing to do with metaphysics or the discovery of "laws,"[66] then at best Pokrovskii, Nechkina, and their seconders in Soviet historiography have come to a defensible conclusion for the wrong reasons. It may, indeed, be wise to shun the term "Kliuchevskii school," or even "Moscow school" (which has the advantage of pushing the heritage back at least as far as Solov'ev, Kliuchevskii's teacher) if only because the influence of both Solov'ev and Kliuchevskii was pervasive throughout Russian historiography of the late nineteenth and early twentieth centuries, as can be seen by examining the work of such outstanding representatives of the "Petersburg school" as S.F. Platonov or A.S. Lappo-Danilevskii.

Nevertheless, certain persistent characteristics of historical scholarship as it was practiced in and around Moscow University in the last two decades of the nineteenth century and the first two or three decades of this century bear the imprint of Kliuchevskii's influence. Some of them are pointed out by Nechkina in her biography of Kliuchevskii: the posing of broad questions, significant chronological scope, distinctive problem-orientation; typically, the study of political forms and relations, but penetrating to the social and economic background; extensive use of archives, and presentation of new "facts." Nechkina also notes the general tendency of Kliuchevskii's pupils to push the chronological boundary forward into the eighteenth century.[67]

These points are well taken, as far as they go. By looking at legal and institutional records as sources for a large variety of social and economic structures and processes, Kliuchevskii's "school" so extended the agenda of historical inquiry, the definition of the "eventworthy" (Veyne's *l'événementiel*) in a single generation as to transform the face of Russian historiography.[68] Some of this work is astonishingly modern in its wide-ranging treatment of the "eventworthy," presaging by about a generation the similar flowering of the *Annales* school in French historiography. If Kliuchevskii's pupils for the most part adhered to a positivist view of history as the accumulation of documentation, which discouraged the kind of bold cultural-anthropological and social-psychological interpretations made by the best practitioners of the *Annales,* they nevertheless greatly expanded the agenda, and it was their fundamental respect for the documents that gave their work its enduring value.

The animadversions of Soviet historiography about "the crisis of bourgeois historiography" notwithstanding, the last two decades of the nineteenth century and the first years of the twentieth before the outbreak of the Great War was a period of great progress in the writing of history, for progress in historical writing over time has been for the most part a matter of what Veyne calls *l'allongement du questionnaire:* the extension of those areas of human experience that are deemed eventworthy, rather than a matter of attaining deeper levels of explanation or a more perfect metaphysics—a horizontal, not a vertical process. Judging from the accounts of his pupils, Kliuchevskii's part in all this was central. Pokrovskii and co. got it all wrong: what Kliuchevskii taught was not "method" with a small "m"—this was a common property of scholarship and could be learned from others—nor was it "Theory" with a capital "T," metaphysics. It was the demonstration, in part through his monographic work but especially through his course, of the breadth of the agenda and the great variety of phenomena—economic, social, political, demographic, geographic—that could be employed in the construction of rational historical explanations; in a word, the very "eclecticism" that Nechkina called his "tragedy."

In the introduction to the first volume of his *Course*, Kliuchevskii justified his "eclecticism" in abstract, sociological terms:

> The endless variety of associations [*soiuzov*] that make up human society arises from the fact that the basic elements of social life in various times and places do not have the same arrangement; they come in various combinations, and the variety of these combinations arises in turn not only from the quantity and arrangement of the component parts, the greater or lesser complexity of the human associations, but from different relations between the same elements—for example, from the dominance of one over the others. In this variety, whose basic cause lies in the endless changes in the interaction of historical forces, the most important thing is that the elements of social life in various combinations and situations display unequal properties and effects, show different sides of their nature to the observer. As a result, one and the same elements behave differently even in the same kind of associations.[69]

"Here," Nechkina interjects in exasperation, "you have a complete rejection of historical monism, in the first place, and in the second a rejection of philosophy of history in general."[70] She was certainly right in the first instance; we can say she was right in the second as well only if we accept her historicist (in Karl Popper's sense), teleological notion of "philosophy of history."

Together with his analytical eclecticism went Kliuchevskii's insistence, also backed by demonstration, on the utilization of the variety of documentation in the archives.[71] It seems to me these were the two elements of his "teaching" that had the greatest impact on his pupils and formed the basic characteristics of the "Kliuchevskii school." Neither the now-apparent inadequacy of some of Kliuchevskii's explanations nor the logical inconsistencies in his periodization scheme should prevent us from appreciating the impact of his approach to the Russian historical past on the following generation of Russian historians.

A secondary characteristic of the "Kliuchevskii school" was its highly critical attitude toward the bureaucratic absolutist state and its ability, historically, to carry out reforms beneficial to the country as a whole. To a considerable extent, this tendency in the historiography of the last decades of the nineteenth century and the first years of the twentieth reflected the declining reputation of the autocracy that reemerged very broadly in Russian educated society (*obshchestvo*) during the period of the so-called "counterreforms" under Alexander III and the first decade of the reign of Nicholas II, which is all part of the story leading up to the revolution of 1905. In academic historiography the line of filiation seems to go straight back to Kliuchevskii, and through him, from what we know of his formative years, to the "realism" of the 1860s; like so much else in *fin de siècle* Russia, it all begins in the turmoil of the reform epoch. (The issue of anti-noble bias, which runs like a thread through the "school" as well, is a related phenomenon that can probably be understood in the same terms.)

A closely related characteristic of the work of Kliuchevskii's pupils— one that points up the present-mindedness of these academics—is the very large amount of attention paid to the search for traditions of decentralization and self-government in Russian history. Like the judgments on the autocracy's capacity for reform, this was part of a broader wave of literature on political theory and the history of Russian political institutions that reached flood stage in 1905, and it is possible, in a few cases quite likely, that these academics saw their weighty monographic researches as, in part, a contribution to the social movement. The inspiration can also be traced back to Kliuchevskii, both to his programmatic statements, as in the introduction to *Boiarskaia duma,* and to his *Course.* Of course, the civic-mindedness of Kliuchevskii's pupils was by no means entirely attributable to their teacher's influence. Some such attitudes were characteristic of a great many Russian academics in these years. But the element of present-mindedness in the research strategies and conclusions of the Moscow historians does appear to have been more pronounced than in the work of their Petersburg counterparts, who tended to hew to the nominalist tradition of K.N. Bestuzhev-Riumin (1829–1897).[72]

These comments about the research strategies of Kliuchevskii's pupils raise the interesting question of the extent to which these strategies were the subject of discussion and coordinated effort. In this respect, the testimonies of Miliukov, Kizevetter, and Got´e suggest that the extent may have been considerable, and that the circle of students and instructors grouped around Miliukov during his nine-year teaching career as a *Privatdozent* in the late 1880s and early 1890s, when all of the group were at the university, was the main forum. It may be that the Kliuchevskii school owed a good deal of its particular identity to the efforts of Miliukov, whose political and ideological activism was already well developed in those years (and led, of course, to his removal from the university in January 1895). This seems to be an interesting subject in need of further inquiry.[73]

Finally, I would like to raise the question of how, if at all, Kliuchevskii's theoretical views, his sociology, affected his students.

We have to begin by asking how they affected Kliuchevskii's own work as a practicing historian. On this score we find that such ideologically divergent critics of Kliuchevskii as G.P. Fedotov and M.V. Nechkina have denied any connection between the two, at least any connection of a positive sort.

Fedotov, the émigré historian of Russian religious thought, wrote that Kliuchevskii "was not, of course, a sociologist; he was not a theoretician at all," but as a man of his time (that is, the 1860s and 1870s) he felt obliged to "justify his work before the tribunal of Sociology." That was the only meaning of the theoretical introduction to his *Course:* "The historian in Kliuchevskii was terrorized by sociology and pretended to accept its social mandate. But only his pupil, Rozhkov, on the basis now of Marxism, made an attempt at a 'sociological' construction of Russian history." The negative side of Kliuchevskii's commitment to "sociology," according to Fedotov, was that it kept him from any kind of adequate treatment of the individual and, therefore, of spiritual culture in Russian history.[74]

Nechkina describes Kliuchevskii's course on methodology (1884–85) and then concludes: "Perhaps the most dramatic aspect of Kliuchevskii's eclectic system was the fact that it was for all practical purposes useless to him. . . . His methodological conception was stillborn in his own creative work, and was of no use to him in his research work.[75] These conclusions are, in my opinion, quite misguided. They amount to acceptance of Pokrovskii's view that Kliuchevskii's "method" was nothing but "divination"; that it was, in the final analysis, some kind of unanalyzable "art," a matter merely of striking images and unexpected connections—a curious conclusion to be coming, in Nechkina's case, from a scholar who spent a considerable part of her very long career analyzing Kliuchevskii's work and capped it off with a six-hundred-page book. All this amounts to a nearly total failure to come to terms with what was in fact a remarkably coherent, sophisticated, and innovative methodology.

It is true, of course, that Kliuchevskii was not very successful in formulating his theoretical–methodological views in abstract terms, as a reading of his lectures on methodology or even the passage from the theoretical introduction to his general *Course* cited above clearly shows: the terminology is derivative (Kliuchevskii's debt to the great historian of law and philosopher, B.N. Chicherin, is especially remarkable), the language stilted, especially by comparison with his usual narrative style. This was due in part, of course, to the need for brevity in the introduction to his general course. But, as Miliukov notes in his memoirs, Kliuchevskii's theoretical views were best developed in the body of his substantive work, in the context of specific historical problems. As S.I. Tkhorzhevskii points out in his 1921 study—to my mind, the best treatment of Kliuchevskii's theoretical views we have—these views comprised a sophisticated and coherent political philosophy, sociology of law, and sociology of ideas, all of which were brought to bear on his main enterprise, which was revealed already in the subtitle of *Boiarskaia duma*—not political history, or economic history, or the history of social classes, but "the history of society," of the nation as an historical entity. From this perspective, Tkhorzhevskii argues—correctly, in my opinion—the problem of the primacy of economics or politics, state or people, ideas or material conditions, in regard to which Kliuchevskii has been accused of eclecticism, is irrelevant.[76]

Kliuchevskii's two attempts to develop his theoretical views in abstract formulations were not simply tributes to the tyranny of the "Sociology" regnant among the Russian intelligentsia during his formative years as a historian.[77] In the introduction to his *Course* published in 1904, when he was over sixty years old, he tells us in so many words that he considers his history of Russian society to be a contribution, of a preparatory kind, to the science of society. His theoretical statements there are a testimony to his abiding commitment to that enterprise, as well as a guide, when compared to his course on methodology, to the honing of his theoretical views through many years of applying them to the historical record. The rather awkward discourse there on "historical forces," "human associations," and "the elements of social life," which was quoted earlier, was not a jejeune attempt to impose externally received concepts on his historical analysis, but an effort to sum up in "scientific" language the results of long years of profound reflection on how things work historically.

The obverse of this proposition would seem to be that sociological concepts and the general idea of a possible science of society had somehow helped the decidedly undogmatic Kliuchevskii to expand vastly the agenda of the "eventworthy" left him by his teachers, to focus on the historical process, rather than the history of forms and institutions as such, and to deal with complex problems of historical explanation with great nuance and originality.

Kliuchevskii was not a sociologist; he made no contribution to sociological theory. He was a historian whose work—written in jargon-free literary Russian of uncommon grace and economy—was informed with a sociological perspective. It is impossible to say much more about the relationship between "theory" and "practice" in Kliuchevskii's work without a detailed analysis of the structure of his historical writing, a task yet to be undertaken.

By the same token, my provisional response to the question about the influence of Kliuchevskii's theoretical views on his pupils is to beg it: that influence is to be found in the body of their work, just as Kliuchevskii's views were for the most part communicated to his students not in formal discourses or theories but, to quote Miliukov once more, in "the very fact of his relation as a researcher to Russian history as a subject of study."

None of his students makes any note of having been influenced by Kliuchevskii's formal theoretical statements. As a matter of fact, it appears that none of them heard his lectures on methodology, and they were all mature scholars by the time the first volume of the *Course,* with its theoretical introduction, was published. Only two of his students showed an abiding interest in sociological theory: Miliukov and Rozhkov; and, as Fedotov noted, Rozhkov was the only one to go on to work out an explicitly "sociological construction of Russian history," carrying on in a highly idiosyncratic way, one might say, Kliuchevskii's commitment to the idea of a science of society. Miliukov came to Kliuchevskii with his own positivist sociological views already well developed, and found Kliuchevskii's views and general orientation compatible with his own. Rozhkov may have owed much to Kliuchevskii in developing his early views on the sociological imperatives involved in the study of history. For the others, their theoretical views, and therefore the answer to the question of Kliuchevskii's influence in purely theoretical matters, must be sought in a detailed analysis of the explanatory structures embodied in their own historical writings.

The story of Kliuchevskii and his pupils is, of course, only part—albeit a very important part—of the story of the great fluorescence of Russian historical scholarship in the late nineteenth and early twentieth centuries. It is a story that involves pathbreaking Russian contributions to world scholarship in the study of the history of the ancient world, of medieval Europe and Britain, and of eighteenth-century France and the French Revolution, among other subjects. A common characteristic of all this work is the expansion of the agenda to problems of social and economic history. The Russian historians' precocious turn to social and economic history can be traced back to a common intellectual–ideological origin in the 1860s and 1870s;[78] it was undoubtedly sustained by the ongoing, rapid transformation of the society in which they all lived.

Notes

A version of this paper was first presented at the 1987 annual meeting of the American Association for the Advancement of Slavic Studies in a session dedicated to the memory of Petr Andreevich Zaionchkovskii (1904–1983). Reprinted here by permission of *California Slavic Studies.*
   1. Hayden White, *Tropics of Discourse* (Baltimore, 1978), p. 40.

2. Paul Veyne, *Comment on écrit l'histoire* (Paris, 1978), p. 9: "Non, l'histoire n'a pas de méthode: demandez donc un peu qu'on vous montre cette méthode."

3. J.H. Hexter, *Doing History* (Bloomington, IN, 1975), p. 48 and ff.

4. M.V. Nechkina has surveyed the memoir literature and the public response to Kliuchevskii's *Course* in her massive biography of the historian. What it makes up for in biographical detail it unfortunately lacks in critical analysis of Kliuchevskii's narrative work. M.V. Nechkina, *Vasilii Osipovich Kliuchevskii: Istoriia zhizni i tvorchestva* (Moscow, 1974).

The four completed volumes of the *Course* were first published between 1904 and 1910, and then underwent numerous subsequent editions. The most recent Soviet edition of the complete course, including the unfinished volume 5, was in the 1956–59 edition of Kliuchevskii's works: *V.O. Kliuchevskii: Sochineniia v vos'mi tomakh*, vols. 1–8 (Moscow, 1956–59); a new edition is currently under way. The only full translation into English of the *Course*, by C.J. Hogarth (New York and London, 1911–31), mangles the sense and style of the original almost beyond recognition. Good English translations exist only of the parts of the *Course* devoted to the seventeenth century and the reign of Peter I: V.O. Kliuchevsky, *A Course in Russian History: The Seventeenth Century,* trans. Natalie Duddington, introd. Alfred Rieber (Chicago, 1968; Armonk, NY: M.E. Sharpe, 1994); V.O. Kliuchevsky, *Peter the Great,* trans. and introd. Liliana Archibald (New York, 1959).

5. Obvious though they are, these questions have been almost completly ignored in the Soviet historiographical literature. The reasons for this neglect are explained below.

6. Nicholas V. Riasanovsky, *A History of Russia,* 4th ed. (New York, 1984).

7. P.N. Miliukov, *Vospominaniia (1856–1917),* vol. 1 (New York, 1955), pp. 89–93.

8. P.N. Miliukov, "V.O. Kliuchevskii," in *V.O Kliuchevskii: Kharakteristiki i vospominaniia* (Moscow, 1912), p. 189. In the English translation by Hogarth, Kliuchevskii's two introductory lectures on theoretical issues were omitted from the first volume and were later added as an Appendix to volume 5.

9. P.N. Miliukov, "Dva russkikh istorika (S.F. Platonov i A.A. Kizevetter)," *Sovremennye zapiski* 51 (1933): 323.

10. P. Miliukov, *Gosudarstvennoe khoziaistvo Rossii v pervoi chetverti XVIII stoletiia i reforma Petra Velikogo,* 2d ed. (St. Petersburg, 1905), p. xiii.

11. On historians' interpretations of Peter's reign, see N.V. Riasanovsky, *The Image of Peter the Great in Russian History and Thought* (New York, 1985), especially pp. 166–76.

12. Miliukov, *Gosudarstvennoe khoziaistvo,* p. xi.

13. V.O. Kliuchevskii, "Boiarskaia duma drevnei Rusi: Opyt istorii pravitel'stvennogo uchrezhdeniia v sviazi s istoriei obshchestva," *Russkaia mysl',* 1880, no. 1, p. 48. The book edition of Kliuchevskii's doctoral dissertation omitted this statement.

14. Ibid., p. 40.

15. This course, "Metodologiia," is the only one of Kliuchevskii's cycle of lecture courses on "historiography" that remains unpublished (mimeographed copies of an auditor's notes are available in several libraries). On Kliuchevskii's special courses, see Nechkina, *Vasilii Osipovich Kliuchevskii,* chapter 6.

16. Cf. P.N. Miliukov, *Ocherki po istorii russkoi kul'tury,* vol. 1, 3d ed. (St. Petersburg, 1898), p. 12; and V.O. Kliuchevskii, *Sochineniia,* vol. 1 (Moscow, 1956), pp. 25–26.

Kliuchevskii: "The individual history of a particular nation can be important because of the uniqueness of its phenomena, regardless of their [universal] cultural significance, when they make it possible for the investigator to observe those processes that reveal the mechanism of historical life especially clearly, processes in which historical forces appear in circumstances that are rarely repeated or are unobserved anywhere else, even though these processes have had no significant influence on the general historical movement. In this respect, the scientific value of the history of any given nation is determined by the quantity of unique local combinations and the qualities of whatever social elements they reveal."

Miliukov: "In its pure form, the inherent tendency of the social process is only an abstract possibility. In order to go from possibility to reality, this tendency must be refracted in the prism of real conditions of historical life. Under the influence of given geographical, climatic, soil, and other conditions, the basic direction of historical life can vary infinitely, to the point that it becomes quite impossible to recognize the presence of the same basic underlying tendency. It is the direct responsibility of the historian, not only to discover the presence of this underlying tendency, but to explain the causes of its manifestation in precisely this given concrete form, in each individual variation."

Both historians thus subscribed to a kind of theory of contrasts, according to which the very peculiarities of Russia's history (vis-à-vis Europe) made it a particularly promising candidate for study by the "historian-sociologist" (Kliuchevskii, ibid.). The issue of scholarly legitimacy for the study of Russian history seems to lie not far beneath the surface of this argument.

17. P. Miliukov, *Ocherki po istorii russkoi kul'tury,* vol. 1, jubilee ed. (Paris, 1937), p. 29.

18. See Iu.V. Got'e, "Universitet," *Vestnik moskovskogo universiteta, Seriia 8. Istoriia,* 1982, no. 4, p. 23, for a contemporary student's opinion.

19. *Sbornik statei, posviashchennykh Vasiliiu Osipovichu Kliuchevskomu ego uchenikami, druz'iami i pochitateliami ko dniu tridtsatiletiia ego professorskoi deiatel'nosti v Moskovskom Universitete (5 Dekabria 1879–5 dekabria 1909 goda)* (Moscow, 1909), pp. ii–iii.

20. M.K. Liubavskii, "Solov'ev i Kliuchevskii," in *V.O. Kliuchevskii: Kharakteristiki i vospominaniia,* pp. 45–68. This point is made by Dorothy Atkinson in an unpublished seminar paper.

21. Karpovich saw this "legalistic reversion" as a significant tendency among the younger generation of historians. Michael Karpovich, "Klyuchevski and Recent Trends in Russian Historiography," *Slavonic and East European Review* 21 (1943): 37. On the "state school," whose most prominent representative on the history faculty had been Solov'ev, see, in English, the work by Riasanovsky cited in note 11. The most interesting piece on the place of the "state school" (or "juridical school") in Russian historiography remains Miliukov's essay, which he gave as his introductory lecture upon becoming a *Privatdozentship* at Moscow University in 1886: "Iuridicheskaia shkola v russkoi istoriografii (Solov'ev, Kavelin, Chicherin, Sergeevich)," in *Russkaia mysl',* 1886, 6 (June), pp. 80–92.

22. M.K. Liubavskii, *Litovsko-russkii seim: Opyt po istorii uchrezhdeniia v sviazi s vnutrennim stroem i vneshneiu zhizn'iu gosudarstva* (Moscow, 1900), p. 1.

23. Kliuchevskii, "Boiarskaia duma," p. 50.

24. M.K. Liubavskii, *Lektsii po drevnei russkoi istorii do kontsa XVI veka,* 3d ed. (Moscow, 1918), "Predislovie." Liubavskii took particular exception in his lectures to Kliuchevskii's characterization of Kievan Rus' as a state founded on trade (pp. 64–69).

25. N.A. Rozhkov, "Avtobiografiia," *Katorga i ssylka* 32 (1927): 161–65.

26. This was G.P. Fedotov's point: G.P. Fedotov, "Rossiia Kliuchevskogo," *Sovremennye zapiski* 50 (1932): 353–54.

27. N. Rozhkov, *Sel'skoe khoziaistvo moskovskoi Rusi v XVI veke* (Moscow, 1899). On the relation to Kliuchevskii's thesis, see V.I. Picheta, *Vvedenie v russkuiu istoriiu (istochniki i istoriografiia)* (Moscow, 1923), p. 174.

28. N.A. Rozhkov, *Gorod i derevnia v russkoi istorii (Kratkii ocherk ekonomicheskoi istorii Rossii),* 3d ed. (St. Petersburg, 1913), pp. 6–7.

29. M.M. Bogoslovskii, "V.O. Kliuchevskii kak uchenyi," in *V.O. Kliuchevskii: Kharakteristiki i vospominaniia,* p. 31.

30. Gosudarstvennyi Istoricheskii Muzei, f. 442, d. 4, l. 230 ob. (Bogoslcvskii's diary, 1917), as quoted by L.V. Cherepnin, *Otechestvennye istoriki XVIII–XX vv: Sbornik statei, vystuplenii, vospominanii* (Moscow, 1984), p. 111.

31. "V.O. Kliuchevskii kak uchenyi," p. 36.

32. Ibid., p. 38.

33. Cherepnin, *Otechestvennye istoriki,* pp. 98–99. The text excerpted by Cherepnin, Bogoslovskii's 1927 memoir about Vinogradov, has recently been published: M.M. Bogoslovskii, *Istoriografiia, memuaristika, epistoliariia (nauchnoe nasledie)* (Moscow, 1987), pp. 69–93.

34. M.M. Bogoslovskii, *Oblastnaia reforma Petra Velikogo: Provintsiia 1719–1727 gg.* (Moscow, 1902); *Zemskoe samoupravlenie na russkom severe v XVII v.,* vol 1: *Oblastnoe delenie Pomor'ia,* vol 2 *Zemlevladenie i obshchestvennyi stroi, Organy samoupravleniia* (Moscow, 1909); *Deiatel'nost' zemskogo mira, Zemstvo i gosudarstvo* (Moscow, 1912); *Petr I: Materialy dlia biografii,* vols. 1–5 ([Moscow], 1940–48).

35. Cherepnin, *Otechestvennye istoriki,* p. 99.

36. *Zemskoe samoupravlenie,* vol. 2, p. 260.

37. On the "gentry theme" in Bogoslovskii's work, see Cherepnin, pp. 102–5.

38. Several colleagues attest to Kizevetter's particular closeness to Kliuchevskii; Kliuchevskii supported Kizevetter's candidacy (over Bogoslovskii's) for the chair in Russian history in 1911. V.O. Kliuchevskii, *Pis'ma, dnevniki, aforizmy i mysli ob istorii* (Moscow, 1968), pp. 216–17.

39. A.A. Kizevetter, "Pamiati V.O. Kliuchevskogo," *Russkaia mysl',* 1911, no. 6, p. 135.

40. Ibid., p. 139.

41. Ibid., p. 135.

42. Miliukov, "Dva russkikh istorika," p. 324.

43. "V.O. Kliuchevskii kak prepodavatel'," p. 167.

44. Got'e testifies to this from personal experience: Iu.V. Got'e, *Time of Troubles: The Diary of Iurii Vladimirovich Got'e, Moscow July 8, 1917–July 23, 1922* (Princeton, 1988), p. 347.

45. Miliukov, "Dva russkikh istorika," pp. 324–25.

46. A.A. Kizevetter, *Posadskaia obshchina v Rossii XVIII st.* (Moscow, 1903). The focus of the work is, to be sure, on relations with the state; it is not a social history of the Russian town in the eighteenth century.

47. A.A. Kizevetter, *Istoricheskie ocherki* (Moscow, 1912), p. 271. (From Kizevetter's speech at his dissertation defense.)

48. Kliuchevskii, *Sochineniia,* vol. 3, p. 12.

49. Kizevetter, *Istoricheskie ocherki,* p. 273.

50. Iu.V. Got'e, "V.O. Kliuchevskii kak rukovoditel' nachinaiushchikh uchenykh," in *V.O. Kliuchevskii: Kharakteristiki i vospominaniia,* pp. 177–182; and "Universitet," cited earlier.

51. "Universitet," p. 21.

52. Ibid., p. 23.

53. Got'e, "V.O. Kliuchevskii," p. 182.

54. Iu.V. Got'e, *Zamoskovnyi krai v XVII veke: Opyt issledovaniia po istorii ekonomicheskogo byta moskovskoi Rusi* (Moscow, 1906; 2d rev. ed., 1937).

55. Iu.V. Got′e, *Istoriia oblastnogo upravleniia v Rossii ot Petra I do Ekateriny II*, vol 1: *Reforma 1727 goda, Oblastnoe delenie i oblastnye uchrezhdeniia 1727–1775 gg.* (Moscow, 1913); vol. 2: *Organy nadzora, Chrezvychainye i vremennye oblastnye uchrezhdeniia, Razvitie mysli o preobrazovanii oblastnogo upravleniia, Uprazdnenie uchrezhdenii 1727 g.* (Moscow, 1941).

56. Got′e, *Time of Troubles*, p. 302.

57. Ibid., p. 303.

58. Ibid.

59. Bogoslovskii, "V.O. Kliuchevskii kak uchenyi," p. 38. Nechkina also remarks Kliuchevskii's abiding fascination with the history of the "first estate."

60. Kliuchevskii, *Sochineniia*, vol. 3, p. 10 et passim.

61. In 1906–08, of the 22 members of the historico-philological faculty, 8 (36 percent) were of *dvorianstvo* background, 8 (36 percent) were from the *dukhovenstvo*, and 3 (14 percent) were of *chinovnik* background. In addition, there was 1 faculty member from the *kupechestvo*, 1 of military background, and 1 foreigner. As it was, that faculty had the lowest proportion of gentry and the highest proportion of clergy of any faculty at the university: the totals for the entire university faculty were 43 percent and 13 percent, respectively. (Data compiled by Mark von Hagen.)

62. See Richard Pipes, *Struve: Liberal on the Right, 1905–1944* (Cambridge, MA, 1980).

63. See Thomas Riha, *A Russian European: Paul Miliukov in Russian Politics* (Notre Dame, IN, 1968).

64. M.N. Pokrovskii, *Marksizm i osobennosti istoricheskogo razvitiia Rossii. Sbornik statei, 1922–1925 gg.* (Leningrad, 1925), p. 76.

65. M.V. Nechkina, "V.O. Kliuchevskii," in M.N. Pokrovskii, ed., *Russkaia istoricheskaia literatura v klassovom osveshchenii*, vol. 2 *(Moscow, 1930), p. 345: "Analysis of the class struggle led him toward new generalizations, but he failed to reach them. That is the tragedy of Kliuchevskii."*

66. Veyne, *Comment on écrit l'histoire*, p. 99 et passim. "Comprendre l'histoire ne consiste donc pas à savoir discerner de larges courants sous-marins par-dessous l'agitation superficielle: l'histoire n'a pas de profondeurs."

67. Nechkina, *Vasilii Osipovich Kliuchevskii*, p. 375.

68. In this frame of reference, the "school" should include a number of important Moscow historians who came along after Kliuchevskii's retirement (that is, approximately between the two revolutions of 1905 and 1917), and probably S.F. Platonov of St. Petersburg, who owed much of the inspiration for his great work on the Time of Troubles to Kliuchevskii. See Picheta, *Vvedenie v russkuiu istoriiu*, chs. 17–18; A.N. Tsamutali, *Bor'ba napravlenii v russkoi istoriografii v period imperializma* (Leningrad, 1986), ch. 2 (S.F. Platonov).

69. Kliuchevskii, *Sochineniia*, vol. 1, pp. 23–24.

70. Nechkina, "V.O. Kliuchevskii," p. 311.

71. Several contributors to the collection, "Kliuchevskii's Russia: Critical Studies," raise questions about Kliuchevskii's mastery of archival sources; the most ardent of these critics goes so far as to argue that Kliuchevskii stopped intense work in the archives after his magister dissertation, that is, in 1872, *before* beginning work on his doctoral thesis, *Boiarskaia duma*. It seems difficult to reconcile that assertion with the virtual unanimity with which Kliuchevskii's pupils expressed awe for his mastery of the sources for old Russian history. (By the late nineteenth century, of course, a great many of the sources for early Russian history had been published.) *Canadian-American Slavic Studies*, vol. 20, nos. 3–4 (Fall-Winter 1986), "Kliuchevskii's Russia: Critical Studies," ed. Marc Raeff.

72. Bestuzhev-Riumin rejected the idea of specifically historical laws and was generally suspicious of broad generalizations, and was a perennial critic of Solov'ev's great history on both accounts. He accordingly steered his students toward archeographic studies. N.L. Rubinshtein, *Russkaia istoriografiia* (Moscow, 1941), pp. 411–414.

73. It may be that the framework for such discussions was laid in Vinogradov's rather formal monthly discussion circles, to which various historians, legal scholars, and economists were invited. Its meetings, which were held regularly throughout the 1890s to 1898, when the university's official Historical Society was established, were customarily devoted to discussions of new works of European history and social science. Miliukov, Liubavskii, Bogoslovskii, and Kizevetter were among the young scholars (*Privatdozents*) who were considered members of the circle. Bogoslovskii, *Istoriografiia, memuaristika, epistoliariia,* pp. 85–87.

74. Fedotov, "Rossiia Kliuchevskogo," pp. 352–55.

75. Nechkina, *Vasilii Osipovich Kliuchevskii,* p. 263.

76. S.I. Tkhorzhevskii, "V.O. Kliuchevskii kak sotsiolog i politicheskii myslitel'," *Dela i dni,* 1921, 2, pp. 152–79. On Chicherin, whose courses at Moscow University Kliuchevskii took in the early 1860s, see Andrzej Walicki, *Legal Philosophies of Russian Liberalism* (Oxford, 1987).

77. See P.S. Shkurinov, *Pozitivizm v Rossii XIX veka* (Moscow, 1980).

78. On Russian scholars of world [*vseobshchaia*] history, including such well-known names as Vinogradoff, Rostovtzeff, and Louchitsky, whose work was part and parcel of the general trend, see V. Buzeskul, *Vseobshchaia istoriia i ee predstaviteli v Rossii v XIX i nachale XX veka,* 2 vols. (Leningrad, 1929–31). Among the many books dealing with intellectual currents of the 1860s–70s—"nihilism," "realism," "subjective sociology," and positivism, *inter alia*—one that concentrates on the origin and development of the idea of a "science of society" is Alexander Vucinich, *Social Thought in Tsarist Russia: The Quest for a General Science of Society, 1861–1917* (Chicago, 1976).

7

The St. Petersburg School
of History and Its Fate

Boris Anan'ich and Viktor Paneiakh

The St. Petersburg historical school evolved throughout the nineteenth and early twentieth centuries. One of its fullest expressions can be found in the work of Leningrad University Professor S.N. Valk (1887–1975), who underlined the importance of studying local conditions and characteristics of academic development at a given university in order to understand their shared destiny. Valk also linked the rise and development of the historical schools of St. Petersburg and Moscow to specific social and political conditions: in particular, St. Petersburg University, located in the capital city, was closer to the government and less involved in sociopolitical life than was Moscow University.[1]

It has been customary to attribute the founding of the St. Petersburg historical school to M.S. Kutorga, while T.N. Granovskii is considered the founder of the Moscow school. Kutorga, a noted expert on sources who specialized in the history of ancient Greece, was a graduate of St. Petersburg University and taught there from 1835 onward; from 1869 to 1874 he taught at Moscow University. Granovskii, also a graduate of the Law Faculty of St. Petersburg University, nonetheless spent his entire pedagogical and scientific career in association with Moscow University. It was there, in 1839, that Granovskii taught his first course on the history of the Middle Ages and Western Europe. A talented speaker, Granovskii became well-known as an educator and public figure. Valk, however, believed that if Granovskii had taught at St. Petersburg University, he would never have achieved the kind of public recognition that he enjoyed in Moscow.[2]

Although Kutorga was one of the sources of the St. Petersburg historical school, Valk noted that it was "the creative efforts of A.E. Presniakov that marked the bright flowering of its creation," saying that "nobody ever represented the basic features of its academic character better than he." Presniakov was interested in general questions of history and sociology from the earliest years of his academic activity, but his first work as a college student "in the traditions of the St. Petersburg school" was devoted to a source study of the "chronicle."[3] Presniakov, naturally, considered himself a representative of the St. Petersburg historical school, and in the remarks he made just before his doctoral defense, he defined its characteristics precisely. The dominant feature of the school, as he characterized it, was "scientific realism as reflected primarily in the specific, direct treatment of the source and the fact—without regard to historiographical tradition": that is, reinstating the rights of sources and facts, according them more complete and immediate importance without subordinating their selection, analysis, and interpretation to a schema developed in advance and without the sociological dogmatism so damaging to any critical treatment of sources. In reference to works by the so-called juridical school (best represented by S.M. Solov'ev and V.O. Kliuchevskii), reflecting their investigation of the process by which the Russian state was formed in the fifteenth century, Presniakov noted: "the theoretical approach to the material . . . turned the primary source data into illustrations of a predetermined schema—but not one that was derived from them—of the historical–psychological doctrine being advocated." As a result, these historians deliberately selected sources that were less reliable. In particular, they gave preference to later sources and refrained from using earlier sources—only because the former "better illustrated the proposed schema." "The dominance of theoretical interpretations . . . has led to such a one-sided selection of data, which allows the elimination from consideration of everything that does not illustrate the preferred schema and fails to confirm its premises." This type of historical thinking, in Presniakov's opinion, developed "under the influence of German idealistic philosophy and represent[ed] a reflection of Hegelianism."[4]

Presniakov specifically contrasted the St. Petersburg historical school with the Moscow school, which he equated with the "juridical school" and which, in particular, was distinguished by a greater amount of ideology and a propensity for systematization, as a consequence of which the material derived from sources did not play the kind of fundamental role that it should. The approaches to that material, therefore, suffered from an excessive tendency to theorize. Presniakov—and, following him, Valk as well—attributed a considerable role in the formation of the St. Petersburg historical school to K.N. Bestuzhev-Riumin, V.G. Vasil'evskii, and S.F.

Platonov, emphasizing the latter's special role in the teaching of Russian history at the university from the 1890s onward, as well as "in the study circle [*kruzhok,* pl. *kruzhki*] of Russian historians" that was formed at St. Petersburg University in the 1880s as an informal association of young scholars.[5]

We find a similar characterization of the two historical schools in the memoirs of P.N. Miliukov. Unlike Presniakov and Valk, however, Miliukov, a Muscovite, reproached the representatives of the St. Petersburg school for their obsession with sources. In Miliukov's opinion, this tradition dated from the time of August Ludwig Schlözer, who asserted that "Russian history cannot be written without first having made a critical study of its sources." According to Miliukov, Schlözer's point of view signaled "a transition from the compilers of the eighteenth century to the scientific study of history," but by the end of the nineteenth century this approach had become obsolete and was "nearing its end" there in St. Petersburg.[6]

Miliukov's remarks were not entirely unfounded. Not only Schlözer but also the other German historians, philologists, and archeographers who had been affiliated with the St. Petersburg Academy of Sciences—for example, Gottlieb Siegfried Bayer or Gerhard Friedrich Müller—had to some extent or other influenced the formation of the St. Petersburg historical school. Miliukov contrasted the accomplishments of the Moscow school to the traditionalism of the St. Petersburg school, and he viewed any instance in which the St. Petersburg historians addressed general issues associated with the historical process as a result of the Moscow school's influence. Thus he discerned signs of "compromise" in S.F. Platonov's study of the seventeenth-century Time of Troubles, because Platonov devoted the first part of his work to source criticism and "in the second part presented the history of the Time of Troubles in the Moscow manner." In the early 1890s Miliukov attended Platonov's kruzhok, where he found that the Moscow participants in the kruzhok, including himself, "gave a new impetus" to the "compromise" orientation already discernible in its approach to history, "with certain St. Petersburg reservations." Among St. Petersburg historians capable of thinking "broadly and abstractly," Miliukov named Platonov himself, A.S. Lappo-Danilevskii, N.P. Pavlov-Sil´vanskii, and A.E. Presniakov.[7]

As we saw, Presniakov defined his own attitude toward the Moscow historical school differently from Miliukov, and his treatment of relations between the two schools is built on the principle of opposition rather than on mutual influence. Regardless of who is right in this dispute, however, one thing is clear: the St. Petersburg school, which traditionally ascribed primary importance to working with sources, was represented not only by such figures as Platonov and Lappo-Danilevskii but also by younger scholars such as Pavlov-Sil'vanskii and Presniakov—all talented historians with broad intellectual horizons and the ability to make analytical generalizations.

In Presniakov's words, representatives of the St. Petersburg historical school did not tend to deceive themselves that an analysis of sources is possible "in the absence of any sociological and historical preconditions: the researcher's thoughts are not a tabula rasa, and the material he studies can yield answers only to the questions to which his thoughts have given rise." However, "scientific realism demands that the questions posed relate to the properties of the material that is being studied rather than imposing something on it that it . . . cannot, owing to its basic nature, provide."[8]

Pavlov-Sil'vanskii passed away in 1908, whereas Presniakov remained the distinguished leader of the new trend within the St. Petersburg historical school until his death in 1929, thus missing by several months the destruction of that school inflicted by the regime.

The October Revolution of 1917 caused an abrupt turn in the fate of both historical schools, as well as in the fate of the scholars who were identified with them. Many of the older representatives died during the Civil War, and a number of historians ultimately emigrated. Some of those who remained in the country and survived began to collaborate with the new regime and continued to work in the universities, libraries, and archives.

The St. Petersburg school of historians demonstrated its viability under the difficult conditions of the early 1920s, making a great contribution to the revival and development of our country's historical discipline. In the early 1920s this viability was manifested in the creation of numerous scholarly kruzhki intensely pursuing the traditions of the St. Petersburg school and meeting primarily at participants' homes, just as they had in the pre-revolutionary period.

From 1918 to 1920 the university was never heated, and many professors—A.E. Presniakov, A.I. Zaozerskii, M.A. Poliektov, I.M. Grevs, and M.D. Priselkov, for example—conducted classes, administered examinations, and discussed graduate students' work with them at their own homes. For this reason, it was perfectly natural for the meetings of the kruzhki to be held at people's homes.

Among the informal scholarly associations in Petrograd in the early 1920s, a special role was played by the "young historians' kruzhok," which consisted primarily of students of S.F. Platonov, E.V. Tarle, N.I. Kareev, A.G. Vul'fius, A.E. Presniakov, and S.V. Rozhdestvenskii. The overwhelming majority of the permanent members of this kruzhok were arrested by the OGPU [secret police] in 1929. The testimony they gave during the investigation, as well as the surviving memoirs of one of the participants in the kruzhok—and even one of its founding members—the female historian and bibliographer N.S. Shtakel´berg, make it possible to reconstruct a general picture of its activity.[9] The kruzhok was by no means formally constituted, and no minutes of the meetings were kept. The functions of the kruzhok's chairman were often also performed by one of its organizers, legal historian S.I. Tkhorzhevskii, a student of Professor L.I. Petrazhitskii. The membership of the kruzhok was not strictly defined. The kruzhok began to function either at the very end of 1920 or in January 1921, and it remained in existence until the end of 1927 or the beginning of 1928.

For the most part, meetings of the kruzhok were held at Shtakel´berg's home, as well as at the university in the facilities of the historical seminar room, the Scientific Workers Club in which S.I. Tkhorzhevskii held the post of secretary, in the House of Scientists, at the house shared by S.F. Platonov and his daughters, and at the homes of other kruzhok members. The meetings were held on Fridays. Usually, twenty or thirty young scholars attended. They not only discussed papers but also exchanged the latest news and arranged parties and teas. "At the first meeting of the kruzhok," N.S. Shtakel´berg recalled,

> each participant brought a piece of sugar, a piece of bread, and a stick of firewood. In 1921 our living room was two degrees below zero, and we didn't have much firewood. . . . People would drop by the day before the meeting with a piece of wood: the doorbell would ring; someone would laugh and hand the log through the door, wrapped in a newspaper or bundled up some other way. Then it was "See you tomorrow," and the deliverer would disappear. . . . I did everything I could to make the living room and dining room cozy. People didn't have to keep their overcoats on, as they did almost everywhere else in the winter of 1920–21—at the university, at the public library, in people's private homes. And this in itself made our gatherings festive.[10]

Most of the people in the kruzhok were young scholars studying Russian history, but there were some legal historians and literature specialists as well. Platonov's two daughters, Natalia Sergeevna and Nina Sergeevna, regularly attended meetings of the kruzhok. Another who visited the kruzhok was Natalia Sergeevna Platonova's husband, the literary scholar N.V. Izmailov, who later became a well-known expert on Pushkin. Among those more or less regular members of the kruzhok who left a definite mark on scholarship and represented the traditions of the St. Petersburg historical school (in addition to those mentioned above), we might also name S.N. Valk, B.A. Romanov, A.N. Shebunin, P.A. Sadikov, A.N. Nasonov, E.Ch. Skrzhinskaia, and I.I. Liubimenko.

Occasional visitors at kruzhok meetings included G.P. Fedotov, who left the USSR in 1925, and P.P. Shchegolev, as well as the following professors: M.M. Bogoslovskii, S.F. Platonov, S.V. Rozhdestvenskii, B.D. Grekov, and A.A. Vasil'ev. A.E. Presniakov and M.D. Priselkov attended a gathering of kruzhok members held at the Iusupov Palace. The jubilees of E.V. Tarle and M.M. Bogoslovskii were celebrated at kruzhok meetings, as was Bogoslovskii's election to full membership in the Academy of Sciences in 1921.

"In general, the political face of the kruzhok was the face of the Russian intelligentsia in those years," Shtakel'berg wrote in her memoirs.

> A great many of us feared both the Reds and the Whites and "did our best to escape in the confusion." Most of us were innocents when it came to Marxism. Formally, members of the kruzhok might belong to different parties. A.N. Shebunin was a Menshevik, M.N. Martynov was an SR [Socialist Revolutionary], S.I. Tkhorzhevskii and M.A. Ostrovskaia had affinities for the Kadets [Constitutional Democrats], and A.A. Vvedenskii favored the Bolsheviks. . . . All of us were members of the third estate—the working intelligentsia—with certain gradations in our social positions or wealth, and all of us wanted to find our place in academia and in life.[11]

Thus members of the kruzhok held various political views. Those university faculty members who attended kruzhok meetings likewise held different political views. In his personal convictions, for example, E.V. Tarle was a long way from S.F. Platonov. This did not, however, prevent them from acting together to support gifted young scholars.

According to Shtakel'berg's memoirs, kruzhok members liked Tarle best among the professors.[12] Tarle attended the parties, joked with the young people, and over a glass of tea talked about his travels abroad and about the new books being published there.

Tarle's "salon," founded after 1920, also played a significant role in the cultural and scientific life of the city; these gatherings were held on Wednesdays. Academicians N.P. Likhachev, V.V. Bartol'd, M.M. Bogoslovskii, and V.P. Buzeskul attended the salon, where abstracts of papers were read. According to testimony N.P. Likhachev gave to OGPU, he met Tarle at such a session in 1924, and Tarle's "most distinguished guest" on Wednesdays was S.F. Platonov, who twice presented abstracts.[13] As many as twenty people attended these Wednesday gatherings, all at Tarle's personal invitation; members of the kruzhok were also present.

The young historians' kruzhok was not the only informal scholarly association in those years to be linked to the traditions of the St. Petersburg historical school. Many of those who belonged to the community of young historians were members of other kruzhki, which were often formed as small groups of scholars who gathered around their teachers or older mentors. In the middle of the 1920s approximately ten people worked, under A.I. Zaozerskii's guidance, on archival materials relating to the history of large landownership in Russia in the eighteenth and nineteenth centuries.

After the death of A.S. Lappo-Danilevskii in 1919, his students did their best to preserve the kruzhok or seminar that he had created and to complete the work he had started: compiling a complete inventory of Russian private deeds. The members of this kruzhok—A.I. Andreev, S.N. Valk, A.A. Vvedenskii, N.I. Sidorov, T.M. Kotliarov, A.A. Shilov, and A.A. Drozdetskii—continued to meet during the 1920s at Sidorov's and Drozdetskii's homes. Sometimes the meetings of the kruzhok were also attended by people from other cities, such as Professor V.I. Veretennikov from Kharkov and A.F. Zlotnikov from Dnepropetrovsk.[14]

In 1921 students of N.I. Kareev, both from the university and from the Bestuzhev courses, formed a kruzhok; the kruzhok met regularly at Kareev's home. Specifically, the members were I.L. Popov, S.M. Danini, P.P. Shchegolev, M.K. Grinval´d, E.N. Petrov, and V.V. Biriukovich.

In 1925 a kruzhok devoted to questions of art and church history was formed at the home of M.D. Priselkov. The formation of the kruzhok was occasioned by M.D. Priselkov's dismissal from the university. The dismissal of I.M. Grevs and his brilliant female student O.A. Dobiash-Rozhdestvenskaia from the university led to the reactivation of Grevs's kruzhok, which had appeared during the early years of the Revolution. Participants in the kruzhok would gather at the homes of Dobiash-Rozhdestvenskaia and Grevs. The kruzhok—composed of V.V. Bakhtin, G.P. Fedotov, E.N. Fedotova-Nechaeva, and E.Ch. Skrzhinskaia—was organized in 1924 or 1925, after the closing of the Historical Research Institute. It met three or four times a year; and A.D. and V.S. Liublinskii, M.E. Shaitan, M.A. Gukovskii, and V.V. Bakhtin were members. Occasionally, N.V. Pigulevskaia, E.Ch. Skrzhinskaia, and M.A. Tikhanova also attended. The kruzhok was devoted to medieval history, paleography, and source study.[15]

In October 1925 former students of the university's Archeology Department formed a kruzhok called New Arzamas. The participants included L. A. Tvorogov and I.A. Pidotti.

Even a simple listing of the kruzhki testifies to the rather lively and informal creative activities of historians in Petrograd-Leningrad during the 1920s. The kruzhki were a natural form of scholarly interaction—one, however, that conflicted with the government's course toward establishing control of the historical discipline and confining it within the rigid channels of official ideology.

The kruzhki were closely linked to historical journals published in

Petrograd/Leningrad during the 1920s, in particular to publications such as *Dela i dni, Russkoe proshloe, Annaly,* and *Russkii istoricheskii zhurnal,* edited by, among others, Presniakov, Tarle, Platonov, and Rozhdestvenskii.

N.S. Shtakel'berg mentioned certain themes addressed in papers read at meetings of the young historians' kruzhok. Almost everything that was discussed by the kruzhok was published. It is sufficient merely to glance at the contents of just the publications listed above to find the work of kruzhok members. Shtakel'berg's own "The Riddle of the Death of Nicholas I" [Zagadka smerti Nikolaia I] was published in the first volume of *Russkoe proshloe* in 1923. The same journal also published B.A. Romanov's "The Concession on the Yalu" [Kontsessiia na Ialu]. The third volume offered articles by S.V. Sigrist and S.I. Tkhorzhevskii. Tarle published not only articles but also reviews that had been discussed by the kruzhok in *Annaly,* a journal that he and F.I. Uspenskii put out together.

Hence a very specific historiographical axis was being developed in Petrograd/Leningrad during the 1920s, one that drew on the academic traditions of St. Petersburg. This group aspired to a special place in our national historiography, and it was already represented not only by professionals of the older generation but also by their students—promising young scholars such as B.A. Romanov, A.N. Shebunin, S.N. Valk, A.N. Nasonov, and others.

A distinct feature of this axis was the substantial expansion of the chronological framework of its representatives' research to include the history of the nineteenth and twentieth centuries, even though most of their teachers (S.F. Platonov, S.A. Zhebelev, I.M. Grevs, and others), following academic tradition, had held negative attitudes toward involvement in modern—and especially in recent—history. Thus in 1922 B.A. Romanov argued the necessity of addressing an array of problems that were new to professional historians and that had previously "never been an object of systematic study and, more important, of free instruction."[16]

Not long after the end of the Civil War, a second new historical school began to take shape. Its basic postulates were expressed by M.N. Pokrovskii, who had received his professional training at Moscow University. In contrast to the principles of the St. Petersburg historical school, this new school was not based on analyzing sources and on facts established as a result of that analysis but rather on the basis of a schema, a doctrine, and predetermined theoretical constructs. In this sense, the new historical school outwardly resembled the Moscow school, but the theory on which it was based was definitely unlike that used in prerevolutionary historiography— and consequently opposed both the St. Petersburg and the Moscow schools in that regard. Instead of Hegelianism, positivism, and Neo-Kantianism, there was the Leninist interpretation of Marxism—which, to be sure, was largely based on Hegelian dialectics.

For Pokrovskii, all history was rigidly determined by the theories of the development of commercial capital and the class struggle. Born from the womb of revolution and a most ferocious civil war, Pokrovskii's school reinterpreted any facts it itself had not confirmed in the spirit of class conflict and antagonism, sought class meaning and impulses not only in the actions of major historical figures but even in those of ordinary people, and denied the statehood of previous epochs, as well as national and universal human values and positive experiences of the past, unless these were associated with the proletariat's struggle against tsarism and the bourgeoisie. Accorded Party support, this school became dominant nationwide. Its adherents extended the class struggle to include even the sphere of history itself, directing their barbed (under Petrograd-Leningrad conditions) attack against the St. Petersburg historical school and its representatives, whom they treated as exponents of "the ideology of the nobility and the bourgeoisie." In the name of combating this ideology, Pokrovskii and his students carried out a policy of liquidation: they managed to stop the teaching of history in the general schools and to close the history faculties at the universities and pedagogical institutes.

In the middle of the 1920s Pokrovskii launched a determined campaign to obtain a historical monopoly for his own school, which represented the state's ideology, subjecting anybody who stood in his way to harsh criticism. In his article "The 'New' Currents in Russian Historical Literature" ["Novye" techeniia v russkoi istoricheskoi literature], which appeared in volume 7 of the journal *Istorik-Marksist* in 1928, Pokrovskii sharply criticized E.V. Tarle's book *Europe in the Epoch of Imperialism* [Evropa v epokhu imperializma], published in 1927, accusing the author of sympathy for the Entente and of "attempting to smash Marxist historical concepts by means of supposedly Marxist techniques."[17]

This criticism was just one sign of the secret political trial of representatives of the academic intelligentsia (primarily people working in the humanities) that was fabricated in 1929–31 on orders from the Politburo by the Plenipotentiary Representative Office of the OGPU in the Leningrad Military District.[18] This, then, was the origin of Case No. 1803, or the "Academic Affair," as it was later dubbed in the literature. The victims of this affair included more than one hundred members of research institutions, as well as four academicians—the historians S.F. Platonov, E.V. Tarle, N.P. Likhachev, and M.K. Liubavskii—and nine corresponding members, including V.N. Beneshevich, a distinguished specialist in Byzantine history. Those arrested also included the well-known Moscow historians Iu.V.

Got´e, S.V. Bakhrushin, and A.I. Iakovlev. All these people were charged with forming a counterrevolutionary organization called the All-People's Union to Struggle for the Revival of a Free Russia, aimed at overthrowing the Soviet regime and restoring the monarchy. Another leader of this alleged counterrevolutionary organization was the well-known orientalist Professor A.M. Mervart, who was also accused of having spied for Germany and of having created a network of informers and secret agents.[19]

But the counterrevolutionary organization, the All-People's Union to Struggle for the Revival of a Free Russia, never existed. There was no antigovernment plot, no military organizations or stockpiles of weapons at the Academy of Sciences. There was no secret deal between the scholars and foreign intelligence agents; there were no conspiratorial meetings involving S.F. Platonov, E.V. Tarle, or V.N. Beneshevich with foreign intelligence agents in Paris, Berlin, or the Vatican Library. All these monstrous accusations were fabricated by OGPU investigators. When the arrests started, the investigators had no materials to justify accusations against the arrested persons. All they had was a scenario for a trial. For this reason, the investigators forced the people they arrested to give false testimony about having taken part in a plot, and on the basis of this testimony they fabricated charges and made new arrests. In this way, those arrested found themselves in the position of serving as the investigators' involuntary "co-authors" in drawing up charges.[20]

The government's goal was to subordinate the Academy of Sciences to itself and to place the Academy at the service of socialist construction. The "Academic Affair" was designed to frighten those who still manifested any recalcitrance. Its victims included not only eminent representatives of national scholarship but also most members of kruzhki. Almost all the organizers and members of the young historians' kruzhok were arrested and convicted.

The OGPU classified the act of belonging to a kruzhok that convened in a private home as illegal counterrevolutionary activity in support of the mythical organization they themselves had concocted, the All-People's Union to Struggle for the Revival of a Free Russia. The OGPU also focused its attention on journals that published articles by kruzhok members. M.N. Pokrovskii was certainly involved in the preparation by OGPU consultant "Stormy Petrel," (Burevestnik, the pseudonym of historian G.S. Zaidel´) of an extensive report on their characters. Especially harsh accusations were directed against *Annaly*. "Reviewing all four volumes of the journal, issued between 1922 and 1924," Zaidel´ wrote, "we can state with particular certainty that this journal was in fact an organ 'in the service of Russian specialists'— but history specialists of a particular persuasion, namely, anti-Marxists. The journal published works by major bourgeois historians, from Tarle, Kareev,

Buzeskul, Grevs, and others to a whole constellation of young people nurtured on the yeast of anti-Marxist reactionary methodology." Named as "active contributors to the journal" were N.S. Platonova, M.K. Grinval´d, S.M. Glagoleva-Danini, B.A. Romanov, M.E. Libtal´, N.S. Tsemsh, and A.N. Shebunin. Zaidel´ pointed out that "in all four volumes of the journal one cannot find a single reference to the historical works" of M.N. Pokrovskii and N.M. Lukin "that were published in those years."[21]

The investigation into the "Academic Affair" ended in 1931. Sentence was handed down by the Collegium of the OGPU. Six members of the Academy of Sciences (former officers thereof) who were convicted in the case were to be shot. The rest were sent to prison camps for various terms ranging from three to ten years or into internal exile. S.F. Platonov, E.V. Tarle, N.P. Likhachev, M.K. Liubavskii, S.V. Rozhdestvenskii, and other eminent historians were exiled to remote places in the USSR for terms of five years. Almost all the representatives of the older generation died in exile. In the middle of the 1930s, their students, after having served their sentences, gradually began to return to Leningrad. And, although it was difficult and sometimes impossible for these people after their release to obtain regular paid work in their specialties and in accordance with their professional qualifications, they did gradually begin to adapt to the new circumstances.

Pokrovskii died in 1932, but his students at the Leningrad Branch of the Society of Marxist Historians and at GAIMK (the State Academy for the History of Material Culture), in cooperation with associates of N.Ia. Marr, continued the fight against proponents of "reactionary ideas," both among the ranks of surviving representatives of the St. Petersburg historical school and in their own ranks. In these research institutions, a view was being developed that all human history could be divided into five successive socioeconomic formations. After Stalin gave a speech to the 1933 Congress of Shockworker Collective Farmers (*kolkhozniki-udarniki*),[22] a new element was added to this schema: that transitions from one formation to another could occur only through revolutionary means. This then became part of the new official doctrine—not yet proclaimed but then being formulated secretly within the Party apparatus to reflect the changing political situation both within and outside the country—that was to replace Pokrovskii's views.

Such changes were becoming more and more evident. Stalin had won a total victory in the intraparty struggle. The Soviet state was being deliberately designed to be one-dimensional and rigidly centralized, headed by the Party apparatus nurtured by Stalin and based on the punitive agencies. The ideas of world revolution and of a particular kind of internationalism had become obsolete. The threat of the restoration of the old regime remained only as part of the standard accusation in fabricated political "affairs." At the same time, Hitler came to power in Germany under the banner of the national idea in its extreme form ("blood and soil"); his foreign policy program called for a *Drang nach Osten* and war against Soviet "Judeo-Bolshevism."

These circumstances led to the formulation of a new policy and to a search for ideological guidelines for implementing it. Stalin began to develop such guidelines as early as 1930. He harshly condemned Dem'ian Bednyi for writing satirical pieces about Russia's past. Stalin accused Bednyi of slandering "the USSR, both past and present."[23] This incipient turn away from the messianism of world revolution and empire building to a strong emphasis on the role of "the Great Russian people" as the "Elder Brother" of other peoples and to the drive toward a powerful state and the proclamation of a direct link to "great ancestors" indicated that a decision had been made: to abandon the classical Marxist postulates of cosmopolitanism, based on proletarian solidarity, as well as the idea that the state would wither away as progress was made toward communism; and to endorse patriotism as a fundamental idea.

This political and ideological shift could hardly fail to affect the discipline of history. Very rapidly, on the orders of the authorities, a partial return to its prerevolutionary sources took place. In 1934 Stalin launched a campaign against the Pokrovskii school.

At the same time, history faculties began to be reestablished at the pedagogical institutes, and a number of scholars who had recently returned from prison camps were appointed as professors. The teaching of history was resumed in the schools; abstract sociological schemas were discarded; but the strict framework of Party guidelines reflecting the new ideological course of action was maintained. Stalin assigned top priority to the preparation of new textbooks for the secondary schools. It was no accident that Stalin, along with A.A. Zhdanov and S.M. Kirov, signed the directive-like "Comments on an Outline of a Textbook on the History of the USSR" [Zamechaniia po povodu konspekta uchebnika po istorii SSSR]. The government announced a competition to develop an elementary textbook on the history of the USSR. The competition was conducted under the supervision of the Central Committee, with Zhdanov, chairman of the Central Committee's and USSR Council of People's Commissars' Commission for the Revision of History Textbooks, acting in its name. It was he who made the basic corrections to the proposed primary-school textbook on the history of the USSR, which had been prepared by a collective under the supervision of A.V. Shestakov, and he wrote whole pages of additions. Stalin himself also examined the textbook very carefully and wrote comments in the margins. This book played a decisive role in establishing the new conception of Russian and Soviet history and in shaping a new historical consciousness.[24]

It served as a virtual template for the development of other textbooks for schools, universities, and institutes.

Quite unexpectedly, the works of historians who had recently been punished were also in demand. One of the most interesting manifestations of the new course of action was the republication in 1937 of S.F. Platonov's famous *Studies in the History of the Troubles in the Muscovite State in the Sixteenth and Seventeenth Centuries* [Ocherki po istorii Smuty v Moskovskom gosudarstve XVI–XVII vv.]. Platonov had died not long before (in 1933), while in exile. His textbook on Russian history, which was also republished, was even authorized for the Party schools.

One by one, many people returned to the discipline who had been subjected to persecution in the 1920s and early 1930s—those who had managed to stay alive and keep working. Stalin decided to harness the experience and professionalism of prerevolutionary history to serve the official ideology. He tried to create a historical school derived in part from Marxist ideology, as that had been adapted to the policies he was implementing, and in part from certain national traditions.

One of the first to return, in 1933, was E.V. Tarle. His title of academician was restored to him in 1938. During the 1939 elections, Iu.V. Got´e was named as academician, and S.V. Bakhrushin as a corresponding member. Those who survived and were able to return to their discipline paid not only with their health, and not only by being persecuted by the authorities in one way or another to the end of their days, but also by damage to their morale, which kept them from completely realizing their professional potential.

After 1934 a new Soviet historiography began to emerge. The publication of *The History of the All-Union Communist Party (Bolshevik): A Short Course* [Istoriia VKP(b): Kratkii kurs] in 1938 reinforced Stalinist priorities in history, making them mandatory. Campaigns of humiliation organized before and after the Great Patriotic War were designed to keep scholars in check while preparing the soil for the adoption of more and more new prescriptions.

Having undergone radical changes, the official view was rapidly transformed into a Stalinist imperial-state, national-Bolshevik doctrine that even genuine scientists did not dare to ignore. Among representatives of the historical school that was considered Marxist-Leninist, moreover, those who, with the support of Party ideologists, tried to replace the St. Petersburg historical school (and the Moscow school as well, incidentally) changed their own theoretical guidelines and unmasked the conceptions of their teacher M.N. Pokrovskii. During the new stage of development of this school, however, the selection of sources and facts and their later interpretation depended entirely on party directives, "theory," and "doctrine"—as it had before, and to an even greater extent.

Turning back to the fate of the St. Petersburg historical school, we should stress that—despite its destruction at the beginning of the 1930s, the rigid ideological framework imposed at the end of the 1930s, and the pogroms of the late 1940s and the early 1950s—its traditions did not disappear without a trace but continued to live on. Those of its representatives who managed to return to academic activity tried to preserve their traditions and to teach their own students in that spirit.

In their works, M.D. Priselkov, A.N. Nasonov, D.S. Likhachev, and Ia.S. Lur'e developed the principles for the use of the old chronicles as sources that A.A. Shakhmatov had formulated.[25] A.S. Lappo-Danilevskii's works had a considerable impact on techniques for preparing critical editions of historical sources (including those of the Soviet period), archeographical theory and practice, critique of memoirs, and studies of private documents. These topics were further developed in the works of A.I. Andreev, S.N. Valk, and their students.[26] In particular, Valk adapted techniques of source study developed by Lappo-Danilevskii to the interpretation of historical documents associated with the Revolution.[27] As a student attending A.E. Presniakov's seminar, B.A. Romanov specialized in the history of ancient Rus', and in the course of analyzing Russia's Far Eastern policies on the eve of the Russo-Japanese War, as he himself asserts, decided that his top priority was "to build a watertight dam of facts"[28] in order to make an unprejudiced presentation of events in the tradition of the St. Petersburg historical school.[29]

These traditions evolved not only in research on Russian history but also in studies of the history of the ancient world and the European Middle Ages. In particular, the students of I.M. Grevs and O.A. Dobiash-Rozhdestvenskaia—A.D. Liublinskaia, V.V. Bakhtin, E.Ch. Skrzhinskaia, A.I. Khomentovskaia, and others—made a deep imprint on the discipline.

Many representatives of the St. Petersburg historical school taught at the university at various times, although they were expelled from there on ideological grounds in the 1920s, the 1930s, the 1940s, and the 1950s. Despite such persecution, Grevs, Presniakov, Priselkov, Valk, Romanov, and Liublinskaia trained a number of talented students and followers.

More time is needed, however, to assess the importance of the St. Petersburg historical school and the results of the clashes in the historiography of the Soviet period between a high level of professionalism and innovation—based on advances achieved in prerevolutionary Russian scholarship, on the one hand, and official ideology, on the other.

Notes

Translated by Kim Braithwaite for publication in *Russian Studies in History*, vol. 36, no. 4, ©1998 by M.E. Sharpe, Inc.

1. S.N. Valk, "Istoricheskaia nauka v Leningradskom universitete za 125 let," in *Trudy iubileinoi nauchnoi sessii Len[ingradskogo] Gos[udarstvennogo] universiteta, Sektsiia istor[icheskikh] nauk* (Leningrad, 1948), pp. 3–79.

2. Ibid., p. 11.

3. Ibid., pp. 56–57.

4. A.E. Presniakov, (1) *Obrazovanie Velikorusskogo gosudarstva XIII–XV stoletii* (Petrograd, 1918), pp. 25–26; (2) *Rech´ pered zashchitoi dissertatsii pod zaglaviem "Obrazovanie Velikorusskogo gosudarstva"* (Petrograd, 1920), pp. 5–6.

5. See S.V. Chirkov, "Arkheografiia i shkoly v russkoi istoricheskoi nauke XIX–nachala XX v.," in *Arkheograficheskii ezhegodnik za 1989 g.* (Moscow, 1990), pp. 22–23. Platonov soon became the actual leader of that kruzhok. Its members gathered at the home of one of Platonov's students –V.G. Druzhinin, the son of a wealthy Old Believer merchant—and wits dubbed the kruzhok members "Platonov's retinue" [a pun on Druzhinin's name, derived from *druzhina*—retinue]. If we can trust the testimony concerning this point extracted under interrogation from Academician N.P. Likhachev, who was arrested during the "Academic Affair," "once Platonov was firmly back on his feet again, a salon was formed at his home, where a second stratum of 'Platonovites' of quite varied composition gathered together, and after the Revolution Platonov gathered around him a third and final stratum of 'Platonovites' with whom he worked and to whom he offered patronage." "I myself joined this third group," Likhachev said, "after thirteen years of enmity or, to put it better, unfriendliness." (See Archives of the Administration of the Federal Security Service for St. Petersburg and Oblast [henceforth AUFSB po SPb. i oblasti]), d. P-65245, t. 7, l. 362).

6. P.N. Miliukov, *Vospominaniia,* vol. 1 (Moscow, 1990), pp. 161–62.

7. Ibid., p. 162.

8. Presniakov, *Rech´,* p. 6.

9. N.S. Shtakel´berg, " 'Kruzhok molodykh istorikov' i 'Akademicheskoe delo,' " in *In memoriam: Istoricheskii sbornik pamiati F.F. Perchenka* (Moscow–St. Petersburg, 1995), pp. 19–77.

10. Ibid., pp. 35–36.

11. Ibid., pp. 42–43.

12. Ibid., p. 36.

13. AUFSB po SPb. i obl. d. P-65245, t. 7, l. 362.

14. The efforts of kruzhok members resulted in the publication, edited by A.I. Andreev, of *Terminologicheskii slovar´ chastnykh aktov Moskovskogo gosudarstva* (Petrograd, 1922). The "Foreword" to this edition (p. xvii) contains information about those who participated in the seminar up to 1919.

15. B.S. Kaganovich, "K biografii O.A. Dobiash-Rozhdestvenskoi," in *Vspomogatel´nye istoricheskie distsipliny: Vysshaia shkola, issledovatel´skaia deiatel´nost´, obshchestvennye organizatsii: Tezisy dokladov i soobshchenii* (Moscow, 1994), pp. 69–71. In addition to Dobiash-Rozhdestvenskaia, the students of I.M. Grevs who represented the St. Petersburg school of medieval studies at the end of the nineteenth and the beginning of the twentieth centuries also included L.P. Karsavin, A.I. Khomentovskaia, and N.P. Ottokar. Kaganovich, who devoted his own candidate's dissertation to the study of their works, wrote that "the works of the medievalists of the St. Petersburg school at the beginning of the twentieth century to a considerable extent laid the founda-

tions for the scientific study of Western European medieval culture in our country. Some of them—in particular O.A. Dobiash-Rozhdestvenskaia and A.I. Khomentovskaia, as well as L.P. Karsavin to some extent, during the early stages of his career—anticipated a number of themes and conclusions of contemporary medieval studies and offered brilliant insight into such problems as social psychology, the 'history of everyday life' and 'history of death,' the spatial-temporal orientations of medieval man, and religiosity among the people" (B.S. Kaganovich, *Peterburgskaia shkola medievistiki v kontse XIX– nachale XX v: Avtoreferat dissertatsii na soiskanie uchenoi stepeni kandidata istoricheskikh nauk* [Leningrad, 1986], pp. 13–14).

16. B.A. Romanov, [review of] A.A. Shilov, *Chto chitat' po istorii russkogo revoliutsionnogo dvizheniia? Ukazatel' vazhneishikh knig, broshiur i zhurnal'nykh statei* (Petrograd, 1922), *Byloe,* 1922, no. 20, p. 295.

17. M.N. Pokrovskii, " 'Novye' techeniia v russkoi istoricheskoi literature," *Istorik-Marksist,* 1928, pp. 3–17.

18. See *Akademicheskoe delo 1929–1931 gg.: Dokumenty i materialy sledstvennogo dela, sfabrikovannogo OGPU,* no. 1: *Delo po obvineniiu akademika S.F. Platonova* (St. Petersburg, 1993).

19. Ibid., pp. v–vi.

20. For more detail on this matter, see B.V. Anan'ich and V.M. Paneiakh, "Prinuditel'noe 'soavtorstvo' (K vykhodu v svet sbornika dokumentov 'Akademicheskoe delo 1929–1931 gg.,' vyp. 1), in *In memoriam,* pp. 87–111.

21. AUFSB po SPb. i obl., d. P-65245, t. 16, ll. 162–63.

22. I.V. Stalin, "Rech' na pervom vsesoiuznom s''ezde kolkhoznikov-udarnikov, 19 fevralia 1933 g.," in I.V. Stalin, *Sochineniia* (Moscow, 1952), vol. 13, pp. 239–40.

23. I.V. Stalin, "Tov. Dem'ianu Bednomu (vyderzhki iz pis'ma)," in ibid., pp. 23–27. This letter did not become widely known at the time; it was not published until 1952. In 1936, however, in the USSR Council of People's Commissars All-Union Committee on Matters of the Arts Decree "On Dem'ian Bednyi's Play *Heroes* [Bogatyri]," the author was publicly accused of defaming the heroes of the Russian folklore epic and of presenting "an antihistorical and mocking portrayal of the conversion of Rus', which was in reality a positive stage in the history of the Russian people" (*Protiv fal'sifikatsii narodnogo proshlogo* [Moscow–Leningrad, 1937], pp. 3–4; A.M. Dubrovskii, "Kak Dem'ian Bednyi ideologicheskuiu oshibku sovershil," in *Otechestvennaia kul'tura i istoricheskaia nauka: Sbornik statei* (Briansk, 1996), pp. 143–51.

24. For more detail, see A.N. Artizov, "V ugodu vzgliadam vozhdia," *Kentavr,* October–December 1991, pp. 125–35; A.M. Dubrovskii, "A.A. Zhdanov v rabote nad shkol'nym uchebnikom," in *Otechestvennaia kul'tura i istoricheskaia nauka XVIII–XX vekov,* pp. 128–43.

25. See M.D. Priselkov, *Istoriia russkogo letopisaniia XI–XV vv.* (Leningrad, 1940); A.N. Nasonov, *Istoriia russkogo letopisaniia XI–nachala XVIII v.* (Moscow, 1969); D.S. Likhachev, *Russkie letopisi i ikh kul'turno-istoricheskoe znachenie* (Moscow–Leningrad, 1947); and Ia.S. Lur'e, *Obshcherusskie letopisi XIV–XV vv.* (Leningrad, 1976).

26. A.I. Andreev, *Ocherki po istochnikovedeniiu Sibiri* (Moscow–Leningrad, 1960–65) nos. 1–2; and S.N. Valk, *Izbrannye trudy po arkheografii: Nauchnoe nasledie* (St. Petersburg, 1991).

27. S.N. Valk, [review of] *Istoriko-revoliutsionnaia biblioteka* (Petrograd, 1920–21), *Dela i dni* (St. Petersburg, 1922), bk. 3.

28. B.A. Romanov, "Rech' na zashchite doktorskoi dissertatsii *Diplomaticheskaia istoriia russko-iaponskoi voiny,*" in Archives of the St. Petersburg Branch of the Institute of Russian History of the Russian Academy of Sciences, f. 298, op. 1, d. 75.

29. B.A. Romanov, *Rossiia v Man'chzhurii (1892–1906): Ocherki po istorii*

vneshnei politiki samoderzhaviia v epokhu imperializma (Leningrad, 1928). See also B.A. Romanov, *Ocherki diplomaticheskoi istorii russko-iaponskoi voiny: 1895–1907* (Moscow–Leningrad, 1947); 2d ed., rev. and enl. (Moscow–Leningrad, 1955); B.A. Romanov, *Liudi i nravy drevnei Rusi* (Leningrad, 1947). A[lfred J.] Rieber, author of a historiographical study of the foreign policy of prerevolutionary Russia, contrasted Romanov, as a representative of the St. Petersburg historical school of the Soviet period, with Pokrovskii, who worked in the traditions of the Moscow school. Rieber specifically noted that Romanov's researches "opened up new prospects for the study of Russia's imperialist policies in the Far East" (Alfred [J.] Rieber, "The Historiography of Imperial Russian Foreign Policy: A Critical Survey," in *Imperial Russian Foreign Policy,* ed. and trans. Hugh Ragsdale and Valerii Nikolaevich Ponomarev [New York, 1993], pp. 376–78).

8

On the Problem of Russia's "Separate Path" in Late Imperial Historiography

Terence Emmons

The hoary question of Russia's destiny in relation to Europe and, more generally, "the West," has once again come dramatically to the fore in the last few years, as the historically innocent predictions of various economists and political scientists about Russia's speedy "transition" to a "market economy" and "democracy" have been pummeled by the realities of Russian existence following the collapse of the Soviet regime in 1991. Given its classic formulation in the so-called Slavophile–Westernizer controversy of the 1840s, the debate about Russia and the West descended in subsequent decades from the empyrean of idealist historiosophy to the prosaic realm of revolutionary politics and professional history writing. The participation in the debate by professional historians illustrates very well the profound inter-penetration of politics and scholarship—especially historical scholarship—that was characteristic of late imperial Russian culture. This was a complex relationship that by no means had only detrimental effects on scholarship. Some of the most enduring monuments of Russian historical scholarship were produced in the last few decades before the Russian revolution, some of it by the most politically active historians. A case in point is Pavel Nikolaevich Miliukov (1859–1943), one of Russia's most accomplished and influential historians, for many years the unchallenged leader of the Constitutional-Democratic Party, and for a brief time in 1917, Russia's leading statesman.

A look at Miliukov's striking (if by no means entirely original) characterization of the Russian historical process in the first volume of his widely read magnum opus, *Essays on the History of Russian Culture* [Ocherki po istorii russkoi kul'tury], and at the evolution of his dialogue with his critics and with his own formulations about Russian history provides an interesting perspective on the relationship between history and politics in late imperial Russia. It also provides some historical perspective on the current discussion about the overall nature and direction of Russia's development in relation to "Europe," particularly in regard to the role of the state in that process.

The debut of Pavel Nikolaevich Miliukov (1859–1943) as a professional historian was made in characteristic fashion: he came out swinging. In his first "trial lecture" (*probnaia lektsiia*), read before the historical-philological faculty of Moscow University on 13 May 1886, Miliukov took on his most illustrious academic predecessors in the business of interpreting the Russian historical process, K.D. Kavelin, S.M. Solov'ev, B.N. Chicherin, and V.I. Sergeevich, criticizing "the juridical school," as he collectively labeled them, in the name of a "sociological" approach: "State authority is one of the manifestations of societal organization, and societal organization itself depends on the elements of which society is constructed. In the scheme [of the juridical school] we see a juridical form whose explanation must be sought in the study of the social material it contains."[1] In his master's dissertation, defended in 1892, Miliukov delivered a major blow to the received view of Peter I, disputing the Promethean role assigned to that individual in the development of Russian statecraft and institutions.[2] A little later, in 1896, in the introduction to the first volume of *Essays on the History of Russian Culture,* Miliukov pronounced himself an adept of the "new direction" (*novoe napravlenie*), which held that the proper subject of history was "the life of the people as a whole" or "the life of the popular masses" (*zhizn' narodnoi massy*). There, too, he invoked (unspecified) universal laws governing societal development that, he held, applied to Russia as much as to anywhere else in general and to Western Europe in particular.[3] These were basic elements of Miliukov's historical worldview that earned him the short-term (and erroneous) reputation of being an early academic Marxist and, along with his anti-Slavophilism, his critique of the "subjective-sociological" foundations of Russian populist philosophy, his liberal-constitutionalist politics, and polyglot cosmopolitanism, the enduring nickname of "the Russian European."[4]

It is ironic that after delivering himself of such a *profession de foi,* Miliukov proceeded in the text of the first volume of his *Ocherki* to give what was to become a classic, striking formulation of the role of the state in Russian history as an independent creative force, indeed "the creator of society" (*tvoritel' obshchestva*), essentially elaborating on the formulation of that great *gosudarstvennik,* B.N. Chicherin, and attracting, eventually, the unwanted accusation of being a proponent of the "Slavophile" idea of Russian uniqueness, or *samobytnost'.*

It is not hard to see how readers could have drawn this conclusion:

> Studying the culture of any western European state [Miliukov wrote in his introduction to "The State System"], we would have to proceed from the economic system, first to social structure, and only then to state organization. For Russia, it is better to proceed in the opposite order; that is, to acquaint ourselves with the state system before [examining] the social order. The fact is that in Russia the state had an enormous influence on societal organization, whereas in the West societal organization conditioned the state order.... In Russia, the historical process developed in the opposite direction—from the top down.[5]

Miliukov accordingly first gives his description of the development of the state in Russia and only then comes the section on the social order. To be sure, first of all comes the section on the economic order. But its purpose is merely to set the stage for the preeminent role played by the state in Russia's social and, yes, economic development: Miliukov claimed to subscribe, with anti-reductionist reservations, to an "economic materialist" view of history—that is, to recognize the importance of the economic factor in Russia's history as elsewhere. Russia, however, proved the rule by negative example: rather than economic development driving political-institutional development, it was precisely the *lack* (*elementarnost'*) of economic development and sparse population (due ultimately to relatively poor soil and climatic conditions) that explain the overriding role of the state in Russian history, together with the existence of external threats and a geography conducive to constant expansion:

> Inexplicable as a process of internal development, the appearance of this central state superstructure—the military-national state—can be explained by external causes. These causes are in part an elemental need for self-defense and self-preservation, and in part a conscious policy of territorial seizures guided by the idea of national unification. The spontaneous and the conscious are so interwoven in the activities of the Muscovite "gatherers" of Rus that it is hardly possible to draw an accurate line between them.... Our present main goal is to elucidate the spontaneous conditions of Russian historical life, those necessary conditions that led, in a certain sense artificially and forcibly, to creation of the military-national state on an elementary economic foundation, and then continued to influence the further growth of the newly created state, again without any correspondence to the economic and social life of the Russian population. We shall see later that all the essential traits of

Russian social history are explained by this preponderance of external growth over internal.[6]

Miliukov then proceeds to identify the five fiscal-administrative revolutions in the life of the state brought on by expanding military needs between the end of the fifteenth century and the death of Peter the Great (1490, 1550, 1680, and 1700–1720).[7]

Summing up his arguments in the conclusion to the first volume of his *Ocherki,* Miliukov wrote these words:

> If we wish to formulate the general impression one gets from comparing all those aspects of the Russian historical process on which we have touched with the same aspects of the historical development of the West, this impression, it would seem, can be reduced to two characteristics. The most striking things about our historical evolution are, first, its extremely elementary character; and, second, its complete peculiarity [*sovershennoe svoeobrazie*].[8]

Miliukov presented this vision of Russia's "complete peculiarity," to be sure, in a matrix of Comtian-positivist rhetoric, claiming that Russian development in the final analysis operated according to the same universal regularities (*zakonomernosti*) as prevailed in the West, and that, in accordance with them, Russia at present was already transcending the stage of state hypertrophy and societal dependence and was developing along lines familiar from the range of European experience; moreover, a cultural level would one day be reached where there would come into play "conscious human activity, striving to take advantage of natural evolution and bring it into harmony with certain human ideals." The past was already tied to the present "only as ballast, pulling us down, but weaker and weaker with every day that passes."

But, as several of his critics later pointed out, these "regularities" or laws remained unspecified in the philosophical preamble to his work, and Miliukov provided no clue as to what they might be by choosing systematically to avoid in the body of his work the problem of the relations in Russian history between the "material base" and the "spiritual superstructure." He explained (much later) his choice as a reflection of his rejection of both idealism (he remained a monist) and "philosophical materialism" (read Marxism: "Philosophical materialism is one of the worst forms of monism"). He opted for what appears to be a variety of "psychological monism":

> The economic factor only appears to be of a "material" character: in fact, the phenomena of human economics occur in the same psychic milieu as all other social phenomena. . . .

One can agree in a certain sense that the entire process of human evolution occurs under the influence of a powerful impulse—the necessity to adapt to the surrounding environment. But man's relations with the surrounding environment are not limited to economic needs alone. In the human psyche these relations are so differentiated that the historian must reject any hope of tracing them back to some primordial unity. He can only study the parallel development and further differentiation of the many and various aspects of human nature in the period of the social process accessible to him.[9]

In practical terms, this meant that he had decided, following Bagehot, to trace the internal evolution of various aspects of human culture, rather than the relations between them: "That is why in our 'Essays' we will now trace the development of Russian theoretical and moral worldviews independently from changes in the satisfaction of economic need." And this is just what he proceeded to do, producing over the next few years the second (*The Church and the School [Faith, Creativity, Education]*, 1897) and third (*Nationalism and Public Opinion*; part 1, 1901, part 2, 1904) volumes of the great work that permanently established Miliukov's reputation as a leading historian of Russia.[10]

The most striking thing about the reception of Miliukov's perspective on the state–society relationship in Russian history is that prior to the revolution of 1905 (by which time volume 1 of *Ocherki* had gone through five editions) it appears to have aroused no serious objections among scholarly reviewers. There was criticism, some of it quite outspoken, on a variety of other issues: the then Marxist Petr Struve, writing in *Novoe slovo,* objected to a few points of a factual nature (such as alleged errors regarding the character of Russia's industrial development, which Miliukov, as one might expect, considered to have been implanted, "artificially," by the state), but concentrated on "gnoseological" criticisms of Miliukov's historico-philosophical preamble (underestimation of the role of the individual in history, "trivialization" of problems of monism, and so on).

The young populist historian V.A. Miakotin, in a long review in *Russkoe bogatstvo,* criticized the author for failing to include pre-Muscovite Rus in his survey, for misinterpreting population and colonization trends in early Russian history, and for his uncritical acceptance of Chicherin's view on the recent, state-induced origins of the peasant commune (*obshchina*). M. Hrushevsky, who reviewed volume 1 in his *Zapyski naukovoho tovarystva im. Shevchenka,* published in Lviv, objected to Miliukov's subscription to what he elsewhere would call "the traditional scheme of "Russian" history"; namely, appropriation of Kievan Rus as the exclusive antecedent of imperial/Great Russian culture—but there was not a word about *samobytnost'* or *svoeobrazie.*[11]

The one apparent exception to the rule was the long essay, published, like Miakotin's review, in *Russkoe bogatstvo,* but a year later, by the veteran *narodnik* publicist of the London emigration, Leonid Shishko, who signed his article "P.B."[12] (Although an autodidact and not a professional historian, Shishko was an erudite and prolific writer on historical themes.)

Shishko clearly saw Miliukov's work as yet another Marxist challenge to Populism in the then ongoing debate between those two perspectives on Russia's past and possibilities for the future, and he set out to demolish it in defense of "subjective sociology." His main attack was on the historiosophical level: for all his qualifications, the author of *Ocherki* was at bottom an "economic materialist" (read: Marxist) who explained historical developments in terms of "objective forces," "necessity," and the like, rejecting the (Lavrovian) philosophy of history, which linked progress to goal-oriented, conscious human action. This was a view of historical causation that either contained an implicit teleology or was circular nonsense, and pernicious nonsense to boot, for it ultimately counseled quietism and passivity:

> We cannot understand the point of view according to which historical phenomena are explained as the results of societal necessity [*obshchestvennoiu neobkhodimost'iu*]. It appears to us that this merger of historical necessity or simply of the complex of sufficient causes with societal necessity is a direct result of the elimination of subjective factors [that is, conscious goal-seeking by concrete individuals]. The so-called materialist understanding of history leads to identifying the subjective factor with "society," that is, an abstract construct to which a conscious role is assigned. . . . If psychic factors [that is, consciousness] are not recognized as independent historical forces, then the dynamic of social life must take on in terms of its theoretical explanation the character of expediency.[13]

Although he went too far in locking Miliukov into the Marxist-objectivist tradition, Shishko's rejection of Miliukov's philosophical stance, as he understood it, led him to reject almost all of Miliukov's explanations of concrete historical phenomena, including his explanation for the rise of the absolutist Muscovite state: It was not in some abstract necessity of national self-defense together with geographic conditions that the explanation for the rise of the Muscovite state should be sought, but in the princely politics of conscious aggrandizement dating back to the days of the "Tatar yoke." He also questioned the "peculiarity" of Russia's "top–down" development: the role of conquest and violence in the early history of western Europe made its development much less "organic" and "internal" than Miliukov allowed.

Shishko's review, however, was the exception that proved the rule: for all its many telling points, it was not really a review at all, but an installment in the polemic between the Populists and the Marxists about whether or not Russia had a separate path in its *future;* and, most tellingly, Shishko did not in the end dispute Miliukov's characterization of Russia's "top–down" development.[14]

New, and newly critical, attention was drawn to Miliukov's conception of Russian peculiarity only in the wake of the revolution of 1905. The principal critics of *Ocherki* were two young historians who were proponents of the idea that Russia had a feudal past: N.P. Pavlov-Sil'vanskii (1869–1908) and Boris Syromiatnikov (1874–1947).[15]

Pavlov-Sil'vanskii, the best-known proponent of the idea of "Russian feudalism" (in the juridico-political tradition of European scholarship, not the Marxist variety), had come to the conclusion by the turn of the century that typical feudal institutions such as vassalage, subinfeudation, and immunities were widespread in Kievan and appanage Rus. He claimed to have reached this conclusion under the influence of new archival discoveries and of new German and French scholarship. It is possible that the liberation movement underway in the first years of the new century played a certain role here, too: Russia is on the way to becoming a constitutional state, that is, a "normal," Western regime. If its future is such, then perhaps its past was not so different from that of the West, after all.

Pavlov-Sil'vanskii entered the revolution of 1905 a quite moderate constitutional monarchist and emerged from it a radical democrat, criticizing from the left the leadership of the Kadet Party with Miliukov at its head. One can see in his 1907 critique of Miliukov's conception of Russian history a connection with his political dissatisfaction with the Kadets, although it was at the same time a continuation of a polemic that had begun with a critical review of Pavlov-Sil'vanskii's notions about feudal relations in early Russian history that Miliukov had published in the Brockhaus-Efron Encyclopedia as early as 1902.[16] In any case, the experience of 1905 confirmed Pavlov-Sil'vanskii in the correctness of his views about the essential similarity of Russian and West European development: Russia was backward, and that's all: In a lecture for schoolteachers in June 1907 Pavlov-Sil'vanskii said:

> The erroneousness of this view [of Russian peculiarity] has been demonstrated most strongly in the last three years, when reality, history itself, correcting the errors of historiography, gave us some practical lessons. . . . Everyone was amazed to see in this example that Russian history, if not in its entirety at least at certain basic turning points, develops quite similarly to Western history. . . . Everyone suddenly learned the comparative method, learned to discern the internal, essential similarity of phenomena under the deceptive veneer of external difference.

But all this was, indeed, new:

> Our historiography, taken en masse, has turned out to be ill-prepared for the demands made of it: to facilitate national self-awareness and understanding of the present and future along with the past.
>
> In the Slavophile–Westernizer controversy over the basic principles of Russian history, the Slavophiles were more convincing [than the Westernizers]. The Slavophiles were strong precisely because they built their whole theory around historical justification for the peculiarity of the Russian historical process. . . . They had a strong position, based on the peculiarity of its development, and from this they drew a logically consistent political conclusion about its development in the future. . . .
>
> Our Westernizers, agreeing with the Slavophiles on this basic point [about the peculiarity of early Russian history], took upon themselves the difficult task of demonstrating that, whatever the peculiar paths taken by Russian history in the past, in the future it will lead to the same destination as the history of the West. This task was difficult because from the peculiarity of the Russian historical process it was necessary to draw a conclusion about its identity with Western development in the future.[17]

The way out of this dilemma for the Westernizers, beginning with K.D. Kavelin and S.M. Solov´ev, was Peter the Great's radical leap onto the new path of Western development, a solution that did violence to the regnant nineteenth-century principle of organic historical development; in other words an unsatisfactory solution, but a solution nonetheless, and one that had allowed most historians until recently to accept the "significant peculiarity" of early Russian history. Kliuchevskii, of course, was a special case, with his view that the *entire* Russian historical experience, in contrast to the Western experience, was determined by the process of colonization, and his constant preoccupation with Russian peculiarities. But Miliukov, whose *Ocherki* carried the contradictions inherent in the Westernizer view of Russian history to their furthest extreme in Pavlov-Sil´vanskii's opinion, was the chief case in point: "His theory relies on the same unsatisfactory leap from former peculiarity to future identity with the West as in Kavelin's theory." But Miliukov went even further than his predecessors in emphasizing the peculiarity of old Russian history—here Pavlov-Sil´vanskii describes Miliukov's characterization of Russia's early history and cites the striking phrase about her "inside-out," "top–down" development: *"Our history proceeded inside out, and Miliukov studies it also inside out: first he examines the state order and then the social [order]. . . . Thus as a result of the sociological study of history, Miliukov came to an antisociological construction of it."*

And his leap from peculiarity in the past to identity with Western development in the future is even less satisfactory than the old reliance on the Petrine revolution; Miliukov had deprived himself of that option with his dissertation about Peter's reforms:

> For justification of the hope for similarity in future development, he refers only to completely hypothetical universal laws of social development, which he nowhere explains. . . . In the sociological introduction, Miliukov talks in detail about this completely hypothetical internal tendency, an internal developmental law of every society. . . , and he seeks salvation in the services of this same hypothetical law when in conclusion he has to go from the contrasts between Russian and Western history that he has explicated to similarity of development in the future, when he, casting off the toga of the historian, puts on the democratic macintosh of a liberal politician.[18]

But, Pavlov-Sil'vanskii concludes, with references to Marx and Maksim Kovalevskii, similarities of development are the result of similarities in economic and demographic conditions, not of hypothetical laws of development: "And the only means of explaining similarity and contrast, and thereby the essence of development, is the comparative method. Miliukov frequently compares Russian ways with those of the West, but incidentally and in their most general features. That is inadequate. Only scrupulous, prolonged comparison will yield a correct perspective on our history."[19]

As if anticipating Pavlov-Sil'vanskii's critique, or more likely in retroprojection of his own growing optimism about the chances of Russia becoming a "normal" state, Miliukov on the eve of the revolution of 1905 had modified some of his characterizations about Russian peculiarity in *Ocherki,* toning down the contrast between Russian and Western historical development, even to the point, in the fifth (1904) edition, of positing the existence of a "feudal way of life" (*feodal'nyi byt)* in early Russia. But as Pavlov-Sil'vanskii took pains to point out in a special section of the 1907 book in which his articles on feudalism in Russia were collected, Miliukov's adjustments were mostly cosmetic and in no way amounted to a rejection of his "theory of contrast" regarding Russian and Western development.[20] In the preface to the sixth edition, written in February 1909, Miliukov assured his readers that "recent events" had in no way contradicted the general construction of *Ocherki* and the basic historical and political views that informed them, but on the contrary had served to "confirm and further develop the author's conclusions."[21]

Pavlov-Sil'vanskii's plan to write a detailed comparative history of Russian and Western feudalism was cut short by his death from cholera in 1908 at the age of thirty-nine. That baton was picked up by another critic of the Miliukovian interpretation of Russian history, Boris Ivanovich

Syromiatnikov. A legal historian who is known to most scholars as the author of a slim volume on the reign of Peter the Great published in 1943, Syromiatnikov before the revolution was a passionate advocate of "the comparative-historical method" and the author of a large, unfinished work, "On the origins of feudal relations in ancient Rus."

Returning in 1905 from an extended study tour in Berlin and Paris, Syromiatnikov began to tout the "new method" that had "in the space of a quarter century completely transformed historical science." For Syromiatnikov, "the comparative-historical method" meant not simply the widening of the historian's field of vision beyond the boundaries of individual states to neighboring countries in space and time so as to perceive the working-out of processes that were underway in a given cultural region before its breakup into national states. Syromiatnikov had in mind much more ambitious, scientistic structural comparisons, a method allegedly justified by the discovery of modern scholarship "that all peoples have developed by an *analagous path,* going through identical historical stages, subjected to one and the same laws of development." "Peoples of totally different chronological zones have met on the same historical level," and so on. The goals of scholarship must change with the discovery of "this great truth": "If the historian previously set himself the task of "national self-awareness," he now strives for a purely *scientific knowledge*; in other words, his ultimate purpose has become the discovery of the laws of historical development."[22]

Having made such a manifesto, Syromiatnikov, of course, would have no truck with notions of "Russian peculiarity." In his view, the failure of Russian historians to understand the fundamental similarity of the Russian and Western historical processes was the result of the backwardness of Russian historiography. In keeping with his scholarly convictions, Syromiatnikov proceeded forthwith to undertake a multivolume work whose purpose was to demonstrate the essential similarity of Russian history and the history of the West, *The Origins of Feudal Relations in Ancient Rus*, the first volume of which was devoted to "the traditional theory of Russian historical development," that is, to the dominant idea in Russian historiography of Russian peculiarity in the relations between state and society:

> The science of Russian history and of the history of Russian law continues even today to be trapped in a vicious circle of traditional schemes and long-held propositions. Two ruling ideas, two despotic principles, still restrain our historical thought, as if in a vise. According to the first of these principles, the basic motor force in Russian history was the all-powerful, all-creating "state power," the government, which created "from above" the modest edifice of Russian "society." . . . This was the logical source of the second

principle, which states that Russia's historical development followed a completely special, "peculiar" path, in contrast to the historical evolution of West European peoples, which developed organically, from within.[23]

These characterizations of the state of Russian historical scholarship were made with Miliukov's *Ocherki* principally in mind, and Syromiatnikov addressed them at the beginning of his work. According to him, *Ocherki* only reproduced, or was at best a further development to, classic formulae and propositions that could be traced all the way back to the *Stepennaia kniga* and the *Khronograf* of the sixteenth century. Despite the sociological packaging and the critical attitude of the author of *Ocherki* toward the "juridical school," his picture of the Russian past is inserted in the old frame, well known to us, of the "state" theory, "and the picture itself, upon closer examination, turns out to be a simple copy of an old original." Applying to Miliukov the formula that Miliukov had applied to Karamzin in his own work on Russian historiography, Syromiatnikov concluded:

> We will hardly be mistaken if we say that the new work of P.N. Miliukov is that same summing up of Russian historical knowledge for the nineteenth century as Karamzin's *Istoriia gosudarstva rossiiskogo* was for the eighteenth century. As the latter clearly expressed the then popular view that turned Russian history into the biography of state power, so in the former that generally recognized historical scheme finds its final expression, according to which the history of Russia is identified with the history of state power, or as the author says, with the history of its *gosudarstvennost'*. But if, on the other hand, Karamzin's work could no longer satisfy his contemporaries, so in the same sense it can be said that the *Ocherki* of P. N. Miliukov in turn no longer satisfy, in their given construction, the scientific demands of our time.[24]

And what sort of construction of Russia's past would meet the "scientific demands of our times"? Syromiatnikov never completed the projected major work he had in mind, and even the first volume, set in type at Moscow University Press but not yet published at the time Syromiatnikov resigned in connection with the infamous Kasso affair in 1911, never saw the light of day. He did write an outline of it in 1912 for the students of the Shaniavskii (Moscow City Public) University, where he had gone to teach with many of his other colleagues who had left the state university in 1911. The Russian state, he told his students, "In historically specific conditions and over more than a thousand years resolved its national task, tardily [*medlitel'no*] passing through the universal human stages of historical life."[25] The general trajectory, in Russia as elsewhere, was from direct democracy to the rule-of-law state (*ot narodopravstva k pravovomu gosudarstvu*) by way of feudalism. Kievan Rus had been the last chapter of an early, direct democracy, a "town-meeting" order (*vechevoi stroi*). Appanage Rus and the Moscow "autocracy" were successive stages of Russia's feudal order (characterized by political splintering and unification, or by "political" and "social" feudalism, respectively). Thus far, the picture is not much different from Miliukov's. Syromiatnikov, however, then went on to emphasize that the "absolutist" monarchy was, essentially, the instrument of the ascendancy of the "middle classes" (*dvorianstva i gorodov*) over the feudal aristocracy of the appanage order. Russia was on the path of transformation into a bureaucratic, centralized, absolute monarchy "on the basis of the state 'enserfment' of the social orders," yet with a ruling class: "the serf-based gentry state" ruled over by a prince embodying the classic state principle: "l'état—c'est moi" (*gosudarstvo—eto ia*). Finally comes the fourth stage, the imperial absolutist monarchy, a typical eighteenth-century "police state," which, again in accordance with the universal law of development, in bringing about the separation of the idea of the state from the monarch and introducing the principle of "regularity," sows the seeds of its own demise and the transition to the modern rule-of-law, constitutional-representative state, a process made long and tortuous by the origins and nature of the imperial autocracy, which was without formal restraints on its arbitrariness yet was at the same time the creature of the nobility with its vested interests in the maintenance of serfdom and other aspects of the old order. Finally, in Russia the strength of the noble reaction determined the revolutionary character of the reform movement.[26]

At the same time as Syromiatnikov was at work challenging the "traditional theory" in general and Miliukov's construction of Russian historical development from an integrationist and constitutional-monarchist perspective (Syromiatnikov was an Octobrist after 1905, though obviously not of the conservative Slavophile wing of the party), the Bolshevik historian M.N. Pokrovskii was hard at work in exile preparing a multivolume general history of Russia that was designed to be a Marxist answer to Miliukov's *Ocherki*. Pokrovskii, with his theory of merchant capitalism, would eventually go much further than Syromiatnikov, denying not only Russia's peculiarity in regard to the relationship between state and society, but also its backwardness.[27] Not all Marxists took such strong exception to the Miliukovian paradigm. Indeed, Trotsky, in his 1908–9 German articles, which were republished in his book *1905* (1922), characterized the development of Russian state and society in terms that are almost a paraphrase of Miliukov's text.[28] It is ironic that the polemical, politically charged exchange set off between Pokrovskii and Trotsky in 1922 over the question of Russia's historical peculiarities, with the publication of Trotsky's book, served as a prelude to the even more profoundly politicized debate over the doctrine of "socialism in one country," in which the "anti-exceptionalist" Pokrovskii sided with Stalin's "peculiar" social-ism, while the "exceptionalist" Trotsky argued against further continuation of Russian exceptionalism.[29]

These Soviet debates take us far afield from the academic historiography of late imperial Russia, but they do testify to the resonance acquired by Miliukov's rendition of the "traditional theory of Russian development." More generally, they remind us that the debate about a Russian *Sonderweg*—which in one way or another always came back to the problem of Russia and Europe (could or should Russia catch up with the West or go its own way?) went far beyond academic circles, was in fact an integral part of the struggle for political power going into and coming out of the Russian revolution; it became acute after the events of 1905 demonstrated to almost everyone that the social forces capable of making a revolution really did exist, that the final showdown with the autocracy was near at hand.

Miliukov made no rejoinder to his post-1905 critics beyond the general remark in the sixth edition (1909) mentioned earlier, although he must have been familiar, at least, with Pavlov-Sil'vanskii's claim to have found a deep contradiction in Miliukov's view of the direction of Russian historical development. A seventh edition, the last to appear in Russia until after the fall of the Soviet Union, came out unchanged in 1918.[30] But this was not the end of the story of Miliukov's *Ocherki,* nor, more particularly, of the evolution of his views on Russian *svoeobrazie.*

In 1929–30, three developments conspired to make Miliukov reexamine the views on Russia's historical development he had first developed in volume 1 of *Ocherki:* (1) the advent of Stalin's revolution from above and the end of NEP, which Miliukov interpreted as a major diversion from the path of Russia's Europeanization, indeed, as a radical regression in the direction of archaic Russian "peculiarity"; (2) Miliukov's growing concern with Eurasianism, a trend he had systematically ignored during the ascendancy of NEP, as a doctrine providing intellectual support for Stalin's "separate path"; and (3) the formation of a fund by Miliukov's admirers on the occasion of his seventieth birthday for the purpose of sponsoring a new, "jubilee" edition of *Ocherki.*

In a lecture he gave in Britain in 1930, Miliukov launched an attack on the Eurasianist movement, rejecting point by point its claims about a special Eurasian civilization (shaped more by Asia than by Europe), decrying its millenarian aspirations for Russia, warning of its sympathies for Bolshevism (as "an unconscious weapon of a renascent statehood"), and, on the positive side of the ledger, emphasizing the essentially European nature of Russia's heritage:

While [the Eurasianists] attempt, with insufficient means, to construe a hypothetic civilisation for some time to come and hope to make use of it for the supposed revival of the Asiatic spirit—or of a sort of tabula rasa, brought about by the Bolshevist revolution,—Russian civilisation does exist and its basis can be no more changed. As a matter of fact, this civilisation is European. It is such by reason of its parallel development with Europe—not with Asia—at the early periods when the basis of national character is usually laid down. It is European by its victory over the Asiatic elements of the steppe. It is European even in its Siberian projection, because it brought to the barbarians and the nomads the elements of European culture. It is especially European in its educated class which was formed since Peter the Great's reign and which substantially contributed to the blossoming of the national creative power. Russian civilisation is European as it is proven by democratic strivings of the elite of its educated class, the Russian "intelligentsia," which since the end of XVIII century, successfully fought against serfdom and autocracy. It is European even in its mistakes and exaggerations. It is European in the initial idea of Russian revolution being a fight for equality and freedom as against the nationalistic tradition of social privilege and political oppression.[31]

This was to be the leitmotif of his revisions of *Ocherki* for the "jubilee" edition.

In October 1930, Miliukov gave a lecture in Berlin entitled "The sociological foundations of the Russian historical process." It handily sums up the state of his thinking about Russian "regularities and peculiarities" at the time he was at work revising his magnum opus. It is especially valuable because the latter work was never completed (see below). Miliukov begins by reaffirming his belief in the existence of "general tendencies" in the development of societies, "drawing together the Russian historical process with others that confronted no hindrances in the development of these tendencies"—this was the foundation that lay under his *Ocherki* from the outset. Beginning with the study of Russian demography, he had established two theses, "which were then confirmed by the study of all other aspects of the Russian historical process": (1) the evolution of the Russian populations repeated the same stages through which other "cultured countries of Europe" had passed, and (2) the process of this development in Russia was slower (*bolee medlen*) than in other parts of Europe. If the first thesis points to similarity, the second "established difference, that which constitutes the *peculiarity* [*svoeobrazie*] of the Russian historical process compared with other European [experiences]." In short, Miliukov has reduced the notion of "peculiarity" to the idea of backwardness or "slowness" (*medlennost'*).

Next came the study of the geographical factor for understanding Russian peculiarity, a sphere of study that had been extensively developed since the first edition of *Ocherki,* both as a matter of anthropogeography (a term

Miliukov borrowed from F. Ratzel) and of "developmental space" (*mestorazvitie*), a term he borrowed, with attribution, from the Eurasians. This study would occupy a special chapter in the new edition of *Ocherki*, but its result would be the opposite of that derived by the Eurasians: "Studying the 'developmental space' of Russian history, we come to the same conclusion as before: This history unfolds on European soil, and along European lines. But this process is powerfully retarded [*sil'no zamedliaetsia*] by the conditions of the 'developmental space' [mostly having to do with climatic conditions]." The interaction of the peculiarities of demography and "developmental space" account for the slowness of Russia's economic development, the late coming of her industrialization, hyperindustrialization once it got underway, and so on. Miliukov then turns to his belief in the fundamental importance of the economic factor ("they were ready to make a Marxist out of me for the above line of thought and for the order of my presentation"), to which he still holds, but with one amendment:

> My amendment simply consists of the fact that peculiarity is not the exclusive legacy of Russia: it shows up in the same characteristics in Europe itself, in a growing progression as we proceed from the Loire and the Seine to the Rhine, from the Rhine to the Vistula, from the Vistula to the Dnieper, and from the Dnieper to the Oka and the Volga, that is, in the direction of the gradual displacement of the maritime climate by the continental.

What about the issue of serfdom? Here Miliukov stood his ground:

> Was there feudalism in Russia? The historian Pavlov-Sil'vanskii, who died young, devoted very valuable works to demonstrate this. Many young scholars have taken up the results of his studies. But to those extremes of the "Europeanization" of Russian history I could not go. The presence in Russia of discrete elements characteristic of the feudal order cannot be denied. They show up everywhere in the absence of a strong centralized governmental authority. But it is characteristic for Russia that there the elements of feudalism were significantly and originally developed not in the period of fragmentation, but precisely with the strengthening of central state power. [Miliukov had in mind here land-based service relations and the enserfment of the peasantry.] The solution to this apparent paradox may be found in the same economic-geographic fact: in the complete impossibility for centralized Russian power to realize its full strength and influence horizontally throughout its territory or vertically into the social strata, given the expanse of Russia and the weak organization of her social elements.

But, as this passage intimates, he had subtly changed his way of presenting the state-society nexus: if in the prerevolutionary version of volume 1 he had presented the state starkly as "the creator of society," he now speaks of their interaction:

For the same reason, the history of the social order in Russia fuses from the time of the strengthening of central authority with the history of Russian statehood [*gosudarstvennost'*]. The estates are put into service to the state, and this service constitutes the *raison* for their existence. . . . And the further history of the estates consists in their gradual unbinding in the XVIII and XIX centuries. . . . But as a result of this unbinding, the social order of Russia returns to its previous amorphousness. And it was in this state that the recent catastrophe overtook [Russian society]. Its destructive force can likewise be explained by the low level of resistance, which could have been mounted by more established and better organized social strata.

And even more to the point:

Turning to the evolution of the state in Russia, we find the explanation for its peculiarity in the evolution of the social order. The fact is that the late breakup of the tribal order and the resultant weakness of a landed aristocracy did not permit the development of a state in Russia from within, organically, so to speak. . . . The imported authority had to organize the country anew. The aim of this organization, naturally, was the support of this same power by means of military defense of the country from the depredations of neighbors. For the elements of the population that had been unable to take shape economically and socially, this task was excessive, and from this came the necessity of using force, to get by force what could not be gotten voluntarily. From this arose the progressive binding of the estate up to the middle of the seventeenth century.

The turn toward Europe led inexorably to the replacement of arbitrariness by the rule of law, and brought Russia into the sphere of political changes taking place elsewhere in Europe, pointing in the direction of constitutional monarchy; but on this shoal the Russian ship of state ran aground (that is, on the resistance of the monarchy to reform), so that when the dynasty disappeared, so, too, did the state.

These remarks brought Miliukov, finally, to explicate his understanding of the contemporary Soviet state under Stalin: "We are presently experiencing a recidivism of that power which a new Herberstein could also call 'stronger than all monarchs' and presidents on earth. He would be, perhaps, more correct than in the case of Vasilii III: now there is the *apparat* of state power that extends to the very depths of society."

Despite this recidivist digression, the development of the Russian state was clearly headed in the direction of European development: witness the rise of public opinion, self-government, and even elements of representative government before the revolution. The same was true of cultural development: "After the incubation period of the eighteenth century there followed the flowering of national creativity from the time of Pushkin and Glinka

(1820–30). Russia got back on the path of European development. She was recognized by Europe precisely in this area of her culture."

But the European line of political development in Russia was interrupted by the world war, which

> stirred up the masses and gave advantage to the extreme political currents. In the process the cultured stratum, not yet firmly ensconced, was swept away. Ancient historical strata came to the surface. With these old habits the masses unconsciously supported a sudden new flowering of autocracy. . . .
>
> The Russian historical process is not ending; it is only being interrupted at this point. All the ascending curves of prerevolutionary statistics since that moment are performing an unimaginably wild dance, down and up, and down again, and in the end statistics themselves are abolished. A characterization of this latest period lies outside the task of this report; I will only remark that even these leaping figures and abrupt changes in life do not contradict history and cannot overthrow the conclusions derived from observation of a centuries-long process. It is not difficult to perceive survivals of the remote past under the new names. The destruction of the Russian intelligentsia, together with the abuse [*utrirovka*] of its doctrine, is only a new episode, the most tragic, in the history of its struggle with authority. Meteorology is familiar with "climatic disturbances" that provoke drought and the hunger of millions. Historical sociology must also include among its factors of analysis this fourth element—earthquakes in the historical foundation and the eruption of political volcanoes. Despite earthquakes and eruptions—more often than not with their help—history goes on.[32]

In hindsight, it is easy to see that the intent of Miliukov's revisions for what was to be the last version of his *Ocherki* would be to emphasize Russia's European credentials and to neutralize, so to speak, those aspects of his text that could be interpreted to support a Russian *Sonderweg* in current conditions: the notion of Russia's "complete peculiarity" would be reduced to backwardness or retardation; the divide between Russia and the West would be replaced by a West–East continuum (the very idea, incidentally, that would later be taken up by Alexander Gerschenkron in his analysis of industrialization); the state–society relationship would be modified to undercut or at least complicate the notion that the state was "the creator of society," and so on. In the end, the "jubilee" edition of the *Ocherki* turned out to be something quite different, in several important respects, from its predecessors.

Miliukov's preoccupations come through clearly in the "Author's Note" to volume 3 of *Ocherki,* dealing with the advent of critical thought in Russia through the reign of Catherine II, which was the first part of the "jubilee" edition to appear—in the same year of 1930 (the "Author's Note" was dated December 1929).[33] After explaining that volume 3 was being published first in the new edition because it had required little change, Miliukov explained to his readers why he had changed its title from *Nationalism and Public Opinion (obshchestvennoe mnenie)* to *Nationalism and Europeanism (evropeizm)*:

> Without rejecting [the former] terminology even now, I would like, however, to avoid a misunderstanding that it might invite. "The critical period" is, of course, not only a period of the destruction of the old but also of the creation of the new. My new title is intended to reflect that nuance. And what positive [value] was opposed to "nationalism" throughout all the debates engendered by that doctrine? Obviously, "Europeanism." . . .
>
> There has recently appeared a term that is meant to perpetuate national peculiarity, which is allegedly unique: Eurasianism [*evraziistvo*]. *Ocherki* did not and do not share that point of view, *although the founders of Eurasianism sometimes refer to the author of Ocherki as a theoretician of Russian "peculiarity" [svoeobrazie], who even introduced this word.* [Emphasis added.] The reader will see from the foreword to the first volume, as from the construction of *Ocherki* as a whole, that along with elements of peculiarity, the author emphasizes elements of commonality between Russia and the more fortunate countries, in terms of culture. Europeanism, from this point of view, is not a principle foreign to Russian life—a principle that can only be borrowed from without—but is its own milieu [*stikhiia*], one of the basic principles on which this life develops—insofar as common European elements of development were provided by its "developmental space" [*mestorazvitie*]. The very term "Eurasianism" points to this idea, if it is used scientifically rather than tendentiously. *Eur-Asia is not Asia, but Europe complicated by Asia.* [*Evr-Aziia ne est' Aziia; a est' Evropa, oslozhnennaia Aziei,* emphasis added]. Incidentally, I will return to this question, which has once again come to the fore, not accidentally, in the new edition of the first volume.

And so he did. The next volume to appear, the following year, was volume 2, the core of *Ocherki* dealing with culture properly speaking (*Faith, Creativity, and Education*). This volume was vastly expanded in two large tomes, mainly by bringing the narrative on cultural developments in all areas treated up to 1930—a prodigious scholarly achievement that synthesized many aspects of Soviet cultural development for the first time. Part I was devoted to the church and religion (including church-state relations to 1930) and to literature; part II treated art and both the institutional and substantive history of education (*shkola i prosveshchenie*). But the author changed nothing in terms of approach or general conclusions.[34]

It was volume 1, of course, that required the most extensive revisions, for two reasons. (1) He intended to beat the Eurasians at their own game, by demonstrating the European origins of the Russian people; this required a detailed inquiry into the "developmental space of Russian culture," the ethnic-cultural origins of the Slavs, the early migrations of the East Slavs, their expansion over eastern Europe, and the colonization of Siberia. (2) It was there that Miliukov had delivered his formulations about Russian peculiarity "inside-out," "top-down" development, had characterized the Russian state as "the creator of society," and had accordingly presented the essay on state development before that on social development—they would have to be revised along the lines he had developed in his Berlin lecture.

Miliukov took up the first of these task with characteristic, almost obsessive thoroughness, transforming what had been the first of four parts of the original wolume 1 ("Population," occupying only forty-five pages; the succeeding parts had been: "The Economic Order," "The State Order," and "Uhe Social Order") into two volumes, changing the work in the process, as he himself acknowledged, into something that could no longer appeal to a broad public. The first of these he published in 1937; it was devoted to "Developmental Space, The Beginnings of Culture, The Origins of Nationalities." The second volume, subtitled *From Prehistory to History*, and containing five sections—"Southern Russia and the Steppe Nomads", "The Forest Zone and the Migration of the Eastern Slavs," "The First Zone of Russian Expansion," "The Conquest of Siberia," and "The Problem of the Russian Anthropological Type"—was completed about 1940 and was published posthumously in 1964.[35] The details of Miliukov's treatment of these issues, replete with interrogations of a mass of now-forgotten literature of the 1920s and 1930s on linguistics, physical anthropology, and racial theories, need not detain us here. Its general import is clear enough: to demonstrate the European origins of the Slavs and to show that the expansion of the East Slavs, then the Russians, eastward, even into Siberia, was essentially a matter of the expansion of European culture into Eurasia.

In the introduction to the first part of the new version of volume 1, Miliukov outlined what he had in mind regarding the second task, to qualify his views on Russian "peculiarity":

In previous editions the forms of Russian state authority were derived [*vyvodilis*] directly from the elementary nature of economic development; [the former] had an extraordinarily great influence (from the top down) on both the economy and the social order. Such an arrangement of the material graphically underlined the peculiarity of the Russian historical process. In the present edition, however, I have preferred to return to the traditional order, presenting the history of state forms [*gosudarstvennosti*] after the history of the economy and of the social order. I have been guided in this by the intention to emphasize this time the other basic characteristic of the local process: the uniformity [*odnorodnost*] of the law-abiding development of [the Russian historical process] with that of other, better-endowed [countries]. In this way, the order of transition from the elemental to the conscious is also restored, insofar as the state is the highest expression of the consciousness of social development. Compared to the state order, the social order is after all more dependent on the economic, and through them the natural, conditions of the "developmental space."[36]

In the end, the revision of the last three parts of volume 1 was never undertaken, nor were they published in unrevised form, either in the "jubilee edition" or thereafter, with a result more radical than the author could have intended with his revisions: his once-famous lapidary formulations about Russian "peculiarity" and his characterization of the Muscovite state as a kind of independent force in Russian history have been largely forgotten.[37]

At the end of the introduction to the first part of volume 1 published in 1937, Miliukov expanded, at a length that will seem curious to those readers who know the work only in the "jubilee" edition, on the evolution of his treatment of the perennial issue of the Russian *Sonderweg:*

> It remains for me to pause on what was one of the basic characteristics of *Ocherki* and remains so, it seems to me, in the present edition as well. In the struggle between two opposing constructions of Russian history, one of which advanced the similarity of the Russian process with the European and carried that similarity to identity, while the other argued Russian peculiarity and carried that peculiarity to complete incomparability and exclusivity, the author occupied a conciliatory position. He constructed the Russian historical process on a synthesis of both characteristics, peculiarity and similarity. *At the same time, however, the features of peculiarity were probably underlined somewhat more sharply than the features of similarity* [emphasis added]. In this there was no doubt to be seen the influence of my teacher, V.O. Kliuchevskii, the most original [*svoeobraznyi*] of Russian historians.[38]

At the time of first writing, Miliukov continued, the issue had seemed unproblematical: the original controversy between the Slavophiles and Westernizers had died down. The Marxists had already renewed the dispute, advancing against the teaching of the Populists about Russian peculiarity the doctrine of similarity with the European economic process, but these opponents of peculiarity were as yet of little influence. Since then, however, the dispute has not died down, but has been renewed with new force by the younger generation of scholars: first came the proponents of feudalism, beginning with Pavlov-Sil'vanskii (who did some very good work, but went too far with the similarities); then, after the war and revolution, came the even younger generation of Eurasianists, arguing, under the impact of the Russian catastrophe and basing their arguments essentially on the geographic factor, the complete peculiarity of Russia:

> My task in the present edition, therefore, was a double one: on the one hand I

had to make use of everything that was positive in the works of both tendencies. On the other hand, I had to eliminate what was artificial in their confrontation and incorporate the remainder that corresponded to the truth into the synthesis of *Ocherki*.

It was particularly the task of the new edition to analyze the conditions of the "developmental space," on which the Eurasianists relied, and the result was (repeating the point made in the English lecture) that the European element had prevailed, that "even in the distant prehistoric period we were able to find the beginning of Russia's ties with Europe."

Finally, there has been a new development animating the old dispute about the peculiarity or similarity of Russian and European development, and that is that the dispute has been renewed, "in another form, of course," within the doctrine that is presently the official doctrine of Russia's rulers:

> Marxism apparently precluded the doctrine of Russian peculiarity in preaching their monistic view of the historical process. However, the facts of life have led to the creation of a new variant of the orthodox doctrine. Somewhat disguised in the teaching of Lenin, but quite openly in the teaching of Stalin, the Russian communist-Marxists have adopted the point of view of Russian peculiarity in the very process, foreseen by their theory, of the transition of Russia from capitalism to socialism. The well-known theory of "socialism in one country" was invented, and the teaching of the Eurasians thereby converged with the nationalized doctrine of Marxism and the experiments of Stalin on the body of Russian reality.[39]

* * *

It is ironic that Miliukov, who from the beginning of his career as a politically committed scholar had cast himself in the role of mediator between the extremes of "exceptionalism" and "identity" in the interpretation of Russia's historical trajectory (for it was the country's *future* that was at stake, and the radical-liberal Miliukov found unacceptable precisely the vision of the *future* held by both extremes), should have found, at the end of his career, that proponents of the two extremes had, as it were, ganged up against his vision of a normal European future for Russia and that he should have found himself obliged to fight a kind of rearguard action against the use of his own work in support of this hybrid form of neo-Slavophilism, as he saw it. It is no less ironic that in the process Miliukov shifted the focus of the debate from the comparative-sociological hypotheses to which he continued to pay ample lip service in the 1937 introduction to questions of cultural identity, expansion, and confrontation.

The history of *Ocherki* and its reception provides a vivid reminder of the power that the image of the Promethean state as the shaper of Russian destiny has played in Russian thought. Syromiatnikov was right: it was an entrenched tradition when he encountered it in the early twentieth century, and not only in academic discourse; but he was wrong to think it could be made to disappear under the scrutiny of "objective"!historical scholarship. Grounded in the reality of Russian historical experience, it came to the fore during the!reign of Peter the Great and has never left the scene. It is the linchpin of the debates about Russian *samobytnost'* and about the relationship between Russia and the West—does Russia have a separate path, is Europe's present Russia's future, do Russia and Europe have divergent pasts but a common future, and so on—which received their classic formulation in the Slavophile–Westernizer disputes of the 1840s. As Miliukov noted with dismay, the debate continued under various guises—Populism v. Marxism, Eurasianism v. Europeanism, "socialism in one country" v. "communist internationalism"—with now one side, now the other in ascendancy, and always with the future at stake.

Of course, both dichotomies—Slavophile–Westernizer and Russia–Europe—were and are polemical constructs. While most professional historians of Imperial Russia, like most other Russian intellectuals, actively rejected the "noble dream" of objectivity entertained by their American contemporaries (in the sense of disinterested scholarship, as opposed to the epistemological question about the discoverability of truth—on the latter issue they shared the positivist outlook of their American colleagues),[40] it is not so easy to classify them according to these dichotomies, as several of the contributors to this volume have pointed out. Even Miliukov, the ultimate "Russian European," is a case in point. Appealing to universal laws of development that dictated an outcome of Russia's historical evolution essentially similar to that of European countries, he proceeded to provide the most striking picture of Russian "peculiarity" in late imperial scholarship. Subsequently, in his effort to distance himself from the Eurasians, Miliukov broke down the Russia–Europe dichotomy by recognizing the existence of many "Europes" and constructing a West–East cultural gradient, which included Russia as the easternmost flank of Europe and, therefore, the most "peculiar" European country, most exposed to "Asiatic" influences, but European nonetheless.

While Miliukov's final word on Russian peculiarity is certainly not the final word *tout court,* it is closer to the truth than the classifications of Russia, going back to Hegel or Marx, as an "oriental despotism." It is a view that is supported by the very persistence of the Russia–Europe debate among Russian intellectuals: the comparison of Russia to the countries lying to its west has been endemic in Russian thought since the Europeanization of the

Russian elite began in a significant way in the eighteenth century and has proceeded apace with the penetration of modern secular culture. It is not a perspective sustained primarily by foreign scholars or observers, so that if a "Russian-centered" perspective on Russian history that is not simply a new edition of Slavophilism is to be developed, it will have to come from within Russia.[41] Was Miliukov right in seeing Soviet experience as a temporary "interruption" or detour from the historically determined path of Russian development? Only time will tell, of course, but his views would seem to merit a hearing in the debate going on in Russia today.

Notes

The general outline of this chapter was presented at a conference in Smolensk in 1992. I am indebted for additional insights and information to the authors of several works that have appeared since then: M.G. Vandalkovskaia, *P.N. Miliukov, A.A. Kizevetter: istoriia i politika* (Moscow, 1992); N.G. Dumova, *Liberal v Rossii, tragediia nesovmestimosti: Istoricheskii portret P.N. Miliukova,* part 1 (Moscow, 1993); Thomas M. Bohn, *Russische Geschichtswissenschaft von 1880 bis 1905: Pavel N. Miljukow und die* Moskauer Schule (Phil. diss., Hamburg, 1995); and Melissa Kirschke Stockdale, *Paul Miliukov and the Quest for a Liberal Russia, 1880–1918* (Ithaca and London, 1996).

1. P. Miliukov, "Iuridicheskaia shkola v russkoi istoriografii (Solov'ev, Kavelin, Chicherin, Sergeevich)," in *Russkaia mysl'*, 1886, bk. 6, pp. 80–92: 91.

2. *Gosudarstvennoe khoziaistvo Rossii v pervoi chetverti XVIII stoletiia i reforma Petra Velikogo* (St. Petersburg, 1892).

3. P.N. Miliukov, *Ocherki po istorii russkoi kul'tury,* part 1: *Naselenie, ekonomicheskii, gosudarstvennyi i soslovnyi stroi, "Vvedenie: Obshchie poniatiia."* (All references to volume 1 are to the 7th ed., Moscow, 1918, unless otherwise indicated.) It should be noted that Miliukov believed that the framework of societal evolution was the individual society (in which statehood was a normal phase of development), not mankind as a whole, "Western civilization," etc.

4. Cf. Thomas Riha, *A Russian European: Paul Miliukov in Russian Politics* (Notre Dame and London, 1969), and the works cited in note 1.

5. *Ocherki,* part 1, pp. 138–39, 148–49.

6. Ibid., p. 149.

7. Ibid., pp. 150–51.

8. Ibid., pp. 291–92.

9. *Ocherki po istorii russkoi kul'tury,* part 2: *Tserkov' i shkola (vera, tvorchestvo, obrazovanie,* 4th ed. (St. Petersburg, 1905), pp. 1–5.

10. *Ocherki po istorii russkoi kul'tury,* part 3: *Natsionalizm i obshchestvennoe mnenie,* no. 1 (St. Petersburg, 1901); *Ocherki po istorii russkoi kul'tury,* part 3: *Natsionalizm i obshchestvennoe mnenie,* no. 2 (St. Petersburg, 1904).

11. *Novoe slovo,* no. 13, October 1897, part 2, pp. 89–94 (Struve); *Russkoe bogatstvo,* 1896, no. 11, section 2, pp. 1–20 (Miakotin); *Zapysky naukovoho tovarystva imeny Shevchenka,* 1896, vol. 13, pp. 2–5. Miliukov answered his principal critics in the foreword to the third edition of volume 1 of *Ocherki* (1898).

12. I.F. Masanov, *Slovar' psevdonimov russkikh pisatelei, uchenykh i obshchestvennykh deiatelei,* vol. 2 (Moscow, 1957), p. 313.

13. "Neskol'ko zamechanii ob 'Ocherkakh po istorii russkoi kul'tury' g. Miliukova," in *Russkoe bogatstvo,* 1898, no. 8, section 2, pp. 1–21. For a list of reviews of Miliukov's work, see the bibliography of Bohn, *Russische Geschichtswissenschaft.*

14. Ibid.

15. See the dissertation of V.A. Murav'ev, "Teoriia feodalizma v Rossii v russkoi istoriografii kontsa XIX–nachala XX vv." (Moscow, 1969). There is an American dissertation on Pavlov-Sil'vanskii: Thaddeus C. Radzilowski, "The Life and Works of N.P. Pavlov-Silvanskii (1869–1908)" (University of Michigan, 1979).

16. "Feodalizm v Rossii (v severo-vostochnoi Rusi)," in *Entsiklopedicheskii slovar',* vol. 35a (Brokgauz-Efron) (St. Petersburg, 1902), pp. 548–50. There is a detailed discussion of the differences between Miliukov and Pavlov-Sil'vanskii over Russian feudalism in Vandalkovskaia, *P.A. Miliukov, A.A. Kizevetter,* pp. 185–210.

17. N.P. Pavlov-Sil'vanskii, "Revoliutsiia i russkaia istoriografiia," in *Istoriia i istoriki 1972* (Moscow, 1973), pp. 356–64.

18. Ibid., p. 362.

19. Ibid., p. 364.

20. Cited from N.P. Pavlov-Sil'vanskii, *Feodalizm v drevnei Rusi,* 2d ed. (Moscow and Petrograd, 1923), "III. Teoriia kontrasta Miliukova," pp. 27–35.

21. *Ocherki po istorii russkoi kul'tury,* part 1, 6th ed., rev. and enl. (St. Petersburg, 1909), n.p.

22. B. Syromiatnikov, "Osnovnye momenty v razvitii istoricheskoi mysli," *Russkaia mysl',* 1906, no. 12, pp. 91, 94.

23. B.I. Syromiatnikov, *Proiskhozhdenie feodal'nykh otnoshenii v drevnei Rusi, Vvedenie: Traditsionnaia teoriia russkogo istoricheskogo razvitiia (istoriograficheskii ocherk)* (Moscow: Tipografiia Moskovskogo universiteta, 1911), pp. 48–49. This work was set in type and a few proof copies were struck before the type was scattered because of the author's resignation from the university. I am beholden to V.A. Murav'ev for the opportunity to consult this work.

24. Ibid., pp. 60–61.

25. B.I. Syromiatnikov, *Kratkii obzor i ukazatel' literatury po istorii gosudarstvennoi vlasti v Rossii* (Moscow, 1913), p. 6.

26. Ibid., pp. 5–26.

27. M.N. Pokrovskii, *Russkaia istoriia s drevneishikh vremen v 5-ti tomakh* (n.p., 1910–14). See Tamas Krausz, "Svoeobrazie russkogo istoricheskogo protsessa: o diskussii L.D. Trotskogo i M.N. Pokrovskogo," in G.D. Alekseev, ed., *Istoricheskaia nauka Rossii v XX veke* (Moscow, 1997), pp. 200–216.

28. L. Trotskii, *1905,* 2d ed. (Moscow, 1922), "Sotsial'noe razvitie Rossii i tsarizm," pp. 17–24.

29. This point is made by Tamas Krausz (see note 27).

30. See note 3.

31. Paul Miliukov, "Eurasianism and Europeanism in Russian History," in *Festschrift Th.G. Masaryk zum 80. Geburtstage: Erster Teil mit einem Bild* (Bonn, 1930), pp. 225–36. The slightly skewed English is Miliukov's own.

32. "Sotsiologicheskie osnovy russkogo istoricheskogo protsessa," Pavel N. Miliukov Papers, box 12: Minor Manuscripts, Bakhmeteff Archive on Russian and East European History and Culture, Rare Book and Manuscript Library, Columbia University.

33. P. Miliukov, *Ocherki po istorii russkoi kul'tury,* Vol. 3: *Natsionalizm i evropeizm,* jubilee ed. (Paris, 1930), pp. 5–6.

34. P. Miliukov, *Ocherki po istorii russkoi kul'tury,* vol. 2: *Vera, tvorchestvo, obrazovanie,* part 1: *Tserkov' i religiia, Literatura,* jubilee ed. (Paris, 1931). P. Miliukov, *Ocherki po istorii russkoi kul'tury,* vol. 2: *Tvorchestvo, obrazovanie,* part 2: *Iskusstvo,*

shkola, prosveshchenie, jubilee ed. (Paris, 1931).

35. P. Miliukov, *Ocherki po istorii russkoi kul'tury*, vol. 1: *Zemlia, Naselenie, Ekonomika, Sosloviia, Gosudarstvo*, part 1: *Vvedenie, Mestorazvitie, Nachalo kul'tury, Proiskhozhdenie natsional'nostei*, jubilee ed. (Paris, 1937); P. Miliukov, *Ocherki po istorii russkoi kul'tury*, vol. 1: *Zemlia; Naselenie, Ekonomika, Sosloviia, Gosudarstvo*, part 2: *Ot preistorii k istorii: Posmertnoe izdanie pod redaktsiei N.E. Andreeva* (The Hague, 1964).

36. *Ocherki*, vol. 1, part 1, p. 27.

37. This observation is based on the recent re-edition of the "jubilee" edition" (plus posthumous supplement), whose editors appear to be oblivious to its incomplete state— P.N. Miliukov, *Ocherki po istorii russkoi kul'tury v 3-x tomakh* (Moscow, 1993)—but also on the lack of reference to Miliukov's earlier views on Muscovite state and society in several recent studies devoted to him.

38. *Ocherki*, vol. 3, part 1, jubilee ed., p. 29.

39. Ibid., pp. 30–31.

40. See Peter Novick, *That Noble Dream: The "Objectivity Question" and the American Historical Profession* (Cambridge, 1988).

41. Cf. Paul A. Cohen, *Discovering History in China: American Historical Writing on the Recent Chinese Past* (New York, 1984). In this respect, foreign, and perhaps especially American, scholarship on Russian history seems to present a clear contrast with China scholarship: if anything, American scholars have been criticized for importing "criteria of significance" *from Russia,* either the statist tradition of prerevolutionary Russia or the Bolshevik perspective of the Soviet era, rather than the other way around, as per Cohen's critique of American China scholarship. This state of affairs reflects a basic difference between the "Russia and the West" and "China and the West" experiences.

9

Remembrance of Things Past

Historians and History in Russia Abroad

Marc Raeff

War, revolution, and civil war shattered Russian society. They not only dramatically transformed the accustomed ways of public life but also revealed depths of cruelty, savagery, depravity, misery, and sheer horror that had not seemed possible. Whatever the idea or picture of a harmonious, idyllic, and cooperative society many may have held on the eves of 1914 and 1917, it was destroyed by the behavior of all classes. True, one had also witnessed instances of heroism, self-abnegation, devotion, and love—but these acts seemed exceptional and isolated islands in the midst of the swirling sea of human suffering and misery. The Horsemen of the Apocalypse had not spared anything that educated society had known before 1914. At the end of the years of horror, a regime had imposed itself that was brutally contemptuous of everything held dear and sacred in the past, and that stopped at nothing to retain its grip on the country and its inhabitants. The Bolsheviks, so it seemed, were bent upon implanting what was most ugly and despicable, and doing so in a most offensive and beastly manner.

For the many who had fled across the border, the old Russia was gone. But even that was not the most painful change: everything good and beautiful appeared to have been smashed; the accumulation of riches, memories, and traditions was irremediably lost as well. It seemed to them that something ugly, coarse, and inhuman had taken over and was in the process of transforming the very nature and soul of the Russian people. Even without answering the questions of how it could have happened, who was to blame, and what could be done, every thinking and educated person in emigration had to shape a new, acceptable image of Russia's past. How could one face life in exile with only the images of death, destruction, and vicious dictatorship in one's consciousness? It was natural to turn to the past and cling to anything that seemed to suggest how things might have gone differently. Émigrés wanted to recall selectively those trends and manifestations of Russia's past that would help them overcome the recent horrors; they sought things that represented the perennially valuable aspects of Russia's true identity. And since the exiles had been raised in the post-Romantic era of modern nationalism, they expected to pinpoint in the past those features that always characterized the Russian nation and its culture, and explained its historical process.

It was an all-too-human reaction. As individual memory selects the pleasant and useful in its own past, so does the group's, especially if its members are educated and can give literary expression to their perception of this past. We find the most dramatic—and effective—example of this in the Great Polish Emigration of 1831. Not only did it nurture the greatest national poets, A. Mickiewicz and J. Słowacki, but also its most influential historian, J. Lelewel. They built their image of Poland from selected periods and events—either the glories of the most remote past or the sufferings of the more recent centuries—and endowed it with a meaning that pointed to their own role in preparing for a great national revival.

Nor did the émigrés from Germany in the 1930s remain content with tracing the roots of the evil that had triumphed in their homeland to the entire course of German history. They felt that some aspects of that history offered an alternative course, and held out the promise, however dim at the time, of the possibility of change and a better future. Rejecting a deterministic reading of the baneful legacies of Luther and Frederickian Prussia, émigré intellectuals turned to the literary and philosophic achievements of Goethe's Weimar, to Germany's contributions to science and scholarship, to the traditions of individual freedom and local autonomy in the Holy Roman Empire.[1]

How did the Russian historians in emigration rise to the challenge of an appropriate and meaningful reading of the Russian past?[2] Let us first turn to their organizations and activities in exile to help us find an answer.

In 1922, after the expulsion on Lenin's orders of more than 100 intellectuals, it was estimated that there were about five hundred active scholars and scientists in emigration.[3] As was true of the entire "Great Emigration" from Russia, these professional scholars were dispersed all over Europe and the Far East; but their centers were in Berlin, Prague, Harbin, and Belgrade and, to a lesser extent, in Riga, Warsaw, and Sofia. As a result of the course taken by the civil war, a proportionately larger number of professors and scholars had been associated with the universities in Ukraine and Siberia, although many had also been connected with Moscow and St. Petersburg at some time in their careers. Of course, not everyone who might have wished to leave was able to do so, as the recently discovered diary of the Moscow historian Iu. Got´e illustrates.[4]

The scholars who found themselves in emigration took immediate steps to secure their material and professional existence. The opportunities of the Duma period and the experiences of the civil war had taught a number of intellectuals how to coordinate their efforts for a common purpose. The scholars and intellectuals who had been politically active in Paris since 1917–1918 took the initiative in setting up so-called academic groups. With the encouragement and modest material help of English academic circles and of the YMCA in Berlin, a number of such academic groups had sprung up in the European centers of the Russian emigration.[5]

The academic groups of Russian scholars set themselves the following tasks. First, they wanted to find material assistance for émigré scholars; second, they hoped to enable them to pursue their professional and scholarly–scientific activities; and, third, they intended to spread knowledge of Russian science, scholarship, and culture among the host societies. A fourth purpose came to be added later, coordinating and cooperating with those organizations that endeavored to give the younger émigrés (and their children) a Russian education, so as to prepare them for an eventual professional role in the motherland.

As we have noted, the most elaborate effort to attain the goals of the Russian academic groups abroad took place in Czechoslovakia. The so-called Action russe involved the establishment of the Russian University in Prague, as well as a series of scholarly institutions. Among the Russian historians prominently active in Prague we should mention A. Kizevetter, E. Shmurlo, V. Frantsev, G. Vernadsky (until his move to the United States in the late 1920s), and the somewhat younger M. Shakhmatov and A. Soloviev. The Russian University also helped train a few "younger" historians—S. Pushkarev, G. Florovsky, N. Andreyev, and (on a temporary visiting basis) M. Karpovich.

The struggle for mere survival all too often absorbed the lion's share of the émigrés' energies. This largely explains why most were in no position to produce large-scale studies and monographs—or did so only when they had some economic security, as was the case of the "successful" lawyers V. Eliashevich and B. Nolde, or P. Miliukov during World War II. A few—e.g., N. Berdiaev—lived on "retainers" provided by sympathizers, usually American, and friends.

But even shorter studies were published with difficulty, for a simple reason: the dearth of sources. There were no adequate collections of Russian materials at the leading European universities. Even printed materials had to be garnered in many places; and under the prevailing technological, legal, and economic conditions, duplication and travel were practically unavailable to émigré scholars. Because of the ethnocentric historiographical tradition of the time, most émigré scholars could not turn to foreign archival sources on the history of Russia. There were notable exceptions: for instance, Shmurlo continued his researches on Italo-Russian contacts, but he added almost nothing to the sources from the Vatican archives he had identified and partially published before 1917; A.V. Florovsky devoted most of his time, from the mid-1920s on, to a monumental two-volume study of Czech-Russian relations in medieval and early modern times. To my knowledge, however, no other émigré scholar tried to plumb the archival holdings in Paris, Berlin, or elsewhere for their *Russica* contents. Partly, perhaps, because access to official archives was not easy for foreigners to obtain in those days; but also, I suspect, because prerevolutionary Russian historians had focused almost exclusively on the internal history of their country, and they did not realize the potential that the view of an outsider *altérité* offered for an understanding of oneself.

An important concomitant of the émigrés' parlous economic and professional situation everywhere, except perhaps in Prague, was the difficulty of finding a venue for the publication of their works. Most scholars abroad were not in a position to write directly in a foreign language—even though some had an excellent passive command of a major Western tongue. The few who could do so found interest only in popular books (*ouvrages de vulgarisation,* as the French call them) on contemporary themes and periods. Translations were expensive and not always easy to arrange. Thus the émigré historians were restricted to the limited forum of publication in Russian. Naturally, such a situation did not encourage them to make material sacrifices for the sake of research.

In Prague, the historians organized their own professional society (Russkoe istoricheskoe obshchestvo v Prage), first under the chairmanship of Shmurlo and later of Frantsev. It sponsored meetings and seminar discussions, and published its own irregular serial *Zapiski russkogo istoricheskogo obshchestva v Prage* (1927–30). The faculty of history of the Russian University in Prague also participated in the "learned notes" of the university and in the notes of the evening school affiliated with it, the so-called Narodnyi russkii universitet (*Uchenye zapiski osnovannye russkoi uchebnoi kollegii v Prage,* 1924–).[6] But as the bibliographic record of these publications makes amply clear, their appearance was neither regular nor very frequent. Since the claims on their space were great, any sizable publication had to be arranged separately. This entailed scraping together money for the printing with much effort and great investment of time. Benefactors were hard to find in the 1920s or early 1930s, especially after the onset of the Great Depression; besides, most of them had their own preferred causes. The correspondence preserved in émigré archives gives a vivid picture of the many appeals, and the few successful responses, that were launched on both sides of the Atlantic. Even the most faithful and dedicated supporter, the YMCA, was not so forthcoming with its funds, especially after the failure of its effort at mass production and mass distribution of Russian textbooks.[7]

I have mentioned that scholars had difficulty in finding an outlet for the publication of their writings. As we have seen, there existed, attached to the several institutions of advanced learning and the academic groups in the major émigré centers, scholarly serials. They appeared more or less regularly and opened their pages to articles in the humanities, law, sociology—and, in some cases, the natural and physical sciences as well. These serial publications offered interesting, original contributions to various aspects of Russian history. By and large, however, they were based on materials the authors had previously found and worked upon in Russia before emigrating. In a few rare cases archives in foreign locations came into play. Because of limitations of space these articles have a narrow focus and deal with a single discrete event or a limited problem.[8] But given the erudition and high technical level, practically all the articles in these "learned notes" are worthy of the professional historian's attention and should be consulted in every case in which they deal with a topic of relevance to the contemporary searcher. Unfortunately, few libraries have full runs of these serials, and they are only partly, and not very satisfactorily, registered in bibliographies. It should also be stressed that these contributions were written in the manner and style of prerevolutionary professional articles, which had little appeal to the educated lay reader. Their impact, therefore, was quite limited and, given the slight interest displayed by foreign scholars in Russian history (and widespread ignorance of the language), they were largely ignored by non-Russian historians, with the exception of the rare specialists. The summaries in French or German appended to some of the serial publications did little to widen their audience. Only articles summarizing significant new findings or interpretations that touched on broad topics of European import were sometimes translated and published in foreign professional journals.

One last general issue remains to be mentioned in setting forth the material and psychological conditions under which the émigré historian had to work. It is the question of the emigration's "receptivity" to historical knowledge and interpretations—in short, its interest in and attitude to history. The émigrés who settled in Europe and the Far East (and in small scattered numbers all over the globe) had just experienced one of the most upsetting, dramatic, and harrowing series of "historical events." Their world had crumbled before their very eyes; a completely new political, social, and cultural order had taken over after years of bloody fratricidal war. All this occurred just after World War I, which most of them had also experienced more or less directly. Is it surprising that the émigrés were "tired of history"? They felt, even more so than did the literary critic M. Gershenzon in his letters to Viacheslav Ivanov, the "burden" of history and civilization.[9] They could not work up much interest in remotely past events, in the kind of issues and sources that excited and fascinated the historian. To be sure, the émigrés had a natural curiosity about the experiences of fellow participants. The memoirs of leading prerevolutionary personalities, as well as those of both prominent and humble participants in the war and civil war, found an eager audience. They were readily published in books or serialized in journals and newspapers. The interest in memoirs was akin to nostalgia, a desire to relive the past—not necessarily a better, but at any rate a memorable past. Not surprisingly, the émigrés asked themselves how it had been possible for the revolution and the civil war to engulf Russia. How had Russia departed from some "normal" path, be it a Russian, or a European, or a universal one? But such questions were better treated, better "digested" in reflective or polemical essays, not in scholarly treatises. And such essays, raising the perennial "accursed question" of Russia's relationship to the West, to Europe, of the peculiar makeup of the Russian national character and experience, were constantly appearing on the pages of émigré journals and newspapers. But these ruminations were far from being an analysis of causes and effects, a kind of analysis that, if undertaken at all, appeared lifeless, dehumanized, to those who had only recently experienced historical events in all their inconclusiveness.

This kind of experience was better conveyed by historical fiction (or memoirs) than by scholarly studies. This goes a long way, to my mind, to explain the popularity enjoyed by the prolific Mark Aldanov's novels and historical sketches. Indeed, Aldanov "relativized," so to speak, the Russian experience by writing about the prehistory and history of the French revolution, and by setting the later prodromes to the Russian revolution in an all-European framework. In second place, he described and explained events as the result of unpredictable consequences of the concatenation of actions taken by individuals. These individuals intended one thing, but, most frequently, what resulted was not what they expected. Consequently, there are no laws of history, no predictability—everything is chance and flux. History is the stage for our activities, nothing more, nothing less. Aldanov's skepticism, detachment—as well as great narrative skill—were like a soothing balm on the raw wounds of his émigré readers. He provided the kind of historical reading that appealed to them, and unintentionally foreclosed their interest in scholarly, "scientific," or "objective" history.

The foreigners among whom the Russian émigrés lived did not evince much interest in the past of their guests' homeland. Most were at best attuned only to recent events—in part to understand how the tragic collapse of Russia could happen, in part to bring the Soviet regime and its policies into some kind of framework. By and large, the feelings toward Russia were unfriendly, either because of the belief that Russia had "betrayed" the Allies in 1917–18 or for having allegedly contributed to the instability of the postwar world. Since there was much ignorance about Russia and its past, the foreigners dismissed the subject in anger or with a contemptuous reference to the incomprehensible "Slavic soul" and Russian "barbarism." Meanwhile, the so-called progressive public opinion—pacifists, socialists, fellow travelers, committed Communists—considered the Bolshevik revolution to have been a positive and necessary event, and they did not want to hear about the evil past of tsarist Russia from the pen (or mouth) of those whom history had deservedly condemned to exile. Given the increasingly pro-Soviet mood of European intellectuals in the 1930s, the historian of Russia, especially of émigré background, had a dwindling foreign audience.

This was surely in contrast to the role played by Adam Mickiewicz, for example, of the Great Polish Emigration in pioneering the study of Slavic languages and literatures at the Collège de France in the 1840s. But it was also very different from the German historians who emigrated to England and the United States after Hitler's accession to power.[10] They were relatively easily and rapidly integrated into the academic establishments of their places of asylum. In the case of the United States, the German refugee scholar played a most influential role in both war and peace, contributing to raising the professional level of universities and colleges. As a glance at the development of historical studies in the United States (and to a lesser degree in England, too) shows, they also made for important historiographical changes, introducing, for example, the history of ideas, bringing a new understanding and expansion of Renaissance history, and revolutionizing art history, not to mention their contribution to the study of Germany and in training specialists in that field. One may well ask what caused this difference from the Russian historians among whom there were equally distinguished scholars. There may have been a difference in numbers, but that was hardly the crucial factor. The most important single factor was that the Russians were and remained émigrés, always hoping to return to the homeland, and therefore unwilling—and unable in the Europe of the time—to integrate. The Germans, in contrast, came to the United States (and England) having made a clear break with the country of their birth; they were committed (with some exceptions, to be sure) to making their permanent home in the new land. In the second place, we should also remember that graduate studies in the United States had developed on the German pattern. Although most Russian scholars before 1914 had also studied in Germany, and their university system was similar to the German, this did not lead to as much interdependence. Anyway, most Russian historians did not settle in Germany but in France and other countries that had different practices and traditions, or that aimed at developing their own academic ways. Finally, Russian history—unlike the German—was more "exotic," more remote for the European academic community. For most Westerners the break in 1917 seemed radical enough to encourage them to ignore what had preceded it. This was far from being the case with Germany—especially after the outbreak of the war, soon after the arrival of refugees from there.

What about the young generation of émigrés? The children of those who had actively fought in the war and civil war spoke Russian and had received an introduction to Russian literature and history. But few were truly interested in deepening this knowledge. There was the predictable negative reaction to their parents' unfortunate past, reinforced by their position as outsiders in the schools and country of asylum by virtue of this very past. The prospects of economic survival, and of securing a socially satisfactory status in the foreign land (once a return to the homeland became virtually impossible), were not furthered by a professional commitment to the study of Russia's past. Of course, some émigré children were interested in history and later pursued that interest at the university; but in this case, too, they turned rather to the history of foreign countries where they could at least do archival work and enlist the guidance and support of established academics.[11]

As a result, the émigré professional historian (with the qualified exception of a few instances in Prague) had no successor, no *relève*, to train, to supervise, and to promote. The Russian University in Prague did grant a few advanced degrees; but they were obtained by scholars who had already reached the last stage of their professional training in Russia—for example, S. Pushkarev and G. Florovsky. Only N. Andreyev, who had been educated in Estonia, received all his graduate training in Prague. Marc Szeftel, who had studied with A. Eck in Brussels, first received a law degree in his native Poland.

At first glance it may appear surprising that the professional historians of the emigration did not turn their immediate attention to chronicling the revolutions of 1917 and the civil war. As a matter of fact, I know of only one serious and comprehensive history of the revolution by an émigré (before 1939). It was written by the indefatigable P. Miliukov, and it partakes as much of the genre of memoir and brief *pro domo sua* as it does of academic history.[12] I think that the reason for this is obvious: the events were too painful and too close to allow dispassionate treatment. Equally important, of course, was the fact that the official archives were not accessible, while the documents of the White Armies, which had been evacuated along with the officers and troops, were dispersed and in a chaotic state; it would take years for the archives in Prague and at the Hoover Institution to be constituted as research instruments, and it would have taken many years more to work up and analyze the material—World War II cut short any effort in that direction.[13] Perhaps it was neither unnatural nor accidental that the first comprehensive account of the revolution and civil war was written by an American journalist, William H. Chamberlain, and it is still the best overall chronicle.[14]

This certainly does not mean that the émigré historians were not interested in the causes and course of events that preceded and followed upon the collapse of the imperial government in February 1917. But their energies went into the writing of memoirs, collecting them and other relevant materials for future scholarly treatment. The memoirs were primarily personal statements, or special pleadings, by all those who had been directly involved in any of the major events of the last decades of the empire, as well as of the "time of troubles" that followed.[15] But they also try to account for the causes that brought about the end of the old regime, although from a personal perspective. Several serial publications were specially founded to provide a vehicle for this memoir output: the best and most comprehensive was the *Archive of the Russian Revolution* [Arkhiv russkoi revoliutsii]; in addition we have the short-lived *The Historian and the Contemporary* [Istorik i sovremennik], and *On Foreign Soil* [Na chuzhoi storone].[16] In addition, as I have already pointed out, the journals of general interest and the better newspapers serialized memoirs of participants and witnesses to the revolution and civil war. As the archival collections abroad show, almost as many memoirs were never published. Quite clearly, in the 1920s and 1930s the émigrés were still too much in a state of shock to face the task of critical analysis, synthesis, and "objective" reconstruction of events.

Naturally, the broader question of the origins and causes of the revolution could not fail to be of great concern to émigré historians. Theirs and their fellow exiles' memoir efforts aimed at suggesting answers. Basically, there were two types of answers: the first consisted in seeing the revolution as an accident that had disturbed the more or less natural, harmonious, and progressive developments of the last decades of the imperial regime (or since 1861), and prevented them from coming to fruition. The "accident" may have been the result of an unexpected series of events, for example, World War I, or a conspiracy by evil men bent upon destroying the greatness of Russia and of its culture—whether to further the interests of Germany or to promote nihilism. The second answer, given by all "liberal-minded" historians among the émigrés, was that the trends operating in the Russian Empire since 1861, or the accession of Alexander III, had created problems of such magnitude that they could not be addressed by a conservative bureaucracy and an obscurantist emperor; society had to be integrated with the government and failing this, the collapse of the imperial regime became inevitable, although the specific events that set off and accompanied the collapse were not predetermined by long-range trends. Except for S.S. Oldenburg's defense of the last tsar as an individual and ruler, there was no one to argue seriously in favor of the ways in which the old regime had responded to the critical issues confronting Russian society. This, however, did not preclude the publication of a large volume of popular, sentimental, and patriotic literature that grieved for the tragic end of the imperial family; it reflected a retrospectively emotional rehabilitation of the last tsar and his wife, which had arisen and grown in the course of the civil war.

The preceding remarks bring me to the crucial aspect of émigré historiography which, in my opinion, goes a long way toward explaining its relatively unoriginal and uncreative character. Émigré historians had received their professional training in the last decade or two of the nineteenth or in the very first decade of the twentieth centuries. This was the period of the dominance of positivism, both in Western Europe and in Russia. The positivist orientation in historiography had two sides to it. One was the belief that the historian's main task was to accumulate all possible facts, preferably those based on archival documentation (for the modern period— for earlier times manuscript sources were used) and dealing with the political and public socioeconomic facets of the past. The mere accumulation of all documented facts, which were critically assessed as reliable, was the ideal toward which the historian should strive, because the interpretation of these facts would follow almost automatically. This is, obviously, an over-simplification of the "fact"-oriented bent of this historical school, but it points to the reason for the lack of popular success of history written in this mode. There is an absence of color, drama, and personalities. And indeed, with the exception of Kliuchevskii, who was an exception in most respects, at least in his lectures and his university course based on those lectures, Russian historians wrote turgidly and displayed no interest in biography, so that their readership was largely restricted to the profession and a few aficionados.[17]

As we all know, however, the mere accumulation of facts does not create a meaningful synthesis; besides, it is impossible to obtain all the facts. Facts are selected, and the choice is determined by certain assumptions. Moreover, the selection and interpretation of facts must be based on some underlying intellectual scheme if they are to have any meaning. The other side of positivist historiography, therefore (and its tenets were first formulated by Auguste Comte, founder of positivism), was the belief that the facts will reveal the specific forms in which the laws of social development manifest themselves. The laws of development are universal, though varying in their specifics and chronological sequence from case to case. However, if one posits the existence of laws of social and historical development, one at once enters the realm of determinism—a determinism that can only partially and inadequately be tempered by individual actions and accidental events.

The scheme of development proposed by positivism has a teleological character in that it presupposes, or sets forth, the next state, or the ultimate goal, of this development. Positivist historians believe that we normally know what the next stage will be, because all humanity has to pass through a similar set of stages in a prescribed order—a belief inherited from the Enlightenment. We, therefore, must know what the immediate goals of development should be in the case of a certain society and historical period, for other societies (or nations) that have reached a subsequent stage provide both a model and a standard. Such a scheme can be associated with geographic, ethnic, racial, or other factors determining the evolution of a given society. Thus Russia, its positivist historians concluded, would pass through the stages that Western and Central Europe had passed or entered, since it, too, belonged to Europe. The peculiarities of Russia's development stemmed from a chronological discrepancy that was largely due to geography and its past evolution. It meant that Russia, too, one day soon—once the artificial barriers had been removed—would become a member of the European social, economic, and political civilization *à part entière*.

I have dwelt at some length on this scheme because it was the scheme adopted by the most influential and significant émigré historian, P.N. Miliukov. It was the leitmotif of his *Ocherki,* more particularly in the "jubilee" edition. And the scheme also underlay the writings of more narrowly focused historians, such as A. Kizevetter, D. Odinets, and P. Bitsilli. It was the conception that was at the basis of the organization, and the few general interpretations, to be found in the three-volume history of Russia published in Paris, in French, and edited by Miliukov, who also wrote a good part of it. His collaborators were V. Miakotin, A. Kizevetter, and several other specialists who wrote the short sections dealing with prehistory, geography, and diplomacy. The history's intellectual sponsor was the French "high priest of positivistic historiography," Charles Seignobos.[18] Their philosophy aside, the three volumes offer a still useful compendium of the essential political and socioeconomic events of Russian history. But they are short on interpretation, and whatever explanations they do offer are mere repetition of the nineteenth-century liberal clichés. Nor is their style very engaging, and if we also mention that there are few, if any, suggestive portraits of leading personalities, it becomes understandable why they are not terribly readable.

The positivist approach, regardless of its philosophical and epistemological problems, presented the émigré historian with a major difficulty in connection with the revolution. Indeed, however one evaluated the "backwardness" of Russia in comparison to the Western and Central European (or North American) pacesetters, the anticipation was that Russia would become a modern society with all the attendant critical issues. The revolution was, therefore, the culmination of Russia's moving in the direction of modernization, and of the old regime's inadequacy in solving the attendant difficulties. This evolution, however, could also be explained as an almost natural, or organic, result of the special path taken by Russia in its earlier historical development (whose determining roots go back still further, ad infinitum). The conclusion imposes itself, therefore, that the revolution had been inevitable and in the natural order of things, given the special circumstances of Russia's history, geography, society, culture, and so on. But was this a palatable, nay possible, conclusion to face for émigrés who had suffered so much as a result of this revolution, and who were still deprived of their homeland because of it?

The alternative to such an interpretative approach was to see the revolution as resulting from the sudden and capricious impact of a historical accident, of a catastrophe along the lines of a meteorological or geological upheaval, which could neither have been foreseen nor prevented. This was not much of an explanation, but in accepting it, one could dispense with any investigation of the past in search for reasonable causes. Many, especially among the uneducated and prejudiced monarchists, were inclined to accept such a view of the recent past, and it explains their impatience with historical literature in general. The unpleasant conclusions about one's own past offered by these alternative schemes were the major barrier to the emigration's enjoyment of history. Similar reactions could be observed among the German liberal professionals who emigrated after 1933, bewildered by the failure of the Weimar Republic. They began coming to terms with the past only after World War II had run its course. The delayed reaction to the Holocaust is another instance of men's preferring to forget the unpleasant immediate past.

The positivist methodology and interpretative scheme dominated almost all émigré historical scholarship in the interwar period. Was there no alternative to them? At one point it seemed that an alternative did emerge. As has been well shown by Nicholas V. Riasanovsky, this alternative, too, had some of its roots in the prerevolutionary cultural atmosphere. It was the so-called Eurasianism. Its tenets, as they pertained to history, may be summarized as follows. The unit for the historical study of Russia is Eurasia—not a combination of Europe and Asia, but a separate entity with basic characteristics of its own. It is defined, first of all, by its geographic location, which also determines its climate, resources, and modes of economic organization; Eurasia is the geographic area of steppes and forests, landlocked, devoid of mountainous massifs (except on its southern and southeastern borders). Its continental climate has stamped its agricultural development.[19] By defining Russia's geographic identity in this way, the Eurasians were in fact equating Eurasia with the boundaries of the Russian Empire on the eve of 1914, or of Soviet Russia—though the latter had been deprived of the Western fringes (Baltic states, Bessarabia, eastern Poland). The social and political development of this Eurasian entity was marked by the struggle between steppe and forest, with the latter eventually subduing the former. But the struggle underscores the importance of the steppe nomads in shaping the civilization—political, material, spiritual—which evolved organically in the territory of Eurasia. Hence, to understand Russia's past one has to pay proper attention to its steppe heritage, and not forget that for many centuries it was facing Asia rather than Europe. From Europe, however, it has received a major element of its identity, Christianity; but characteristically it was the Christianity of the East. This explains why the Western elements of modern Russian culture are so alien to it—they were mechanically imposed on Russia (by Peter the Great and his successors). The Bolshevik revolution, among other things, was a revolt of Eurasia against this alien intrusion. It proved, once again, that Russia's cultural specificity is anti-Western, even if modern science and technology are compatible with it. Here we need not take up the question of the political consequences the Eurasians drew from this interpretation—it belongs to another book.

On closer examination, however, the Eurasians did not offer an adequate alternative to the positivist scheme either. Their interpretation, too, led to a deterministic view of Russian history, a determinism based on geographic and climatic factors. Any determinism, however, implied the inevitability of the Bolshevik revolution, and the Soviet regime's "legitimate" and lasting character.[20] This was a conclusion that few émigrés were prepared to accept. Nor did it make for an interesting history, because its teleological nature deprived epochs, events, and actors of their singularity and individuality and—consequently—of their fascination for both student and reader. For all these reasons Eurasianism did not have the impact on historical writing that one might have expected at first. The only professional historian to be, and to remain, "converted" to Eurasianism was G. Vernadsky. In fact, however, except for acknowledging the importance of the Mongol invasion and domination, something that Russian historiography had indeed tended to downplay or to ignore (e.g., the curious omission in Kliuchevskii's course), Vernadsky's account of the process of Russian history was hardly different from the one found in earlier general surveys of Russian history (or from the three-volume history in French, for that matter). To be sure, specific issues of the prehistory and the early Kievan period were given by Vernadsky new interpretations based on hypotheses rooted in philological considerations that argued for the unity of the Slavic (Russian) and "Turanic" (Eastern) cultures. But these hypotheses (and his arguments in their favor) have been contested and, on the whole, rejected by both historians and linguists. (In all honesty, it should also be acknowledged that Vernadsky lacked the ability to organize his material effectively, and even in Russian his prose did not inspire.) His most significant contribution, five volumes on pre-Petrine Russia, was written and published after World War II and, except for the chapters on the Mongols, these books owe more to traditional positivism than to Eurasianism. In spite of the stimulation it provided, for a brief period, to émigré discussions on the nature of Russia, its past, its culture, and the revolution, Eurasianism had no significant impact on Russian historiography.

Both the positivist scheme—with its standards of interpretation derived from the Western and Central European experiences—and the Eurasian theory, in its fascination with the steppe and nomadic elements of Russia's past, confronted a crucial problem of definition: what was subsumed under the rubric "history of Russia"? In other words, what was Russia? The political unit known since Peter the Great as the All-Russian Empire? But what was its relationship to Muscovy, the appanages, Kiev? And what about all those areas—Ukraine, Byelorussia, the Baltic and the Caucasus or Central Asia—which became part of the empire; how was their history to be treated and fitted into the evolution of the empire? Since by common consent neither geography nor the political events of state building were an adequate base for the study of the past, and more specifically for its transmission to the young after the revolutionary upheaval, what methods should one use? To be sure, the process of state and empire building was an important aspect of Russia's past. But this was a very ambiguous heritage; could it also be considered a permanent element in defining the national identity of the Russians (not to speak of Ukrainians, Caucasians, Jews, and others who were also part of the emigration)?

After all, had not the events of 1917 and the aftermath revealed the brittle-ness of the imperial establishment and brought it to a permanent end? There was no going home again; the past was a closed chapter. Finally stressing the political aspects would only run up against the political divisions of the emigration, become the source of bitter disputes, and fragment still further the émigré community. And this at a time when the stress should be on what united the exiles and what was valuable in their heritage and could be passed on to the generation of children born abroad.

Not only the political but also the traditional social structures of Russia had disintegrated in the course of 1917–21, and new ones had been fash-ioned by the Bolsheviks. It was, therefore, difficult to speak of Russia in the usual, primarily political, terms. True, with the introduction of the New Economic Policy, and even more so after Stalin had restored some of the nationalist and historical heritage of the past, it seemed that the Soviet government had re-created a politically powerful state—another "imperial" Russia. This development elated chauvinists in exile; even liberals, includ-ing Miliukov, could think again in the traditional terms of a Russian state in a historical continuum from Kiev, by way of Moscow and St. Petersburg, to the Red Kremlin. But this return to politically determined historical conti-nuity in approaching Russian history came late, on the eve of World War II, when most émigré historians had passed their active, creative period.

It can be readily observed that whenever a traditional political or sociopo-litical unit suffers a major catastrophe, or collapses altogether, the tendency is to look for those manifestations of public life that seem to provide a longer perspective, and a more permanent foundation for a sense of historical conti-nuity and identity.[21] For example, the collapse of the Weimar Republic, or of Germany after 1945, led scholars in exile (and not only there) not to view their country's past in customary political terms but to search for another coherence-giving concept. In the case of the Germans it was the "humanis-tic" heritage of the classical period of Schiller and Goethe. After 1945, for many, it was the notion of Western Christendom. For the Poles of the Great Emigration it was the idea of Poland as the bulwark of Christendom, home of political freedom, and martyr destined to be the future savior of Western civilization. What concept could replace the political idea of the All-Russian Empire? One possible suggestion was to define Russia as the society of Orthodox Christianity and of the institutions that issued from Prince Vladimir's conversion of Rus' in 988. The suggestion was taken up by some émigré scholars, especially those of a conservative bent who settled in Yugo-slavia. They contributed to and published a few books of essays, and sup-ported an effort to have the feast day of St. Vladimir (8 July) celebrated as a symbol of the unity and purpose of the emigration.[22]

But they had no appreciable impact on the scholarly writing of the emigration's historians. Indeed, for most the approach was too closely connected with the failings and, in their opinion, reactionary role of the Russian Orthodox Church in its subservience to the Muscovite and imperial state establishments. Moreover, most of the émigré historians were positivists of mildly liberal persuasion, and, consequently, also profoundly secularist. Whatever their personal religious feelings and faith, and some were pious churchgoing individuals, they advocated the separation of church and state. Firm believers in the Enlightenment ideas of progress and human rights, they scorned the "obscurantism" and "barbarism" of Muscovy, let alone Kiev and the so-called appanage period that preceded it. We should also remember that although all émigré scholars possessed Russian language, culture, and education, not all were ethnic Russians or Orthodox Christians.

Something that clearly united all émigré scholars, as well as their audience, and tied them to the past was language, language in the wider sense of the aesthetic, spiritual, and moral values that the Russian word, through its great literature, had created. The Great Polish Emigration had been the cradle of modern Polish literature—and its greatest achievements came about because of the exiled writers Mickiewicz and Słowacki. It also was contemporary with the Romantic period, when art and nationalism combined to create the very notion of a distinct national culture. The Russian emigration, for its part, could draw on a great literature, with its own traditions and seminal role in defining the cultural values and national consciousness of Russians of all persuasions and classes. (Soviet successes in education showed how this great literary tradition could help cement the entire population.) It was natural, therefore, for the émigrés to adopt as their unit of discourse modern Russian literature—the creation of the St. Petersburg period. The poet Alexander Pushkin was its most glorious symbol, as had been publicly acknowledged ever since the famous celebration of 1880.

The notion of culture was not precisely defined; it was a somewhat hazy concept tinged with sentimentality and nostalgia. Culture, in the usage of émigré historians, essentially referred to the great works of Russian literature and their moral and spiritual message, as interpreted by the intelligentsia. The function of literature as the almost exclusive element in defining both culture and national historical identity was given additional prominence because many historians were also active as literary scholars, lecturers, and critics. This was the case of Kizevetter, as well as Miliukov, while Bitsilli, Florovsky, and Fedotov devoted almost as much attention to literary themes as they did to historical topics. This was also true of philosophers and theologians such as Berdiaev, Shestov, Frank, and Zen'kovskii. "Russianness" was thus seen and defined in terms of the accomplishments of the greatest figures of Russian letters, from M.V. Lomonosov and G.R. Derzhavin to the great novelists of the nineteenth century.

The émigrés perceived Russian history as characterized by a series of profound and radical breaks—particularly noticeable in aspects of culture—each of which defined and determined a new period. The perception of the deep and irrevocable character of these breaks was much more intense in the case of Russian historians, before the revolution and after, than in any other historiography. Be that as it may, Russian history was traditionally seen as a succession of very distinct periods whose relationship to one another gave rise to a great deal of acrimonious debate. The Kievan period was sharply contrasted to the era of the appanages and of the Mongols, both assessed very negatively; fifteenth- to seventeenth-century Muscovy, with its several great crises, was marked off by the Petrine "revolution" from the St. Petersburg period which, in turn, ended in the brutal revolution and civil war that the emigration had experienced. It may be a generalization, but not an overly rash one, I think, to say that every Russian historian not only preferred one or the other of these major periods in his country's history, but tended to dismiss or ignore those he did not like. The most striking instances of this selectivity were the appanage and Mongol periods—they were downplayed, deplored, or even ignored. The prerevolutionary historiography, under Romantic and Hegelian inspiration, had concentrated on the process of state building, of the formation of the centralized state of Moscow and St. Petersburg. It had paid little attention to Kiev, and generally ignored the scattering of political sovereignty and the cultural poverty of the appanage and Mongol centuries. In contrast, it had extolled the grand princes of Moscow for their "gathering of Russian lands," for patronizing church culture. It also had praised the Petersburg era that had issued from the Europeanizing efforts of Peter the Great. The Slavophiles, like the Eurasians in emigration, had little use for the Petersburg era and the turn to Europe that it had signified, but they had few representatives in the historical guild; and anyway, they could not help but praise the imperial and cultural accomplishments of Peter and his successors.

The majority of the recognized émigré historians also had distinct preferences when it came to the Russian past. With the exception of mainly ecclesiastical writers, Kiev was treated cursorily; even Vernadsky before 1945 wrote about it only as an instance of Eurasia's steppe connection. Miliukov, in the posthumously published volume of his *Ocherki,* dealt at length with the prehistory and the migrations of the Slavs but evinced little interest in the Kievan "state." The appanage and Mongol periods remained neglected or ignored, as had been the case in most prerevolutionary treatises. On the other hand, the émigré scholars displayed a distinct lack of sympathy for the Muscovy of 1400–1600, although they acknowledged its positive contribution in "gathering the Russian lands."[23] Even when the amateur historian I. Bunakov (Fondaminskii) branded Muscovy an "Asiatic," centralized state, a negative label for most intellectuals, the rebuttal merely consisted in pointing out that not everything in Muscovy was the result of the tsar's (and his court's) autocratic direction but that, as a matter of fact, it was the autonomous organizations of Russian society on the local level that had been responsible for whatever positive accomplishments occurred in that period.[24]

The tsardom of Muscovy was excoriated by émigré historians (and their liberal predecessors before the revolution) because it was identified with the church's domination over all culture and the origin of entrenched autocracy. The allegedly absolute power of the tsar, as displayed in the brutal conquest of the free cities of Novgorod and Pskov, and in the capricious and barbaric tyranny of Ivan IV's *oprichnina*—so reminiscent of the Bolsheviks—stood irremediably condemned in their eyes. To make matters worse, the autocracy proved so powerful that its stamp was indelible on all following centuries, down to 1917. As Miliukov had proven in his first scholarly monograph (and as Kliuchevskii had also stressed), Peter the Great's manner of rule was inconceivable without the background of Muscovy. Autocracy was the handy tool Peter seized to carry out his policies, and this is what gave a warped twist to his reforms and transformations and split Russia into two nations.

There was a distinct ambivalence about the St. Petersburg period. Its major accomplishments had been to serve as the matrix and taproots of modern Russian culture, especially its glorious literature. It also deserved praise for having set Russia on the path of modernization and intensive Europeanization—a path that was so abruptly disrupted by war and revolution. On the other side of the ledger, however, was the fact that Imperial Russia's autocracy had been the major stumbling block in the liberalization and modernization of public life. It withheld freedom of expression from the intelligentsia. The revolution had thus been largely prepared by the Romanovs on the Neva—by their stubborn clinging to bureaucratic autocracy and their perverted and limited cultural outlook.

What conclusions can we draw regarding the focus of interest and themes of émigré historians, as compared to those of their prerevolutionary predecessors? In reaction to the dominant influence of the so-called statist school in Russian historiography, beginning in the 1890s there had been a marked shift to the study of the social and economic aspects of Russia's past—Kliuchevskii's university course was a dramatic and popular instance of the new trend. This shift of focus encouraged scholars to find new fields of investigation (on the basis of new materials, of course), e.g., the fate of the peasantry, not only in its relationship to the state, but primarily with respect to the serf system as an all-encompassing socioeconomic phenomenon and to its subsequent impact on the agrarian problems. The role of the bureaucratic apparatus was displaced from the center of attention it had occupied to the benefit of the "root processes" on the local level. This line of thought continued to be pursued to the extent possible in emigration. Those who had managed to bring along their research notes were able to write monographs of which the magisterial study of V. Miakotin on the transformation of the Ukrainian peasantry in the late seventeenth and early eighteenth centuries is the best illustration. Another instance was the set of articles by A. Florovsky that complemented his major monograph on the elections to the Great Commission of 1767, which he had published in Russia before the revolution.[25] In exile, the peasantry continued to hold the attention of historians, although it became more difficult to study the subject abroad. If archives were out of reach, a fresh reading of the published documentation might yield new insights. Such was the approach taken by the "younger" historian S. Pushkarev, who completed his degree work and became active in Prague and published a suggestive thesis on the repartitional commune. In the same vein, the jurist V. Eliashevich took advantage of his enforced leisure under the German occupation of France to complete a two-volume juridical investigation of the principles and practices of land tenure rights from the sixteenth to the eighteenth centuries. A few articles dealing with the peasantry and serfdom were published in the Festschrift in honor of P.B. Struve, and Struve himself worked in his last years on an economic history of Russia, concentrating on agrarian issues.[26]

The experience of the civil war had brought many émigrés into closer contact with the Russian provinces. Some scholars had been active in various provincial universities (Saratov, Tomsk, Irkutsk, Odessa, Rostov) or local public organizations. They had had occasion to witness not only anarchy and disintegration but also impressive displays of local initiatives and resourceful energy, once St. Petersburg's (or Moscow's) grip had loosened or disappeared altogether. This reinforced a historiographic trend that had been noticeable since before 1914, the discovery and recovery of the elements of local and regional autonomy and initiative that the previous historiographic perspective had neglected. Thus a greater interest in and familiarity with the border areas of the old empire resulted in several monographic studies by historians in emigration. Fulfilling an assignment of the Cossack émigré establishment, S. Svatikov wrote a comprehensive general history of the Don Cossack Host, stressing the autonomous and independent development of the territory it occupied, all the while strongly emphasizing the Russian character and orientation of Cossack society. On the basis of his research in the 1920s and 1930s, B. Nolde, during World War II, undertook the writing of a comprehensive history of the acquisition and incorporation of the border territories into the Muscovite and St. Petersburg Empire. His work remained incomplete, and only a fragment of it was published posthumously in French after the war. But it is a seminal and magisterial monument of émigré historiography, which bears witness to the transformation of the emigration wrought by the 1940s, and to the de facto integration of émigré scholarship into their lands of asylum. We should also mention the studies of V. Riasanovsky on Mongol law, to some extent a product of his Siberian experience during the civil war and his association with the Chinese and Manchurian milieu of Harbin.[27]

* * *

We are now in a better position to offer some general observations on the issues raised at the beginning of this chapter. What was the emigration's attitude to Russia's past and how did the scholarly émigré community respond to it? As a group, the emigration was ambivalent about its country's past. The burden of experiencing such dramatic historical events had totally "soured" history for the émigrés. They implicitly rejected, and showed little enthusiasm for, Russia's history as it had been presented in prerevolutionary historiography. To the extent that the émigré scholars carried over the methods, assumptions, and major interpretations that had held sway in happier times, they elicited little interest and received scant support from the émigré communities.

The difficulties of carrying on original work and the limited possibilities for publication discouraged émigré historians from striking out along new paths. This helps explain the great success among the émigré public of the historical novel, a genre that combined nostalgic descriptions, absorbing plots, enviable characters, and skepticism about one's ability to foresee and understand, let alone control, events. It accounts for the popularity of Mark Aldanov—a past master of the genre. Aldanov's novels, despite their stylistic and technical brilliance, have not stood the test of time, although a revival of his popularity is occurring among the third wave emigration and more recently in Soviet Russia for probably the same reasons.

A major factor in the ineffectualness, as well as the sterility, of émigré historians at the time was their inability to find a responsive echo in the host countries. In the 1920s and 1930s, whatever curiosity existed about Russia was about the "Soviet experiment." It did not extend to a desire to understand better the past experiences of the country where the experiment was taking place. Those who were enthusiastic about it shared the antihistorical mood of the early Bolshevik years. They were to be disappointed and shocked when Stalin reintroduced respect for the Russian past. Those foreigners who were anti-Bolshevik had little use for the country; they were resentful that Russia had withdrawn from World War I, reneged on its foreign debt, and supported all kinds of modernistic and nihilist trends in politics, the arts, and literature. They could approve of those liberal émigré historians who wrote of Russia's backwardness in relation to Western Europe, and leave it at that.

To be sure, a few academic circles or institutions (mainly in Germany) were concerned with Russia. But they were unreceptive to new approaches and showed no interest in new interpretations. Theirs were all too frequently narrow utilitarian concerns—of a political, military, or economic kind—and they stood to benefit from factual information about contemporary Russia. They did not feel the need to understand the country's past.

For their part, the émigrés endeavored to concentrate on aspects of Russia's past that would be soothing to them in their difficult circumstances and might offer some prospect as building blocks for the future. This double purpose was served on the one hand by an almost reverential interest in modern Russian literature as symbolized by Pushkin, and, on the other hand, by a renewed commitment to their religious past. . . .[T]he latter resulted in the most notable and innovative contributions of émigré scholarship, for it was an area that could not be studied in the Soviet Union. The seminal works of Florovsky and Fedotov, illuminating Russia's religious traditions, proved to be of lasting value both for Western and Russian (including Soviet) interpretations.

What can we say about the Russian intelligentsia's attitude to the past of their country on the basis of their émigré experience? It seems to me that émigré historiography shows that basically the Russian intelligentsia saw history in mainly "instrumental" terms, as a tool for the ongoing critique and struggle against autocracy, which in the 1920s and 1930s was automatically redirected against the Bolshevik regime. There was little interest in the past as something meaningful on its own. True, the émigrés did experience nostalgia for the more recent past; witness the popularity of memoirs and historical fiction. But they turned to literature for inspiration and exemplary lessons. And as had been true of the prerevolutionary intelligentsia, Russian literature of the 1800s, beginning with the Golden Age of Pushkin and concluding with the titanic opuses of Tolstoi and Dostoevsky, was their wellspring of moral and spiritual support and intellectual nourishment.

The Silver Age, it is true, added a significant element: a lively concern for spirituality, philosophy, and religion. However, it also consolidated the rift between those educated as professionals, who were moving away from political engagement and who were receptive to new trends, and those who were politically committed, who maintained the traditions of the positivist, materialist, and ideologically instrumentalist notions of the nineteenth century. The rift was carried over into emigration—as illustrated by the discussions about the relative role of aesthetic and sociopolitical values, or by the emergence of new tastes and norms on the part of those who had matured in Russia Abroad.

Paradoxically, both traditionalism and innovation were to be of seminal influence in the revival of scholarly interest in things Russian in the West in the decades following World War II. This was largely the consequence of the integration into the American (and to a lesser degree English and French) academic world of émigrés who came to the United States in the early 1940s. Only then did Russian scholars find themselves in a position comparable to that of the German–Austrian Jewish émigrés of the 1930s. By the 1940s, the Russians had been absorbed into academe or the professions and could participate and contribute, *à part entière,* to the war effort and subsequent scholarly developments.

Notes

Reprinted here from Marc Raeff, *Russia Abroad: A Cultural History of the Russian Emigration, 1919–1939* (New York: Oxford University Press, 1990): 156–73, 185–86, with the permission of the author.

1. People of the "Great Emigrations" that preceded the Romantic period and the rise of modern nationalism—for example, the Huguenots—did not share this need and problem. Their exile was motivated by religious beliefs, and their frame of reference remained totally religious: the suffering of exile had to be borne as a witness to God's will and for the sake of salvation, not because of some human, historical, secular process. In addition, their sense of "nationality" lacked a historical dimension. Finally, the refugees from Louis XIV's persecution, for example, moved into an international community that readily integrated them. *Im*migration to America, even when triggered by religious or political persecution, was different in essence from an *em*igration of the kind we are concerned with here. We know too little about the scale and nature of "mass" exile or emigration in the still remoter past, from Byzantium or in antiquity, for example, to make any meaningful comparison.

2. I shall not deal with those scholars who took the history of other countries and periods as their professional province—for example, M. Rostovtsev, the historian of antiquity, or A. Vasiliev, the Byzantinist.

3. On this expulsion, see M. Heller, "Premier avertissement: Un coup de fouet (L'histoire de l'expulsion des personnalités culturelles hors de l'Union soviétique en 1922)," *Cahiers du monde russe et soviétique* 20: 2 (April–June 1979): 131–72.

4. Iu. Got′e, *Time of Troubles,* transl. and ed. T. Emmons (Princeton, NJ: Princeton University Press, 1988).

5. *S''ezdy russkikh akademicheskikh organizatsii za granitsei* (Prague, 1923), pp. iii, 3, 5–6.

6. S. Pushkarev, "Russkie v Prage," *Novyi zhurnal* 149 (1982): 150–63. *Russkie v Prage 1918–1928,* ed. S. Postnikov (Prague, 1928).

7. Paul B. Anderson Papers, University Archives, Univ. of Illinois at Urbana-Champaign, Box 10, Edgar McNaughton to Ethan T. Colton, 16 December 1931.

8. Closely related to this form of scholarship were the *Festschriften* in honor of émigré or foreign colleagues. The two most important volumes dedicated to émigré scholars were *Sbornik statei, posviashchennykh Pavlu Nikolaevichu Miliukovu 1859–1929* (Prague, 1929), and *Sbornik statei posviashchennykh Petru Berngardovichu Struve ko dniu tridtsatipiatiletiia ego nauchno-publitsisticheskoi deiatel'nosti 1890 30 ianvaria 1925* (Prague, 1925). An early overview of all this scholarly historical production can be found in Antoine Florovskij, "La littérature russe en émigration—Compte rendu 1927–1929," *Bulletin d'information des sciences historiques en Europe orientale* 3, fasc. 1–2 (Warsaw, 1930), pp. 25–79, and for the years 1921–1926, ibid., 1, 1928, pp. 83–121. See also Wolff Leppmann, "Die russische Geschichtswissenschaft in der Emigration," *Zeitschrift für osteuropäische Geschichte* 1: 2 (1931): 215–48.

9. Viacheslav Ivanov and M.O. Gershenzon, *Perepiska iz dvukh uglov* (Peterburg: Alkonost, 1921) (English trans. by G. Vakar, in *Russian Intellectual History: An Anthology,* ed. M. Raeff [New York: Harcourt Brace, Jovanovich, 1978]).

10. On the German, and generally European, academic immigration to the United States, see *The Intellectual Migration: Europe and America 1930–1960,* ed. D. Fleming and B. Bailyn, vol. 2 of *Perspectives in American History* (Cambridge, MA: Harvard University Press, 1968); Lewis A. Coser, *Refugee Scholars in America: Their Impact and Their Experiences* (New Haven, CT: Yale University Press, 1984); Laura Fermi, *Illustrious Immigrants: The Intellectual Migration from Europe 1930–41,* 2d ed. (Chicago: University of Chicago Press, 1971); and the "soured views" of Anthony Heilbut, *Exiled in Paradise: German Refugees and Intellectuals in America from the 1930s to the Present* (Boston: Beacon Press, 1983).

11. This was the case of M.M. Shtrange, who joined a Communist resistance group during the war and became an agent of the Soviet intelligence establishment in France before returning to Soviet Russia where he gained professional recognition at the Institute of History of the Academy of Sciences as a historian of the French revolution and of its impact on Russia. A.F. Damanskaia, manuscript memoirs, Bakhmeteff Archives.

12. The "history-memoir" of General A. Denikin, *Ocherki russkoi smuty,* 5 vols. (Paris, 1921–26) also belongs to this category. P. Miliukov, *Istoriia vtoroi russkoi revoliutsii,* 3 vols. (Sofia: Rossiisko-Bolgarskoe knigoizdatel'stvo, 1921–24), and *Rossiia na perelome,* 2 vols. (Paris, 1927).

13. Postnikov, *Russkie v Prage; Bibliografiia russkoi revoliutsii i grazhdanskoi voiny, iz kataloga biblioteki russkogo zagranichnogo arkhiva v Prage,* ed. Ia. Slavik, and comp. S. Postnikov (Prague: Rusky, Zahraniční Historicky Archiv v Prage, 1938). Carol A. Leadenham, comp., *Guide to the Collections in the Hoover Institution Archives Relating to Imperial Russia, the Russian Revolution and Civil War, and the First Emigration* (Stanford, CA: Hoover Institution, 1986).

14. W.H. Chamberlain, *The Russian Revolution, 1917–1921* (Princeton, NJ: Princeton University Press, 1987).

15. The historians also contributed memoirs on their own lives and careers, for example, A.A. Kizevetter, *Na rubezhe dvukh stoletii* (Prague: Orbis, 1929); and N. Miliukov, *Vospominaniia, 1859–1917,* 2 vols. (New York: Chekhov Publishing, 1955).

16. *Arkhiv russkoi revoliutsii* 1–22. (ed. I. Gessen, Berlin, 1921–37); *Istorik i sovremennik* 1–5 (ed. I. Petrushevskii, Berlin, 1922–1924); *Na chuzhoi storone* 1–13 (S.

Mel'gunov, ed., Berlin, Prague, 1923–25). The first title was a kind of parallel to the Soviet publication *Krasnyi arkhiv,* whereas the latter was the continuation of the pre-revolutionary *Byloe.*

17. A. Amfiteatrov, "V.O. Kliuchevskii kak khudozhnik slova," *Literaturnyi al'manakh Grani,* 2 vols. (Berlin: Grani, 1922–23), 1: 173–79.

18. Paul Milioukov, C. Seignobos, and L. Eisenmann, *Histoire de Russie,* 3 vols. (Paris: Librairie Ernest Leroux, 1932–35), trans. Charles Lam Markmann as *History of Russia* (New York: Funk and Wagnalls, 1968–69).

19. O. Böss, *Die Lehre der Eurasier* (Wiesbaden, 1961); Nicholas V. Riasanovsky, "The Emergence of Eurasianism," *California Slavic Studies* 4 (1967): 39–72. P. Savitskii developed a theory of spatial movements of civilization depending on the mean yearly temperatures.

20. The New Economic Policy raised the hopes for taming the Bolshevik regime and for greater "legitimacy" of the revolution. But the policies adopted in 1928 left only the "statist" and imperial character of Soviet Russia as a positive element.

21. As E. Gellner put it, "If citizenship, effective membership, 'belonging' but also less sentimentally, effective enjoyment of rights, depends on culture, it follows that loyalties will also be expressed in terms of it. . . . Nationalism hasn't created the situation in which culture defines groups and provides the criterion in which membership and loyalty can be expressed. It is, on the contrary, a consequence of this situation obtaining independently." Ernest Gellner, *Thought and Change* (Chicago: University of Chicago Press, 1964), p. 157.

22. *Vladimirskii sbornik* (Belgrade), 1938, Hoover Institution Archives, S.N. Paléologue Papers.

23. The process itself was viewed more critically in line with A. Presniakov's interpretation in his *Obrazovanie velikorusskogo gosudarstva: Ocherki po istorii XIII–XV stoletii* (St. Petersburg, 1918).

24. Report on discussion in *Poslednie novosti* (Paris), no. 5100, 10 April 1935, p. 3, signed by N.P.V. (Vakar), and the article by D. Odinets, *Sovremennye zapiski* 59 ("Moskovskoe tsarstvo") (1935): 297–317.

25. A.V. Miakotin, *Ocherki sotsial'noi istorii Ukrainy v XVII–XVIII vekakh,* 3 vols. (Prague: Vataga-Plamia, 1924–1926); A. Florovsky's articles are scattered in *Uchenye zapiski uchevnoi kollegii v Prage* and *Nauchnye trudy russkogo narodnogo universiteta v Prage.*

26. S. Pushkarev's studies were republished in a revised edition, *Krest'ianskaia pozemel'no-peredel'naia obshchina v Rossii* (Newtonville, MA: Oriental Research Partners, 1976); V.B. El'iashevich, *Istoriia prava pozemel'noi sobstvennosti v Rossii,* 2 vols. (Paris, 1948–1951); P.B. Struve, *Sotsial'naia i ekonomicheskaia istoriia Rossii* (Paris, 1952). Struve also wrote the chapter on Russian serfdom in the first volume of *The Cambridge Economic History of Europe,* 1st ed. (Cambridge: Cambridge University Press, 1941).

27. S. Svatikov, *Rossiia i Don, 1549–1917* (Belgrade, 1924); Boris Nolde, *La Formation de l'empire russe: Etudes, notes et documents,* 2 vols. (Paris, 1952–1953); V.A. Riasanovskii, *Mongol'skoe pravo* (Harbin, 1931), his *Obychnoe pravo mongol'skikh plemen* (Harbin, 1924), and his *Fundamental Principles of Mongol Law* (Tientsin, [Tianjin] 1937). His historical survey of Russian culture was written and published after World War II in the United States.

II

The Individual Practitioners

10

Christianity, Science, and Progress in Sergei M. Solov'ev's *History of Russia*

Ana Siljak

Sergei M. Solov'ev, the Russian participant in the grand tradition of nine-teenth-century national history, is best known today for his attempt to write the definitive, multivolume work on the history of Russia. His *History of Russia from the Earliest Times,* begun in 1851, had reached an immense twenty-nine volumes by 1876 and was still unfinished when he died in 1879. Both his careful use of documentary material and his search for unifying themes within Russian history influenced an entire generation of Russian historians. Solov'ev's importance in Russian historiography is dif-ficult to exaggerate—he was in many ways analogous to the classic nine-teenth-century historians of the West, such as Gardiner, Macaulay, or Michelet. His student V.O. Kliuchevskii said of Solov'ev that all later Rus-sian historians began where his work ended; he characterized Solov'ev as the "lighthouse" that guided the progress of Russian history.[1]

While Solov'ev's importance is uncontested, the precise nature of his influence has eluded commentators. Traditionally, historians have placed Solov'ev squarely within the "state school" of Russian history, arguing that the most salient aspect of his historical approach was a Hegelian emphasis on the Russian state as the most important factor in the modernization of the Russian nation. This interpretive line argues that, like Hegel, Solov'ev fo-cused almost exclusively on high politics and viewed the Russian autocracy as the instrument propelling Russian history. For many, Solov'ev typifies the conservative approach to history that can be so sharply contrasted to his populist and progressive contemporaries.[2] Other historians have added to the portrait of Solov'ev as a conservative by emphasizing his Romantic nationalism: they argue that Solov'ev primarily strove to create through his history an organic national consciousness in the wake of the Napoleonic wars.[3] Some historians have found Solov'ev's conservatism mitigated by positivist tendencies within his work and have suggested that he was influenced by such English positivists as the historian Henry T. Buckle and by Herbert Spencer. To these (mostly Soviet) historians, Solov'ev was elevated from the "conservative-reactionary" historical school into the "bourgeois-liberal" school by the fact that he accepted the characterization of society as an organism governed by laws of nature, and the accompanying characterization of the historian as scientist.[4] The existing literature on Solov'ev thus variously declares him to be a statist, a Romantic, or a positivist and seeks to reconcile these characterizations with his seemingly indisputable conservatism and nationalism.

Part of the confusion as to Solov'ev's place within the Russian historiographical tradition stems from Solov'ev's general reticence on the matter of intellectual influences. He wrote few essays that dealt with his views on history in general, and he rarely referenced the ideas of other historians in his purely historical writings. Historians have thus been free to speculate about the impact of various ideas on Solov'ev's historical approach. It is, perhaps, natural to assume that Solov'ev was a Hegelian historian, since the philosopher had a tremendous impact on Russian intellectual life during Solov'ev's university years. In that sense he could not escape the indirect, pervasive influence of the philosopher's ideas. In his own memoirs, however, he does hint at his own doubts about the Hegelian approach to history. He found Hegelian abstractions insufficiently historical, and he felt Hegelianism to be ultimately incompatible with his Christian faith. "From Hegel's works I read only the 'Philosophy of History,' " he wrote, "it made a great impression on me and for a few months I became a Protestant, but it did not go further than that; religious sentiment had rooted itself too deeply within my soul."[5] Equally speculative is the oft-remarked influence of the positivists Herbert Spencer and Henry Buckle on Solov'ev's historical thought. Solov'ev's descriptions of society as an "organism" subject to "laws of development" are definitely comparable with those of Herbert Spencer and Henry Buckle, but the works of both men had been published after Solov'ev had already substantially formulated his historical approach.[6]

A fuller picture of Solov'ev's historical thought must include themes that have been substantially underemphasized in the existing historical literature. One such neglected theme is Solov'ev's firm belief in history as the narrative of continuous development, improvement, and "progress." It is with this ostensibly conservative historian that we first find a deep faith in the beneficial and inevitable qualities of human progress. Solov'ev's conviction that Russia was a member of those chosen European nations destined continually to perfect their social and political systems lay at the base of all his writings on Russian history. A related and similarly underemphasized premise of Solov'ev's work was the importance of the natural-scientific method in historical writing. Solov'ev believed that all societies, like all natural phenomena, were governed by the same fundamental "laws," and thus the historian had to approach any society using the methods of the natural scientist. For Solov'ev, the history of any given nation was "the science of national self-consciousness," and world history was "the science of the self-consciousness of all humanity."[7] Finally, the importance of Solov'ev's deeply Christian faith for his approach to history has been consistently ignored. "It occurred to me to study philosophy so that I could use its methods in order to affirm religion, Christianity," he wrote about the effect of reading Hegel as a student at Moscow University, "but abstraction was not for me; I was born a historian."[8] For Solov'ev, history could be used as a means of proving the superiority of the Christian faith.

Solov'ev's belief in progress and science and his Christian faith were intimately connected into a single historical worldview. To understand the strong connection between these three elements of his historical thought, it is necessary to explore the historical writings of the man Solov'ev admired most: the French historian François Guizot. Guizot, a devout Christian himself, had set himself the task of elucidating the importance of science, progress, and Christian belief for historical study in his lectures on *The History of Civilization in Europe*. It is not surprising, then, that Solov'ev characterized himself as a "follower" of Guizot. Solov'ev's student V.O. Kliuchevskii declared in stronger terms that "of all the representatives of European historiography of the nineteenth century, [Solov'ev] did not respect anyone as much as Guizot."[9] A comparison between the work of Guizot and Solov'ev can shed light on the important premises upon which Solov'ev constructed his history of Russia, and it can better elucidate the significance of Solov'ev's writings for future generations of Russian historians.

Sergei Solov'ev was born in 1820, the son of a clergyman and a nobleman's daughter. Through the influence of his mother, Solov'ev was encouraged to aspire to a position beyond the limits of the clerical estate, and he received a gymnasium education instead of the seminary education usually provided for sons of the clergy.[10] Solov'ev himself had a negative opinion of his father's profession, and he began his autobiography with a strident critique of the Russian Orthodox clergy. He complained that priests were ill-educated, backward, poor, and unwashed, and thus never respectable in polite company. The monastic clergy were even worse, entering the monastic orders in order to achieve positions of power and thus leave their "slave status."[11] But Solov'ev's opinions about the Orthodox clergy had little effect on his commitment to the Orthodox Christian faith. Solov'ev recalled that even as a gymnasium student he had sought various means to express his deep piety, desiring, even then, to "construct a philosophical system which . . . would put an end to atheism." It is unclear how much Solov'ev knew about Orthodox theology, for he rarely discussed theological matters in his works. Nonetheless, despite what he thought to be the sorry state of the Orthodox Church, Solov'ev did believe that Orthodox Christianity had a promising future. Eventually, he believed, both Protestants and Catholics would grow disenchanted with their respective religions, and the Russian people, emerging out of their backwardness, would proclaim the power of the Orthodox faith in the world.[12]

Solov'ev's interest in history began at a very young age (he claimed to have read Nikolai Karamzin's *History of the Russian State* twelve times before the age of thirteen), and it was therefore of no surprise that he chose to study Russian history under M. Pogodin at Moscow University.[13] After graduating from the university in 1842, he accompanied the Stroganov family as a tutor on a nearly two-year tour of Europe and it was on this trip that he became more closely acquainted with Western historical thought, attending lectures in Paris and Berlin and meeting with a group of Czech Slavophiles in Prague.[14] According to his own memoirs, the combined influences of his fervent Orthodoxy, his encounters with what he believed to be the corrupt and "foreign" nature of the Russian aristocracy, and his experiences as a Russian traveling abroad led to his initial fascination with the ideas of the Slavophiles, particularly with their romantic notions of the importance of the Russian peasantry and their glorification of the values of Russian Orthodoxy.[15]

Very quickly, however, Solov'ev's religious and historical views led him to reject the Slavophile conception of Russia. In the first place, he was suspicious of the Slavophile use of Orthodox Christianity to prove the uniqueness of the Russian national idea, distrusting those who, "without believing in Christ," spoke of "the superiority of Orthodoxy over other confessions." In the realm of Russian history, Solov'ev was continually amused by the Slavophile misunderstandings of Russian history; and he was particularly offended by their insistence that Russia was not European, by their "endless phrases about the decay of the West, about the superiority of the East, of Orthodoxy."[16] He had a special hatred for the minister of education under Nicholas I, Sergei Uvarov, whom he called a "lackey" for inventing the supposedly Russian national principles of "Orthodoxy, Autocracy, Nationality." Solov'ev believed that Uvarov, like many other Russian nationalists, was dedicated to the values of "Orthodoxy—as an unbeliever, failing to believe in Christ even in the Protestant sense; autocracy—as a liberal; and nationality—having read not a single Russian book in his life, writing constantly in French and German."[17] Solov'ev claimed that it was particularly his immersion in Russian history that "saved him from Slavophilism" and helped to contain his patriotism "within the necessary limits."[18] By the time he had defended his thesis for the master's degree in 1845, Solov'ev had fully embraced the ideas of the Russian "Westernizers" about the backward and primitive nature of Russia's past and the need for Russia to continue to modernize its institutions, laws, and culture according to the Western model. Although these opinions initially led Solov'ev into conflict with his Slavophile advisor, M. Pogodin, other Westernizers in the Department of History at Moscow University were delighted by his views, and in 1845 Solov'ev had received an appointment as lecturer in Russian history at the university.

In 1847, Solov'ev published his dissertation on "The History of the Relations between the Russian Princes of the House of Riurik," and from then on he continued diligently writing and lecturing until the end of his life. In 1851, a year after being appointed as full professor at Moscow University, he began to publish his *History of Russia from the Earliest Times,* and finished with his twenty-ninth volume in 1876. Although the focus of his writing career was always his *History,* he wrote a number of essays and lectures in which he sketched out many of the broader themes that would later be used in his main work. He retired from the university in 1875 because of the Ministry of Education's attack on "liberalism" among professors in that year, and he died in 1879.[19]

Solov'ev's attacks on the Slavophile conception of Russian history, and his criticism of Romantic nationalism in general exposed the premises upon which his own historical worldview was founded. His "Historical Letters," written in 1858, directly attacked both German and Russian Romantic nationalism, characterizing it as "Buddhism."[20] Buddhism, as Solov'ev understood it, originated in India as a result of that culture's simple inability to "struggle with life." Due to its "fear of progress," India clung to a religion that preached contentment and peace with things as they were. A similar fear of progress could be found in various other nations at various times in history, and corresponding "Buddhist"-like doctrines arose as a response. Solov'ev even traced the decline of the ancient Greek world to the same desire to stop the clock and return society to its "original simplicity." In his view, Plato's *Republic* was an expression of the yearning to keep society under strict discipline.[21] Modern-day "Buddhists," as Solov'ev termed both the German Romantic nationalists and the Slavophiles who imitated them, also desired to avoid the difficulties and evils of progress and therefore mistakenly sought perfection in a medieval past where they believed life was rural, simple, family-oriented, and moral.[22]

For Solov'ev, Romantic nationalist views of the past were simply a reflection of historical ignorance. Anyone who truly understood medieval life in Germany or in Russia knew the poverty and barbarism of those times and knew that fear of violence and lack of education forced people to live narrow lives confined to the class and place in which they were born.[23] A truly historical view of the world would encourage people to understand the concept of progress, of the movement from a dark, unenlightened, and dangerous existence into a world where "the walls that separated people came down," and people were able to live more open and free lives, "not fearing for their safety, able to travel and act freely." Through historical progress, Solov'ev wrote, men freed themselves from "tight, closed communities" and joined the larger and more benevolent state that protected them from arbitrary violence and allowed them to trade, own property, and develop culturally.[24] Furthermore, only in a society that was progressing could a person become increasingly independent of his class or his community and become an individual endowed with both rights and responsibilities.[25]

This conception of history as the chronicle of progress, with its emphasis on the tight connection between the power of the state and the freedom of the individual, bears unmistakable resemblance to Hegel's concept of world history; and this evidence has been used to prove the connection between Hegel and Solov'ev.[26] But a closer look at the writings of François Guizot demonstrate that what seems to be the influence of Hegel can be more accurately interpreted as the result of the impact of the French historian on Solov'ev's thought.

Guizot, born in 1787 into a Protestant family, had a distinguished career as both a politician and a historian.[27] The most intense period of his scholarly career occurred between 1820 and 1830, when he published his most famous works: *Essays on the History of France, History of the Revolution in England,* and the compilations of his lectures *History of Civilization in France* and *History of Civilization in Europe.* He was a contemporary of Hegel's, lecturing in history at the Sorbonne at the same time that Hegel was lecturing in Berlin. There is evidence that he may have been familiar with Hegel's works, for apparently his knowledge of and fascination with German philosophy caused him to be accused of being "too German."[28]

Like Hegel, Guizot believed that world history should be understood in terms of gradual human progress or, in his terms, the growth of "civiliza-tion." Civilization, for Guizot, was both a process of historical development through which societies passed and a goal to which all societies had to aspire. A civilized society was one in which both the life of the individual and the relationships between individuals were constantly improving—ma-terially, morally, and intellectually. Societies on the road to civilization could be distinguished by their continual understanding and respect for the freedom of the individual, combined with a growing understanding of the necessity for a harmonious interrelation among individuals in a free society governed by a free state.[29]

In this sense, Guizot certainly shared Hegel's conviction that the historical process was governed by universal laws of development, with Western Europe as the culmination of this historical process. In contrast to Hegel, however, Guizot was careful to explain that the concept of civilization could not remain a purely abstract idea, since people had to transform "ideas into facts." Truly harmonious interactions between the individual and society could always be measured in terms of concrete effects, such as political, social, and economic institutions. In fact, Guizot criticized the ineffectuality of German philosophy, claiming that the French capability of transforming ideas into concrete social progress was far superior to any abstract German intellectual achievement.[30]

More substantively, Guizot took issue with the Hegelian metaphysical approach to history and its use of concepts such as "Spirit" and "Idea." He much preferred the work of the natural scientists of his day, who emphasized that no grand notions could be arrived at without "facts." "In every direc-tion," he wrote, "the scientific method is extending and establishing itself; in every direction the necessity is more and more felt of taking facts as the basis and rule of our proceedings. Facts are now in the intellectual order, the power in authority."[31] According to Guizot, the historian had to imitate the scientists and similarly regard facts as the most durable aspects of the past and use them to build the historical narrative.[32] Rather than launching grand philosophical schemes, the historian had to generalize "slowly, progres-sively, concurrently with the ascertainment of facts." Only through the pains-taking accumulation of evidence could historians eventually develop a "physiology" of history, which would consist of "the secret laws which preside over the course of events." Guizot believed that just as scientists had begun to understand the laws that governed astronomy, so historians could begin to understand the laws that governed human development.[33]

Solov'ev, as we have seen, shared with Guizot and Hegel the concept of history as progress and the belief in Western Europe as the culmination of the historical process. For Solov'ev, the great task of the Russian historian was to determine Russia's place in the history of European civilization.

Even though Solov'ev could not write as confidently of Russia as Guizot did of France, Solov'ev firmly believed that Russia followed Europe along the path of progress. Civilization, for Solov'ev, came later for Russia, moving, as he put it "from West to East." But the advent of civilization for Russia was inevitable, because, in Solov'ev's words, "civilization had thrown its net upon the Russian people."[34]

In his methodological approach to Russian history, Solov'ev sided with Guizot in rejecting the abstract, metaphysical method of Hegel's history. Solov'ev could not see history as the unfolding of a metaphysical "Idea," because he found such "abstraction" to be dangerously inaccurate. He shared Guizot's belief that the correct historical method had to begin with the facts and then proceed toward the larger generalizations. "In history," he wrote, "as in the natural sciences, only the most careful, exact and microscopic observations of all phenomena at various times and various places can free one from drawing untrue conclusions about the general laws of observed life."[35] Solov'ev believed that all phenomena, biological and historical, were governed by the same universal principles or laws. Societies and nations could not be excepted from the laws of nature: "Nations live and develop according to known laws, pass through known stages, like individual people, like all that is living, all that is organic."[36] In terminology strikingly similar to that of Guizot, Solov'ev wrote of the necessity for the historian to be a "physiologist," who could show "the connections between events, . . . unifying separate parts into one organic whole."[37]

Solov'ev followed Guizot in using biological metaphors in his historical writing. Just as biology had determined that different organisms were destined to develop differently, so historians had to see that different human societies had different histories—some were destined to progress, while others were not. "An organic body, the nation," Solov'ev wrote, "grows, . . . finding hidden within itself health or sickness, strength or weakness, and at the same time is subject to beneficial or harmful external conditions."[38] Knowing this, Solov'ev believed that the historian was required to put the same questions to a society that a natural scientist might ask in order to understand the life of a plant or animal. The historian had to determine for each society "the nature of the country which it inhabits, the nature of the tribe to which it belongs; and the course of external events, influences, which come from the nations that surround it."[39]

Solov'ev's interest in natural-scientific methods shed new light on his insistence on the importance of geography in history. For him, the question of "the nature of the country"—the geographical environment in which a society lived—was the one with which the historian had to begin. It was here that Solov'ev found one of the first clues to Russia's backwardness: it was of no small importance that the Russian climate and geography were less favorable for human life than the European. Europe was blessed by many beneficial natural phenomena: "the proximity of the sea, of long mountain chains, the ease of internal lines of communication . . . the mild nature of the climate without African heat and Asian frost." Russia, by contrast, was a wide expanse without natural frontiers to thwart invaders; its very size meant difficulty in communication; and the soil and climate were particularly harsh. Solov'ev's metaphorical formulation of the difference between European and Russian geography was that in Europe, nature was a "mother," whereas in Russia, it was a "stepmother."[40] Nonetheless, if the organism was strong enough to withstand it, such a set of natural conditions could have beneficial effects on development. "Nature that is more frugal with its gifts," he wrote, "demands constant, difficult work from a man and keeps him constantly active."[41]

From understanding the geographical environment of a given society, the historian had to turn to the innate characteristics of the society itself. Again, Solov'ev used biological metaphors in describing the characteristics of Russian society. Some societies and cultures, like some biological organisms, were destined to develop more fully than others. The Russians, for Solov'ev, were capable of flourishing despite their difficult environment, because they were a "young, fresh, and powerful nation."[42] The advantage for Russia lay in the fact that Russia was of European, "Arian" stock; and the "Arian race" was, according to him, "beloved of history."[43]

Again, this conception of an inherent, organic, and, in the end, racial distinction among different cultures was shared by Solov'ev and Guizot. Guizot, like Hegel, made a fundamental distinction between what he called "Asian" and "European" societies; but unlike Hegel, he described the distinction using natural-scientific terms. Just as in biology one learned that simpler or more "primitive" organisms were characterized by their "unity" of form, so ancient and primitive populations such as the Asian were, for Guizot, characterized by their "unity." A primitive society, Guizot believed, attached itself to "a solitary, dominant principle, which determined its institutions, its customs, its creeds"—such a principle could be a particular religion or a particular political system. A unitary society was despotic by nature, concentrating all political and social power into the hands of one man or one idea, denying any freedom or respect for the human individual, and careful to "stifle . . . the principle of liberty." Moreover, such societies were stagnant: they did not progress, did not move forward; and in them, "immobility" characterized the morality of the people.[44] By contrast, just as more advanced biological organisms were more complex and diverse, so Guizot believed that Europe, unlike Asia, developed an incredible diversity throughout its history and was composed of a variety of creeds, political views, and classes. The battles between these various elements energized European society, caused it to grow and develop, and prevented the dominance of any one principle for too long. Thus Europe was governed by a balance of diverse forces, and from this diversity came a respect for the human individual, for "the development of man himself, of his faculties, his sentiments, his ideas."[45]

Solov'ev took this idea of a fundamental, organic distinction between Asian and European societies and used it to explain the course of Russian history. He agreed with Guizot that just as growth from "a seed to a tree, or an egg to an animal" were the characteristics of all biological organisms, so human societies developed from the simple to the more complex, from uniformity to "division of tasks" and "separate organs of society."[46]

For Solov'ev, the primary stage of social organization, in all societies, was clan life (*rodovoi byt*). In such societies, the extended family came before all else and was the primary unit of allegiance for all individuals. Through patriarchal relations, a hierarchy was set up which placed the father over the son, the older over the younger, the man above the woman. Such society was "conservative" in its preference for the "customs of the fathers," and it insisted on the complete subordination of the individual to the family in rights, actions, and property. This division of society into clans welcomed the appearance of a single ruler, who, like the patriarch of the clan, subordinated all of society to his personal will. Society then surrendered all of its freedom to this one man and demanded only to be left in peace. Like Guizot, Solov'ev characterized Asian society as simple or unitary, or in his words, "centralized and all-powerful." Clan life agreed with the Asian conception of passivity and indolence; it left the individual alone to pursue his modest private needs and never demanded activity, movement, or progress.[47]

In Europe, in contrast, dissatisfaction with the passive and immobile clan form of social organization rescued societies from the threat of stagnation. As far back as ancient Greece and Rome, the historian could find the development of the militia (*druzhina*), a form of political and social organization that challenged the clan. A *druzhina*, according to Solov'ev, was composed of people who broke away from their families due to their dissatisfaction with their modest, "peaceful existence," and who sought to satisfy their existential needs "through battle." Such men banded together into a company, in which the organizing principle was no longer hierarchy, but the equality of "comradeship." When the *druzhina* chose its leader, it did so not in order to become "subjects," but rather to find someone who would respect its members' equality. In Solov'ev's words, in a *druzhina* "everyone knows his power, everyone knows his worth, even the leader, whose relationship to his fellow *druzhina* is that of the older comrade."[48] In ancient Greece, where the *druzhina* first appeared as a phenomenon, the effects of this type of social organization were extremely beneficial. For Solov'ev, the *druzhina* introduced the principles of diversity, complexity, and movement that helped society to break away from the stagnant, primitive clan form of life. The despotism of a single individual was unknown; and, when the *druzhina* settled down and became a legitimate government, its members demanded that the previous free relations between individuals be preserved. The notion of equality became codified into a legal system in which all are subject to law as something "firm, eternal, godly." The urge for continual movement led to the development of diverse, independent cities in Greece, as well as to trade and economic growth. Finally, the respect for all individuals was great in ancient Greece, leading to the "powerful development of the human personality." Thus the settled *druzhina* was transformed into a legitimate state in which reigned law, autonomy, and freedom of the individual.[49]

These fundamental, organic distinctions between Asia and Europe, between the clan and the *druzhina,* were the basic concepts Solov'ev used in formulating his narrative of Russian history. Russia's past, for Solov'ev, unmistakably contained elements of Asian unity and European diversity. For Solov'ev, Russia had always been on the outskirts of Europe, on the border between "European quality" and "Asian quantity."[50] The consequences of such proximity were grave. Not only did Russia have to defend itself from the continuous attacks on its borders by Asian tribes, but Russia itself embodied the conflict between the Asian and the European forms of social and cultural life. Russian history was shaped, in part, by the struggle to conquer the remnants of the Asian forms of life within.

Solov'ev argued that the clan system of social organization existed in Russia from the earliest times: long before the formation of the Russian state, Slavic tribes had lived in clans.[51] This type of social organization had negative consequences for Russia's growth. Not only did the clan forms of communal property and communal agriculture spell, in Solov'ev's words, "economic and general underdevelopment and an equality of poverty," but before the Russian state developed, clashes between clans had led to general chaos and civil strife within the countryside. In comparing medieval Russia to medieval Europe, the historian had to see that Russian society had to leave "such a way of life behind in order to develop."[52] If Russia was to avoid the stagnation of its Asian neighbors, other principles had to be introduced into society, including "the development of the individual . . . a division of tasks . . . social principles other than blood ties."[53]

Fortunately, Russia was also blessed with the presence of the social institution of the *druzhina*. It is perhaps fitting that Solov'ev construed the entrance of the European phenomenon of the *druzhina* into Russia literally as the invasion of the Norman militias onto Russian soil. The Slavic tribes, he argued, had realized the dangerous chaos that their clan life had brought them; they therefore "invited" a foreign tribe to act as "a single, general authority to bring together the various clans into a united whole."[54] Thus, with the arrival of the first Norman *druzhina* in Russia, the Russian state was born. As in ancient Greece, the *druzhina* was organized around a prince, who was not an absolute ruler, but rather acted as an "older brother." Members of the *druzhina* were free to serve the prince as long as they wished, and if disagreements arose, they were equally free to join the company of another prince. According to Solov'ev, this principle of sociopolitical organization existed in Russia until the fifteenth century: Russia was ruled by princes and their armed companies, who lived in a state of continual movement from city to city. As Solov'ev had argued in the case of ancient Greece, the sociopolitical principle of the *druzhina* had beneficial consequences for Russian society. It served to break up the stagnant quality of clan life, and it introduced the principles of movement, action, and individual freedom into society. It prevented the formation of a centralized, despotic, "Asian" form of government.[55]

Nonetheless, this move toward a freer, livelier, and more diverse form of social organization was not without its harmful consequences. As Guizot had warned in his *History of Civilization in Europe,* complex social organisms, like complex biological organisms, required more vigilant effort in order to keep the different aspects of the organism in harmony. For Guizot, the history of ancient Rome demonstrated how the development of diversity within society and the greater respect for the individual could potentially lead to social fragmentation.[56] Even those Germanic barbarians so beloved by Hegel exhibited this tendency toward destructive individualism. According to Guizot, the lesson to be learned from observing the medieval Germanic tribes was that "wherever man considers no one but himself, . . . society . . . becomes for him almost impossible."[57] Excessive individual freedom, too much movement from place to place, and the absence of bonds holding individuals together could also hasten the disintegration of society.

According to Solov'ev, such difficulties precisely characterized the history of Russia well up until the fifteenth century. The *druzhina* principle meant that princes and their militias moved from place to place, individual members of the militia went from prince to prince, and elites never settled down sufficiently to build long-lasting institutions—to invest in land, agriculture, and the building of cities and towns. Moreover, satisfied with their primitive freedoms, members of a *druzhina* were never forced to develop a sense of their corporate rights and privileges.[58] Although Solov'ev believed that the *druzhina* had the necessary effect of breaking up the stagnant qualities of the original Slavic clans, he also saw the *druzhina* principle as a chaotic force that prevented the development of a stable Russian governmental system.[59]

To become a stable, unified, advanced, and fully European state, Russia had to move beyond both the clan and *druzhina* principles and develop what he called "the state [*pravitel'stvennyi*] principle" of government and the "civic" form of social structure.[60] The ruling elite had to be bound together not by the ties of kinship but rather with relations of an official, "administrative" nature. This would end the inevitable clashes between clans in their struggles for power. At the same time, the freedom of movement allowed by the *druzhina* principle also had to be curtailed: elites had to settle down, take up agricultural activities, and invest in the development of cities and trade. Finally, the Russian individual had to break out from subordination to the family and understand his or her own independent worth, both demanding the protection of individual rights and offering individual loyalty to the society that was beyond that of the immediate clan.[61]

Russian history was thus the struggle to conquer both the clan and *druzhina* principles in government and society, and the struggle was not an easy one. Conflicts between the elements of Asian and European culture within Russia led to strife and discord. Resorting again to organic metaphors, Solov'ev argued that Russian history, perhaps well up until the time of Peter the Great, was a chronicle of the diseases of the Russian organism: "Strong were the illnesses in the unsettled young body, but thanks to that youth strong were also the forces that could counteract that illness, protecting the body from destruction."[62] Russian history was also the story of how Russia was able to conquer its "illnesses" and finally enter into European civilization, the story of "the growth of the state together with the development and growth of the people."[63]

What stands out most clearly in this account of Russian history is the belief that Russia, as a European country, was destined to progress, regardless of difficulties encountered along the way. The belief was justified through the use of natural-scientific metaphors—comparing Russia to a biological organism living in a harsh environment and beset by diseases, which nonetheless, through its physical hardiness, was able to survive and flourish. In Solov'ev, there is a strong sense of an emerging faith, in the inevitable and beneficial qualities of progress for those societies destined to experience it, combined with a faith in the power of empirical, scientific research to confirm the results of human progress at every level of social and political life. Solov'ev's affinity with Guizot stems from their shared conviction that science and progress were intimately intertwined and confirmed the beneficial and rational order of human history. For both men, exhaustive study of the material building blocks of history would serve to confirm the universality of the laws that govern human life and would prove conclusively that these laws were designed for human benefit.

This shared faith in science and progress, for both Solov'ev and Guizot, cannot be fully understood without recognizing the religious sentiment that propelled it. For both men, the inevitability of progress and the success of scientific method were unthinkable without a guiding Christian faith. And it was their particular interpretation of the Christian religion that led them to believe that faith in the benevolence of God could translate, on earth, into the beneficial arrangement of the material world. Guizot believed that it could be specifically proven that progress toward civilization was accomplished only through the advent and spread of Christianity, and that science would serve only to confirm the intentions of God. For this reason, in his *History of Civilization* Guizot sought to prove that Christianity had practical benefits for the nations that accepted it. In the first place, Christianity placed great value on the individual, for it "changed the internal man, creeds, sentiments, and . . . it regenerated the moral man, the intellectual man." As a faith, Christianity placed great moral responsibilities upon the individual and simultaneously respected his free will. But Christianity also prevented the social fragmentation that could accompany the excessive emphasis on individual freedom. Faith bound society together by teaching the individual that "there was a law superior to human laws," and by directing the individual to something transcending personal interests. Because Christians voluntarily united in the name of a higher principle, this unity could become the basis of a harmonious, free society.[64] Most importantly, however, with the acceptance of Christianity, Christian nations were endowed with "the idea of progress." Guizot explicitly argued that progress and civilization were the gifts of Providence to Christian nations and that they were a blessing of God. "European civilization," he wrote, "has entered, if we may so speak, into the eternal truth, into the plan of Providence; it progresses according to the intentions of God." The history of European civilization, for Guizot, was thus "the rational account" of Europe's "superiority."[65]

Solov'ev's deep Christian faith similarly supported his faith in progress. Like Guizot, Solov'ev interpreted Christianity as having practical, material benefits for the societies that espoused it. Christianity, for example, gave a society good warriors. Since the Christian religion required of the individual "love for his neighbor," Solov'ev argued, every man had to understand this in the most practical sense: "Love for the neighbor not in words, but in actions. . . . If the neighbor is attacked, the responsibility of the Christian is to defend him to the last drop of blood." The Christian, required to serve his state, was visibly more patriotic: "A second demand of Christianity is the fulfillment of all given responsibilities, faithful and diligent service to existing authority." Thus the modern, Christian European proved his superiority to the pagan through his victories in battle and his patriotic sentiment. Furthermore, Christianity beneficially regulated family relationships. In the first place, it protected the woman from being treated as an "object," specifically by preventing polygamy and bride capture. In the second place, it laid the foundation for the development of society through the division of tasks between men and women, giving men the "external, social activities" and women "the internal and domestic." As Solov´ev explained, this division of labor was "the blessing of civilization."[66] Finally, Christianity encouraged the growth of respect for the individual, not only by asserting the importance of individual rights, but also by giving each person "the consciousness of his moral strength, his need for continuous development."[67]

In writing his accounts of the history of Russia, Solov´ev gave many concrete examples where the Russian Orthodox Church had been a particularly beneficial influence throughout Russian history. Again using organic metaphors, he argued that Christianity was the very "medicine" that counteracted the diseases of the Russian organism and gave it the "extraordinarily powerful spiritual forces" that it needed to survive its difficult environment.[68] In the first place, the Church had struck at the root of the clan system by regulating family life. No longer could the head of the clan act as a quasi-religious figure, for the Church made sure that the rights of all members of the clan were respected and demanded that the family open itself up to the wider Christian community. This, according to Solov´ev, meant that the Church facilitated the transformation "from the old forms of clan life to the new, civic forms."[69] The Orthodox Church also played a great role in mitigating the effects of the *druzhina*. In the Kievan period of Russian history, while the *druzhina* was moving from place to place, the clergy remained "with their flock," exercising a stabilizing effect on the Russian population. In the later, Muscovite period, the Orthodox Metropolitan bishops supported the rise of a centralized and unified state authority within Moscow "with all their resources."[70] The Orthodox Church in Russia also exerted its influence in order to bring education and enlightenment to the Russian people, and monasteries and churches took on the task of helping the Russians out of their ignorance.[71] Finally, it was the Church that consistently gave the Russian people the spiritual strength to withstand all their trials, reminding the population that "the foundation of society is sacrifice."[72]

More importantly, however, Solov´ev followed Guizot in believing that the crucial distinction between Russia and the rest of the world lay in the fact that Russia, as a Christian nation, was destined to be a part of the eternal and inevitable progress toward civilization, regardless of the obstacles it encountered along the way. Solov'ev believed that the Christian religion, through its insistence on the moral perfection of the individual, held up a virtually impossible, unattainable standard to its believers. In Solov'ev's words, Christianity held up to man "a being that was perfect and demanded moral perfection of man." In trying to achieve this standard, Christians constantly sought to perfect their society, to unite it through religious precepts, and to respect their fellow men, according them equality and freedom. This search for perfection never allowed for contentment, for reconciliation with the present; rather, it encouraged forward movement and progress. And it was this constant desire to progress that formed a civilized country. "Civilization" was a mark of distinction of those societies that refused to remain static, that were continuously struggling with their imperfections. Solov'ev, using Guizot's exact words, declared that a civilized society was motivated by this "idea of progress" that could only have come from a Christian faith.[73]

It was erroneous, Solov'ev wrote, for Russian historians to attempt to prove the civilized nature of Russian society by pointing to the presence of laws, trade, and industry in Russia's medieval past. After all, Solov'ev argued, "Indians and Chinese" had the same things, and yet they remained barbarian. "A barbarian people," he explained, "is one that has befriended the deficiencies of its social structure ... and does not wish to hear of anything better." Russia might look uncivilized on the surface, because there was no doubt that it was backward, poor, and "at the borders of Europe." Nonetheless, Russia was European, because Christianity gave it the will to be dissatisfied with the backwardness of its own society and gave it the power to move forward, improve, and progress. By reminding the Russians of the fact that there was always a higher ideal to which to aspire, Christianity had kept the Russians in a state of constant dissatisfaction with their present lot, and had urged them to improve themselves both materially and morally. Russia had left its barbarianism behind; it had understood the principle that "others have it better." This turn from "good to evil" was possible only because of Christianity, which had continuously reminded the Russians of "the higher spiritual principles with which the society could be saved."[74] Like Guizot, Solov'ev believed that Russian progress was a gift of Providence to a believing nation. Progress, then, was the destiny of the chosen Christian nations and the mark of their faith; it was "the flag, upon which it is written, 'the golden age is ahead.'"[75]

Because of their faith in Christianity and its power to bring civilization to society, both Solov'ev and Guizot were confident that the scientific method would confirm the inevitability of Christian progress through a patient accumulation of facts. Since the world was organized according to God's will, all aspects of that world could confirm the providential nature of growth and progress. Just as biologists could determine the processes of the growth of an organism, and point to the inexorable paths that this growth had to take, so historians, according to Guizot and Solov'ev, could map out the course of social progress and similarly find the laws that determined the nature of that progress. Forward movement, development, growth—these were all the beneficial qualities possessed by healthy natural organisms, and this meant that healthy societies had to have these qualities as well. Neither man had any doubt that the scientific study of history would prove that progress was the material manifestation of God's benevolence. Guizot went so far as to declare that science was therefore a "moral" discipline, and its study an aspect of religious faith. In his words:

> Science is a beautiful thing, undoubtedly, and of itself well worth all of the labor that man may bestow upon it; but it becomes a thousand times grander and more beautiful when it becomes a parent of virtue. This, then, is what we have to do . . . to discover the truth, to realise it . . . in external facts, for the benefit of society; in ourselves to convert it into a faith capable of inspiring us with disinterestedness and moral energy, the force and dignity of man in this world.[76]

This faith in science and progress, so closely connected to religious faith, was one of the most significant contributions of Solov'ev and Guizot to the Russian historiographical tradition. Indeed, it is not accidental that the work of both men so closely resembles that of positivists in both France and Russia.[77] Particularly in Russia, Solov'ev's admiration for Guizot was shared by writers of various convictions. Nikolai Chernyshevskii called Guizot a "first-class mind," and was inspired from his works to believe, like Solov'ev, that historians could "clarify the laws to which the fate of humanity is subject." His conclusion, after reading Guizot, was that "History is faith in progress."[78] Similarly, when Vasilii Kliuchevskii was asked how he developed his "social-historical" views, he first mentioned "*The History of Civilization* of Guizot."[79]

The works of Solov'ev also had a similar effect on a diverse range of writers and thinkers. Later historians such as Kliuchevskii and Sergei Platonov were influenced precisely by Solov'ev's conception of history as a science of human progress. Indeed, Kliuchevskii remembered very clearly that Solov'ev's lectures convinced students of the need to study history as "a scientific subject," showing how events followed the path of "historical logic."[80] Similarly, in his own lectures, Sergei Platonov discussed the nature of the historical endeavor in Solov'evian terms: "History is a science, studying concrete facts within the conditions of time and place, and its main goal is the systematic depiction of the development and transformation of the life of individual societies and of all mankind."[81]

By understanding Solov'ev's faith in progress and science, the fascination of populist and revolutionary writers with his works becomes clear. Reacting to the appearance of the first volume of Solov'ev's *History of Russia,* the revolutionary journal *Sovremennik* called it "a scholarly event of the first importance." The famous revolutionary writers Nikolai Chernyshevskii and Nikolai Dobroliubov believed that Solov'ev had ushered in a new era in historical writing, because he had demonstrated that history was a process governed by "universal laws."[82] This view of Solov'ev's works can also shed light on the claim that Solov'ev was influenced by positivists such as Henry Buckle and Herbert Spencer. It is true that in the 1860s, the explicitly positivist history found in the work of Henry T. Buckle became extremely popular in Russia. But it is now possible to see that, rather than being influenced by such histories, Solov'ev may have helped to foster the faith in science and progress that led to the fascination with the English positivist. When the Russian Nihilists and Populists began to see the "idea of progress" as one of the utmost social importance, and the knowledge of science as the key to understanding progress, they were, in a sense, continuing the passionate faith in progress and science that was so linked to the Christian faith as exemplified by Solov'ev and Guizot.[83] Solov'ev and Guizot bequeathed to a new generation their unquestioning faith that continual movement forward, continuous dissatisfaction with the present, and a desire for a better future combined to create a fundamentally beneficial phenomenon, granted by God to his chosen faithful. They proposed that natural science, both its methods and laws, would serve only to confirm the beneficial nature of human progress, because science could only further prove their faith.

But the faith of the new positivists became increasingly secular, detached from the Christian religion. Both Guizot and Solov'ev became disturbed as scientific method turned against Christianity itself, declaring that there was no need to believe in God in order to believe in the beneficial qualities of science and progress. In the late 1860s, both men were thus forced to reexamine their beliefs about the harmonious relations among the scientific method, the belief in inexorable progress, and the Christian religion.

By the end of his life, Guizot realized that his ideas about progress and science had taken a turn he had not anticipated. In his *Meditations on the Essence of Christianity,* written in 1867, Guizot sought to preserve Christianity from the positivist onslaughts of Comte and others. In doing so, he did not seek to deny the discoveries and methods of science but merely to set up boundaries between these and the Christian spiritual world. He sought to explain that "the enlargement of our knowledge in all of the natural sciences, so far from adding to our presumption, should only give a more profound sense of our natural incapacity and ignorance."[84] For Guizot, it was necessary to separate the "finite from the infinite," to understand that "the limits of the finite world are also those of science." Guizot now sought to declare that the scientific method was not all-powerful, that it was useful only in the "material realm."[85] Beyond the material world, scientists had to understand that there was a place where scientific method was no longer applicable, where faith had to step in. Man had to recognize that knowing the "material Universe" did not mean that someone was any closer to understanding "the Moral and Spiritual universe," which could only be accepted as "a revelation of an order of things different from the facts and laws of the finite world." For this, man needed "superhuman assistance."[86]

Only a year after Guizot published his *Meditations,* Solov'ev wrote his essay "Progress and Religion."[87] Ten years before, he recalled, he had believed it necessary to defend progress against those who found it difficult to accept. Now, however, he felt the need to protest against a growing problem among Russian intellectuals—"the idolization of progress, to which all has to be subjected, and to which religion must be subjected." He was disturbed by the new belief that scientific study of the material world would provide for the totality of human knowledge.[88] Like Guizot, Solov'ev sought to make a distinction between the material and the spiritual worlds. "I know that which I completely understand, that which my reason appropriated through my own means," he wrote. "I believe in that which I do not understand, that for which my reason is insufficient." That which was understood through the "senses," that which "materially" existed, was all subject to the laws of science. But, he continued: "For a thinking man it is necessary to understand the cause of causes . . . the existence of another world which we call spiritual. The relationship of this world to the world of the senses is for us unattainable, and this is the realm of faith."[89] Positivists were denying the need for faith, and were proclaiming that humanity could progress beyond the need for religion. Solov'ev countered that progressing beyond Christianity was impossible, for only Christianity could demand perfection and could hold up the ideal to which all humanity must strive. Progress arose through "the understanding of that idea and from the impossibility of achieving it." For Solov'ev, all defenders of progress had to understand that Christianity was the "eternal religion," because "progress is sanctified through Christianity and cannot contradict it."[90]

Solov'ev was ultimately unsuccessful in returning positivism to what he believed were its religious foundations. Indeed, future Russian religious thinkers, including his own son Vladimir Solov'ev, felt the need to battle against the positivist agenda of the Russian intelligentsia by countering it with a more romantic and mystical view of human knowledge. In this sense, Sergei Solov'ev and his French counterpart, François Guizot, occupied a peculiar place in the narrative of European historical writing; they wrote during a transitional period, before the secularizing tendencies of professionalized, positivistic history became clear. They both saw potential in the newly emerging scientific methodology to confirm historical truths that were essentially aspects of their religious faith. Solov'ev's own writings crossed the threshold of the sociological history that would come to dominate the writings of progressive Russian historians in the second half of the nineteenth century. But his faith in historical progress and the scientific method was built upon his faith in Christianity, and for him, there was no doubting the harmony between science and Christian religion. He must have been disturbed to find that he had contributed significantly to a project that turned science and progress against his religious beliefs, a project that limited the positivistic faith to the secular, material world.[91]

Notes

1. V.O. Kliuchevskii, "Solov'ev, kak prepodavatel'," in *Ocherki i rechi, vtoroi sbornik statei* (Petrograd, 1918), pp. 26–36, especially pp. 33–34.

2. J.L. Black, "The 'State School' Interpretation of Russian History: A Reappraisal of its Genetic Origins," *Jahrbücher für Geschichte Osteuropas* 21 (1973): 509–30; see especially pp. 516–17 for a discussion of Solov'ev and Hegelianism. See also N.I. Tsimbaev, "S.M. Solov'ev i ego nauchnoe nasledie," in A.A. Levandovskii and N.I. Tsimbaev, eds., *S.M. Solov'ev: Izbrannye trudy: Zapiski.* (Moscow: Izd. Moskovskogo Universiteta, 1983), pp. 353–80, esp. pp. 367, 371–72. N. Rubinshtein is particularly critical of Solov'ev's inability to break away from his "idealistic worldview"; see his "S.M. Solov'ev i russkaia istoricheskaia nauka," *Voprosy istorii* 3–4 (1945): 57–71, p. 58. David Saunders further argues that Imperial Russian historiography can be divided into two opposing camps, "statists" and "populists," in "The Political Ideas of Russian Historians," *The Historical Journal* 27, 3 (1984): 757–71.

3. Carl W. Reddel, "S.M. Solov'ev and Multi-National History," *Russian History/Histoire Russe,* 13, 4 (Winter 1986): 355–66; Mark Bassin, "Turner, Solov'ev, and the 'Frontier Hypothesis': The Nationalist Signification of Open Spaces," *Journal of Modern History* 65 (September 1993): 473–511.

4. N.P. Pavlov-Silvanskii was the first to argue that Solov'ev came under the influence of Henry T. Buckle. See his *Feodalizm v drevnei Rusi* (St. Petersburg, 1907), especially pp. 8–11. Z. Lozinskii places Solov'ev in the state school, but also claims that Solov'ev read Herbert Spencer and was influenced by Buckle's and Spencer's notions of "organic development." Z. Lozinskii, "Istorik Velikoderzhavnoi Rossii: S.M. Solov'ev," in M.N. Pokrovskii, ed., *Russkaia istoricheskaia literatura v klassovom os-*

veshchenii, 2 vols. (Moscow: Izd. Kommunisticheskoi Akademii, 1927), 1: 205–76, especially pp. 211, 217–18, 225. See also A.M. Sakharov, "Istoriia Rossii v trudakh S.M. Solov'eva," *Vestnik Moskovskogo Universiteta,* Series 9 (May–July 1971): 73–87. A few historians have tried to reconcile these arguments, as did Solov'ev's biographer, V.E. Illeritskii, who claimed that Solov'ev tried to combine "idealism with positivism." V.E. Illeritskii, *Sergei Mikhailovich Solov'ev* (Moscow: Nauka, 1980), especially pp. 60–63. Mark Bassin also suggests that Solov'ev was deeply influenced by Hegel, but that he found it no problem to join this with Spencer's positivism. See Bassin, "Turner, Solov'ev, and the 'Frontier Hypothesis,' " p. 482.

5. Sergei Solov'ev, "Moi zapiski dlia detei moikh, a esli mozhno, dlia drugikh," in Sergei Solov'ev, *Sochineniia,* eds. I.D. Kovalchenko and S.S. Dmitriev, 18 vols. (Moscow: Mysl', 1996), 18: 530–660: especially p. 572. Hereafter, this collection of Solov'ev's works will be referred to as *Sochineniia.*

6. Buckle published his *History of Civilization in England* between 1857 and 1861. Solov'ev had, in fact, read Buckle in the 1860s and wrote a critique of his approach in the essay "Nabliudeniia nad istoricheskoi zhizniu narodov"; see *Sochineniia,* 17: 6–202. Solov'ev claimed that Buckle had failed to see that the state, rather than being a hindrance to the progress of a nation, was instead the concrete manifestation of that progress. See pp. 9–16. I have found no mention of Spencer's philosophy in any of Solov'ev's works.

7. "Nabliudenie," p. 6.

8. "Moi zapiski," p. 573.

9. The Russian historian V.M. Dalin was the first to make this important connection in his "F. Gizo i razvitie istoricheskoi mysli v Rossii," in Dalin, *Liudi i idei: Iz istorii revoliutsionnogo i sotsialisticheskogo dvizheniia vo Frantsii* (Moscow: Nauka, 1970), pp. 354–86. Dalin bases his article on a chronicle of the life of the historian composed by N.A. Popov using Solov'ev's diary and notebooks. The quote from Kliuchevskii is found on p. 376. Unfortunately, Dalin did not discuss the connection between the ideas of Solov'ev and Guizot in great detail, nor did he notice the significance of their shared Christian faith. In his memoirs, Solov'ev openly claimed to "feel a connection" with the French and to enjoy reading French far more than reading German. "Moi zapiski," pp. 581, 584.

10. Most of the important details about Solov'ev's life are found in his autobiographical essay, "Moi zapiski dlia detei moikh, a esli mozhno, dlia drugikh." In fact, almost all accounts of his life are exclusively based on this essay. See V.E. Illeritskii, *Sergei Mikhailovich Solov'ev,* and S.S. Dmitriev and I.D. Koval'chenko, "Istorik Sergei Mikhailovich Solov'ev: Ego zhizn', trudy, i nauchnoe nasledie," in *Sochineniia,* 1: 7–48.

11. "Moi zapiski," pp. 534–35.

12. Ibid., p. 542. Laurie Manchester has noted the phenomenon of the retention of faith among the sons of clergymen, even after leaving the clerical estate, and demonstrates the persistence of a religious worldview in their future professions. Laurie Manchester, "Secular Ascetics: The Mentality of Orthodox Clergyman's Sons in Late Imperial Russia," Ph.D. dissertation, Columbia University 1995; especially pp. 520–23.

13. "Moi zapiski," p. 532.

14. Ibid., pp. 574–89. In his account of his travels, Solov'ev lists all the lectures he attended, but unfortunately, he only gives short accounts of his impressions of the lectures, often including many superficial details about the dress and outward appearance of the lecturers, so that it is hard to tell which ideas influenced him most.

15. Ibid., p. 554. For examples of his writing during this Slavophile phase, see the recently published S.M. Solov'ev, *Pervye nauchnye trudy: Pis'ma,* ed. A.N. Shakhanov (Moscow: Arkheograficheskii tsentr, 1996).

16. Ibid., pp. 541, 562. Solov'ev wrote that he had endless fun with Konstantin Aksakov, with whom he had friendly relations, because Aksakov delighted in Solov'ev's ability to write letters in the seventeenth-century style. Solov'ev claimed that Aksakov knew particularly little about Russian history. Ibid., pp. 610–11.

17. Ibid., p. 571.

18. Ibid., pp. 592–93.

19. Ibid., pp. 597–98.

20. S.M. Solov'ev, "Istoricheskie pis'ma," *Sochineniia,* 16: 354–404.

21. Ibid., pp. 356–57.

22. Ibid., pp. 364–65.

23. Ibid., pp. 360–61.

24. Ibid., p. 361.

25. Ibid., p. 357.

26. Both Illeritskii and Black claim that Solov'ev emphasized the history of the Russian state over the history of the Russian people, and both authors argue that Solov'ev developed such an approach through reading Hegel. Illeritskii, *Solov'ev,* pp. 61–63; Black, "The 'State School' Interpretation," p. 516.

27. Some works on Guizot include Douglas Johnson, *Guizot: Aspects of French History* (London, 1963); Dirk Hoeges, *Francois Guizot und die Französische Revolution* (Bonn, 1973); Rut Keiser, *Guizot als Historiker* (Saint-Louis, 1925); Pierre Rosanvallon, *Le moment Guizot* (Paris, 1985); Madame de Witt, *Monsieur Guizot in Private Life, 1787–1874,* trans. M.C.M. Simpson (London, 1880). The best summary of Guizot's historical thought can be found in Mary Consolata O'Connor, *The Historical Thought of Francois Guizot* (Washington, D.C.: Catholic University of America Press, 1955).

28. O'Connor, *Historical Thought,* pp. 21, 31.

29. F. Guizot, *History of Civilization in Europe,* found in F. Guizot, *History of Civilization,* trans. William Hazlitt, 4 vols. (New York, n.d.), 1: 107; O'Connor, *Historical Thought,* p. 40.

30. Guizot, *History of Civilization in Europe,* p. 104; O'Connor, *Historical Thought,* p. 41.

31. F. Guizot, *History of Civilization in France,* found in F. Guizot, *History of Civilization,* trans. William Hazlitt, 4 vols. (New York, n.d.), vol. 1, p. 283; For contrast with Hegel, see G.W.F. Hegel, *Philosophy of History,* trans. J. Sibree (New York, 1899), pp. 4–5, 8.

32. *History of Civilization in France,* p. 283.

33. F. Guizot, *History of Civilization in Europe,* p. 9; O'Connor, *Historical Thought,* p. 29. See also Hegel, *Philosophy,* p. 16.

34. Solov'ev, *Istoriia Rossii s drevneishikh vremen, v piatnadtsati knigakh* (Moscow, 1959–62), 7: 135. This collection will hereafter be referred to as *Istoriia Rossii.*

35. Solov'ev, "Nachala russkoi zemli," *Sochineniia,* 17: 705–35, p. 712. "Publichnye chteniia o Petre Velikom," *Sochineniia,* 18: 5–152, p. 31; Solov'ev, "Shletser i antiistoricheskoe napravlenie," *Sochineniia,* 16: 315–52.

36. "Publichnye chteniia," p. 7.

37. *Istoriia Rossii,* 2: 654.

38. "Publichnye chteniia," p. 12.

39. He reiterated this in several of his articles. The quote is found in "Nachala russkoi zemli," p. 706. Similar formulations are found in "Nabliudenie," p. 7; "Vzgliad na istoriiu Rossii do Petra Velikogo," *Sochineniia,* 16: 5–42, pp. 6–7.

40. *Istoriia Rossii,* 7: 7–8, For a very complete and interesting analysis of Solov'ev's understanding of the Russian geographical environment, see Bassin, "Turner, Solov'ev, and the 'Frontier Hypothesis,' " especially pp. 491–95.

41. "Vzgliad na istoriiu," p. 30.

42. "Drevniaia Rossiia," *Sochineniia,* 16: 261–76, p. 264, "Nachala russkoi zemli," p. 708.

43. "Nabliudenie," pp. 101–2; "Publichnye chteniia," p. 74.

44. Guizot, *History of Civilization in Europe,* pp. 9, 26; here Guizot's ideas are remarkably similar to Hegel's. Hegel also speaks (without using organic metaphors) of a unity of thought pervading Chinese culture, but he contrasts this with Indian culture, which he claims to be pervaded by "diversity." Hegel, *Philosophy,* pp. 106–7, 166–67.

45. *History of Civilization in Europe,* pp. 13, 26; Hegel, interestingly enough, claims that there is a certain turn "inward" of the individual in Greek culture, but he also claims that this is not analogous to natural phenomena because, for him, the Greeks were the first to free themselves from their natural environment. Hegel, *Philosophy,* pp. 230–33.

46. "Istoricheskie pis'ma," p. 354.

47. "Nabliudenie," pp. 48, 101–2.

48. Ibid., p. 49.

49. Ibid., pp. 47, 102.

50. "Drevniaia Rossiia," pp. 261–62; "Nabliudenie," p. 102.

51. Solov'ev had an almost Freudian explanation for the origins of clan life in Russia. He argued that when the father of a family died, the sons, not wishing to part with him, made him into a deity—the originator of the clan and its name. Thus the head of the clan became a quasi-religious figure. "Nachala russkoi zemli," p. 711.

52. Ibid., pp. 714, 719.

53. Ibid., p. 713.

54. *Istoriia Rossii,* 1: 55.

55. Ibid., 7: 18.

56. *History of Civilization in Europe,* pp. 33–35.

57. Ibid., p. 65.

58. *Istoriia Rossii,* 7: 18.

59. Solov'ev also argued that the remnants of clan structure could mitigate the chaotic qualities of the *druzhina.* He sometimes stated that Russia was saved by the fact that the Russian princes, even in their wanderings from city to city, never entirely lost their attachment to the larger clan to which they belonged. Therefore, the Russian ruling elite retained its unity only by considering itself an enormous clan/dynasty, "whose indivisible property was the Russian land." "Vzgliad na istoriiu," pp. 12–13. *Istoriia Rossii,* 1: 55–6, 7: 14–15.

60. *Istoriia Rossii,* 1: 55–56; "Vzgliad na istoriiu," p. 27.

61. *Istoriia Rossii,* 1: 58, 7: 29–31; "Nabliudenie," p. 74; "Drevniaia Rossiia," p. 263.

62. "Publichnye chteniia," p. 72; "Drevniaia Rossiia," pp. 264, 266.

63. *Istoriia Rossii,* 7: 15–16.

64. Guizot, *History of Civilization in Europe,* pp. 14, 45.

65. Ibid., p. 32.

66. "Publichnye chteniia," p. 107.

67. Ibid., p. 357.

68. "Publichnye chteniia," p. 72; *Istoriia Rossii,* 7: 9, 15–16.

69. *Istoriia Rossii,* 7: 13; "Vzgliad na istoriiu," pp. 18, 25.

70. *Istoriia Rossii,* 7: 15, 21, 32.

71. "Vzgliad na istoriiu," p. 42; *Istoriia Rossii,* 7: 33.

72. *Istoriia Rossii,* 7: 52; "Drevniaia Rossiia," p. 269.

73. "Nabliudenie," p. 115.

74. "Drevniaia Rossiia," pp. 264–65, 272, 274.

75. "Nachala russkoi zemli," p. 714.

76. *History of Civilization in France,* p. 288.

77. In France, Guizot's history had a significant impact on the work of Auguste Comte. Comte had written in 1824 that Guizot was the man with which he had "the most numerous and the most important points of contact." Moreover, Comte was impressed by Guizot's *History of Civilization in France,* calling it a "positivist" work. Mary Pickering, *Auguste Comte: An Intellectual Biography* (Cambridge: Cambridge University Press, 1993), pp. 270–71.

78. Dalin, "F. Gizo," pp. 363, 366.

79. Ibid., pp. 379, 385.

80. Kliuchevskii, "Solov'ev, kak prepodavatel'," pp. 26–36, especially pp. 33–34. For the influence of Solov'ev on Kliuchevskii, see also M.K. Liubavskii, *S.M. Solov'ev i V.O. Kliuchevskii* (Moscow, 1913).

81. S.F. Platonov, *Lektsii po russkoi istorii* (Moscow: "Vysshaia shkola," 1993), pp. 39–40.

82. A.N. Tsamutali, who described the course of Russian history as a "battle" between different currents, and who divided historians into "revolutionaries" and "liberals," also noted this sympathy of *Sovremennik* for Solov'ev's works. See his *Bor'ba techenii v russkoi istoriografii vo vtoroi polovine XIX veka* (Leningrad: Izdatel'stvo "Nauka," 1977), pp. 4, 113–14, 125–26. In his book *Ocherki demokraticheskogo napravleniia v russkoi istoriografii 60–70-kh godov XIX v.* (Leningrad, 1971), he also argues that, while the "democrats" saw Solov'ev's praise of the state as problematic, they thought of him as the founder of "historical science," see pp. 32, 146–47. V.E. Illeritskii has trouble with Chernyshevskii's praise of Solov'ev, feeling compelled to explain that he "could not always clearly and carefully determine and expose the class basis of [the bourgeois historians'] views." See his *Istoriia Rossii v osveshchenii revoliutsionerov-demokratov* (Moscow, 1963), p. 83n, and his *Revoliutsionnaia istoricheskaia mysl' v Rossii* (Moscow, 1974), p. 227 (quote).

83. Alexander Vucinich, *Science in Russian Culture, 1861–1917* (Stanford, CA: Stanford University Press, 1970), pp. 23, 26. Interestingly enough, Vucinich writes that both Nihilists and Populists believed that the "idea of progress" included the notion of "a gradual perfection of morality." Ibid., p. 29.

84. M. (François) Guizot, *Meditations on the Essence of Christianity and on the Religious Questions of the Day* (New York: Scribner and Co., 1867), p. 147.

85. Ibid., p. 179.

86. Ibid., pp. 152, 162.

87. "Progress i religiia," *Sochineniia,* 16: 674–92.

88. Ibid., pp. 674–75.

89. Ibid., pp. 676–77.

90. Ibid., pp. 679–80, 682.

91. The role of Christianity in the development of modern historical thought is a vast subject, much commented upon. The historical and teleological aspects of Christianity as incorporated into positivist historical thought have been discussed by such historians as R.G. Collingwood, *Idea of History* (Oxford: Oxford University Press, 1946), pp. 46–52 and Karl Löwith, *Meaning in History: The Theological Implications of the Philosophy of History* (Chicago: University of Chicago Press, 1949). Lowith particularly argues that, in the case of positivism, "the very doctrine of progress had to assume the function of providence"; and he claims that positivists, in contrast to Hegel, saw this progress as manifested through the "physical, chemical and biological conditions of the white race," pp. 60, 67–68.

11

Kliuchevskii's View of the Flow of Russian History

Robert F. Byrnes

V.O. Kliuchevskii (1841–1911), whom most observers consider the greatest historian of Russia that Russia has produced, was a giant in the flowering of Russian culture in the nineteenth century, one who stood with Tolstoy and Chaliapin as symbols of Russia's highest achievements. An extraordinarily stimulating teacher in Moscow University and four other institutions, he encouraged the study of history among thousands of students, hundreds of whom as teachers carried his affection for history and his emphasis upon geography, the nation and national character, and economic and social forces throughout European Russia. He also attracted into advanced study thirty men who became scholars. These men helped train the first generation of Soviet historians and even participated in writing textbooks for schools and universities after 1934. Two won Stalin prizes and five became members of the Soviet Academy of Sciences. Two others who began advanced study with him, Michael Karpovich and George Vernadsky, placed his stamp upon many American historians through their work at Harvard and Yale after 1927, the formative years of American scholarship on Russia.

A prolific and insightful scholar whose research Russian and Western specialists still admire and use, Kliuchevskii spent much of his last decade converting his famous course on the full sweep of Russian history into five volumes. Hundreds of thousands of copies of *A Course in Russian History* have been published in his homeland: the most recent edition of 250,000 copies in 1987–89 became a rarity almost as soon as subscriptions closed. The volumes have been translated into eleven languages. Their enduring popularity among students and readers of all ages and scholars everywhere has made them the most widely read study of Russian history ever published. The quality of Kliuchevskii's writing, his quiet and moderate nationalism, and his view of the long, organic Russian historical process together exert a compelling attraction upon generations confused by the decline and fall of the Soviet system. This surge and the popularity of other nineteenth-century historians suggest that Kliuchevskii has remained a maker of modern Russia and provides a foundation for Russian's renewed faith in their country and for a new nationalism.

Although most educated Russians of his era were attracted by political philosophy and the philosophy of history, Kliuchevskii had no concern with or knowledge of philosophy and was disinterested in political thought and politics. Confessing that his mind was feeble when confronting abstractions, he rarely used philosophical terms or even words such as nationalism and patriotism. He considered his effort to construct a coherent philosophy of history in a methodology course in 1884 a failure and concluded history "must not be philosophical if it wishes to remain history." Its study was an art, not a science: determining what had happened and describing that accurately and lucidly were a scholar's goals. Trying to find laws behind history, even in the record of one nation, was illusory. In short, he would have rejected Hayden White's dictum that there is "an irresistible ideological component in every historical account of reality" and that every historian develops a philosophy of history, although it may be inconsistent and unclear.[1]

Kliuchevskii's course on methodology used Bossuet and Hegel as targets when he declared that no philosophy of history could identify laws explaining what had happened and what was likely. Late in life, both his diary and most famous volumes reiterated that position, concentrating then against the Slavophile interpretation. He accepted evolution but noted that continuity did not mean advance. "Progress in some spheres of life is accompanied by losses in others," and no political system or period of time was superior to another. After his death, his successor in Moscow University and the Moscow Ecclesiastical Academy summarized his mentor's approach: "His mind always needed concrete factual material, as a fire needs fuel. For him, facts seemed to take the place of logical constructs. That is why he was organically incapable of setting himself the task of extrapolating the entire course of Russian history from any kind of abstract principle."[2]

In spite of these disclaimers, Kliuchevskii subtly advanced a philosophy of history, one that explained the past of all societies and in some detail the history of his homeland, the only country with which he was fully acquainted. He was not consistent, in part because he was so knowledgeable concerning the complications of Russia's past and in part because the massive changes affecting Russia during his last decades influenced his view of the long past. These modifications, far more evident in his essays and lectures than in the major work millions have read, suggested that individuals in modern times have played important roles and that Western influence was undermining traditional Russian values and institutions. Moreover, the element of change he had found constant in history was beginning to undermine the factors he found "permanent" in Russia's past. But these views appeared late and he did not articulate them fully in his masterpiece. However, they help explain the pessimism that grew throughout his last twenty years.

A populist and moderate nationalist, Kliuchevskii emphasized the role of location and geography, economic and social forces, national character, and the slow, organic flow of history. He ignored intellectuals when he did not ridicule them, rejected the Slavophiles' glorification of Russia's allegedly unique culture, and quietly pointed out the perils of Westernization.

Fundamentally, Kliuchevskii found a clear and coherent pattern, "a regularity of the historical process" marking the past, one in which "an eternal law" of gradual change was a central part. Indeed, every element or "reality" in every society was in a constant process of change. Moreover, each alteration of each element produced modifications in the other structural materials. Consequently, the historical process is "an endless series of facts in an endless variety of combinations." The "complicated interaction of shifting bundles of building materials" generated slow and gradual changes of society itself in a course that was not logical, rational, moral, providential, or predetermined, but "national psychological."[3]

In addition, Kliuchevskii concluded that "the same general laws govern the history of mankind." These laws were hidden to his generation and its immediate successors: they were collecting the raw materials for national histories, from which scholars would one day create a science of history, based on geography and sociology. One general historical law was already apparent, the gradual disappearance of social inequality in every society: "Political community begins with distinctions within society that gradually disappear as history moves on."[4]

Continuity and change were both evident throughout history, and change gradually reshaped institutions, customs, and values. A draft compared this process to successively superseding concentric circles formed when a stone falls into water. Change was so inexorable that "nothing is accidental." He often used "natural and necessary," a phrase popular with his mentor, Sergei M. Soloviev, who inherited it from Guizot. Sometimes he substituted "sociological determinism," particularly when he referred to the effects geography and economic conditions produced. Thus, Riurik had no alternative but to establish the Kievan kingdom, just as a tenor had to remain a tenor, even though he preferred to be a bass. Sometimes, wise men who lack a scholar's training understand the flow of history better than historians: "To know one's history is to understand why it was so and the consequences to which earlier periods inevitably led. This is why someone who understands the past is not always a historian."[5]

In sum, Kliuchevskii assumed that providing a historical account of an institution constituted both a definition and an explanation: "History is the main cause of history." The past was a seamless web in which every development was the consequence of previous events in new conditions. Every era quietly ripened into its successor. The rise of Moscow, the establishment of serfdom and its abolition, and all such events were part of an inexorable organic movement and had deep historical roots. One answers a question not by defining terms but by providing a historical account.

History has few sharp breaks, saints, heroes, or devils. It lacks a beginning and an ending. It is organic and continuous, unspectacular and gradual, flowing like a river and sometimes spilling over the banks. "Inherited administrative deposits," not the judgment or will of men such as Ivan the Terrible or Peter the Great, over centuries transform institutions, habits, and values. "The past does not move forward without influence. Only the people have gone on, but they have left everything to us as inherited property. . . . We are in great part their content and feelings. . . . Consequently, the history of our native land is our biography. . . . The object of history is the historical process."[6] Changes that some label reforms are "the products of all the previous history of a people" and grow from widely recognized needs. Peter the Great's Northern War was a powerful engine of reform, but change would have occurred without that war. Often a society appears to advance. At other times, it seems to retreat. But where one historian sees advance, another sees retreat, because their judgments are subjective and they have different views of the same process. Those who conclude that change produces unforeseen or apparently paradoxical consequences are simply uninformed. Education is an important cause of gradual change, but efforts to hasten or direct modifications through "violent interruption of the established political tradition" rest upon the illusion that man can control the flow. Such attempts inevitably fail. Reconstruction after such a failed endeavor is slow and painful, but the stream of history invariably returns within established banks, of course affected by the interference and violence.[7]

Examples abound to demonstrate this. Thus, the original harsh circumstances affecting Russian history gradually lost authority as man acquired mastery over some geographical elements and reduced the effects of climate. Pressure from the steppe and Asia declined or ceased as Russia became stronger and sturdier. "National religious unity" had constituted a major force shaping the people and their institutions until the sixteenth and seventeenth centuries. As the Church declined, the autocratic state assumed leadership of a secular drive for national unity.

His most important scholarly volume, *The Boyar Council of Old Russia,* published early in 1882, traced the undramatic and organic rise and decline of an institution from the tenth century until the late seventeenth century, the councils first helping manage small princedoms and later helping direct the Moscow state. This volume emphasized the role of families and family alliances, the immense power of customs and traditions, and the continuous way changing elements and combinations transformed the council. Later tsars' departments and colleges simply modified the inherited institution as it faded away.

Kliuchevskii's studies of social structures and the rise and decline of the *zemskii sobor* ("land assembly") analyze similar processes. He divided Russian history into four periods, but "the idea of the Russian land" and colonization linked the segments and helped each period grow into its successor. Even the organization of *A Course in Russian History* reflects this approach: few chapters have precise headings or titles, and the paragraphs and chapters flow into each other.

His treatment of historiography, the rise of the state and the Muscovite autocracy, and the origins and abolition of serfdom illustrates his philosophy of history as well as his eclectic explanations. Even the process through which he created the course on historiography casts light both upon the way transformations occur and the effort to record them. In its first year, he taught students how to use primary sources. He then added lectures on the first collectors and editors of documents and on eighteenth-century amateur historians. Finally, he moved back in time to the first Russian historians, who appeared during the Time of Troubles. In sum, the amended course showed that Russian historiography had developed at the same pace as the nation's history. Moreover, his students learned that historiography was an essential part of the national past, one of the "bundles of realities" that underwent constant modifications and transformed the country's other elements. Historians are as important as rulers: they reflect the laws of history, influence other elements of society, and enable a people to understand itself by explaining its origins and development.[8]

One of Kliuchevskii's central tenets was that everyone connected with recording and describing the past participated in an eternal and almost sacred order. The historiography course sought to ensure that budding scholars understood and appreciated their predecessors' contributions to that permanent chain of change. The twelve public lectures and essays he produced on contributors to historical scholarship were part of that campaign, as were the ten he prepared on the anniversaries of the university, the Society for History and Antiquity, and the abolition of serfdom. Similar lectures and articles commemorating the birth or death of scholars, saints, rulers, and writers helped make Russians aware of the continuities that bound past and present.

In Kliuchevskii's judgment, the state's origins lay in primary or natural unions. The tribe succeeded the family and clan when changes made them inadequate instruments, and the secondary or artificial union known as the state then replaced the tribe. The foundations of the state and Russian nationality both lay in Kiev, which also produced the crucial "idea of the Russian land." The early Russians divided geographically, but Great Russian leadership brought the Great Russians, Belorussians, and Little Russians together in a unified state and people. As this process gathered momentum in the fifteenth century, Muscovy, "the Great Russian national state," emerged at the center.[9]

The process through which Moscow became the creator of national unity and defender of the national interest and Russia became an autocracy was also slow and gradual. First, history passed by Kiev, the original capital and center. Kliuchevskii did not identify any major turning points, but described an inexorable and impersonal series of steps reflecting a variety of forces that led to Moscow's slowly and almost secretly replacing Kiev and its successor, the appanage system. Ideas, except for "the idea of the Russian land," played no role. A section of the lithographed editions of his university lectures that he omitted from A *Course in Russian History* compared Moscow to an anthill, a huge, lifeless collective body "without any traces of individual happiness," from which emerged a powerful, unified Russia.

The foundation was faith in national unity, which legitimized the centralized power's replacing the contractual agreements and freedoms of the appanage centuries. Location and geography were significant factors. Moscow's early isolation offered protection, and its position at the center of a river network provided commercial advantage. The *pomestie* system contributed: the ruler granted land to those who agreed to fulfill military service under central leadership against Asia, the steppe, and the Germans. The land of northeastern Russia was so poor that the nobles tended to gather around the ruler, not live on their estates. The prince or tsar then rewarded them by grants from conquests, making them "the earliest shareholders in the Russian state." The Tatars helped Moscow against Tver, and Moscow's leadership in the battle of Kulikovo against the Tatars in 1380 was a symbolic step in the long process.

The rulers' part in Moscow's rise was minor, but their promotion of growth through Mongol grants, purchase, and seizure of property contributed to the state's gradual eminence. Indeed, the mediocrity of its princes, more products than causes of its success, was an important reason for Moscow's selection and rise. The system of succession also kept the land together. Constant migration and colonization then helped fill the huge, poor, and sparsely populated land over which Moscow gradually tightened control.[10]

The same eclectic description of Moscow's emergence also explained the rise of the autocratic system. Kliuchevskii almost derisively eliminated Novgorod and Pskov as possible centers or as precursors of another form of government than autocracy. They were growths on the margins that geography and the course of history together created and destroyed. "Fictional democracies doomed by history," they had briefly possessed more independence and freedom than other parts of the country. However, these "unnatural oligarchies" ruled by merchants were not harbingers of democracy. Location, geography, social disunities, and the power of nationalism together condemned them to become permanent and indistinguishable parts of a Russia ruled autocratically from Moscow.[11]

Maintaining control over expanding territory and defending open boundaries tended to concentrate power. Indeed, Russia's defense of Europe against Asiatic pressure was responsible to some degree for developing a form of government different from those of the West. In this defense, Moscow used the boyar council and land assembly until late in the seventeenth century, making autocracy the natural and apparently inevitable system of Russian rule.[12]

The crucial period for enthroning the state and establishing autocracy was that between the middle of the sixteenth and the middle of the seventeenth centuries, a plateau that both separated and joined early and modern Russian history, with the Time of Troubles as a hinge. It included part of the reign of Ivan the Terrible, the Time of Troubles, and the years before the religious schism. During that period, the autocracy and serfdom together became dominant forces, with roots in both cases extending deep into Russian history. Neither Ivan's reign nor the Time of Troubles nor any other individual or event was a turning point: they were all parts of the seamless web, of the continuing undramatic flow.

Kliuchevskii indirectly demonstrated his philosophy of history by the way he resolved a simple academic problem, selecting the point at which to divide the survey course of Russian history, which Soloviev had done with Peter the Great, whose reign he considered a sharp turning point. In Kliuchevskii's view, no clear break existed. When he began teaching in Ger'e's Women's Higher Courses in 1872, he ended the first semester of the one-year course in the middle of the sixteenth century. When he inherited Soloviev's two-year survey at the university, he completed the first year in 1613, the end of the Time of Troubles and the center of the plateau.

During the plateau century, Russians gradually recognized that the state was more important than the dynasty. As the national will emerged late in the Time of Troubles, they accepted an unencumbered state as the expression of the people's will and the instrument for achieving the general welfare. The boyar council gradually lost its effectiveness and share of government. The land assemblies, which had helped create the sense of nation, faded because they too proved unnecessary. By the middle of the sevententh century, as Russia recovered from the crisis and faced other problems, the government was no longer the absolute monarchy of Ivan the Terrible tempered by an aristocratic administration but gradually became an autocracy, "the natural and necessary" consequence of a process that flowed from historical circumstances. The new dynasty then established a firm grip on power, the structure of society changed, the nobility began its ascent, and expansion westward resumed.[13]

Kliuchevskii also emphasized the role of constant, slow change in the long articles published in 1885 on the origins and consequences of serfdom, the series in 1886 on Peter the Great's poll tax, and the summary accounts in *A Course in Russian History*. The essays unfolded slowly and gradually; their organization and style seemed examples of the historical law.

Most Russian historians of serfdom before 1917 supported his analysis. Scholars in the twentieth century have saluted him for assigning economic factors major responsibility and identifying the critical character of the economic crisis in the second half of the sixteenth century. However, most have rejected his "brilliant attempt" to identify the gradual growth of peasant indebtedness as the primary cause of serfdom, in part because new sources have provided additional insights. Instead, they ascribe enserfment directly to "the primacy of the role of state power," expressed in a series of state actions. The most thorough analysis of the "dread institution" termed the culminating step, the 1649 Code, "the greatest legal act directed toward the final enserfment of the peasants."[14]

The roots of Kliuchevskii's interest in serfdom lay in the abolition decree of 1861, which he proclaimed the most important event in his life. The university classes he attended in the early 1860s devoted little attention to serfdom or the momentous decree, and the slow growth of his engagement almost symbolized his view of the way history unfolded. Teaching a survey course in Russian history in 1872 renewed his understanding of serfdom's central significance, and he began to collect documents on its history. Research on the boyar council then elucidated some of serfdom's causes and effects, particularly the declining role of the council and land assemblies and the establishment of autocracy.

In 1881, he wrote that serfdom "was prepared by centuries and molded by the unsatisfactory conditions of our life" and that dismantling it would be an equally slow process. For example, abolition had not touched 15 percent of the serfs twenty years after the edict.[15] The university seminars he launched then produced insight into the peasant's position before serfdom. Finally, a book he read in 1884 by Professor I.E. Engelman of Dorpat led him to undertake intensive study. Engelman argued that a series of state decrees in the first half of the seventeenth century and the 1649 Code had established serfdom. This "state school" thesis collided with Kliuchevskii's judgment that Russian history was far more complicated than Engelman appreciated. He set out to demonstrate that the origins of serfdom lay deep in history and that its establishment represented an imperceptible change without clear definition of time.

In his judgment, many factors explained serfdom's rise and long survival. The fundamental reason was the low level of cultural and political life caused by centuries of difficult circumstances, external pressures, and intellectual inadequacies. He expressed this most precisely in the popular 1892 lecture and essay on "The Good People of Ancient Russia," which asserted that the peasants' personal freedom was "one of the sacrifices" necessary to ensure the nation's survival.

The immediate reasons were primarily economic. In the second half of the sixteenth century, poverty, inflation, and continuous borrowing forced thousands to default on their financial obligations, cease their grueling effort to survive independently, abandon the right to move, and drift into serfdom. The turmoil and dislocation the Time of Troubles created, foreign intervention, and the heavy financial burdens of wars in the first half of the seventeenth century then hastened both serfdom's spread and the state's formal acknowledgment of it. Perhaps the state promoted the process, but it did not initiate it and certainly did not decree it. Indeed, the state lacked the authority and competence for such action. It simply accepted serfdom and established its boundaries: the 1649 Code was "belated recognition of what life itself had already enacted."[16]

After 1649, serfdom expanded and deepened. It protected the treasury and landowners, who accepted responsibility for collecting state revenues from peasants fixed to the land. The owners' powers over the peasant's person, work, and even posterity then grew gradually. Peter the Great's poll tax to support a peacetime regular army gave serfdom a "double foundation" by amalgamating its forms and blending slavery and serfdom. Conditions worsened after Peter. The "third formation" in 1762 and Catherine the Great's policies provided Russia with the most deeply rooted and vicious form of serfdom Europe had seen, just when the last "justification" of serfdom had disintegrated. For Kliuchevskii, the poll tax darkened Peter's image, while the history of Catherine's Russia was that of serfdom.[17]

The institution affected every aspect of Russian life. It corrupted the nobility, a goal Kliuchevskii thought Catherine sought. The nobles became a slothful, worthless class who wasted their time on petty disputes and their funds on frivolous luxuries. Enjoying dissolute lives in an elegant but artificial social regime, they formed a cancer feeding on their fellow citizens.[18] Set apart from others, they became politically indifferent, although they should have led in promoting change.

The economic consequences of serfdom were just as disastrous. Serfdom led owners to exploit the peasants rather than the land. It wrecked the natural distribution of labor and capital, undermined entrepreneurial spirit, and destroyed incentives to create capital. The predominance of backward agriculture in an economy that the state shackled guaranteed stagnation. Russia remained mired in a backward rural economy without the sturdy urban classes that provided initiative in other societies. Instead, enterprising non-Russians dominated Russia's weak industry and feeble internal trade, leading many to despise energy and enterprise as foreign qualities. The national income remained static and living standards low. Consequently, the state became a hungry debtor and retrogressive taxes crippled the economic system. Russia spiraled downward economically and became "a colossus on serf legs" at a time when European states were becoming more productive, prosperous, and free.

The effects of "civilized barbarism" extended far beyond legal and economic arrangements binding the peasant to the land. Serfdom weakened Christianity, placed injustice and cruelty at the heart of Russian life, and lowered a civilization already humble. Serf owners became dependent upon the state and opposed all change. The character and quality of education remained at the lowest level in Europe. Every aspect of Russian culture tilted away from freedom and responsibility toward passivity and arbitrary rule. This strengthened the submissive, servile attitude Kliuchevskii considered a central aspect of the national character and political system and destroyed the slim possibility that the land assembly might become an effective representative assembly: how could a serf participate in representative government? In addition, making noble landowners tax collectors ensured that peasant dissatisfaction would turn against the state rather than against the landowner. This helped Kliuchevskii understand why the violent assaults upon the nobility in the seventeenth century became rebellions against the state a century later.[19]

From the time he began teaching, Kliuchevskii planned to make abolition in 1861 the culminating point of his major course because it completed the process of estate formation and class landowning that had begun in the tenth century. When he died, the pages on the period after 1796 were scrappy and unfinished. He had commented, sometimes in detail, on early criticisms of serfdom and had drafted essays on approaches to abolition that men such as Kiselev had considered. But he described the steps that led to abolition only in the last article he drafted, published first in 1958. This unfinished essay is unusual because it provides a detailed factual account but contains little analysis of the issues engaged or the forces pressing for and against action. Similarly, the materials on the period after 1861 consist largely of details, with little analysis.

Even so, the abundant materials on abolition and its aftermath express the thesis that change is constant and slow and that abolition was the result of the same process that had brought an end to slavery almost a century and a half earlier. Alexander II needed almost six years to reach a decision and prepare the decree. Fifty years later, little change had occurred.[20]

In Kliuchevskii's view, the first criticisms of serfdom and suggestions for abolition appeared late in the seventeenth century. Eighteenth-century imperial rulers snuffed out comments, but men such as Speransky under Alexander I and Kiselev under Nicholas I proposed study of ways to abolish it. Nicholas I recognized that serfdom weakened Russia as a power but did not comprehend the problem's magnitude. He "approached serfdom as though he were a doctor who treated his patient's scabs individually, moving from one scab to another only after ointment had completely healed the first." Lacking a concept of the national interest and resolution, he established committees to study serfdom but kept them secret and introduced only minor revisions.[21]

After the Crimean War, men of good will such as Samarin proposed liberation with a garden plot for each family, gestures that showed they considered serfs the owners' private property, guests, or lodgers. For them, serfdom was a legal issue, not a central national problem rooted in history that would disappear no more quickly than it had risen. In short, even liberal reformers of good will did not comprehend the cancer that "remained in our customs like a mortal illness."[22]

An early admirer of Alexander II, Kliuchevskii as a mature scholar was deeply critical of the tsar. He thought the tsar indecisive, ignorant, and self-centered and his aides incompetent. Alexander II was not a statesman: he acted out of fear and gave little thought to the long-term consequences of his action. He proceeded so slowly and ineptly that the nobles were able to reduce the effectiveness of abolition. His policies toward the Poles constituted a series of errors. Other changes were shallow and tardy, and he reverted to inaction after only a decade of reform.

Emancipation began completion of a process that had roots deep in ancient Russia's social structure that other fundamental changes had gradually affected. Economic forces were decisive, as always. Slow or stagnant economic growth, an incompetent government staffed over centuries by urban bureaucrats blind to the need to assist crafts, promote industry, and modernize the economy, and the population's steady growth were other significant causes. While Christianity had contributed to weakening and ultimately eliminating slavery, he assigned it no credit for abolition. Curiously, he failed to mention Radishchev or the impact of Western ideas or models. The immediate cause, but only the immediate cause, for Alexander's tardy initiative was the increasing number of ever more vigorous uprisings. "The nobles feared the peasants, the peasants hated the nobles, neither had any confidence in the state, and the state feared both."[23]

Because the government failed to comprehend and resolve the long-term causes, the problems responsible for abolition worsened after 1861. Population pressures raised land prices. The commune, designed to protect less-enterprising peasants from their aggressive neighbors and city slickers, to ease collection of recruits and taxes, and to help control the countryside, instead denied peasants the advantages of freedom and drove the most able and ambitious into resentment and hostility. Nonetheless, Stolypin's program to dismantle it after 1906 was too drastic. Kliuchevskii in his last months doubted whether Russia had time or the will to avoid an explosion.[24]

The fundamental causes of the successive modifications that occurred in all societies were "the human spirit" and "physical nature," in Russia as in any country.[25] Within his native land, the most volatile structural material was migration or colonization, an elemental national force that helped produce mastery of the land and bind Russia together but that was also the principal visible source of change.

Economic elements, the social interests and groups that created them and then reflected them, and administration were among the principal building materials that constituted a society. Indeed, they were "more important than the building itself," and "political facts grow from economic facts." No community could survive unless individuals were willing to sacrifice themselves to the common good, to a new political system in which private and general interests would achieve some balance.[26] Thus, an armed merchant class helped establish the state in Kiev, replacing the tribe, just as economic factors had led to the clan's superseding the family and the tribe's replacing the clan. Economic elements were mainly responsible for the rise of Moscow and autocracy, the origins of serfdom, and its abolition. Economic and social transformations since 1861 constituted the fundamental reasons for the revolution of 1905. The 1909 edition of Kliuchevskii's outline history barely mentioned the Russo-Japanese War: it was only the immediate cause of the revolution. Similarly, he assigned more significance to completion of the

Trans-Siberian railroad and the Stolypin land program than to the cataclysmic events of 1904–5. This epitomizes his relegating political systems to a secondary role. They reflect a society. They are responsible neither for backwardness nor for achievements.[27] Late in life, he recognized that the stagnant economy's inability to satisfy the most basic human needs created discontents affecting every aspect of Russian life. Although he lacked the statistical information available to later scholars and could not identify the propellants behind this explosion, he appreciated that the population's rapid growth was a critical factor.

On the role of rulers and other prominent leaders Kliuchevskii was ambivalent. He considered social processes the decisive element, although he recognized rulers affected the character and timing of change. But history recorded no miracles or miracle workers. No one, even a tsar, could exercise significant influence, except through character and promoting education. Even Robinson Crusoe did not modify the society into which circumstances thrust him. Moreover, individuals' efforts to divert or direct the flow of human affairs were almost inevitably unsuccessful and destructive: Russia's autocrats caused heavy damage when they tried to force or hasten change.

Dozens of his aphoristic statements and analyses of trends and events minimize the importance of individuals. Leaders were "lampposts that light the path to change in times of peace and on which people hang errant rulers" in times of trouble. A society's moral level depends as much on its separate members as the temperature depends on the thermometer. Similarly, "life is like a church procession. Those in the front ranks should not conclude that they lead the others." Princes are drops of water, symbols and figureheads, products of conditions, not agents of change. Muscovy's early rulers did not enlarge the state: it grew because of factors beyond the control of such mediocrities. Peter the Great's achievements were due to his responding to national needs at the appropriate time, not to his foresight, energy, or genius. The changes for which many gave him credit had been underway for more than two generations. In fact, reforms are "the product of all the previous history of a people," national responses to long-recognized needs.[28]

Nonetheless, he recognized that leaders often contributed to directing and even creating peaceful change in stable, well-governed societies such as England's.[29] He also assigned some individuals an important place in the flow of Russian history, particularly in the period after 1500, when more information was available concerning individuals and they played more distinctive roles than earlier. By that time, the "harsh circumstances" of earlier times had lost some of their authority, and pressures from Asia, the steppes, and later the West had helped concentrate power at the center in the hands of one man. The inexorable flow of impersonal forces bore fundamental responsibility for the rise of the Muscovite state, the religious schism, the origins and abolition of serfdom, and other fundamental aspects of Russian history. However, he awarded much of the liability for dynastic crises, wars, and extravagant waste to individual rulers, as though they were aberrations from the historical process.

Kliuchevskii may have given increased prominence to particular persons as a teaching device. His artistry in character analysis and storytelling marks some of the most engaging and informative sections of his lectures and of *A Course in Russian History*. His most effective and renowned public lectures and essays described the role individuals had played in the flow of history, not so much as men or women who constituted turning points, but as individuals who reflected the spirit of an age. The essays on Pushkin, Lermontov, Boltin, and Saint Sergei were illustrative of this technique. Similarly, analyses of men such as Prince Dmitrii M. Golitsyn and Speransky provided insight into the forces pressing for continuity and change. Thus, the immensely gifted Golitsyn failed to limit the powers of Empress Anna because no accretions from other necessary economic and political changes existed in 1730. He devoted seven chapters in *A Course in Russian History* to individuals and only two to the Church: the Russian editor of the most recent edition of his works termed his masterpiece "a gallery of portraits" and in 1990 arranged a printing of two million copies of Kliuchevskii essays entitled *Historical Portraits*.[30]

Kliuchevskii's use of individuals as an instructional technique was especially obvious in the courses he taught at the Alexandrovskoe Military School and in Ger'e's program for women. Thus, the course on the origins of the French Revolution demonstrated that France had benefited from the wisdom of Richelieu, Colbert, and Louvois. Discerning "builders," they helped create a strong government that maintained close ties with the country through the aristocracy and church. However, Louis XIV drew the aristocracy and high clergy away from their estates and bishoprics into Versailles. There, "the court lolled in luxury, while the people lived in misery." He abused absolute power, neglected the general welfare, and wasted national resources trying to conquer Europe. He unleashed destructive religious persecution, drove some of the nation's most sage and productive men and women abroad, and united much of Europe against France. His successors were even less intelligent. They ignored the rising middle class creating much of the national wealth, drove the prosperous peasantry into rebellion, launched half-hearted reforms that further alienated those they were seeking to aid, and encouraged demagogues.[31]

The 1873–74 course on Russian history in Ger'e's program assigned Ivan the Terrible some credit for enlarging Muscovy's territory and strengthening central power. Kliuchevskii's character sketch and psychological analysis also attributed to Ivan's personal qualities, especially his mental and moral instability, some responsibility for conflict with the nobles. The analysis of Ivan in a manuscript he drafted in 1894 and the one published in the second volume of *A Course in Russian History* in 1906 do not differ in substance from the early one, except that the last version is the most sharp and clear in expression. In any case, Ivan the Terrible, like Louis XIV, emerged as a force in history.[32]

Similarly, the essays and famous chapter on Peter the Great emphasize the significance of character and personality, although they also assert that the changes he introduced were only technical and rose from roots deep in the past. The 1896 essay on the hundredth anniversary of Catherine the Great's death, the pages devoted to her borrowing from the West, and the section on her in *A Course in Russian History* also emphasize the significance of character. The analyses of Tsars Paul and Alexander I stress to an even greater degree the ruler's psychology.[33]

Kliuchevskii produced as many brilliant lectures and essays on "quiet heroes" as he did on dramatic rulers. Their role in the flow of history was less visible, but they represented permanent forces and were more significant than leaders. Thus, at the time "the state grew fat and the people grew lean," millions of individuals, most of them invisible, were producing changes underneath the surface that led to gradual transformations. A long draft statement in his archives described the sixteenth and seventeenth centuries as a haze through which one could envision the forms of Peter the Great and Pushkin, shining like lighthouses on a rocky coast. In this era, the state fulfilled its basic functions, external security and internal order, while millions of "good people" and small groups of high character, patriotism, and faith fed the poor and built churches. By leading decent lives, spreading literacy, and educating children to love their country and honor their faith, they helped create the national character and make Russia a sound society. "This energy, this creative work does not derive from inspiration from above, like snow falling on one's head: it is the product of successive work-loving generations who adapt themselves to national circumstances, morals, and life." They constitute the creative force of the nation, the quiet motor that drives the other mutually dependent variables or "realities" that form society. Those in the great chain who produced the historical record were among those unassuming but important men and women. When historians utilized the product of other unsung heroes to provide their countrymen an account of the past, they established the national consciousness that helped make Russia.[34]

Intellectuals occupied the lowest rung in Kliuchevskii's assessment of factors fundamental in the historical process: he expressed scorn for this group throughout his life, and he even criticized use of the word "intellectual." Above all, his major works, especially *A Course in Russian History,* ignore this group. He did not participate in the attack upon radical intellectuals in the volume *Landmarks* [Vekhi] in 1909, for such an action would have been out of character. Moreover, he was not acquainted with any of the nine who contributed. Nevertheless, his archive contains an incomplete short story drafted then that assails intellectuals in the same way as do the *Landmarks* articles.

Although Soloviev's course on the French Revolution at the military school had assigned much responsibility to Rousseau and Voltaire, Kliuchevskii ignored those men and their ideas when he taught it. Only in the early 1880s did he suggest that "theories without substance" had helped demolish a social order that had served France for centuries. In these lectures, he termed Speransky a "Voltaire in Orthodox theological garb."

From that point, his published works and even more his unpublished essays and aphorisms excoriated intellectuals. An early lecture announced that the survey course excluded them: their place was in biographies and studies of philosophy. He even ignored Pushkin and Lermontov. His study of the abolition movement failed even to mention Radishchev and his famous work.[35]

In his judgment, intellectuals failed to recognize that society was a living organism with its own language and ways. "Educated fools" who did not realize that reason is a method of thought, not a way of life, they used logical concepts, artistic forms, daydreams, and limited personal experience to explain history.[36] An untrained diagnostician who could identify and treat the portents of disease was superior to the physician who scorned preventive medicine and tried to cure those already ill.[37] Kliuchevskii did not venerate the peasant, but he valued highly the common sense of the ordinary Russian and declared many illiterate Russians intelligent and sensible: instinct was a more certain guide than advanced education and intellectual attainment.

For him, Russian intellectuals were a noisy, publicity-seeking handful of political ideologues, a small and isolated band who sought self-aggrandizement and rapid social change, the source and substance of which they did not understand. Ignorant of a homeland they despised, "the colored Russian dolls of Western civilization" were more foreign than Russian. Superficial and unpatriotic demagogues, they produced dangerous proposals for "milk and honey socialism." While claiming to be individualistic, they herded together and rushed like blind lemmings from one extreme to another. In many ways, they resembled toy windmills turning harmlessly in whatever direction the wind blew. They reminded him of leaves falling from a tree: "they felt sorry for the tree, which did not miss them and instead grew other leaves."[38]

Moreover, an idea, the product of an individual mind, usually that of a political ideologue, "becomes an active social factor only when it is recognized as a generally accepted rule of belief" and an essential element of the national culture. It resembles a flash of lightning, ephemeral and useless until harnessed as electricity, when it acquires enormous power. Thus, "the idea of the Russian land" was the essential spark for national unity. A comment he contributed at the Peterhof meeting on the Bulygin constitution in 1905 expressed this view as a canon of life: the wise statesman adopts those ideas that possess vitality and have secured general acceptance because they will triumph in the end.[39]

As he matured and devoted increasing emphasis to the period after 1500, he concluded that the factors that had shaped Russian character in its first centuries had gradually lost their potency. At the same time, increasing participation in European affairs and the flow of Western influences enlarged the European dimensions. In the first centuries, Russia had easily assimilated Byzantine influence, including Christianity. Similarly, until the middle of the seventeenth century, it had integrated Western foods, fashion, habits, and weapons without significant effect upon its cultural integrity. However, the imported scholarship that helped create the religious schism produced vastly different consequences, in particular weakening the national religious unity that had been the nation's principal strength. In short, Western influence gradually became one of the most significant "structural materials" and threatened Russia's cultural individuality.

Kliuchevskii's analyses of the boyar council, origins of serfdom, land assemblies, and religious schism, in the chronological order completed, suggested that the West was in some ways superior to Russia. The West emphasized learning and critical thought, rather than ignorance and conceit. It abolished serfdom and its deadly poison long before Russia did. The gradual transformation of the West's political institutions into representative processes helped make it more lively, free, prosperous, and powerful than Russia. Europeans endured some costs to achieve these gains, but he noted that influence flowed just one way: Russia followed Europe's path and exercised little impact upon the outside world.

Russia's increasing engagement in the Balkans since Catherine the Great represented another form of Western influence and helped modify state policy, the character and direction of Russian nationalism, and Kliuchevskii's definition of his country. Thus, a Russia concerned with the Balkan Slavs and Orthodox Slav unity had extended its ambitions beyond the "idea of the Russian land" and no longer retained the peaceful national character that had been a predominant structural material. Similarly, the fading of institutions such as the boyar council and the Church indicated that apparently permanent institutions and values were temporary elements in the flow of events, while the role of the West was growing. In sum, modern history registered increasing flux.

Examples of this abound. Kliuchevskii informed a class in 1886 that there had been times and would again be periods when there were no estates or classes. A decade later, he noted in a public lecture on Alexander II that one day the land assembly might reappear. He also suggested that even the colonization that distinguished Russia's past might not be permanent.[40] Moreover, just as serfdom and the autocracy had developed in long, slow processes and abolition had begun the end of the servile mentality, so autocracy might disappear as part of the endless, "natural and necessary" change that characterized history. But the successor system, whether constitutional or some other form of governance, would also be transitory in the flow of history.

Some of Kliuchevskii's views, especially his determinism, emphasis upon economic factors and social classes, and belief that scholars would one day discover the laws that govern all society suggest that Marx may have influenced him. The first Russian translation of Marx was published in 1872, and his ideas circulated quite freely in the university later in the century. However, Kliuchevskii rejected friends' suggestions that he read Marx, whose ideas he ranked with Tolstoy's as useless and even harmful. Indeed, he declared Marxism "a hastily read theory," one that "lay upon our thought like a dog in our lap or Paris wigs on the heads of our remote ancestors." Moreover, as Soviet critics frequently pointed out, the most central qualities of his life and thought separated him from Marx.[41]

However, he did prepare the way for some Russians' acceptance of Marx's ideas, just as his teaching and publications persuaded or confirmed others in quite different directions. Some Kliuchevskii students, especially Michael Pokrovskii, who studied six years with him, played prominent roles as Communists in the Soviet historical scene, in some cases until after Stalin's death. Kliuchevskii interceded with the minister of the interior in 1899 to obtain the release from prison of a Marxist undergraduate whose intellect had impressed him. Alexei I. Iakovlev, who returned to study with him and whose father was a friend of Lenin, proudly proclaimed himself a member of "the Kliuchevskii school" until his death in 1951 ended his long career as a Communist scholar.[42] However, some, like Michael M. Bogoslovskii and Matvei K. Liubavskii (who died in confinement in 1936), remained monarchists. Others, such as A.A. Kizevetter and Paul N. Miliukov, became constitutional democrats and were forced to spend their last years abroad. Peter Struve and George Plekhanov have admitted that *The*

Boyar Council awakened them to the significance of economic factors before they read Marx. But these men and the millions of others Kliuchevskii reached through his teaching and writing were only among the most well-known whose views concerning the historical process he deeply affected.

Notes

Reprinted from "Kliuchevskii's View of the Flow of Russian History," *Review of Politics* 55, 4 (Fall 1993): 565–91, with permission of the publisher.

1. Archives of the Institute of History, Academy of Sciences, Moscow (hereafter ANIIM), Vasilii O. Kliuchevskii (hereafter VOK) archives, f. 4, op. 1, d. 27, "Metodologiia i terminologiia: Programma i kurs lektsii chitannyi v Moskovskom universitete v 1884–1885 gg.," pp. 65–66; VOK, *Pis'ma, dnevniki, aforizmy i mysli ob istorii* (Moscow, 1968), pp. 283, 343; Hayden White, *Metahistory: The Historical Imagination in Nineteenth-Century Europe* (Baltimore, 1973), pp. ix–xx, 192, 428. Fernand Braudel, whose approach to the study of history resembles Kliuchevskii's, agreed: "Narrative history is not an objective method, still less the supreme objective method, but is itself a philosophy of history" (Braudel, *On History* [Chicago, 1980], p. 4).

2. VOK, "Metodologiia russkoi istorii 1884–85 ak. god," *Sochineniia v deviati tomakh* (Moscow, 1987–89), VI: 3–55, 57–72, 87–92, especially 2–4, 7–8, 24–26, 32–35, 59–66; VOK, "Prilozhenie k kursu 'Metodologiia russkoi istorii,'" ibid., pp. 392–95; VOK, *Pis'ma*, pp. 89–92, 265; Mikhail M. Bogoslovskii, "Professor Vasilii Osipovich Kliuchevskii," *Pamiati pochivshikh nastavnikov* (Sergiev Posad, 1914), pp. 347–50; Bogoslovskii, "V.O. Kliuchevskii kak uchenyi," in *V.O. Kliuchevskii: Kharakteristiki i vospominaniia* (Moscow, 1912), pp. 36, 38; Boris I. Syromiatnikov,"V.O. Kliuchevskii i B.N. Chicherin," ibid., p. 61; Sergei A. Golubtsov, "Teoreticheskie vzgliady V.O. Kliuchevskogo," *Russkii istoricheskii zhurnal* VIII (1922), 178–82; Vadim A. Aleksandrov and A.A. Zimin, "Kommentarii," in VOK, *Kurs russkoi istorii, Sochineniia* (Moscow, 1956), III: 374; Marc Raeff, *Russia Abroad: A Cultural History of Russian Emigration, 1919–1939* (New York: 1990), pp. 165–66, 176.

3. VOK, "Metodologiia i terminologiia," pp. 3–8, 31–35, 81–86, 91–92; VOK, *Kurs, Sochineniia,* I: 13–14, 18–25, 31–40, 284–86; II: 128–29; VOK, *Boiarskaia duma drevnei Rusi* (Moscow, 1902), pp. 40, 163–68, 240–43; VOK, *Lektsii po russkoi istorii professora Moskovskogo universiteta V.O. Kliuchevskogo* (St. Petersburg, 1902), I: iii; VOK, "Boiarskaia duma drevnei Rusi," *Russkaia mysl'* 1, no. 1, part 2, 1880, 48; VOK, "Istoriia soslovii v Rossii," *Sochineniia,* VI: 285–88, 297–98, 305; VOK, *Pis'ma,* pp. 283–84; Pavel S. Shkurinov, *Pozitivizm v Rossii XIX v.* (Moscow, 1980), pp. 312–13; Aleksandrov and Zimin, "Kommentarii," I: 411.

4. VOK, "Metodologiia i terminologiia," pp. 88–92, 104; VOK, *Kurs Sochineniia,* I: 18–19; VOK, "Istoriia soslovii," pp. 285–86; VOK, *Pis'ma,* pp. 24, 207–208, 282–83, 287–90; Aleksandrov and Zimin, "Kommentarii," I: 380–82; Golubtsov, "Teoreticheskie vzgliady," pp. 199–200.

5. ANIIM, VOK archive, f. 4, op. 1, d. 28; VOK, *Kurs, Sochineniia,* I: 24–5; IV: 368; VOK, "Metodologiia i terminologiia," pp. 3–8, 31–38, 132–33; VOK, "Terminologiia russkoi istorii," *Sochineniia v deviati tomakh,* VI: 180–82; VOK, *Pis'ma,* pp. 241, 246, 282–84; Aleksandrov and Zimin, "Kommentarii," I: 410–12; III: 371–72; Vadim A. Aleksandrov, A.A. Zimin, and Raisa A. Kireeva, "Kommentarii k kursu lektsii po istochnikovedeniiu," in VOK, Kurs VI: 475; Seymour Becker, *Nobility and Privilege in Late Imperial Russia* (De Kalb, IL, 1988), pp. 55–56; Shkurinov, *Pozitivizm,* pp. 315–18.

6. ANIIM, VOK archives f. 4, op. 1, d. 93, "Konspekt 3-kh klassov vvodnykh lektsii po russkoi istorii, Uchilishche Vaianiia i . . ."; d. 94, "Lektsii (4 vecher) o krasotie i pom. v drevnei Rusi"; VOK, "O vzgliade khudozhnika na obstanovku i ubor izobrazhaemogo im litsa," *Istoricheskie portrety* (Moscow, 1990), pp. 29–39; VOK, "Nabroski," *Sochineniia v deviati tomakh,* IX: 466–67.

7. VOK, *Kurs, Sochineniia,* II: 13–30,105–13,139–50; VOK, "Istoriia soslovii," pp. 285, 294–96, 464; VOK, "Lektsii po russkoi istoriografii," *Sochineniia,* VIII: 181–86; VOK, *Pis'ma,* pp. 152, 241, 282–83.

8. VOK, *Boiarskaia duma drevnei Rusi* (Moscow, 1882); VOK, *Kurs, Sochineniia,* I: 31–34; VOK, "Istoriia soslovii," pp. 472–73; Aleksandrov, "Posleslovie," VOK, *Kurs, Sochineniia,* I: 379–81; Raisa A. Kireeva, *Izuchenie otechestvennoi istoriografii v dorevoliutsionnoi Rossii s serediny XIX v. do 1917 g.* (Moscow, 1983), pp. 30–40, 114–19; Kireeva, "Posleslovie," VOK, *Kurs, Sochineniia,* VI: 433–35; VII: 432–35, Zimin and Kireeva, "Iz rukopisnogo naslediia Kliuchevskogo," pp. 307–9; A.A. Kizevetter, "Klyuchevsky and His *A Course in Russian History,*" *Slavic Review* 1 (1922): 510–11; Hans Torke, "Kliuchevskii's *Istoriia soslovii,*" *Canadian-American Slavic Studies,* XX, no. 3–4 (1986): 311; Nicholas V. Riasanovsky, *The Image of Peter the Great in Russian History and Thought* (New York, 1985), pp. 175–76.

9. VOK, *Kurs, Sochineniia,* II: 5–7, 105–28, 330–68; VOK, *Boiarskaia duma,* pp. 75, 83–71, 163–68, 240–43; VOK, "Metodologiia i terminologiia," pp. 3–8; VOK, "Terminologiia," pp. 131–35; Aleksandrov, "Posleslovie," VOK, *Sochineniia v deviati tomakh,* II: 379–81; Aleksandr Lappo-Danilevskii, "Istoricheskie vzgliady V.O. Kliuchevskogo," *Kliuchevskii: Kharakteristiki i vospominaniia,* p. 112.

10. VOK, *Kurs, Sochineniia,* II: 3–42, 49–53, 105–38, 151–56, 208, 271, 320, 330–32, 395–97, 436; III: 207–9; IV: 405–8; VOK, *Boiarskaia duma,* pp. 73–74; VOK, "Istoriia soslovii," pp. 366–71, 376; VOK, *Posobie dlia podgotovleniia k polukursovomu ispytaniiu po russkoi istorii* (Moscow, 1897), pp. 196–200; A.A. Zimin, "Kommentarii," VOK, *Kurs, Sochineniia,* II: 402, 414–17; Lev V. Cherepnin, *Obrazovanie russkogo tsentralizovannogo gosudarstva v XIV–XV vekakh* (Moscow, 1960), pp. 77–79.

11. VOK, *Kurs Sochineniia,* II: 55–76, 87–88, 97–104, 107–8; VOK, *Boiarskaia duma,* pp. 73–74, 182–84; VOK, "Pskovskie spory," *Sochineniia,* VII: 45; VOK, "Metodologiia russkoi istorii," pp. 7–8, 24–26, 32–5; Georges P. Fedotov, *The Russian Religious Mind* (Cambridge, MA 1966), I: 186; George Vernadsky, *The Mongols and Russia* (New Haven, 1953), 242–44.

12. VOK, *Kurs russkoi istorii* (Moscow, 1937), II: 146; VOK, *Kurs, Sochineniia,* II: 42–44; VOK, *Boiarskaia duma,* 12–3, 240–42; VOK, "K.N. Bestuzhev-Riumin," *Neopublikovannye proizvedeniia* (Moscow, 1983), p. 155; VOK, "Znachenie prepodobnogo Sergeia dlia russkogo naroda i gosudarstva," *Bogoslovskii vestnik* 4, no. 11 (1892): 201–2; Iurii V. Got'e, "Primechaniia," VOK, *Kurs* (Moscow, 1937), II: 427; Cherepnin, *Obrazovanie russkogo tsentralizovannogo gosudarstva,* pp. 72–74; Donald Ostrowski, "The Mongol Origins of Muscovite Political Institutions," *Slavic Review* 49, no. 4 (1990): 525–42.

13. VOK, *Kurs, Sochineniia,* II: 172–89; III: 213.

14. VOK, "Proiskhozhdenie krepostnogo prava v Rossii," *Opyty i issledovaniia: Pervyi sbornik statei* (Moscow, 1912), pp. 212–310; VOK, "Podushnaia podat' i otmena kholopstva v Rossii," ibid., pp. 311–16; Mikhail A. D'iakonov, "Zadvornye liudi," *Zhurnal Ministerstva narodnogo prosveshcheniia,* no. 12, 1897, 391–98; Got'e, "Primechaniia," p. 433; Aleksandrov and Zimin, "Kommentarii," II: 403–4; Aleksandrov, "Posleslovie," II: 388–89; Boris D. Grekov, *Kievskaia Rus'* (Moscow, 1953),

pp. 171–75; Grekov, *Krest'iane na Rusi s drevneishikh vremen do XVII veka* (Moscow, 1952–54), I: 11, 143–45, 164, 172, 183, 263–65; Lev V. Cherepnin, "V.O. Kliuchevskii," Academy of Sciences, Institute of History, *Ocherki istorii istoricheskoi nauki* (Moscow, 1955–1985), II: 155–56; Richard Hellie, *Enserfment and Military Change in Muscovy* (Chicago, 1971), pp. 1–9, 276–77; Hellie, *Slavery in Russia, 1450– 1725* (Chicago, 1982), pp. 1–9, 141–42, 374–75.

15. VOK, "Proiskhozhdenie krepostnogo prava," pp. 226, 258–68, 308–10; VOK, "Krepostnoi vopros nakanune ego zakonodatel'nogo vozbuzhdeniia," *Otzyvy i otvety: Tretii sbornik statei* (Moscow, 1914), pp. 310–20; VOK, *Boiarskaia duma*, pp. 225–31; 304; VOK, "Istoriia soslovii," pp. 328–33, 427–34.

16. VOK, *Kurs, Sochineniia,* II: 287–96, 309–28; III: 162–73, 185, 187–200, 213– 20, 280–84; IV: 92–100, 311; V: 83–84; VOK, "Proiskhozhdenie krepostnogo prava," pp. 230, 262; VOK, "Dobrye liudi drevnei Rusi," *Ocherki i rechi: Vtoroi sbornik statei* (Moscow, 1913), p. 157; VOK, "Krepostnoi vopros," pp. 301–2; Militsa Nechkina, *Kliuchevskii*, pp. 586–87.

17. VOK, *Kurs, Sochineniia,* IV: 102–6, 317–29; V: 80–108, 136–37; VOK, "Proiskhozhdenie krepostnogo prava," pp. 300–301, 310–12, 410–14; VOK, "Istorii soslovii," p. 328; VOK, "Podushnaia podat'," pp. 322–24; Evgenii V. Anisimov, *Podatnaia reforma Petra I: Vvedenie podushnoi podati v Rossii, 1719–1728* (Leningrad, 1982, pp. 3–9, 147–50, 274–75; Aleksandrov and Zimin, "Kommentarii," V: 395–98.

18. VOK, *Kurs Sochineniia,* III: 187–200; VOK, *Kurs russkoi istorii* (Moscow, 1921), V: 99–125, 136–37; VOK, *Kratkoe posobie po russkoi istorii* (Vladimir, 1909), 171–73.

19. VOK, *Kurs Sochineniia,* III: 187, 213–20; V: 99–125, 136–37, 273–75, 468.

20. ANIIM, VOK archive, f. 4, op. 1, d. 26, 27, 223; f. 44; Manuscript Division Lenin Library (hereafter GBL), VOK archive, f. 131, op. 23, d. 3, "Aleksandr II: Lektsii po istorii tsarstvovaniia," pp. 57–66, VOK, *Kurs Sochineniia,* I: 38: IV: 225–32, 311– 15; V: 188–91, 225–32, 264–71, 371–78, 468, 486; VOK, "Noveishaia istoriia Zapadnoi Evropy v sviazi s istoriei Rossii," *Neopublikovannye,* pp. 285–89; VOK, "Otmena krepostnogo prava," *Sochineniia,* V: 371–93; VOK, *Kratkoe posobie,* pp. 175–76; Nechkina, *Kliuchevskii,* pp. 563–68.

21. Aleksandrov and Zimin, "Kommentarii," V: 464–88.

22. VOK, "Krepostnoi vopros," pp. 301–20; VOK, "Pravo i fakt v istorii krest'ianskogo voprosa. Pis'mo k redaktoru," *Rus',* no. 28, May 23, 1881, pp. 14–17; VOK, "Russkaia istoriografiia 1861–1893 gg.," *Neopublikovannye,* pp. 181–83; Nechkina, *Kliuchevskii,* pp. 207–209, 212–18.

23. ANIIM, VOK archive, f. 4, op. 1, d. 223, 224; f. 26, d. 73; VOK, *Kurs, Sochineniia,* I: 38; IV: 311–15; V: 468; VOK, *Kurs* (Moscow, 1921), V: 270–71; VOK, "Otmena krepostnogo prava," pp. 380–89; VOK, *Kratkoe posobie,* pp. 179–83; VOK, "Noveishaia istoriia Zapadnoi Evropy," pp. 285–89; VOK, *Pis'ma,* p. 332.

24. ANIIM, VOK archive, f. 4, op. 1, d. 26, 223; VOK, *Kurs, Sochineniia,* II: 247–50, 297–308; V: 271–80; VOK, "Metodologiia russkoi istorii," p. 398; VOK, *Kratkoe posobie,* pp. 171–76; VOK, "Krepostnoi vopros," pp. 300–308.

25. VOK, *Kurs, Sochineniia,* I: 20.

26. Ibid., pp. 37–38; V: 271–79; VOK, "S.M. Solov'ev kak prepodavatel'," *Ocherki i rechi,* pp. 24–35; VOK, "Terminologiia," p. 183; VOK, "Istoriia soslovii," pp. 259, 358–59; VOK, "Metodologiia russkoi istorii," pp. 44–45; VOK, "Noveishaia istoriia Zapadnoi Evropy," pp. 277–81; Grekov, "Kievskaia Rus' i problema proiskhozhdeniia russkogo feodalizma u M.N. Pokrovskogo," *Izbrannye trudy* (Moscow, 1957–60), II: 442–53; Bogoslovskii, "Kliuchevskii," pp. 347–50; Cherepnin, "Kliuchevskii," p. 153; Golubtsov, "Teoreticheskie vzgliady," pp. 191–92.

27. VOK, *Kratkoe posobie,* 152–54, 192, 199–200.

28. VOK, *Kurs, Sochineniia,* III: 319–29; IV: 203–4; VOK, "O vzgliade khudozhnika," pp. 296–305; VOK, "Vospominaniia o N.I. Novikove i ego vremeni," *Russkaia mysl'*, 16, no. 1 (1895): 55; Iulii I. Aikhenvald, "Kliuchevskii: Myslitel' i khudozhnok," *Kliuchevskii: Kharakteristiki i vospominaniia,* p. 141; Veniamin M. Khvostov, "Istoricheskoe mirovozzrenie V.O. Kliuchevskogo," *Nravstvennaia lichnosti i obshchestvo: Ocherki po etike i sotsiologii* (Moscow, 1910), pp. 38–40; Basil Maklakov, "Klyuchevsky," *Slavic Review* 13 (1935): 327–28; George H. Bolsover, "Ivan the Terrible in Russian Historiography," *Transactions of the Royal Historical Society,* Series V, 7 (1957): 82; Riasanovsky, *The Image of Peter the Great,* pp. 175–76.

29. VOK, *Noveishaia istoriia: Lektsii chit. V3–m Voen. Aleksandrovsk. uchilishche, Kurs 1882–1883 ucheb. goda* (Moscow, 1883), pp. 13–15.

30. Vadim A. Aleksandrov, ed., *V.O. Kliuchevskii: Istoricheskie portrety, Deiateli istoricheskoi mysli* (Moscow, 1990), p. 8.

31. GBL, VOK archive, f. 131, op. 40, d. 13, "Zapiski po vseobshchei istorii: Lektsii chitannye v Aleksandrovskom voennom uchilishche v 1871–72 i 1872–73 gg.," pp. 4–21, 57–69; Aleksandrov, "Kliuchevskii," p. 18.

32. ANIIM, VOK archive, f. 4, op. 1, d. 150; VOK, *Kurs, Sochineniia,* II: 170–71, 183–89; III, 27–28, 362–64; VOK, "Kn. V.V. Golitsyn. Podgotovka i programma reformy," *Istoricheskie portrety,* pp. 139–50; "Chestvovanie V.O. Kliuchevskogo," *Istoricheskii vestnik* 87, no. 2 (1902): 751–52; A.A. Kizevetter, "Pervyi kurs V.O. Kliuchevskogo, 1873–1874," *Zapiski* 3 (Russkii istoricheskii institut, Belgrade,1931), 292–97.

33. VOK, *Kurs,* IV: 273–93; VOK, "Petr Velikii sredi svoikh sotrudnikov," *Ocherki i rechi,* pp. 474–76; VOK, "Imperatritsa Ekaterina II, 1729–96," ibid., pp. 312–88; VOK, "Zapadnoe vliianie v Rossii posle Petra," *Neopublikovannye,* pp. 45–50.

34. VOK, *Kurs, Sochineniia,* II: 319–29; VOK, "Kurs lektsii po istochnikovedeniiu," *Sochineniia,* VI: 26–32; VOK, "V.N. Tatishchev," *Neopublikovannye*, p. 129; VOK, "O vzgliade khudozhnika," pp. 296–304.

35. VOK, "Avtobiografiia," *Neopublikovannye,* pp. 342–47; Aleksandrov and Zimin, "Kommentarii," V: 431.

36. VOK, *Noveishaia istoriia,* pp. 11–15; VOK, "Ob intelligentsii," *Neopublikovannye,* pp. 298–302; VOK, "Pis'mo frantsuzhenki," ibid., pp. 326–33; VOK, "Prilozhenie k kursu 'Noveishaia istoriia Zapadnoi Evropy v sviazi s istoriei Rossii," ibid., pp. 367–70; VOK, "O vzgliade khudozhnika," pp. 174–89; VOK, "Avtobiografiia," pp. 342–47; VOK, *Pis'ma,* pp. 228–29, 260, 333, 336, 342, 347, 374; Elpidifor Barsov, "Mnenie V.O. Kliuchevskogo o Maksime Gor'kom: Zapisano 25 sent. 1907 g." *U Troitsy v Akademii, 1824–1914* (Moscow, 1914), pp. 692–93; Sergei I. Smirnov, ed., "V.O. Kliuchevskii v ego ponimanii natsional'nogo vospitaniia," ed. Vladimir Volzhenin, V.F. Dinze, and S.D. Smirnov, *O natsional'noi shkole: Sbornik* (Petrograd, 1916), pp. 68–72; Samuel D. Kassow, "The Russian University in Crisis, 1899–1911" (Ph.D. diss., Princeton University, 1976), p. 712.

37. VOK, *Pis'ma,* pp. 260, 336.

38. Ibid., pp. 228–41, 338, 342, 379.

39. VOK, *Kurs, Sochineniia,* I: 34–37; III: 126–27; VOK, "Vechernie chteniia v Abastumane," *Neopublikovannye,* p. 296; VOK, "Ob intelligentsii," pp. 300–301; VOK, *Pis'ma,* p. 322; Bernard Pares, "The Peterhof Conference (On the Draft Project of the Imperial Duma), August 1–5, 1905," *Russian Review,* November 1913, p. 116.

40. VOK, "Istoriia soslovii," *Sochineniia v deviati tomakh,* VI: 233–36; VOK, "Aleksandr II," p. 62.

41. Nikolai K. Karataev, *Ekonomicheskie nauki v Moskovskom universitete, 1755–1955* (Moscow, 1956), pp. 194–202; Iziaslav Kh. Shteingauz, *Sotsiologicheskie vzgliady V.O. Kliuchevskogo* (Irkutsk, 1974), II; Sergei I. Tkhorzhevskii, "V.O. Kliuchevskii kak sotsiolog i politicheskii myslitel'," *Dela i dni* II (1921): 204–5; Nechkina, *Kliuchevskii,* pp. 176–77, 262, 592–93.

42. Archives of the Academy of Sciences, Moscow, Alexei I. Iakovlev archive, f. 640, op. 1, d. 40, "Vospominaniia o V.O. Kliuchevskom"; Iurii V. Got'e, *Time of Troubles: The Diary of Iurii Vladimirovich Got'e, Moscow, July 9, 1917–July 23, 1922,* trans., ed., and intro. Terence Emmons (Princeton, 1988), pp. 133–34; VOK, *Pis'ma,* pp. 269, 465–66; Iakovlev, "Primechaniia," VOK, *Kurs* (Moscow, 1937), I: 385–90; Nechkina, *Kliuchevskii,* pp. 41–42, 372, 381–82, 607.

12

The Idea of Development in Miliukov's Historical Thought

Melissa K. Stockdale

The nation is adaptable.
—*P.N. Miliukov to the State Duma, December 4, 1909*

In the introductory lecture of his course on Russian history, first delivered in 1892, Miliukov told his students he would not be offering them a narrative history such as they were accustomed to from their schooldays. The sort of history that set itself no further goal than the "possibly true reproduction of that which was" might be interesting and instructive but had very little in common with history as a science. The subject of scientific history was not changes in dynasties and the conduct of wars but the study of the "internal, fundamental processes of a people's development in all its fullness and animation." Its goal was not only to ascertain the process of development but to understand it.[1]

While characterizing the discipline of history in more theoretical terms than was its wont, Miliukov's remarks epitomize the views of the Moscow school of historiography. For Miliukov's own individual interpretation of Russian history, the phrase "a people's development" is critical. His interests and methodology were too diverse and his oeuvre too vast to be reduced to one fundamental issue.[2] Still, explaining the process of development—the means by which societies change in general, and the exceptionally changeable nature of Russia in particular—was the goal informing virtually all of Miliukov's work. For that reason, in the following discussion of his sociological orientation, major works, and historiographic contributions, his treatment of the dynamism of the Russian state and the adaptiveness of the Russian nation will take pride of place.

Pavel Nikolaevich Miliukov was born in Moscow in 1859 to a family of modest means and somewhat indeterminate social status: though the Miliukovs claimed to be of the noble *soslovie,* they did not have a patent of nobility. Miliukov received a classical education at Moscow First Gymnasium, graduating with a silver medal in 1877, and enrolled in the history–philology *fakul'tet* of Moscow University with the intention of studying classics. He was to spend some seventeen years at the university, earning kandidat's and magister's degrees in history in 1883 and 1892, respectively, as well as teaching courses in Russian history and historiography from 1886 until his expulsion on political grounds in 1895.

V.O. Kliuchevskii's inspiring achievements decided Miliukov upon graduate study in Russian history, but Miliukov's interest in history and approach to its study had already been shaped in significant ways by the time Kliuchevskii joined the faculty in 1879. In the 1870s a remarkable circle of young professors coalesced at Moscow University, including Maksim Kovalevskii, dean of Russian sociology; Vsevolod Miller, a linguist specializing in Sanskrit; the jurist I.V. Ianzhul; Paul Vinogradov, a lecturer in world history recently returned from research at Oxford; N.I. Storozhenko and Aleksei Veselovskii, from the literature department; and S.A. Muromtsev and A.I. Chuprov, from the law school. No single orientation characterized the entire group, but their empiricism and hostility to "metaphysics," multidisciplinary and comparative approach to the history of culture, law, and beliefs, and search for "regularities" or laws (*zakonomernost'*) in history and social life all left their imprint on Miliukov's mature sociological views.[3]

It was Kovalevskii who introduced Miliukov to the work of Auguste Comte, and Miliukov remained throughout his life a self-proclaimed positivist. From Comte he took his belief in mankind's development from a theological to a metaphysical and thence to a rational and scientific mode of thinking, and his belief in the growing complexity and interrelatedness of all social phenomena. Again following Comte, Miliukov believed that all social phenomena were subject to laws of causality and that scientific history could properly seek and hope to identify these laws. For Miliukov, differences between the methods of the natural and social sciences were differences of degree rather than kind.[4]

Miliukov felt that empirical observation made the idea of the "regularity" or "lawfulness" of the historical process virtually inescapable. The numerous similarities observable among different human societies at comparable stages of development required explanation. Once reference to a providential plan or anything external to the human world was excluded as a tenable mode of explanation of human history, the historian had to suppose the existence of sociological laws. Methodologically, he first assumed, following the British historian Thomas Buckle, that those laws should be discerned inductively. By 1895, however, with the serial publication of volume one of his *Studies of Russian Culture,* he was advocating a deductive approach. Historians could draw on the known laws of other disciplines, above all psychology, and apply them to the explanation of the historical process.[5]

The idea of any key causal factor seemed to him too narrow and dogmatic—this was the problem with Marxism's materialistic monism.[6] His own perspective on causal relationships was a pluralist one. "From the point of view of science there are not primary and necessary, secondary and accidental causes," but only causes turning out to have a larger or smaller sphere of influence in any given case.[7] Insisting that the many aspects of human culture were interdependent, but at the same time too differentiated and complex to be reduced to any "primordial unity," Miliukov was skeptical of overly schematic approaches to cultural history. He in fact never attempted an overall schema of the history of Russian culture, instead offering separate periodizations, for example, of the evolution of the state, spirituality, and social consciousness.

In the second place—and it is here that Miliukov was most original—he accommodated operation of the unique and individual within an overall regular framework by seeing regularity as only one of three factors constituting the historical process. Alongside the operation of the sociological "law" there was the fact of its realization in a given milieu in a given time and place. Milieu included what might be called structural or "necessary" conditions, such as climate and geography, and slightly more variable or accidental conditions, such as the presence of hostile neighbors. Finally, there was a third element, the most truly ephemeral and accidental, and that was the role played by individual human personalities. "Constituting one indivisible whole, all these sides develop in closest connection and interdependence."[8]

This tripartite theory of the functioning of the historical process largely determined the structure of Miliukov's three-volume *Studies of Russian Culture,* being most apparent in the volume detailing the formulation of the Russian "national ideology." In this volume Miliukov addressed the question of the origins of Russia's definition of itself as a distinct nation and people. The sociological process of self-definition was one undergone by every people. In Russia, however, the process of self-definition was set in motion when the society was at a relatively low level of cultural and economic development, with the result that Russians borrowed a great deal of their "national idea" from other, more advanced cultures. This was the effect of milieu on the operation of the universal law. Finally, the choice of what cultures were to be borrowed from, what elements of a given culture were borrowed, and how constituted the most "accidental" factor in the development of the national idea and the one most susceptible to influence by human will, such as the character and inclinations of a given ruler and his advisers.

In this way, Miliukov accommodated the structural and the dynamic, the universal and the particular, strict causality and the adventitious in his explanation of the functioning of the historical process. The joint action of universal law and particular milieu preserved his explanation from being overly abstract and ahistorical, a shortcoming he had detected in Marxist and Populist perspectives of the 1890s: "The Marxite view seems to ignore the idiosyncratic peculiarities of Russia and appears no less fallacious than the Populist view, which is inclined, on the contrary, to exaggerate the importance of these peculiarities."[9]

It also allowed him to steer a middle course between the conception of a totally unconscious, elemental social development offered by Spencerian evolution, on the one hand, and the pronounced voluntarism of the Russian "subjective school" of sociology, on the other. Spencer's model of social evolution ignored the factor of human consciousness and left no historical role to individual human actors, Miliukov felt, while he detected in subjective sociology's idea of the "critically thinking individual" Carlyle's great man in more up-to-date costume. Miliukov's characterization of the historical process did accord a place to individual will and action, though its sphere was limited, since human will did not exist independently of the influences and constraints of both milieu and sociological "laws." Individuals were motivated by instincts and unconscious desires—riddles that Miliukov thought psychology might one day unravel—and by conscious ideals, which were socially generated, historical in nature, and whose origins and evolution historians could discover.

Such a perspective was critical to avoiding an ahistorical conception of the human personality which inflated the role of human will in history. In his opinion, philosophers of history frequently overlooked the huge gulf separating an individual purposeful act "from its social consequences, from a purposeful social result; a whole series of conditions existing fully only at the highest rungs of societal life are necessary for the bridging of this gulf." Examples of the gap between intentions and results appear repeatedly in Miliukov's historical work, one of the best being his analysis of Catherine the Great's unsuccessful effort to create a "new man" by radically recasting Russia's educational system.[10]

The importance Miliukov attached to making this point about the role of human will becomes clearer when it is considered as part of a larger debate about the meaning and uses of history. Miliukov was an impassioned opponent of any normative or ethical interpretation of history. He wanted to demarcate scientific history from "metaphysics," an approach shared by the Moscow young professors and generally typical of the Russian sociological orientation of the time.[11] In his view, the chief difference between an approach that was truly scientific as compared to a philosophical one was that the former undertook to *explain* history while the latter sought to evaluate it. A philosophical or "metaphysical" approach looked for the meaning of history. For Miliukov, this question was entirely improper to a scientific viewpoint: the historian was an investigator, not a judge.[12]

The scholar's choice of subject matter was as important as was the approach to it: events, being by nature more accidental, were less amenable to scientific methods of investigation and less likely to yield "scientific" knowledge. With other proponents of the new sociological orientation in history, Miliukov believed that the focus of inquiry should shift from politics and the actions of individuals, which he called "a sort of dust on the surface of the historic ocean," to the more "immobile" and substantive, that is, to the institutions and life of the whole people. But this view on topics reflected normative as well as methodological considerations: demanding that historians not "extravagantly" expend their energies on studying what need not be studied, Miliukov implicitly used the criterion of usefulness to society in determining what subjects merited scholarly investigation.[13]

What, then was the use of history? Scientific history sought to know human society, to establish what it was and has become, and explain why it has done what it has done. The value of this, for Miliukov, was connected to his conviction that "knowledge of the truth will set us free."[14] The burden of the past would be lightened immensely when the past became truly known, for much of that burden was the accumulated detritus of times dead and gone: "It is clear that our own conscious activity should be directed not at preservation of this archeological remnant of a remote antiquity, but toward creation of a new Russian cultural tradition corresponding to contemporary social ideals."[15]

Miliukov did, increasingly, believe in progress. He understood progress to be the gaining of knowledge of and mastery over the material world, the shedding of superstition, and the advancement toward genuine, scientific knowledge of the workings of human society. He believed that human society was becoming more enlightened and thereby "conscious," and that it was in the full consciousness of an entire people and not just its elite that the possibility of truly "making" history reposed. When a common goal had been worked out, transmitted over generations, and disseminated by education and upbringing so that it truly constituted a cultural "tradition," society could at last hope to bridge the gap between articulation of social ideals and achievement of those ideals.[16]

In terms of social organization, progress meant democracy. In Miliukov's reading of the historical process, European states in the modern period increasingly experienced the participation of lower social estates and classes in the governing process, concomitant with the penetration of enlightenment and culture to those classes. The result was not only political democratization but also the increased concern of the state with domestic welfare and, more abstractly, greater rationality and less scope for the element of the accidental in the movement of history as "consciousness" characterized more and more of the citizenry. From approximately 1900 onward, much of his research and writing was dedicated to explaining why Russia, for all that was unique in its experience, was no exception to this process.

This belief in progress was in part predicated upon confidence that the picture of social evolution yielded by a scientific history was not simply another species of transferring "a golden dream of the future" onto the past. He did not doubt the possibility, in principle, of arriving at genuine knowledge of the past; epistemological considerations in Miliukov's work were conspicuous by their absence.

The confidence that humanity can gain objective knowledge of its past has been called a characteristically "nineteenth-century" view: Stuart Hughes contrasts it with a view which he sees as more typically twentieth-century in its heightened intellectual self-consciousness and recognition of the disparity between external reality and internal appreciation of that reality.[17] At the same time, the Annales school, one of the most influential historical orientations of the twentieth century, approaches the study of the past with a set of positivist assumptions remarkably similar to those of Miliukov and the Moscow school of historiography. The nomological approach of the Annales school, its belief in the possibility of obtaining direct, objective knowledge of the past, its interest in both structure and dynamic in history, and its commitment to *histoire totale* and relative lack of interest in political history are all highly reminiscent of the Moscow school.

The major difference, at least in the case of Miliukov, lies in the annalistes' resistance to any attempt to impose a theory of progress, or even of discernible direction, on history. Arguably, it was Miliukov's mature conviction in the near inevitability of progress, based on a Eurocentric model and resulting in more democratic government and greater social justice, that most clearly marks him as a product of the nineteenth century.

Less characteristic of the Moscow school of historiography was Miliukov's abiding interest in the history of ideas. Kliuchevskii was typical of Russian historiography as a whole in separating intellectual history from political, social, and economic history, and in neglecting the former. Miliukov held that ideas, representing "spiritual forces," were as important a factor in the historical process as material conditions. However, in studying ideas one could not divorce them from the social, political, and economic realities of the time in which they were formulated and gained currency. Neither should they be looked at abstractly: one must study how people attempted to realize ideas in practice and, especially, how those ideas changed when confronted with "real life."[18]

Miliukov's interest in ideas extended to ideas *about* history. One of the most theoretically minded historians of his generation, he introduced the first course in Russian historiography at Moscow university. Future historians, among them Aleksandr Kizevetter and Iu.V. Got′e, took his classes and were profoundly influenced by his methodological and theoretical training. Like his mentor Paul Vinogradov, he was an enthusiastic and "hands-on" teacher, sharing with students his excitement over his archival discoveries, guiding them in their own research, and inviting them home for lively discussions where they jointly worked out "common views on history as science." This pedagogic role was one of Miliukov's most important contributions to the formation of the Moscow school of historiography.[19]

Major Works and Themes

Miliukov's scholarly career divides roughly into three parts. The earliest period, from 1886 to 1893, was that of scholarship strictly conceived, directed to a specialized audience. From 1894 to 1905 he was more present-minded in his approach, increasingly writing for the broader educated public on historical topics with contemporary political implications. After a twelve-year hiatus caused by his shift to political activity, Miliukov returned to scholarship in emigration, but now focusing almost exclusively on the sort of narrative, political history he earlier eschewed.

Even with the long interruption in his scholarly writing he was an enormously prolific historian, publishing fourteen original book-length works in addition to numerous reviews, articles, encyclopedia pieces, public lectures, and an edited textbook. As amazing as the sheer volume of output was his erudition and the range of his interests: his writing displayed familiarity with topics as diverse as the origins of the Slavs, Byzantine influence on Russian ideas of sovereignty, the history of Russian art, and nineteenth-century agrarian policy.[20]

Miliukov's magister thesis, *State Economy and the Reforms of Peter the Great,* caused an immediate stir upon publication in 1892. The assertion that Peter's reforms were neither an abrupt break with the past nor a consciously thought-out whole was not new. Solov'ev had first argued that the Petrine reforms were the outgrowth of the gradual Westernizing of the seventeenth century, while Kliuchevskii had demonstrated the ad hoc nature and underlying military motivations of most of Peter's administrative and financial reforms. What was novel was the way Miliukov tried to shift discussion from intentions to results, by moving the focus of the investigation to reforms whose results were more readily quantifiable. In Miliukov's opinion, the Slavophile–Westernizer debate as to whether Peter had created modern Russia or betrayed the country's traditions had played out its usefulness for scholarly knowledge. It was time to plant the study of Peter on firmer, more scientific ground by recasting the questions asked about his reign and returning to the primary sources. Miliukov therefore decided to explore the fiscal policies and financial institutions of the Petrine period, undertaking a huge investigation of unpublished archival documents, many of them never before consulted by scholars.[21]

He drew two very controversial conclusions. Whereas Solov'ev and Kavelin had asserted that the Petrine reforms were "necessary" and "organic," in this work the question of the necessity of the reforms was answered in somewhat ambivalent fashion. Miliukov concluded that while the international situation had indeed demanded creation of a military capability such as that wrought by Peter, the country was not financially capable of supporting it: "The price of raising Russia to the rank of a great power was the ruination of the country."[22]

Miliukov's conclusion reflected the dilemma Peter's activities posed for him. As a thoroughgoing proponent of European culture and "European" state administration, he could not but sympathize with Peter's efforts to make Russia a great European power. But as an opponent of autocratic government he criticized the sacrifice of the welfare of the people to the interests of the state. In effect, he defended the goals while deploring the means and many of their indirect results. Yet his own research seemed to suggest that, given the low level of development of productivity in Petrine Russia, there was no way Russia could have achieved great-power status which would not have entailed wholesale privation for the masses.

The second controversial area had to do with Miliukov's negative assessment of Peter's role as a reformer. The absence of visible evidence of Peter's participation in various administrative and institutional reforms led Miliukov to assert that Peter not only lacked an initial, overall plan but was not even the architect of most of the reforms, which were actually the creation of trusted subordinates. This evaluation reflected the "temper of the times," the hostility of the radical intelligentsia toward the tsarist system, but also the sources consulted; the discovery of new archival evidence modified Miliukov's views. In subsequent works touching on Peter, he increasingly expanded his picture of the first emperor's personal role in reform, emphasizing the correspondence of Peter's means to the conditions of the day, the more "conscious" long-term goals of the last reforming years, and Peter's right to be considered the creator of an intellectual class in Russia.[23]

State Economy and the Reforms of Peter the Great remained for some seventy years the most comprehensive and authoritative account of the Petrine financial reforms. Miliukov also succeeded in this work in giving an impetus to the "new history" based on extensive archival work. M.M. Bogoslovskii's dissertation on the regional reform of Peter the Great and Aleksandr Kizevetter's book on the provincial reform of Catherine are among the best of the works inspired by the achievement of Miliukov's pioneering monograph.[24]

Miliukov's second monograph, *Controversial Questions in the History of Muscovite State Finances,* retained the financial–institutional focus of his work on Peter's reforms but revealed more pronounced theoretical views on the study of history. The book grew out of a review of A. Lappo-Danilevskii's monograph on seventeenth-century financial institutions, *The Organization of Direct Taxation in the Muscovite State.* Miliukov warmly praised Lappo-Danilevskii's achievement without entirely supporting his conclusions; what is of interest to this discussion, however, is Miliukov's remarks on the author's historical approach.[25]

Miliukov took issue with Lappo-Danilevskii's assertion that "the specialist in the history of a given people should study in its history primarily *specific* phenomena peculiar to the national type, and not features it has in common with other peoples." Miliukov found this statement in itself highly disputable but directed his main critique to a second assertion, based on this initial assumption of a national type, that "the most specific phenomenon of Russian national history is the Muscovite state of the seventeenth century."[26]

In rejecting the idea of a "type" as an abstraction from reality, Miliukov showed his preference for the study of "social dynamics" over "social statics" in sociological history. "This primary concentration of attention on an idea of a type, worked out in advance, does not presage anything good," he averred. "Exaggerating the 'stability' of phenomena, the investigator risks losing the necessary flexibility of thought and acuteness of view; following the unity of a type, the historian risks missing the main thing underlying historical study, the diversity, complexity and mobility of the historical process." A typological perspective, Miliukov concluded, cannot accommodate the dynamic of historical development.[27]

Main Currents in Russian Historical Thought represented a departure from Miliukov's first two monographs in terms of subject and approach, as his focus shifted from the history of institutions to the history of ideas and culture. Although it did not generate the sort of attention produced by his study of the Petrine reforms, it is one of his finest works. Certainly, it is the least dated: no book on Russian historiography, written before or after, rivals its treatment of the period 1700–1836. The work actually has two subjects, for Miliukov here consciously used the history of historiography as a vehicle for tracing the evolution of the worldviews of Russian society at large.

Main Currents begins with a brief overview of the *Synopsis* of 1688 and ends with an examination of the initial influence of German Idealism on Russian thought. A projected second volume, which would have taken the exposition to Miliukov's own day, was never completed. Two premises underlie the book. Miliukov advanced the proposition that all scientific work, consciously or unconsciously, was directed by theories, and that these theories were the product of the prevailing worldview of the given period in which they were advanced. The scholar who ignored theory became the involuntary tool of outdated theory, and his work suffered in consequence. At the same time, appreciation of the cultural context informing earlier scholarly work had a liberating effect, "freeing contemporary thought from the aggregate of historical axioms taken on faith from old historical productions."[28]

Second, by asserting the existence of an "uninterrupted connection between science and learning" Miliukov's history of historiography became a larger history of Russian thought. The general current of Russian historiography, he held, "is always in more or less close connection with the development of the general worldview."[29]

Miliukov divided the development of Russian historical writing over the last two centuries into two periods. The first, from Tatishchev through Karamzin, was the period of the practical or ethical understanding of the tasks of the historian. The second period, extending from the mid-1820s to his own day, was that of history looked on as a science. He identified four subperiods in the eighteenth-century development of historical study and, by extension, in the evolution of Russian thought, by examining four outstanding representatives of the Russian Enlightenment—Tatishchev, Lomonosov, Shcherbatov, and Boltin.

Between the two periods of Russian historiography stood Karamzin, and Miliukov was at pains to rout forever the myth of Karamzin as "the Peter the Great of Russian historians." This was the most controversial section of his study. In Miliukov's opinion, Karamzin profited by his predecessors' work without managing to correct their faults. Even his views on the course of Russian history were largely borrowed from a schema worked out by eighteenth-century historians, and they had discovered it laid out for them in the sources. In Karamzin, Moscow appeared as the natural continuation of Kiev, and the rise of Moscow was presented as something necessary in the general course of Russian history. The actions of the rulers were the prime mover of history: princely will plunged Russia into the depths and raised it to greatness. Miliukov here explored the way in which this understanding of Russian history was formulated and incorporated into the original sources themselves in the fifteenth and sixteenth centuries. This reading of the sources would become the provocative central thesis on the foreign origins of national ideology in the *Studies of Russian Culture.*

The second, "scientific" period of Russian historical science had its genesis in the huge sea change in worldview wrought by German Romanticism. Particularly influential, in Miliukov's opinion, was Schelling's nature philosophy, with its insistence upon a "living, dynamic unity of life permeating the universe." With the generation of the 1820s the prevailing concentration on external history—that is, political history—gave way to the study of "internal" history, "the history of the mind and heart of mankind."[30] Chief among the disputes engendered by the new orientation was the question of what gave the Russian nationality its ordained place in world history, a dispute Miliukov illustrated by looking at the way N.A. Polevoi, M.P. Pogodin, I.V. Kireevskii, and P.Ia.Chaadaev addressed this issue.

Main Currents was a study of gradual and not uninterrupted progress, for advances in historiography in one area often occasioned neglect of previous advances in others. By the time of Kireevskii and Chaadaev, Russian scholarship had experienced but not succeeded in uniting the three elements which, taken all together, constituted truly scientific history in Miliukov's eyes: the rigorous, critical methodology and insistence on subject matter drawn from "real life" that distinguished the approach of the eighteenth century, and the dynamic, "lawful," theoretical view of the historical process introduced in the nineteenth.

Main Currents was also the story of the joint contribution of Western and Russian influences to the development of native historiography. If French and German scholarship were mainly responsible for scientific theory and methodology, it was Russian scholars who uncovered sources and provided the historical schema. And theories foreign in origin were revised, added to, transformed—and sometimes distorted—in the hands of Russian scholars, in order to suit them to the realities of the Russian experience. What might be called the "subplot" of the work, the larger intellectual history of the period 1700–1836, unfolded in parallel fashion. The "main currents" examined were all European imports, but the story of their acceptance and reworking was one of increasingly widespread cultural attainments and of increasingly sophisticated thinking.

Although Miliukov never wrote the projected second volume of this work, his views on the further development of Russian thought and historiography may be found in lectures, scattered articles, and the third volume of *Studies of Russian Culture*. In a seminal 1886 essay on the extended generation of Russian historians preceding that of his own day, Miliukov identified a "juridical school" of Russian historiography exemplified in the work of Sergei Solov'ev, K.D. Kavelin, B.N. Chicherin, and V.I. Sergeevich. For all their differences in emphasis and periodization, he believed these scholars constituted a meaningful school distinguished by its Hegelian-inspired focus on the origins of "political juridical forms" and their transformation into the state. In the work of Solov'ev, a society organized by kinship began to give way to one based on political relationships when the center of Russian life shifted from the south to the north. Kavelin added an intermediate stage in the development from clan to state organization, one based on family relationships and a transition from communal to private property, while Chicherin believed that princely relationships were guided as much by personal interests as by clan ties, causing him to see the intermediate stage as a period of private law that was eventually replaced by one of state law.

The juridical school made several important contributions to the study of Russian history, Miliukov suggested, not least of which was its replacement of the old ahistorical concept of the state as a conscious contract of individuals by a more organic and dynamic concept, that of the state as a historically evolving system of relationships. The problem he had with the approach was not so much its identification of the state as the engine of the historical process in Russia, but rather the predominance of system over content: the juridical school did little research into the "social material" making up the organization of society that it sought to explain.[31]

Also worth noting is Miliukov's work on Slavophilism, a current of thought that fascinated him and on which he developed considerable expertise. Although he appreciated the originality of Slavophilism, regarding it as the first truly creative Russian reworking of European philosophy, he took it to task for being internally inconsistent as well as simply bad history. Slavophilism attempted to combine particularism and universalism, the idea of unique nationality and that of world-historical significance. In seeking national characteristics that were distinctly "Russian" and that would furthermore promise Russians a world-historical significance, the Slavophiles hit upon the integrated spiritualism of peasant Orthodoxy and the practical communalism of peasant institutions. By virtue of these qualities, they believed, the Russian people would help humanity transcend the atomizing rationalism of Western civilization. For all their esteem for tradition, however, the Slavophiles were profoundly ahistorical in their thought. In Miliukov's view, this ahistoricism encompassed more than idealization of certain features of the Russian past, including the Muscovite autocracy. Slavophiles erroneously construed inalterable "absolutes" from temporary historical phenomena—assuming, for instance, that communalism was an inalienable trait of the Russian people—and then compounded the error by attributing a *causal* significance to what was a product of social development.[32]

Studies in Russian Culture was, until publication of Kliuchevskii's *Course,* the most widely read interpretation of Russian history since Karamzin's. Over the course of seven editions, from 1896 to 1918, it underwent significant revision and supplementation, reflecting the suggestions and criticisms of Miliukov's colleagues, new discoveries in historical scholarship, and, under the influence of developments in the political realm, his changing conception of the connection between the Russian past and present. The phenomenal success of *Studies* was due in part to the fact that it answered a need for an interpretative history of Russian culture, broadly defined, for the growing educated public. Miliukov's explicit goal was to "explain the present in terms of the past." This was not, in his view, strictly scholarly history; in *Studies* he undertook to present "what was most essential and elementary in the process of Russian history," in readable and accessible form.

Studies grew out of a course of lectures Miliukov first gave at the Moscow Pedagogical Institute in 1892–94. The treatment is thematic and methodological rather than chronological. Its three volumes deal, respectively, with material culture, spiritual culture, and the origins and development of the "national idea." Three major premises connect all three volumes: the changeability of Russia throughout its existence, due to its own internal dynamic; the external nature of the formative influences on the state order, culture, and national ideas; and the fact of the imposition of borrowed culture from above. Also of great importance was the novel decision to exclude Kievan history from the history of the state order and of national ideas, since "in the northeast there were entirely different conditions of historical development than in the south."[33]

Miliukov's treatment of material culture included demographic history, economic history, and development of the whole institutional and social structure of the Russian state. Russia's harsh climate, short growing season, and vast expanses meant, first, that only low levels of population could be supported by primitive economy and, second, that the population was peripatetic, naturally inclining to the easier course of extensive rather than intensive agriculture. The huge difference in population density between European Russia and Western Europe had enormous significance for the history of the Russian state. Because the population was not only numerically small but "wandering," productivity was low and the potential pool of recruits for the army small. Given these factors, in the face of the threat posed by hostile and aggressive neighbors, the state had to become hyperactive, summoning into existence and harnessing social estates, urban settlement, and industry in the interests of self-defense. The Russian state developed in a fashion opposite to the course of development of the state in Europe, being created from the top down rather than from the bottom up. This, in Miliukov's interpretation, was the single most important fact of Russian history.

Its consequences were enormous. In the West, Miliukov said, the existence of entrenched aristocratic landed interests forced the developing modern state to recognize, from the start, legitimate interests separate from and independent of its own. The existence of cities with corporate interests and traditions of independence gave birth to the idea of political freedom. In Muscovite Russia, in contrast, cities had their origins in the princely *dvor* or military settlements, and there was no entrenched landed interest. As a result, there was no conception of political freedom nor participation of citizens in government. Instead, the state became a "military camp" and conscripted every social order to its service.[34]

Miliukov's analysis of spiritual culture addressed religiosity and high culture. His fundamental concern was to chronicle the history of the break between the elite and the people, which he saw, above all, as a product of the evolution of the official church. Informing the whole work was a refutation of both the Slavophile and "official" view of religiosity as a distinctively Russian characteristic, in his assertion that "despite the generally accepted opinion, we can say that Russian life in the past was not too much but too *little* penetrated by the foundations of faith."[35]

According to Miliukov, there has been a break between the intelligentsia and the people in every European country, and this break is always evoked by changes in the state of religious belief [*verovanie*]. In Russia, the joint factors of material circumstances and the nature of the Eastern Orthodox church eventually resulted in indifference toward the church, which in turn helped explain the difference in the character of the break of Russian and European society with their past.[36]

Miliukov argued that, for a variety of reasons, Christianity did not genuinely penetrate to the masses of the population for centuries after the formal conversion of the Eastern Slavs. In the sixteenth century, when the people began to demonstrate greater spiritual awareness and needs, the church hierarchy saw only cause for alarm, and turning to the government for help, it stamped them out. The church thus lost any chance to foster and direct creativity; Russians would turn to other secular and borrowed sources.

One could say that, with Chaadaev, Miliukov found Russia's choice of Eastern Christianity a fateful one. It was not Peter who divided the intelligentsia from the people, but the evolution of the official church—the hundred years from the Stoglav council to the Schism marked the great watershed in the creative and spiritual life of Russia. The consequences of this rupture for cultural development were disastrous. Russian art and literature became secularized too abruptly and, lacking a native secular tradition of high culture, merely imitated foreign ways. Not until the nineteenth century, as men of the people began to penetrate the upper social echelons and those in "society" began to seek out the sources of their native cultural heritage did a truly indigenous and creative Russian culture begin to flourish again. In this way, the course of development of high culture paralleled that of the state and social order, being primarily shaped by external factors but only in response to changes generated internally, by the people.

The heart of *Studies of Russian Culture* was volume three, which many consider Miliukov's masterpiece. First published serially in 1899–1900, it was informed by Miliukov's Balkan research into Slav national movements as well as by his continuing work with Russian historical sources. His subject in this volume was the genesis and evolution of "popular consciousness," which he defined as consisting of two successive processes or periods, those of national consciousness and social consciousness. Miliukov argued that in all countries nationality was a product rather than a cause of the historical process, and that it carried the unmistakable stamp of the period in which its characteristics came to be recognized. Such an understanding of nationality and national consciousness had far-reaching implications.

When nationality was identified as a phenomenon of natural science— speaking of blood or race—or as an "anthropological–geographical" one, it assumed the character of an absolute, something unchanging. From this followed the romantic concept of a national genius or national tradition that was equally unalterable, which allowed scholars to search the past for the "genuine" national tradition, one perhaps deviated from over the course of time, that should serve as the touchstone for nationally minded policies. For example, followers of Kostomarov could identify the *veche* period as the expression of a truly Russian democratic tradition, blaming subversion of this tradition on the influence of the Mongol yoke. Whether one's outlook was conservative or progressive, however, the usual view of popular consciousness made it possible to look to an absolute national tradition to legitimate social and political programs in the present.

The sanction of tradition disappeared when nationality was understood as a sociological phenomenon, the first moment in the evolution of popular consciousness. In Miliukov's dry definition, "Nationality constitutes a social group that has at its disposal language, as the singular and necessary means for uninterrupted psychological interaction and which elaborates for itself a permanent fund of unique psychological experiences that regulate the correctness and the recurrence of the phenomena of this interaction."[37]

In dividing the evolution of popular consciousness into two successive processes or periods, Miliukov also distinguished them as being expressed by different social groups with different desiderata, so that national consciousness assumed a basically traditional character, while social consciousness was primarily reformist. National consciousness, since it is evoked by recognition of an "other," arises from the clash of nations and is most often worked out during the process of a people's struggle for unification and independence. The customs, religion, and language of that period, which developed during earlier, unconscious eras, are taken to be what is distinctively indigenous and truly national, though in fact the group has already absorbed much that was foreign. The transition to the period of social consciousness is accompanied by a struggle which ends, in the most favorable circumstances, with replacement of the traditional system of social relations by a system founded on the conscious choice of the majority—in other words, by democracy. "National 'tradition' retires to the background before victorious 'public opinion'."[38]

The history of popular consciousness yielded the same double conclusion arrived at in the analysis of material and spiritual history: the Russian experience was both universal and unique. That the formative period of national consciousness was influenced by an external threat of danger was in no way singular. What Miliukov saw as unique or accidental, in the case of Russia, was that the activity of the factor of external danger to the state coincided with a given—and low—degree of development of internal "social" forces.[39]

Class struggle, religious thought, and the territorial aspirations of the grand princes of Moscow were among the important factors shaping the "national idea" from the time of Ivan III to Peter I, but in Miliukov's exposition foreign influence played the primary role. It was European ideas that were responsible for "the rapid ideological metamorphosis that clothed the grand prince of the appanage period in the costume of the tsar." Bulgarian and South Slav theories, for example, were the source of the Muscovite rulers' claim to be the "sole Orthodox tsar in the entire universe" and of the representation of Moscow as the "new Tsargrad and the third Rome."[40] These theories and legends underwent revision in Russian hands, reconciling the South Slavic formula for Muscovy's political role as heir of the Byzantine tsars with native Muscovite pretensions to the lands of their Kievan "ancestors."[41]

The emergence of a new class, the service gentry, was another important factor in determining the shape of the "national idea." Beholden to the autocratic order for its status and well-being, the gentry proved very conservative. The Time of Troubles had taught it to fear an insufficiency of power rather than an excess; it therefore did nothing to impede the monopolization of political power by the ruler and his burgeoning bureaucracy. In this way, the early seventeenth century saw the triumph of a national ideology that justified the absolutist idea of an all-Russian "tsar," one imposed by the state and greatly influenced by foreign ideas.[42]

Miliukov's interest was always piqued more by the business of explaining how things came to be than by establishing what they had been, the approach he saw as a defining characteristic of the Moscow school of historiography, as compared to that of St. Petersburg. He found plenty of scope for this interest in the problem of determining why, during Peter's reign, the triumphant "national program" was so swiftly succeeded by a critical program under the auspices of the state itself and, above all, why a reform that was "necessary" was accomplished violently and arbitrarily.

By the beginning of Peter's reign, Miliukov argued, increased contact with the West had already made it clear that reform was unavoidable. The violence and extremism of the Petrine reforms stemmed from Russia's low level of cultural and social development, which made virtually impossible a conscious combination of borrowed elements and viable national traditions. For proponents of change, the choice seemed clear-cut: reform along Western lines *or* preservation of the "national" tradition. With corporative society still weakly developed, it was once again the dynamic state that determined the course of action and ruthlessly imposed it on the population. Only later, from roughly the 1780s onward, did an independent, vital, genuinely "social" consciousness arise, one created not by the state but by the intelligentsia that the state had created and enlightened.[43]

Publication of *Studies of Russian Culture* engendered a lively debate over the evolution of the state and social structure in Russia. Critiques varied widely in both approach and interpretation, but most argued for the existence of internal obstacles to the untrammeled development of the autocratic Muscovite state. Several scholars objected to Miliukov's disavowal of the influence of indigenous traditions, such as the institution of the *veche* of the appanage period and the whole tradition of Novgorodian spiritual culture. Several others held that Miliukov ignored the existence of social forces with which the developing state had had to contend. Pavlov-Sil'vanskii, for example, argued that Muscovite Russia had experienced a feudal period and that Miliukov exaggerated both the mobility of the early Russian population and the "immobility" of populations in the West; Russia was, therefore, much more "European" in its development than Miliukov maintained.

These objections underscore the rather abstract quality of Miliukov's characterization of state development—excessive abstraction being the very flaw he had detected in the juridical school—and in subsequent editions of *Studies* he somewhat modified his exposition. He came to agree with Pavlov-Sil'vanskii that northeastern Rus' had evolved a sort of feudalism, although he saw it as a weakly developed one. He also took greater care to emphasize that the rulers' consciousness of the tasks of state building was a developing one: the Moscow princes at first acted solely in their own interests, only gradually articulating, with the aggrandizement of their position, a genuine political program and its ideological foundation.[44]

Miliukov was less accommodating on the issue of the influence of native traditions. In his opinion, the state order of Muscovite Russia was not the product of struggle between competing, dissimilar traditions, but simply the product of the development of the old forms of governance of northeastern Rus'. Only the uninterrupted existence of institutions, such as the boyar duma and *zemskii sobor,* could allow them to be considered "tenacious traditions" handed down from earlier eras, and Miliukov saw no such continuity. In this sense, Russia did not have a "usable past."[45]

Studies of Russian Culture clearly carried the stamp of its time. This is discernible in its overall positivistic conception, in Miliukov's preservation of an "us/them" dichotomy in his treatment of the later conflict between "social forces" and the state, in his use of anachronistic terminology, and in his extreme Europhilism. His recognition of the extent to which the context of the time had colored his interpretation was only partial. In emigration, he changed the title of the revised volume three from *Nationalism and Social Consciousness* to *Nationalism and Europeanism.* He did so because he no longer posited the dichotomy between nationalism and progressive social views implied in the original subtitle, having come to recognize that nationalism could be a genuinely democratic phenomenon. He did not change, however, the contrast of "society" and "state."[46]

Whatever its shortcomings, *Studies* was a brilliant and pioneering work. It far surpassed such Russian efforts in this field as preceded it and compared favorably with similar works being written in this period in England and Europe. Using a strongly comparative approach, Miliukov made the first sustained effort to reconcile the old debate on the particularity or universality of the Russian experience on sociological grounds. Despite its initially over-abstract formulation, his explanation of the genesis of autocracy was original and persuasive, while his thesis concerning the long-term effects of the "hyperactive state" continues to influence scholarly discussion today.[47] Also original was his thesis on the foreign origins of the national idea, including his exposition of the South Slav and Bulgarian roots of the

Third Rome theory, based on his identification of the first formulation of a national ideology in the Muscovite sources.

Perhaps the most novel contention of the work was its emphasis on the protean and dynamic nature of the Russian state, not only institutionally and in terms of geographic extent but even regarding its own self-definition. "Official nationalism" of the nineteenth century proclaimed Russia to be, and to have been, more or less immutable. In reality, Miliukov argued, Russia had been in a state of constant change, disequilibrium, and transformation since at least the middle of the sixteenth century, and more nearly since the gathering of the lands. This perspective very subtly shifted understanding of Russia's relationship to the West, from a strictly reactive one to a more complex mixture of indigenous change, impact, and response.[48]

Miliukov was increasingly drawn into oppositional activity in the seven years during which he composed *Studies,* and its line of interpretation—especially in volume three, some of which was written in prison—had obvious political implications. In his 1905 book, *Russia and Its Crisis,* based on lectures he gave in America and published there, he was free to develop his themes concerning the dynamism and adaptiveness of Russian culture in more explicitly political fashion. The book is interesting for a number of reasons, including its structure, a sophisticated joining of cultural history over the *longue durée* and contemporary, event-driven history. Three chapters examine the centuries-long evolution of autocracy, orthodoxy, and nationality, followed by two chapters of more limited chronological scope on the development of liberalism and socialism in Russia. A final chapter, still more immediate and chronologically focused, details Russia's political and economic crisis right up to the event of Bloody Sunday.

The import of the book was to show Russia's readiness for a more democratic political order along European lines. Tracing the process of modernization—"civilization" is the word he used—Miliukov concentrated on the internal dynamic of Russian social and political culture, with an emphasis on the development of public opinion. The result of ceaseless change, abrupt secularization, and an accelerating pace of cultural and political borrowing from abroad, was the absence in Russia of organic, "national" traditions connecting past and present. Moreover, these circumstances had generated a national type whose chief feature was its "plasticity" and adaptiveness.[49] In consequence, Russia was, in effect, free of the burden of the past: it could remake itself wholly on the basis of the needs of the present and, by implication, relatively rapidly.

Miliukov wrote almost nothing of a scholarly nature between 1906 and 1917, although the activities and upheavals of those years profoundly shaped his three major historical works in emigration.[50] His three-volume

study of the Russian revolution from February to October 1917, published
in 1921, was an almost purely political history of a type he had never before
undertaken. Influenced by Hippolyte Taine's study of the French revolution, Miliukov presented Russia's "second revolution" as a political one
tragically distorted by socialist mistakes, Bolshevik extremism, and a general insufficiency of "state consciousness" (*gosudarstvennost'*). His second
work on the revolutionary period, *Russia at the Turning Point,* published in
1926, extended the treatment to include the civil war and the NEP era.
Despite weaving more social and economic discussion into the analysis,
however, Miliukov deliberately preserved the focus on the state and the
exercise of power.[51]

His most original and least-known work of the emigration was also his most
sociological in approach. In *The National Question* Miliukov drew on his
earlier work on the Russian national idea, investigations into the history of the
nationality question connected with his work in the Duma, and the national
movements and wars of 1912–1919 to produce a work that was both a history
and a theoretical overview of thinking about nationality. Tracing the process of
the evolution of national self-consciousness through three stages, each stage
becoming more political and involving more of the population, Miliukov argued that once "national consciousness" spread from the intelligentsia to become a democratic phenomenon it could not be suppressed or eradicated.
Appreciating the changeability, as well as the constructed quality, of *all* "national ideas," Miliukov finally came to regard "plasticity" as a feature less
singularly Russian than he had first maintained.[52]

* * *

Throughout his life, Miliukov refused to call his approach a "philosophy of
history" as such; for him this had overtones of the despised "metaphysical"
approach, with its assumption of absolute ethical values and search for
"meaning" in history. His view of history was pluralistic and avowedly
sociological, with Comtean positivism the most formative element. His
choice of subject matter was extraordinarily wide-ranging, embracing everything from state finances to the love life of the idealists. His methods
were no less diverse, drawing on linguistics, archaeology, anthropology,
psychology, and economics for both theory and evidence. And in all his
works he preserved a view of history that sought to reconcile the unique and
the universal, the "lawful" and the accidental, the structural and the dynamic to account for everything in the historical process.

A "scientific" approach to history was necessarily a historicist one, and it
can be argued that at least *consciously* Miliukov avoided normative inter-

pretations. In the larger sense, he failed here completely, since his reading of Russian history was based on the assumption that a socially conscious society in the ideal "European" mode—democratic, secular, enlightened—was not only the superior form of social organization but the state toward which all Western peoples evolve. But in the narrower sense of not passing judgment on historical eras or individual actors on the basis of externally imposed criteria, Miliukov practiced the historicism he preached. He did not, for example, deprecate the seventeenth-century gentry servitors for failing to institutionalize their role in the governing process because such was not their interest or concern at the time.[53]

In the context of the history writing of the day, both Miliukov's sociological approach and his eclecticism were consistent with the approach of what was called "new history" in western Europe and the United States. This approach stressed a dynamic, generative view of history, a change in subject toward more institutional and social history, and greater flexibility in methods of investigation. Viewed more specifically in the context of the "Kliuchevskii legacy" or the Moscow school of historiography, Miliukov fit the tradition not only in his interest in sociology and economics but also in his relative lack of attention to political and diplomatic history and to biography. Also in keeping with the tradition of Kliuchevskii was Miliukov's neglect of the influence of non-Western cultures on the course of Russian development.

Where Miliukov diverged from his professor's tradition was in his comparative approach, his employment of theory, and his interest in ideas and "spiritual" culture. Kliuchevskii had no interest in philosophy and consciously excluded the history of ideas from study of the past; Miliukov made ideas, and the efforts to realize them in practice, one of his chief concerns. Those works devoted to the history of ideas were his most original and compelling.

Notes

Reprinted from Melissa Stockdale, *Paul Miliukov and the Quest for a Liberal Russia, 1890–1918.* Copyright © 1996 by Cornell University. Used by permission of the publisher, Cornell University Press.

1. Miliukov, "Lektsii po 'vvedeniiu v kurs russkoi istorii,' " (Moscow, 1894–95), pp. 2, 4. Hectograph version of his 1892–94 lectures at the Moscow Pedagogical Institute.

2. The most detailed study of Miliukov's historical work is M.G. Vandalkovskaia, *P.N. Miliukov, A.A. Kizevetter: Istoriia i politika* (Moscow, 1992); see also Melissa Kirschke Stockdale, *Paul Miliukov and the Quest for a Liberal Russia, 1880–1918* (Ithaca, N.Y., 1996) and Thomas M. Bohn, "Russische Geschichtswissenschaft von 1880 bis 1905: Pavel N. Miljukov und die *Moskauer Schule*" (unpublished diss., Universität Hamburg, 1996).

3. On the Moscow young professors, see M.M. Kovalevskii, "Otryvki iz vospominanii," and P.N. Miliukov, "Moi universitetskie gody," in *Moskovskii universitet, 1755–1930: iubileinyi sbornik,* ed. V.B. El'iashevich et al. (Paris, 1930), pp. 275–93 and 262–74, respectively.

4. P.N. Miliukov, "Istoriosofiia g. Kareeva," *Russkaia mysl'* (November 1887), pp. 92–93, and *Ocherki po istorii russkoi kul'tury,* vol. 1, 2d ed. (St. Petersburg, 1896), p. 7. (All references to vol. 1 are to this edition, unless otherwise noted.)

5. Miliukov, *Ocherki,* vol. 1, pp. 7–9, and "Istoriosofiia g. Kareeva," p. 91.

6. For his later expanded views on economic materialism, see Miliukov, *Ocherki,* vol. 1, p. 14, preface to the third edition of vol. 1, reprinted in 6th ed. (St. Petersburg, 1909), p. 308, and vol. 2, 2d ed., p. 3.

7. Miliukov, *Ocherki,* vol. 1, pp. 13–14. The pluralist views of Kovalevskii greatly influenced Miliukov's sociological ideas: Alexander Vucinich, *Social Thought in Tsarist Russia: The Quest for a General Science of Society, 1861–1917* (Chicago, 1976), p. 164 (henceforth, *Social Thought*) and Miliukov, "Novaia kniga po sotsiologii," *Mir Bozhii* (December 1899), pp. 196–215.

8. See the section on *Studies in Russian Culture* below for this tripartite theory in action. Miliukov, *Ocherki,* vol. 1, p. 15, and vol. 2, p. 5. His trilogy of sociological laws, milieu, and individual action resembled somewhat Kliuchevskii's triad—the human individual, human community, and physical environment; the key difference was the idea of universal laws. See V.O. Kliuchevskii, *Sochineniia,* vol. 1 (Moscow, 1959), p. 21.

9. Miliukov, "Russia," *The Athenaeum* (London), July 4, 1896, p. 26.

10. Miliukov, *Ocherki,* vol. 1, p. 7; on Catherine, see *Ocherki,* vol. 2, pp. 304–28.

11. On the typicality of this attitude for contemporary Russian social theorists, see Vucinich, *Social Thought,* p. 233.

12. Miliukov, *Ocherki,* vol. 1, p. 7; his dissertation defense comments are in *Istoricheskoe obozrenie,* no. 5 (1892), p. 203.

13. Miliukov, *Ocherki,* vol. 1, p. 19.

14. See his introductory remarks in Miliukov, *Glavnye techeniia russkoi istoricheskoi mysli,* 2d ed. (Moscow, 1898), p. 2; see also Miliukov, *Ocherki,* vol. 2, 2d ed., pp. 2–7, and vol. 3, 2d ed., pt. 1, pp. 15–17.

15. Miliukov, *Ocherki,* vol. 1, p. 222.

16. Miliukov, "Lektsii," pt. 1, p. 14, and *Ocherki,* vol. 1, p. 7.

17. H. Stuart Hughes, *Consciousness and Society: The Reorientation of European Thought, 1890–1930* (New York, 1977), p. 16.

18. This contextual approach to the study of ideas was first discussed in his unsigned review of *Vlast' Moskovskikh gosudarei: Ocherki iz istorii politicheskikh idei drevnei Rusi v kontse XVI veka,* by M. D'iakonov, in *Russkaia mysl'* (October 1889), pp. 425–27.

19. On Miliukov as a teacher, see Iu. V. Got'e, "Universitet (Iz zapisok akademika Iu. V. Got'e)," *Vestnik Moskovskogo universiteta, seriia 8: Istoriia,* no. 4 (July–August 1982), pp. 13–27, and A.A. Kizevetter, *Na rubezhe dvukh stoletii (vospominaniia 1881–1914)* (Prague, 1929), p. 87.

20. For a list of Miliukov's unsigned history reviews in *Russkaia mysl'* (1886–94), see *P.N. Miliukov: Sbornik materialov po chestvovaniiu ego semidesiatiletiia, 1859–1929* (Paris, 1929), ed. S.A. Smirnov, pp. 313–51.

21. P.N. Miliukov, *Gosudarstvennoe khoziaistvo Rossii v pervoi chetverti XVIII stoletiia i reforma Petra Velikogo,* 2d ed. (St. Petersburg, 1905), pp. xi–xii and 544, and Miliukov, *Vospominaniia,* p. 105.

22. Miliukov, *Gosudarstvennoe khoziaistvo,* p. 546. His severe estimates of population decline were contested by contemporaries. See M. Bezobrazov, *Russkoe obozrenie,*

April 1892, cited in an unsigned review essay, "Novyi trud o petrovskoi reforme," *Vestnik Evropy,* no. 8 (1892), pp. 813–33.

23. Several years after publication of Miliukov's dissertation, Pavlov-Sil'vanskii discovered archival materials proving that Peter had in fact helped draft the reforms. See N.V. Pavlov-Sil'vanskii, "Proekty reform v zapiskakh sovremennikov Petra Velikogo," in *Zapiski istoriko-filologicheskogo fakul'teta Imperatorskogo S. Peterburgskogo universiteta,* no. 42 (St. Petersburg, 1897), especially pp. 50–52, 55–56, 76–77. Miliukov acknowledged these findings in his "Petr velikii," *Entsiklopedicheskii slovar',* vol. 23–a (St. Petersburg, 1898), pp. 487–95. See also Miliukov, *Ocherki,* vol. 3, pt. 1, 2d ed. (St. Petersburg, 1903), pp. 134–86; *Ocherki,* vol. 3, jubilee ed. (Paris, 1930), pp. 157–217; and P.N. Miliukov, Charles Seignobos, L. Eisenmann, et. al., *Histoire de Russie,* vol. 1 (Paris, 1932), pp. 267–427.

24. M.M. Bogoslovskii, *Oblastnaia reforma Petra velikogo v provintsii* (St. Petersburg, 1902); A.A. Kizevetter, *Posadskaia obshchina v Rossii XVIII stoletiia* (Moscow, 1903).

25. P.N. Miliukov, *Spornye voprosy finansovoi istorii moskovskogo gosudarstva* (Moscow, 1892), responded to A.S. Lappo-Danilevskii's *Organizatsiia priamogo oblozheniia v moskovskom gosudarstve* (St. Petersburg, 1892).

26. Miliukov, *Spornye voprosy,* pp. 2, 4.

27. Ibid., pp. 5–6. Miliukov rejected the use of "ideal types" and his only reference to Max Weber is to the article on "pseudo-constitutionalism" and the Russian liberation movement, "Russlands Übergang zum scheinkonstitutionalismus"; see *Ocherki,* vol. 1, 6th ed., p. 219.

28. Miliukov, *Glavnye techeniia,* pp. 1–2.

29. Ibid., p. 1.

30. Ibid., pp. 259, 292, 311–22, 338.

31. P. Miliukov, "Iuridicheskaia shkola v russkoi istoriografii (Solov'ev, Kavelin, Chicherin, Sergeevich)," *Russkaia mysl'* (December 1886), pp. 80–92. A critique of the validity of Miliukov's influential notion of a juridical or "state" school of historiography is contained in Gary Hamburg, "Inventing the 'State School' of Historians, 1840–1995," chapter 5 in this volume.

32. Miliukov's most detailed analyses of Slavophilism were his 1893 public lecture "Razlozhenie slavianofil'stva," the text of which is reproduced in Miliukov, *Iz istorii russkoi intelligentsii,* 2d ed. (St. Petersburg, 1903), pp. 266–306, and P. Miliukov, "Slavianofil'stvo," in F.A. Brokgauz and I.A. Efron, *Entsiklopedicheskii slovar',* vol. 30 (St. Petersburg, 1900), pp. 307–14.

33. Miliukov, *Ocherki,* vol. 1, p. 17. Usually considered the first fully articulated scholarly objection to the connection of Kievan and Russian history is Mychaylo Hrushevsky's 1902 article, "The Traditional Schema of 'Russian' History," in *From Kievan Rus' to Modern Ukraine: Formation of the Ukrainian Nation* (Cambridge, 1984), pp. 355–64.

34. Miliukov, *Ocherki,* vol. 1, pp. 114–15, 164–67, 177–80. J. Michael Hittle, *The Service City: State and Townsmen in Russia, 1600–1800* (Cambridge, Mass., 1979), p. 7 notes that Miliukov ignored the circumstance that many European cities had their origins as the administrative centers of medieval rulers.

35. Miliukov, *Ocherki,* vol. 2, 5th ed. (St. Petersburg, 1909), pp. 1, 398 (emphasis in the original).

36. Miliukov, *Ocherki,* vol. 2, pp. 9, 391–93, 399.

37. Miliukov, *Ocherki,* vol. 3, pt. 1, 2d ed., pp. 7, 10; he also stresses the religious coloration of national distinctions as they first come to be recognized.

38. Ibid., pp. 11–12.

39. Ibid., p. 24.

40. Miliukov, *Ocherki,* vol. 3, pt. 1, 3d ed. (St. Petersburg, 1909), pp. 25–26, 35–46. The discussion of the Third Rome theory was one of the features of *Ocherki* considered most novel and compelling by contemporaries; for a more recent favorable appraisal, see Dmitri Stremooukhoff, "Moscow the Third Rome: Sources of the Doctrine," in *The Structure of Russian History,* ed. Michael Cherniavsky (New York, 1970), p. 117.

41. Hrushevsky allowed for more Kievan influence on Muscovy than did Miliukov, but their views on the nature of Kiev's connection to "Russian" history are strikingly similar. Like Miliukov, Hrushevsky saw that connection as an anachronism derived from the old Muscovite history writing. See Hrushevsky, "The Traditional Scheme of Russian History," pp. 356–57.

42. Miliukov, *Ocherki,* vol. 3, pt. 1, pp. 75–78, 92.

43. This is the subject of the entire second part of volume three. The exposition in *Ocherki* stopped at the end of Catherine's reign, perhaps out of censorship considerations, but in the lecture course upon which it was based Miliukov traced the development of social consciousness up to his own day, concluding with a survey of the penetration of this thought from the capitals to the provinces.

44. Miliukov, *Ocherki,* vol. 3, pt. 1, 2d ed. (St. Petersburg, 1903), p. 26.

45. Ibid., p. 18.

46. Miliukov, *Ocherki,* vol. 3, parts 1 and 2, jubilee edition (Paris, 1930).

47. Miliukov's influence can be seen in Richard Pipes, *Russia Under the Old Regime* (New York, 1974), and Robert Tucker's treatment of state building in Soviet Russia, including his "Stalinism as Revolution from Above," in *Stalinism: Essays in Historical Interpretation,* ed. Robert C. Tucker (New York, 1977), pp. 77–108.

48. An interesting treatment of "impact-response" models of change in Western historiography on China is contained in Paul A. Cohen, *Discovering History in China* (New York, 1984); there are a number of suggestive parallels for the Western student of Russian history.

49. Paul Milyoukov, *Russia and Its Crisis* (Chicago, 1905), pp. 13–29 and 546–64, where he identifies the fundamental feature in the Russian historical process as "the lack of continuity and the insufficient development of any binding social tradition."

50. A partial exception is his book-length essay on the Russian intelligentsia, rebutting the critique of the intelligentsia launched in the controversial symposium *Vekhi,* since it is as much polemic as history; see P.N. Miliukov, "Intelligentsiia i istoricheskaia traditsiia," in *Intelligentsiia v Rossii,* ed. K. Arsen'ev et al. (St. Petersburg, 1910), pp. 89–191.

51. P.N. Miliukov, *Istoriia vtoroi russkoi revoliutsii,* 3 vols. (Sofia, 1921–24) and *Rossiia na perelome* (Paris, 1927); this work first appeared as *Russlands Zusammenbruch* (Berlin, 1926).

52. P.N. Miliukov, *Natsional'nyi vopros, (Proiskhozhdenie natsional'nosti i natsional'nye voprosy v Rossii)* (Prague, 1925). Originally published in Prague, Miloslav Hroch's *Social Preconditions of National Revival in Europe: A Comparative Analysis of the Social Composition of Patriotic Groups Among the Smaller European Nations,* trans. Ben Fowles (Cambridge, 1985), identifies three stages similar to Miliukov's, making it tempting to speculate that he was familiar with Miliukov's work.

53. Miliukov, *Ocherki,* vol. 3, pt. 1, 3d ed., pp. 91–92.

13

Aleksandr Aleksandrovich Kizevetter

Margarita Georgievna Vandalkovskaia

Affiliation with a school within a discipline has a great impact on a scholar's life. It was natural for Kliuchevskii's contemporaries and students to assimilate not only his extensive scholarship and the particular skills he adopted in his approach to historical materials, already achieved and amplified by him, but also his manner of historical writing and his skills as a lecturer.

Naturally, the students adapted all these weapons from their teacher's academic arsenal in different ways, filtering them through their own individuality. According to his contemporaries, A.A. Kizevetter assimilated his teacher's precepts more than anybody else. This was manifested both in his fidelity to Kliuchevskii's scholarly traditions and in his skills as a speaker. At the same time, although a worthy successor to Kliuchevskii, Kizevetter also had his own, unique talents as a historical researcher and teacher.

Kizevetter's name was forgotten in Soviet historiography. He received only an occasional mention in works on historiography and in specialized studies on eighteenth-century Russian history. During the Soviet era, historical knowledge served ideological purposes: scholars who did not share the Bolsheviks' views were treated primarily as political adversaries; their scholarly endeavors were subjected to politicized assessments and painted in dark hues. Now the time has come for an objective examination of the historical discipline in prerevolutionary Russia, including Kizevetter's role.

Aleksandr Aleksandrovich Kizevetter was born on 10 May 1866, in St. Petersburg, in the building that housed the Chief Military Staff. At the time, Kizevetter's father, who was in charge of the Staff Archives, had an official apartment in one wing of the building. "Could this be the source," Kizevetter was to wonder later, "of the love of working in the archives with historical documents that overpowered my soul? Because sitting in the archives, immersed in the reading of documents, is the occupation I love best, an occupation that holds indelible charm for me."[1]

Kizevetter came from a talented, upwardly mobile family. His ancestors had come from Thuringia, and a great-grandfather on his father's side had been a blacksmith in Sonderhausen. His grandfather was a musician who settled in Russia and made his living by giving music lessons in St. Petersburg. Kizevetter's father, "now a thoroughly Russianized German," graduated from the law faculty of St. Petersburg University and worked as an inspector at the Commercial School in St. Petersburg, as well as at the Staff Archives. His mother, A.N. Turchaninova, graduated from the Smol'nyi Institute (the prestigious school for daughters of the nobility); her grandfather had been an archpriest and a well-known composer of liturgical music, and her father was a graduate of the Theological Academy, a teacher of history, and the author of a book about church synods in Russia.

Kizevetter's family influenced him greatly, of course. His literary and oratorical abilities came from his maternal grandfather.[2] From his father Kizevetter inherited his forthright opinions and his sense of dignity and honor. His mother taught her children (besides Aleksandr, the family included an older sister named Anna, a younger boy named Ivan, and the mother's niece Natal'ia) tractability and tact. These traits determined Kizevetter's moral character.

In the middle of the 1860s the family moved to Orenburg, where Kizevetter's father served in the military department of the council under the governor-general of Orenburg. The family lived in Orenburg for sixteen years—that is, until Kizevetter enrolled at Moscow University. During his time at the gymnasium, Kizevetter became passionately fond of reading, nurtured a special interest in history, and made his choice of a life path: Kliuchevskii's *The Boyar Duma of Old Rus'* [Boiarskaia duma drevnei Rusi] was constantly on his desk. In 1884 Kizevetter enrolled in the history and philology faculty at Moscow University. "I entered the university," he recalled, "with an almost religious feeling, as if it were a cathedral, full of sanctity."[3]

The professors at the history and philology faculty during those years included V.O. Kliuchevskii, P.G. Vinogradov, V.I. Ger'e, S.F. Fortunatov, M.M. Trotskii, N.S. Tikhonravov, A.N. Veselovskii, P.N. Miliukov, and I.V. Tsvetaev. Of Kliuchevskii, Kizevetter later wrote that he "captivated" the students with his "extraordinary combination of powerful scholarly thinking and the exquisite artistry of his exposition, plus his skillful performer's enunciation. Those who listened to this course from the mouth of Kliuchevskii himself," Kizevetter related, "know well how the virtuoso intonations of his voice served as a wonderful enhancement to his words."[4]

Vinogradov's lectures and seminars constituted a virtual school in scholarly endeavor. He taught courses on the history of the Middle Ages and of Greece. "Vinogradov had a gift for gathering dedicated students around him and forming a school that was united by shared scholarly interests. At the time, P.G. Vinogradov's hospitable home, in the small house of Father Slavtsov on Mertvyi Pereulok, was the center of an animated association of Moscow historians. At these gatherings we listened to papers by Miliukov, Fortunatov, Vipper, A. Guchkov, Korelin, Ivanov, Shamonin, Beliaev, Kudriavtsev, Petrushevskii, Gusakov, Brune, Manuilov, and many others. . . . At such times we saw Kliuchevskii in relaxed, friendly surroundings and enjoyed his flashes of wit; we saw Miliukov, then thoroughly engrossed in the archives, presenting his discoveries on the history of Peter's reforms."[5]

After graduating from the university, Kizevetter stayed on to prepare himself for a professorship. He also taught history at a secondary school, in what were known as "collective classes," as part of Ger'e's Higher Courses, to the Society of Female Teachers and Governesses, and at pedagogical institutes. He taught history and geography at the Lazarev Institute of Oriental Languages, the history of Russian literature at the Moscow Art School of Painting, Sculpture, and Architecture. In 1898 he was appointed a private tutor at Moscow University. According to M.V. Vishniak's recollections, in his first lecture courses at the university he stood "erect, wearing a black frock coat, with a celebrated 'Chernomor' beard and wobbly pince-nez on a black string, somewhat imposing and a bit fastidious. When he came down from the rostrum, he seemed to lose height but gain in ordinariness."[6]

During those years, Kizevetter began to involve himself in civic education work on behalf of the Moscow Committee for Literacy and the Commission for Literacy established by the Education Department of the Society for the Spread of Technical Knowledge. The commission included many prominent academics such as Kliuchevskii, V.I. Vernadskii, A.I. Chuprov, and others. It operated under the supervision of P.G. Vinogradov and devoted its time to publishing textbooks and handbooks. Under the sponsorship of the commission's lecture office, Kizevetter lectured on Russian history in Nizhnii Novgorod, Tver', and other cities.

Even as Kizevetter gave lectures and university courses and engaged in civic education work, he did not neglect his research, and this work was always most important to him. He began his research under Kliuchevskii's supervision as early as his third year of study at the university. By then he was already "completely absorbed in the mementoes of historical antiquity," studying the history of service-class landownership in Russia in the sixteenth and seventeenth centuries. With Kliuchevskii's help, he chose the topic of his master's dissertation: *The Urban Community in Eighteenth-*

Century Russia [Posadskaia obshchina v Rossii XVIII stoletiia], later published under the same title.

In his memoirs, Kizevetter recalled: "Almost every day for seven years I sat in the archives from 9 o'clock in the morning to 3 o'clock in the afternoon ... and then spent two years processing the material."[7] Hence work on his dissertation lasted from 1895 until 1903. The hours he spent in the archives, Kizevetter wrote, "I will always remember as the most satisfying hours of my life."[8] Reviewing his entire past in his mind's eye, he continued, "I can say, 'with a sound mind and in full possession of my memory,' that I experienced a source of spiritual satisfaction only there in the archives, immersing my mind in the significance of the old texts, trying not to miss the smallest hint, the tiniest line that might give me a glimpse of light into the historical questions that concerned me."[9]

Kizevetter explained his scholarly interest in the history of the eighteenth century and the urban community in two ways. First, he gave a purely academic reason. He believed that the historical works of L.O. Ploshinskii, A.P. Prigara, and I.I. Ditiatin on state acts and political institutions were "inadequate," because they failed to account for the rise and development of social relations themselves. The second motive was dictated by his conviction that, as a constitutionalist, which he believed himself to be and in fact was, he should search for the historical preconditions of representative institutions in Russian history. Added to these motives was another that, he wrote, was connected "not with the possible results but rather with the process . . . of the work itself. What most attracted me was the kind of work in which I would have to reconstruct the familiar picture of the historical process on the basis of a mosaic selection of the most minute facts."[10] It was scholarly impulses, then, that predominated in the author's approach to his topic.

As he began his study of the urban community, Kizevetter tried to find an individual, new angle from which to explore it, "to determine the actual conditions under which the urban community actually lived."[11] This required a study of the "social ground" on which the central and oblast-level governmental institutions were built, as well as of the social forces "that set its wheels in motion or stopped them."[12] The enormous archival material extracted from the Chief Magistracy and the town magistracies, the Camer-College and the Senate, the Trade Commission, and so forth, provided the documentary base for his research. Kizevetter studied the urban community of the Russian town from three angles: its social composition, state service and taxes, and self-government. Kizevetter restricted the chronological framework of his study to the period from the municipal reforms of Peter I to the publication of Catherine II's Charter to the Towns in 1785.

At the conclusion of the study, the categories of the urban population established by Kizevetter coincided with the division of the community into economic groups—that is, merchants of the three guilds, members of the crafts guilds, and "people of the lower orders." This conclusion allowed Kizevetter to sketch "the everyday social physiognomy" of the urban community and to discern trends in its socioeconomic development and the actual economic level of the Russian town as a whole. His analysis of the services and payments owed by the urban community led him to conclude that the community was completely dependent on the "people of first rank" who "shifted" the burden of the poll tax to the lower orders of the population and took into their own hands "the role of direction and command" in administrative bodies. Urban self-government, in Kizevetter's view, was also "thoroughly" dependent on the taxes levied on the urban community. His study of archival data on the personal composition of the local assemblies gave him grounds to state that "while legally representing the entire urban community, in actuality the assembly turned out to include primarily taxpayers of the first rank,"[13] which attested to the low level of legal awareness of the town as a whole.

Kizevetter's work was innovative. He studied the social organism (the urban community) from the standpoint of its social composition, and, through the use of documentary material that he introduced into scholarly circulation for the first time, he demonstrated the close connection between various social categories of the population and their economic situations, as well as the association between the population's legal status and the level of its socioeconomic development.

His dissertation was very well received. V.O. Kliuchevskii and M.K. Liubavskii took part in his dissertation defense.[14] Kliuchevskii made only a few critical remarks, and, as Kizevetter wrote, "my best reward" was Kliuchevskii's "nonsarcastic tone,"[15] which indicated his acknowledgment of the candidate's scholarly merits. Once published as a book, Kizevetter's views on the urban community had a widespread scholarly resonance. The Society of Russian History and Antiquities awarded Kizevetter the G.F. Karpov Prize, and it awarded gold medals to his reviewers, M.M. Bogoslovskii and E.V. Petukhov.[16] Not long afterward, the Academy of Sciences asked Kizevetter to prepare the 1785 Charter to the Towns for a series on Russian legal documents. The text was prepared but never published.

During those years, research occupied a predominant place in his life. In addition to his book-length dissertation, he published articles in journals such as *Russkaia mysl'*, *Russkoe bogatstvo*, *Obrazovanie*, *Zhurnal dlia vsekh*, and others. His articles on "Domostroi," "Ivan the Terrible and His Opponents" [Ivan Groznyi i ego opponenty], the reforms of Peter I, and the urban mandates of the Catherinian Commission of 1767, among others, grew out of his special courses and lectures and testified to his profoundly scientific approach to his tasks as a lecturer and teacher. In 1903 Kizevetter was invited by V.A. Gol'tsev to join the editorial board of *Russkaia mysl'*, and he became its head after Gol'tsev's death in 1907. From 1905 onward, he also worked with *Russkie vedomosti*. His activities on these editorial boards brought Kizevetter into close contact with numerous civic and political leaders and writers.

Kizevetter attended Teleshov's celebrated Wednesday salons. He met L[eonid] Andreev, I[van] Bunin, M[axim] Gorky, B[arfolomei] Zaitsev, and F[edor] Shaliapin; he was also on friendly terms with A[nton] Chekhov, who was in charge of the literary section of *Russkaia mysl'*. On journal business, Kizevetter visited Chekhov in Yalta in 1904. "We had a simple and relaxed conversation," he recalled, "which made a strong impression on me, and it seemed to me that as I observed all Chekhov's habits that evening I grasped the key to the principal motive behind the creative endeavors of this elegant bard of the Russian 'twilight.' "[17] Chekhov longed for an elegant life, a life based "on the kinship of human souls, on people's subtle understanding of another's intimate impulses of the soul," and he pitied people. Kizevetter's penetrating and subtle mind caught the deep-seated meaning of Chekhov's creative work, the intelligence and poetry of his thinking. Kizevetter also maintained his connections with the literary community as an émigré, when he joined the Union of Writers and Journalists of Czechoslovakia.

Kizevetter's special proclivity for the arts and his fascination with the theater, which dated from his youth, also brought him into close contact with a broad circle of theatrical personages. He was friends with M.N. Ermolova, G.N. Fedotova, A.P. Lenskii, and A.I. Iuzhin-Sumbatov. They often met in the home of N.V. Davydov, who was a close friend of L.N. Tolstoy—in fact, Davydov gave Tolstoy the themes for his plays *The Reign of Darkness* [Vlast' t'my] and *The Living Corpse* [Zhivoi trup].[18] Davydov long served as the chairman of the Moscow District Court, then became the rector of Shaniavskii University (Kizevetter was invited to work there); he was also chairman of the literary–theatrical committee of the Malyi Theater and an actor. Kizevetter recognized that Davydov had a special talent—bringing people together.

Kizevetter recalled that at his home on Levshinskii Pereulok, Davydov "used to host a lengthy dinner party every Friday . . . , where the flower of science, literature, and the arts sat together in crowded but jovial circumstances. . . . At one end of the table Kliuchevskii always sat next to the actor Lenskii. Alternating further down the table were Lopatin the philosopher; Fedotova the actress; actors named Iuzhin, Fokht, Sadovskaia, and

Iablochkina; and Professor Manuilov."[19] Kizevetter's affection for the theater led him to create works on the history of the theater, as well as word portraits of well-known actors and actresses such as Fedotova, Savina, and others in his notes on theater performances and elsewhere.[20]

In the revolutionary years of 1905–7, Kizevetter was involved in active political work. A confirmed constitutionalist, he worked on the journal *Osvobozhdenie* and took a stance very close to that of Petr Struve. In October 1905 Kizevetter joined what was to become the leading party of Russian liberalism, the Constitutional Democratic Party (Kadets). Together with P.D. Dolgorukov, V.A. Maklakov, and F.F. Kokoshkin, Kizevetter was a leader of the Moscow Provincial Committee and a member of the City Committee of the Kadet Party. He was extremely active in support of the Kadet Party. Kizevetter wrote an essay about the Kadet leader, P.N. Miliukov, as well as several articles and pamphlets about the Kadets and their program. After the Manifesto of 17 October 1905 was issued, he wrote a leaflet expressing the Kadets' reaction to it. Later, during the election campaign to the Second Duma, he collaborated with V.A. Maklakov to create a kind of handbook for Kadet speakers. This work came to be known as "Kizevetter's Catechism."[21] As an advocate of parliamentary forms of state, Kizevetter, along with F.F. Kokoshkin and V.A. Maklakov, was one of the most outstanding speakers during the campaign for elections to the First and Second State Dumas.

Kizevetter was elected to the Second Duma as a deputy from Moscow.

Political activity, however, never absorbed Kizevetter completely. "By nature I am not a politician at all. I am a scholar and a writer," he insisted. In his own words, Kizevetter never had an "internal taste" or "immediate propensity" for political activity, but he did consider it his duty to take part in public life during difficult periods of history.[22]

Kizevetter had started work on a new topic associated with Catherine II's legislation as early as 1904, but it was interrupted by his political activities and he did not return to it until 1908. Then he "immersed" himself in his favorite work. His book *Catherine II's Charter to the Towns: A Historical Commentary* [Gorodovoe polozhenie Ekateriny II: Istoricheskii kommentarii] was ready in 1909. He defended this book as his doctoral dissertation.

The work represented a logical continuation of his research on the urban community. The author himself called his work a historical commentary. Essentially, *Catherine II's Charter to the Towns* is a study of sources. The author analyzed numerous rough drafts and editions of the Charter to the Towns. Through a meticulous reconstruction of the process by which the royal legislator composed and edited her work, he set himself the task of determining the sources of the Charter to the Towns. The sources turned out to be the Charter to the Nobility (*Zhalovannaia gramota dvorianstvu*), foreign laws and bills (Baltic German, Swedish, German, etc.), and business correspondence of private companies gathered by the Legislative Commission (*Ulozhennaia komissiia*) of 1767. Kizevetter was able to determine what each of these sources had contributed to the Charter to the Towns, how Catherine had utilized them, and how this legislation had actually been implemented. His study of the factual material convinced Kizevetter of Catherine II's pronobility policies and her tendentious interpretations of foreign sources to favor those in power while she was composing the Charter to the Towns. The author showed that in actuality the business council was the merchants' and artisans' institution, and that its activities, like those of the six-man council (*shestiglasnaia duma*), was completely dependent on the provincial board and the royal administration.[23]

Taking the role of critic at Kizevetter's defense, Iu.V. Got´e commented that Kizevetter unquestionably deserved credit for having, "for almost the first time," applied the "scientific, objective method of processing archival materials" to events of history not remote from modern times and, most important, for having thoroughly understood the task of critical research. Such comprehensive analysis of sources made it possible to answer particular historical questions such as how Catherine thought, what cultural and legal borrowings went into the Charter to the Towns, and how society implemented the gist of the law in practice.[24] A. Iziumov, a student of Kizevetter's who became a well-known journalist and who emigrated with Kizevetter, made the following comment about Kizevetter's doctoral defense: "Neither of his official critics, M.K. Liubavskii and Iu.V. Got´e, were very gifted speakers. Aleksandr Aleksandrovich gave apt and dignified answers and obviously exceeded his critics in his ability to speak from the rostrum."[25]

Many of Kizevetter's later works, published both in Russia and abroad, testified to the steadfastness of his scholarly interest in the eighteenth century, the reign of Catherine and her legislative and social policies, and these works continued the themes begun in his master's and doctoral dissertations. Kizevetter's works offered a new assessment of Catherine II's activities. Kizevetter argued against the generally accepted view—expressed in works by V.A. Bil´basov, A.G. Brückner, and in part P.N. Miliukov—that Catherine, captivated by Enlightenment ideas, perceived the goal of her political program as equalizing the classes and eliminating despotism and serfdom, so that not until the second period of her reign did she truly become "the tsaritsa of the nobility."

On the basis of his thorough study of Catherine's legislative measures and social policies, Kizevetter argued that Catherine II defended the nobility's interests from the very beginning of her reign and had never even considered abolishing serfdom. In this she followed in the footsteps of Peter I, Anna Ivanovna, and Elizabeth. Her receptiveness to the ideology of enlightened absolutism did not conflict with the noble and autocratic orientation of her policies.[26]

Kizevetter had a keen interest in one sociopsychological problem: what was the source of Catherine II's triumphs? He suggested that it was Catherine's passionate nature and calculating self-possession in choosing the means by which she would accomplish her goals, as well as the advertising, directed not at subtle observers but at the masses, which created a firm foundation for the empress's triumphant accomplishments. Feelings of doubt and disillusionment were foreign to Catherine II—a characteristic of creative natures. "Oversights and failures were not part of the formula that drove her actions,"[27] and her ability to write journalistic and dramatic works constituted no more than dilettantism. "All these were just good enough," he wrote, "not to allow her to fall below the generally accepted literary requirements of her time."[28]

Kizevetter also paid considerable attention to matters of social consciousness, culture, and ideology. Thus, for example, in sketching his portrait of F.V. Rostopchin, who personified the reign, Kizevetter said that he combined the ideals of the independent citizen with the idea of political slavery, the conviction that the welfare of society was achieved through unequal rights. The causes of such judgments, Kizevetter argued, lay in the defense of the inviolability of noble privileges and the feudal dependency of the peasants.[29]

In his study of the eighteenth century, Kizevetter showed particular interest in the history of popular movements. He wrote several articles on E[milian] Pugachev's rebellion, which he viewed as a combination of Cossack and peasant revolts. The latter he called the Russian jacquerie, and he linked its defeat to the lack of preparation, plan, and union with the Cossacks and to the incompetent leadership of Pugachev, whom Kizevetter considered an ordinary man who was incapable of leading a major movement. It is characteristic of him that he perceived the Cossacks' and peasants' actions as a result of the social tension generated by the entire Russian system at that time.[30]

It is of considerable interest to examine his thoughts on the peasantry and peasant uprisings. From his point of view, the Russian peasantry never manifested anarchic tendencies but rather always had a consciousness of statehood and a desire for state order. The peasants' struggle against serfdom was not a struggle against the state. All the peasant uprisings were undertaken under the banner of political loyalty, which accounted for the particular thought process formulated by peasant consciousness: serfdom was seen as an invention of the nobles but not of the authorities. For this reason, peasant uprisings were launched under the slogan "Against the nobles in the name of the tsar." This was how Kizevetter accounted for the increase in peasant disturbances during a change of rulers, as well as the popularity of pretenders among the people.

In Kizevetter's view, the mixed composition of uprisings, which involved peasants, Cossacks, workers, and slaves—that is, representatives of various social categories, each with its own interests—did not prove the strength of these uprisings but rather the contrary: that they were mechanical unions that did not produce a concerted movement.

As for the peasants' demands, these were not limited to the struggle for land: they always included demands for personal freedom and political rights. At the same time, the slogan associated with the struggle for land changed as time went on: as land scarcity became more common (especially after 1861), demands for increasing land allotments began to predominate.[31]

Kizevetter was awarded his doctorate in Russian history on 30 May 1909. He continued to work at Moscow University, which he combined with teaching at Shaniavskii University. Kizevetter taught general and specialized university courses on Russian history in the eighteenth and nineteenth centuries.

Characteristic of Kizevetter's lectures was the way they reflected contemporary advances in scholarship in a popular and eloquent form, as well as their own, in essence, profoundly scholarly nature. In his courses and lectures Kizevetter devoted considerable space to the theory and methodology of history. He also taught a special course called "Introduction to History," which has, unfortunately, been preserved only as fragments of rough drafts. Kizevetter classified himself as an advocate of scientific realism and a follower of positivism. The task of history, as he perceived it, was that of studying genuine patterns of connections linking elements of the historical process and the many ways in which they were combined.[32] In the tradition of his predecessors and teachers (Solov'ev, Kliuchevskii), Kizevetter recognized general patterns governing historical development as an organic, objective process, yet at the same time he emphasized its uniqueness, conditioned by specific historical circumstances (territory, population, geography, colonization processes, etc.). Kizevetter believed that the problem of the individual in history was important; he denied the importance of individuals as creators of the historical process even as he warned against underestimating that importance.

In his lectures Kizevetter questioned the necessity of following the scientific approach in interpreting historical material. He emphasized the particular importance of historico-philosophical generalizations closely connected to researchers' worldviews and set for himself the complicated methodological task of determining the connections between such generalizations and the detailed study of historical events. He considered the application of the comparative historical method of research as a genuinely scientific approach to the process of maintaining horizontal and vertical analysis of phenomena under examination, thus ensuring the use of the empirical historical approach and the principle of historicism.[33]

According to Kizevetter, any genuinely scientific and relatively complete knowledge must be based not only on source study but also on various interpretations of sources, various viewpoints. For this reason, scientific thinking cannot develop without debate. "Disputes," he wrote, "express the internal content of the advance of science,"[34] and he believed that the end of argument meant "the death of scientific progress." It seemed to him that the study of scientific controversies was a useful way to reveal the essence of the subject being studied.

Take, for example, the history of Russia. It seemed to Kizevetter that the views of those who argued in favor of the uniqueness of Russian history, like those who believed that Russia's history was identical to that of the West European countries, represented "opposite extremes" that were incompatible with "the foundations of the scholarly worldview."[35] In Russian history he perceived the same processes that characterized the European countries. At the same time, he believed that those processes proceed "at a comparatively slower pace and are comparatively more blurred in their outline."[36] It was his belief, then, that Russian history constituted a local variation of the historical process taking place throughout the countries of European culture.

The overall canvas of Russian history, as Kizevetter envisioned it, looked as follows. The eighth and ninth centuries of Old Russian history were characterized primarily by processes of colonization, and he perceived in the history of the ancient Slavs the beginnings of a state form, rejecting the view that the Slavs' way of life was base and "bestial." He acknowledged the summoning but not the conquest of the Varangians. Kizevetter derived his history of Old Russian statehood not from the Rus′ along the Dnieper but rather from northeastern Rus′. To him Kievan Rus′ was purely of archeological interest. In political associations of the state type he discerned only the beginning stages of feudalism, which he understood as a political and social plan; he assigned the monarchy's final victory in its struggle with the appanage to the sixteenth century. Kizevetter's interest in the topic of the Muscovite tsardom, which he viewed as expressing all-Russian (national) interests, and in the particular stages of its development was conditioned by his desire to understand the process of evolution of the Russian state, its byways and characteristics. In his opinion, the sixteenth century, and in particular the reign of Ivan the Terrible, was "one of the paramount moments" of state development. Following the tradition of the statist school, he asserted that from the middle of the fifteenth century onward, the whole Russian population was bound to the state: the higher classes were required to carry out the tasks of administration and foreign policy; the lower classes were to provide the means for maintaining them. The way the administration was organized, centralization, social policy, the religious and nationalistic worldview ("Moscow, the Third Rome"), and foreign policy doctrines all fostered the formation of "a purely military monarchy," in which militarism became a fundamental element.

In his assessments of Ivan the Terrible, Kizevetter disagreed with established views. He dismissed as one-sided the opinions of M.M. Shcherbatov and N.M. Karamzin, who focused on the tsar's spiritual drama while ignoring state forms and conditions of national life, as well as those of K.D. Kavelin, for whom the tsar represented "a crowned propagandist of the idea of statehood" and "an idealistic terrorist operating in an unreal atmosphere." He called for a comprehensive and in-depth study of the reign of Ivan the Terrible, one that took preceding historical development into account.

"Peter I and his reforms" was, for Kizevetter—as for all Russian historians, incidentally—"the key theme of Russian history." He singled out three stages in the historiographical treatment of Peter's reign: the period of "naive rationalism," when Peter's reign was viewed solely through the lens of his personality; the period of "philosophical symbolization," when Peter's reforms were regarded as a dramatic breakthrough in Russian life; and the "scientific-realistic" period, in which Peter's transformations were viewed as but one link in Russia's logical historical process.[37] Naturally, Kizevetter shared the latter point of view. He argued for the organic origins of Peter I's reforms, the idea that the preceding period had laid the ground for them. Kizevetter rejected the view that Peter I's reforms represented an "acrobat's leap" or a "sudden turn," instead seeing Peter's activity as a "major, decisive step" that was "strongly rooted" in Russia's national soil, in Russia's ongoing development. In examining the broad range of questions associated with Peter I's reforms, Kizevetter acknowledged the Europeanization of Russia, the enhancement of its technological and cultural level, and the preparation of conditions that were to lead to the emancipation of society under Catherine II.

Kizevetter worked through nineteenth-century history both in his general courses and in his *History of Russia in the Nineteenth Century* [Istoriia Rossii v XIX veke], published in 1909. According to Kizevetter, the nineteenth century had inherited a police state, a privileged landowning nobility, and a predominantly subsistence economy. Kizevetter called the peasant reforms "a great social reform," the achievements of which included liberating the peasants and providing them with land—"an incomplete and protracted" process, to be sure. In his opinion, the zemstvo, municipal, and judicial reforms represented a logical continuation of the peasant reform, although he acknowledged their limited and truncated character. Recognition of the imperfections of the zemstvo reform and the obvious benefits it conferred on the nobility did not prevent him from acknowledging the importance of the reforms from the legal standpoint. In the zemstvos he discerned the "definite beginnings of a legal system." Kizevetter attributed the "major success" of the judicial reforms to the fact that they did not encroach on estate interests, they did not provoke an acute class struggle, and they wound up in "good professional hands."[38] Kizevetter was also keenly interested in social movements, especially the Decembrist movement. In the course of studying the Decembrist societies, their programs, their connections with the general European liberation movements (the Carbonari in Italy and the Tugendbund in Germany), and their practical activities, Kizevetter perceived in them a fine example of renunciation of narrow class-based interests and, at the same time, an instructive lesson on the dangers of political radicalism.

Both in his lectures and in his articles Kizevetter created brilliant portraits of historical figures such as Ivan the Terrible, Peter I, Catherine II, Alexander I, Speranskii, Arakcheev, Alexander II, and the leaders of the reforms of the 1860s and of the social movements of the twentieth century. The historian's scholarly positions reflected the advanced level of the Russian historical discipline at the end of the nineteenth and the beginning of the twentieth centuries. The accomplishments of scholarly thought were expressed in Kizevetter's teaching.

In one of his articles Kizevetter sketched the ideal portrait of a historian, the kind of ideal toward which every professional ought to strive. "One ought not to be a historian," he wrote, "unless one knows how to sort through the motley hurly-burly of life events to discern the patterns that unify them. Without this gift one cannot become a historian but can only become a narrator, because merely experiencing the past in one's imagination is not the same as being able to understand it." Continuing this line of thought, Kizevetter said that it is also impossible to be a historian "unless one is able to envision for oneself and to re-create for others in words the events of the past in all their specificity, in all their individual uniqueness, in all the succulence of their vivid colors. Without this gift of concrete reconstruction of bygone times one cannot be a historian, one can only be a resonating dialectician."[39] It takes a combination of "the generalizing power of thought" and the ability to reconstruct events to make a historian a professional.

In Kizevetter's view, very few historians exemplified "these two gifts, heterogenous as they are," in equal proportions. It goes without saying that Kizevetter himself possessed the full measure of these characteristics of the intellectual frame of mind. He valued the historical fact and knew how to understand its meaning and its place in the interpretation of historical material.

It was only natural that Kliuchevskii wanted Kizevetter to succeed him in the Department of Russian History at Moscow University. We have a character description written by Kliuchevskii for Kizevetter in 1910 in connection with the latter's proposed appointment as professor: "We have the honor," Kliuchevskii wrote,

> of recommending private tutor A.A. Kizevetter to the History and Philology Faculty to fill the position of professor extraordinary in the Department of Russian History.... The faculty recognizes Kizevetter as a fine, well-educated, experienced, and talented instructor.... Two major studies on Russian history and twenty-one years of teaching, of which eleven years have been devoted to Moscow University, I venture to say, provide sufficient proof that in Mr. Kizevetter the faculty is gaining a tested and completely reliable member.[40]

Kizevetter's term as the successor to Kliuchevskii at Moscow University proved to be all too brief. Russian universities had experienced grave turmoil from the turn of the century and especially during the revolutionary years of 1905–7. This turmoil continued during 1910–11 as a result of the so-called Kasso Affair (named after the minister of education). Kasso severely curtailed Moscow University's autonomy, and a large group of distinguished professors, including Kizevetter, resigned in protest. The feelings of protest against pressure from above, the feelings of solidarity and honor that were characteristic of these scholars, were clearly manifested in these events.

Kizevetter later taught mainly at Shaniavskii University and at the Commercial Institute. Kizevetter considered Shaniavskii People's University "a remarkable event in the history of Russian culture," in the history of Russian education, a venue that organically combined the missions of science and education.[41] The university, established by A.L. Shaniavskii with the help of A.I. Chuprov and M.M. Kovalevskii in 1905, operated for more than ten years. Shaniavskii University consisted of a popular science branch (serving as a secondary school) and an academic branch. The academic branch, a "higher educational institution," was divided into two groups: the natural sciences and the sociophilosophical disciplines. In addition, there were also special courses on library science, education, the history of the cooperative movement [*kooperatsiia*], local government, and so forth. "I taught my courses," Kizevetter recalled, "in the big main auditorium...."

What a varied picture it was; what a mixture of ages, clothes, and types! Seated next to one another I saw an officer of the General Staff and a city tram conductor, a university tutor and a clerk from Miura and Meriliz, a lady with a fur boa around her neck and a monk in his cassock."[42]

During those years Kizevetter published two collections—*Historical Sketches* [Istoricheskie ocherki] in 1912, and *Historical Comments* [Istoricheskie otkliki] in 1915. He basically compiled these works from previously published articles on Russian history in the eighteenth and nine-teenth centuries. The year 1915 also saw the publication of his book *The Guild of Moscow Merchants* [Gil'diia moskovskogo kupechestva], written at the request of the Moscow Merchants Society. The book further explored topics touched on in his studies of the urban community and the Charter to the Towns. On the basis of archival materials, the author argued that the activities of municipal institutions over the course of the eighteenth and nineteenth centuries had been determined by the role that the elite merchants had played, thanks to their economic position.

Kizevetter greeted the February Revolution of 1917 with great joy. In her diary entry of 3 March 1917, Kizevetter's wife recorded these impressions of the revolutionary events of those days: "Everything that has happened seems like a dream. In three days everything has been swept away! Nothing remains of the old regime. . . . Just received the latest report by telephone from *Russkie vedomosti*. Rozenberg reports, 'Nicholas has abdicated the throne. . . . Sasha is sitting and hurriedly writing the appeal from the committee of the People's Freedom Party . . . and reading the title of his article to me: *The Abdication of Nicholas II.'* "[43]

That article was published on 4 March 1917 in *Russkie vedomosti.* Kizevetter declared the abdication of Nicholas II a "red-letter day" in the country's history, marking its liberation from despotism. In his own newspaper articles during that time, he repeatedly argued in favor of a parliamentary republic and bourgeois freedom. He condemned Bolshevism and its program, and he added his voice to those who advocated bringing the imperialist war to a victorious conclusion.[44]

It is obvious that the logic of Kizevetter's convictions could not allow him to recognize the Bolshevik Revolution. He was a principled opponent of revolutionary methods of transforming Russian reality.

He continued his teaching and educational work during the first years of Soviet rule, until his emigration in 1922. In March 1917, after Manuilov had come back to serve as rector of Moscow University, Kizevetter also returned there. In 1920 Kizevetter, Vipper, and Bogoslovskii were banned from giving lectures at higher educational institutions, for they were viewed as vehicles of the old bourgeois culture. Their activities were restricted to working with beginning scholars. For a certain amount of time, financial difficulties forced Kizevetter to work as a clerk at the Archives of the Ministry of Foreign Affairs. As a member of the Cultural and Educational Division of the Moscow Branch of the Alliance of Cooperative Associations, he traveled around the country giving lectures to small audiences (Yaroslavl, Tver, Tula, and elsewhere).

Kizevetter took part in a cooperative publishing house called Zadruga. In response to financial difficulties, the publishing house opened a bookstore, where it sold journals with lists of recommended self-help literature and programs in history and literature. It also offered professional advice. V.A. Miakotin, S.P. Mel'gunov, B.K. Mlodzevskii, and Kizevetter worked behind the counters as sales clerks and consultants. Bookselling was accompanied by some curious and rather extraordinary episodes. V[alerii] Briusov, the poet, once visited the store. When he saw his acquaintance Kizevetter standing behind the counter, he recited: "Unwittingly to These Sad Shores." Kizevetter, who did not share Briusov's Bolshevik orientation, responded: "Look, Valerii Iakovlevich, you are a Pushkin expert. Pushkin spoke those words after his betrayal."[45]

The complicated circumstances of the first years of Soviet rule and the persecutions suffered by the old prerevolutionary intelligentsia had a significant impact on Kizevetter's life. As a former member of the Central Committee of the Kadet Party he was an object of close scrutiny by the VChK [Cheka, secret police]. Between 1918 and 1921 he was arrested three times. During one of his incarcerations in Butyrskaia Prison, a period of three and a half months, he translated into Russian Charles Poux's book *Napoléon II, Alexandre II, et Gortchakoff* (the book was accepted by Sabashnikov Publishers but never published). According to A. Florovskii, one of Kizevetter's close companions during his years abroad, when Kizevetter was arrested for the second time his wife turned to M.N. Pokrovskii for help. Pokrovskii, however, advised her to "compose herself; all her efforts were in vain, and they weren't going to let Kizevetter go anyway."[46] Kizevetter himself, however, believed that this time the efforts of D.B. Riazanov might facilitate his release from prison (Riazanov revered Kizevetter as a major scholar and teacher), as might the efforts of the doorkeepers and servants at Shaniavskii University, who were well acquainted with the famous professor and were attracted by his democratic ideals.

Kizevetter was arrested for the third time in 1922 at Ivanovo-Voznesensk, where he was giving lectures at Riga Polytechnic, which had been evacuated there. Kizevetter was escorted to Moscow and spent about one month in confinement. In August 1922 Kizevetter's apartment was searched once more, and he himself was placed under house arrest.[47] At the end of 1922 preparations were made to deport a large group of the old intelligentsia from Soviet Russia. This measure was part of a series of steps being taken by the Soviet regime—the trial of V.N. Tagantsev, which resulted in N[ikolai] Gumilev being shot, the trial of the Central Committee of the Socialist Revolutionary Party, and others. Dissidents were being persecuted. The Soviet authorities considered the deportation a "humanitarian measure."

N.M. Mendel′son, a historian of literature who was well acquainted with Kizevetter, made these entries in his diary on 27 August and 3 September 1922: "Around sixty people are being deported from Moscow. Very likely Berdiaev, Kizevetter, [and others] will be exiled. The reason is that in the five years of the Soviet regime's existence they have never actively shown any sympathetic attitude toward it." He went on: "They say ... that Kizevetter has been forgiven and will not be deported. But he has sold everything he owned and given his apartment away, and now he doesn't know how he will get by."[48] And, in fact, a receipt dated 10 September 1922 confirms that A.A. Kizevetter "sold his apartment and its contents" to V.A. Kudriavtsev (Kizevetter's stepson was remaining in Russia) "and received 200,000 1922 rubles."[49]

Kizevetter, as one of a group of Moscow professors, was shipped to Petrograd, and on 28 September 1922 he sailed from there to Stettin, Germany, on the German steamship *Oberburgomeister Haken.* On 15 October, in a letter to N.I. Astrov, he wrote: "To me, all of Moscow was nothing more than a prison, although the regimen was somewhat freer than in the Butyrka. . . . As I left Moscow, I was well aware that I was leaving it for a very long time."[50]

From Stettin everybody was sent to Berlin, after which they all went to different countries. The University of Berlin and the University of Leipzig offered Kizevetter the opportunity to teach classes in Russian history, but he declined on account of the difficulty of giving lectures in German. Kizevetter waited anxiously for an answer from Prague, where he was hoping "to find a way to use his abilities before a Russian audience."[51] Kizevetter arrived in Prague on 1 January 1923 and lived the remaining ten years of his life there. "We have been living for a week now in the capital city of Czechoslovakia," he wrote to V.A. Rozenberg. "We drove directly to Vernadsky's home and are staying there. . . . The population strikes me as very pleasant, but how the outward circumstances of our lives will develop, we do not know, and this is very important for weary bodies and spirits."[52]

Czechoslovak president T[omáš] Masaryk's policy of giving asylum created very favorable conditions for Russian émigrés. The principle of "Russian action" was established in 1921 by the Committee to Aid Russian Students and the Independent Scholars' Commission, whose task was to find work for Russian professors and scholars. Several professional associations were set up in Prague, including the Union of Russian Academic Organizations Abroad, the Pedagogical Bureau for Higher and Secondary Educational Affairs, the Association of Russian Teachers' and Students' Organizations, and so forth. Other Russian associations founded in Prague included the Russian Law Faculty, on the principle and with the rights of the Russian state universities; the Russian People's (Free) University; the Cooperative Institute; a School for Transportation Engineers; commercial and bookkeeping courses; vocational gymnasiums; and so forth.

Kizevetter immediately became involved in all this activity. He joined the Academic Group and the Pedagogical Bureau; served as the chairman of the History and Philology Department of the Educational Commission; joined the Russian Institute in Prague; and became a professor of Russian history at the People's University, the Russian Pedagogical Institute, and the Russian Law Faculty, which was headed by his friend P.I. Novgorodtsev. Kizevetter taught a history course at the Philosophy Faculty of Charles University. The university's archives still contain a file on Professor A. Kizevetter; it includes his service record and a notice of his death, in Czech.[53]

In the classroom at Charles University Kizevetter also had the occasion to lecture before the high assembly of the Theological Academy, which included Metropolitan Eulogius. Kizevetter discussed the cultural role of the church.[54] At the Russian People's University Kizevetter headed the History and Philology Department, where he not only engaged in teaching and was a member of the Council of Instructors as well as the Presidium of the Council, but was also involved in publishing. He participated directly in the publication of the university's scholarly works.

Kizevetter traveled around Czechoslovakia a great deal, wherever there were Russian or Russian-Czech cultural associations, giving lectures on Russian history and culture. He also had occasion to give lectures to the local population through teacher's courses in towns of Carpathian Rus' and the Baltics. As a member of the Russian Research Institute in Berlin, he lectured on Russian history; in 1929 he spent more than a month at the Russian Research Institute in Belgrade. Kizevetter's lectures were extremely successful and attracted numerous large audiences of teachers, students, and lovers of history who greatly admired his talents as a speaker. His contemporaries recognized Kizevetter as one of the most popular speakers and lecturers in Prague, and in the whole Russian colony.

In contemplating the characteristic features of Kizevetter's extraordinary speaking skills, A. Florovskii wrote that his lectures were not characterized by bombastic enthusiasm and "random words," but by internal discipline and restraint; "the reserve of inspiration and inner fervor in his speeches was subordinated to the restraining control of external harmony and moderation."[55]

Recalling Kizevetter, Miliukov said, "His merits and talents, his scintil-lating wit and brilliant talent for exposition, inevitably drew him to emulate our incomparable Vasilii Osipovich [Kliuchevskii]."[56] The moral side of Kizevetter's personality was characterized by his faithfulness to his teacher's memory and traditions. During his life as an émigré, Kizevetter devoted more than thirty articles to Kliuchevskii.

Kizevetter did not become actively engaged in political activity while in Czechoslovakia—a trait characteristic, incidentally, of Miliukov, Mel'gunov, and many others as well. His political convictions remained as before. He advocated the democratic, parliamentary form of state govern-ment, partially condemned Soviet rule, and worried about Russia. An article entitled "From the Editors" appeared in the newspaper *Rul'* on 29 March 1931. It was signed by A.A. Argunov, A. Bem, I.V. Gessen, A.I. Kaminka, G.A. Landau, S.S. Maslov, V.E. Tatarinov, and A.A. Kizevetter. The article proclaimed the newspaper's independence from parties and political organi-zations, acknowledged the "destructiveness" of Bolshevism and the neces-sity of struggling against Soviet rule. The article discussed the necessity of establishing a democratic system, an order based on the rule of law, and so forth in Russia after the overthrow of Bolshevism. Kizevetter was deeply concerned about all these matters, but he "failed to find" an answer to the question of how to help Russia "from a single foreign Russian journalist."

His primary mission, in his own eyes, was to propagandize Russian science and culture. Not a single major event of cultural significance among the émigré community took place without Kizevetter's participation. In September 1928 he attended a congress of scientists and a congress of writ-ers in Belgrade. Along with twelve other members of the congress of scien-tists, Kizevetter was awarded the Star of Saint Savva, one of Yugoslavia's highest awards. In 1930 he was elected chairman of the Fifth Congress of Russian Scientists Abroad—attended by I. Kuprin, P. Struve, E.F. Shmurlo, and S.V. Zavadskii. These congresses were of enormous importance to the Russian émigré community—offering meetings, opportunities to reminisce, and united efforts in propagandizing Russian science and culture. In 1930, in connection with the celebration of the 175th anniversary of the founding of Moscow University, Kizevetter joined N.I. Astrov, M.M. Novikov, A.V. Iziumov, and V.A. Miakotin in organizing the celebration of Tat'iana's Day.

In March of that year, when all of Czech society was observing Masaryk's eightieth birthday (Masaryk was greatly admired by the entire Russian émigré community), Kizevetter published several articles about him, and at an assembly of all-Russian and Russian-Czech organizations he delivered a paper entitled "Masaryk as a Political Leader."[57]

Kizevetter regularly took part in Russian Culture Days, which were held at the initiative of committees that had been established for the purpose in thirteen countries. For the émigré communities, this day—solemnly observed on the anniversary of A.S. Pushkin's birth—had enormous moral significance. "Here we have a very particular and urgent task of today," Kizevetter stated on 4 October 1928 on the occasion of Russian Culture Day in Belgrade. "And that task is to maintain in our souls, in times of trouble, the unquenchable light of our national consciousness. That's what Russian Culture Day is all about."[58] At gatherings of this sort memoria were dedicated to Pushkin and Tolstoy; Shaliapin sang *Boris Godunov,* and Bunin spoke on Russian literature.

Another important cultural and scientific event was the creation of the Russian Historical Archive Abroad in Prague. The purpose for creating the archive was to gather together materials on the history of the Russian revolutions of 1905 and 1917 and World War I, as well as documents relating to the Russian emigration. Kizevetter was in charge of the Archive Council and its Scientific-Administrative Commission. V.A. Miakotin, E.F. Shmurlo, A.V. Florovskii, and D.I. Meisner also participated in such work. Their endeavors led to the gathering of a huge fund of both prerevolutionary and Soviet-era Russian newspapers and journals; Russian émigré publications with centers in Paris, New York, Prague, Berlin, Belgrade, Sofia, and elsewhere; and journals in Slavic and other languages. A special division of the archives contained sources on various questions of Russian history. After the Great Patriotic War [World War II], the Russian Historical Archive Abroad was turned over to the Academy of Sciences of the USSR by the Czechoslovak government. Among the archive employees who assisted the transfer was D.I. Meisner.

Kizevetter also found scholarly and patriotic meaning in his activities with the Russian Historical Society, organized in Prague in 1925. One of the founders of the society, he served as a member of its presidium and as assistant to the chairman, and when he stepped down from that post, E.F. Shmurlo became chairman. The Russian Historical Society in Prague was actively concerned about the scholarly life of émigré historians, trying to organize them, to preserve the "Russian historical school" and its scholarly traditions in emigration, and to transmit these to the younger generation.

Kizevetter wrote a great deal while in exile. He published his articles in a collection entitled *Peasant Russia* [Krest´ianskaia Rossiia]; in journals such as *Na chuzhoi storone, Volia naroda,* and *Slavia;* and in newspapers like *Rul´, Segodnia,* and others. He was a regular contributor to the "thickest" of the émigré journals, *Sovremennye zapiski;* he published articles on historical topics and regularly contributed reviews to the journal. M.V. Vishniak, who was one of the founders and editors of the journal, reminisced about the reviews that Kizevetter wrote, often fifteen to sixteen pages or longer, with unfailing good will toward the journal as well as with criticism—both harsh and kindly-ironic. "He wrote simply and clearly, perhaps, indeed, in a style that was a bit old-fashioned."[59] Vishniak was highly appreciative of Kizevetter's contributions to the journal.

Kizevetter published a second edition of his book about the actor M.S. Shchepkin, and he published a book in Czech about outstanding Russian performers—a tribute to his passionate interest in the theater. He published a pamphlet about Moscow University and participated in the preparation of a jubilee (175th anniversary) edition on the history of Moscow University. He also took part in the development of a course on Russian history for French readers, a work edited by P.N. Miliukov, C. Seignobos, and L. Eisenmann. The year 1931 saw the publication in Berlin of his book *Historical Silhouettes: People and Events* [Istoricheskie siluety: Liudi i sobytiia]—which consisted basically of studies earlier published in Russia on Catherine II, Potemkin, and Granovskii—as well as several articles about Tolstoy's *War and Peace* [Voina i mir] and A. Griboedov's *Woe from Wit* [Gore ot uma].

Of considerable scientific interest was Kizevetter's article "On General Interpretations of Russian History in Modern Literature" [Ob obshchikh postroeniiakh russkoi istorii v sovremennoi literature] and on Eurasianism (*evraziistvo*). He argued against the viewpoints held by B.E. Nol'de and I. Bunakov. The former declared that the Russian people was not capable of "statehood endeavor," that it was apathetic and anarchical. The latter stated that the characteristic property of the Russian soul was its proclivity for serfdom, as exemplified by the tsardom of Muscovy. Kizevetter did not share the view that Russian history was accomplished without the Russian people, which had no history. He was keen and decisive in his condemnation of the idea that Russia should be considered part of Eurasia. He wrote a great many articles on this theme. Kizevetter viewed Russia's history as one in which the people participated and that developed within the context shared by the countries of Western Europe, with all its specific characteristics.

Life in exile as an émigré, naturally, was not easy (either in financial or in morale terms) for a scholar who was already fifty-seven years old. Still, Kizevetter's energy, industry, and enormous erudition and tact helped him to become comfortable in the life of Prague and to win the admiration of Prague natives as well.

In 1929 Kizevetter moved into a comfortable new home, built with the émigrés' own funds.

D.I. Meisner, the author of an interesting memoir entitled *Mirages and Reality* [Mirazhi i deistvitel´nost´], depicted Kizevetter during that period as follows: "The people who lived in the houses," he wrote, saw this talented lecturer and speaker . . . leave the house every morning with a bold, quick, but not entirely confident step on his by now already aging legs. Kizevetter used to hurry to the trolley to attend a lecture or a meeting, to visit the library, or, with a small folding chair under his arm, to head for Prague's big Stromovka Park, where he used to find a comfortable spot in the shade, surrounded by books and manuscripts. Sometimes thoughtfully, sometimes very temperamentally he talked to himself as he strolled the paths in the park. At other times, as he hurried along the streets of Prague, he softly sang some rather bravura little song. A little old man with a big beard, now snowy white, he had lively, restless eyes and the inexhaustible eloquence with which fate had endowed him.[60]

The last years of Kizevetter's life brought both financial problems and diabetes. On 2 November 1932 he wrote to M.V. Vishniak, "You ask how I live. I inject myself with insulin twice a day. God knows when it will all end! On account of this I am not able to go to public lectures, and I have to turn down various invitations to speak—which is to say, I have no means of earning money."[61]

Kizevetter's last important work was his elegant memoirs, *At the Cusp of Two Centuries* [Na rubezhe dvukh stoletii], a summation of his life and a loving tribute to Moscow University and to Russia. His life as an émigré, so filled with constant labor, could never extinguish his longing for Russia.

His trip to Riga in 1927 evoked old associations with Russia. "I walk along the streets," he wrote, "and enjoy it so much—everything covered in snow, the sun shining and ten to fifteen degrees of frost. Russia."[62] In a letter to his daughter from Iur'ev in 1929 he wrote: "When I woke up this morning I had a remarkable feeling—it was as if I had been magically transported to Russia. In the hallway I could hear Russian voices, and the sound of the bells of an Orthodox church wafted in from the street."[63]

On his sixtieth birthday Kizevetter wrote a poem profoundly expressing the state of his soul:

> Again the circle of the year is closing,
> And, hiding the sorrow in my soul once more,
> A melodious, tuneful chirping.
> Want to or not, I stand stock still,
> But the sorrow in my soul goes deeper,
> Tormenting me to the point of pain, and
> I would hasten to Russia forthwith.[64]

Kizevetter never did go back to Russia, however. He died suddenly in Prague, in his apartment, on 9 January 1933.

"I feel inexpressible sadness," an émigrée wrote in her condolences to Kizevetter's daughter, "that Aleksandr Aleksandrovich had to die in a foreign land, loving Moscow so ardently, loving Russia so faithfully and tenderly."[65]

Kizevetter was buried in Prague's Olšansky Cemetery on 11 January 1933. There is a monument on his grave, erected using funds from the Russian émigré community, collected by the Russian Historical Society.

Notes

Translated by Kim Braithwaite for publication in Russian Studies in History, vol 36, no. 4, ©1998 by M.E. Sharpe, Inc.

1. Manuscript Division of the Russian State Library (henceforth RO RGB), f. 566, k. 3, d. 6, l. 1.

2. Ibid.

3. A.A. Kizevetter, *Na rubezhe dvukh stoletii (Vospominaniia. 1881–1914)* (Prague, 1929), p. 31.

4. Ibid., p. 51.

5. Ibid., p. 71.

6. M.V. Vishniak, *"Sovremennye zapiski": Vospominaniia redaktora* (Bloomington: Indiana University Press, 1957), p. 170.

7. Kizevetter, *Na rubezhe*, p. 276.

8. Ibid., p. 275.

9. Ibid.

10. Ibid., pp. 267–68.

11. A.A. Kizevetter, *Posadskaia obshchina v Rossii XVIII st.* (Moscow, 1903), p. iv.

12. A.A. Kizevetter, "Rech' pered disputom," *Russkaia mysl'*, 1904, bk. 1, p. 159.

13. A.A. Kizevetter, "Posadskaia obshchina v Rossii XVIII stoletiia," in *Istoricheskie ocherki* (Moscow, 1912), p. 260.

14. "Disput A.A. Kizevettera," *Istoricheskii vestnik*, February 1904, pp. 803–7; *Russkie vedomosti*, 19 December 1904.

15. Kizevetter, *Na rubezhe*, pp. 277–78.

16. *Chteniia v Istoricheskom obshchestve istorii drevnostei rossiiskikh pri Moskovskom universitete: Otchet ob odinnadtsatom prisuzhdenii premii G.F. Karpova* (Moscow, 1906), bk. 4.

17. Kizevetter, *Na rubezhe*, p. 363.

18. Ibid., pp. 358–66; N. Teleshov, *Zapiski pisatelia* (Moscow, 1952), p. 33.

19. A.A. Kizevetter, "Na moskovskom zhurfikse," *Rul'*, 7 September 1930.

20. A.A. Kizevetter, *Pervyi obshchedostupnyi teatr v Rossii* (Moscow, 1901); A.A. Kizevetter, "Teatral'nye zametki: Anatema—Tsezar' i Kleopatra," *Russkaia mysl'*, 1909, no. 11; A.A. Kizevetter, "Teatral'nye zametki: Moskovskaia dramaticheskaia stsena," *Russkaia mysl'*, 1911, no. 5, 12, and 1912, no. 2, 5; A.A. Kizevetter, "Teatr v Rossii v epokhu Otechestvennoi voiny," *Russkaia mysl'*, 1912, no. 11; A.A. Kizevetter, *M.S. Shchepkin: Epizod iz istorii russkogo stsenicheskogo iskusstva* (Moscow, 1916); A.A. Kizevetter, *Teatr: Ocherki, razmyshleniia, zametki* (Moscow, 1922); and others.

21. A.A. Kizevetter, *Napadki na partiiu narodnoi svobody i vozrazhenie na nikh* (Moscow, 1906); A.A. Kizevetter, "Vtoraia Gosudarstvennaia duma," *Russkaia mysl'*, 1907, no. 7; A.A. Kizevetter, *Partiia narodnoi svobody i ee ideologiia* (Moscow, 1917); A.A. Kizevetter, *P.N. Miliukov* (Moscow, 1917); Kizevetter, *Na rubezhe*, pp. 390–466.

22. Kizevetter, *Na rubezhe,* p. 466.
23. A.A. Kizevetter, *Gorodovoe polozhenie Ekateriny II* (Moscow, 1909).
24. Iu.V. Got'e, "Gorodovoe polozhenie Ekateriny II," *Zhurnal ministerstva narodnogo prosveshcheniia,* September 1909, pp. 206–19.
25. A. Iziumov, "Stranichka vospominanii," *Zapiski russkogo istoricheskogo obshchestva v Prage,* bk. 3 (Prague: Cheshska-Narva, 1937).
26. A.A. Kizevetter, "Ekaterina II kak zakonodatel'nitsa: Rech' pered doktorskim disputom," *Russkaia mysl',* 1909, no. 12; A.A. Kizevetter, "Istoricheskoe znachenie tsarstvovaniia Ekateriny Velikoi," *Obrazovanie* (St. Petersburg), 1896, no. 11.
27. A.A. Kizevetter, "Ekaterina II," in *Istoricheskie siluety: Liudi i sobytiia* (Berlin, 1931), p. 24.
28. Ibid.
29. A.A. Kizevetter, "F.V. Rostopchin," in *Istoricheskie otkliki* (Moscow, 1915).
30. A.A. Kizevetter, "Rossiia," in *Entsiklopedicheskii slovar' Brokgauz i Efron,* vol. 55, bk. 27 (St. Petersburg, 1899); A.A. Kizevetter, "Krest'ianstvo v istorii Rossii," in *Krest'ianskaia Rossiia: Sb. statei po voprosam obshchestvenno-politicheskim i ekonomicheskim* (Prague, 1923), bk. 3; A.A. Kizevetter, "Pugachevshchina," in *Istoricheskie siluety,* pp. 55–92; and others.
31. A.A. Kizevetter, "Krest'ianstvo v istorii Rossii," in *Krest'ianskaia Rossiia,* bk. 3, pp. 9–10; Kizevetter, "Pugachevshchina"; A.A. Kizevetter, "K istorii krest'ianskikh dvizhenii v Rossii," in *Krest'ianskaia Rossiia* (Prague, 1924), bks. 13–19.
32. RO RGB, f. 566, k. 7, d. 12, ll. 27, 35; A.A. Kizevetter, *Istoriia Rossii XIX veka: Kurs, chitannyi v Moskovskom universitete v 1908–1909* (Moscow, 1909), pt. 1, p. 6.
33. RO RGB, f. 566, k. 4, d. 15, l. 3; k. 7, d. 3, l. 23; k. 7, d. 12, ll. 1–3, 7, 11, 20, 35.
34. RO RGB, k. 7, d. 12, ll. 27, 35; Kizevetter, *Istoriia Rossii XIX veka,* pt. 1, p. 6.
35. Kizevetter, *Istoriia Rossii XIX veka,* pt. 1, pp. 3–6; A.A. Kizevetter, *Rossiia na rubezhe XVIII i XIX stoletii: Vstupitel'nye lektsii professorov Moskovskogo imperatorskogo universiteta* (Moscow, 1909), pp. 15–18; RO RGB, f. 566, k. 9, d. 3, l. 1; k. 4, d. 18, l. 1; f. 218, d. 822, ll. 1–10.
36. Kizevetter, *Rossiia na rubezhe,* p. 17.
37. RO RGB, f. 261, k. 16, d. 7, l. 141.
38. Kizevetter, *Istoriia Rossii XIX veka,* pt. 2, p. 69.
39. A.A. Kizevetter, "V.O. Kliuchevskii kak prepodavatel'," in *V.O. Kliuchevskii: Kharakteristiki i vospominaniia* (Moscow, 1912), pp. 164–76.
40. V.O. Kliuchevskii, *Pis'ma, dnevniki, aforizmy i mysli ob istorii* (Moscow, 1968), pp. 457–58.
41. A.A. Kizevetter, "A.L. Shaniavskii i universitet ego imeni," *Russkaia mysl',* December 1915; A.A. Kizevetter, "Universitet imeni Shaniavskogo," in *Na chuzhoi storone* (Berlin and Prague, 1923), bk. 3.
42. Kizevetter, "Universitet imeni Shaniavskogo," pp. 175–76.
43. RO RGB, f. 566, k. 19, d. 1, l. 486.
44. A.A. Kizevetter, "Amnistiia," *Russkie vedomosti,* 8 March 1917; A.A. Kizevetter, "Partiia narodnoi svobody i respublika," *Russkie vedomosti,* 18 March 1917; A.A. Kizevetter, "Partiia narodnoi svobody i Vremennoe pravitel'stvo," *Russkie vedomosti,* 9 (22) July 1917; A.A. Kizevetter, "Iz dumskikh vpechatlenii," *Russkie vedomosti,* 25 July (7 August) 1917.
45. RO RGB, f. 165, k. 1, d. 8, l. 38; d. 9, l. 1; V. Ozeretskovskii, "Kul'turnaia rabota v Sovetskoi Rossii," in *Golos minuvshego na chuzhoi storone* (Paris, 1926), no. 4; A.A. Kizevetter, "Kak ia byl prikazchikom," *Segodnia,* 20 September 1931.
46. A. Florovskii, "Aleksandr Aleksandrovich Kizevetter," in *Zapiski Russkogo istoricheskogo obshchestva v Prage* (Prague and Narva, 1937), bk. 3, p. 191.

47. Ibid., pp. 190–95.

48. RO RGB, f. 165, k. 1, d. 1, l. 2, 4–8.

49. RO RGB, f. 566, k. 4, d. 2, l. 1.

50. M. Raev [Marc Raeff], "Pis'ma A.A. Kizevettera N.I. Astrovu, V.I. Vernadskomu, M.V. Vishniaku," *Novyi zhurnal,* 1988, nos. 71/73, p. 464.

51. Iziumov, "Stranichka vospominanii," pp. 212–13.

52. GA RF [State Archives of the Russian Federation], f. 5978, op. 1, d. 256, l. 77.

53. Archives of Charles University, f. 12, d. 5, 2/1.

54. *Poslednie novosti,* 3 December 1924.

55. Florovskii, "Aleksandr Aleksandrovich Kizevetter," p. 196.

56. P. Miliukov, "Tri pokoleniia," in *Zapiski Russkogo istoricheskogo obshchestva v Prage,* bk. 3, p. 16.

57. *Rul',* 7 and 9 March 1930.

58. *Den' russkoi kul'tury* (Belgrade, 1928).

59. Vishniak, *"Sovremennye zapiski,"* pp. 172, 174, 176.

60. D. Meisner, *Mirazhi i deistvitel'nost'* (Moscow, 1966), pp. 206–7.

61. Raeff, "Pis'ma," p. 523.

62. RO RGB, f. 566, d. 54, l. 6.

63. Ibid., d. 52, l. 26.

64. Ibid., l. 11.

65. Ibid., k. 32, d. 8, l. 4.

14

Sergei Fedorovich Platonov (1860–1933)

A Life for Russia

Aleksei Nikolaevich Tsamutali

The family in which the eminent Russian historian Sergei Fedorovich Platonov was born and raised could well exemplify how the most competent persons from the peasantry, despite all obstacles and thanks to their abilities and industry, gradually not only filled the educated segment of Russian society but even became an ornament to it. According to family tradition, Platonov's ancestors were originally peasants from the Kaluga area. Evidently, they were given their freedom even during the period of serfdom, and they settled in Moscow. Not only were the parents of the future historian "native Muscovites" but all their kin "were concentrated in Moscow." Fedor Platonov, trained as a typographical engineer, was sent by the "government service" to the Ukrainian town of Chernigov, where he served as head of the provincial press. It was there, in Chernigov, that Sergei F. Platonov was born on 16 (28) April 1860. In 1869 Fedor Platonov was transferred to St. Petersburg, and nine-year-old Sergei Platonov also traveled to St. Petersburg, together with his whole family. From then on, his entire life was linked to St. Petersburg. During his childhood and adolescence, however, the future historian felt close spiritual ties with Moscow. In his declining years he wrote, "Whenever I visited Moscow during my childhood, in the home of my grandfather on the northern edge of the city . . . I felt as if it were my real home," even though the family homestead "was not there but in St. Petersburg." Recalling the "Great Russian element" that reigned in his family and with which he "was reared and imbued," and which, he believed, gave him the right to consider himself "a pure representative of the southern (Moscow) branch of the Great Russian tribe," Platonov concluded: "Not only our origins but also our conscious devotion to Moscow, with its shrines, history, and way of life made my parents, and hence me as well, Great Russian patriots." Sergei Platonov was greatly influenced by his father, "an intelligent, able, and humane man who stood head and shoulders above those around him in terms of intelligence and morality." The father instilled a love for reading in his son and "gave him his first understanding of history and literature." Sergei Platonov "started to read Karamzin and Pushkin at around the age of eight or nine, and dearly loved to listen to his father's stories about happenings in his own youth, which took place in close contact with student circles [*kruzhki*] in Moscow."[1]

By his gymnasium years, Sergei Platonov already had a sense of what Moscow and St. Petersburg universities were like, of the professors who taught there and their courses. He knew about Moscow University from his relative E.P. Berkut (née Kalaidovich) and her husband V.P. Berkut. He was well informed about St. Petersburg University thanks to V.F. Kenevich, a teacher at the gymnasium. Through his conversations with the Berkuts and Kenevich, Platonov became interested in philosophy while still at the gymnasium, and he read the works of J[ohn Stuart] Mill, G[eorge] Lewes, H[ippolyte-Adolphe] Taine, and Fr[iedrich (Ludwig)] Büchner.[2]

In 1878 Platonov enrolled in the history and philology faculty at St. Petersburg University. His original intent was to "acquire a literary education on a philosophical foundation." However, the courses in the history of literature that he took during his first year of study were "not all that brilliant; the lectures of most of the professors were not attractive to the young student." Meanwhile, the law and history professors immediately drew Platonov to them "both by their personal talent and by the subject of their lectures." First place in this regard went to K.N. Bestuzhev-Riumin, a professor of Russian history who, in Platonov's words, was "a thoroughly educated man freely conversant with all spheres of the humanities and with a magnificent knowledge of his discipline," a man who raised his students "to the heights of abstract conjecture" and introduced them "to the subtleties of specialized scholarly controversy." Platonov, who recalled Bestuzhev-Riumin as the person who had "the greatest influence" on him, emphasized that the course in Russian history given by this professor "was so constructed that he not only set forth historical facts but rather explained the history of their scholarly treatment, the successes and attainments of scholarly endeavor and wit."[3] The attention to historical facts that

Bestuzhev-Riumin inculcated in his students was also closely connected with the requirement that they engage in meticulous study of historical sources. Thanks to Bestuzhev-Riumin's lectures, Platonov absorbed the importance of comprehensive historical source study in his very first year, as well as the importance of strictly validating historical facts, and he became even more convinced of this in the classes conducted by V.G. Vasil'evskii, who taught medieval history and was already well known for his works on the history of Byzantium. Platonov wrote that when Vasil'evskii was examining some particular episode from the history of Byzantine–Gothic or Byzantine–Russian relations, he had the knack of bringing students "face to face with the text of the primary source" and of demonstrating "graphically ... how the historical conclusion was derived from that text, a conclusion that was sometimes of great interest and substantial importance." Thanks to such training, the students "entered into the actual process of scholarly research and creative endeavor and began to understand the seductive charm of successful scholarly endeavor."[4] The students also received a sound historiographical foundation from Bestuzhev-Riumin and Vasil'evskii. Bestuzhev-Riumin encouraged this, and not only as an author of historiographical works. According to Platonov, the professor had a constant "urge ... to present every issue in terms of historiography."[5] Before examinations, Vasil'evskii had his students "read a number of historical works (Guizot, Thierry, Granovskii)" in addition to his own course work.[6]

During his student years, Platonov also came under the influence of law professors A.D. Gradovskii and V.I. Sergeevich. In lectures given by Gradovskii, who taught the state law of Russia and of foreign countries, Sergei Platonov first developed "a conception of the state and society, of the purposes of the state, of relations between the state and the individual, and of the value of personal freedom and independence." Sergeevich's lectures attracted Platonov because the professor's "resonant and smooth phrasing always incorporated a thought that was precise and vital, and the force of his analysis was astonishing when he was examining ancient documents and characterizing ancient legal relations."[7]

The professors under whom Platonov studied also affected the shaping of his personality. This influence was manifested in various ways. Under Sergeevich, according to Platonov, "one wished to learn to be a lecturer"; however, "there was nothing in him of the tutor or the moral guide—nothing but a consummate technique, a beauty of method and style." In the teaching of Bestuzhev-Riumin and Gradovskii, in contrast, "the element of morality was strong"; "both of them penetrated the heart and the conscience, awakened the soul, and compelled one to search for the ideal and for moral foundations." At the same time, Gradovskii and Bestuzhev-

Riumin differed from one another in their political sympathies. According to Platonov, "They gravitated to different sides—Gradovskii was clearly a 'Westernizer,' while Bestuzhev-Riumin was closer to the 'Slavophiles.' "[8]

In addition to his professors in St. Petersburg, Platonov's formation as a historian was greatly influenced by the ideas contained in the works and lectures of V.O. Kliuchevskii, then a quite young professor at Moscow University. The older generation of St. Petersburg historians greeted Kliuchevskii's early works with caution. Bestuzhev-Riumin himself was restrained, and in private conversation he smilingly described *The Boyar Duma* [Boiarskaia duma] as a "huge, enormous freak."[9] Platonov did not agree with that assessment, or, especially, with the attacks against Kliuchevskii. He believed that Kliuchevskii's critics were not familiar with his lithographed courses and had no interest in the new chapters of *The Boyar Duma,* published in *Russkaia mysl',* chapters that "revealed all the charm of Kliuchevskii's talent." What attracted Platonov in Kliuchevskii's works and lectures was not "his inclination toward the economic point of view" but rather "the multidimensionality and breadth of his historical understanding," in what Platonov took to be his independence from the leading lights of the historical-juridical school. Platonov acknowledged that the influence of Kliuchevskii's ideas on him was powerful and deep. At the time, although Bestuzhev-Riumin said enviously to Platonov, "I can see that you are more of a pupil of Sergeevich," Platonov himself said that he had "learned first from Bestuzhev-Riumin and Gradovskii, then from Vasil'evskii and Kliuchevskii."[10]

Bestuzhev-Riumin recommended that Platonov, who had successfully completed his course of study in 1882, remain at the university to train for the rank of professor. Indisputable proof that Platonov deserved this honor was his candidate's essay, on the basis of which Platonov wrote and soon published an article entitled "Notes on the History of the Moscow Assemblies of the Land" [Zametki po istorii moskovskikh zemskikh soborov].[11] This article proved not only that Platonov was a competent young researcher but also that he had developed a special interest in the history of Russia at the beginning of the seventeenth century. One might reasonably anticipate that research on this subject would yield important results. He was not, however, able to enroll in the university, for financial reasons. To earn money, Platonov had to teach. When Bestuzhev-Riumin fell ill, Platonov replaced him as lecturer for the Higher Courses for Women. Later, Platonov began to teach at a gymnasium, and from 1886 onward he taught at the Alexander Lyceum. Meanwhile he was preparing himself for his examinations and writing his master's dissertation.

Having envisioned his dissertation as a historical and sociological study, Platonov soon realized that to write it he would not only have to "seek out new historical material" in "archives that had yet to be put in order," but also have "to perform a critical analysis of familiar historical and literary materials that historians have utilized without necessary caution."[12] As a result, he started to prepare a source study, as he reported in a letter to Bestuzhev-Riumin, then recuperating in Italy. Bestuzhev-Riumin wholeheartedly supported Platonov's plans. In his reply he wrote: "The topic of your dissertation is one I heartily approve. I am definitely of the opinion that the use of sources is an excellent topic for a master's or even a doctoral dissertation. I hope that for the doctorate you will survey foreign sources on the Time of Troubles. Without source criticism we will never know anything; in other words, we have to know them. Do your work and all will be well."[13] Bestuzhev-Riumin's injunction to pay special attention to historical sources was an instruction close to Platonov's heart. V.G. Vasil'evskii's seminar had instilled in him this very precept. Many years later, in 1920, A.E. Presniakov, in his critique of the "Moscow historical school," which he believed suffered from "an approach that is too theoretical," wrote the following: "The Petrograd historical school gave a different direction to its students. This was the school of V.G. Vasil'evskii, of which our own school of Russian historians, nurtured in Platonov's classroom, also became an organic branch. I would define its characteristic feature as one of scholarly realism, reflected above all in the specific and direct appeal to the source and the fact, without regard to historical tradition."[14]

After painstaking effort, Platonov prepared and submitted his master's dissertation, entitled *Old Russian Legends and Tales About the Seventeenth-Century Time of Troubles as a Historical Source* [Drevnerusskie skazaniia i povesti o Smutnom vremeni XVII veka, kak istoricheskii istochnik]. Platonov not only undertook to study published documents but also to seek out manuscripts scattered throughout various repositories, not only in St. Petersburg and Moscow but also in many other cities, and even the documents that were frequently kept in the archives of distant monasteries. In all, he managed to gather more than sixty chronicles, stories, legends, and other Russian writings devoted to the Time of Troubles, which he studied "on the basis of approximately 150 manuscripts."[15] Platonov separated original documents from the mass of compilations and imitations, then studied the original documents in chronological order. The first two chapters of his book consisted of works written before the end of the Troubles. The third and fourth chapters included very important works on the Troubles written during the reign of Tsar Mikhail Fedorovich [1613–1645]. In his fifth chapter Platonov investigated "secondary and later works concerning the Troubles": "documents of a biographical character," "compiled documents," and "local legends." These included, in his estimation, "approximately thirty, if not more, works that are completely original; the number of compiled works, on the other hand . . . cannot be determined with precision."[16] Platonov himself, and almost everybody who reviewed his work, viewed his book primarily as a critical study of historical sources. Kliuchevskii agreed with this assessment. Not only did he give Platonov's book a positive review,[17] but he also used it in preparing a special course on source analysis and investigation.[18] Platonov's book was favorably reviewed by K.N. Bestuzhev-Riumin,[19] P.N. Polevoi,[20] V.S. Ikonnikov,[21] and E.N. Shchepkin.[22] V.I. Lamanskii, the well-known Slavicist, had a particularly noteworthy reaction: he declared Platonov's study to be important for the history of literature as well, showing how the Troubles had served as a major topic of seventeenth-century Russian literature.

Platonov, who became a private tutor after his successful defense of his master's dissertation in 1888, was appointed acting head of the Department of Russian History when E.E. Zamyslovskii fell ill. For one who had become a private tutor only recently and who had not yet earned his doctoral degree, this was quite an honor. Contrary to the formal rules, the faculty petitioned to have Platonov appointed as acting professor. That petition was granted by the Ministry of Public Education, and in the autumn of 1890 Platonov became a full member of the faculty. Platonov himself believed that he owed his appointment primarily to V.G. Vasil'evskii. In 1890 Vasil'evskii, then editor of the *Zhurnal ministerstva narodnogo prosveshcheniia,* invited Platonov to join the editorial board and made him his assistant. Platonov's permanent appointment in the Department of Russian History helped to improve his financial position and created the necessary conditions for further scholarly work. From 1891 onward, Platonov served as a permanent staffer (in 1894 he became a member) of the Archeographical Commission. He was assigned the job of preparing and publishing the materials that he himself had gathered and researched, and the result was *Monuments of Old Russian Literature Relating to the Time of Troubles* [Pamiatniki drevnei russkoi pis'mennosti, otnosiashchiesia k Smutnomu vremeni]—volume 13 of the Archeographical Commission's *Russian Historical Library* [Russkaia istoricheskaia biblioteka]. The Archeographical Commission then assigned Platonov the job of publishing and editing the Nikon Chronicle [Nikonovskaia letopis'], the official and comprehensive sixteenth-century chronicle compilation that became one volume of the *Complete Collection of Russian Chronicles* [Polnoe sobranie russkikh letopisei].

In his capacity of acting professor, Platonov's duties included conducting a Russian history survey, as well as more specialized courses and a seminar. Platonov's seminar produced a number of talented historians. The older generation of Platonov's pupils included S.V. Rozhdestvenskii, A.E. Presniakov, I.I. Lappo, M.A. Polievktov, N.P. Pavlov-Sil'vanskii, P.G. Vasenko, and E.F. Turaeva-Tsereteli. Platonov's seminars were attended not only by historians but also by historians of literature such as S.A. Adrianov. Platonov established and maintained close relations with historians working in other cities. He began an amicable correspondence with V.O. Kliuchevskii. Platonov helped a young Moscow historian and pupil of Kliuchevskii's, P.N. Miliukov, to publish his dissertation in *Zhurnal ministerstva narodnogo prosveshcheniia*. All that Platonov needed to do to consolidate himself in his position at St. Petersburg University was to write and defend his doctoral dissertation. To gain more free time, in 1895 Platonov quit his post as assistant editor of *Zhurnal ministerstva narodnogo prosveshcheniia*.

At the beginning of 1896, Platonov began work on his doctoral dissertation. He did not follow K.N. Bestuzhev-Riumin's suggestion to make his doctoral dissertation a study of foreign sources on the history of the Time of Troubles; instead, he undertook to reconstruct in all its complexity the history of the Time of Troubles in Muscovy. Fulfilling the difficult task that Platonov had set for himself was made easier, first, because he had already completed a considerable amount of painstaking work on these sources, and, second, because in his lectures he had focused considerable attention on the Time of Troubles, attempting to explore its causes and shed light on the course of events and their consequences. As he tried to interpret the Time of Troubles, Platonov made critical assessments of the works of his predecessors—in particular, historians such as S.M. Solov'ev and K.D. Kavelin. In Platonov's opinion, these historians deserved credit primarily for showing that the reforms of the beginning of the eighteenth century, usually linked with the name of Peter I, did not represent a sudden and major shift, and that not Peter's reign but rather the Time of Troubles, with its political catastrophes and social upheavals, should be considered to mark the beginning of modern Russian history. Platonov found useful Solov'ev's idea that the Time of Troubles represented the "final moment of struggle between the old, clan-based [*rodovye*] 'foundations' and the new, state-based ones," the moment after which "the state-based 'foundations' triumphed once and for all." At the same time, Platonov thought that this formula, which had acquired "great certainty from the viewpoint of the Solov'ev school," nevertheless failed to give historians of his generation "any realistic basis for understanding."[23] A substantial contribution to the historical study of the Time of Troubles was made by S.M. Solov'ev's pupil V.O. Kliuchevskii, who focused attention on the necessity of studying the Troubles as a complex crisis that encompassed all spheres of life—political, social, and economic. At the same time, Kliuchevskii emphasized that all classes of Russian society had taken part in the Troubles, becoming involved "in the same order they occupied in the hierarchy of Russian society at the time, as they were placed in terms of comparative importance in the state according to the social ladder of ranks."[24] Taking Kliuchevskii's interpretation as his basis, Platonov created a new concept that in its final form contained several elements that differed from Kliuchevskii's views. Platonov titled his study *Studies in the History of the Troubles in the Muscovite State in the Sixteenth and Seventeenth Centuries (An Attempt at a Study of Social Structure and Class Relations in the Time of Troubles)* [Ocherki po istorii Smuty v Moskovskom gosudarstve v XVI–XVII vv. (Opyt izucheniia obshchestvennogo stroia i soslovnykh otnoshenii v Smutnoe vremia)].

Gradually, in the course of his work on the Time of Troubles, Platonov came to recognize the necessity of a more detailed study of the period preceding the Troubles. As a result, the first part of his book included two long chapters. The first chapter, entitled "Regions of the Muscovite State" [Oblasti Moskovskogo gosudarstva], represented a meticulous study of historical geography. Many years later, M.N. Tikhomirov characterized that chapter as "a brief outline of the historical geography of Russia in the sixteenth century, written from a great knowledge of affairs."[25] In the second chapter, "The Crisis of the Second Half of the Sixteenth Century" [Krizis vtoroi poloviny XVI veka], Platonov, following Kliuchevskii, focused on the struggle Ivan IV waged against the princely elite. He paid special attention to the *oprichnina* policies of Ivan IV. He defined the *oprichnina* as a group of measures directed against the aristocracy that undermined its social and political influence and fostered the growth of lesser service (gentry) landownership, which depended on the power of the sovereign. The *oprichnina* and the terror to which it gave rise resulted not only in the physical extermination of the previous elite but also in the establishment of small landownership, which was linked to the growth of enserfment among the peasantry. The peasants, trying to escape enserfment, fled from the center of the Muscovite state. Many of them swelled the ranks of the free Cossack bands. Because of the manpower drain, the lands of the Russian center were depopulated, and the government lost revenues and could no longer muster the small landowners who had been given that land in return for government service. At the moment of Ivan IV's death, Platonov argued, "the economic crisis in the central regions was in full flower," with the government openly acknowledging that a "time of great leanness" had befallen its servants.[26] It was in this atmosphere of economic crisis, aggravated by the dissatisfaction of many population strata, that the Troubles began, and Platonov discerned three stages in their development.

A detailed analysis of the events of the Time of Troubles itself was presented in the second part of his *Studies in the History of the Troubles,* consisting of three chapters, each of which was devoted to one period of the Troubles. In his division of the Troubles into three periods, Platonov called the first "dynastic," because in his view it encompassed the period in which various pretenders contended for the throne of Muscovy, ending with the reign of Tsar Vasilii Shuiskii. The second stage, in Platonov's view, was marked by "internecine strife among the classes of society and intervention in this struggle by foreign governments." The third and final period was the time of "the struggle of the people of Muscovy against a foreign state until the creation of the national government with M[ikhail] F[edorovich] Romanov at its head."[27]

In *Studies* Platonov focused considerable attention on the economic situation and on social conflict. While he emphasized the importance of the conflict between the service estate and the serfs, Platonov wrote that this conflict was not manifested in its "pure form." He pointed out that "the supporters of Tsar Dmitrii" demanded "not only the reinstatement of the rights of the deposed tsar but also radical social changes."[28] Among these followers he singled out the most loyal allies of Ivan Bolotnikov, allies who constituted "a mass Cossack and serf opposition."[29] The actions of the Cossacks, whom Platonov perceived as "bandits," resulted in the destruction of the state. In his opinion, in the second half of 1612, after the "Cossack camp" that had seized power near Moscow "became, for a time, the governmental focus of the whole country," "the most critical moment in the internal history of Muscovite society occurred."[30]

The resolution of the crisis, in Platonov's view, came about through the reawakening of religious feelings and national forces. The people who formed the second militia [in 1611–12], according to Platonov, were tradesmen, the "lower classes subject to taxation [the *tiaglo*]," followed by the "service estate and the clergy."[31] It was these "middle strata" of Muscovite society, Platonov argued, who "won the game" after "the upper and bottom strata had lost it." Quoting Isaac Massa, Platonov regarded "one of the principal victories of the tsar" as having defeated the Cossack regime.[32] The election of Mikhail Romanov as tsar, in Platonov's eyes, both marked the restoration of the autocracy and signaled the triumph of "order," after which "the Troubles came to an end."[33]

Platonov's *Studies in the History of the Troubles in the Muscovite State*—published first in *Zhurnal ministerstva narodnogo prosveshcheniia* and later, in 1899, as a book—became an important event both in the life of its author and in the field of Russian history.[34]

Several historians viewed the appearance of *Studies in the History of the*

Troubles as an important historiographical event, indicating that the historiographical schools of St. Petersburg and Moscow had reached a rapprochement. P.N. Miliukov wrote that since the time of Shlözer, the St. Petersburg school had adhered to the principle that "Russian history cannot be written without a preliminary study of its sources." While acknowledging the value of this principle for the study of "ancient history," Miliukov gave preference to the Moscow school, which, in his estimation, dealt with "historical materials of a later time," and not only "advanced much further," but also "did not dwell on the study of the ancient period," rather incorporating in its work vast quantities of archival materials from which one could draw direct conclusions about the history of daily life [*byt*] and institutions. Despite the influence of the Moscow school, in Miliukov's estimation, the St. Petersburg school had maintained its ties to the older generation in its approach. In Miliukov's opinion, Platonov had made a compromise with the Moscow school and "resolved it brilliantly, devoting the first part of his work on the Troubles of the seventeenth century to a critique of the sources (which by their very nature demanded this) and not presenting the history of the Troubles in the Moscow manner until the second part."[35] By "first part" Miliukov had in mind Platonov's *Old Russian Legends and Tales About the Seventeenth-Century Time of Troubles,* and by the "second part" he meant *Studies in the History of the Troubles.*

On 3 October 1899 Platonov defended *Studies in the History of the Troubles* as his doctoral dissertation. The defense took place at St. Vladimir University in Kiev.[36] Awarding the doctoral degree to Platonov signaled more than just the high esteem in which his scholarly works were held. Not long after his doctoral defense, a new period of Platonov's life began, one marked not only by scholarship and teaching but also by his being appointed to responsible administrative posts. From 1900 through 1905 Platonov served as dean of the history and philology faculty of St. Petersburg University. The Women's Pedagogical Institute was formed in 1903, and Platonov was appointed its director. Not only was he called upon to compile syllabi and choose professors and instructors, but he was also involved in the construction of buildings and the equipping of offices and laboratories. A women's gymnasium was attached to the institute. As director of the pedagogical institute, S.F. Platonov worked closely with Grand Duke Konstantin Konstantinovich, who was an honorary trustee of the institute as well as president of the Imperial Academy of Sciences.

Teaching played a major role in Platonov's life. He lectured on Russian history at various higher educational institutions—St. Petersburg University, the Women's Pedagogical Institute, the Academy of the General Staff, and the Academy of Military Law. He also conducted classes at the women's gymnasium attached to the pedagogical institute. The historian B.A. Romanov, who attended Platonov's lectures at the university, commented on Platonov's characteristic "literary manner of lecturing in class" as follows: "What was fascinating about his manner was that in the classroom it always seemed as if the lecture were being delivered from notes, yet one noticed with astonishment that one was really hearing free conversation."[37] Among the students who attended Platonov's lectures at the Academy of the General Staff in 1907–8 was B.M. Shaposhnikov, who later became a marshal of the Soviet Union. In his memoirs he wrote: "Russian history to the period of Alexander III was taught by Professor of History Platonov. What can one say about this erudite historian? His lectures were supremely rich in content, intelligent, and meticulously prepared." Comparing Platonov's lectures with those given by G.V. Forsten, a professor of world history, Shaposhnikov noted that in contrast to Forsten, whose "lectures were full of zeal and represented particular philosophical views," Platonov's lectures were attractive in their simplicity. "His words flowed casually down from the lectern and captivated the whole class. Inveterate readers of newspapers, primarily Guards officers, used to set their newspapers aside to listen to the lectures given by this professor, this storyteller of Russian history, especially when he climbed onto his hobby horse—the Time of Troubles."[38] The students published the notes they took of Platonov's lectures in lithograph form. Beginning with the sixth edition, Platonov himself verified the text of the lectures. The tenth edition of S.F. Platonov's *Lectures in Russian History* [Lektsii po russkoi istorii], revised and amended, came out in 1917.[39]

In addition to his survey of Russian history, Platonov also taught specialized courses. These included a course on source study offered through the Institute of Archeology.[40] In that course, Platonov distinguished between "external" and "internal" source criticism. "External" meant the dating of a document, the establishment of its authenticity, and so forth. "Internal" criticism, in Platonov's opinion, did not constitute part of the competence of archeography and paleography; rather, it was the concern of "pure history," inasmuch as its purpose was to determine "who had written [the text], to what party he belonged, what his point of view was, what influences acted upon him, and what his passions, tendencies, and sentiments were."[41] This kind of attention to "internal" criticism, in the opinion of modern historians,[42] marked a step forward compared with historians like N.P. Likhachev, who insisted that "external" criticism ought to play the chief role, that auxiliary historical disciplines, which constitute "theory," stand above history and historical narrative, which represent "practice."[43] Platonov's attitude may have developed under the influence of A.S. Lappo-Danilevskii, to whose source studies he had paid diligent attention. A.E. Presniakov wrote that early in his career as an instructor, Lappo-Danilevskii had won the respect of other professors, and that "during those years Professor S.F. Platonov was already including among his injunctions to his students on how to study: 'Listen to Professor Lappo-Danilevskii.'"[44]

This advice from Platonov to his students, telling them to pay careful attention to the lectures given by A.S. Lappo-Danilevskii, is extremely significant. It reminds us that many historians who began as students at St. Petersburg University at the end of the nineteenth and in the early twentieth centuries were greatly influenced by several professors. For example, B.D. Grekov, who studied at Warsaw University and later attended Moscow University before winding up in St. Petersburg, considered himself primarily a pupil of M.M. Bogoslovskii and D.M. Petrushevskii, but he also emphasized the great influence that S.F. Platonov and A.S. Lappo-Danilevskii had on him. Platonov's students included A.I. Andreev and S.N. Valk, who considered themselves students of A.S. Lappo-Danilevskii, and B.A. Romanov, a student of A.E. Presniakov. B.A. Romanov, in comparing the influence of the schools of S.F. Platonov and A.S. Lappo-Danilevskii, later wrote that "the first generations of students of Kliuchevskii and Platonov, naturally, 'were schooled' in the works of Kliuchevskii and Platonov."[45] Another of Platonov's students was G.V. Vernadsky, who graduated from university not long before the Revolution and emigrated in 1920. As an émigré, Vernadsky taught first in Prague, and after 1927 in the United States, where he was considered one of the most knowledgeable specialists in Russian history.

Another very popular work prepared by S.F. Platonov was his *Textbook of Russian History for Secondary Schools* [Uchebnik russkoi istorii dlia srednei shkoly], which went through several editions starting in 1909. Under Alexander III [1881–1894], Platonov was invited to teach history to the tsar's children, Grand Duchess Ol'ga Aleksandrovna and Grand Duke Mikhail Aleksandrovich. He also taught history to Alexander III's nephews, Grand Duke Dmitrii Pavlovich and Grand Duke Andrei Vladimirovich. Despite Platonov's loyalty, however, attitudes toward him in ruling circles, especially under Nicholas II, were not equable. In Platonov's own words: "After 1917 a 'memorandum concerning professors of Russian history' was found among the papers of Nicholas II and made public. It included these lines: 'Another very decent man is Professor Platonov, who possesses enormous erudition, but he is dull and definitely has little sympathy for the cult of Russian heroes. The study of his works, naturally, cannot evoke either a feeling of affection for the Fatherland or a sense of national pride.' " Concerning this expression of "monarchical attention," Platonov wrote, "Fortunately, I more frequently encountered a different opinion."[46]

In addition to his considerable teaching load and administrative work, Platonov also continued his scholarly endeavors. In 1903 and in 1910 he republished his *Studies in the History of the Troubles in the Muscovite State.* Platonov also wrote a substantial number of articles. In 1903 he published a collection of articles written between 1883 and 1902.[47] The year 1912 saw the publication of S.F. Platonov's *Works* [Sochineniia] in two volumes.[48] Volume 1 included the second edition of *Articles on Russian History (1883–1912)* [Stat'i po russkoi istorii (1883–1912)]; volume 2 included the second edition of his master's dissertation *Old Russian Legends and Tales About the Seventeenth-Century Time of Troubles as a Historical Source.* The range of topics addressed in Platonov's work written at the beginning of the twentieth century was quite extensive. First of all, he wrote a number of articles that introduced amendments and revisions to the study of the history of the Time of Troubles.[49] Seventeenth-century Russian history was the subject of Platonov's articles on the seventeenth-century assemblies of the land[50] and the Muscovite government under the first Romanovs,[51] as well as his book on Tsar Aleksei Mikhailovich.[52] Several of Platonov's articles also indicated that he had begun to pay more attention to eighteenth-century Russian history.[53] Platonov also focused attention on Russian history at the beginning of the nineteenth century. In addition, in an article devoted to the hundredth anniversary of the War of 1812, Platonov went beyond the bounds of a jubilee essay. He emphasized that even though the "calamity of the War of 1812 crushed the French empire rather than Russia," "Russia did suffer a number of profound consequences of the Patriotic War." Prominent among these consequences was the Decembrist movement. "Having returned to their Motherland from the war," the Decembrists "brought back the idea that serfdom must be abolished and the state structure based on serfdom must be changed."[54] The articles and obituaries that Platonov wrote and dedicated to Russian historians had the same character as his historiographical essays. Historians in this category included N.M. Karamzin, K.N. Bestuzhev-Riumin, V.G. Vasil'evskii, and V.O. Kliuchevskii.[55] Platonov enjoyed considerable prestige in the scholarly community. Evidence for this can be seen both in his election as a corresponding member of the Academy of Sciences in 1909[56] and in the collection of articles published in his honor, to which numerous historians contributed.[57]

In June 1916 S.F. Platonov earned the right to a pension, and he retired. He resigned as director of the Women's Pedagogical Institute. All that remained to him were a few lectures at the university and at the Women's Pedagogical Institute. "It was with great pleasure that I spent the winter of 1916–17 as a gentleman of leisure. But this pleasure was to be short-lived: the 1917 coup returned me to the ranks of ordinary workers,"[58] Platonov wrote many years later. The Revolution disrupted the familiar rhythm of life in the section of society to which Platonov belonged. The feelings of the people with whom Platonov associated can be judged from a letter that he received from M.K. Liubavskii in 1917. Liubavskii wrote: "All that is happening is God's retribution—against the bourgeoisie because it took advantage of the war to enrich itself and against the intelligentsia because its members, with typical frivolity, shattered the foundations by confusing the idea of autocracy with the name of the monarch."[59] The civil war that followed further increased the difficulties of life that befell the educated segments of Russian society. Some of Platonov's colleagues at the university died—A.S. Lappo-Danilevskii in 1919 and A.A. Shakhmatov in 1920. N.P. Kondakov left Petrograd in 1917 and later emigrated. Platonov's own fate, however, took an apparently paradoxical turn during the years of revolution and civil war. Having retired not long before the February Revolution, soon after the October Revolution he became actively involved in the archival establishment and in the Russian Academy of Sciences. In the spring of 1918, S.F. Platonov, in his own words, "was appointed by the university to serve on an interdepartmental commission for safeguarding and organizing the archives of abolished institutions." This commission later became the Main Directorate for Archival Affairs, headed by D.B. Riazanov, a Bolshevik. Platonov became his assistant. From 1918 through 1923 Platonov managed the Petrograd branch of the Main Directorate for Archival Affairs. It was under his direction that the archives of those Russian state institutions that were abolished after the Revolution were collected and combined into the Unified State Archival Holdings. To assist him in organizing the work on the archives, S. F. Platonov enlisted his closest associates, both corresponding members of the Russian Academy of Sciences—A.E. Presniakov and S.V. Rozhdestvenskii. Several young historians also took part in the job of saving and systematizing the archival materials. These included one of A.S. Lappo-Danilevskii's students, S.N. Valk, who headed the division that received and handled documents formerly belonging to the Police Department and other institutions and containing information on the history of the revolutionary movement in Russia; and A.E. Presniakov's student B.A. Romanov, who processed documents from the former Ministry of Finance.

After the Revolution, S.F. Platonov also became deeply involved with the Russian Academy of Sciences. From 31 December 1918 onward, Platonov served as chairman of the Archeographical Commission, which, after first being assigned to the People's Commissariat of Education, was transferred to the jurisdiction of the Academy of Sciences in 1922. In 1926, after merging with the Permanent Historical Commission, it became the Permanent Histor-

ical–Archeographical Commission of the Academy of Sciences of the
USSR. It was largely thanks to Platonov's efforts that from 1920 to 1927 the
Commission published the next four volumes of *The Russian Historical
Library,* continued the publication of the *Complete Collection of Russian
Chronicles,* and printed the *Records of the Proceedings of the Archeographi-
cal Commission* [Letopis' zaniatii Arkheograficheskoi komissii].

In April 1920 Platonov was elected to full membership in the Academy
of Sciences, after which his participation in the work of the Russian Academy of Sciences increased further. From 1 August 1925 he served as director of Pushkin House (now the Institute of Russian Literature); from 1925
through 8 October 1928 he was in charge of the Academy of Sciences
Library; and from 7 March through 8 November 1929 he was acting academic secretary of the Department of Humanities and became a member of
the Presidium of the Academy of Sciences of the USSR. Thus, even though
he was by then in his declining years, Platonov not only worked hard but
also held high posts in Academy of Sciences institutions. After the civil war
ended, contacts were resumed between the Academy of Sciences and scholarly and scientific institutions in Western Europe, and Platonov made several official trips abroad. In 1924 he visited Germany and spent time in
Berlin and Leipzig, where he tried to restore cooperation with German
scholars who studied Russian geography and history. In 1926 Platonov
went to Paris. There he filed a request and began to conduct negotiations
aimed at securing for Pushkin House the Pushkin expert A.F. Onegin's
unique collection, which contained manuscripts by A.S. Pushkin as well as
other materials concerning Pushkin's life and work. Platonov's trip to
France made possible a reunion with one of his daughters, Nadezhda
Sergeevna Kraevich, who had emigrated with her husband. In 1928
Platonov attended Russian History Week, held in Berlin, in which context
he presented a paper entitled "On the Study of the History of the Russian
North" [Ob izuchenii istorii Russkogo Severa]. Also in 1928 Platonov
began a correspondence with German scholars—Professor F.A. Braun of
the University of Leipzig (who had been a professor at St. Petersburg University before the Revolution), Doctor Schmidt-Otto, chairman of the Society for the Advancement of German Science, and the latter's secretary. In
the course of their correspondence they discussed the possibility of German
scholars taking part in archeological excavation of the ruins of the cave city
of Eski-Kerman not far from Bakhchisarai in Crimea, the site, according to
assumptions current at the time, of the principal city of the Crimean Goths.

From all appearances, then, Platonov's position was quite secure even
after the Revolution. Nonetheless, the highest circles of the Soviet leadership were not unambivalent toward him. On the one hand, Platonov had

excellent relations with men who were well known in the Bolshevik Party at the time, such as D.B. Riazanov and P.L. Voikov. In recent years A.V. Lunacharskii's favorable description of his character has come to light. On 9 March 1921, in response to a secret memorandum from the Board of the Council of People's Commissars containing a request from the chairman of the Council of People's Commissars, V.I. Lenin, to "characterize" a number of eminent cultural figures, People's Commissar of Education A.V. Lunacharskii wrote as follows: "Academician Platonov is a very bright man. Apparently he has now been elected president of the Academy; he is a remarkable historian of right-wing convictions. Yet in spite of this, he has worked with us from the beginning. First he was in charge of the Archives of the People's Commissariat of Education, and later Riazanov appointed him as his assistant in managing the archives in Petrograd. He is currently supervising the archives more or less single-handedly under the general supervision of M.N. Pokrovskii. He conducts himself in a supremely loyal and courteous manner."[60] This reference contained an error: Platonov was not elected president of the Academy of Sciences. But the important feature of this document was its tone: A.V. Lunacharskii's letter was generally favorable with regard to Platonov.

This, however, was just one side of the coin. The other side was the negative view of Platonov held by M.N. Pokrovskii, who was Lunacharskii's deputy. Pokrovskii was openly hostile to members of the old intelligentsia. In 1922, in an article which attacked the *spetsy* (that is, specialists of the old intelligentsia), Pokrovskii wrote that "the door to the Cheka must always be left hospitably open for them."[61] Pokrovskii and others like him managed to have the university history and philology faculties closed. In their place came the faculties of social sciences (FONs). Even this, however, was not enough. In May 1923, while lecturing at Zinov'ev Communist University in Petrograd, Pokrovskii complained about the necessity of keeping "the old faculties of social sciences" while "gradually communizing, or perhaps I should say Sverdlovizing and Zinov'evizing, them from below."[62]

Meanwhile, the old professors whom Pokrovskii hated so much continued not only to write but also to publish their works. In general, they were able to live something of an independent life.[63] A major collection of articles in honor of S.F. Platonov was published in 1922.[64] Also during the 1920s Platonov was able to publish a substantial number of articles and even books. Various publishing houses in Petrograd/Leningrad published the following books by Platonov: *Boris Godunov* in 1921; *Ivan the Terrible* [Ivan Groznyi], *The Time of Troubles* [Smutnoe vremia], and *The Past of the Russian North: Essays on the History of the Colonization of the White Sea Coast* [Proshloe russkogo Severa: Ocherki po istorii kolonizatsii

Pomor'ia] in 1923; *Social Crisis in the Time of Troubles* [Sotsial'nyi krizis v Smutnoe vremia] in 1924; *Muscovy and the West in the Sixteenth and Seventeenth Centuries* [Moskva i Zapad v XVI–XVII vv.] in 1925; and *Peter the Great* [Petr Velikii] in 1926. Some of these works were also published abroad: *Boris Godunov* in Prague in 1921; *Ivan the Terrible* in Berlin in 1923; and *The Time of Troubles* in Prague in 1923. Platonov's *Lectures* and *Textbook* were used in educational institutions abroad attended by Russian émigrés.

Pokrovskii did not hesitate to write a very critical review of Platonov's book *Boris Godunov;* the review was published in the journal *Pechat' i revoliutsiia* (1921, no. 3). In it he sarcastically dubbed Platonov a "well-bred historian" and an "inveterate connoisseur of Muscovite Rus'," and he charged that Platonov's "class affiliation" made him afraid to acknowledge that "it is not individual persons but classes that make history"—attempting to prove, instead, that "history has always been made by individual persons who bear full moral responsibility for the events of history." In commenting on Platonov's book, Pokrovskii characterized it as a work that presented neither any new facts nor a new point of view. Pokrovskii failed to grasp the point of Platonov's proposed treatment of the personality and the state activities of Boris Godunov.[65]

Quite different in character from Pokrovskii's review was the detailed analysis of Platonov's book offered by B.A. Romanov in the journal *Dela i dni* (1921, bk. 2). Romanov saw Platonov's book as "a biography that decisively incorporates all that might serve to elucidate the life and fate of Godunov," a biography written in such a way that "the vibrancy of life resonates for the reader on every one of its pages." Platonov, Romanov remarked, "takes the historiographical approach to Godunov and vigorously undertakes his defense."[66] Platonov's book, moreover, while it "may not refute all the charges that have been leveled at Godunov," at least "makes it possible for Boris Godunov's next biographer to dispel them utterly." Romanov saw in this "the fundamental scholarly importance" of Platonov's book on Boris Godunov.[67] During the 1920s Pokrovskii still had to reckon with historical journals whose authors and editors found it possible to express their points of view. B.A. Romanov's review was not the only review of Platonov's works to appear in journals over which M.N. Pokrovskii had no control. In 1924, for example, the journal *Veka* published A.E. Presniakov's review of Platonov's *Ivan the Terrible.*[68]

Pokrovskii's attacks might have warned Platonov. To Platonov, however, it seemed that on the whole, despite the difficult years of revolution and civil war, his life was going well. In his 1926 autobiography he wrote: "The coup of 1917 and the breakdown of the old order that began in 1918 spared me and my family, and in the midst of the general privations from which Russian society suffered during the blockade and the famine, I did not lose my library and my familiar surroundings."[69]

It so happened, however, that Platonov became one of the victims of the "Academic Affair" that was fabricated by OGPU [the secret police] under direct orders from the Politburo. During the night of 12–13 January 1930 Platonov and one of his daughters were arrested. He was accused of counterrevolutionary activity. M.N. Pokrovskii was quick to express his pleasure that these "inveterately reactionary historians" who had "sat" in the Second Department of the All-Union Academy of Sciences—that "lofty citadel of the old historiography"—had been "removed from their posts," and to express regret that it had not been done earlier.[70] Pokrovskii's allies parroted him.[71] At a session of the Academy of Sciences held on 11–12 February 1930, Platonov was stripped of his membership and of the rank of academician. After being imprisoned for a year and a half, on 8 August 1931 Platonov was sentenced to exile in the city of Samara by a decree of the Special Conference [*Osoboe soveshchanie*] under the OGPU. There he settled on the outskirts of the town; he was now deprived of not only his library but his familiar surroundings as well. A severe illness shortened his life. S.F. Platonov passed away on 10 January 1933.

Pokrovskii and his associates believed that they had successfully consigned Platonov's works to oblivion. In the first half of the 1930s, however, a significant change in the assessment of historical works was begun by I.V. Stalin and his associates. This time the principal target of criticism was the works of M.N. Pokrovskii, who had died in 1932. Under these circumstances, attitudes toward the scientific legacy of scholars of the old school were revised. Works by V.O. Kliuchevskii, M.M. Bogoslovskii, Iu.V. Got'e, and P.V. Liubomirov were reissued. The year 1937 saw the publication of the fourth edition of S.F. Platonov's *Studies in the History of the Troubles in the Muscovite State in the Sixteenth and Seventeenth Centuries.* The same year also saw the publication, with a press run of one thousand copies, of Platonov's textbook on Russian history, for the internal use of the Higher School of Propagandists under the Central Committee of the All-Union Communist Party (Bolshevik), later to be known as the Higher Party School.[72]

Considerably later, in 1967, the Military Board of the Supreme Court of the USSR reviewed the charges against S.F. Platonov and others convicted in the case of the alleged "All-People's Union to Struggle for the Revival of a Free Russia." Platonov was completely rehabilitated, as were others. In 1993 came the publication of volume 1 of *The Academic Affair of 1929–1931: Documents and Materials of an Investigation Fabricated by the OGPU* [Akademicheskoe delo 1929–1931 gg: Dokumenty i materialy sledstvennogo dela, sfabrikovannogo OGPU].[73] New research was conducted on the persecutions suffered by the Academy of Sciences in 1929,[74] and this investigation demonstrated the absurdity and falsehood of the charges leveled against S.F. Platonov and the others who fell victim to the "Academic Affair."[75]

Notes

Translated by Kim Braithwaite for publication in *Russian Studies in History*, vol 36, no. 4, ©1998 by M.E. Sharpe, Inc.

1. S.F. Platonov, "Avtobiograficheskaia zapiska," in *Akademicheskoe delo 1929–1931 gg.,* no. 1 (St. Petersburg, 1993), p. 256.

2. S.F. Platonov, "Neskol'ko vospominanii o studencheskikh godakh," *Dela i dni,* 1921, bk. 2, pp. 104–5.

3. "Avtobiograficheskaia zapiska," p. 257.

4. Ibid., p. 260.

5. S.F. Platonov, "Konstantin Nikolaevich Bestuzhev-Riumin," in *Sochineniia,* vol. 1: *Stat'i po russkoi istorii (1883–1912),* 2d ed. (St. Petersburg, 1912), p. 175.

6. Platonov, "Avtobiograficheskaia zapiska," p. 261.

7. Ibid., p. 258.

8. Ibid., pp. 262–63.

9. Platonov, "Neskol'ko vospominanii," p. 130.

10. Platonov, "Avtobiograficheskaia zapiska," p. 262.

11. S.F. Platonov, *Sochineniia,* vol. 2: *Stat'i po russkoi istorii (1883–1912),* 2d ed. (St. Petersburg, 1913), pp. 1–25.

12. Platonov, "Avtobiograficheskaia zapiska," p. 265.

13. "K.N. Bestuzhev-Riumin—S.F. Platonovu, 14 (26) ianvaria 1883 g.," quoted in A.N. Tsamutali, *Bor'ba napravlenii v russkoi istoriografii v period imperializma* (Leningrad, 1986), pp. 76–77.

14. A.E. Presniakov, "Rech' pered zashchitoi dissertatsii pod zagolovkom 'Obrazovanie velikorusskogo gosudarstva'," *Letopis' zaniatii Arkheograficheskoi komissii* (Petrograd, 1920), p. 7.

15. Platonov, "Avtobiograficheskaia zapiska," p. 268.

16. S.F. Platonov, *Sochineniia,* vol. 2: *Drevnerusskie skazaniia i povesti o Smutnom vremeni XVII veka, kak istoricheskii istochnik,* 2d ed. (St. Petersburg, 1913), p. 432.

17. V.O. Kliuchevskii, *Otzyvy i otvety: 3-i sbornik statei* (Petrograd, 1918).

18. M.V. Nechkina, *Vasilii Osipovich Kliuchevskii* (Moscow, 1974), p. 291.

19. *Russkii vestnik,* 1888, no. 7, pp. 228–38.

20. *Istoricheskii vestnik,* 1888, no. 11, pp. 485–92.

21. *Universitetskie izvestiia* (Kiev), 1889, no. 5, pp. 114–66.

22. *Golos minuvshego,* 1913, no. 10, pp. 279–84.

23. Platonov, "Avtobiograficheskaia zapiska," p. 271.

24. V.O. Kliuchevskii, *Sochineniia,* 9 vols. (Moscow, 1988), vol. 3, p. 27.

25. M.N. Tikhomirov, *Rossiia v XVI stoletii* (Moscow, 1962), p. 4.

26. S.F. Platonov, *Ocherki po istorii Smuty v Moskovskom gosudarstve XVI–XVII vv.,* 3d ed. (St. Petersburg, 1910), p. 179.

27. Ibid., p. 180.

28. Ibid., p. 320.

29. Ibid., pp. 320, 326, 332–33.

30. Ibid., p. 495.

31. Ibid., pp. 501, 503.

32. Ibid., pp. 536–37.

33. Ibid., p. 534.

34. A review of the first edition of *Ocherki po istorii Smuty v Moskovskom gosudarstve* by V.S. Ikonnikov appeared in *Zhurnal ministerstva narodnogo prosveshcheniia,* 1900, no. 2, pt. 2, pp. 367–99; no. 3, pp. 165–89.

35. P.N. Miliukov, *Vospominaniia,* vol. 1 (Moscow, 1990), pp. 161–62.

36. "Disput S.F. Platonova," *Istoricheskii vestnik,* 1899, no. 12, pp. 1282–83.

37. B.A. Romanov, "Akad. S. F. Platonov, Boris Godunov: Obrazy proshlogo (Petrograd: K-vo Ogni), 157 pp.," *Dela i dni,* 1921, bk. 2, p. 213.

38. B.M. Shaposhnikov, *Vospominaniia: Nauchnye trudy* (Moscow, 1974), p. 134.

39. S.F. Platonov, *Lektsii po russkoi istorii,* 10th ed. (Petrograd, 1917).

40. S.F. Platonov, *Obzor istochnikov russkoi istorii letopisnogo tipa* (St. Petersburg, 1905). Lithographed.

41. Ibid., pp. 10–11.

42. *Ocherki istorii istoricheskoi nauki v SSSR,* vol. 3 (Moscow), p. 575.

43. N.P. Likhachev, *Diplomatika: iz lektsii, chitannykh v S.-Peterburgskom arkheologicheskom institute* (St. Petersburg, 1901), p. 1.

44. A.E. Presniakov, *Aleksandr Sergeevich Lappo-Danilevskii* (St. Petersburg, 1922), p. 28.

45. Quoted in V.M. Paneiakh, "Boris Aleksandrovich Romanov: Pis'ma druz'iam i kollegam," *Otechestvennaia istoriia,* 1993, no. 3, p. 149.

46. Platonov, "Avtobiograficheskaia zapiska," p. 281.

47. S.F. Platonov, *Stat'i po russkoi istorii (1883–1912 gg.)* (St. Petersburg, 1903). A review of this collection by V.N. Storozhev appeared in *Mir bozhii,* 1903, no. 9, pt. 2, pp. 86–88.

48. Platonov, *Sochineniia,* 2d ed., vols. 1–2.

49. S.F. Platonov, "Vopros o proiskhozhdenii pervogo Lzhedmitriia," in *Sochineniia,* 2d ed., vol. 1, pp. 267–78.

50. S.F. Platonov, "K istorii moskovskikh zemskikh soborov," in *Sochineniia,* vol. 1, pp. 279–338.

51. S.F. Platonov, "Moskovskoe pravitel'stvo pri pervykh Romanovykh," in *Sochineniia,* vol. 1, pp. 339–406.

52. S.F. Platonov, *Tsar' Aleksei Mikhailovich* (St. Petersburg, 1913).

53. S.F. Platonov, (1) "K dvukhsotiletiiu Peterburga," in *Sochineniia,* vol. 1, pp. 249–57; (2) "K istorii poltavskoi bitvy," ibid., pp. 435–43; and (3) "Stoletie konchiny imperatritsy Ekateriny II," ibid., pp. 234–48.

54. S.F. Platonov, "Sviashchennoi pamiati dvenadtsatyi god," in *Sochineniia,* vol. 1. p. 518.

55. S.F. Platonov, (1) "Slovo o N.M. Karamzine," in *Sochineniia,* vol. 1, pp. 504–12; (2) "Konstantin Nikolaevich Bestuzhev-Riumin," ibid., pp. 163–80; (3) "Vasilii Grigor'evich Vasil'evskii," ibid., pp. 189–94; and (4) "Vasilii Osipovich Kliuchevskii," ibid., pp. 495–503.

56. M.A. D'iakonov, A.S. Lappo-Danilevskii, V.V. Latyshev, [reviews of the scholarly works of S.F. Platonov], *Izvestiia Akademii nauk, Seriia 6,* 1910, no. 1, pp. 34–35.

57. *S.F. Platonovu ucheniki, druz'ia i pochitateli* (St. Petersburg, 1911).

58. Platonov, "Avtobiograficheskaia zapiska," p. 281.

59. Quoted in Tsamutali, *Bor'ba napravlenii,* p. 126.

60. "V.I. Lenin i A.V. Lunacharskii," *Literaturnoe nasledstvo* (Moscow, 1971), p. 258.

61. M.N. Pokrovskii, "Nashi spetsy v ikh sobstvennom izobrazhenii," *Krasnaia nov'*, 1922, no. 1(5), p. 154.

62. M.N. Pokrovskii, *Bor'ba klassov i russkaia istoricheskaia literatura* (Petrograd, 1923), p. 5. S.O. Schmidt has pointed out that this passage was omitted when the lectures were republished in the first volume of Pokrovskii's collected works, entitled *Istoricheskaia nauka i bor'ba klassov* (Moscow, 1933), and in vol. 4 of Pokrovskii's *Izbrannye proizvedeniia* (Moscow, 1967).

63. On Pokrovskii's campaign against Platonov, see S.O. Schmidt, "Doklad S.F. Platonova o N.M. Karamzine 1926 g. i protivoborstvo istorikov," *Arkheograficheskii ezhegodnik za 1992 god* (Moscow, 1994), pp. 39–76.

64. *Sbornik statei po russkoi istorii, posviashchennyi S.F. Platonovu* (St. Petersburg, 1922).

65. Pokrovskii, *Istoricheskaia nauka i bor'ba klassov,* no. 2, pp. 87–93.

66. B.A. Romanov, "Academician S.F. Platonov, *Boris Godunov,*" p. 213.

67. Ibid., p. 214.

68. A.E. Presniakov, "Platonov, S.F., *Ivan Groznyi* (Petrograd, 1923)," in *Veka: istoricheskii sbornik,* vol. 1 (Petrograd, 1924), pp. 179–82.

69. Platonov, "Avtobiograficheskaia zapiska," p. 284.

70. Pokrovskii, *Istoricheskaia nauka i bor'ba klassov,* no. 2, pp. 388–91.

71. G. Zaidel' and M. Tsvibak, *Klassovyi vrag na istoricheskom fronte: Tarle i Platonov i ikh shkoly* (Moscow and Leningrad, 1931), p. 110; S.A. Piontkovskii, *Burzhuaznaia istoricheskaia nauka v Rossii* (Moscow, 1931), p. 33.

72. *Materialy iz uchebnika po russkoi istorii professora S.F. Platonova dlia klassnykh zaniatii v Vysshei shkole propagandistov im.* A.M. Sverdlova pri TsK VKP(b) (Moscow, 1931), pts. 1–2.

73. *Akademicheskoe delo 1929–1931 gg.,* no. 1: *Delo po obvineniiu akademika S.F. Platonova.*

74. F.F. Perchenok, (1) "Akademiia nauk na 'velikom perelome'," in *Zven'ia: Istoricheskii al'manakh,* no. 1 (Moscow, 1991), pp. 163–235; and (2) " 'Delo akademii nauk'," *Priroda,* 1991, no. 4, pp. 96–104.

75. B.V. Anan'ich and V.M. Paneiakh, "Prinuditel'noe soavtorstvo (K vykhodu v svet sbornika dokumentov 'Akademicheskoe delo 1929–1931 g.' Vyp. 1," in *In memoriam: Istoricheskii sbornik pamiati F.F. Perchenka* (Moscow and St. Petersburg, 1995), pp. 87–111.

15

Mykola Kostomarov as a Historian

Thomas Prymak

Mykola Kostomarov (1817–1885) made significant contributions to Ukrainian and Russian culture both as a writer and ethnographer and as a political ideologue and public figure. But he considered himself to be first and foremost a historian, and it is as a historian that he is best remembered. He was a formidable scholar indeed. His collected *Historical Monographs and Studies* [Istoricheskie monografii i izsledovanii] fill some twenty-one volumes in eight bulky books, even though many of his seminal works are not included in this collection. Although Kostomarov's scholarly legacy was long ignored or deprecated by the Soviet historical establishment, he is today universally acknowledged as a major Ukrainian and Russian historian, and his works are being printed and reprinted both in Kyiv and in Moscow. His histories are once again widely read, and he has been fully "rehabilitated" in the leading Ukrainian and Russian historical journals.[1]

In view of Kostomarov's renewed popularity, it is fitting to ask about his place in the history of Ukrainian and Russian historiography. What was his approach to history and his methodology? Did his scheme of Russian history differ from the schemes of his predecessors, his contemporaries, and his successors? Were his terms of reference and his vocabulary conventional or original? What was the source of his enormous popularity? Exactly who was Mykola Kostomarov and what is his significance as a historian?

Kostomarov was born and raised in Voronezh province, near the Ukrainian–Russian ethnolinguistic frontier. His father was a Russian nobleman; his mother originally a Ukrainian serf. He was brought up, it seems, in the rationalist traditions of the eighteenth century, and at first paid little attention to the rich Ukrainian folk culture that surrounded him. But during his university studies in Kharkov he became acquainted with the values and ideals of the romantic movement and immediately applied them to his personal experience. Under the influence of one of his professors, M.M. Lunin, who in turn was influenced by Herder and Sir Walter Scott, he became interested in history. His conversion to history and the Romantic movement was sudden and complete. Many years later he described it thus:

> History was my most beloved subject. I read a great many history books of every type, reflected upon them and arrived at the following question. . . . Why is it that all the history books talk about the extraordinary historical characters, and occasionally about laws and institutions, but at the same time ignore the lives of the masses of ordinary people? The poor peasant, the working farmer, as it were, does not exist in history. Why does history not tell us about his way of life, his spiritual world, his feelings, and the means by which he expresses his happiness and his sadness? I soon became convinced that history must be studied not only from dead chronicles and writings but also among living people. Could it not be that the bygone ages are also reflected in the lives and memories of their heirs? It was merely necessary to seek, and certainly much would be found that scholarship had up to now overlooked. But where was one to begin? Naturally enough, with the study of my own Russian people. But in so far as I then lived in Little Russia I would begin with its Little Russian [that is, Ukrainian] branch. This idea turned me towards the reading of the monuments of the national heritage. For the first time in my life, I got hold of the Little Russian songs published by [Mykhailo] Maksymovych in 1827 and the Great Russian songs of [I.P.] Sakharov, and I began to read them. I was struck and then carried away by the sincere beauty of Little Russian popular poetry. I had never suspected that such eloquence, such depth and fresh feelings, could be found in the creations of the [common] people who were so close to me and about whom I unfortunately knew nothing.[2]

There are three basic points that Kostomarov makes in this passage: firstly, his love for history; secondly, his interest in the common people; and thirdly, his belief that folk songs, especially historical folk songs, were a potentially rich source for understanding the history of the common people. In other words, the historian Kostomarov was proposing a new methodology for Russian history; he was proposing to use an "ethnographic method" in his professional work.

The young man wasted no time in beginning. In his first dissertation for the master's degree at Kharkov University, he used the published collections of Ukrainian historical songs that were available to him to elucidate the causes and nature of the Union of Brest (1596), by which the Orthodox Church in the old Polish–Lithuanian Commonwealth accepted the Roman primacy while retaining its autonomous structure and traditional rites and usages.[3] For political reasons unrelated to his ethnographic method, Kostomarov's dissertation was rejected before he could defend it, and it was officially burned on the university premises, but he was allowed to undertake a second dissertation on a new subject.

Undaunted by the unusual experience—even in the Russia of Nicholas I—of having his scholarship committed to the flames, Kostomarov selected a second topic which even more closely revealed his conversion to the Romantic movement. In his second dissertation, which was entitled *On the Historical Significance of Russian Popular Poetry,* Kostomarov once again turned to the experiences of the common people and argued that folk song could to some limited degree help establish a chronicle of historical events, could reveal general facts about the people's way of life, could be used as a source for the history of a language, and most importantly of all, was an excellent source for examining the people's view of itself; that is, folk song said something concrete about national psychology and national character. Although several of the Kharkov professors objected to Kostomarov's innovative emphasis upon the common people and social history rather than upon tsars, princes, and international relations, his thesis was accepted, and he successfully graduated.[4]

During the years that followed, Kostomarov continued to collect and to analyze folk songs and to use them in his historical work. For example, on the basis of such materials he authored an innovative book on ancient Slavic mythology[5] and began to reconstruct the social history of the great Cossack revolt against the Poles led by Bohdan Khmel'nyts'kyi. In 1847, however, he was arrested, imprisoned, and then exiled to Saratov for his participation in the illegal pan-Slavic Cyril–Methodian Brotherhood. Although Kostomarov managed to continue to write during his exile, he was forced to rely increasingly upon old chronicles, travellers' reports, and other published documents to complete his work, and this, of course, influenced his composition and style. He did, however, use the published corpus of historical songs and the folk material that he had already collected, and he enlivened his narrative with frequent dialogue, anecdote, and direct quotation from the chronicles. His use of new Polish material was especially remarkable, and when some ten years later his book *Bohdan Khmel'nyts'kyi* was finally published, it was enthusiastically received by both professional reviewers and the general reading public.[6]

During those same years in Saratov, Kostomarov interested himself in the social history of that Volga province and gathered material for a history of revolt of the Russian Cossack leader Stenka Razin. Once again, folk materials played an important role in his major theme. Kostomarov's *Revolt of Stenka Razin* holds an honorable place as the first full monograph on popular revolt in the history of Russian historiography.[7]

The era of the Great Reforms saw Kostomarov teaching at St. Petersburg University and contributing historical compositions to the first journal of Ukrainian studies published in the Russian Empire. In a detailed cycle of historical articles in this journal, *The Foundation* [Osnova], Kostomarov outlined his general scheme of Russian history and articulated the contemporary problem of Ukrainian–Russian relations. He further elaborated his scheme in seminal writings on Novgorod and the *veche* system and on Muscovy and the beginnings of central government.

In all these writings two main themes emerged. First, there was a clear division between old Russian history and recent Russian history—that is, between the period of Kievan Rus' and the subsequent *udel*, or appanage, period, and the period which began with the Tatar conquest and the rise of Muscovy. The older period Kostomarov drew in bright colors as one of individual freedom, religious tolerance, and national concord. There were no firmly centralized state structures—there was in fact no real "state"—but rather decentralized forms. The "federal principle" was ascendant. The powers of the princes were limited, and the *veche*, or popular assembly, reigned supreme. This was true in "Southern Rus'," to use Kostomarov's exact vocabulary, but it was also true in "Northern Rus'."

The Tatar conquest shattered this idyll of early Slavic happiness. As in Western Europe, so too in Rus' did foreign conquest bring statehood, centralized government, and oppressive rulers. First the Mongol khans and after them the Muscovite tsars established central rule in northeastern Rus'. The *veche* system and popular rule—Kostomarov probably did not dare to call it "republicanism" out of fear of the government censors—lived on in Novgorod, which, Kostomarov believed, had always been especially close to Southern Rus' by virtue of ethnic ties. But Muscovite aggression eventually put an end to the *veche* system of Novgorod, and the victory of statehood, central rule, and monarchy was assured. The new principles of autocratic rule, religious conformity, and national exclusivity came to the fore. The old principles of individual liberty and religious and national tolerance disappeared from Muscovy and the lands it conquered.[8]

But the old principles did not disappear elsewhere. They lived on in Southern Rus'—what Kostomarov's contemporaries called "Little Russia" and what we today call "Ukraine"—most notably among the Zaporozhian Cossack brotherhood, which was headquartered in the middle of Southern Rus', and among the Don Cossacks, who lived in the southern borderlands of the Muscovite state. According to Kostomarov, the revolt of Stenka Razin and his Don Cossacks was a flashback to the golden liberties of earlier times. The principal facts of Ukrainian history also gestured back to these times. In fact, Kostomarov's perception of the continuity between the history of ancient Southern Rus´ and Cossack history was so strong that it became the basis of the second great pillar of his historical thought, the existence of what he called "the two Russian nationalities."

Kostomarov gave the essence of his interpretation of Russian history in his pathbreaking essay "Two Russian Nationalities" and in a series of related books and articles. According to this interpretation, the ancient Rus´ polity *(russkii materik)* and the modern Russian people *(russkii narod)* had never been an undivided, organic whole but had always been composed of more than one nationality *(narodnost´)*. Ancient tribal differences had taken hold in various principalities, and by the fifteenth century the Slavic tribes of the territory that later became Russia *(Rossiia)* had been grouped into four: Novgorod, Muscovy, Lithuania (that is, Belarus´), and Rus´ (that is, the later Little Russia or Ukraine). These four nationalities were later reduced to two: Northern Rus´ and Southern Rus´. This clear distinction, which Kostomarov traced back to the most ancient times, was formed by geography and historical circumstances and was revealed in the different characters of the two nationalities in question. Thus, according to Kostomarov, the Great Russians of the northeast were practical and materialistic with little poetry or love for nature, and the Little Russians of the south were impractical and poetic with a great love for nature. The Great Russians *(Velikorussy)* were stiff, formal, and intolerant, and this disposition gave rise to schisms and heretical sects of various sorts; by contrast, the "South Russians" *(Iuzhnorussy)* were flexible and tolerant, and sectarianism did not appear in their land. The Muscovites were suspicious of foreigners and sealed them off; but Southern Rus´ was filled with Poles, Jews, and Tatars and for centuries tolerated them well. The Great Russian had autocracy, the village commune, and the ability to found a state; the Southerner had personal freedom and individual ownership but was weak in the management of a state. The Northerners were autocratic, the Southerners democratic. But both peoples shared a common religion, a common book language, and, in the early days, a common ruling house, the house of Riurik. They needed each other and had qualities that complemented each other's. Together the two separate nationalities formed the Russian people, the Russian nation, and had made Russia what it was.[9]

Kostomarov's general scheme of Russian history differed greatly from the approach to Russian history prevalent in his day. Before Kostomarov, the unitary, conservative, monarchical, and state-centered scheme of Nikolai Karamzin (1766–1826) had dominated Russian historical thought. For Karamzin and most of his contemporaries a separate Ukrainian people simply did not exist. Stressing the old Muscovite genealogical claims to the heritage of Kievan Rus´, Karamzin had traced the Russian state back through Muscovy and the principality of Vladimir–Suzdal to Kiev. Karamzin was critical of Kievan freedom but was an admirer of the Muscovite tsardom and a supporter of the Russian autocracy. He thought that the Tatar conquest had actually strengthened the Russian autocracy and that this was good. With his emphasis upon state, politics, and religion, Karamzin had space in his presentation for only one Russian tsar, one Russian state, and one undivided Russian nation.[10]

Kostomarov's historical ideas were a direct challenge to Karamzin's scheme. Where Karamzin postulated one undivided Russian nation and traced the state in a direct line from Kiev to Moscow to St. Petersburg, Kostomarov did not. Rather Kostomarov divided what he called "contemporary Russia" into two distinct parts: Southern Rus', to which belonged the history of Kievan times and Cossack Ukraine, and Northern Rus', which eventually became centered on Muscovy. Moreover, where Karamzin saw Kievan Rus' with its personal freedom and loose political structure in a negative light and contrasted it to orderly, autocratic, and powerful Muscovy, which he saw in a positive light, Kostomarov painted the history of Kievan Rus' in bright colors and the history of Muscovy in darker ones. Where Karamzin thought the Tatar conquest beneficial because it strengthened autocracy and the state, Kostomarov thought of it in negative terms for exactly the same reasons. Karamzin was a partisan of the state; Kostomarov a partisan of the people.

However, in looking closely at the history and life of the people, Kostomarov discovered that this people was clearly divided into two easily discernible parts. Today we would call them Ukrainian and Russian; Kostomarov called them South Russian (*Iuzhnorusskii*) and Great or sometimes North Russian (*Velikorusskii* or *Severnorusskii*). In fact, Kostomarov's nomenclature was quite innovative in its day, for not all Russians—even some Russians of Ukrainian origin—would then agree that the "South Russians" actually formed a nationality of their own. But in his essay on the "Two Russian Nationalities" Kostomarov daringly applied his Herderian-derived ideas about national character to the Russian people and, in the eyes of the majority of his nationally conscious "South Russian" compatriots at least, convincingly demonstrated that these two Russian nationalities, each with its own specific character, did, in fact, exist.[11]

Of course, Kostomarov's ideas about the South and Great Russian nationalities differed in content as well as in nomenclature from present-day conceptions; that is, Kostomarov distinguished between nationality (*narodnost'*) and nation (*natsiia*) and claimed that the South Russians, or the Great Russians for that matter, formed only a nationality and not necessarily a nation. Rather, in Kostomarov's view it was the South and Great

Russian nationalities put together that formed the Russian "nation." Statements about the Russian "nation," however, are very rare in Kostomarov's works and are, in general, confined to his polemical rather than his historical writings.[12] In his historical corpus (as for example in the introductory pages of his masterpiece on Bohdan Khmel'nyts'kyi) and in his illegal writings (as, for example, in *The Books of the Genesis of the Ukrainian People* and his letter to Alexander Herzen), Kostomarov clearly distinguished between Great and South Russian and put the latter on an equal plane with other recognized peoples of the world. Although today one might well stress the moderation and limited nature of Kostomarov's statements about the existence of an independent "South Russian" or Ukrainian nationality, in their own day these statements were a clear defense of the uniqueness of Kievan Rus', Cossack Ukraine, and Little Russia. They divided Russian history into two clear lines: one for the South, beginning in ancient times and continuing to the end of the Cossack era; and one for the North, beginning somewhat later and continuing into modern times. This was not, especially in vocabulary, the clear division of "Russian" history into a threefold ethnolinguistic "history of the East Slavic peoples" such as that proposed by the great Ukrainian historian, Mykhailo Hrushevs'kyi, some forty years later. Hrushevs'kyi discarded Kostomarov's "South Russian" and "North Russian" within the context of "contemporary Russia" and used the clear-cut terms "Ukrainian," "Belorussian," and "Russian" within the context of the three "East Slavic" peoples, a vocabulary that makes more sense to most twentieth-century scholars. Nevertheless, Kostomarov's break with the unilinear, monarchical, and state-centered scheme of Karamzin was so profound that as late as the 1920s Hrushevs'kyi himself called it "a full revolution in the historical thought of Eastern Slavdom."[13]

If Kostomarov's approach to "Russian" history and his conceptualization were new and interesting in their day, so too were his subject matter and his style. Kostomarov was the first to write specialist monographs on Bohdan Khmel'nyts'kyi and the great Cossack revolt against the Poles, the first to deal in depth with Stenka Razin and popular revolt in Russia, the first to praise openly Novgorod and the *veche* system, and the first to make extensive use of Polish and Western sources to write a full history of the Time of Troubles and the fall of the Polish–Lithuanian Commonwealth. Kostomarov's writings on Old Russian domestic life and Muscovite economic history were also very innovative, being pioneering works on Russian social history. Thus in his choice of topics as well as his conceptualization, Kostomarov clearly shifted the focus of Russian history away from tsars and rulers toward the history of the common people.

Kostomarov was equally innovative in his writings on Ukrainian history.

This comes out most clearly in his work on Bohdan Khmel′nyts′kyi, which was his masterpiece and which he revised time and again throughout his long career. Kostomarov differed from his "Little Russian" predecessors, country gentlemen who glorified the great Cossack leader who had cast off Polish rule, created a new Ukrainian landed class, and laid the foundation of an autonomous new polity, which historians now usually call the "Hetman state." He criticized Khmel′nyts′kyi and focused his attention upon the masses of Cossacks and common people who rose up against what he believed to be the social injustice, religious intolerance, and estate pride of the Polish gentry. Where his Ukrainian predecessors, the Cossack chroniclers and their gentlemen successors, praised the Cossack leaders or Hetmans and defended the autonomy of Little Russia on the basis of their historic rights derived from the Treaty of Pereiaslav (1654), according to which Ukraine turned to Russia, Kostomarov focused his attention upon language and people and thus boldly stepped forward into the modern world of ethnolinguistic rights and claims. In doing so, he became the first to formulate clearly the contemporary problem of Ukrainian–Russian relations. In his works on the successors of Khmel′nyts′kyi— Ivan Vyhovs′kyi, Iuryi Khmel′nyts′kyi, Petro Doroshenko, Ivan Mazepa, and others—Kostomarov maintained this focus and was critical of all those Ukrainian Cossack leaders who dared to take up arms against the integration of Ukraine into the Muscovite state. To what degree this criticism derived from his mistrust of Ukrainian statehood and to what degree it was necessary in order to get controversial Ukrainian subject matter past the tsarist censors is still an open question. The fact remains, however, that Kostomarov's prolific writings on Ukrainian Cossack history, which included his systematic collection of primary sources, practically created a new field, a field primarily defined by "national" rather than "estate" interests, a field we today call "Ukrainian history." His ideological and professional successor, the Kiev historian Volodymyr Antonovych, when considering this phenomenon, concluded: before him there was chaos; after him came order.[14]

Kostomarov's innovative conceptualization was a contributing factor, but not the sole reason for his enormous popularity among the general reading public in the Russian Empire: there was also the matter of his style. Kostomarov's penchant for telling an interesting story and bringing his subject matter to life was truly astounding. He achieved this by a close reading of chronicle, folklore, and contemporary source to extract from them everyday details, local color, and dialogue with which to garnish his story. In fact, his use of short direct sentences, dialogue, and direct quotation was systematic and pervasive. They invariably succeeded in bringing to life the events and personalities portrayed in his histories. He developed this technique to such a degree that he quickly acquired the reputation of being Russia's leading "historian-artist."[15]

Of course, there were severe limitations to what Kostomarov could achieve by using these techniques. He could paint masterful portraits of various rebels, Cossacks, and popular figures, but he did not have the methodological and technical expertise to join them together into a synthetic history of Russia or of Ukraine. His principal attempt to write such a history of Russia, his *History of Russia in the Lives of Its Principal Figures,* was left incomplete at the time of his death and was a step back from the conceptualization he had earlier developed in his essay on the "Two Russian Nationalities."[16] His attempt to write a complete history of Ukraine on the basis of folk materials was similarly incomplete and not entirely successful.[17] Although the former is now once again widely read among the general reading public and the latter remains a rich source for the folklorist interested in history, neither had the intensity and the impact of his specialist monographs or his historical polemics. Kostomarov was a master painter of historical icons and an innovative ethnographer, but these icons based on chronicle or folklore were frozen in time as it were, without a past and without a future. That is, his histories lacked process and development and revealed the limitations of his method and his style.

There is one further point to be made with regard to Kostomarov's style. That point concerns his stress upon narrative at the expense of analysis, his consistent refusal to write inquiring introductions and incisive, summarizing conclusions—indeed, any conclusions at all—and his general reluctance to make historical judgments. To get Kostomarov's view on a question, it was, and still is, invariably necessary to read closely his entire work, and even then one is never quite positive about what he was actually saying and what its implications were for current politics. Contemporaries invariably thought that Kostomarov was letting the facts speak for themselves and was thus promoting historical objectivity. The entire process, however, was frustrating for his friends and his publishers, who at times could not make head or tail of what he was trying to say. On one occasion, his publisher simply refused to print one of his works until he had rewritten it with some kind of conclusion.[18]

However, with the passage of time this reticence on Kostomarov's part can be seen in an entirely different light: Kostomarov was a democrat and a patriotic Ukrainian writing Russian and Ukrainian history in an autocratic Russia which tried to censor systematically all historical materials. Indeed, how would it have been possible for Kostomarov openly to condemn the development of autocratic government or to praise Cossack revolts against this government? How would it have been possible for him to openly condemn Khmel′nyts′kyi's turn to Moscow or to praise Vyhovs′kyi or Mazepa's turn away from it? Given the censoring mechanisms of nineteenth-century tsarist Russia, such historical judgments would have been totally unprintable. As it was, Kostomarov was getting away with a lot by praising Novgorod and Cossack liberty and condemning individual tsars such as Ivan the Terrible or Peter the Great whenever he could. Whether consciously or unconsciously— and which, we cannot be absolutely certain—Kostomarov's great skill at weighing contradictory facts concerning controversial questions and weaving them into his narrative while simultaneously refusing to draw general conclusions was a response to the system of censorship within which he was writing. Of course, this system of censorship pales in comparison with the Soviet one which was to succeed it, but this did not mean that it did not exist. Even a casual perusal of the historian's autobiography reveals how much he suffered at the hands of the tsarist censors.[19] Kostomarov's unusual style, as well as his innovative conceptualization, was a product of nineteenth-century autocratic Russia, and of the Romantic age within which he lived and worked.

Kostomarov was, in fact, very much a man of his age. He was a leading representative of the Romantic movement in Ukrainian and Russian historiography and was clearly wedded to the principal assumptions of this movement. In subject matter, methodology, concept, style, and temperament he was a Romantic historian and was acknowledged as such by his contemporaries. A century ago, Volodymyr Antonovych compared him to the great French Romantic historian Augustin Thierry, and the comparison clearly has stood the test of time.[20]

National in his interests, democratic and egalitarian in his beliefs, ethnographic in his method, and engaging in his style, Kostomarov and his works are a monument to his age and place. The terms of reference and the vocabulary of his ideas about Ukrainian and Russian nationality, as well as his methodology, were not those of the twentieth century, nor could they be, but they succeeded in shifting the focus of "Russian" history from the rulers to the ruled and from diplomatics and international relations to social history. In the process, they were a tremendous impetus toward the creation of a new nineteenth-century field: "Ukrainian" history. Thus they were a definite step in the direction of modernity. Both present-day Ukrainian and contemporary Russian historiography owe him a great debt.

Notes

1. For a long time, the fullest treatments of Kostomarov in English were those by Dmytro Doroshenko, "A Survey of Ukrainian Historiography," in *Annals of the Ukrainian Academy of Arts and Sciences in the US,* vols. V–VI (New York, 1957), pp.

132–45, which was the most serious treatment, and Anatole G. Mazour, *Modern Russian Historiography,* 2d ed. (Princeton: Van Nostrand, 1958), pp. 152–57, which was more impressionistic. The most recent work on him is Thomas M. Prymak, *Mykola Kostomarov: A Biography* (Toronto: University of Toronto Press, 1996), which treats his "rehabilitation" on pp. xx–xxi. In Ukrainian see Iu.A. Pinchuk, *Mykola Ivanovych Kostomarov* (Kiev: Naukova Dumka, 1992) and in Russian idem, *Istoricheskie vzgliady N.I. Kostomarova* (Kiev: Naukova Dumka, 1984). The fullest and most available edition of his collected works is *Sobranie sochinenii,* 21 vols. in 8 bks. (St. Petersburg: Stasiulevich, 1903–6; photoreprinted, The Hague: Europe Printing, 1968). Most of this collection is currently being reprinted under various titles by the Moscow firm Charli, 1994ff.

2. N.I. Kostomarov, *Istoricheskie proizvedeniia: Avtobiografiia,* ed. V.A. Zamlinskii (Kiev: Izdatel'stvo pri Kievskom Gosudarstvennom Universitete, 1989), pp. 446–47.

3. The original text of Kostomarov's *O prichinakh i kharaktere Unii v zapadnoi Rossii* (Kharkiv, 1841), a few copies of which were preserved, is reprinted in *Naukovpublitsystychni i polemichni pysannia Kostomarova,* ed. M. Hrushevs'kyi (Kiev: Derzhavne vydavnytstvo Ukrainy, 1928), pp. 1–40. Later in life, Kostomarov revised his dissertation and had it printed under the title "Iuzhnaia Rus' v kontse XVI veka." This work has been recently reprinted in *Istoricheskie proizvedeniia: Avtobiografiia,* pp. 108–97.

4. For the text of Kostomarov's second dissertation, which was entitled *Ob istoricheskom znachenii russkoi narodnoi poezii,* see M.I. Kostomarov, *Slov'ians'ka mifolohiia: Vybrani pratsi z folklorystyky i literaturoznavstva* (Kiev: Lybid, 1994), pp. 44–200.

5. N.I. Kostomarov, *Slavianska mifologiia* (Kiev, 1847) is reprinted in ibid., pp. 201–56.

6. N.I. Kostomarov, *Bogdan Khmel'nitskii,* 2 vols. (St. Petersburg: Kozhanchikov, 1859); revised edition reprinted in Moscow by Charli, 1994. For an analysis of the reception of this work, see Prymak, *Mykola Kostomarov: A Biography,* pp. 72–77.

7. For a recent edition, see N.I. Kostomarov, *Bunt Stenki Razina* (Moscow: Charli, 1994), which also contains a number of other works.

8. See, in particular, N.I. Kostomarov, "O znachenii Velikogo Novgoroda v russkoi istorii," in *Sobranie sochinenii,* bk. I, vol. I, pp. 199–214; reprinted in the *Bunt Stenki Razina* collection, pp. 239–58, and idem, "Nachalo edinoderzhaviia drevnei Rusi," in *Sobranie sochinenii,* bk. V, vol. XII, pp. 5–94.

9. For the most recent edition of Kostomarov's "Dve russkie narodnosti," see *Bunt Stenki Razina,* pp. 41–83.

10. On Karamzin as a historian, see J.L. Black, "Karamzin's Scheme for Russian History," in *Eastern Europe: Historical Essays,* ed. H.C. Schlieper (Toronto, 1969), pp. 16–33, and idem, *Nicholas Karamzin and Russian Society* (Toronto: University of Toronto Press, 1975).

11. At this point it should be noted that Kostomarov actually attempted to change the Russian terms for the national names during his day. Thus he replaced the term "Little Russians" (*Malorossiany*) with the term "South Russians" (*Iuzhnorussy*), which was a clear break. This might have been an attempt to replace a historical and *legal–administrative* term, which was mostly applied to the lands of the formerly autonomous Hetmanate in Left Bank Ukraine but only very infrequently to Right Bank Ukraine and Galicia, with a new *ethnolinguistic* term which could be equally applied to all lands where the Ukrainian nationality lived. Or alternatively, it might have been an attempt to replace an originally innocuous national term which had gained pejorative overtones

over the course of a century or so, with a fresh new term that would give new *dignitas* to the Ukrainian people. Kostomarov was inconsistent in his use of the term "Ukrainians" (*Ukraintsi*) and in his essay on the two "Russian" nationalities rejected it because he thought that it displayed sharp regional overtones; that is, that it was primarily applicable to what today would be called central Ukraine but not to Galicia and other areas.

Similarly, Kostomarov rejected the traditional term used for "Great Russians" (*Velikorossiany*) and replaced it with the new term *Velikorussy* for which we also use the translation "Great Russians." Perhaps Kostomarov did this simply to parallel his innovative *Iuzhnorussy*. At any rate, the term did catch on and by the end of the nineteenth century there was a lengthy article under this heading in the foremost encyclopedia published in imperial Russia. See D.N. Anuchin, "Velikorussy," *Entsiklopedicheskii slovar'*, vol. X (St. Petersburg: Brokgauz-Efron, 1892; reprinted Yaroslavl', 1990), pp. 828–43, who acknowledges Kostomarov's role in the propagation of this term.

12. In fact, I have found only one reference to the Russian "nation" in his entire corpus. This was in a very conservative piece appealing to the ruling circles of imperial Russia to permit the unfettered printing of literature in the Ukrainian language. The appeal was unsuccessful. See N.I. Kostomarov, "Kniaz' Vladimir Monomakh i Kazak Bogdan Khmel'nitskii," in *Naukovo-publitsystychni i polemichni pysannia Kostomarova*, pp. 149–55.

13. M. Hrushevs'kyi, "Z publitsystychnykh pysan Kostomarova," in ibid., p. x.

14. V.B. Antonovych [Antonovich], "N.I. Kostomarov kak istorik," *Kievskaia starina*, XXI, 5 (1885): xxx–xxxi.

15. This term was first applied to Kostomarov by A.A. Kotliarevskii (O.O. Kotliarevs'kyi' in Ukrainian) who was reviewing his *Bogdan Khmel'nitskii*. See Prymak, *Mykola Kostomarov: A Biography*, p. 74.

16. That is, it did not divide Russian history into two parallel lines: one for the South and another for the North. See N.I. Kostomarov, *Russkaia istoriia v zhizneopisaniiakh ee glavneishikh deiatelei*, 3 bks. in 7 pts. (St Petersburg: Stasiulevich, 1873–88; photoreprinted Moscow: Kniga, 1990–91). This work, which was dictated from memory to a secretary, also contains many factual inaccuracies.

17. N.I. Kostomarov, "Istoricheskoe znachenie iuzhnorusskogo narodnogo pesenogo tvorchestva," *Sobranie sochinenii*, bk. VIII, vol. XXI. For a brief discussion of this work in English, see Thomas M. Prymak, "Mykola Kostomarov and East Slavic Ethnography in the Nineteenth Century," *Russian History*, XVIII, 2 (1991), 163–86, especially 183–84.

18. Prymak, *Mykola Kostomarov: A Biography*, pp. 175–76. This work, *The Ruin* [Ruina], about the political chaos in Ukraine after the death of Khmel'nyts'kyi, is still the best work on the subject. Even in its revised form it did not really contain any conclusion. For the most recent edition, see N.I. Kostomarov, *Ruina* (Moscow: Charli, 1995).

19. See the discussions in Prymak, *Mykola Kostomarov: A Biography*, pp. 14–15, 68, 72, 84, 195–96.

20. Antonovych, "Kostomarov kak istorik," p. xxvii.

16

Introduction to Mykhailo Hrushevsky's *History of Ukraine-Rus'*

Frank E. Sysyn

The History of Ukraine-Rus' constitutes the most comprehensive account of the ancient, medieval, and early modern history of the Ukrainian people. Written by Ukraine's greatest modern historian, Mykhailo Hrushevsky, the *History* remains unsurpassed in its use of sources and literature, even though its last volume was written sixty years ago. In the development of the Ukrainian national movement, it constitutes the scholarly proof that Ukrainians are a people with its own historical process. For Ukrainians the work is comparable in significance to František Palacký's *History of Bohemia* for the Czechs. The great work of Czech national historiography was published in the early nineteenth century, but its Ukrainian counterpart did not appear until the turn of the twentieth. To a considerable degree, the delay reflects the difficulties Ukrainians faced in demonstrating that they were not a subgroup of the Russians or Poles and that they had their own history.

By the end of the nineteenth century, the histories of Russia and Poland had already received academic treatment. The twenty-nine volumes of Sergei Solov'ev and the four volumes of Michał Bobrzyński were the culmination of a series of efforts that stretched back into the eighteenth century. Nevertheless, each of these two "national" historiographies had considerable difficulty in integrating the Ukrainians and the Ukrainian lands into its account.[1]

In the eighteenth and early nineteenth centuries, Russian history was defined as a development over nine hundred years of a Russian state and a Russian nation. The historians Vasilii Tatishchev (1686–1750) and Nikolai Karamzin (1766–1826) established the view that the polity and culture that emerged around Kyiv in the tenth century was the beginning of Russia and downplayed the discontinuities between Kyivan Rus´, the Vladimir–Suzdal principality, Muscovy, and the Russian Empire. In the nineteenth century, Russian historiography evolved without delineating clearly the distinction between the Russian state and the "Russian" nation. Russia's link to Kyivan Rus´ was primarily dynastic: the ruling house of Riuryk and the state that emerged under its Muscovite descendants' rule were the central theme of Russian history. Yet for centuries the dynasty (and its successors) and the state did not control the core area of the old Kyivan polity and did not hold sway over the millions of Ukrainians and Belarusians who were clearly heirs of Kyivan Rus´. Modern Russian historians considered these people Russians, but until the Second Partition of Poland (1793), the majority lived outside the Russian state. Even in the nineteenth century, the Habsburgs, not the Romanovs, held the allegiance of the descendants of the ancient Rus´ principality of Halych. To include these purported "Russians" in the rubric of Russian history meant to expand Russian history to encompass the histories of the Grand Duchy of Lithuania, the Kingdom of Poland, the Polish–Lithuanian Commonwealth, the Principality of Moldavia, the Cossack Hetmanate, the Zaporozhian Sich, and the Habsburg domains. It required including institutions and events of no significance to the development of the Muscovite state and the Russian Empire. It also posed the question of how to treat the "non-Russians"—the Poles, the Jews, the Armenians, the Hungarians—of these "Russian" lands.

Historians such as Sergei Solov´ev (1820–1879) and Vasilii Kliuchevsky (1841–1911) sporadically included events from the Ukrainian and Belarusian past in what was essentially a combination of the history of the Russian state and of an "all-Russian" people with the "Great Russians" at the core. Ukrainians challenged these views throughout the nineteenth century. Indeed, the debate over the legacy of Kyivan Rus´ between the Russian historian Mikhail Pogodin (1800–1875) and the Ukrainian historian Mykhailo Maksymovych (1804–1873) in the 1850s even caused Pogodin to put forth the ultimately untenable thesis that the "Great Russians" had originally inhabited the Kyiv region and that only after they moved northeast in the eleventh and twelfth centuries did the Ukrainians ("Little Russians") migrate into the area. In general, however, Russian historians could ignore Ukrainian viewpoints, in part because the government's political persecution muted expression of the Ukrainian historical perspective.

The quandary faced by those writing Polish history was more obvious, because no Polish state existed in the nineteenth century. Therefore historians of "Poland" wrote the history of the "Polish lands," usually defined as the pre-1772 Polish–Lithuanian Commonwealth. They also wrestled increasingly with the question of who the "Poles" were both in the present and in the past. While the question of the present was complicated by changing and multiple identities ("Polish" Jews became "Russian" Jews) and emerging national consciousness (peasants in Silesia became Poles just as nobles in Samogitia decided that being Lithuanian excluded being Polish), they also faced problems in identifying the Polish national past. Having accepted the Commonwealth of 1772 as the territorial limit of Polish history, historians had to decide how they would treat these territories before 1569, when the Commonwealth was formed, or before 1386, when the Grand Duchy of Lithuania and the Kingdom of Poland entered into a dynastic union. They had to determine whether the history of the Grand Duchy was "Polish" history in the same sense that the history of the Kingdom of Poland was. They also had to define Polish history from the tenth to the fourteenth centuries, when the Piast domain fractured and reassembled in an altered geopolitical space.

In any account of the Polish lands, the Ukrainians (or Ruthenians) and the Ukrainian territories posed special problems. The annexation of the Halych principality in the fourteenth century had changed the composition of the Polish state. Polish historians had to decide to what extent the pre-fourteenth-century history of Western Ukraine was Polish history and to what degree Ruthenian culture and Eastern Orthodoxy were Polish. The transfer of the central and eastern Ukrainian lands from the Grand Duchy of Lithuania to the Kingdom of Poland in 1569 further complicated the issue. The most difficult questions were the Khmelnytsky revolt and the formation of the polities of the Cossack Hetmanate and the Zaporozhian Sich. Were Kyiv and Poltava to be considered part of Polish history in 1610, when they were in the Commonwealth, but not in 1690, when they were not? If Polish history were confined to the 1772 borders, the history of the Ukrainians would be divided along the Dnipro, even though the close relations of Chyhyryn and Pereiaslav as late as 1700 were obvious. The insistence that Ruthenians were a mere branch of the Polish nation could prevail only if one accepted the late seventeenth-century demarcation line of the Dnipro as somehow definitive in the long perspective of history.

The Russian and Polish interpretations of the Ukrainian past clashed in the nineteenth century, and each pointed to the other's inconsistencies. That these interpretations could be maintained so long was due in part to the political and cultural situation that retarded the emergence of a Ukrainian historical interpretation of the past. Indeed, the quite auspicious beginnings of Ukrainian historiography in the eighteenth and early nineteenth centuries did not develop into an academic synthesis of Ukrainian history during the second half of the nineteenth. The eighteenth century had produced the Cossack chronicles and the tracts on the rights of "Little Russia" that posited a claim for a Ukrainian historical process centered on, but not limited to, the Hetmanate. The political ramifications of this vision of the past were most forcefully expressed in *Istoriia Rusov* [History of the Rus´], which circulated in numerous early nineteenth-century manuscripts and found its way into print in 1846. If late eighteenth-century texts concentrated on the political entity of "Little Russia" (the Left-Bank Hetmanate), the early nineteenth-century histories by Dmytro Bantysh-Kamensky (1788–1850) and Mykola Markovych (1804–1860) provided accounts of "Little Russia" in the broader Ukrainian sense, in part because the narrower "Little Russian fatherland" no longer existed. From the 1830s, Mykhailo Maksymovych claimed a Ukrainian history before the Cossack period and underlined the Ukrainian character of Kyivan Rus´. By the mid-nineteenth century, the Cyrillo-Methodians, above all Mykola Kostomarov, conceived of Ukraine as a unique cultural entity with its own historical past and its own political future.[2]

The clash of historical vision with contemporary politics, along with a language prohibition, arrested the development of Ukrainian historical studies. As the Russian authorities declared Ukrainian activities politically seditious, they censored historical writings and discouraged historians from undertaking general works that might have developed into academic syntheses. Indeed, because the very word "Ukraine" was banned, scholars had to cloak their discussions in such terms as "Southwestern Russia" or "Little Russia" so as to avoid charges of disloyalty. Consequently, historians could most easily make contributions by dealing with regional topics or fields such as numismatics and archaeology, or by publishing documents. Since writing in Ukrainian was banned by the Valuev decree (1863) and the Ems ukase (1876), historians could not even develop Ukrainian as a scholarly language.

In this environment, Kostomarov's *Bogdan Khmel´nitskii* (first edition, 1857), which dealt with mid-seventeenth-century Ukraine rather than with the person of the hetman, stood out as one of few synthesizing works. Most historians, including those grouped around the excellent journal *Kievskaia starina* [Kyivan Antiquity; 1882–1907], collected a mass of information on specific people and incidents, albeit not equally on all periods and fields of history. Volodymyr Antonovych (1834–1908), the leading specialist in Ukrainian history at Kyiv University and founder of the documentary school, wrote outstanding studies on questions of demographic, social, and religious history. The "documentary school" emphasized the collection and publication of sources, an activity invaluable for Ukrainian historical studies that was also a strategy to demonstrate the existence of the Ukrainian people in the past without openly challenging the imperial authorities. The only general work by Antonovych to appear was an outline of his private lectures, which was published in Ukrainian, but in Habsburg Bukovyna, without his express permission.

By the 1890s, Ukrainians had still not produced a history comparable to Palacký's *History of Bohemia,* which had established Czech history as an academic discipline and furthered the Czech national movement. While the impetus behind the writing of the *History of Bohemia* was to provide the Czech nation with a past, the subject of the work was the history of the Bohemian polity, which Palacký brought down only to 1526, when its integration into the Habsburg domains began. The writer of Ukrainian history faced the problem that the unity of the Kyiv-based polity had collapsed in the twelfth century, and independent political entities had disappeared in the fourteenth century. More comparable to the Ukrainian experience was the formation of Czech culture, which developed in resistance to the dominant Germans and the Catholic church in the fourteenth and fifteenth centuries, and the Hussite movement and wars, which Palacký saw as the quintessence of the Czech spirit. The revival of the Eastern Church in the sixteenth century, the resistance to the Union of Brest, and the Cossack revolts that culminated in the Khmelnytsky movement could be seen as having a similar function in Ukraine.

Ukraine found its Palacký in the person of Mykhailo Hrushevsky.[3] From 1894 to 1934, Hrushevsky not only wrote the *magnum opus* of Ukrainian historiography, but also organized and led the two most productive schools of Ukrainian historical studies in modern times, the Shevchenko Scientific Society of Lviv, from 1894 to 1914, and the Institute of History of the All-Ukrainian Academy of Sciences, from 1924 to 1930. Hrushevsky's more than two thousand works in history, literary history, and other fields were matched in accomplishment by his inspiration of scores of younger scholars and his leadership of the Ukrainian national movement. But while the individuals he trained and the institutions he nurtured were destroyed in the vortex of Stalinism, his *History of Ukraine-Rus´*—except for the lost volume ten, part two, left in manuscript—survived. It weathered the Soviet assault on Ukrainian culture because no collective of specialists commanded by Soviet bureaucrats was able to produce a comparable work.[4]

Born in 1866 to the family of an educator, the descendant of Right-Bank clerics, Hrushevsky spent most of his formative years outside Ukraine, in the Caucasus.[5] Financially secure because of the success of his father's textbook of the Church Slavonic language, Hrushevsky was able to follow the career of his choosing. Living in an environment so varied in culture, religion, and national traditions, and so different from the Ukraine of his parents' reminiscences and of his own observations during visits to relatives, Hrushevsky soon saw the national issue as a fundamental question of his age. As a young gymnasium student in Tbilisi, he was strongly impressed by the classic works of Ukrainian ethnography, history, and literature. This impression was reinforced by the appearance in 1882 of the journal *Kievskaia starina,* which contained an abundance of material on Ukrainian affairs. After initial attempts to work in Ukrainian literature, the young Hrushevsky decided to go to Kyiv, the center of Ukrainophile activities, to study history.

The elder Hrushevsky agreed to his son's decision on condition that he refrain from student political activities. In the age of Alexander III, all student organizations were under suspicion, and manifest Ukrainian sympathies could call forth police surveillance. The Ukrainian movement, organized in the Kyiv Hromada, was still reeling from the Ems ukase and the banishment of Mykhailo Drahomanov (1841–1895), the leading Ukrainian intellectual of his generation. Although from abroad Drahomanov served as a spokesman for the Ukrainian movement and kept up a stream of criticism of the oppressive policies of the Russian government, the Hromada and Ukrainian leaders in Kyiv were withdrawing from political activities. Their goal became the mere survival of the Ukrainian movement. Professor Volodymyr Antonovych typified the trend with his decision that continuing to research and teach would be of more long-term significance than any hopeless political protest. His student Hrushevsky would prove to be the vindication of that decision.

Under Antonovych's supervision, Hrushevsky received a firm grounding in the examination of extensive sources in order to describe Ukrainian social and economic institutions of the past. Antonovych's work concentrated on the vast sources for the history of Right-Bank Ukraine in the sixteenth to eighteenth centuries, a time when, significantly, the area had not been part of a Russian state. Hrushevsky followed his mentor's lead in brilliant studies of the medieval history of the Kyiv region and of the early modern nobility and society of the Bar region. He might have been expected to follow Antonovych in making an academic career in the difficult political situation of Imperial Russia, but developments in the neighboring Habsburg Empire were to provide him with a much more conducive environment for furthering Ukrainian historical studies.

In 1890, the dominant Poles of Austrian Galicia showed a willingness to reach an accommodation with the growing Ukrainian national movement in the province. In the 1880s, partly under the influence of Drahomanov and other Eastern Ukrainian intellectuals, the populist or Ukrainian movement had demonstrated new dynamism among the Ruthenians of Galicia. Challenging the more conservative Old Ruthenian movement, which had a pro-Russian wing, the populists thought in all-Ukrainian terms and were open to the liberal and radical political ideas of the Ukrainophiles in the Russian Empire. The Ukrainian leaders in the Russian Empire found the growing Ukrainian–Polish conflict in Galicia regrettable, both because Polish–Ukrainian relations were relatively better in tsarist Russia and because they saw the dispute as weakening resistance to Russian pressure. Antonovych and other Eastern Ukrainian leaders played a role in Polish–Ukrainian negotiations that resulted in the New Era of 1890, a brief lull in the Polish–Ukrainian struggle in Galicia. Although the Polish–Ukrainian accommodation proved abortive, it did yield some concessions to the Ukrainians, the most important of which was the establishment of a chair intended to be in Ukrainian history with Ukrainian as the language of instruction. The Austrian minister of education, Otto von Gauch, did not permit use of the words "Ukrainian history" in the name of the chair, because, he asserted, "Ruthenian history is not a concrete scholarly field." Nonetheless, the chair in universal history with specialization in Eastern Europe was de facto in Ukrainian history. Professor Antonovych was called to the chair, but he proposed that his student Mykhailo Hrushevsky be appointed instead.

Hrushevsky's arrival in Lviv was the culmination of the process whereby the Ukrainian intelligentsia in the Russian Empire circumvented the imperial authorities' restrictions on Ukrainian activities by transferring them to the Habsburg Empire. Drahomanov, the most prominent political émigré, had greatly advanced this process by becoming a mentor to the more radical Galician populists, albeit from Switzerland. The symbiosis that emerged among the Ukrainian intellectuals furthered the formation of an all-Ukrainian perspective. Galicia offered the advantages of a territory where publishing could take place in Ukrainian, ideas could be expressed relatively freely, and political movements could be organized. Competition with the nationally minded Poles and the example of national movements throughout the Habsburg Empire stimulated interest in national issues. Galician Ukrainian society was in general more European than Ukrainian society in the Russian Empire, though its Europeanness was of a conservative, Central European, and Catholic kind. The Ukrainians of the province also possessed a religious structure, the Greek Catholic or Uniate Church, which differentiated them from the Poles and could be used in disseminating the national movement.

Galicia benefitted through its contacts with the Ukrainians of the Russian Empire in other ways. Galicia was an economic and, in some ways, a cultural backwater of the Habsburg lands. Ukrainians in the province were disadvantaged, comprising a peasantry and a small group of clergy and professionals. By contrast, Eastern Ukraine included areas and cities of considerable economic dynamism. Although primary education lagged behind that in Austrian Galicia, higher education and intellectual life in Eastern Ukraine, often closely connected with that in St. Petersburg and Moscow, was more advanced in many fields. While most Ukrainians in the Russian Empire were peasants, significant groups of nobles and urbanites, especially in the territories of the former Hetmanate, were ethnically Ukrainian. Ukrainians also had greater chances for social advancement than in Galicia. This explains why modern Ukrainian culture developed first in Eastern Ukraine and why a greater number of intellectuals of stature emerged there than in Galicia.

The Russian imperial authorities prevented the emergence of a broad-based Ukrainian movement in the Russian Empire, but in so doing they forced Ukrainian activists to direct their attention to the Ruthenians of Galicia. These activists provided a great deal of the intellectual and cultural substance of the Ukrainian movement in Galicia, which became a mass phenomenon in Galicia before World War I.

The young Hrushevsky's inaugural lecture at Lviv University in 1894 reflected the cultural and intellectual issues of the region.[6] Since the proclamation of Galician autonomy in 1868, the dominant Poles of Galicia had turned the university into a Polish institution not only in language of instruction but also in political attitudes. The Ukrainian students, primarily in theology, had become increasingly alienated from the university. Yet if Hrushevsky represented a field whose academic credibility was questioned and a language and people whose position was subordinate in the city and province, he also had reasons to be confident. He came from a historical school in Kyiv that had accomplishments equal or even superior to those of the Polish historians of Lviv.[7] For all the organizational accomplishments of the Ukrainian leaders and clergymen gathered in the auditorium to hear him, they realized that no local scholar was the equal of Professor Antonovych's student. Most important, Hrushevsky was confident of his broad and modern vision of history.

In his inaugural lecture Hrushevsky sketched an image of Ukrainian history as the evolution of the Ukrainian people from ancient times to the present. He called for the application of methods and data from all scholarly fields, from anthropology to archaeography, to that endeavor. Addressing the audience in Ukrainian, he demonstrated that a scholarly language appropriate to both sides of the Zbruch River could be forged.[8] In practice, Hrushevsky was initiating his life's project, the writing of a history of Ukraine. He was to use his lectures at Lviv University to compose this work. He attracted students to seminars where research papers filled the gaps in the project. He reshaped the Shevchenko Scientific Society into a scholarly academy with a library and a source publication program that provided materials for his history. By 1898, he had published the first volume of the *History of Ukraine-Rus´*, which went up only to the end of the tenth century rather than to the end of the Kyivan Rus´ period, as he had originally planned. The last of the published volumes would appear, posthumously, in 1937, bringing the project up only to the 1650s.

The very title of Hrushevsky's work was a programmatic statement. A history of Ukraine-Rus´ emphasized the continuity between Kyivan Rus´ and modern Ukraine. Written at a time when most Western Ukrainians still called themselves *Rusyny* (Ruthenians), the title served to ease the transition to the new name, Ukraine. In selecting a geographic name, Hrushevsky was defining the categories of his contemporaries. Ukraine was not an administrative entity at that time. In Russia the term was forbidden, and even the accepted "Little Russia" often did not encompass all the territories inhabited by Ukrainian majorities. To Galician Ukrainians, Ukraine often meant the territories in the Russian Empire. The term "Great Ukraine," applied by Galicians to these territories, implied in some way that the Habsburg Ukrainian lands were "Small Ukraine." Hrushevsky defined the borders of his Ukraine as the lands in which Ukrainians had traditionally constituted the majority of the population, the object of the striving of the Ukrainian national movement. Most importantly, his use of the term Rus´ and the emphasis on continuity with Kyivan Rus´ also challenged the monopoly that Russians had on that name and tradition in scholarship and popular views.

The subject of Hrushevsky's history was the Ukrainian people and their evolution, both in periods when they possessed states and polities and when they did not. Hrushevsky rejected the view that history should deal only with states and rulers. Deeply imbued with the populist ideology of the Ukrainian national movement, he saw simple people as having their own worth and history. This meant that elites in Ukrainian society, who had often assimilated to other peoples, were of little interest to him. He sought to write the history of the *narod,* and in his conceptualization it was relatively easy to conflate its dual meanings of populace and nation. This conflation has always made it very difficult for commentators to identify his orientation as either left- or right-wing on national or social issues.

In addition to his populist sentiments, Hrushevsky relied on his Kyiv training in the documentary school. He sought out all sources and perused masses of literature. His notes were replete with the latest Western works in archaeology, linguistics, and anthropology. He weighed and dissected sources in reaching a conclusion on any issue. His reader was drawn into the kitchen of scholarship and shown the full array of ingredients and utensils.

Between 1898 and 1901, Hrushevsky published three large volumes. The first was issued in the year that Galician Ukrainian society celebrated the one hundredth anniversary of the first work of modern Ukrainian literature, Ivan Kotliarevsky's *Eneïda* (the travestied *Aeneid*).[9] Hrushevsky, fully recognizing the significance of the occasion, wrote in the preface to volume one: "It is pleasing to me that the appearance of this book falls on the centenary of our national rebirth. Let it be a greeting to that event." Having taken three large volumes to cover Ukrainian history just up to the time of the Galician–Volhynian principality, Hrushevsky realized that his initial plan to encompass Ukrainian history in five to six volumes would have to be revised. In 1901, Hrushevsky wrote volume four, dealing with the political situation in the Ukrainian lands under Lithuanian and Polish rule from the fourteenth to the sixteenth century. He began work on the fifth volume in 1902, but the remarkable tempo of publication slowed, in part because Hrushevsky was seeking additional ways to disseminate his research. His works could not be distributed in Russian-ruled Ukraine because they were in the Ukrainian language, and they could not be read by most Western scholars, who did not know Ukrainian. In 1900, Hrushevsky began to search for a German-language publisher in order to circumvent the Russian ban (German was not proscribed) and to increase the resonance of his work in the West. In early 1903, he found a way to increase the dissemination of his views: he accepted an invitation to lecture at the Russian school in Paris. Although he found Russian students little interested in the Ukrainian question, he used the opportunity to prepare a Russian-language outline of his lectures. He also traveled to London, Berlin, and Leipzig, where he became more familiar with Western scholarship and arranged for the publication of volume one in German. He immediately embarked on a substantial revision of that volume, incorporating recent scholarship for a new Ukrainian edition that would serve as the text for the German version. Even before the German version appeared, Hrushevsky began the revision of volumes two and three. In 1904 he had been informed that the Russian minister Petr Sviatopolk-Mirsky had reacted to his protests and given permission to import the *History* into the Russian Empire. Volumes two and three were out of print, so Hrushevsky revised them. Volume four had appeared in 1903. Deciding that he could not finish volume five under the prevailing circumstances, Hrushevsky issued its first part in early 1905, followed by the new versions of volumes two and three.

Political changes further slowed the pace of writing the *History of Ukraine-Rus'*. The 1905 Revolution in the Russian Empire improved the situation for the Ukrainian movement and for scholarship on Ukraine. Following the lapse in the ban on publishing in Ukrainian, these events offered an opportunity to repeat the Galician advances in the lands where most Ukrainians lived. During the revolutionary events Hrushevsky took an active role as a publicist. His Russian-language outline was reissued with a summary of more recent events. Hrushevsky began to transfer Ukrainian cultural and scholarly activities to Kyiv. The journal *Literaturno-naukovyi vistnyk* [Literary-Scientific Messenger] made the move, and Hrushevsky established a scholarly society in Kyiv. Ultimately the political reaction in the Russian Empire after 1907 and the relatively less favorable conditions for the Ukrainian movement there than in Galicia—above all, the ban on Ukrainian in schools—undermined some of these initiatives. One indication of the continued opposition to the Ukrainian movement was the refusal to give Hrushevsky the chair at Kyiv University for which he applied in 1908. Beginning in the late 1890s, Russian nationalist circles had begun to see Hrushevsky as the architect of "Mazepist separatism," and his manifest scholarly achievements infuriated them. They succeeded in denying him the chair. Taking advantage of whatever opportunities were available to him, Hrushevsky divided his energies between Kyiv and Lviv (and, to a degree, St. Petersburg) and turned his attention to writing popular histories of Ukraine.

Hrushevsky did not, however, abandon his major scholarly work. In 1905, he published the second part of volume five, followed by volume six in 1907, thereby completing his account of the Polish and Lithuanian period. Next Hrushevsky began his discussion of what he saw as the third period of Ukrainian history, publishing volume seven under the title of a subseries, "The History of the Ukrainian Cossacks," in 1909. This volume, which covered events to 1625, was followed in 1913 by the first part of volume eight, dealing with the years 1625 to 1638. The increasing source base, due in part to Hrushevsky's vigorous archaeographic activities, was overwhelming him. In addition, mindful of the importance of public opinion for the acceptance of his ideas and interpretations in the Russian Empire, Hrushevsky issued part of volume one in Russian translation in 1910; in the course of doing so, he revised the work and put out a third Ukrainian edition of that volume in 1913. In 1913–14, Russian translations of volume seven and the first part of volume eight also appeared.

The outbreak of World War I found Hrushevsky, a Russian citizen, vacationing in the Ukrainian Carpathians of Austrian Galicia. Realizing that his presence abroad would provide propaganda for reactionary Russian forces, who had already begun a campaign against the Ukrainian movement before the war, Hrushevsky decided to return to Kyiv. He was immediately arrested. The intervention of highly placed friends changed his place of exile from Siberia to Simbirsk. Later he was permitted to take up residence in the university city of Kazan. In 1916 the intervention of the Russian Academy of Sciences succeeded in gaining permission for him to live in Moscow under police surveillance.

Before the war, Hrushevsky had written a draft of his history up until the Zboriv Agreement of 1649. In Simbirsk he was unable to continue research on the primary sources needed for the *History,* so he had turned his attention to writing a world history in Ukrainian. In Kazan, however, he had returned to his major project, revising and publishing volume eight, part two, for the years 1638 to 1648. With access to the archives and libraries of Moscow, Hrushevsky continued to expand his draft to cover the period up to the spring of 1650 and prepared it for publication. Volume eight, part three, was printed, but the copies were destroyed during the revolutionary events in Moscow and the book reached the public only in 1922, when it was reprinted in Vienna from a single preserved copy.

The Russian Revolution of February 1917 gave Hrushevsky his political freedom. It also resulted in his becoming the president of the first independent Ukrainian state, which took him away from scholarship. During 1917 he headed the Ukrainian Central Rada, which developed into the autonomous and then the independent government of Ukraine. In taking the city of Kyiv in early 1918, the Bolshevik artillery specifically targeted Hrushevsky's house, thereby destroying his library, priceless manuscripts, and museum, as well as the materials he had prepared for the *History of Ukraine-Rus'.* On 29 April 1918, he was elected president of the Ukrainian People's Republic (UNR), which evolved out of the Central Rada, but the German military authorities, whom he called in to protect Ukraine from the Bolsheviks, supported a coup by General Pavlo Skoropadsky to depose Hrushevsky and the UNR and to establish the monarchist Hetmanate. The fall of the Central Rada at the end of April removed Hrushevsky from power and the subsequent loss of Kyiv by its successor, the UNR Directory, in January 1919, made him a political refugee. He then served as the foreign representative of the Ukrainian Party of Socialist Revolutionaries, which he had supported since 1917. After extensive travels through Western Europe, he settled near Vienna, the initial center of the Ukrainian political emigration. He had lost considerable political authority among the tens of thousands of Ukrainian political émigrés, in part because of his failure to back the UNR fully and because of his political move to the left. He was, however, looked upon as the greatest Ukrainian scholar and was expected to organize Ukrainian scholarly and intellectual life.

Initially Hrushevsky fulfilled these expectations. He organized the

Ukrainian Sociological Institute and published a French version of his general history, a discussion of early social organization, and an account of the development of religious thought in Ukraine. In 1922, he turned his attention to his second monumental work, the *Istoriia ukraïns'koï literatury* [History of Ukrainian Literature], and published the first three volumes in Lviv. Nevertheless, Hrushevsky was increasingly out of tune with the major trends in Ukrainian historical studies outside Soviet Ukraine. Already in the decade before World War I, the younger generation of Hrushevsky's students in Galicia had departed from their teacher's populist convictions. They instead saw political formations and elites as playing positive roles in historical development, and they studied these phenomena in the Ukrainian past. Thus, while Western Ukraine under Polish rule was open to Hrushevsky's activity, he was increasingly alienated from the dominant historical views. In any event, Lviv under Polish authorities hostile to Ukrainian aspirations, where academics had been forced to establish an underground university and members of Ukrainian armies were denied civil rights, including the right to study, was a far cry from Habsburg Lviv. It was Prague, then rapidly becoming the center of Ukrainian political and scholarly life, that would have seemed the likely place of residence for Hrushevsky. There the Ukrainian Free University, transferred from Vienna in 1922, was developing rapidly with support from Thomas Masaryk and the Czech government.

Hrushevsky's attention, however, was already directed to events in Soviet Ukraine. Although the Ukrainian movement had failed to maintain an independent state, it had succeeded in institutionalizing its view that Ukraine should be a distinct administrative entity and that the Ukrainian nation had its own language and culture. While the Bolsheviks had accepted these tenets, they remained a group with relatively few ethnic Ukrainians in their leadership and even fewer followers versed in Ukrainian culture. When the Soviet leadership adopted a policy of indigenization, accompanied by a reversal of its more radical ideological and social policies, the government in Kyiv sorely needed cadres who would be perceived as legitimately Ukrainian.

In 1923, Hrushevsky began seriously to consider returning to Kyiv. Rumors to that effect caused consternation in Ukrainian political circles, which saw such an action by the first president of the Ukrainian state as a major blow to the cause of Ukrainian independence. Hrushevsky was offered a professorship at the Ukrainian Free University and a number of other posts in hopes that he would abandon his plans. In 1924, however, he decided that he would go to Kyiv instead of Prague. The reasons for his decision have been debated to the present day. Certainly his assertion that he planned to bring his *History of*

Ukraine-Rus' up to 1917 and could do so only with access to libraries and archives in Ukraine weighed heavily in his decision.[10]

Accepting an offer by the Kharkiv government, Hrushevsky returned to Kyiv to take up a position at the Ukrainian Academy of Sciences. He showed his customary energy in organizing scholarship. Reinvigorating the academy's *Zapysky* [Annals], Hrushevsky also revived the journal *Ukraïna* [Ukraine]. He gathered a talented group of co-workers and launched a number of new series, including *Za sto lit* [In one hundred years], a publication devoted to the nineteenth century. New journals specializing in unearthing and studying sources, such as *Ukraïns'kyi arkheografichnyi zbirnyk* [Ukrainian Archaeographic Collection] and *Ukraïns'kyi arkhiv* [Ukrainian Archive] were launched.[11] He also continued his work on the *History of Ukrainian Literature,* publishing volumes four and five. Returning to his *magnum opus,* he prepared volume nine on the period 1650 to 1658, publishing it in two separate, massive parts in 1928 and 1931. Hrushevsky's research on the *History* was indeed stimulated by his return to the academic environment and archives of Kyiv, but the city did not long provide a conducive environment for his work.

The very sweep of Hrushevsky's activities threatened the Communist leadership. They had sought legitimacy by inviting Hrushevsky to return, but then found his revitalization of non-Marxist Ukrainian historiography dangerous, particularly at a time when the Ukrainianization policy presented opportunities for the old Ukrainian intelligentsia to reach the masses. Attempts to obviate Hrushevsky by promoting the newly developing Marxist cadres led by Matvii Iavorsky did not have the desired effect. Ultimately the Communist authorities in Kharkiv did not decide the fate of Hrushevsky's historical school, for the rising tide of centralization accompanying the ascent of Joseph Stalin engulfed them, too. Ukrainian national communism was judged to be as dangerous as more traditional Ukrainian nationalism in a Soviet state that was increasingly becoming a successor to the Russian Empire. Beginning in 1928, Hrushevsky came under mounting attack by Party officials. As arrests and trials of the Ukrainian intelligentsia proceeded, Hrushevsky became an isolated figure.[12] After an all-out attack by V.P. Zatonsky, Hrushevsky was warned to leave for Moscow. Departing in early March 1931, he was arrested in Moscow and sent back to Kyiv, but then returned to Moscow. As Hrushevsky was exiled to Russia, the Institute of History was dismantled and its scholarly programs halted. Deprived of his Ukrainian context, Hrushevsky nevertheless continued his scholarly work, publishing in Russian journals and completing volume ten of his history. Illness overtook him during a trip to Kislovodsk in 1934, and he died under somewhat mysterious circumstances, as the result of an operation. The best testimony of the power of his name was that he was accorded a state funeral in a Ukraine devastated by famine and terror. His daughter Kateryna even succeeded in printing the first part of volume ten of his *History,* dealing with the years 1658–60, before she herself was arrested in the new terror. The second part, sometimes called volume eleven, which covered the period to 1676, remained in manuscript in Kyiv until the 1970s, when it disappeared.

Hrushevsky did not complete his history, but he had written more than six thousand pages outlining his vision of the Ukrainian past.[13] His shorter histories allow us to see how he would have treated subsequent periods. He viewed the Ukrainian past as a process in which a people had evolved on a given territory under differing political rulers. Although he discussed the territory from the most ancient times, he dated the origins of the Ukrainian people to the fifth century, to the Antae, whom he viewed as Slavs. His goal was to use all available evidence to study periods of the Ukrainian past for which written evidence was sparse. Just as the nineteenth-century historians had turned to ethnography and folklore to understand the past of the common folk who had left few written records, so Hrushevsky turned to the rapidly developing disciplines of historical linguistics, archaeology, anthropology, and sociology to penetrate the distant past of the entire Ukrainian people.

Hrushevsky considered the study of the people, rather than of rulers and states, to be the major advance of nineteenth-century historiography. He was rooted in the nineteenth-century populist tradition that saw Ukrainian history as, above all, an examination of the dispossessed. Indeed, populists considered Ukrainians as doubly dispossessed. As a primarily peasant and initially serf population, Ukrainians and their history were seen as essentially a populist subject. As a people who had frequently lacked a state of their own and who had been ruled by neighbors, they were excluded from the usual historical discussions. Historians such as Kostomarov, Antonovych, and Lazarevsky had even taken great pride in this dispossession and argued that Ukrainians would not, by nature, form repressive states and elites. This view even influenced the study of periods when Ukrainians had possessed political entities and elites, so that they were described in a negative light. This tradition viewed its defense of Ukrainian nationality as intrinsically democratic and progressive, but spent little time examining the phenomenon of nation per se—how Ukrainians had evolved as a national community—or analyzing whether the traits it saw as endemic to Ukrainians could provide the basis for a modern national community. The backward political and economic life in the Russian Empire and the persecution of Ukrainian activities partially explain how this rather idealized version of Ukrainian identity was maintained. Even the increasing tempo of urbanization and industrialization at the end of the century did not have as great an impact as might be expected in changing these views, because Ukrainian peasants played a relatively limited role in that process.

The political and social conditions of the Russian Empire explain in part Hrushevsky's link to this rather antiquated Ukrainian political tradition, but the connection also stemmed from his own intellectual formation. In general, radical political movements, including revolutionary populism and, by the 1890s, Marxism influenced his generation. By contrast, the Ukrainophile literature of the early nineteenth century and the Ukrainian populism of the 1860s formed Hrushevsky. The organic-work culturalism that typified the Kyiv Hromada of the 1880s and the journal *Kievskaia starina* strengthened this link. These traditions remained vital even as Hrushevsky set out to accomplish the "nationalist" enterprise of writing a national history. Undoubtedly the move to Galicia reaffirmed Hrushevsky in the enterprise, since it placed him in an intellectual context where national issues were considered basic and where an increasingly awakened peasantry played an active role in political and cultural life. After all, Hrushevsky's close collaborator in Lviv was the literary titan of peasant stock, Ivan Franko. Yet this situation probably postponed any examination of where the populist ended and the national began. For, in practice it was primarily national history that Hrushevsky wrote. In doing so, he did not see the Ukrainian nation as a constant throughout the ages. Indeed, in contrast to his peers among Russian historians, who largely disregarded the question in writing Russian history, Hrushevsky discussed the development of nationality in historical context. He saw the Ukrainian nationality as emerging late and under difficult historical circumstances. The vision of a long process comprising leaps forward and setbacks, but with the Ukrainian people at its core, was essential to his view of history.[14]

Hrushevsky also brought a Hegelian structure to his vision of the Ukrainian past. He conceived of Ukrainian history as a thesis, antithesis, and synthesis. He saw Kyivan Rus' as the Ukrainian people's first historical creation, their thesis. He viewed the Cossack period as an antithesis. Both thesis and antithesis had an element of instability. In the Kyivan Rus' period he saw the tension between the princes and their retinue and communal institutions as unresolved. In the antithesis he saw the Cossacks as embodying elements of national-cultural renewal and social justice. They had led the Ukrainian people in a great surge during the Khmelnytsky revolt, but ultimately these vital forces had dissipated. In the *History of Ukraine-Rus'* he did not reach the decline, in the mid-eighteenth century, of Cossack Ukraine. Nor did he deal with what he saw as the synthesis, the modern national revival.

Around the time of his trip to Paris (1903), Hrushevsky also became interested in social theory, above all that of Durkheim.[15] This interest in the newly developing discipline of sociology grew, so that in the period after the failure of Ukrainian state building Hrushevsky devoted considerable attention to establishing a Ukrainian school of sociology, even encouraging his daughter, Kateryna, to work in that field. He began to refer to himself as a "historian-sociologist." Certainly the field gave him an opportunity to examine primitive societies, and he could feel that he had a better tool for understanding the popular masses, as well as the earliest societies on Ukrainian territory. This new interest helped him in the redrafting of volume one and may have provided an underpinning for his discussion of the Ukrainian Cossacks. Durkheim's method of describing matters in great detail and avoiding synthesis may have influenced Hrushevsky's presentation in volumes nine and ten.[16]

In launching his history, Hrushevsky sought to challenge the accepted view on the origin of the Ukrainian and Russian peoples. Inherent in his work and broached in a number of reviews that he wrote at the turn of the century, Hrushevsky's new scheme for the study of Rus´ history, or East Slavic history (a term he popularized), was most comprehensively presented in an article published in St. Petersburg in 1904. This short piece, perhaps the best known of all his writings, argued that the current, accepted framework for studying "Russian" history was illogical.[17] Based on the claims of Muscovite bookmen, it accepted the theory of dynastic descent from Kyivan Rus´ to Vladimir to Moscow to St. Petersburg as an appropriate framework for historical study. Hrushevsky maintained that while this approach may have had some applicability for the history of states, it was totally inadequate for the study of peoples and cultures. After the early period, it dealt with the Belarusians and Ukrainians episodically. It also did not permit examination of the Russians and their origins. Hrushevsky maintained that by appropriating Kyivan Rus´—which properly belonged to Ukrainian history—to Russian history, the traditional scheme did damage to Russian historical studies. Without denying that a collective history of all the East Slavic peoples could be written, Hrushevsky emphasized the need to reexamine each people's history. He declared that he was in the process of doing so for the Ukrainians, and that a similar project was needed for the Belarusians. He stated that the Russian historical past had generally been studied and that once the issue of the Russians' origins was reexamined, a proper national history could emerge. In issuing the third edition of volume one in 1913, Hrushevsky commented on how much acceptance his vision of Ukrainian history had gained since he had begun his project.

Hrushevsky's schema was as controversial as his opinion on the great

debate over the role of the Varangians in the formation of the early Rus'
state. Deeply committed to the view that rulers had only superficial influence and that Rus' society had developed organically out of ancient roots
that went all the way back to the Antae, Hrushevsky almost inevitably
chose the anti-Normanist side.

The *History of Ukraine-Rus'* contains relatively few great men or heroes.
Even Volodymyr and Danylo do not stand out for heroic deeds. The most
troublesome figure for Hrushevsky was Hetman Bohdan Khmelnytsky. In
some of his popular writings, he expressed rather favorable opinions of the
hetman's accomplishments. In the *History of Ukraine-Rus'*, however,
Hrushevsky seemed to develop an aversion to the hetman as his lengthy
account of Khmelnytsky's age progressed. In this he diverged from the
centuries-old Ukrainian tradition that viewed Khmelnytsky as the father of
the nation. He also polemicized with contemporaries who belonged to the
statist school of Ukrainian historiography, in particular Viacheslav
Lypynsky. This younger generation saw Ukrainian elites and polities as
positive and considered Khmelnytsky a great statesman. Hrushevsky an-
grily replied that for him the Ukrainian masses were the only heroes of the
Khmelnytsky revolt.

Hrushevsky did, however, accept the traditional Ukrainian attitude toward the Cossacks. He began his subseries on the history of the Ukrainian
Cossacks with a document that had just been published by the church historian Platon Zhukovich. In the document, a protest from the early 1620s,
Metropolitan Iov Boretsky described the Cossacks as descendants of the
warriors of the tenth-century prince Oleh who had campaigned in their
boats on the Black Sea. The metropolitan cast them as heroes of Christendom and defenders of the Rus' Orthodox church. With this epigraph,
Hrushevsky affirmed a national role for the Cossacks and justified his label-
ing of the entire age as Cossack.

The initial reaction to the *History of Ukraine-Rus'* differed greatly between Ukrainian historians and activists, on the one hand, and foreign
scholars, on the other. When Hrushevsky's colleagues and students celebrated his fortieth birthday in 1906, they were fulsome in their praise of his
accomplishments. The editorial board, including Volodymyr Hnatiuk,
Denys Korenets, Ivan Krevetsky, Stefan Tomashivsky, and Ivan Franko,
went so far as to call the *History* "that great basis of Ukrainian historical
scholarship and inexhaustible source of national-political and social-politi-
cal self-understanding and consciousness, which for the first time truly
brings us into the family of European peoples."[18]

Hrushevsky had unequivocally become the foremost Ukrainian historian.
In Western Ukraine his schema was soon universally accepted. In Russian-

ruled Ukraine the *History*'s influence was also great. In 1916, Mykola Vasylenko asserted that despite the ill will with which Russian nationalists such as Timofei Florinsky had greeted the work, all had to come to terms with Hrushevsky's erudition, as well as his success in what many had viewed as the questionable enterprise of writing Ukrainian history.[19] Some of the most convincing testimonies to the work's significance came from the attempts of the opponents of Hrushevsky and the Ukrainian movement to discredit it. The Russian nationalists in Kyiv who plotted to deny Hrushevsky a chair at the university in 1908 argued that his work could not be evaluated because it was written in an incomprehensible jargon. A fellow student of Antonovych, Linnychenko, wrote a brochure in 1917 against Ukrainian autonomy in which he devoted considerable attention to refuting Hrushevsky's *History*. Arguing as a loyal "Little Russian," he maintained that Ukrainian history could be seen only as part of all-Russian history, in particular because, lacking a state, the Ukrainians had neither a history or culture of their own.[20] These were largely reactions against the political and cultural successes of the Ukrainian movement, but they testified to what degree Hrushevsky's *History* had served as an underpinning.

Hrushevsky commented that initially Russian and Polish historians had met his work with silence. Perhaps the linguistic medium he chose explains this, for the Ukrainian language obviously made his *History* less accessible to most other historians. Therefore Hrushevsky's strategy of arranging a German translation was well-justified, even though it was initially devised as much to promote access to his work in Eastern Ukraine, where Ukrainian-language books were banned, as to reach Western scholars. The publication in German of volume one seemed to have the desired effect: a major Polish scholar reviewed the work. Aleksander Brückner gave eloquent testimony to Hrushevsky's erudition and phenomenal mastery of literature. He paid Hrushevsky a great compliment: "Regrettably, we cannot take pride in a similarly voluminous, fundamental and intelligent work about Polish history. Would that its example might influence our historians, so that in this field they do not remain behind Rus′."[21] He criticized Hrushevsky's linguistic observations, however, and lamented his adherence to anti-Normanism. He did not mention the issue of the origin of the Ukrainian people. Favorable notice of Hrushevsky's work also appeared in the Czech publications of Karel Kadlec.[22] However, although the *Kwartalnik Historyczny* had published a positive review of Hrushevsky's inaugural lecture, Polish scholars came to see Hrushevsky's historical vision, as well as his political activities, in a negative light.[23] Still, Ludwik Kołankowski's negative assessment, which focused on volumes four to six, testified to the increasing attention being paid to the *History*.[24] Certainly the Russian translations of three volumes of the history increased its currency in Russian historical circles, and its influence was apparent in the work of Sergei Platonov, Vasilii Storozhev, and Matvei Liubavsky.[25] In 1929, Aleksandr Presniakov even took up Hrushevsky's proposal to write the history of the origin of the Russian state and nation.[26]

By the 1920s, the reception of the *History of Ukraine-Rus'* had changed considerably. The publication of eight volumes had added to the *History*'s authority, in particular since they were usually the most extensive and bibliographically up-to-date studies yet published on a broad array of topics and questions dating up to the mid-seventeenth century. In addition, the manifest rise of the Ukrainian movement and the attempt to establish a Ukrainian state had transformed the Ukrainian question from an obscure problem to a widely recognized issue. Finally, Hrushevsky's importance in the Central Rada had turned the historian into an internationally known figure. In 1922, the Ukrainian historians of Lviv issued another celebratory volume for Hrushevsky. His former student Vasyl Herasymchuk wrote a laudatory evaluation of Hrushevsky as a historian; indeed, the schema worked out by Hrushevsky and the data presented in his *History* were considered fundamental by all Western Ukrainian historians.[27] Yet, in attitude and approach, Ukrainian historians in Western Ukraine and in the emigration were increasingly alienated from Hrushevsky's populist views and negative attitudes toward Ukrainian leaders. Similar views were also held by some of the historians who gathered around Hrushevsky after his return to Kyiv in 1924.

The success of the Bolsheviks raised the prestige of Marxist thought, either because historians were influenced by the triumph of the revolution or because they were subjected to pressure. Initially the Marxists did not feel secure enough to criticize Hrushevsky directly, though Matvii Iavorsky produced his own, albeit popular, history of Ukraine. The most authoritative critical evaluation came, instead, from Dmytro Bahalii, a student of Antonovych, senior to Hrushevsky and formerly a professor at Kharkiv University.[28] Bahalii described the *History* as the culmination of prerevolutionary Ukrainian historiography and predicted that all future advances would come from the Marxists. More substantively, he disputed whether Kyivan Rus' belonged to Ukrainian history alone. He questioned whether there was a Cossack age in Ukrainian history. Bahalii also disputed some of Hrushevsky's statements about the context in which the *History* was written. He maintained that the professors of Kyiv University must have had a more positive influence than Hrushevsky ascribed to them. He asserted that the Kyiv circle had understood the need for a general history and had initiated a competition in 1895 that Aleksandra Efimenko had won. In the end, Bahalii did not complete the history he himself was working on. His prediction that Marxist historiography would become dominant proved all too true, although its accomplishments have been of questionable value.

Communist forces had always seen accommodation with Hrushevsky as tactical. In 1925, the Soviet political police (GPU) in Moscow had sent out a secret circular describing the *History of Ukraine-Rus'* as "falsely scientific history, dangerous, and harmful to Soviet rule" and calling on local police units to identify all those who showed interest in the work or distributed it.[29] By 1926, when Bahalii published his evaluation, the campaign against non-Marxist scholarship had already begun. Led initially by Iavorsky, it gained increasing intensity in 1928 when Communist Party members were forced on the Ukrainian Academy. Simultaneously, prerevolutionary historical views were reemerging in the Moscow center, as could be seen from the publication of Aleksei Tolstoy's novel on Peter I and Boris Grekov's work on Kyivan Rus'. That development and the drive for ideological purity explains the campaign against Iavorsky and his school of Kharkiv Marxists. Iavorsky publicly recanted his views in early 1930. The campaign against him included charges of failing to act vigorously enough against Hrushevsky's influence.

The Marxist attack on Hrushevsky and his historical work attained great momentum in 1930. In articles published in Moscow and in Ukraine, Mykhailo Rubach pressed charges that would later evolve into the standard Soviet interpretation of Hrushevsky.[30] As one might have expected, Hrushevsky was attacked for failing to use Marxist periodization. To this was added the charge that he propagated the concept of the classlessness of the Ukrainian nation—a twisted interpretation of his populist sympathies and his statements to the effect that Ukrainians had frequently lacked upper classes and in modern times had a weakly developed bourgeoisie and proletariat. Rubach also charged Hrushevsky with attempting to sow discord between the Russian and Ukrainian peoples by overemphasizing the historical differences between them. He maintained that Hrushevsky had paid excessive attention to European influences in the Ukrainian past. By 1932, the destruction of historical studies and the atmosphere of terror had gone so far that such charges did not even need a semblance of veracity. Lev Okinshevych insisted that Hrushevsky had been fixated on the issue of Ukrainian statehood and the upper classes, and that there was no substantive difference between the views of Lypynsky and Hrushevsky.[31] The Soviet process of demonizing Ukrainian "nationalism" as if it were a unified camp had begun. As Hrushevsky's works were removed from library shelves in Ukraine, and copies of the posthumous volume that, paradoxically, was published in 1937 were almost entirely destroyed, the public could know Hrushevsky only through these attacks.

Abroad, the reputation of Hrushevsky and his *History* had grown greatly. In his obituary André Mazon expressed a widely held sentiment in stating "L'Ukraine a perdu son historien."[32] Otto Hoetzsch described Hrushevsky's influence on him as a friend and historian. Calling the *History* "a great achievement," Hoetzsch maintained that it was "the first to present the Muscovite and the Ukrainian historical process as separate. It worked out the first schema, the first truly scholarly synthesis of Ukrainian history."[33] In a warm personal obituary, Hans Koch called the work an "enormous synthesis of an abundance of details that are not overlooked despite their microscopic size and are masterfully turned to account. Everything available in printed sources and contributions to the literature, including the most recondite gymnasium and provincial reports of every language and culture, including Turkic and Arabic sources, and the collected data of archaeology, palaeontology, linguistics, even ethnology and theology, is here united and brought up to date with astonishing industry."[34]

In the New World, George Vernadsky wrote admiringly of Hrushevsky's work in an introduction to an English translation of his popular history: "It is the work of a great scholar, based upon exhaustive research, pervaded by the spirit of keen criticism, and displaying a wealth of information with regard not only to the Ukrainian people, but to the general history of the period, as well."[35] Appropriate praise was rendered by Ukrainian scholars outside Soviet Ukraine, such as Ivan Krypiakevych and Myron Korduba, even though they now belonged to a different historical school and had not agreed with Hrushevsky's political accommodation with the Left.[36] World War II destroyed the historical centers in Central and Eastern Europe where Hrushevsky had made his greatest impact, and the Soviet victory and absorption of Western Ukraine decreased interest in Ukraine's history. Still, as soon as Stalinism receded, Polish scholars began citing Hrushevsky with admiration and Russian historians began including him in footnotes. In Ukraine, however, his works could not be cited and his name appeared only as an object of political vituperation.

The outcome of World War II also resulted in a large emigration of Ukrainian historians and intellectuals from prewar Western Ukraine and Soviet Ukraine to the West. Many eventually went on to North America, where there were well-established Ukrainian communities. Most of these historians worked in an émigré environment. They usually found Hrushevsky's historical views lacking in statist perspective. But they carried on his general schema and the tradition of his national historiography. One of the great achievements of the Ukrainian diaspora in the 1950s was the reprinting of the *History,* which made it widely available in Western research libraries. Borys Krupnytsky wrote an introduction explaining the importance of Hrushevsky and his work, but also presenting the statist school's divergence from his views.[37] In the 1960s, the Ukrainian Historical Association and contributors to its journal, *Ukraïns'kyi istoryk* [The Ukrainian Historian], in particular Lubomyr Wynar, began publishing large numbers of source materials and bibliographies as well as studies on Hrushevsky. In 1968, the Ukrainian community funded a chair in history at Harvard University named in Hrushevsky's honor. The Shevchenko Scientific Society, reestablished in the West after its abolition following the Soviet annexation of Western Ukraine, announced a project to translate the *History* and commissioned a number of translations, but it lacked the resources to carry out the enormous undertaking.

In Ukraine, Hrushevsky and his works remained taboo. This taboo served as a symbol of the provincial, colonial nature of Ukrainian culture. In the period of de-Stalinization and the subsequent Thaw, Russian scholars republished the histories of the "reactionary" Solov'ev and Kliuchevsky, but Ukrainian historians could not even discuss the contributions of the "leftist" Hrushevsky. In Moscow historians could cite Hrushevsky in scholarly discourse, while in Ukraine his name appeared only as a vehicle for denunciations of Ukrainian bourgeois nationalism. This did not stop a select circle of historians from using his *History* in writing their works, and, in the degraded environment of Soviet scholarship, they felt free to appropriate his notes without attribution. At the end of the cultural thaw of the late 1950s and 1960s, Fedir Shevchenko attempted to return Hrushevsky's name to historical discussion, but that effort was soon suppressed.[38] After the pogrom against Ukrainian culture in 1972, Russian centralizing trends strengthened, suppressing Hrushevsky and his ideas even more. It was during the 1970s that the manuscript of volume ten, part two, of the *History* disappeared from the Ukrainian archives. By the mid-1980s, the state of Ukrainian historical studies was so lamentable that historians, in contrast to writers and literary specialists, were slow to react to glasnost, which in any event came later to Ukraine than to other parts of the Soviet Union.

In the late 1980s, Hrushevsky's name returned to public discussion in an increasingly free press, largely under the prompting of activists such as Serhii Bilokin and Zynoviia Franko, who had attempted secretly to preserve Hrushevsky's legacy.[39] By 1989, Ukrainian literary and cultural journals began publishing Hrushevsky's works: the journal *Vitchyzna* [Native Land] printed volume seven and part of volume eight of the *History* in installments, and *Kyiv* similarly began printing volume one.[40] In February 1989, the Academy of Sciences supported a decision of a meeting of Ukrainian archaeographers to publish a photo-offset edition of the *History*. In 1991, the first volume appeared, in an edition of one hundred thousand copies.[41]

Plans were made to conclude the reprint with a volume of indexes and bibliographic information. To date, six volumes have appeared.

The preface to the new Ukrainian edition emphasized the cooperation of Ukrainian specialists in the West in the project. The Ukrainian Research Institute of Harvard University and the newly formed Peter Jacyk Centre for Ukrainian Historical Research at the Canadian Institute of Ukrainian Studies, University of Alberta, joined as sponsors of the edition. The preface also announced that the Peter Jacyk Centre had undertaken to produce an English translation of the entire *History*.

The translation of Hrushevsky's *magnum opus* into an international scholarly language is being realized ninety years after the historian sought to arrange the German translation. In issuing a work begun nearly a century ago by a scholar who died more than six decades ago, one must consider whether the work continues to have relevance and whether there is a need for a version other than the Ukrainian original. New archaeological finds have been made, new and better editions of sources have been published, new literature has appeared, and new theories and methods have emerged.

Hrushevsky's *Istoriia Ukraïny-Rusy* is the major statement of a historian of genius. In breadth and erudition it still has no equal in Ukrainian historiography, and its examination of many historical questions remains unsurpassed. In some ways this is due to the unfortunate history of Ukraine, above all, the Soviet policies that not only imposed official dogmas but also discouraged study of pre-modern Ukrainian history and the publication of sources. This policy, as well as the relative neglect of Ukrainian history in surrounding lands and in the West, have made new source discoveries and expansion of information more limited than might have been expected. The tragic fate of Ukrainian archives in the twentieth century—above all, the losses occasioned by wars and revolutions—frequently means that Hrushevsky's discussions and citations are the only information extant. The reprinting of the *History* in Ukraine demonstrates to what degree Hrushevsky's work is the starting point for rebuilding historical studies there. Indeed, in the period after the proclamation of Ukrainian independence in 1991, a Hrushevsky cult emerged in Ukraine, as could be seen in the luxuriously published collection of Hrushevsky's essays and materials about him entitled *Velykyi ukraïnets'* [A Great Ukrainian]. Leonid Kravchuk, Ukraine's president, wrote the introduction.[42] For most, the *History of Ukraine-Rus'* will be the basis for understanding the period up until the seventeenth century, but others will use it as a tool to examine the thought of the Ukrainian national revival and the views of one of its greatest leaders.

The unfavorable situation of the Ukrainian language in the twentieth century also reinforces the need for a translation. Although for most of this century Ukrainian has been the second most widely spoken language within one of the major linguistic groups in Europe, it has not received the currency one might assume is its due. In Ukraine itself it has been under siege, so that large numbers of Ukrainians have lost it as a native tongue. In the last decades of Soviet rule Ukraine became a country in which all postgraduate theses had to be written in Russian and most scholarship appeared in Russian. In essence, Ukrainian was returning to the status it had had in the Russian Empire, with the additional disadvantage that Galicia had been annexed to this reconstituted empire. Thus, even in the lands neighboring Ukraine, there was little need to pay attention to the Ukrainian language. In Western Europe and North America, university Slavic departments have given Ukrainian very low priority in their programs, and graduate students in Russian and Eastern European history have rarely developed even a reading knowledge of it. The modern-day scholar who does undertake the challenge of reading the Ukrainian original must cope with many quotes in Slavonic, middle Ukrainian, Muscovite chancery language, Polish, and the classical languages. Students of Western and Central European history, Middle Eastern history, and Eastern European history have generally not had access to this major account of the history of Ukraine. Yet the reassertion of Ukrainian independence has increased general interest in Ukrainian history and in the work of Hrushevsky.

The publication of *Istoriia Ukraïny-Rusy* in Ukraine has given the lie to the twisted representation of the work in Soviet discussions. The appearance of the English translation now permits a wider scholarly community, which has often only known of Hrushevsky as a "nationalist" historian, to examine the type of national history that this great scholar wrote. In Ukrainian historical circles in the West, Hrushevsky is often called a populist, with little attempt to see whether the actual text of the *History* indeed reflects that self-description by its author.[43] Some have questioned the advisability of translating the *History* because it is out of date, which usually means that it does not reflect the statist school now dominant in the Ukrainian diaspora. Fortunately, the possibility of pursuing pluralistic approaches in Ukraine and the development of Ukrainian historiography in the West beyond the Ukrainian diaspora among a wider group of historians and students of varied descent are bound to break down the ideological nature of the field. For all, Hrushevsky's work will be a first point of reference.

In preparing the English edition, the issue of obsolescence had to be addressed and decisions had to be made about correcting "errors," providing information on current views of scholarly questions, and updating information on subsequent literature and source publications. It was decided to render the text as Hrushevsky presented it, and to ask specialists to place his work in the context of the field in their introductions to each volume. The English version has one advantage over the Ukrainian original: bibliographies with complete bibliographic information are appended to each volume. These bibliographies permit closer analysis of the scholarly context of the *History*.

The need to continue Hrushevsky's work has frequently been broached. For those who would see such a continuation as one individual picking up where Hrushevsky left off, the example of Palacký would seem instructive: attempts to find a successor to carry on the Czech historian's work failed. A genius and titan of industriousness like Hrushevsky is a rare phenomenon among us. Then, too, the methods and style of writing history have changed, so that the grand national history based on examination of massive sources is rare. The collective history, practiced so poorly in the Soviet period, offers one possibility for a voluminous continuation, but it will always lack the spirit of one person's work. It is more likely that monographs and survey histories will prove to be the continuation of Hrushevsky's *History*. These works will undoubtedly devote considerable attention to the scholarly legacy of Hrushevsky in dealing with the period from the mid-seventeenth to the mid-nineteenth century, and they will go on to document and assess the legacy of the political and national leader Mykhailo Hrushevsky in the late nineteenth and early twentieth centuries.

Notes

Originally published as the introduction to Mykhailo Hrushevsky, *History of Ukraine-Rus'* (Edmonton: Canadian Institute of Ukrainian Studies, 1997), pp. xxii–xlii, with permission of the publisher.

1. For Russian and Polish writings on Ukrainian history, including an extensive bibliography, see Stephen Velychenko, *National History as Cultural Process: A Survey of the Interpretations of Ukraine's Past in Polish, Russian, and Ukrainian Historical Writing from the Earliest Times to 1914* (Edmonton, 1992).

2. On Ukrainian historiography, with some attention to Polish and Russian writings, see the special issue of *The Annals of the Ukrainian Academy of Arts and Sciences in the U.S.*, vols. 5–6 (1957), including Dmytro Doroshenko, "A Survey of Ukrainian Historiography," and Olexander Ohloblyn, "Ukrainian Historiography, 1917–56."

3. This comparison was made in a review of Hrushevsky's *Istoriia Ukraïny-Rusy* by Dr. Karel Kadlec, *Sborník Věd Právních a Státních* (henceforth *SVPS*) 9 (1909): 298.

4. On Hrushevsky's life and political career, see Thomas M. Prymak, *Mykhailo Hrushevsky: The Politics of National Culture* (Toronto, 1987), as well as the concise account by L. Wynar and O. Ohloblyn in *Encyclopedia of Ukraine* 2: 250–53. For his activities as a historian, see Liubomyr Vynar (Wynar), *Naivydatnishyi istoryk Ukraïny Mykhailo Hrushevs'kyi (1866–1934)* (n.p., 1985). On Hrushevsky and his works, see the bibliographies by Lubomyr Wynar, *Mykhailo Hrushevs'kyi, 1866–1934. Bibliographic Sources* (New York, 1985) and *Mychajlo Hruševs'kyj:*

Biobibliographische Quelle, 1866–1934 (Munich, 1984), and the extensive bibliography in Prymak's book.

5. Information on Hrushevsky's early life comes largely from an autobiography that he wrote in 1906 and revised in 1926. Both of these texts are reprinted in *Velykyi ukraïnets'* (Kyiv, 1992), pp. 197–213 and 220–40.

6. For the inaugural lecture, see *Zapysky Naukovoho tovarystva im. Shevchenka* (henceforth *ZNTSh*) 4 (1894): 140–50.

7. Indeed, whereas the excellent scholarly journal *Kievskaia starina,* devoted primarily to Ukrainian history, had been issued in Kyiv since 1882, the Polish historical journal in Lviv, *Kwartalnik Historyczny,* was founded only in 1886.

8. This did not mean that Hrushevsky was a good stylist in Ukrainian. Ivan Franko called Hrushevsky's prose "cold" and full of abstractions. He pointed out that there were frequent jumps and lapses in presentation, as well as russicisms and polonisms. Ivan Franko, "Prychynky do istoriï Ukraïny-Rusi," in *Zibrannia tvoriv u p'iatdesiaty tomakh,* vol. 47 (Kyiv, 1986), pp. 417–55, especially 453–55.

9. The 50th anniversary of the abolition of serfdom in Galicia, the 25th anniversary of the literary activity of Ivan Franko, and the 250th anniversary of the Khmelnytsky uprising were all marked the same year. Each event was testimony to the growth of national consciousness and the mobilization of the national movement.

10. See the account by Matvii Stakhiv of his mission in 1923 to dissuade Hrushevsky from returning to Ukraine. Matvii Stakhiv, "Chomu M. Hrushevs'kyi povernuvsia v 1924 rotsi do Kyieva? (Zhmut faktiv i uryvok zi spohadiv)," and *Mykhailo Hrushev'skyi u 110 rokovyny narodzhennia 1876* [sic]*–1976* (New York, 1978) (=*ZNTSh,* vol. 197), pp. 109–47, especially 133.

11. On Hrushevsky's archaeographic achievements, see B. Krupnyćkyj, "Die Archäographische Tätigkeit M. Hruševśkyjs," *Jahrbücher für Kultur und Geschichte der Slaven,* n.s. 11 (1935): 610–21.

12. On the destruction of Ukrainian scholarship, see Mariia Ovcharenko, ed., *Zbirnyk na poshanu ukraïns'kykh uchenykh znyshchenykh bol'shevyts'koiu Moskvoiu* (Paris and Chicago, 1962) (=*ZNTSh,* vol. 173), in particular N. Polons'ka-Vasylenko, "Istorychna nauka v Ukraïni za soviets'koï doby ta dolia istorykiv," pp. 7–111.

13. On Hrushevsky's historical thought, see Leo Bilas, "Geschichtsphilosophische und ideologische Voraussetzungen der geschichtlichen und politischen Konzeption M. Hruševśkyjs: Zum 90. Geburtstag des ukrainischen Historikers (29 September 1956)," *Jahrbücher für Geschichte Osteuropas,* n.s. 4 (1956–57): 262–92; Illia Vytanovych, "Uvahy do metodolohiï i istoriosofiï Mykhaila Hrushevs'koho"; Omelian Pritsak, "Istoriosofiia Mykhaila Hrushevs'koho," in Mykhailo Hrushevs'kyi, *Istoriia Ukraïny-Rusy,* vol. 1 (reprint: Kyiv, 1991), pp. xl–lxxiii.

14. For Hrushevsky, the concept of a nation or nationality as a collective of individuals united by common characteristics in the present, a communality in the past, and a common set of tasks and aspirations in the future, independent of territorial, political, or confessional divides, was a nineteenth-century phenomenon. He saw earlier concepts of nationality or people as often related to political, religious, and cultural unity. He believed these criteria had often worked against the emergence of the Ukrainian nation (*narod*). For his views, see his "Razvitie ukrainskikh izuchenii v XIX v. i raskrytie v nikh osnovnykh voprosov ukrainovedeniia," in *Ukrainskii narod v ego proshlom i nastoiashchem,* vol. 1 (St. Petersburg, 1914), pp. 1–36, especially 1–2.

15. Illia Vytanovych asserts that Hrushevsky became aware of Durkheim's work through contacts with Maksim Kovalevsky and directly, during his trip to Paris, but his misdating of the trip to 1905 casts doubt on his assertion. "Uvahy," p. 51.

16. This is suggested by Illia Vytanovych in "Uvahy," p. 51.

17. "Zvychaina skhema 'russkoï' istoriï i sprava ratsional'noho ukladu istoriï skhidnoho Slov''ianstva," in *Stat'i po slavianovedeniiu,* pt. 1, ed. V.I. Lamanskii (St. Petersburg, 1904).

18. 'Peredmova' [Introduction] in *Naukovyi zbirnyk prys'viachenyi profesorovy Mykhailovy Hrushevs'komu uchenykamy i prykhyl'nykamy z nahody Ioho desiatylitn'oï naukovoï pratsï v Halychynï (1894–1904)* (Lviv, 1906), p. vii.

19. See the evaluation of Hrushevsky's historical work by Mykola Vasylenko in 1916, in which he discusses Florinsky's reaction and compares Hrushevsky's accomplishment to Solov'ev's, but points out that Hrushevsky had to search more widely for archival sources and discusses a much greater body of secondary literature. N. Vasilenko, "M.S. Grushevskii kak istorik," *Ukrainskaia zhizn',* 1916, p. 43.

20. See O.P. Tolochko, "Dvi ne zovsim akademichni diskusiï (I.A. Linnychenko, D.I. Bahalii, M.S. Hrushevs'kyi)," *Ukraïns'kyi arkheohrafichnyi shchorichnyk,* n.s. 2 (1993): 97–103.

21. A. Brückner, "Dogmat normański," *Kwartalnik Historyczny* 20 (1906): 679 (the review appears on pp. 664–79).

22. See Kadlec's review in *SVPS,* pp. 298–305, in which he states: "Professor Hrushevsky's work is written with such unusual erudition, and is based on such a large literature and such a wealth of sources, that it belongs to the most distinguished products of Slavic literature of the past decade" (pp. 301–2). Also see his article "Mychajlo Hruševśkyj," *Slovansk Přehled* 11 (1909): 163–67.

23. See the review of A. Lewicki in *Kwartalnik Historyczny* 9 (1893): 565–67.

24. *Kwartalnik historyczny* 27 (1913): 349–65.

25. Hans Koch, "Dem Andenken Mychajlo Hruševśkyj's (29 September 1866–25 November 1934)," *Jahrbücher für Kultur und Geschichte der Slaven* n.s. 11 (1935): 3–10.

26. A.E. Presniakov, *The Formation of the Great Russian State: A Study of Russian History in the Thirteenth to Fifteenth Centuries,* trans. A.E. Moorhouse (Chicago, n.d.), pp. 6–9. Also see Viktor Novyts'kyi, "Istorychna pratsia prof. O.Ie. Priesniakova i rozmezhuvannia velykorus'koï ta ukraïns'koï istoriohrafiï," *Ukraïna* 40 (March–April 1930): 55–65.

27. Vasyl' Herasymchuk, "Mykhailo Hrushevs'kyi iak istoriograf Ukraïny," *ZNTSh* 133 (1922): 1–26.

28. Akadem. D.I. Bahalii, "Akad. M.S. Hrushevs'kyi i ioho mistse v ukraïns'kii istoriohrafiï (istorychno-krytychnyi narys)," *Chervonyi shliakh,* 1927, no. 1, pp. 160–217.

29. Prymak, *Mykhailo Hrushevsky,* p. 215.

30. See M.A. Rubach, "Burzhuazno-kurkul's'ka natsionalistichna ideolohiia pid mashkaroiu demokratiï 'trudovoho narodu' (Sotsiial'no-politychni pohliady M.S. Hrushevs'koho," *Chervonyi shliakh,* 1932, nos. 5–6, pp. 115–35; 1932, nos. 7–8, pp. 118–26; 1932, nos. 11–12, pp. 127–36. Rubach later wrote the entry on Hrushevsky in the Soviet historical encyclopedia: M.A. Rubach, "Grushevskii, Mikhail Sergeevich," *Sovetskaia istoricheskaia entsiklopediia* 4 (Moscow, 1963): 857–59.

31. L. Okinshevych, "Natsional-demokratychna kontseptsiia istoriï Ukraïny v pratsiakh akad. Hrushevs'koho," *Ukraïna,* 1932, nos. 1–2 (January–June), pp. 93–109.

32. "Nécrologie," *Revue des études slaves* 15 (1935): 185–87.

33. Otto Hoetzsch, "Michael Hruševśkyj," *Zeitschrift für Osteuropäische Geschichte* 9 (n.s. 5) (1935; reprint, 1966): 160–64.

34. Hans Koch, "Dem Andenken Mychajlo Hruševśkyj's (29. September 1866–25. November 1934)," *Jahrbücher für Kultur und Geschichte der Slaven,* n.s. 11 (1935): 3–10.

35. George Vernadsky, preface to Michael Hrushevsky, *A History of Ukraine,* ed. O.J. Frederiksen (New Haven, n.d.), pp. v–vi.

36. See Miron Korduba, "Michael Hruševśkyj als Forscher und als Organisator der wissenschaftlichen Arbeit," *Zeitschrift für Osteuropäische Geschichte* 9 (n.s. 5) (1935; reprint, 1966): 164–73; and Ivan Kryp''iakevych, *Mykhailo Hrushevs'kyi: Zhyttia i diial'nist'* (Lviv, 1935), reprinted in *Velykyi ukraïnets'. Materialy z zhyttia ta diial'nosti M.S. Hrushevs'koho* (Kyiv, 1992), pp. 448–83.

37. B. Krupnyts'kyi, "M. Hrushevs'kyi i ioho istorychna pratsia," in *Istoriia Ukraïny-Rusy,* vol. 1 (New York, 1954), pp. i–xxx.

38. F.P. Shevchenko, "Chomu Mykhailo Hrushevs'kyi povernuvsia na radians'ku Ukraïnu?" *Ukraïns'kyi istorychnyi zhurnal,* 1966, no. 2, pp. 13–30.

39. Establishment historians such as V. Sarbei and R. Symonenko opposed "rehabilitation." See Bohdan W. Klid, "The Struggle over Mykhailo Hrushevs'kyi: Recent Soviet Polemics," *Canadian Slavonic Papers* 33, no. 1 (March 1991): 32–45.

40. *Vitchyzna,* 1989, nos. 1–12, and 1990, nos. 1–8; *Kyïv,* 1989, no. 12, and 1990, nos. 1–10.

41. The reprint is also important for the process of integrating Hrushevsky's legacy into post-Soviet Ukrainian historiography. See the introduction by V.A. Smolii and P.S. Sokhan', "Vydatnyi istoryk Ukraïny," pp. viii–xxxix.

42. Fedir Shevchenko, who had attempted to secure Hrushevsky's rehabilitation in the 1960s, wrote the afterword (pp. 486–89).

43. For a discussion asserting that the populist label is an oversimplification, see Liubomyr Vynar (Wynar), "Mykhailo Hrushevs'kyi i derzhavnyts'kyi napriam v ukraïns'kii istoriohrafiï," in his *Naivydatnishyi istoryk,* pp. 33–54.

17

Volodymyr Antonovych

Ukrainian Populist Historiography and the Cultural Politics of Nation Building

Bohdan Klid

Volodymyr Antonovych made fundamental contributions to the development of Ukrainian scholarship in the second half of the nineteenth century. As a historian, he wrote pioneering works on the social history of Right-Bank Ukraine and on Lithuanian Rus'. He was, as well, a founder of archeology in Ukraine. As professor of Russian history at St. Vladimir University in Kyiv, he was a mentor for a generation of historians and founded a historical school. Antonovych was also instrumental in the establishment of Ukrainian scholarly publications and institutions. In civic and public life, Antonovych was an acknowledged leader of the populist Ukrainophile intelligentsia in Russia, and his impact on the cultural politics of this group was often decisive.[1]

One could not, however, have easily predicted such a remarkable destiny for Antonovych, for his cultural and social backgrounds were rooted in the *szlachta* (Polish gentry) of Right-Bank Ukraine.[2] It was only following a dramatic intellectual odyssey in search of an identity and commitment to a cause during his years as an adolescent and young man that Antonovych rejected his Polish nationality and social class.

According to official records, Volodymyr Antonovych was born on January 6, 1834, in Makhnivka, county of Berdychiv, Kyiv gubernia.[3] His mother, Monika Górska, was married to Bonifacy Antonowicz. Both were of landless *szlachta* (gentry) background. However, Monika had not lived with her husband for some time when she met Volodymyr's biological father, Janos Dzhidai, the son of a Hungarian revolutionary.[4]

Monika, who was responsible for Antonovych's early education, strived to bring him up as a Polish patriot and gentleman. Dzhidai, who lived in Odesa, took over responsibility for Volodymyr's upbringing in 1844. In Odesa, in addition to receiving a solid secondary-school education, Antonovych did much independent reading, often under the direction of his father, who was a freethinker and democrat. His readings included the works of the eighteenth-century French encyclopedists and philosophers, "under the influence of whom," Antonovych later wrote, "my views were formed."[5]

In 1850, Antonovych moved to Kyiv, where he enrolled in St. Vladimir University Faculty of Medicine. After completing his medical studies, and following his mother's death in 1855, he again enrolled at the university, this time in the Historical–Philological Faculty, from which he graduated in 1860.

While it can be said that Antonovych left Odesa a convinced democrat, his search for an identity, a profession, and a cause to which he could devote his life was completed while at the university. It was during these years that he read what was available in Ukrainian historiography and learned about the Cyrillo-Methodian Society, a secret organization of young Ukrainian intellectuals centered in Kyiv in 1845–47, who advocated the peasantry's liberation from serfdom, popular education, and a democratic union of Slavic states, in which Ukraine would be an autonomous polity.[6]

Antonovych's study of history coincided with the political thaw and initiation of reforms of Alexander II. By the late 1850s, Polish students at Kyiv University had become politically active. Antonovych was widely known at this time as leader of a Polish Ukrainophile student group known as *khlopomany* (peasant lovers).[7]

Antonovych's search for identity also led him to ethnographic fieldwork. Toward the end of the 1850s and in 1860, he and other *khlopomany* spent their summers traveling about the Ukrainian countryside dressed in peasant garb. It was during these "going to the people" excursions that Antonovych became a Ukrainian populist.[8]

The *khlopomany* were radicals within the Polish student body at Kyiv University because their Ukrainophilism was linked to the defense of the peasantry's social interests. This social Ukrainophilism put them on a collision course with the Polish *szlachta,* who had great influence in society and on the local and gubernia administrations. It was not until preparations for the 1866

Polish insurrection had begun in earnest, however, that Antonovych had to face the question of choosing between two causes and identities.

The crisis came in the fall of 1860, when it became clear that the majority of Polish students would support the resurrection of historical Poland—to include the three Right-Bank gubernias of Volhynia, Podillia, and Kyiv—as well as mute their criticisms of the *szlachta* in the interests of national solidarity. Antonovych and his closest followers decided then to break with the Poles and form their own Ukrainian group.[9]

This split coincided with the activation of Ukrainian students at Kyiv University, which was in great part stimulated by and was a reaction to the activities and politics of the Polish students. Claims by Polish students to Right-Bank Ukraine aroused national passions and led to fierce arguments between Ukrainian and Polish students. By the fall of 1861, Ukrainian student groups from Left-Bank Ukraine, who had been involved in promoting popular education as teachers in Sunday schools, merged with Antonovych's *khlopomany* to form a semiclandestine organization—the Kyiv *Hromada* (Commune).[10] Antonovych became a leading member of the Kyiv *Hromada,* which soon became the organizational and intellectual nucleus of the Ukrainian national movement in Russian-ruled Ukraine. He remained active in the politics of the Ukrainian intelligentsia until late in life.

Antonovych formalized his break with Polish society in a polemical article, "My Confession," which was published in January 1862 in the Ukrainophile journal *Osnova.*[11] Written in response to being labeled a turncoat for betraying the Polish cause in Ukraine, Antonovych not only gave his reasons for defecting, but also expounded on his views on nationality, politics, history, society, and culture. The ideas expressed in the article were accepted by his Ukrainophile contemporaries as a political and cultural credo.

In his essay, Antonovych accused the Poles of aiming to destroy the Ukrainian nation through forced assimilation and of defending the social and economic domination of the *szlachta,* who were unwilling to treat the peasants as humans. He wrote that Poles in Ukraine had but two choices: "Either one was to love the people among whom one lived, become imbued with its interests, . . . compensate the people for the evil done to it," or leave Ukraine for lands inhabited by ethnic Poles to avoid being labelled "a colonist and a planter." Because he had chosen to stay in Ukraine and work for the benefit of its people, he concluded: "I am a turncoat and proud of it, just as I would be proud in America if I had turned from a planter into an abolitionist, or in Italy, if I had become enlightened and from a papist had become an honest and hardworking servant of the national cause."[12]

Antonovych clearly saw his role, then, as a proponent of the national and social liberation of the Ukrainian people, a process he placed within a

European and North American historical context. Similar anticolonial views, as they related to Polish rule in Ukraine, are abundantly found in Antonovych's historiography.

Volodymyr Antonovych's early historical writings were associated with his work in the Kyiv Archeographic Commission, which was established in 1843 in part for political purposes: to collect and publish documents that would show that the Right-Bank lands were not Polish but Russian. Despite this overtly political mandate, the commission became an important institution of Ukrainian scholarship.[13]

Mykola Ivanyshev, a jurist, historian, and chief editor of the Commission, was instrumental in establishing its credentials as a scholarly institution. In the late 1850s, he began publishing the first volumes of *Arkhiv Iugo-Zapadnoi Rossii* (*AIuZR*). These collections of thematically organized documents, prefaced by monograph-length introductions, were taken, for the most part, from Right-Bank Ukraine's municipal and court record books (*aktovi knyhy*) of the fifteenth to eighteenth centuries.[14]

Antonovych was Ivanyshev's student, and he began working in the Central Archive of Old Acts at Kyiv University in the late 1850s, where the *aktovi knyhy* were kept.[15] Ivanyshev was also instrumental in hiring Antonovych in 1862 as editor of the third series of *AIuZR* on the history of the Ukrainian Cossacks.[16] Following Ivanyshev's resignation as chief editor in 1863, Antonovych was chosen in his place and served in this position to 1880.[17] Ivanyshev's influence on Antonovych was especially evident in the direction of his research and the sources with which he worked. He also influenced Antonovych's views on the peasant communes' traditions of self-government.[18]

The other historian who had a great influence on Antonovych's historiography was Mykola Kostomarov. Kostomarov's sympathetic treatment of the common people and critical approach to rulers, leaders, the traditional upper classes, and states must have confirmed Antonovych's own populist views. Importantly, Kostomarov, in his writings, tied the medieval town assemblies of Rus' (*viche*) to the ideals of democracy and self-government, treated Rus' as a federation, wrote that Ukrainian Cossacks were the continuators of the Kyivan Rus' heritage, and indicated that there was continuity in the national ideals and sociopolitical organizations of Ukrainians from medieval Rus' to the Cossack period.[19] In his writings, Antonovych continued to build on these ideas but went beyond Kostomarov's romanticism towards positivism, which was characterized by a more critical approach to the use of documents and a focus on internal, social history.

During Antonovych's tenure as chief editor of the Kyiv Archeographic

Commission, twelve volumes of *AIuZR* were published, seven of which he compiled and edited himself.[20] Antonovych also compiled and published important documents outside of the *AIuZR* series.[21] In addition, he wrote articles and reviews, many of them commentaries to documents, most of which appeared in the journal *Kievskaia starina.*

While working on the commission, Antonovych also prepared to enter the teaching faculty at St. Vladimir's University. In 1870, he was appointed lecturer of Russian history at the university and in 1878, professor.[22] He continued teaching until 1901.

At the university, Antonovych taught courses in medieval and early modern Russian history, some of which were treated as surveys of Ukrainian history. He also introduced specialized courses on sources in Ukrainian history.[23] Antonovych also headed and organized collections of the university's archeological and numismatic museums.[24]

Antonovych's greatest legacy as a professor was that he was a mentor to a group of historians who made valuable contributions in Ukrainian and Belarusian historiography. Antonovych encouraged his students to write regional histories, which, taken together, created the basis for a synthesis of medieval Ukrainian history.[25] It was not fortuitous that his best student, Mykhailo Hrushevs'kyi, wrote the first scholarly synthesis of medieval and early modern Ukrainian history, the ten-volume *Istoriia Ukrainy-Rusy.*[26]

Antonovych also wrote popular history. In 1883, he co-authored a collection of biographical sketches of historical figures of Ukraine.[27] In 1897, a popular history of the Ukrainian Cossacks, based on a series of private lectures he delivered to students at his home in 1895–96, was published in Austrian-ruled Ukraine.[28] Antonovych also promoted the publication of writings on Ukrainian history in Austrian-ruled Galicia in the semipopular series *Rus'ka istorychna biblioteka.*[29]

In addition to his historical writings, Antonovych co-authored an introduction and commentaries to a collection of historical songs of the Ukrainian people, which remains an important source in Ukrainian ethnography.[30] In the 1870s, he began archeological work and wrote as well in the fields of historical geography and numismatics.[31]

Antonovych also promoted the establishment of scholarly institutions and combined these activities with the achievement of Ukrainophile goals. In 1873, the Kyiv *Hromada* succeeded in chartering the Southwestern Section of the Russian Geographical Society, which, during its brief period of existence to 1876, did much to promote Ukrainian scholarship.[32] In 1882, Antonovych was instrumental in establishing the outstanding journal of Ukrainian studies, *Kievskaia starina.*

Tsarist suppression of Ukrainophile activities, however—the first time in

1863, and the second in 1876—made it virtually impossible to build scholarly institutions in Russian Ukraine that would promote Ukrainian studies.
To circumvent this, Antonovych and other *Hromada* members, beginning in
the 1870s, began to establish close ties to and aid their compatriots in
Austrian-ruled Galicia to build Ukrainian institutions there. In the late
1880s, Antonovych was instrumental in negotiating cultural concessions for
Ukrainians from Polish ruling circles in Galicia.[33] Among the concessions
was an agreement to establish a chair of East European (de facto Ukrainian)
history at L'viv University, which was filled by Hrushevs'kyi in 1894. He
was also involved in reform of the Galician-based Shevchenko Scientific
Society in 1892, turning that institution into an unofficial Ukrainian academy of sciences.

Antonovych's Philosophy of History

While his scholarly work became more focused on politically neutral topics
in archeology and numismatics toward the end of his career, Antonovych
never lost interest in contemporary affairs and could never be labeled a
detached scholar. His engagement was reflected not only in Ukrainophile
activities but also in his historical writings.

In his inaugural lecture as professor of Russian history in 1878, Antonovych tried to square the circle between engagement and objectivity in
historiography. The historian, he wrote, should strive for objectivity, maintaining a critical view of the past based on a thorough study of facts.
Although objectivity was most difficult to achieve when writing on one's
own nation, even strong patriotic feelings could be reconciled with objectivity, Antonovych continued, as long as these were based on conscious convictions. "I am convinced," he wrote, "that, remaining objective, rejecting a
priori conceptions and passions, the historian not only does not repudiate
his rights to his personal convictions and sympathies, but, on the contrary,
forges and fixes them on a solid factual background by way of strict scholarly analysis."[34]

Antonovych linked the study of the past with patriotic civic activity in
the present: "Each educated representative of the Russian nation in the
southern Russian lands [Ukraine] will for a long time to come continue—
through peaceful, civic activities—that struggle which his forefathers began
with arms in their hands. This last episode of the people's struggle will end
that much sooner and will be that much more successful the more each
Russian citizen of that land will be filled with the conviction of the righ-
teousness of his nation's cause, based on a conscientious study of the historical fate of his people."[35]

For Antonovych, then, the study and writing of history were inseparably linked to one's convictions and served as a guide to civic action. According to Hrushevs'kyi, Antonovych's scholarly interests were not easily separable from his social and political interests. Impulses for scholarly work came largely from them, and in return, his scholarly work confirmed those views he held on contemporary affairs.[36]

In his writings on Ukraine, Antonovych interpreted events and the actions of individuals and social groups in the context of his views on universal history, which he viewed in quasi-Hegelian terms as the development of certain principles or leading ideas, including their interrelations and struggles with one another. He believed that each nation was guided in its actions through history by its own leading idea. Following the appearance of this idea on the historical stage, it was subjected to various influences; at times it was thwarted, at others it developed rapidly and flowered. The coming to fruition of this idea was the historical process itself, which was also related to achieving consciousness.

Antonovych maintained that the carriers of leading ideas were social groups, not individuals. This was why social history—to Antonovych the study of social groups and their interrelations—was so important. Antonovych believed that the social life of a nation was dependent on the leading idea, but also on the consciousness of the people, their cultural level and education. Only after the people had reached a high level of culture, including a well-developed system of popular education, could the leading idea be realized. Attempts to implement the idea prior to this would inevitably end in failure.[37]

Antonovych's Interpretations of Ukraine's Past

In his writings on Ukraine, Antonovych based his conclusions on the thesis that the communal principle was the dominant or leading idea in its history. According to Antonovych, the communal principle in Ukraine was based on the ideas of participatory democracy and equality of social status. Throughout their history, Ukrainians were never able to fully realize their ideal, but always, even if instinctively, moved toward it.[38]

In his writings, Antonovych tried to identify this idea as it manifested itself in history. In the Kyivan Rus' era, the communal principle was manifested in the *viche,* in religious life by the election of church officials, and in the village communes by people's assemblies or courts (*kopni sudy*). The communal idea, Antonovych concluded, was most vividly expressed in the Cossack period. The Ukrainian nation saw the fulfilment of their ideals in Cossackdom, especially in the Zaporozhian Sich, where communal traditions were most closely kept and where the people believed that the ideal social and political order existed. People there could put into practice "their ancient *viche* instincts: here all were free, equal in rights, [and] here there were no estates other than the Cossack [estate]. All positions, both secular and religious, were held by elected people, and all matters were decided by the will of the assembly—the Cossack *rada* or the village commune."[39]

According to Antonovych, there were three forces within medieval Rus´ that struggled among themselves to assert preeminence: the commune, the prince's retinue (*druzhyna*), and the prince himself. The prince's retinue was a force diametrically opposed to the commune, and it represented the power of the individual and his striving to rise above others. The struggle between these two groups and principles, in their various forms, constituted, according to Antonovych, the main theme of Ukraine's history.[40]

According to Antonovych, the Mongol conquest froze Ukraine's social development but did not destroy communal ways of life. Wealthier aristocrats fled central Ukrainian lands to the north and west, and Ukraine's "center of life" was transferred to Galicia and Volhynia. With some exceptions, only the communal settlements remained in the central regions. While they paid a tribute to the Mongols, the communes, Antonovych concluded, still retained their rights of self-government.[41]

Antonovych was a pioneer in the study of Lithuanian rule, which he viewed as benevolent towards Ukrainian communal life. Resistance to the Lithuanian takeover of Ukraine in the fourteenth century, he noted, came only from the princes and aristocrats; the communes were either indifferent or welcomed Lithuanian rule.[42]

Antonovych wrote approvingly that the Lithuanian state at first fell under Rus´ influence. Although Lithuania had adopted a feudal military–political structure to fight off German crusaders, Antonovych noted that Old Rus´ traditions of equality were still dominant. This ideal fit in well in the new order, which allowed for social mobility, rewarding gifted individuals and state service. Communes continued to govern themselves through their assemblies, and towns retained rights of self-government until the Magdeburg laws were adopted. In the villages, communes governed themselves and were able to retain land ownership, which rights were sanctioned by law. The principle of self-government continued to exist within religious institutions as well, where the hierarchy was chosen at assemblies (*sobory*).[43]

Although he treated Lithuanian rule sympathetically, Antonovych noted that the state was based on a military–feudal principle, which came into conflict with the old communal order, largely over landownership.[44] Conflicts grew more acute following Lithuania's union with Poland. Antonovych concluded that Prince Jogaila's (Jagieło's) acceptance of the Polish crown and his attempts to introduce the Polish political, religious, and social order into Lithuanian Rus´ contradicted normal development and forced the Ukrainian people to waste its energies defending its "national spirit."[45]

In his analyses of Lithuania and Poland, Antonovych distinguished sharply between the two. The Polish knights evolved out of the old Slavic commune, and therefore accepted the idea of the equality of its members, but combined this with the Germanic feudal–aristocratic idea in its relations to the nonmilitary estates, which Polish historians labelled *szlachta* democracy.[46] The Polish political and social order in the mid-sixteenth century, he concluded, was characterized by the equality of members of the *szlachta,* their control over the monarchy and unconditional powers over the peasantry.[47] The dominant principle behind the organization of the Lithuanian state was German feudalism. A noble estate was formed, but distinctions between the lower orders of the nobility and the rest of society were not rigidly cast.[48]

Antonovych stressed that there was a great difference in the position of the peasantry in the two states. In Poland the peasantry had been enserfed, whereas in Lithuania, peasants remained, by and large, owners of land and free into the sixteenth century. These differences constituted one of the major distinctions between the two states prior to the 1569 Union of Lublin. With its promulgation, the peasantry, unable to fight enserfment on the political level, fled to open steppe lands.[49]

Under Lithuanian rule, because of the constant dangers from Tatar raids, members of communes took up arms and became skillful warriors. Lithuanian princes made arrangements for tribute and military services from the communes; in return, communes received lands and rights of self-government. Peasants fleeing from Polish landowners strengthened the communes. These free, partially militarized communes, Antonovych concluded, were the first Ukrainian Cossack communities. They eventually received broad powers of self-government, including the right to elect their own officers.[50]

Whereas Antonovych speculated that the Lithuanian and Ukrainian principles could have become reconciled with one another, this certainly was not possible between the Polish and Ukrainian leading ideas. Following the Union of Lublin, which led to the incorporation of Lithuanian–Ukrainian lands into Poland and the introduction of Polish law, Ukrainian social structures were threatened. The Cossack estate was not recognized in Poland, which forced the Cossacks into opposition. Noblemen began to enserf peasants, which led to their fleeing to the steppes. Communes also lost the right of self-government when their members became enserfed. Tensions increased when the Polish crown gave lands to the *szlachta* in Ukraine that were already settled by Cossacks and free peasants.[51]

Following the Union of Brest of 1596, a religious dimension was added to the struggle between the Cossack and *szlachta* estates. The Ukrainian people, Antonovych concluded, opposed the union because it changed the church from one controlled by the community to one that was autocratic.[52]

In its essence, Antonovych viewed the struggle between the Ukrainian Cossacks and the Polish *szlachta* as one between the democratic–communal and aristocratic–individualistic principles. Early Cossack risings of the late sixteenth and early seventeenth centuries were unsuccessful because they were fought for Cossack rights only. Hetman Bohdan Khmel'nyts'kyi's revolt succeeded because he called the enserfed peasants to arms, promised them Cossack status, and agreed to chase the *szlachta* out of Ukraine.[53]

Antonovych explained the inability of Ukrainians to realize their communal ideals following Khmel'nyts'kyi's victories over the Poles largely by cultural factors. One could not blame Khmel'nyts'kyi, Antonovych wrote, for not being able to establish institutions and laws in line with the people's communal aspirations. Khmel'nyts'kyi, he concluded, was a man of his time and a product of the low cultural level of the people. The people followed him and rose to drive out the hated *szlachta*, but were not ready for political life, and did not as yet understand what could be built in place of the old system. They were, therefore, not able to gain their rights or implement their ideals.[54] Antonovych continued that one could understand, therefore, why at critical moments Khmel'nyts'kyi was indecisive, and why he failed to establish an independent state.[55]

True to his populist convictions, Antonovych was critical of the hetman on one crucial point: his treatment of the peasantry and rank-and-file Cossacks. When the revolt began, the peasantry soon swelled the ranks of the Cossacks. Antonovych wrote that Khmel'nyts'kyi instituted "an outright injustice" in ordering these new Cossacks to return to their previous dependent status following the uprising.[56]

This criticism raises the question of Antonovych's overall treatment of the Cossacks. While he idealized the Cossacks, Antonovych also recognized that they constituted a separate estate, some of whose members, especially the officers, promoted their own narrow, estate-based interests, opposing those of the commoners.

In Antonovych's view, the estate interests of the Cossack officers were assimilated from the *szlachta*. While the officers fought with the commoners against the *szlachta*, their aim was to become a landowning estate based on the Polish model. While the commoners rejected a society of estates, their low cultural development prevented them from formulating their goals concretely.[57]

The absence of a high level of culture, Antonovych postulated, was the underlying reason why the "individual egoism" of estate interests held sway over the communal cause among the Cossacks. He noted the concrete manifestations of this "egoism" in the attempts of Cossack officers to obtain *szlachta* privileges, in the actions of government administrators to seize lands for themselves, and in the attempts to force ordinary Cossacks into the commoner's estate in order to enserf them.[58]

In comments on the aftermath of the Khmel′nyts′kyi period, known as "The Ruin," Antonovych again stressed cultural factors. Soon after Khmel′nyts′kyi′s death, two parties crystallized in Ukraine. The first wanted to build a society on the Polish model, form a privileged estate like the *szlachta* from the officers, and join a reconstituted Polish federal state. The people opposed this goal. However, the second party, based on support of the rank-and-file Cossacks, soon abandoned them and decided to emulate the first group, but with the support of the Muscovite state. Battles between the two were fought not over principles, but for or against individuals and their interests. These struggles were typical of a low level of cultural development, where "egoistic forces" held sway over the common cause. "The Ruin," Antonovych concluded, was the result of the low level of culture among the Ukrainian masses and its leaders.[59]

During "The Ruin," Cossack officers began to coalesce into a noble estate. Antonovych viewed this as a negative phenomenon, emphasizing the dishonest and rapacious nature of the process, such as when Cossack officers seized lands from ordinary Cossacks and peasants and then had these confiscations confirmed by the government. The new Cossack nobility, he concluded, neglected to defend the autonomy of the country and the democratic wishes of the people, caring only for their own personal interests.[60]

Antonovych placed great weight on the cultural factor in history to interpret events and evaluate the actions of the commoners as well as of great men in Ukrainian history. In his judgments of individuals, Antonovych always sided with those whom he felt promoted the well-being of the commoners. This is evident in his comparison of two Ukrainian leaders of the late seventeenth and early eighteenth centuries—the Cossack colonel Semen Palii and Hetman Ivan Mazepa.

Despite his characterization of Mazepa as a sincere patriot and talented politician, Antonovych's assessment of him was ambivalent. He noted that Mazepa was educated in Poland, where his social and political ideals were formed. Thus, Mazepa based his support on the Cossack officers and promoted the process of their transformation into a landowning nobility.[61]

Mazepa's policies resulted in many peasants and rank-and-file Cossacks fleeing to Right-Bank territories, where independent Cossack regiments were being established, the best-known under Colonel Palii. These regiments were, Antonovych approvingly noted, organized on democratic principles, and their leaders "had as their goal not the enrichment of themselves but the people."[62] According to Antonovych, Palii was the last Cossack leader who achieved solidarity with the people's social and political goals, and was honored by the people: whereas Palii was called "Cossack father," Mazepa was hated.[63]

Following the suppression of the Cossacks in Right-Bank Ukraine, popular armed resistance to Polish rule continued in the form of the *haidamaka* uprisings. On the one hand, Antonovych saw this as a new form of the Cossack movement. On the other hand, he recognized its negative qualities that manifested themselves in vengeful, arbitrary, violent acts. But, Antonovych concluded, one could not expect much from the masses because of their low cultural development, which was a consequence of *szlachta* policies.[64]

Although critical of the *haidamaky,* Antonovych placed the blame for the uprisings squarely on the shoulders of the *szlachta*. They were, he concluded, captives of their own narrow estate, religious, and national interests, too egoistic and shortsighted to make concessions to the people and open the door to progress in Poland. Antonovych concluded that by denying all human and civic rights to the masses, the *szlachta* brought upon themselves a great tragedy.[65]

The source of the tragedy, Antonovych insisted, was to be found in the abnormal structure of Polish society. The peasant masses were enserfed, deprived of land and all elementary rights, and exposed daily to abuses by the *szlachta*. In addition, the Polish state persecuted their religion and did not provide for any type of elementary education. The masses, then, were ready to explode at any time. This outburst, in the absence of civic development and a humane education, expressed itself in extreme cruelty and bloody acts. While the masses could be excused for this violence, Antonovych concluded, the cruel, repressive measures taken by the *szlachta* against the rebellious peasantry could not.[66]

Antonovych's scholarly writings on Ukrainian history ended with the *haidamaka* uprisings. However, in private lectures given to students at his home in 1895–96 which were later published, he commented on more recent and contemporary developments.

Antonovych stressed that the characteristic trait of eighteenth-century history was the rebirth of stateless nations. This process, Antonovych believed, took place in a way that was universally valid, the first step being the demand for cultural rights in order to protect the emerging nation's culture by law. The first nationality to begin this struggle among the Slavs were the Czechs, from whom the movement spread to other Slavs.[67]

In Ukraine, the Cyrillo-Methodians were the first to combine cultural tasks with political goals, although weakly and unclearly stated. With the introduction of a constitutional regime in Austrian Ukraine, Ukrainians there gained the opportunity to fight legally for their national rights. Antonovych predicted that the winning of national rights in Russian Ukraine would come later, but that the national movement would spread among the masses and cultural rights would be won. Self-interest, he noted, was forcing the great powers to make concessions to the emerging nationalities whenever they raised demands grounded in contemporary, universally valid, progressive principles.[68]

Antonovych's Views on the State

Antonovych's critical views of elites were carried forward in his treatment of the state. He was especially critical of the role of the Polish state and of Polish historiography, which had failed to incorporate European progressive ideas and to be critical of its own past.[69]

Antonovych's critiques exposed the imperial ideology underlying the works of most Polish writers on Ukraine. These writers, he wrote, believed that the Polish state, supported by the *szlachta,* had a great cultural mission in Ukraine: to civilize the Rus' regions that fell within Polish borders. In a devastating indictment of this thesis, Antonovych concluded that the Polish *szlachta* "did not represent culture and order, but sooner the backwardness and the cultural aberration of Polish society itself."[70]

Hrushevs'kyi wrote that Antonovych held a negative attitude toward even the idea of the state. It was based on: historical Ukrainian opposition to domination by foreign states; assimilation of the traditional distrust of the Polish *szlachta* toward a strong state power; opposition to the authoritarian Russian state that was shared by many liberals and radicals of the Russian intelligentsia; and the ideas of the Cyrillo-Methodians and Russian Slavophiles, especially of the opposition of state and society.[71]

Hrushevs'kyi's conclusions seem one-sided. Antonovych was certainly skeptical of state power and critical of the role the state had played as an instrument of traditional elites, yet, he also expressed the desire that the state play a positive role in history.

In a critique of Polish writings on Ukraine, Antonovych wrote that the state represented one of the higher forms of public life. Contemporary European states were institutions that protected not only the material well-being of society but moral values as well, such as freedom of conscience and full intellectual development. The state, he argued, should be judged in light of the presence or lack of just and impartial relations toward its citizens, without regard to social group, nationality, or an individual's position in society.[72]

Antonovych should not be viewed, therefore, as implacably anti-statist, but rather as a severe critic of the state, which is compatible with his uncompromising views on elites. His attitude toward the state could be described as ambivalent.

In a polemical essay published posthumously in 1928, Antonovych postulated the possibility of the existence of a federal multinational state, provided that state would guarantee universal rights and defend the equality, including the national equality, of its citizens. A federal state, he noted, would be weak if the dominant nationality took on the role of conqueror and proprietor towards others, and tried to realize the utopian goal of forcibly assimilating the other peoples within that state.[73]

Antonovych's attitude toward the formation of an independent Ukrainian state was also ambivalent. Hrushevs'kyi wrote that Antonovych, having negative views on the state, found it easier to accept the statelessness of the Ukrainian nation in the past as well as in the present as a positive trait. Ukrainians were, in his view, not interested in forming a state of their own. This anti-statist position, Hrushevs'kyi wrote, ran through all Antonovych's writings, in which he counterposed a free and vibrant society of communes to state institutions, which strangled and oppressed society.[74]

Indeed, Antonovych did not believe that the nonexistence of Ukrainian statehood in the past was important. He also did not regard the establishment of an independent state as a paramount task of the Ukrainian movement. Questions of cultural standards and of cultural tasks were of far greater importance to him.

Antonovych was consistent in applying exacting standards toward Ukraine's elites and their state-building efforts. He exhibited little sympathy for Ukraine's most talented political leaders, such as Prince Danylo of the Galician–Volhynian principality, or Hetman Mazepa, because they went against the masses.[75] Antonovych praised the Cossacks as defenders of the national rights of Ukraine as long as they also defended the principle of the equality of its members and encouraged the liberation of the peasant masses from serfdom. However, the moment that the Cossacks, especially the officers, began to build a new social order and state based on the social and economic privileges of the Cossack officers, he turned from being an apologist of the Cossacks into their critic.[76]

As an antithesis to the idea of the state, Antonovych proposed the idea of the *hromada* and the ideals for which it stood in Ukrainian history. For Antonovych and other Ukrainian populists, the ideas of wide-ranging democracy and social equality of the historical Ukrainian communes served as a source of inspiration and guide for their activities as leaders of and participants in the Ukrainian national movement.[77]

Conclusions

In his writings, Antonovych expressed views that were clearly anti-imperial and anticolonial. Yet, he was able to work professionally in imperial Russia's scholarly and quasi-scholarly government institutions and used them to promote and build Ukrainian scholarship. Antonovych's scholarly work and activities were tied especially closely to two imperial institutions: St. Vladimir University and the Kyiv Archeographic Commission. His relationship with Russian authorities and the Russian state, however, was never more than a marriage of convenience for him and was never free from tension. The authorities distrusted him as a known Ukrainophile, and there were occasions when he was nearly relieved of his duties as professor or exiled.[78]

One must agree with Hrushevs'kyi's assessment that the inspiration and source of Antonovych's scholarly work lay in his sincere love of the Ukrainian people, with whose revolutionary, albeit still instinctive and elemental uprisings against feudalism and privilege he sympathized. He idealized what he saw as their high cultural and social instincts and their struggle for the establishment of a just society. He was so captivated by these enviable characteristics that he was ready to forgive this nation its less admirable characteristics, both in the present and in the past, which he saw as caused by their low level of consciousness, culture, and education. All the defeats suffered by the Ukrainian people he also attributed to their lack of cultural and political education.[79]

Antonovych can be classified as a Ukrainian populist historian in a broader East European populist school of historiography: in Polish historiography it was represented by Joachim Lelewel; in Russian historiography by Afanasii Shchapov and Vasilii Semevskii; in Ukrainian historiography by his predecessor and older contemporary Mykola Kostomarov, as well as by his contemporary Oleksander Lazarevs'kyi.[80]

In Ukrainian historiography Antonovych can be seen as a transitional figure. The ideas of romantic populism clearly influenced his writings, but so did the writings of the French rationalists and encyclopedists, and he was also strongly influenced by positivism.[81] Both Antonovych and Lazarevs'kyi represented a new generation of historians, reared on rationalism and positivism, who used statistics, paid attention to economic developments, and based their work on strict documentation.[82]

Within the framework of Russian historiography, Antonovych was a regional historian. However, in Ukrainian historiography he is known as the creator of a national-democratic conception of Ukrainian history. In Antonovych's philosophy of history, the historical process was a struggle between ideas, in which nations, largely through social groups, were the carriers of these ideas. In many of his works, Antonovych tried to show that the Ukrainian people had their own national ideal for which they fought throughout their history.[83] The Ukrainian historical process, therefore, was an organic one of centuries-long duration, centered around a leading idea.[84]

As a leader of the Ukrainian populist intelligentsia, Antonovych saw that his primary task and that of his contemporaries in the Kyiv *Hromada* was to continue and participate in the movement to realize these ideals. This involved, first and foremost, the achievement of cultural goals, which explains why *hromada* members focused largely on cultural work. In the early 1860s, they participated in activities linked to popular education, such as teaching in Sunday schools or preparing popular educational materials. When tsarist authorities banned the use of Ukrainian in popular education and took repressive measures against the *hromady,* the members continued their cultural work in scholarship, in teaching, in literature and in other ways, such as work in the *zemstva*. In the evenings, *hromada* members, often at Antonovych's home, worked with students on the compilation of a Ukrainian dictionary and a historico-geographic dictionary.

The achievement of cultural goals, then, was the foundation that was needed for Ukrainians to be able to realize their cherished communal ideals. Statehood, in and of itself, Antonovych believed, was not a goal that Ukrainians should strive for as important. These policies, and their underlying ideology, were later labeled as apolitical Ukrainophilism by younger generations of Ukrainian activists and intellectuals.

Yet Antonovych's cultural work as well as that of his compatriots had political consequences and did lay the groundwork for Ukrainian statehood. The Ukrainian national movement, which Antonovych had tried to keep focused on cultural work, was becoming a mass movement by the early twentieth century, complete with political parties, which advocated autonomy and even independence for Ukraine. Following the 1905 revolution and shortly before his death in 1908, Antonovych became convinced that the time had come to support the political struggle.[85] Fittingly, when the Russian Empire began to collapse in 1917, it was his best student and Ukraine's foremost historian, Mykhailo Hrushevs'kyi, who emerged to lead Ukraine to autonomy and then independence.

Notes

1. The best study on Antonovych is still D. Doroshenko, *Volodymyr Antonovych: Ioho zhyttia i naukova ta hromads'ka diial'nist'* (Prague: Vydavnytstvo Iuriia Tyshchenka, 1942). See also V. Ulianovs'kyi, "Syn Ukrainy (Volodymyr Antonovych: hromadianyn, uchenyi, liudyna)," in V.B. Antonovych, *Moia spovid': Vybrani istorychni ta publitsystychni tvory* (Kyiv: Lybid', 1995), pp. 5–76. For a Polish conser-

vative view, see Fr. Rawita-Gawroński, *Włodzimierz Antonowicz: Zarys jego działności społeczno-politycznej i historycznej* (Lviv: Gebethner i Ska w Krakowie, 1912).

2. See the two studies on the Polish nobility in Right-Bank Ukraine by Daniel Beauvois: *Le Noble, le serf, et le révizor: La noblesse polonaise entre le tsarisme et les masses ukrainiennes (1831–1863)* (Paris: Éditions des Archives Contemporaines, 1985); and *La bataille de la terre en Ukraine 1863–1914: Les Polonais et les conflits socio-ethniques* (Lille: Presses Universitaires de Lille, 1993).

3. One of Antonovych's students, Vasyl' Liaskorons'kyi, wrote that Antonovych was actually born in Chornobyl' in 1830. See his "V.B. Antonovich (Nekrolog)," *Zhurnal ministerstva narodnogo prosveshcheniia,* 1908, New Series, Part 15, pp. 51–52, note 1.

4. V. Antonovych, "Memuary," in his *Tvory,* vol. 1 (only volume published) (Kyiv: Vseukrains'ka Akademiia Nauk, 1932), p. 10.

5. Ibid., p. 40.

6. Ibid., pp. 60–61. On the Cyrillo-Methodian Society, see George S.N. Luckyj, *Young Ukraine: The Brotherhood of St. Cyril and Methodius, 1845–1847* (Ottawa: University of Ottawa Press, 1991).

7. On the activities of Polish students at the University of St. Volodymyr in the second half of the 1850s, and especially on the *khlopomany,* see chapter 2 of my Ph.D. dissertation, *Volodymyr Antonovych: The Making of a Ukrainian Populist Activist and Historian* (University of Alberta, 1992), pp. 45–66.

8. Antonovych described his newly found appreciation of the virtues of the peasantry as follows: "The people appeared before us not as described by the *szlachta,* but as they really were. We noticed their very strong natural logic and highly developed popular ethics, which manifested itself in their willingness to help and in a friendly attitude to all who were in need." Antonovych, "Memuary," pp. 45–46.

9. See B. Poznanskii, "Vospominaniia," *Ukrainskaia zhizn',* 1913, no. 3, pp. 20–21.

10. On the events leading up to the formation of the Kyiv *Hromada,* see chapter 4 of my Ph.D. dissertation, *Volodymyr Antonovych,* pp. 119–75.

11. "Moia ispoved' " was reprinted in Antonovych, *Tvory,* pp. 100–15.

12. Ibid., pp. 113–14.

13. On the commission, officially called *Vremennaia Komissiia dlia razbora drevnikh aktov pri Kievskom, Volynskom i Podol'skom General Gubernatore,* see O.I. Zhurba, *Kyivs'ka arkheohrafichna komisiia 1843–1921* (Kyiv: Naukova dumka, 1993).

14. On Ivanyshev, see A.V. Romanovich-Slavatinskii, *Zhizn' i deiatel'nost' N.D. Ivanisheva* (St. Petersburg, 1876). Ivanyshev's greatest legacies to Ukrainian historiography were that he organized the gathering and preservation of *aktovi knyhy* as well as devised the publications plan for *AIuZR,* based largely on these documents.

15. See I. Kamanin, "Trudy V.B. Antonovicha po istorii Kozachestva," *Chteniia v Istoricheskom Obshchestve Nestora-letopistsa,* 1909, book 21, section 1, no. 1–2, p. 44.

16. See M. Tkachenko, "Arkheohrafichni studii Volodymyra Antonovycha," *Ukrains'kyi arkheohrafichnyi zbirnyk,* 1930, vol. 3, p. 332.

17. Antonovych was relieved of his position in 1882 for Ukrainophile activities. See the September 16, 1882, memorandum of M.V. Iuzefovych to Governor-General Drentel'n in Zhurba, *Kyivs'ka arkheohrafichna komisiia,* pp. 153–54.

18. See N.D. Ivanishev, "O drevnikh sel'skikh obshchinakh v iugozapadnoi Rossii, *Russkaia beseda,* 1857, vol. 3, book 7, section 2, pp. 1–57. Antonovych was also influenced by the Polish historian Joachim Lelewel, who wrote much on the Slavic commune. See M. Hrushevs'kyi, "Z sotsiial'no-natsional'nykh kontseptsii Antonovycha," *Ukraina,* 1928, book 5, pp. 9, 12, note 1.

19. On Kostomarov, see Thomas M. Prymak, *Mykola Kostomarov: A Biography* (Toronto: University of Toronto Press, 1996).

20. These volumes were: *Akty ob unii i sostoianii pravoslavnoi tserkvi v Iugo-Zapadnoi Rossii vo 2-oi polovine XVII iv XVIII st. (1648–1798)* (Kyiv, 1871); *Akty o kazakakh, 1500–1648 gg.* (Kyiv, 1863); *Akty o kazakakh, 1679–1716* (Kyiv, 1868); *Akty o gaidamakakh (1700–1768)* (Kyiv, 1876); *Akty o proiskhozhdenii shliakhetskikh rodov v Iugo-Zapadnoi Rossii (1442–1760 gg.)* (Kyiv, 1867); *Akty otnosiashchiesia k istorii gorodov i mestechek v Iugo-Zapadnoi Rossii (1432–1798 gg.)* (Kyiv, 1869); *Akty o krestianakh v XVIII st. (1700–1799)* (Kyiv, 1870).

Following his dismissal as chief editor, Antonovych completed two more volumes: *Akty o zaselenii Iugo-Zapadnoi Rossii (1386–1700 gg.)* (Kyiv, 1886), Introduction by M.F. Vladimirskii-Budanov; *Akty o mnimom krest'ianskom vosstanii v Iugo-Zapadnom kraie v 1789 g.* (Kyiv, 1902).

21. Some of the more important are: volume IV of *Letopisi Samuila Velichka* (Kyiv, 1864); *Gramoty velikikh kniazei Litovskikh s 1390 po 1569 god* (Kyiv, 1868) (co-compiled and edited); *Sbornik materialov dlia istoricheskoi topografii Kieva i ego okresnostei* (Kyiv, 1874) (Sections I and III); *Sbornik letopisei, otnosiashchikhsia k istorii iu.-z. Rossii* (Kyiv, 1888); *Memuary, otnosiashchiesia k istorii Iuzhnoi Rusi* (Kyiv, 1896).

22. These appointments followed the successful defense of his M.A. thesis, "Posledniia vremena kazachestva na pravoi storone Dnepra po aktam c 1679 po 1716 god," and Ph.D. dissertation, "Ocherk istorii Velikogo kniazhestva Litovskogo do smerti Ol'gerda." See Ulianovs'kyi, "Syn Ukrainy," pp. 26–27.

23. Some of these courses appeared as lithographic editions of student notes: *Istoriia Litovskoi Rusi* (1877 and 1882); *Istoriia Galitskoi Rusi* (1879); *Istochniki dlia istorii Iugo-Zapadnoi Rossii* (1884).

24. See V. Danylevych, "Prof. V.B. Antonovych ta Arkheolohichnyi Muzei I. N. O.," *Zapysky Kyivs'koho Instytutu Narodn'oi Osvity,* 1928, book 3, pp. 7–20, and Fedir Sliusarenko, "Numizmatychna pratsia prof. V.B. Antonovycha," *Pratsi Ukrains'koho Istorychno-Filologichnoho Tovarystva v Prazi,* vol. I, 1939, p. 190.

25. The regional histories written under Antonovych's direction by his students resulted in a series of monographs on Ukrainian and Belarusian lands of the Kyivan and Lithuanian Rus' periods. These include works by: O. Andriiashev (Volhynian lands); D. Bahalii (Siverian lands); V. Danylevych (Pins'k lands); M. Dashkevych (lands ruled by the Bolokhovian princes); M. Dovnar-Zapol'skyi (Krivechian and Dregovichian lands); P. Holubovs'kyi (Siverian lands), M. Hrushevs'kyi (Kyiv lands); O. Hrushevs'kyi (Turov-Pins'k lands); V. Liaskorons'kyi (Pereiaslav lands); I. Lynnychenko (Galician lands); N. Molchanovs'kyi (Podillian lands).

26. On Hrushevs'kyi, see Thomas M. Prymak, *Mykhailo Hrushevsky: The Politics of National Culture* (Toronto: University of Toronto Press, 1987).

27. V.B. Antonovich and V.A. Bets, *Istoricheskie deiateli iugo-zapadnoi Rossii v biografiiakh i portretakh,* no. 1 (Kyiv, 1883). He also co-authored a series of popular lectures with P.Ia. Iarmashevskii, *Publichnye lektsii po geologii i istorii Kieva* (Kyiv, 1897).

28. *Besidy pro chasy kozats'ki na Ukraini* (Chernivtsi, 1897).

29. See Oleksander Barvins'kyi, *Spomyny z moho zhyttia,* vol. 2 (L'viv: Ia. Orenshtein, 1913), pp. 317–18.

30. *Istoricheskie pesni malorusskogo naroda s obiasneniiami V. Antonovicha i M. Dragomanova,* 2 vols. (Kyiv, 1874–75).

31. In the 1890s, he completed three important archeological studies: *Raskopki v strane drevlian* (St. Petersburg, 1893); *Arkheologicheskaia karta Kievskoi gubernii* (Moscow, 1895); and *Arkheologicheskaia karta Volynskoi gub. s kartoi, ukazatelem imen geograficheskim, predmetnym* (Moscow, 1900). For an assessment of Antonovych as archeologist, see Valeriia Kozlovs'ka, "Znachinnia prof. V.B. Antonovych v

ukrains'kii arkheolohii," *Zapysky Vseukrains'koho arkheolohichnoho komitetu,* 1931, vol. 1, pp. ix–xxi. On Antonovych's work in historical geography, see Leonyd Dobrovol'skyi, "Pratsia V.B. Antonovycha na nyvi istorychnoi heohrafii," *Zapysky istorychno-filolohichnoho viddilu Ukrains'koi akademii nauk,* 1926, book 9, pp. 185–207. On his work in numismatics, see Fedir Sliusarenko, "Numizmatychna pratsia prof. V.B. Antonovycha," *Pratsi Ukrains'koho Istorychno-Filologichnoho Tovarystva v Prazi,* 1939, vol. 2, pp. 183–91.

32. On the Kyiv branch of the Russian Geographical Society, see Fedir Savchenko, *Zaborona ukrainstva 1876 r.,* rep. ed. (Munich: Wilhelm Fink Verlag, 1970).

33. On the Polish-Ukrainian compromise, see Ihor Chornovil, "Pol'sko-ukrains'ka uhoda 1890–1894 rr.: geneza, perebih podii, naslidky" (Candidate's dissertation, Institut ukrainoznavstva im. I Kryp'iakevycha Natsional'noi akademii nauk Ukrainy, 1994).

34. "Vstupna lektsiia V. Antonovycha, vstupyvshy na kafedru rus'koi istorii," *Tsentral'na naukova biblioteka,* Fond 1, no. 7895, l. 6.

35. Ibid., ll. 9–10.

36. Mykh. Hrushevs'kyi, "Volodymyr Antonovych: Osnovni idei ioho tvorchosty i diial'nosty," in Mykhailo Hrushevs'kyi, *Volodymyr Bonifatiiovych Antonovych 1834–1908–1984* (New York: LOGOS, 1985), pp. 13–14.

37. See V. Antonovych, *Korotka istoriia kozachchyny,* 3d ed. (Winnipeg-Dauphin, Manitoba, 1971), p. 1 (reprint of *Besidy pro chasy kozats'ki na Ukraini*). See also O. Hermaize, "V.B. Antonovych v ukrains'kii istoriohrafii," *Ukraina,* 1928, book 5, pp. 20–21; and M.V. Dovnar-Zapol'skii, "Istoricheskie vzgliady V.B. Antonovicha," *Chteniia v Istoricheskom Obshchestve Nestora-letopistsa,* 1909, book 21, section 1, nos. 1–2, pp. 31–32.

38. Fascination with old Slavic communal institutions and their contemporary forms was widespread among nineteenth-century Russian and Ukrainian intellectuals. Antonovych's praise of Ukrainian communal traditions falls within this broad spectrum. However, in Antonovych's view, as well as those of other Ukrainian populists, the Ukrainian commune (*hromada*) differed substantially from the Russian commune (*obshchina* or *mir*).

The greatest difference between the two, according to Kostomarov, was that the Ukrainians owned property as individuals, whereas in Russia, the commune, not individuals, owned land. See his "Dve russkiia narodnosti," in *Sobranie sochinenii,* book 1, vol. 1, rep. ed.) (The Hague: Europe Printing, 1967), pp. 60–62. This view is also expressed in a manifesto co-authored by Antonovych and other Kyiv *Hromada* members in 1862. See "Otzyv iz Kieva," in D. Bahalii, ed., *Materiialy dlia biohrafii V.B. Antonovycha, z pryvodu dvadtsiatoi richnytsi z dnia ioho smerty* (Kyiv: Vseukrains'ka Akademiia Nauk, 1929), p. 41.

39. Antonovych, *Korotka istoriia kozachchyny,* p. 45. See also his "Proizvedeniia Shevchenka, soderzhanie kotorykh sostavliaet istoricheskie sobytiia," in *Tvory,* pp. 155–56.

40. V. Antonovich, "Soderzhanie aktov o kazakakh 1500–1648 god.," *AIuZR,* part 3, vol. 2, pp. 2–3; "Izsledovanie o gorodakh iugo-zapadnago kraia," in *Monografii po istorii Zapadnoi i Iugo-Zapadnoi Rossii,* vol. 1 (only volume published) (Kyiv, 1885), p. 136.

41. Antonovich, "Soderzhanie aktov o kazakakh," pp. 9–11. See also his "Kiev, ego sud'ba i znachenie s XIV po XVI stoletie (1362–1569)," in *Monografii,* pp. 224–27.

42. Antonovich, "Soderzhanie aktov o kazakakh," pp. 11–14.

43. Antonovich, "Kiev, ego sud'ba i znachenie," pp. 229, 232, 253–55, 261. See also his "Soderzhanie aktov o kazakakh," pp. 14–18.

Antonovych stressed the communal character of cities in Kyivan Rus' and showed the progressive decline of towns in Ukraine under Lithuanian and then Polish rule. The granting of Magdeburg rights to the towns, he concluded, represented the victory of the feudal military order over the communal. See his "Izsledovanie o gorodakh iugo-zapadnago kraia," in *Monografii,* pp. 138, 165–66, 185. See also S. Tomashivs'kyi, *Volodymyr Antonovych: Ioho diial'nist' na poli istorychnoi nauky* (L'viv: Naukove Tovarystvo im. Shevchenka, 1906), pp. 32–33.

44. Antonovich, "Izsledovanie o gorodakh," pp. 136–38.

45. Antonovich, "Kiev, ego sud'ba i znachenie," p. 230.

46. V. Antonovych, "Predislovie," in *AIuZR,* part 6, vol. 2 (Kyiv, 1870), pp. 1–4.

47. Ibid., pp. 7–8.

48. Ibid., pp. 8–10.

49. Ibid., pp. 5–6, 11–18, 24–27.

50. Antonovych summed up his thesis as follows: "The Cossacks are none other than that which remained of the old Slavic communes, which appear with military features, called forth by local conditions, with a new name, originating in those same military-like conditions." See his "Soderzhanie aktov o kazakakh," p. 117.

51. Antonovych, *Korotka istoriia kozachchyny,* pp. 23–29, 38, 40–43.

52. Antonovych, "Soderzhanie aktov o kazakakh," pp. 37–38, 41. See also his "Ocherk sostoianiia pravoslavnoi tserkvi v Iugo-zapadnoi Rossii s poloviny XVII do kontsa XVIII stoletiia," in *Monografii,* p. 282.

53. V. Antonovych, "Soderzhanie aktov o kazakakh na pravoi storone Dnepra (1679–1716)," *AIuZR,* part 3, vol. 2, pp. 23–24. The historian O. Hermaize wrote that, in Antonovych's view, the Cossacks' struggle was supported by the peasants and townspeople, who recognized the Cossacks as carriers of the national idea. Therefore, the Cossack–Polish wars were deeply rooted historical conflicts, representing a struggle between two national principles. See his "V.B. Antonovych v ukrains'kii istoriohrafii," p. 26.

54. Antonovych, *Korotka istoriia kozachchyny,* pp. 109–11, 120–21. See also his "Kharakteristika deiatel'nosti Bogdana Khmelnitskago," pp. 103–04.

55. Antonovich, "Kharakteristika deiatel'nosti Bogdana Khmelnitskago," p. 102.

56. Antonovych, *Korotka istoriia kozachchyny,* p. 124.

57. Ibid., pp. 112–14. See also his "Soderzhanie aktov o kozakakh na pravoi storone Dnepra," pp. 24–25.

58. Antonovych, *Korotka istoriia kozachchyny,* p. 6.

59. Ibid., pp. 136–40.

60. Ibid., pp. 152–56.

61. See his "Soderzhanie aktov o kazakakh na pravoi storone Dnepra," pp. 69–70. See also his *Korotka istoriia kozachchyny,* pp. 156, 158–59.

62. Antonovych, *Korotka istoriia kozachchyny,* pp. 161–62.

63. Antonovich, "Soderzhanie aktov o kazakakh na pravoi storone Dnepra," pp. 61, 72.

64. V. Antonovich, "Izsledovanie o gaidamachestve po aktam 1700–1768 g.," *AIuZR,* part 3, vol. 3 (Kyiv, 1876), pp. 1–5.

65. Ibid., pp. 1–2. See also his "Proizvedeniia Shevchenka," p. 157.

66. See Antonovych, "Otvet g. Korzonu," in *Tvory,* pp. 234–35.

67. Antonovych, *Korotka istoriia kozachchyny,* p. 230.

68. Ibid., pp. 230–31. See also his "Istorychni baiky p. Mariiana Dubets'koho," p. 212.

69. Antonovich, "Pol'sko-russkie sootnosheniia XVII v. v sovremennoi pol'skoi prizme," in *Tvory,* p. 162. See also his "Istorychni baiky," p. 212.

70. Antonovich, "Pol'sko-russkie sootnosheniia," pp. 162, 176.

71. Hrushevs'kyi, "Volodymyr Antonovych," pp. 18–19.

72. Antonovich, "Pol'sko-russkie sootnosheniia," p. 164.

73. Antonovych, "Pohliady ukrainofiliv," in *Tvory,* p. 248.

74. Hrushevs'kyi, "Volodymyr Antonovych," p. 19.

75. Antonovich, "Kharakteristika deiatel'nosti Bogdana Khmel'nitskago," pp. 102–3.

76. Mykhailo Hrushevs'kyi, "Z sotsial'no-natsional'nykh kontseptsii Antonovycha," *Ukraina,* 1928, book 5, pp. 13–14.

77. Ibid., p. 8.

78. Antonovych wrote that he was questioned by the authorities regarding his Ukrainophile activities on twelve different matters in a two-year period in the early 1860s. See his "Memuary," p. 54.

79. Hrushevs'kyi, "Volodymyr Antonovych," p. 17. See also his "Z sotsial'no-natsional'nykh kontseptsii Antonovycha," p. 8.

80. On Lazarevs'kyi, see V. Sarbei, *Istorychni pohliady O.M. Lazarevs'koho* (Kyiv: Akademiia nauk Ukrains'koi SSR, 1961).

81. Hrushevs'kyi, "Z sotsial'no-natsional'nykh kontseptsii Antonovycha," p. 12.

82. Hermaize, "V.B. Antonovych v ukrains'kii istoriohrafii," pp. 27, 30–31.

83. Ibid., pp. 21–22, 29.

84. See Antonovych, "Pohliady ukrainofiliv," p. 246. See also Hermaize, "V.B. Antonovych," pp. 30–31.

85. Doroshenko, *Volodymyr Antonovych,* pp. 156–57.

III

Non-Russian Historical Visions

18

On Russian-Jewish Historiography

Benjamin Nathans

The historiography of Russian Jewry offers a rich example of the challenges—narrational, political, and epistemological—of representing the past of a stateless, nonterritorial people. In this respect, it speaks to the experience of many other groups, not least in the multinational Russian and Soviet empires, who have similarly passed through long periods of collective subordination.

Like the history of Russian Jews themselves, their historiography resists simple boundaries. Just as Russian Jewry was part of the larger body of world Jewry (and saw itself as such), its historiography cannot be fully understood without consideration of factors outside Russia. During the late imperial period, when historical works on Jews in the Russian Empire first appeared, "Russian" Jewry itself was a relatively recent phenomenon, an unintended result of the partitions of Poland at the end of the eighteenth century, in the course of which some half a million Jews were transformed into subjects of the Romanovs. The historiography of Jews living on the territory of the Russian Empire found expression in Jewish languages (Hebrew and Yiddish), in Polish and German, and above all in Russian. Its practitioners included Christians as well as Jews. Created almost entirely outside the academy, Russian-Jewish historiography emerged within a force field of intense debate over the so-called "Jewish Question," and its genres therefore ranged well beyond the monograph and scholarly article.

Rather than impose *a priori* criteria of what and who constituted Russian-Jewish historiography, I have chosen to make contemporary discussions of its boundaries and its proper content a central part of my essay.[1] By tracing the development of this branch of historical inquiry from its emergence in the 1860s to its demise in the 1930s, I seek to analyze the sources of its remarkably rapid growth, its passage through chronologically overlapping paradigms (archetypal, juridical, nationalist, and Marxist), and its role in transforming the historical consciousness of Russian Jews themselves.

History and Memory

"Does a historiography of Russian Jews exist?" When the thirty-one-year-old Simon Dubnov posed this question in 1891, he offered a straightforward and less than sanguine response: "We Russian Jews have practically no knowledge of our history in the land where we have resided for eight centuries and, apparently, do not feel any particular need to become acquainted with it."[2] These remarks, from the man who would soon become the most widely read historian of Russian Jewry, suggest a useful point of entry into our subject: namely, that a modern historical consciousness came comparatively late, and largely in the form of an intellectual rupture, to the Jews of Russia.

At first glance, this may seem a surprising characterization of a people whose unbroken textual tradition stretched back thousands of years. That tradition, moreover, had cast the Jews themselves as the protagonists in a profoundly historical narrative, centered around their attempts to create a society ruled by divine law, their repeated failure, and their periodic punishment. The biblical narrative, and the subsequent layers of rabbinic commentary and supercommentary, placed the meaning and memory of the past at the heart of postbiblical Jewish existence. But it was precisely the pervasive attachment to their *ancient* past that led generation after generation of Jews, from the Middle Ages until well into the nineteenth century, to view all subsequent history through the prism of biblical and talmudic archetypes, whether of individuals, events, or modes of explanation. As a historical record, Scripture looked not only backward but forward; all historical developments could, through proper exegesis, be found to be implicit in it from the outset. For Jews, therefore, the sacred commandment to remember was fulfilled not primarily through historiography in the modern sense, but through cycles of liturgy and ritual in which a sacred history was continually experienced anew.[3]

Nowhere was the Jewish propensity to telescope the distant and recent past more evident than in the experience of persecution and violence. The revolt of Cossacks and peasants led by Bogdan Khmelnitskii in 1648, for example, was understood by non-Jews and Jews in strikingly divergent ways. The former, depending on their perspective, tended to understand the uprising as a protest by followers of the Eastern Orthodox Church against

Catholic incursions, or as a Ukrainian strike against the hegemony of the Polish aristocracy (and its Jewish estate managers), or as a move toward consolidation of the Russian Empire. By contrast, East European Jews who pondered the destruction of tens of thousands of Jewish lives across Ukraine and Poland in 1648 heard distinctly biblical echoes. Even a nonliturgical, comparatively empirical account of the event, Nathan of Hannover's *Yeven Metsulah* [Deep Mire, 1653], began with a numerological demonstration that the date of the uprising and the names of the perpetrators were encoded in the Bible itself.[4] In nearly all the subsequent chronicles and liturgical poems composed by Jews, the slaughter was represented as a reenactment of previous instances of martyrdom. As another chronicler, Rabbi Yom-Tov Lipmann Heller, put it, "What has occurred now is similar to the persecutions of old, and all that happened to the forefathers has happened to their descendants. It is all one."[5] The urge to collapse historical time, to understand the recent past not as a unique outcome of more or less immediately antecedent causes, but as yet another incarnation of an ancient archetype, found expression in the prayerbooks of many East European Jewish communities, where references to the events of 1648 took their place beside those concerning other catastrophes going back to the destruction of the Temple in Jerusalem in the sixth century B.C.E.

Not only collective catastrophes but the everyday fabric of their existence and their relations with neighbors and political authorities tended to be perceived by Jews through a biblical lens. Levi Yitzhak of Berdichev, one of the early leaders of the mystical-pietist Hasidic movement that swept across Jewish Eastern Europe at the end of the eighteenth century, provides the following example:

> Look how powerful is the law of Moses. The tsar has many policemen and many soldiers and he is alive and well and rules his kingdom with an iron hand. This tsar has said that one may not import liquor or certain other articles except by license, yet his whole empire is flooded with smuggled goods. The son of Amram [i.e., Moses] has been dead for many centuries and has no Cossacks and no divisions, yet he said one may not have leavened bread in one's home for seven days and in all Jewish homes there is no leavened bread during Passover.[6]

To be sure, Jews were hardly the only people whose perception of the past was grounded in religious archetypes. What was distinctive, however, was the force of these archetypes in Jewish culture (elite as well as folk), their origins in a text centered on the Jews' own ancestors, and the degree to which that text was directly accessible to the relatively literate Jewish population.[7] Long after Christian elites had begun to develop, or rediscover, a nontheologically driven historiography, Jewish scholars in Eastern Europe, who after all were almost exclusively rabbis, retained their trans-historical view of the past.

The first cracks in this worldview came with the spread of the *Haskalah,* or Jewish Enlightenment, from its birthplace in Berlin to the scattered outposts of Jewish literati in the Russian Empire during the early decades of the nineteenth century.[8] Like their counterparts in Prussia and Austrian Galicia (and for that matter, like the European Enlightenment as a whole), the followers of the *Haskalah* in Russia were not especially interested in history. Rather, they sought to bring Judaism into fruitful contact with present-minded subjects such as science, mathematics, and philosophy, often attempting to harness the power of the Russian state to assist them in the reform of Jewish schools. The works they produced regarding Jews in the Russian Empire were mostly satirical attacks on their "unenlightened" Jewish opponents, or brief chronicles of local communities.[9] But by chipping away at the traditional East European Jewish antipathy toward secular education, the "Enlighteners" began indirectly to expose the Jewish population to new conceptions of historical time and causality.[10] Moreover, in their two-front struggle—against the separatism and perceived backwardness of the Jews and against anti-Jewish prejudice in the surrounding society—the "Enlighteners" prefigured the position of the Russian-Jewish historians who followed them.

It was again in Germany, now under the sign of historicism, that a modern, critical Jewish historiography was born. The so-called *Wissenschaft des Judentums* (the scientific study of Judaism) was born in 1819 as a loose confederation of university-trained Jews intent on seeing the Jewish past in terms of development rather than archetype, and on applying a conceptual rather than an exegetical mode of analysis. But the *Wissenschaft des Judentums* was devoted almost exclusively to the artifacts of high culture, and in its eagerness to demonstrate the compatibility of Judaism and modernity, it either ignored or dismissed the relatively isolated and backward Jews of Eastern Europe. Not until the 1860s did a Russian Jew, the Hebrew writer Peretz Smolenskin, challenge the *Wissenschaft des Judentums* by calling for a new kind of historiography that would underscore the social and national dimensions of Jewish life. Writing from Vienna in his journal *Ha-Shahar* (The Dawn), Smolenskin outlined his conception of a history of the Jews as a people, without, however, producing such a history himself. In fact, not until the 1880s did both the *Wissenschaft des Judentums* and Smolenskin's critique thereof gain influence among Jewish historians in Russia, and by then Russian Jews had begun to critically examine their own past, in a manner shaped to a considerable degree by conditions in Russia itself.

The Russian Setting

The primacy of ritually grounded memory over historiography persisted among Russian Jews well into the second half of the nineteenth century. Its gradual weakening began in the 1840s with the establishment of government-sponsored Jewish primary schools in the spirit of the *Haskalah,* and it greatly accelerated as a result of the rapid influx of Jews into Russian gymnasiums and universities in the 1860s. Under Tsar Alexander II, select categories of "useful" Jews became eligible to live and work outside the Pale of Jewish Settlement, the broad swathe of territory at the western and southwestern peripheries of the empire to which the Jewish population was legally confined. This carefully contained experiment in selective emancipation was extended in 1861 to Jewish graduates of Russian universities, and in 1879 to Jewish graduates of all institutions of higher education, thereby enormously stimulating the spread of secular education among Jews.[11] By the late 1870s contemporaries were already noting a fundamental realignment of the Jewish intelligentsia, bringing it for the first time within the orbit of its Russian counterpart.[12] The challenge to aristocratic "fathers" by plebeian "sons" (and daughters) within the Russian intelligentsia, as a result of which intellectual life became socially as well as ethnically more open, had also paved the way for such a realignment.[13]

The first and most visible effect of the Russian setting on Jewish history writing was in the realm of language. Whereas the few local histories penned by followers of the *Haskalah* had been in Hebrew (and therefore aimed at traditionally educated Jews), the majority of subsequent Russian-Jewish historiography (until the 1920s) was in Russian.[14] This not only tells us about the intellectual milieu in which historians of Russian Jewry came of age, but alerts us to the fact that the turn to history came simultaneously with the need to present the Jewish case to non-Jewish society.[15]

A second effect of the late imperial Russian setting was to impose an immediate contemporary relevance on research concerning the Jewish past. Russia was, of course, not the only country where polemics over the so-called "Jewish Question" constantly shadowed and illuminated representations of Jewish history.[16] As had happened in Europe, debates in Russia tended to proceed from the common assumption that Jews in their present "degraded" condition were not suited for full membership in society. The "Question" took the form of a chicken-and-egg dispute over which came first: the Jews' ostensibly low moral level and fanatical separatism, or the dense apparatus of legal discrimination directed against them. If the Jews' alleged negative qualities were a result of centuries of persecution and discrimination, then the granting of legal equality would cause those qualities to fade away. If, by contrast, those very qualities had pre-dated and inspired official discrimination, then the Jews would first have to be transformed—assuming this was even possible—in order to "earn" equality. In either case, the focus on cause and effect, on the mutability and therefore historicity of the Jewish condition, created an inescapable link between historiography and the highly charged contemporary discussions of Jewish emancipation. Indeed, the unstable mixture of partial integration and enduring pariah status colored the everyday experience of Russian-Jewish historians themselves. As one remarked, only half jokingly, Russian Jewry "does not yet have a history, since its entire past is still alive in the present."[17]

The late imperial period witnessed a dramatic rise in the scope and temperature of debates over the "Jewish Question." In the government and in society at large, it seemed to many that the Jews had failed to shed their peculiarities and their group allegiance, even as rapid social change was giving them unprecedented access to the institutions of an emerging capitalist economy and civil society. While pogroms and accusations of ritual murder periodically heightened concern over alleged Jewish "exploitation" of non-Jews, it was Jacob Brafman's sensational *Kniga kagala* [The Book of the Kahal] that, more than any other work, set the terms for late imperial Russian anti-Semitism.[18] According to the historical documents presented by Brafman, the executive council (known as the *kahal*) of each Jewish community had long functioned in secret as a kind of mini-government, promoting Jewish interests at the expense of the surrounding society and mercilessly suppressing internal dissent. With Russia now experiencing unprecedented social dislocation, the Jews were supposedly poised to expand their control into all branches of Russian society. During the late imperial period the "Jewish Question" became permanently intertwined with other potent social issues such as the development of capitalism, Russian national identity, and the revolutionary movement. In the words of a comprehensive recent study of Russia as a multinational empire, "By the end of the nineteenth century, the Jewish Question stood at the center of discussion [about nationality], and the Jews became the most important object . . . of nationality policy."[19] These circumstances help account for the frequency, perhaps even the inevitability, of political engagement among historians of the Russian-Jewish past. For some, engagement took the form of a heavily normative approach in their historical works; others crossed over to journalism and advocacy. Most, in fact, practiced both.

A third consequence of the Russian setting for Jewish historiography was, paradoxically, an obsession with "the West." The primacy of Europe in the Russian imagination, coupled with the fact that Jews and the "Jewish Question" were a pan-European phenomenon, all but guaranteed that the

Russian-Jewish past would be compared and contrasted not so much with that of other minority groups in the Russian Empire—the Poles, say, or Muslims or Armenians—as with that of Jewish communities in Germany, France, and England. It was the European examples of Jewish emancipation, upward social mobility, and (by the end of the nineteenth century) renewed anti-Semitism that offered the most compelling paradigm—desired or not—for historians of Russian Jewry.

Fourth and finally, the Russian context had important consequences on an institutional level. While growing numbers of Jewish intellectuals took part in the informal circles (*kruzhki*) of the Russian intelligentsia, they were excluded from employment in academies and universities (and for that matter gymnasiums), the classic homes of professional historians in the nineteenth century. Prior to the revolution of 1917, not a single unconverted Jew held a professorship in a historical–philological or law faculty in the Russian Empire.[20] While conditions in Germany were only slightly better, the presence there of modern rabbinical seminaries provided an institutional haven for a number of prominent Jewish historians. In Russia, by contrast, Jewish higher education—that is, the training of rabbis—was still the exclusive prerogative of fiercely traditional yeshivas.[21] The near-impossibility of a career in the academy or other branches of the civil service, and the attractive prospect of self-employment in the liberal professions, led the vast majority of Jewish university students to study law or medicine.[22] Thus, when a historiography of Russian Jewry emerged in tsarist Russia, it was almost completely outside the training and employment structure of professional academic history, and instead developed in the hands of laymen.

The handful of scholars of Russian Jewry who did not follow this pattern were, tellingly, either non-Jews or ex-Jews. Fedor I. Leontovich (1833–1911), a Christian whose published work included a history of legislation regarding Jews in early modern Lithuania as well as in the Russian Empire, was a professor of Russian legal history at Odessa and then at Warsaw University.[23] His student, Sergei A. Bershadskii (1850–1896), also a Christian, produced a series of pioneering studies of the legal status of Jewish communities in the Polish–Lithuanian commonwealth, and was professor of jurisprudence at St. Petersburg University.[24] Finally, one of Bershadskii's colleagues in St. Petersburg, Daniel A. Khvol'son (1819–1911), was a Russian Jew who had converted to Christianity in order to assume a professorship of Semitic philology. He authored an influential work on the history of the blood libel in Europe and Russia, in response to contemporary accusations by Russian anti-Semites.[25] The singularity of Khvol'son's career, and the extreme rarity of gentile academics who produced historical works on Russian Jewry (as distinct from the many nonacademic writers and journalists who addressed the "Jewish Question" in its contemporary manifestations), only highlight the extent to which Russian-Jewish historiography remained a predominantly Jewish pursuit, remote from the academy.

The Centrality of Law

While the study of the Russian-Jewish past was largely an extra-academic pastime, it certainly did not develop in a conceptual vacuum. Beginning in the 1860s, historians of Russian Jewry took as their central concern the Jews' legal standing—which is to say, the development of official legislation regarding the Jewish population. There were more than a sufficient number of reasons for this. Insofar as the contemporary "Jewish Question" demanded an "answer," that answer was usually articulated in terms of legal status. The emancipation debate that hovered over the development of Russian-Jewish historiography, while touching on a broad spectrum of issues ranging from national identity (Russian as well as Jewish) to economic reform, was implicitly directed at the state, and therefore at the law. It is also possible that the then-dominant "state school" of Russian historiography, which emphasized the role of law and the state in Russia's development, influenced even lay historians who lacked formal training.[26] Finally, the most accessible historical source materials—especially for nonprofessionals—were the voluminous, published, and relatively organized imperial law codes.

But most significant was the fact that, though by and large laymen, historians of Russian Jewry formed a highly distinctive group: nearly all were lawyers by training, occupation, and outlook.[27] Many works on the Russian-Jewish past produced in the late imperial period were in fact hardly "histories" as we understand the term today, but analyses of legislative acts culled from successive volumes of the law codes. Their primary purpose was to give practical guidance to Jews as well as to tsarist bureaucrats attempting to navigate their way through the enormous maze of legislation and court rulings concerning Jews and Jewish issues.[28] Despite their often modest self-descriptions as "handbook" (*rukovodstvo*), "collection" (*sbornik*), or "index" (*ukazatel'*), the best of these works offered a considerable depth of historical interpretation. Instead of tracing the development of official Jewish policy chronologically across successive reigns, the manuals were organized by topic (residence law, property law, commercial law, etc.), within which the analysis moved roughly chronologically. If measured in terms of sheer number and variety of publications, the manuals appear to have reached nearly as many readers as more conventional histories of Russian Jewry.[29]

The first attempt at a narrative history of Russian Jewry came from the

pen of Il'ia Grigor'evich Orshanskii (1846–1875), a precocious and respected expert on civil law whose refusal to convert to Christianity had cost
him an academic appointment at Odessa's Novorossiiskii University. Instead, he went into private practice in Odessa while pouring his academic
ambitions into a broad range of articles, including a series of essays that,
taken together, comprise the first analytical history of the legal status of
Russian Jewry.[30]

Though ultimately aimed at demonstrating the social, economic, and
moral costs of anti-Jewish discrimination, Orshanskii's works took on the
burden of explaining that discrimination's genesis. The protagonist in his
history is therefore not so much the Jews as the tsarist government. Two
conflicting considerations had guided the government's efforts to regulate
the Jews' legal status, according to Orshanskii: traditional Christian prejudice, and the desire to profit from Jewish commercial activity. As religious
hostility waned during the nineteenth century, Orshanskii argued, the main
issue became how best to put the Jews to use—that is, whether to increase
or decrease their regulation by the state. An unabashed proponent of integration and individual as opposed to corporate rights, Orshanskii's analysis
culminated in a call for the abolition not only of external restrictions on
Jewish residence and employment but of state-sanctioned intramural Jewish
taxes and rabbinic control over Jewish marriage and divorce.[31] "The ideal
toward which we strive," he wrote with characteristic vividness, "consists
precisely of expelling the Jews once and for all from the legal codes."[32]

In organizing his analysis around the Jews' legal standing, Orshanskii
established what became an enduring pattern of treating anti-Jewish legislation as an anomaly within the larger framework of Russian law.[33] A talented polemicist with an affinity for abstraction, Orshanskii argued that

> Our legislation regards the Jews from precisely the opposite perspective that
> it does all other classes of the population. With respect to the latter, the law
> operates on the entirely correct principle that everything not prohibited by
> law is permitted.... Thus nowhere in the law will you encounter a ruling
> that a Greek, a Tartar, or a Mordvinian has the right to practice all branches
> of commerce, to acquire property. . . , to educate his children in public
> schools, and so on. All this is assumed as a matter of course, as a result of the
> general human and civil rights of every Russian subject. But with regard to
> Jews the law takes as its point of departure the idea that they, as Jews, do not
> have any rights in Russia and therefore that everything not explicitly permit-
> ted them by law is forbidden.[34]

Orshanskii could point to numerous examples of Russian laws declaring
that "Jews are permitted to engage in agricultural labor," "Jews may over-

see all kinds of factories in the areas where they are allowed to reside," and "Jewish children enjoy unrestricted access to public schools." Moreover, Jewish citizens of other countries visiting or residing in Russia had never shared the legal status of other foreigners, but rather were subject to many of the restrictions imposed on Russian Jews.[35]

While Orshanskii's analysis of the jurisprudential logic at work in the examples he cited was compelling, it ignored numerous historic counterexamples of anti-Jewish discrimination based on a different logic. Just as often, in fact, tsarist law would outline the privileges and obligations of a given estate or social group, only to introduce the qualifier "*krome evreev*" (except Jews). To take a single but prominent example, the landmark decree of February 19, 1861, ending the institution of serfdom, stated that owners of landed estates might henceforth lease their lands to members of all estates, "except Jews."

More significantly, Orshanskii's assertion that the non-Jewish population was protected by "the general human and civil rights of every Russian subject" betrayed an imagined standard, a uniformity in the legal status of the rest of the empire's population, that had more to do with Western legal theory than with the actual legal hierarchy of the Russian *soslovie* (estate) system. Orshanskii appeared at times to recognize the fictitious nature of this uniformity without successfully resolving the tension in his analysis of it:

> The Jews are not the only class of people for whom there exist exclusions from and limitations on general laws. . . . Our legislation allows for an enormous and varied mass of exceptions from general laws for different territories and classes of the population. It is well known that in no other European legislation is the principle of uniformity and equality so weakly applied as in that of Russia. . . . The fundamental abnormality [of the Jews' legal status] lies in the character and quality of [their particular] limitations.[36]

To assess properly the degree of anomaly in the Jews' legal status, one would have had to compare their position systematically to that of other groups. Except for occasional allusions to Old Believers and to groups who shared the Jews' classification as "aliens" (*inorodtsy*), however, such a comparative approach was absent from Russian-Jewish historiography. This is hardly surprising, given that Russia's Jews themselves had barely begun to receive scholarly attention, and in any event the implicit comparative framework was much more likely to be the experience of Jews in Central and Western Europe.

The larger point, however, is that the underlying tension in Orshanskii's work between, on the one hand, presenting the Jews' legal standing as utterly unique, and on the other, viewing the Jews within an imperial Russian context in which legally inscribed inequalities were the norm, never disappeared from Russian-Jewish historiography. This tension often existed not only among historians but—as in the case of Orshanskii—within one and the same historian. In the works of Orshanskii's successors such as Menashe G. Morgulis (1837–1912), Pesakh S. Marek (1862–1920), Genrikh B. Sliozberg (1863–1937), Shaul M. Ginzburg (1866–1940), Leontii M. Bramson (1869–1941), Solomon V. Pozner (1876–1946), and Grigorii Ia. Krasnyi-Admoni (1881–1970)—all lay historians trained in the law—one finds a similar pattern of official legislation regarding Jews analyzed as an arena unto itself, governed by an autonomous ebb and flow of official anti-Semitism, and yet, on a different level of the narrative, utterly in sync with the general rhythms of reform and reaction.[37] In his study of Jews and tsarist educational policy, for example, Pozner presented the Jews' legal status both as distinctive and as a finely calibrated "barometer" of changes in the larger political climate: "General political shifts here [in Russia] have always affected Jews earlier than anyone else."[38] Quite apart from its explanatory value, this point of view may well derive from two contrasting needs on the part of Russian-Jewish historians: to preserve a sense of uniqueness in the Jewish experience of discrimination, while seeing the Jews as bound up and participating in the fortunes of Russian society as a whole.

Usable Pasts

By the 1880s the *Haskalah* had largely receded from the mental horizon of the Russian-Jewish intelligentsia, and with it the rather one-sided veneration of West European Jewry. The struggle for Jewish equality favored the construction of a specifically *Russian*-Jewish past, a past that would demonstrate the Jews' rightful place in and allegiance to the Russian motherland. In this category belong works by S.M. Ginzburg on Jewish participation in the defense of Russia against Napoleon, by S.V. Pozner on Jews in Russian educational institutions, and by M.L. Usov on Jews in the Imperial Russian army.[39] Written with the explicit intention of refuting contemporary charges of Jewish disloyalty and separatism, these studies were nonetheless remarkable for the way they combined apologetic representations of Jewish patriotism and usefulness with trenchant criticism of certain official policies regarding Jews. If Jews were cast as loyal but unappreciated sons, Russia often took the part of the "stepmotherland" (*rodina-machekha*).[40]

In reality, however, the construction of a specifically *Russian*-Jewish past was no simple matter in a region where political boundaries had repeatedly and dramatically shifted over the centuries, producing a kind of multiple exposure, in which local, national, and imperial identities were superimposed on each other.[41] Indeed, the term "Russian Jew" (*russkii evrei*) did not become part of Russian or Jewish discourse until the 1850s.[42] Unlike most Central and East European states, Russia had no medieval tradition of settling foreign Jewish communities on its territory, and instead had acquired its Jewish population—the largest in the world—as an unintended result of imperial conquest. Even at the beginning of the twentieth century, most "Russian" Jews lived in ethnically non-Russian territories that had been conquered by the Romanovs scarcely a century before, and thus had far longer historical ties to vanished states like Poland and Lithuania, or to the Ottoman Empire, or to borderlands like Ukraine, than to Russia proper. To complicate matters further, Jewish communities in Crimea, the Caucasus, and Central Asia, while relatively small, possessed a lineage that reached as far back as the Hellenic era and were culturally distinct from the Ashkenazic, Yiddish-speaking Jews of the Pale of Settlement.

How were diverse Jewish communities, having come under Russian suzerainty during different eras and as part of widely diverging societies, to be made part of a single "Russian-Jewish" history? In what way was "Russian-Jewish" history a coherent unit within the chronologically and geographically much broader history of the Jews as a people? When could "Russian-Jewish" history be said to have begun? Each of these questions had far-reaching historiographical implications. For Orshanskii and many of his successors, whose narratives focused on Russian laws regarding Jews, "Russian-Jewish" history involved only those Jews who lived within the borders of the Russian Empire at any given time. For the period prior to the Polish partitions at the end of the eighteenth century, when relatively few Jews could be found in Russia, this meant analyzing the motives behind the repeated tsarist bans on Jewish immigration as well as such episodes as the Judaizer heresy of the fifteenth century. The Russian state as imperial center and lawmaker was the focal point.

A different approach emerged in the works of Abraham Harkavi (1835–1919), a philologist interested in early Slavic contacts with Semitic peoples (Muslim as well as Jewish). Harkavi was exceptional among Jewish historians in that he held a doctorate from the Oriental Studies Faculty of St. Petersburg University (with periods of graduate study in Berlin and Paris), and was professionally employed in the Division of Ancient Near Eastern Manuscripts in the Imperial Public Library.[43] This background may in part explain his innovative approach to the Russian–Jewish encounter (broadly understood), which all but ignored the Russian state and its laws, turning instead to themes such as the Hebraic influence on early Slavic chronicles, the allegedly Slavic dialect spoken by Jews who lived on the shores of the

Black Sea in late antiquity, contacts between Kievan Rus´ and the Khazar kingdom (whose leaders converted to Judaism in the eighth century), and other aspects of cross-cultural contact.[44]

Early in his scholarly career, Harkavi became embroiled in a historical controversy that gained a certain public notoriety. His work on ancient Jewish inscriptions from Crimea brought him into contact with Abraham Firkovich, a representative of a Jewish sect known as the Karaites. The Karaites preached an exclusive allegiance to the Hebrew Bible, rejecting postbiblical Jewish tradition as codified by the rabbis in the Talmud and other works. Over the course of the nineteenth century, the Karaites had persuaded the Russian government to exempt them from many of the burdens imposed on "rabbinic Jews," principally military conscription and special taxes, and to declare them a distinct nationality, separate from Jews. Firkovich, for his part, published a book in 1872 arguing that Karaites were not even of Semitic origin, but instead had descended from Khazar (Turkic) converts to Judaism. The implication was clear: Karaites were not of the same stock as those who had handed Jesus over for crucifixion, and therefore should not bear the brunt of Christian wrath.

In his published rebuttal of Firkovich's argument, Harkavi raised accusations of forgery and scholarly incompetence, which Firkovich was unable to refute.[45] But for our purposes it is Harkavi's revisionist counter-thesis that holds the greatest interest. For Harkavi proceeded to make an elaborate case that not only the tiny sect of Karaites but the majority of Russia's millions of Jews could trace their origins to the Khazars, and that from the ninth to the seventeenth century, the ancestors of Russian Jewry had spread west from the Black Sea and the Caucasus (not east from Central Europe), speaking a Slavic dialect that only later absorbed Germanic elements and became the tongue known as Yiddish.

Whatever the scholarly merits of this rather strained argument—which nonetheless has proponents even today[46]—the controversy that it generated demonstrates the growing significance of historical consciousness for Russian-Jewish identity. Harkavi was in effect participating in the fashioning of a foundation myth, a narrative that would establish the antiquity and by implication the legitimacy of the Jewish presence on Russian (understood as *rossiiskii,* that is, pertaining to the empire as a whole) soil.[47] To be sure, historians of Russia had long cited the account of how the tenth-century pagan prince Vladimir invited representatives of Christianity, Islam, and Judaism to Kiev to present the virtues of their respective religions. But this account was neither historically reliable nor very flattering to Jews, insofar as Vladimir was said to have rejected Judaism as the religion of a defeated and exiled people. By contrast, Harkavi offered substantial evidence for

Slavic–Jewish contacts well before Vladimir, in fact prior to the historic dawn of the Russian state. Jews, it would seem, had been living on Russian soil since before it became Russian.

The antiquity of Jewish life on the territory of the Russian Empire proved an irresistible idea for many Russian-Jewish historians who followed in Harkavi's wake. But even those most eager for the dividends implied by such a pedigree could not alter the fact that the evidence connecting the ancient Jewish communities of the Black Sea to the contemporary Jews of the Pale of Settlement was exceedingly thin. The ambiguous nature of Harkavi's thesis can be traced across the various editions of one of the great synthetic histories of Russian Jewry, that of Iulii I. Gessen (1871–1939).

Gessen was profoundly influenced by the juridical tradition of Il'ia Orshanskii and Sergei Bershadskii, among others.[48] His *History of the Jews in Russia* (1914), the fruit of decades of research, began with the partitions of Poland and reached the end of the nineteenth century.[49] Like Orshanskii, Gessen harnessed his narrative to the development of Russian state policy toward the Jews, and struggled to articulate both the Jews' unique legal standing and their barometer-like function in the larger political climate. In the post-1905 era, however, the ideologically mobilized Jewish reading public was no longer in the mood for such an old-fashioned, externalist approach. One critic argued that Gessen "has given us a history not of what the Jews did, but of what was done to them."[50] While appreciative of the work's pioneering synthesis, many critics questioned Gessen's use of the Polish partitions as the point of departure, as if a shift in external political rule were the most decisive factor in Jewish history.[51]

Responding to his critics, Gessen published a revised and expanded version of his magnum opus two years later, now called *History of the Jewish People in Russia* (1916).[52] As the change in title hints, Gessen was at least paying lip service to a more nationally oriented historiography. The origins of Russian-Jewish history were now located in the ninth century, precisely along the lines proposed by Harkavi. But the artificial narrative splicing was short-lived. In the final, still further revised edition of *History of the Jewish People in Russia* (1925–27), Gessen referred only cursorily to the premodern period, noting that it "lacked an organic connection" to the history of Polish–Lithuanian, and later Russian, Jewry.[53]

None of this should obscure Gessen's considerable achievements. Though conceptually within the tradition pioneered by Orshanskii, Gessen himself had no legal training. Ironically, this fact may help account for his remarkable extension of the source base of Russian-Jewish history beyond the realm of law. In essence, Gessen brought Russian-Jewish historiography into the archives of the imperial Russian state and thereby broke through the often unreliable facade of published legislation in order to get at a much richer landscape of political motives, internal government rivalries, and state–society relations. While he was not the first to use Russian archival documents for the writing of Jewish history, Gessen utterly eclipsed his peers in the range and depth of material he uncovered and drew upon.[54] In the late 1920s, when the Soviet Union inaugurated a sixty-year de facto ban on serious research on nationality issues, Gessen was unmatched in his knowledge of imperial Russian archival sources pertaining to the Jews. The same could be said even today.[55]

Legal Emancipation and National Autonomy

If Orshanskii's state-centered approach to Russian-Jewish history, even in Gessen's more sophisticated rendering, appeared less and less adequate by the turn of the century, it was in no small part a result of the pioneering work of Simon Dubnov (1860–1941). We are now in a position to contextualize Dubnov's alarming claim in 1891 that neither a Russian-Jewish historiography nor a Russian-Jewish historical consciousness yet existed. In a literal sense this was not at all true: a generation of lay historians and a handful of professionally trained scholars of law and philology had begun to fill in some of the blanks, descriptive as well as analytical, of the Russian-Jewish past. What troubled Dubnov was the absence of a specific *kind* of historiography, the kind that would cast the Jews as a collective subject rather than a passive object of history, and that would deliberately cultivate in the Jewish reading public a *national* historical consciousness as the cornerstone of a modern, secular, Jewish identity. In Dubnov, Russian Jewry found its own version of the nineteenth-century European ideal: the historian as nation builder and culture-hero. How he arrived at this remarkable position is worth a closer look.[56]

Dubnov was perhaps the most striking exception to the pattern of the Jewish lawyer-historian: he had no formal higher education whatsoever, studied non-Jewish subjects and languages completely on his own, and made his living exclusively from writing. As with Harkavi and Gessen, it seems plausible that the absence of legal training facilitated Dubnov's reconceptualization of the Russian-Jewish past beyond the confines of tsarist legislation. In Dubnov's case, this meant situating Russian Jewry in two larger contexts: vertically, with respect to the four-thousand-year-trajectory of Jewish history, and horizontally, within the specifically nineteenth-century East European landscape of stateless nationalities striving for various forms of self-government.

After a traditional Jewish education whose metaphysical mooring had been unhinged by exposure to positivist thought, Dubnov began his professional life as a book reviewer for *Voskhod* [The Dawn], the leading Jewish journal in the Russian language. His subsequent contributions to Russian-Jewish historiography can be understood largely as a series of dialectical responses to his wide-ranging reading in the literature of the *Wissenschaft des Judentums,* European romantic nationalism, and Russian populism. These intellectual currents were filtered through Dubnov's own traumatic experience of what appeared to be the failure of Jewish integration in Russia, beginning with the wave of pogroms in 1881–82, followed by the introduction of residential restrictions even within the Pale, quotas on Jewish admission to institutions of higher education and the liberal professions, and the forcible expulsion of some fifteen thousand Jews from Moscow in 1891. The effect of the state's retreat from emancipation on Dubnov and many other Russian-Jewish intellectuals has been compared to the psychology of failed revolution, and as in the Czech case after 1848 and the Polish case after 1863, one of its consequences was a turn to the consolations of history.[57]

From German-Jewish scholarship, and above all from the sweeping panorama of Heinrich Graetz's eleven-volume *History of the Jews from the Oldest Times to the Present* (1853–76), Dubnov absorbed a passion for grand synthesis and a conviction that in the modern era, Jewish identity had to be grounded in historical consciousness. Graetz himself had tempered the *Wissenschaft des Judentums*'s tendency to treat the Jews strictly as a religious confession and had insisted that, despite their lack of a state and a territory, neither persecution nor integration could alter the continuity of Jewish nationhood. But where Graetz invoked divine Providence as the guiding force behind Jewish nationhood, the more overtly secular Dubnov insisted that the nation itself was the irreducible core, whether it expressed itself through statehood (as in the ancient period), religion (as codified by the rabbis following the loss of Jewish political sovereignty), or historical consciousness (in the modern era). Dubnov ingeniously took the Romantic definition of nationhood, according to which nations have collective souls and are bound together by spiritual attributes, and used it to argue that the Jews had evolved the purest and most enduring form of nationhood, free of the external trappings of territory and state power.

Dubnov was by no means the first to realize that the absence of statehood and territorial unity made the job of narrating postbiblical Jewish history exceedingly complex. In many ways, the problem of constructing a Russian-Jewish past that could somehow stretch across the dramatic realignments of political space in Eastern Europe was merely a subset of this larger phenomenon. How could one write a "national" history of a people that had lived on several continents and within vastly different civilizations, had spoken a dozen different languages and occupied a wide range of social roles over the course of time? In response to this narrative dilemma, Dubnov developed a theory of "hegemonic centers" in Jewish history, whereby at any given time one or two Jewish communities—whether in ancient Israel, Babylonia, or medieval Spain—dominated the rest of the Jewish world. In his own time, Dubnov insisted, Russian Jewry was the heir to this tradition, the living reservoir of Jewish civilization. West European Jewry—outwardly so successful in the wake of its emancipation—had committed the fatal error of sacrificing Jewish nationhood on the altar of assimilation. Not unlike the Slavophiles, Dubnov insisted that it was Russian Jewry that had preserved an authentic communal organization and spiritual life.

Within the field of Russian-Jewish historiography, Dubnov's most important innovation was to displace tsarist legislation from the center of the narrative (without removing it entirely, however) and to give pride of place to the history of Jewish communal life. A pioneer in the use of internal Jewish communal records (*pinkasim*) as a historical source, Dubnov insisted that the long existence of kahals, rabbinical courts, Jewish craft guilds, and intercommunal councils amounted to a history of collective Jewish autonomy, even in the absence of political sovereignty. The boldness of this claim can be appreciated only when one recalls that the specter of a Jewish "state within the state," of the kahal as a kind of collective Jewish conspiracy against the rest of society, was nothing less than the mantra of Russian anti-Semitism. Not only Brafman's influential anti-Semitic tract *The Book of the Kahal* (and many others like it), but much of tsarist policy toward the Jews was aimed at delegitimizing and dismantling all remnants of Jewish internal self-government in the name of "merging" the Jews into the hierarchy of Russian social estates.

Dubnov's revalorization of the kahal was bold in another way as well. The idea of Jewish emancipation, whether actualized or not, was originally predicated on the assumption that Jews would renounce all claims to collective self-rule, and instead join the surrounding society as individual citizens equal before the law. Only as a community of faith would Jewish collective identity continue to exist. This, in fact, was precisely the agenda of most Russian-Jewish historians: to "expel the Jews once and for all from the legal codes," as Orshanskii put it.[58] In classic Whig fashion, their histories highlighted the march of individual rights against the forces of tsarist discrimination, on the one hand, and rabbinic coercion, on the other. In his critique of Brafman's book, for example, the lawyer-historian Menashe Morgulis rejected the charge that the Jews always formed a "state within the state," insisting instead that it was the early modern state that had promoted and perpetuated collective Jewish self-regulation (for purposes of taxation and social control). Morgulis's assumption, however, was not all that different from Brafman's: Jewish self-government was undesirable and anachronistic.[59] Other historians chose simply to downplay the significance of the kahal, or to cite its formal abolition by the Russian government in 1844 as evidence that it was no longer an important issue.

In this approach Dubnov saw nothing less than a deliberate campaign of silence and dissimulation. The Jewish intelligentsia, he wrote in 1891 in his programmatic statement *On the Study of the History of Russian Jews,* was afraid to expose the Jewish past: "And do you know the source of this fear? The concern that the uncovering of age-old communal *pinkasim* will arouse the anti-Semitic press to intensify its screaming about the kahal, about the Jewish 'state within the state.' . . . This is the thinking of many of those in whose hands lies the sacred task of saving our past from oblivion!"[60]

It was a sign of the Jews' high level of social and cultural development, Dubnov insisted, that they had created and sustained their own autonomous institutions, even in the most hostile environments. Without such a tradition of solidarity, they would never have survived. Dubnov appealed to his readers to gather old *pinkasim,* personal letters, folk sayings, tombstone inscriptions, and other materials documenting the full range of Jewish culture and communal life, in order to build up an archive of sources that could balance and complement the well-mined law codes of the Russian, Polish, and Lithuanian states. To preserve and interpret such materials, Dubnov continued, Russian Jewry should follow the pattern set by Jews in France, Germany, and elsewhere, and establish its own historical society (open to Jews and gentiles alike), scholarly journals, and public lecture series.[61] "To construct the history of our eight-century-long life," he wrote, "in the land where, by the will of fate, we live even up to the present day, is one of our most sacred national duties."[62]

Having cast national consciousness and national institutions—rather than legal status—as the cornerstone of Jewish history, Dubnov made the case for a new periodization of Russian-Jewish history. Despite shifting borders and sovereignties, the Jews of the present-day Russian Empire could look back on a continuous national development that originated with the first Jewish migrations from Western to Eastern Europe in the late eleventh century, brought on by the atrocities of the Crusades. "It is impossible," Dubnov wrote, "to separate the history of Jews in Russia from their history in Poland and Lithuania, because the Jews of all these countries, for all their local variations, comprise a single sociocultural unity, possess a common past, and have experienced and continue to experience one and the same fate."[63]

As a historian, Dubnov aimed for and reached a mass audience. It is no exaggeration to say that, in terms of sheer influence during his own lifetime, he eclipsed all other historians of Russian Jewry combined. "History is a science about the people and for the people," he wrote, "and therefore cannot be a guild discipline." With his own exclusion from the academy undoubtedly in mind (as well as that of Russian-Jewish historiography generally), Dubnov proclaimed, "Its place is not under the academic cap, but in the open forum. We work for the people's self-recognition, and not for the sake of our own intellectual sport."[64]

In addition to several hundred pamphlets and articles that appeared in journals and the periodical press, Dubnov authored the *Textbook of Jewish History for Schools and Self-Study,* whose three volumes together sold over 120,000 copies in seventeen reprintings between 1898 and 1917 (and more thereafter).[65] In a 1910 survey of over one thousand Jewish students enrolled in institutions of higher education in Kiev, 43 percent of the respondents listed Dubnov among the authors who had shaped their knowledge of Jewish history—a level of influence unmatched by any other historian.[66] In its various incarnations, his popular three-volume *Modern History of the Jewish People* covered European and Russian Jewry from the French Revolution to the end of the nineteenth century. Finally, his monumental ten-volume *World History of the Jewish People* fulfilled Dubnov's ambition to integrate Russian-Jewish history into the long arc of Jewish history per se.[67] It was Dubnov's answer to the *Wissenschaft des Judentums,* the first "sociological history" of the Jews that emphasized the continuity of collective identity and national institutions rather than great texts by outstanding individuals, and it was a showcase for his theory of hegemonic centers within the Jewish diaspora, including, in his own time, that of Russian Jewry.

By the turn of the century, the radical recasting of Russian-Jewish historiography was a necessary but no longer sufficient modus operandi for Dubnov. His ideological opponents now included not just "assimilationist" historians who treated Jewish self-government as a medieval relic doomed to extinction with the spread of emancipation and individual rights, but Zionist thinkers (there was as yet no real Zionist historiography of Russian Jewry) who insisted that the two-thousand-year Jewish exile was an uninterrupted tale of powerlessness and passivity, and that the only way to return the Jews to their history was to reconstitute full-blown political sovereignty in the land of Israel. To be sure, the perceived failure of emancipation had also triggered Dubnov's re-envisioning of the Jewish past; but his engagement with that past shaped his view of the Russian-Jewish future in a manner fundamentally different from that of the Zionists. Between 1897 and 1906, Dubnov published a series of historical–political essays that culminated in a remarkable proposal: the kahal should be revived and reconstituted as a secular institution of Jewish autonomy within a federated Russian state.[68] The influence on Dubnov of other stateless nationalities' struggle for autonomy in Eastern Europe, especially in the Austro-Hungarian Empire, was unmistakable. When these essays were collected and published in book form as *Letters on Old and New Jewry* (1907), Dubnov added a postscript outlining the program of a new Jewish political party. Neither socialist nor Zionist, his *Folkspartei* (People's Party) advocated "diaspora nationalism" and "autonomism." Russian-Jewish historiography had reached its zenith of political engagement.[69]

As Robert Seltzer has observed, Dubnov's view of the past (and future) of the kahal bears a striking resemblance to the Russian populists' glorification of the peasant commune. Like Alexander Herzen's "discovery" of the peasant *mir* as an indigenous Russian form of socialism, Dubnov found in the kahal a unique, authentically Jewish institution, maligned as obsolete by modern standards, that appeared to offer the basis for solving a burning social question.[70] A reconstituted secular communal authority would save Russian Jewry not from capitalism (to which Dubnov had no objections) but from assimilation, whose destructive effects were already apparent in West European Jewry. And like the peasant commune, the kahal would form the basis of a decentralized, federative form of government.

As Dubnov himself conceded, his "sociological" conception of Jewish history had little to do with sociology per se (he made virtually no use of the work of Ferdinand Tönnies, Max Weber, or other contemporary social thinkers). Rather, it reflected a commitment to the essentially Romantic idea that Jewish history was the history of "a living national organism," an indissoluble people with enduring institutions (above all, in Russia, the kahal).[71] Indeed, the search for continuities across vast stretches of time occasionally led Dubnov to formulations strikingly reminiscent of the archetypal approach to Jewish history. In one such passage, Dubnov remarked that the 1887 quotas on Jewish enrollment in institutions of secondary and higher education, which targeted male students only, "followed strictly the ancient rule of the Pharaohs: 'If it be a son, then ye shall kill him; but if it be a daughter, then she shall live'." Though hardly meant to explain cause and effect (as they had in early modern Jewish chronicles), such biblical allusions, I suspect, were designed to evoke meanings beyond the merely rhetorical.[72] Similarly, the need to emphasize the unity of the Jewish "organism" led Dubnov to underrepresent conflict *within* Jewish society, especially Russian Jewry in the nineteenth century, in which such conflict—economic, religious, and political—was abundant. With the emergence of a Marxist Jewish historiography in the Soviet Union, these weaknesses would come under severe attack.

If the encounter with Graetz during the traumatic 1880s dialectically transformed Dubnov's vision of the Russian-Jewish past, and through him the historical consciousness of much of Russian Jewry, then in a curious way it may also be said that Russian Jewry transformed Graetz in return. Or rather, in translation: many readers in Russia encountered Graetz through the remarkable Hebrew translation by Shaul-Pinhas Rabinovich (1845–1910), which went through three editions between 1888 and 1899. Rabinovich's translation, in fact, was virtually a new version of Graetz, with substantial additions and footnotes, particularly in sections relating to the history of Russian and Polish Jewry, by Rabinovich, Abraham Harkavi, and other Russian-Jewish historians. Thus the Graetz who reached Hebrew readers—and Rabinovich's "translation" was probably the most widely read work of Hebrew historiography ever produced in Russia—had already been adapted to the new currents of Russian-Jewish historiography.

Institutions

Dubnov's call for the creation of institutions to support Russian-Jewish historiography quickly bore fruit. Previously, the only remotely scholarly Russian-Jewish organization was the Society for the Spread of Enlightenment Among the Jews of Russia, founded in 1863 by wealthy Jewish merchants and bankers in St. Petersburg to promote education in the spirit of the *Haskalah* and knowledge of Russian language and culture. Characteristically, the society had sponsored the publication of a laudatory history of Russia in Hebrew, but not Russian-Jewish historiography, least of all in the nationalist spirit championed by Dubnov.[73] The sole existing forums for the publication of research articles and historical documents with commentary were the Jewish "thick journals."[74]

The formation at the turn of the century of an institutional matrix for Russian-Jewish historiography was the work of that ever-dynamic group within Jewish society: lawyers. Since the late 1880s a circle of young Jewish lawyers in St. Petersburg, stung by the introduction of quotas on Jewish admission to the Bar, had begun to assemble yet another collection documenting the history of the Jews' inferior legal status. As one of them (Maksim M. Vinaver [1862–1926], future Kadet leader and Jewish activist) recounted some years later, the appearance of Dubnov's *On the Study of the History of Russian Jews* in 1891 radically reoriented the group's thinking: "We accepted Dubnov's challenge. We gladly committed ourselves, and in our youthful zeal widened our scope. We decided to form an organization that would embrace history, customs, and legislation—everything that, within the scope of the internal life of the Jewish community, ought to be systematized and studied."[75] The study of such sources opened up "the intimate depths of the folk mind and folk life," the "rich new world of our native past [*rodnaia starina*]."[76] "In all these explicit expressions of a way of life," continued Vinaver, "so much was your own that you felt a blood relationship with them, even before you realized consciously that this relationship was called 'nationality'."[77]

By the turn of the century, having published the first of several volumes of documents illuminating the history of Jewish life in Poland, Lithuania, and Russia, this loose conglomeration of lay historians decided to attach itself to the Society for the Spread of Enlightenment under the title of "Historical-Ethnographic Commission." With the significant relaxation of laws governing the incorporation of public bodies after the revolution of 1905, the Commission was transformed in 1908 into the fully independent Jewish Historical-Ethnographic Society, headquartered in St. Petersburg. The unmistakably populist strain in Dubnov's approach to the Jewish past, itself a reflection of Russian influence, made it natural that the society's interests would encompass both history and ethnography, and in fact blended the two.[78] The society sponsored public lectures, research projects, a Jewish ethnographic museum, and most importantly, a scholarly journal devoted exclusively to Jewish history (as opposed to the eclecticism of the previous "thick journal" format), especially Russian-Jewish history. Under Dubnov's editorship, *Evreiskaia starina* [Jewish Antiquity] appeared annually from 1909 to 1917.[79] Complementing *Evreiskaia starina* was another journal, *Perezhitoe: Sbornik, posviashchen obshchestvennoi i kul'turnoi istorii evreev v Rossii* [The Past: A Journal Dedicated to the Social and Cultural History of the Jews in Russia], four volumes of which appeared between 1908 and 1913. Under the editorship of S.M. Ginzburg (a lawyer by training) and Israel Tsinberg (1873–1939; a chemical engineer), *Perezhitoe* specialized in the publication of primary sources, especially memoirs and folklore.

The Society for Jewish Scholarly Publications, founded in St. Petersburg in 1907, sponsored the monumental sixteen-volume *Evreiskaia entsiklopediia* [Jewish Encyclopedia], among whose contributors were virtually all the historians mentioned in this essay.[80] On the eve of World War I, the society commissioned a massive five-volume narrative history of the Jews of Russia, intended as the culmination of a planned fifteen-volume survey of Jewish history. Due to the exigencies of war, revolution, and emigration, only the first volume of the final unit, covering the Jews of Poland–Lithuania up to the partitions, was ever published (in 1914). Like the idea of the series itself, the first volume offers eloquent testimony to the sea change that had occurred in Russian-Jewish historical consciousness. Less than a quarter century after Dubnov's pessimistic assessment in 1891, the volume's editors cited Russian Jewry's "ever more noticeable growth of interest in studying its own past" and concluded that "the idea of publishing a complete 'History of the Jews in Russia' scarcely requires extensive explanation or justification."[81] With chapters devoted to Jewish self-government, internal and external taxation, artisan guilds, rabbinic thought, Hasidism, popular literature, family structures, and ornamental art, this ambitious volume marked the triumph of Dubnov's autonomist approach.

Thus, during the relatively short period between the two Russian revolutions Russian-Jewish historiography developed an institutional framework closely resembling that of the mainstream historical profession in nearly all respects but one: its enduring exclusion from the academy. Russian-Jewish historiography had become in effect a subculture, parallel to but separate from Russian historiography as a whole. Concentrated for the most part in the city of St. Petersburg, it was also removed, in another sense, from the centers of Jewish life in the Pale of Settlement. As was common among stateless minorities in Eastern Europe, the Jewish intelligentsia first conceived a national-historical consciousness outside its ethno-linguistic territory, in the imperial Russian capital, and from there attempted to propagate it to the Jewish masses of the Pale.[82] To be sure, a Jewish national tradition hardly needed to be "invented" by distant elites; but the notion of a specifically Russian-Jewish past, subject to fruitful scrutiny by secular scholarship, was something genuinely new.

Nation and Class

The revolutionary year of 1917 fundamentally altered the conditions of Russian-Jewish life. In March the Provisional Government annulled all elements of tsarist legislation that discriminated on the basis of religion or nationality, effectively fulfilling in one stroke Orshanskii's liberal agenda of "expelling the Jews from the legal codes." With the Bolshevik seizure of power in October, however, this European-style emancipation was superseded by a policy that officially recognized the Jews as a nationality with implied national "rights," including a limited form of autonomy. Russian-Jewish historiography experienced a similarly radical change in status. What had formerly been a marginalized pursuit shut off from institutions of higher education, driven to a considerable degree by the struggle for equality and the need to combat openly anti-Semitic opponents, suddenly found itself embraced, financed, and regulated by the new Soviet state.[83]

The historiography of Russian Jewry in the 1920s can be divided into two basic currents: one whose orientation and institutional locus derived entirely from prerevolutionary traditions, and another that attempted to combine Marxist historical materialism with the shifting ideological imperatives of Soviet nationality policy. To the first belongs the continuing work of the Historical-Ethnographic Society and the Society for the Spread of Enlightenment. Although a brief burst of Bolshevik fervor temporarily shut down the two "bourgeois" societies in 1918, both were allowed to resume operations during the relatively tolerant 1920s. A short-lived "Jewish People's University" in Petrograd employed Dubnov and other "bourgeois" historians on its faculty, though not without ideological difficulties. The Historical-Ethnographic Society continued to sponsor public lectures and to publish *Evreiskaia starina* (if only sporadically) under Dubnov's editorship until his emigration in 1922 and thereafter under that of the ethnographer Lev Shternberg. The 1920s also witnessed publication of the more popular journal *Evreiskaia letopis'*, whose focus was prerevolutionary memoirs, as well as assorted collections and anthologies, all of which built on the traditions of prerevolutionary historiography.[84] The most significant "bourgeois" work from this period was literally a holdover from before 1917, the final two-volume version of Iulii Gessen's *History of the Jewish People in Russia* (1925, 1927). One of the few prerevolutionary Jewish historians to remain in the Soviet Union (Dubnov was joined in the emigration by Bramson, Pozner, Ginzberg, Elias Cherikover, Mark Vishnitser, Jacob Leshtchintsky, and others), Gessen ceased thereafter to publish work on Russian-Jewish history, devoting himself instead to studies on labor and industry.

In institutional terms, the Marxist current in Jewish historiography during the early Soviet period broke radically from the old St. Petersburg school. No longer reliant on private philanthropy from wealthy Jewish patrons, the "new" Jewish historians could proudly turn for support to organs within the government (the Jewish Department of the People's Commissariat for Nationality Affairs, the Jewish Historical Section of the Ministry of Education) as well as the Party (the Jewish Section, or *Evsektsiia*). One can hardly overstate the impression among Jewish intellectuals—both within the Soviet Union and among sympathizers abroad—created by the fact of state support for Jewish scholarship, a phenomenon without precedent anywhere in the world. For Marxist Jewish historians, liberation from the apologetics and class-tainted patronage of prerevolutionary historiography seemed to promise a kind of epistemological breakthrough to an objective—though hardly neutral—analysis of the Russian-Jewish past.[85]

Linguistically and geographically, too, the new Marxist Jewish historiography departed sharply from the old patterns. Since early Soviet nationality policy encouraged ethnic minorities to develop local cultural institutions using native languages, the *Evsektsiia* strove to make Yiddish rather than Russian the language of Jewish scholarship, shifting the implied readership from acculturated Jews and the Russian-reading public at large to the Jewish masses.[86] Soviet nationality policy, however, was designed with territorially concentrated ethnic groups in mind. Had they conformed to this model, Jews would have been encouraged to create a Yiddish university and academy in an autonomous Jewish republic. But fostering territorial concentration of the Jews was not initially part of official policy, and when it became so in 1928, the resulting autonomous region in Birobijan (near the Chinese border) fell far short of the hoped-for results.[87] In contrast to prerevolutionary Jewish historiography, with its center in the imperial capital, far from the Pale of Settlement, the institutions of the new Jewish historiography were based in the two Soviet republics with the largest Jewish populations, Ukraine and Belorussia. Interestingly, local (non-Jewish) promoters of Soviet-style "Ukrainianization" and "Belorussianization" supported the creation of separate Jewish cultural institutions within their republics, in the hopes of stemming the prerevolutionary trend toward Russification among their Jewish populations. The main centers of Soviet-sponsored Jewish historiography were established in 1925 in Minsk (the Jewish Department of the Institute for Belorussian Culture, led by the historian Israel Sosis [1878–after 1936]), and in 1926 in Kiev (the Institute for Jewish Culture of the Ukrainian Academy of Sciences, led by the historian Joseph Liberberg [1897–1937]).

We have touched on patronage, language, implied audience, and geography. What of the content, the conceptual and methodological tools, the categories and assumptions of the two currents within early Soviet Jewish historiography? Historians on both sides of the divide tended to stress their differences, which essentially involved competing claims for the primacy of national versus class loyalties or, in methodological terms, an eclectic approach that privileged human consciousness versus one grounded in historical materialism. Precisely this dispute lay at the heart of the first major work of postrevolutionary Jewish historiography, a synthetic survey by Tevye Heilikman (1873–1948) entitled *History of the Social Movement Among Jews in Poland and Russia* (1926).[88] In large measure a polemic against Dubnov, Heilikman's study attacked the idea of a uniquely Jewish "spiritual nationhood" as so much scholarly window dressing for the hoary theological doctrine of the Jews as the Chosen People. In Heilikman's rendition, the kahal's legislative, juridical, and fiscal powers were instruments not of national preservation but of class oppression of the poor Jewish masses by the Jewish "ruling class." Indeed, according to Heilikman, Jewish elites deliberately used persecution from without to justify their attempts to mute class conflict.[89]

A similar approach, with variations, was taken by other Soviet Jewish historians. Israel Sosis's *History of Jewish Social Trends in Russia in the Nineteenth Century* (1929) cast the *Haskalah* in Russia as an ideology reflecting the interests of the nascent Jewish merchant class.[90] In 1930 Asher L. Margolis (1891–1976) published his *History of the Jews in Russia: Studies and Documents,* in which he elaborated on Heilikman's treatment of the kahal as an instrument of class oppression, while attempting to analyze legal restrictions on the Jews as deriving from both tsarist colonialism and the Russian bourgeoisie's efforts to avoid competition.[91]

Despite the fierce polemic between the two branches of Jewish historiography in the 1920s—Dubnov was well known for his biting remark that "historical materialism has gained many adherents within the nation whose entire history is a violent protest against this doctrine"[92]—it is worth considering their continuities and shared qualities as well. For the roots of the polemic extend back to the prerevolutionary period, to arguments between the Jewish workers party known as the Bund and the larger Russian Social-Democratic Workers Party. At the beginning of the twentieth century these arguments had begun to take on a historical dimension, revolving around the question of whether or not conditions in Russia had made a separate Jewish workers movement necessary and/or desirable.[93] For its part, the Bund had developed the doctrine of the "double oppression" of Jewish workers by tsarist anti-Semitic legislation, on the one hand, and by the Jewish bourgeoisie, on the other. After the 1917 revolution, former Bundists such as Heilikman, Sosis, Moisei Rafes (1883–1942), and Avram Kirzhinits (1888–1940) made the theme of "double oppression" a cornerstone of their works. Only now, with the political landscape utterly transformed, their opponents were no longer Bolsheviks on the left but "bourgeois nationalist" historians on the right.[94]

With the benefit of hindsight, moreover, it is possible to trace a number of affinities between Dubnov and his Marxist opponents.[95] It was Dubnov, after all, who dethroned the individual religious thinkers celebrated by the *Wissenschaft des Judentums* and who displaced Orshanskii's emphasis on the Jews' external legal status. In their stead he created the first social history of Russian Jewry, making possible a mode of historical continuity that bridged the divide between the periods of Polish and Russian rule—and that became an axiom for Soviet Jewish historians in the 1920s. And although he wrote almost exclusively in Russian, it was Dubnov who championed the idea of a historical literature for and about the Jewish masses.

The undeniable contrasts between the two schools of Jewish historiography were therefore not solely the result of methodological or conceptual disagreements. Of considerable importance was the difference in their relationship to the Soviet state. For while the remnants of the prerevolutionary Jewish historiographical tradition sought little more than to survive under the adverse conditions of Soviet rule, Marxist historians, precisely because of their ideological and institutional ties to the Soviet state, felt the shifting winds of official policy much more keenly. For them, to take one example, the Soviet regime's initial opposition to "Great Russian chauvinism" and the reorganization of the empire into ethnic republics made the inherited rubric of "Russian-Jewish" history untenable. Once again, a realignment of political space posed fundamental challenges to the writing of Jewish history: not even the Jewish historians at the Institute for Belorussian Culture in Minsk could claim that there was such a thing as "Belorussian-Jewish history."[96]

With Stalin's rise to power in the late 1920s, the Soviet regime began to draw ever-sharper limits around expressions of minority national identity, and Jewish historiography found itself pushed further and further into an ideological dead end. The emerging Stalinist orthodoxy, whereby all Soviet scholarship was to serve the working class in its epic struggle with the bourgeoisie, made using the category of nationality a highly risky venture. This was certainly the case with the Jews, whom both Lenin and Stalin had previously declared—in the course of their pre-1917 polemics with the Bund—not to be a bona fide nation.[97] By the time of its publication in 1929, Sosis's *History of Jewish Social Trends in Russia in the Nineteenth Century* was already passé: critics savaged the work for its "nationalist opportunism." Sosis's use of phrases such as "Jewish social trends" rather than "social trends among the Jews" was said to obfuscate the mechanisms of class conflict. By the early 1930s merely using the expression "Jewish people" was enough to provoke charges of bourgeois nationalism.[98]

As part of the general campaign against "bourgeois" historians, the citadels of prerevolutionary Jewish historiography—the Historical-Ethnographic Society and the Society for the Spread of Enlightenment in Leningrad—were liquidated in 1929, with the enthusiastic support of their rivals in Minsk and Kiev. The latter, however, were to follow close behind: in the mid-1930s they too were silenced, and many of their leading cadres fell victim to the purges. With the liquidation in 1936 of the Institute for Jewish Culture in Kiev (by then somewhat desperately renamed the "Institute for Jewish Proletarian Culture"), the historiography of Russian and East European Jewry ceased to exist in the Soviet Union, and would not return for over a half century.[99]

Dispersion and Legacy

Although it disappeared from the Soviet Union, the historiographic tradition whose development I have attempted to trace in this essay continued to evolve elsewhere, transplanted by émigrés to other centers of Jewish life. Of these, the most important were Jerusalem, Vilna, Warsaw, and eventually New York. In both personnel and scholarly approach, the Institute of Jewish Studies founded in 1924 as one of three original departments of the Hebrew University in Jerusalem, drew significantly on Russian-Jewish scholarship and indeed regarded itself as a successor to the Russian-Jewish "center" as conceived by Dubnov. An even greater debt was owed by the Institute for Jewish Research (known by its Yiddish acronym, YIVO), founded in Polish Vilna in 1925. Here Dubnov and other Jewish historians, demographers, and linguists from the former Russian Empire continued their research on Russian and East European Jewry; here the doctrines of "diaspora nationalism" and "Yiddishism" found full expression. Despite the virtual annihilation of East European Jewry in the Holocaust, YIVO managed to reestablish itself after the war in New York, where it remains an active center of research. The Institute for Jewish Studies in Warsaw, founded by the historian Majer Balaban and others in 1927, was also strongly influenced by prerevolutionary and early Soviet Jewish historiography, and was reconstituted, though in greatly diminished form, after 1945.[100]

Beginning in the Gorbachev era and especially since the collapse of the Soviet Union, Jewish historiography has again emerged, tentatively, in Russia, Ukraine, and other former Soviet territories. Like its previous incarnations, it is confronting the difficulties of tracing Jewish history across yet another recasting of political boundaries. Conferences, scholarly journals, and newly founded Jewish institutions of higher education are generating a scholarly infrastructure, while the prerevolutionary Russian-language *Jewish Encyclopedia* and works by Dubnov and Gessen are being reprinted for a new generation of readers.[101] Whether these activities represent a genuine revival of historiography or are part of an ephemeral wave of nostalgia for the pre-Soviet past remains to be seen.

Notes

I would like to thank David Myers, Eli Nathans, and Robert Weinberg for their comments on earlier versions of this essay. Generous financial support during the period when the essay was written came from the National Council for Soviet and East European Research and the Social Science Research Council, both under authority of a Title VIII Grant from the U.S. Department of State. Additional support was provided by the Memorial Foundation for Jewish Culture.

1. The following categories of works, however, are not discussed here: works on Russian-Jewish history written by individuals outside the territory of the Russian Empire, and works produced in Russia concerning other areas and periods of Jewish history, such as that of ancient Israel. Studies of pre-partition Polish and Lithuanian Jewry

are considered only when they treat their subject as part of the history of Jews in the Russian Empire. I recognize that these decisions may occasionally appear arbitrary, but they have been taken with considerations of space and coherence, as well as thematic unity with the other essays in this volume, in mind.

2. S.M. Dubnov, *Ob izuchenii istorii russkikh evreev i ob uchrezhdenii russko-evreiskogo istoricheskogo obshchestva* (St. Petersburg: A.E. Landau, 1891), pp. 1, 19.

3. On the tension between history and memory in Jewish tradition, see Yosef Hayim Yerushalmi, *Zakhor: Jewish History and Jewish Memory* (New York: Schocken Books, 1989 [1982]). See also Ismar Schorsch, *From Text to Context: The Turn to History in Modern Judaism* (Hannover: University Press of New England, 1994) and the useful introduction in Michael A. Meyer, *Ideas of Jewish History* (Detroit: Wayne State University Press, 1987 [1974]), pp. 1–42.

4. David Roskies, *Against the Apocalypse: Responses to Catastrophe in Modern Jewish Literature* (Cambridge: Harvard University Press, 1984), p. 48.

5. Quoted in Yerushalmi, *Zakhor,* p. 50.

6. Quoted in Meir Tamari, *'With All Your Possessions': Jewish Ethics and Economic Life* (New York: Free Press, 1987), p. 13.

7. On the "traditionalness" of Jewish culture in early modern Europe, see Jacob Katz, *Out of the Ghetto: The Social Background of Jewish Emancipation, 1770–1870* (New York: Schocken, 1978), pp. 4–7.

8. On the Jewish Enlightenment in the Russian Empire, see Emanuel Etkes, ed., *Ha-dat ve-hahaim: tenuat ha-haskalah be-mizrah eiropah* (Jerusalem: The Zalman Shazar Center, 1993); David Fishman, *Russia's First Modern Jews: The Jews of Shklov* (New York: NYU Press, 1995); Michael Stanislawski, *Tsar Nicholas I and the Jews: The Transformation of Jewish Society in Russia, 1825–1855* (Philadelphia: Jewish Publication Society, 1983), pp. 49–96.

9. The anti-Hasidic literature of the Haskalah, while not directly historical, was put to historical use by later writers; see Israel Bartal, "The Imprint of Haskalah Literature on the Historiography of Hasidism," in Ada Rapaport-Albert, ed., *Hasidim Reappraised* (Portland: Vallentine, Mitchell & Co., 1996), pp. 367–75. Examples of local chronicles, which were little more than compilations of primary sources, include S.I. Fin, *Kiryah ne'emanah* (Vilna, 1860), on the Jews of Vilna; S. Fridenshtein, *Ir gevorim* (Vilna, 1880), on the Jews of Grodno; and L. Fainshtein, *Ir tehilah* (Warsaw, 1886), on the Jews of Brest-Litovsk.

10. These issues are explored in detail in Shmuel Feiner, *Haskalah ve-historyah: toldoteha shel hakarat-'avar yehudit modernit* (Jerusalem: Merkaz Zalman Shazar, 1995).

11. See Benjamin Nathans, *Beyond the Pale: The Jewish Encounter with Late Imperial Russia* (forthcoming, University of California Press), chapter 1.

12. See for example Israel Sosis, "Obshchestvennye nastroeniia 'epokhi velikikh reform'," *Evreiskaia starina* vol. 6, no. 3–4 (1914), p. 360; Shaul M. Ginzburg, *Amolike Peterburg: Forshungn un zikhroynes vegn yidishn lebn in der rezidents-shtot fun tsarishn rusland* (New York: Bikher Farlag, 1944), p. 29; S.M. Dubnov, *Kniga zhizni: Vospominaniia i razmyshleniia: Materialy dlia istorii moego vremeni* (Riga: Jaunatnes Gramata, 1934), vol. 1, p. 103.

13. S.L. Tsinberg, "Arkadii (Avram-Uri) Kovner: Pisarevshchina v evreiskoi literature," *Perezhitoe* vol. 2 (1910), p. 133; and idem, "Assimiliatsiia," in *Evreiskaia entsiklopediia: Svod znanii o evreistve i ego kul'ture v proshlom i nastoiashchem* (St. Petersburg: Brockhaus-Efron, 1906–1913), vol. 3, p. 334.

14. There were several important exceptions, including works by Abraham Harkavi in Hebrew and German (discussed below) and Ben-Zion Katz's *Le-korot ha-yehudim*

be-rusyah u-polin ve-lita (Vilna, 1898), one of the first works to employ rabbinical responsa as a historical source. "Counter-histories" composed by Orthodox Jews in response to the emerging secular Russian-Jewish historiography were also written in Hebrew, and began to appear at the beginning of the twentieth century. See Israel Bartal, " 'True Knowledge and Wisdom': On Orthodox Historiography," *Studies in Contemporary Jewry,* vol. 10 (1994), pp. 178–92. As Bartal makes clear, these "histories" rejected many of the methodological assumptions of the secular works to which they responded; in fact, they typically declined to cite nonreligious works lest faithful readers be led astray. Another body of quasi-historical literature, also in Hebrew, can be found in the hagiographies produced by the Habad branch of Hasidism; see Ada Rapoport-Albert, "Hagiography with Footnotes: Edifying Tales and the Writing of History in Hasidism," *History and Theory,* no. 27: *Essays in Jewish Historiography* (1988), pp. 137–99.

15. The roughly simultaneous flowering of a rich fictional literature in Yiddish—the first language of the Jewish masses—serves only to highlight the absence of a Yiddish-language historiography (except in translation). Only in the 1920s, with official support from the new Soviet state, did a body of original historical works begin to appear in Yiddish (see below).

16. In Germany, for example, even the ultrascholarly *Wissenschaft des Judentums* was implicated in the contemporary struggle for Jewish emancipation. See Schorsch, *From Text to Context,* pp. 266–302. On Russian public debates concerning the "Jewish Question," see John D. Klier, *Imperial Russia's Jewish Question, 1855–1881* (Cambridge, UK: Cambridge University Press, 1995).

17. See the article by David Pasmanik in the newspaper *Rassvet,* no. 48 (1913), p. 11, quoted in R.Sh. Ganelin and V.E. Kel´ner, "Problemy istoriografii evreev v Rossii, 2-ia polovina XIX veka–1-ia chetvert´ XX veka," in Marina Agranovskaia, ed., *Evrei v Rossii: istoriograficheskie ocherki* (Moscow and Jerusalem: Nauka/Gesharim, 1994), p. 197.

18. The charge of ritual murder, a central tenet of Christian anti-Semitic mythology, dates back to the early medieval period. It alleges that Jews use the blood of Christian children when preparing unleavened bread for the Passover holiday. Brafman's *Kniga kagala: materialy dlia izucheniia evreiskogo byta* was first published, with official sponsorship, in Vilna in 1869. Revised and expanded editions appeared in 1875, 1882, and 1888. Like several of the leading anti-Semitic ideologues of late imperial Russia, Brafman was an apostate from Judaism who gained added credibility from his alleged inside knowledge of Jewish life.

19. Andreas Kappeler, *Russland als Vielvölkerreich: Entstehung, Geschichte, Zerfall* (Munich: C.H. Beck, 1992), p. 220.

20. Among those Jews who were offered faculty appointments at the price of conversion, and who declined, were the lawyer-historians Il´ia Orshanskii and Genrikh Sliozberg. See the chapter on Jews in the Russian legal profession in Nathans, *Beyond the Pale.*

21. On conditions in Germany (Prussia), see Schorsch, *From Text to Context,* pp. 51–63. Two government-sponsored rabbinical seminaries existed briefly in Russia, from 1847 to 1873, and only a single, minor historian of Russian Jewry (S.I. Fin; see note 9) ever graced their faculties. See *Evreiskaia entsiklopediia,* vol. 13, pp. 257–62.

22. See the distribution by faculty of Jewish students at various Russian universities during the 1870s in *Rossiiskii gosudarstvennyi istoricheskii arkhiv* (RGIA), f. 733 (*Ministerstvo narodnogo prosveshcheniia*), op. 226, d. 27, ll. 8–148.

23. *Evreiskaia entsiklopediia,* vol. 10, p. 159; see the works listed there.

24. *Evreiskaia entsiklopediia,* vol. 4, pp. 341–47; see the works listed there. See also Paul E. Soifer, "The Bespectacled Cossack: S.A. Bershadskii (1850–1896) and the

Development of Russo-Jewish Historiography" (unpublished Ph.D. dissertation, Pennsylvania State University, 1975). Bershadskii was the guiding spirit behind the publication of several important collections of archival documents, including some concerning the internal administration of early modern Jewish communities. In this he anticipated the documentary approach of Simon Dubnov in the 1890s (see notes 72 and 73).

25. D.A. Khvol'son, *O nekotorykh srednevekovykh obvineniiakh protiv evreev: Istoricheskoe izsledovanie po istochnikam* (St. Petersburg, 1880 [1861]). Among Russian Jews, Khvol'son was well known for an offhand remark concerning his career as historian: when asked whether he had converted to Christianity out of conviction, he was supposed to have replied, "Yes, I was convinced that it was better to be a professor in St. Petersburg than a *melamed* [teacher in a Jewish primary school] in Eyshishok." Quoted in Lucy Dawidowicz, ed., *The Golden Tradition: Jewish Life and Thought in Eastern Europe* (New York: Holt, Rinehart, and Winston, 1967), p. 335. On Khvol'son's career and image among Russian Jews, see Shaul Ginzburg, *Meshumodim in tsarishn rusland* (New York: Bikher Farlag, 1946), pp. 119–56, and *Evreiskaia entsiklopediia,* vol. 15, 584–87.

26. This is only a hypothesis, since the evidence for such influence is sparse. Dubnov and other contemporary Jewish historians rarely cited the major Russian historians, and when they did, it was often with a complaint about the scant and unfavorable attention they had devoted to the Jews. See Dubnov, *Ob izuchenii istorii russkikh evreev,* p. 29.

27. Michael Stanislawski makes this point in *Tsar Nicholas I and the Jews,* p. 6.

28. Over twenty such manuals were published between 1860 and 1917, and several went through multiple editions. The most comprehensive—in part because they were published toward the end of the imperial period—are I.V. Gessen and V. Fridshtein, eds., *Sbornik zakonov o evreiakh s raz"iasneniiami po opredeleniiam Pravitel'stvuiushchago Senata i tsirkuliaram Ministerstv* (Petersburg, 1904); Ia.I. Gimpel'son, comp., L.M. Bramson, ed., *Zakony o evreiakh: Sistematicheskii obzor deistvuiushchikh zakonopolozhenii o evreiakh,* 2 vols. (St. Petersburg, 1914–15); and M.I. Mysh, comp., *Rukovodstvo k russkim zakonam o evreiakh,* 3d ed., (St. Petersburg, 1904).

29. One of the bestselling manuals was N.D. Gradovskii's *Torgovye i drugie prava evreev v Rossii v istoricheskom khode zakonodatel'nykh mer* (Petersburg, 1885), which went through twelve editions.

30. Orshanskii's essays on Jewish issues, which initially appeared in the periodical press, were collected in two volumes published shortly after his death at age twenty-nine: I.G. Orshanskii, *Evrei v Rossii: Ocherki ekonomicheskogo i obshchestvennogo byta russkikh evreev* (St. Petersburg: I.O. Bakst, 1877), and idem, *Russkoe zakonodatel'stvo o evreiakh: Ocherki i izsledovaniia* (St. Petersburg, 1877). Four additional volumes of Orshanskii's writings on Russian civil law were also collected and published posthumously. For a survey of his writings on Russian-Jewish history, see Yitshak Maor, "Eliahu Orshanskii u-makomo ba-historiografyah shel yehudei rusyah," *He-Avar,* vol. 20 (1973), pp. 49–61.

31. Orshanskii, *Russkoe zakonodatel'stvo o evreiakh,* pp. 137–56.

32. Ibid., p. 336.

33. Stanislawski, *Tsar Nicholas I and the Jews,* pp. 5–8.

34. Orshanskii, *Russkoe zakonodatel'stvo o evreiakh,* pp. 3–4.

35. Ibid., pp. 4–6.

36. Ibid., p. 3.

37. Examples of this dissonance can be found in treatments of the extension of military conscription to the Jews (in the context of Nicholas I's general militarization of Russian society), the policy of selective Jewish emancipation (and its place within the

Great Reforms), as well as the establishment of quotas for Jewish students in the late 1880s (within the general reintroduction of estate-based university admissions).

38. S.V. Pozner, *Evrei v obshchei shkole: K istorii zakonodatel'stva i pravitel'stvennoi politiki v oblasti evreiskogo voprosa* (St. Petersburg: Razum, 1914), p. xii.

39. S.M. Ginzburg, *Otechestvennaia voina 1812 goda i russkie evrei* (St. Petersburg: Razum, 1912); Pozner, *Evrei v obshchei shkole;* M.L. Usov, *Evrei v armii* (St. Petersburg: Razum, 1911).

40. Examples of this formula can be found in Pozner, *Evrei v obshchei shkole,* pp. 56 and 185; L.B. [L.M. Bramson], "Sudebnaia reforma i evrei," *Voskhod,* nos. 11–12 (1889), p. 8; M. Morgulis, "Iz moikh vospominanii," *Voskhod,* no. 2 (1895), p. 108; and in works of contemporary Jewish fiction and journalism. The image of the stepmother evoked both the manner by which Russia acquired its Jews (unintentionally, through imperial expansion) and the memory of the "real" motherland, the land of Israel.

41. For a thoughtful discussion of similar issues as they relate to the historical representation of Ukraine, see Mark von Hagen, "Does Ukraine Have a History?," *Slavic Review,* vol. 54, no. 3 (Fall 1995), pp. 658–73, and the responses that follow.

42. Benjamin Nathans, "Conflict, Community, and the Jews of Late Nineteenth-Century St. Petersburg," *Jahrbücher für Geschichte Osteuropas,* vol. 44, no. 2 (Spring 1996), p. 179, n. 2.

43. *Evreiskaia entsiklopediia* vol. 6, pp. 180–83. Harkavi was denied a teaching position because of his refusal to convert, but in the 1890s the tsarist government made him a hereditary nobleman in recognition of his international scholarly reputation.

44. See the following works by Harkavi [Garkavi]: *Ob iazyke evreev, zhivshikh v drevnee vremia na Rusi* (St. Petersburg, 1865); *Ha-yehudim u-sfat ha-slavim* (1867); *Skazaniia evreiskikh pisatelei o khazarakh i khazarskom tsarstve* (St. Petersburg, 1874); *Altjüdische Denkmäler aus der Krim* (1876); *Istoricheskie ocherki Karaimstva* (St. Petersburg, 1897).

45. Harkavi [Garkavi], "Po voprosu o iudeiskikh drevnostiakh, naidennykh Firkovichem v Krymu," *Zhurnal Ministerstva narodnogo prosveshcheniia* (1877) vol. 192, no. 7.

46. See Arthur Koestler, *The Thirteenth Tribe: The Khazar Empire and Its Heritage* (New York: Popular Library, 1978), and on a more scholarly level, Paul Wexler, *The Ashkenazic Jews: A Slavo-Turkic People in Search of a Jewish Identity* (Columbus, Ohio: Slavica Publishers, 1993).

47. On Jewish foundation myths, see Bernard Dov Weinryb, "The Beginnings of East European Jewry in Legend and Historiography," in idem et al., eds., *Studies and Essays in Honor of Abraham A. Neuman* (Leiden, 1962), pp. 445–502. At roughly the same time that Harkavi and others were constructing a foundation myth for Russian Jewry, Jewish scholars in England, France, Germany, and the United States were embarking on similar efforts in their respective countries. See Schorsch, *From Text to Context,* pp. 354–55.

48. See Gessen's acknowledgment of this debt in the preface to his *Istoriia evreiskogo naroda v Rossii* (Leningrad: Gublit, 1925), vol. 1, p. 3.

49. Iu.I. Gessen, *Istoriia evreev v Rossii* (St. Petersburg: Pravo, 1914).

50. Quoted in Ganelin and Kel'ner, "Problemy istoriografii evreev v Rossii," p. 197.

51. Ibid., p. 197.

52. Gessen, *Istoriia evreiskogo naroda v Rossii* (Petrograd: Pravo, 1916). Due to the upheavals of war and revolution, the planned second volume did not appear until 1927, and then only in abridged form, following the second, abridged version of the first volume (1925).

53. Gessen, *Istoriia evreiskogo naroda v Rossii,* 2 vols. (Leningrad: Gublit, 1925

and 1927); the quotation is from vol. 1, p. 6. For a complete bibliography of Gessen's publications, see the appendix of the recent reprint of *Istoriia evreiskogo naroda v Rossii* (Moscow: Evreiskii Universitet v Moskve, 1993), pp. i–vi.

54. The handful of earlier works that drew on archival sources include A.V. Beletskii, *Vopros ob obrazovanii russkikh evreev v tsarstvovanii imperatora Nikolaia I* (St. Petersburg: Russkaia shkola, 1894); O.M. Lerner, *Evrei v Novorossiiskom krae* (Odessa: G.M. Levinson, 1901); P.S. Marek, *Ocherki po istorii prosveshcheniia evreev v Rossii* (Moscow: Obshchestvo dlia rasprostraneniia pravel'nykh svedenii o evreiakh i evreistve, 1909); Kh.D. Ryvkin, *Evrei v Smolenske: Ocherk po istorii evreiskogo poselenii v Smolenske s drevneishikh vremen v sviazi s obshchestvennom polozheniem evreev v drevnei Rusi* (St. Petersburg: Bussel, 1910).

55. Only in 1990 did the enormous volume of materials relating to Jewish history housed in archives of the former Soviet Union become available to scholars. For a preliminary overview of such materials, see G.M. Deych, comp., and Benjamin Nathans, ed., *Arkhivnye dokumenty po istorii evreev v Rossii v XIX–nachale XX vv: Putevoditel'* (Moscow: Blagovest', 1994), and D.A. Eliashevich, comp., *Dokumental'nye materialy po istorii evreev v arkhivakh SNG i stran baltii: predvaritel'nyi spisok arkhivnykh fondov* (St. Petersburg: Akropol, 1994).

56. Because of his wide influence, Dubnov has received more attention than all other historians of Russian Jewry combined. The most sophisticated treatment of his historical thought is to be found in Robert M. Seltzer, "Simon Dubnow [Dubnov]: A Critical Biography of His Early Years" (unpublished Ph.D. dissertation, Columbia University, 1970). See also idem, "From Graetz to Dubnow: The Impact of the East European Milieu on the Writing of Jewish History," in David Berger, ed., *The Legacy of Jewish Migration: 1881 and Its Impact* (New York: Brooklyn College Press, 1983), pp. 49–60; Koppel S. Pinson, "Simon Dubnow: Historian and Political Philosopher," in idem, ed., *Nationalism and History: Essays on Old and New Judaism by Simon Dubnow* (Philadelphia: Jewish Publication Society, 1958), pp. 3–65; Raphael Mahler, "Shitat Dubnov u-mif'alo be-historiografyah ha-yehudit," in Aaron Steinberg, ed., *Simon Dubnow: The Man and His Work* (Paris: World Jewish Congress, 1963); Yehudah Rozental, "Ha-historiografyah ha-yehudit be-rusyah ha-sovyetit ve-Shim'on Dubnov," in Simon Rawidowicz, ed., *Sefer Shim'on Dubnov* (London: Ararat Publishing Company, 1954), pp. 201–20; and most recently, David H. Weinberg, *Between Tradition and Modernity: Haim Zhitlowksi, Simon Dubnow, Ahad Ha-Am, and the Shaping of Modern Jewish Identity* (New York: Holmes and Meier, 1996), pp. 145–216.

57. This idea is developed by Isaiah Trunk, "Historians of Russian Jewry," in Jacob Frumkin et al., eds., *Russian Jewry (1860–1917)* (New York: A.S. Barnes, 1966), pp. 464–65. See also S. Levenberg, "Simon Dubnov, Historian of Russian Jewry," *Soviet Jewish Affairs,* vol. 12, no. 1 (1982).

58. Orshanskii, *Russkoe zakonodatel'stvo o evreiakh,* p. 336.

59. M. Morgulis, "Kagal: ego proiskhozhdenie i uchrezhdenie magdeburgskogo prava: Po povodu 'Kniga kagala' g. Brafmana," in idem, *Voprosy evreiskoi zhizni: Sobranie statei* (n.p., 1903 [1889]), p. 343. This argument reflects what I refer to above as the chicken-and-egg debate in contemporary discussions of the "Jewish Question."

60. Dubnov, *Ob izuchenii,* pp. 52–53.

61. In addition to the Russian original (*Ob izuchenii istorii russkikh evreev*), Dubnov published his programmatic statement in an abridged Hebrew version, "Nahpesa ve-nahkora," *Pardes,* vol. 1 (1892), pp. 221–42.

62. Dubnov, *Ob izuchenii,* p. 56.

63. Ibid., p. 38.

64. Dubnov, *Kniga zhizni,* vol. 1, p. 282.

65. These data come from Dubnov's "auto-bibliography," in Steinberg, *Simon Dubnow: The Man and His Work,* p. 235. They concern only the Russian version of Dubnov's textbook, and do not include sales of the popular Yiddish and Hebrew translations used in Jewish schools in Russia and Palestine.

66. Twenty-five percent of the respondents listed Dubnov alone; an additional 18 percent listed both Dubnov and Graetz. Only 5 percent of the respondents listed any other authors. See *K kharakteristike evreiskogo studenchestva, po dannym ankety sredi evreiskogo studenchestva g. Kieva v noiabre 1910 g.* (Kiev: Rabotnik, 1913), p. 28.

67. Though composed in Russian, Dubnov's magnum opus first appeared in German as *Weltgeschichte des jüdischen Volkes,* 10 vols. (Berlin: Jüdischer Verlag, 1925–1929) and has since been translated and published in several languages, although not in Russian.

68. The idea of Jewish autonomy in the diaspora had also developed among Jews in the fin-de-siècle Austro-Hungarian Empire, but as a political platform, without the historiographic component. See Oscar Janowsky, *The Jews and Minority Rights, 1898–1919* (New York: Columbia University Press, 1933).

69. The Folkspartei itself had little impact in Russia, but the theory of autonomism was enormously influential among non-Zionist and non-Orthodox Jewish political parties, including socialist ones. Offshoots of the Folkspartei achieved notable influence between the world wars in the sizable Jewish communities of Latvia, Lithuania, Poland, and Romania.

70. Seltzer, "Simon Dubnow: A Critical Biography," p. 217.

71. Dubnov, "The Sociological View of Jewish History" (introduction to his *Weltgeschichte*), reprinted in Pinson, *Nationalism and History,* p. 351.

72. S.M. Dubnow [Dubnov], *History of the Jews in Russia and Poland from the Earliest Times until the Present Day* (Philadelphia: Jewish Publication Society, 1916), vol. 3, p. 30. Dubnov's works on modern Jewish history are sprinkled with references to latter-day pharaohs, Hamans, etc. The risk of such analogies is well illustrated in the example of Jewish admission quotas: as Dubnov later acknowledges, the quota system was soon extended to several of the elite institutions of higher education for women.

73. See Dubnov's withering review of the society's activities during its first three decades, "Literaturnaia letopis': Itogi Obshchestva prosveshcheniia evreev," *Voskhod* (1891), vol. 10, pp. 41–55 and vol. 11, pp. 13–24.

74. The most important "thick journals"—anthologies of poetry, fiction, journalism, and travel literature—for the publication of historical works were *Evreiskaia biblioteka* (ten volumes between 1871 and 1903), *Voskhod* (monthly between 1881 and 1906), *Budushchnost'* (four volumes between 1900 and 1903), *Sefer ha-shana* (four volumes between 1900 and 1903), and *Ha-Shiloah* (monthly, with gaps, from 1902 to 1919). For a brief survey of the polyglot Jewish press in the Russian Empire, see *Encyclopedia Judaica* (Jerusalem: Keter, 1972), vol. 13, pp. 1044–47.

75. M.M. Vinaver, "Kak my zanimalis' istoriei," *Evreiskaia starina,* vol. 1, no. 1 (1909), pp. 48–49. Vinaver mentions the assistance and inspiration provided to the group by S.A. Bershadskii and the renowned Russian Orthodox philosopher Vladimir Solov'ev.

76. See the introduction to the annotated document collection produced by this group of Jewish lawyers: M.M. Vinaver, A.G. Gornfel'd, L.A. Sev, M.G. Syrkin, eds., *Regesty i nadpisi: Svod materialov dlia istorii evreev v Rossii (80 g.—1800 g.)* (St. Petersburg: Obshchestvo rasprostraneniia prosveshcheniia mezhdu evreiami v Rossii, 1899), vol. 1, p. vi. Two previous volumes under nearly the identical title, edited by S.A. Bershadskii, had appeared in 1896 and 1897; subsequent volumes, published in 1910 and 1913, drew significantly on material gathered by Bershadskii.

77. Vinaver, "Kak my zanimalis' istoriei," p. 49. Another member of the group and

disciple of Dubnov's, Mark L. Vishnitser (one of the few nonlawyers), noted that in contrast to the *Wissenschaft des Judentums,* "here there was a stronger feeling of closeness to the life of the people." See Mark Wischnitzer, "Reminiscences of a Jewish Historian," in Frumkin, *Russian Jewry,* p. 474.

78. On the growth of Russian-Jewish ethnography and folklore at the turn of the century, see Mark Kiel, *A Twice Lost Legacy: Ideology, Culture, and the Pursuit of Jewish Folklore in Russia* (forthcoming, Stanford University Press). For the early Soviet period see Paul Soifer, *Soviet Jewish Folkloristics and Ethnography: An Institutional History, 1918–1948* (New York, 1978).

79. See V. Lukin, "K stoletiiu obrazovaniia peterburgskoi nauchnoi shkoly evreiskoi istorii," in D. Eliashevich, ed., *Trudy po iudaike,* vol. 1 (1993), pp. 13–26. As Lukin makes clear, the designation of a "Petersburg school" (his term) of Jewish historiography reflects geographical placement more than conceptual or thematic unity.

80. *Evreiskaia entsiklopediia: Svod znanii o evreistve i ego kul'ture v proshlom i nastoiashchem,* 16 vols. (St. Petersburg: Brockhaus-Efron, 1906–1913).

81. A.I. Braudo, M.L. Vishnitser, Iu.I. Gessen, S.M. Ginzburg, P.S. Marek, and S.L. Tsinberg, *Istoriia evreev v Rossii* vol. 1 [= *Istoriia evreiskogo naroda,* vol. 11] (Moscow: Mir, 1914), p. i.

82. Nataliia V. Iukhneva, "Peterburg kak tsentr natsional'no-kul'turnykh dvizhenii narodov Rossii," *Etnografiia Peterburga-Leningrada,* no. 1 (1987), pp. 4–12.

83. In the discussion that follows I rely heavily on the excellent study by Alfred A. Greenbaum, *Jewish Scholarship in Soviet Russia, 1918–1953* (Jerusalem: Hebrew University of Jerusalem, 1978).

84. See, for example, the various collections edited by S.M. Ginzburg: *He-avar* (Moscow, 1918); *Evreiskaia mysl',* 2 vols. (Petrograd/Leningrad, 1922 and 1926); *Evreiskii vestnik* (Leningrad, 1928); *Minuvshee* (Petrograd, 1923); and also V.I. Binshtok, ed., *Voprosy biologii i patologii evreev,* 3 vols. (Leningrad, 1926–29).

85. Greenbaum, *Jewish Scholarship,* p. 91.

86. An important exception, however, was the substantial number of works in Russian on the history of the Jewish labor movement which, because of its intimate ties to the history of the revolutionary movement as a whole, was thought to appeal to non-Jewish audiences as well. Examples include M. Rafes, *Ocherki po istorii "Bunda"* (Moscow: Moskovskii Rabochii, 1923), and idem, *Ocherki istorii evreiskogo rabochego dvizheniia* (Moscow-Leningrad, 1929); N.A. Bukhbinder, *Istoriia evreiskogo rabochego dvizheniia v Rossii* (Leningrad: Akademicheskoe izdatel'stvo, 1925); L. Deich, *Rol' evreev v russkom revoliutsionnom dvizhenii* (Moscow-Leningrad: GIZ, 1925); A.D. Kirzhinits, ed., *1905. Evreiskoe rabochee dvizhenie: Obzor, materialy i dokumenty* (Moscow-Leningrad: GIZ, 1928); and S. Dimanshtein, ed., *Revoliutsionnoe dvizhenie sredi evreev* (Moscow: Vsesoiuznoe obshchestvo politkatorzhan i ssyl'no-poselentsev, 1930). Several of these works were translated into Yiddish.

87. Greenbaum, *Jewish Scholarship,* p. 25.

88. *Geshikhte fun der gezelshaftlekher bavegung fun di yidn in poyln un rusland* (Moscow: Tsentraler farlag far di felker fun G.S.S.R., 1926). A Russian translation appeared as *Istoriia obshchestvennogo dvizheniia evreev v Pol'she i Rossii* (Moscow, 1930).

89. Heilikman, *Geshikhte fun der gezelshaftlekher bavegung,* p. 8.

90. Israel Sosis, *Di geshikhte fun di yidishe gezelshaftlekhe shtremungen in rusland in 19. y.h.* (Minsk, 1929).

91. A. Margolis, *Geshikhte fun yidn in rusland (1772–1861)* (Moscow, 1930).

92. Dubnov, "The Moral of Stormy Days," in Pinson, ed., *Nationalism and History,* p. 210.

93. See, for example, B.N. Krichevskii, *Istoriia evreiskogo rabochego dvizheniia v*

Rossii i Pol'she (Geneva: Soiuz russkikh sotsial-demokratov, 1901), and the Bund's *Materialy k istorii evreiskogo rabochego dvizheniia,* 2 vols. (St. Petersburg: Tribuna, 1906–07). The fundamental theoretical issue at stake here was embodied in Marx's ambiguous declaration in the *Communist Manifesto* that "though not in substance, yet in form, the struggle of the proletariat with the bourgeoisie is at first a national struggle." Much of the debate between the Bund and the RSDRP (and in fact within the Bund itself) revolved around the question of whether Russian Jewry constituted a "nation" and, if so, how long the "at first" stage should last.

94. For works by Rafes and Kirzhinits, see note 86. The direct link between pre-revolutionary Bundist historiography and that of Soviet Jewish scholars in the 1920s suggests that Greenbaum's characterization of Jewish historiography during the Soviet period as "a hothouse plant produced by Soviet nationality policy" (*Jewish Scholarship,* p. 135) requires qualification. Fundamental conceptual and methodological aspects of Soviet-Jewish scholarship trace their origin to the pre-revolutionary period, and can also be found in Marxist-Jewish scholarship in interwar Poland, where a very different political climate prevailed.

95. This issue is raised by Aleksandr Lokshin, "Rossiiskaia iudaika," *God za godom,* vol. 6 (1991), p. 409.

96. Greenbaum, *Jewish Scholarship,* pp. 86–95.

97. See V.I. Lenin, "Critical Remarks on the National Question" (1912), reprinted in Hyman Lumer, ed., *Lenin on the Jewish Question* (New York: International Publishers, 1974), and Joseph Stalin, "Marxism and the National Question" (1913), in idem, *Marxism and the National Question* (Moscow: Foreign Language Publishing House, 1934).

98. Greenbaum, *Jewish Scholarship,* pp. 94–98.

99. On the general campaign against "bourgeois" historiography, see George Enteen, "Marxist Historians During the Cultural Revolution: A Case Study of Professional In-Fighting," in Sheila Fitzpatrick, ed., *Cultural Revolution in Russia, 1928–1931* (Bloomington: Indiana University Press, 1978), pp. 154–68. On the Jewish component, see Greenbaum, *Jewish Scholarship,* pp. 18–23.

100. On the "Jerusalem School" of historians, see David N. Myers, *Re-Inventing the Jewish Past: European Jewish Intellectuals and the Zionist Return to History* (New York: Oxford University Press, 1995). On YIVO, see the collection of essays commemorating the institute's fiftieth anniversary in *Yivo Bleter,* vol. 46 (1980), especially Y. Trunk, "Yivo un di yidishe historishe visnshaft," pp. 242-54, and also Lucjan Dobroszycki, "YIVO in Interwar Poland: Work in the Historical Sciences," in Yisrael Gutman et al., eds., *The Jews of Poland Between Two World Wars* (Hanover: University Press of New England, 1989), pp. 494-518. Currently, Cecile Kuznitz of Stanford University is preparing a doctoral dissertation on the history of YIVO. On the Warsaw school, see Artur Eisenbach, "Jewish Historiography in Interwar Poland," in Gutman, *The Jews of Poland,* pp. 453-93.

101. Jewish institutions of higher education have been established in Kiev, St. Petersburg, and Moscow. Their publications include the quarterly *Vestnik evreiskogo universiteta v Moskve* (Moscow, 1992–), and the annual *Trudy po iudaike: istoriia i etnografiia* (St. Petersburg, 1993–), both devoted largely to the history of Jews in the Russian Empire and Soviet Union. Iulii Gessen's *Istoriia evreiskogo naroda v Rossii* has been reprinted (see note 53), and a reprint of Dubnov's superb memoirs, *Kniga zhizni,* is forthcoming. For a recent overview, see David Fishman, "The Rebirth of Jewish Scholarship in Russia," *American Jewish Year Book* (1997).

19

The Emergence of
a Modern Central Asian
Historical Consciousness

Adeeb Khalid

Central Asia, the last major territorial annexation of the Russian empire, was an integral part of the Muslim world at the time of its conquest. Its literary culture, and the historical vision that informed it, were intimately connected to patterns of cultural practice in the broader Muslim world. The short period of imperial Russian rule—practically coterminous with the postreform era—ushered in the forces of modernity in the region, which transformed the historical imagination of its elites. The new historical imagination lay at the bottom of the intense politics of identity that marked the first decade of Soviet rule.

In this essay, I seek to sketch this transformation and the politics of identity of the 1920s. I begin with an examination, at some length, of the established literary tradition of the nineteenth century and the context within which it was (re)produced. This is an important task, because all too often the nineteenth century is depicted as a dark age in Central Asia, during which little of cultural value was accomplished. Dismissing the nineteenth-century background allows the dominant narratives of Central Asian history—whether Soviet, post-Soviet, or émigré-nationalist—to appear as "natural," existing beyond the reach of history themselves, when indeed they are fully rooted in the same processes that displaced older visions of history and identity. I then proceed to a description of the transformations wrought in this historical imagination at the turn of the twentieth century by

Central Asia's transition to modernity, which, under the impact of socioeconomic changes inaugurated by the Russian conquest, profoundly altered the manner in which knowledge was produced in Central Asia. Crucial in this regard was the Jadid movement of modernist reformers who, basing their activities on such unmistakably modern forms of cultural practice as journalism, textbook publishing, and elementary education, reconfigured their world in significant ways, moving from the sacral historical landscape of the Central Asian Islamic tradition to a historicized, desacralized historical consciousness in which the essence of identity was seen to reside in language and community rather than in faith. Moreover, as print displaced script, Central Asian intellectuals were exposed to new intellectual currents, while a deeper intellectual reorientation led them to assimilate ideas of progress that were fundamentally transformative of their worldview. All this existed, however, in the context of social practice, and when the Soviet regime drastically altered the social and political context of that practice, the effects on historiographical practice were also far-reaching.

Traditional Historiography in Nineteenth-Century Central Asia

The considerable literary production—including historiography—of Central Asia of the so-called Uzbek period (between the demise of the Timurid order at the turn of the sixteenth century and the Russian conquest in the mid-nineteenth) has been little studied. Much of the material remains in manuscript form in repositories in Central Asia and Russia. Historical works from this period have sometimes been used as mines for factual information but seldom as keys to understanding the historical imagination of premodern Central Asians. Although no specialized studies exist, we may nevertheless divide historical production of this period into two streams: a tradition of dynastic history, profoundly influenced by Persian models and practiced under royal patronage at the courts of the three khanates, and a tradition of sacred history, operating both at court and beyond, which provided a vision of group identity. These two streams shared a common historical vision but differed in the manner of their production and, perhaps more important, consumption.

Dynastic histories were produced at the court. Patterned after late medieval Persian histories, which in turn were deeply influenced by the narrative structure and technique of the *Shāhnāma,* Firdawsi's tenth-century epic rendering of pre-Islamic Iranian history,[1] dynastic histories were commissioned by royal patrons (or presented to them in expectation of favors), and this was reflected in both their style and content. They sought to recount the deeds of the dynasty while elevating it over its competitors. As I argue below, larger dynastic histories connected the dynasty into universal history through lengthy descriptions of the genealogies of the dynasts. Other histories (*akhbār* [reports] or *ahwāl* [conditions]) had more modest aims, such as the description of the events of an individual reign or even individual campaigns.[2] Until the nineteenth century, when the court in Khiva began to patronize translations and original compositions in Chaghatay Turkic, the language of dynastic histories remained Persian.

Sacred history included hagiographies of pre-Islamic prophets, Muslim saints, and mystics. Unlike dynastic histories, sacred history was more concerned with recording the lives and deeds of the pious and the miracles associated with them. The Qur'an includes some stories of the pre-Islamic prophets, but as a separate genre, *qisas ul-anbiyā* (tales of the prophets) had emerged only in the second Islamic century.[3] By the later Middle Ages, these stories had incorporated elements of Muslim mysticism and become staples of popular piety. The fourteenth-century account of Rabghuzi was widely read, recited, and memorized. Similarly, hagiographical accounts (*maqamāt, tabaqāt,* and *tazkira*s) of the lives of saints and prominent Sufis circulated widely, both in oral and written forms. Hagiography was produced by the religious elite in colleges (*madrasa*s) or mystic lodges (*khānqāh*s) to recount the deeds of pious forebears as well as the intellectual and spiritual descent of individual mystical orders. By the nineteenth century, hagiography was as likely to be written in Turkic as in Persian.

Rather than being a distinct subject, history formed a part of the broad education an educated individual received.[4] Both streams of historiographical production therefore shared a common historical imagination. The world they described was highly sacralized, one in which the boundaries between the natural and the supernatural were porous, and divine intervention in human affairs routine. This historical imagination also provided the framework for the articulation of group identities, which were defined through genealogical links to figures important in the religious history of the region. Traditional historiography was thus concerned primarily with providing a coherent explanation of the origin of the community, as well as genealogical and cultural markers of distinction to elites within that community. It was not concerned with producing a documentary record of human progress.

This historiographical imagination was firmly rooted in specific cultural practices. Since historiographical production remained in manuscript form, the market was scarcely a consideration in this situation and the production of historical works (original compositions as well as copies) was by necessity tied to patterns of patronage, which in turn determined to a large extent the claims made by works of history. Moreover, the display of the author's virtuosity and his mastery of various literary traditions prized by Central

Asian elites was at least as significant a purpose behind the writing of history as historical accuracy.

These practices remained vibrant in the nineteenth century. The courts at Kokand, Bukhara, and Khiva were active centers of patronage of the writing of history. But it was at Khiva, where Chaghatay Turkic had early displaced Persian as the medium of bureaucratic and intellectual discourse, that perhaps the most substantial work of nineteenth-century Central Asian historiography, the *Firdaws ul-Iqbāl* of Sher Muhammad Munis (and continued by his nephew Muhammad Riza Āgahi), was produced. A brief analysis of this work highlights the points made above.

This work was commissioned in 1805 by the Eltüzer Khan, the ruler of Khiva, who asked the author, a court functionary,

> to place our august genealogy on a throne in the *dīvān* [chancery] of words and to set the names of our glorious ancestors into the seal of history, and you have to string fine pearls on the thread of verses and to scatter multicolored ornaments on the carpet of prose with the events of our life and some of our victories, which are an embellishment of legends and an abrogation of the *Shāh-nāma,* so that until the leaves of ages are scattered by the whirlwind of non-existence and the dwelling of this world is destroyed by the torrent of annihilation, our excellent qualities will remain on the pages of time and mention of our [name] with praise will stir excitement at the feasts of the sultans in the gatherings . . . of the world.[5]

The glorification of the dynasty required appropriately florid language, exemplified in the excerpt above. The text is also—literally—adorned with numerous verses, which according to the count of the modern editor of the text account for 16 percent of the total.[6] The florid style, with its rhymed prose and numerous verses, was connected to the manner in which the text was to be consumed. Histories, like epics, were read aloud at gatherings, where rhymed prose and poetry served to show off the erudition of the author and the magnificence of his patron. The form as well as the content signified the greatness of the dynasty. The mention of the *Shāhnāma* indicates the frame of reference in which the greatness of kings as well as of histories was judged.

Munis proceeded to compose a lengthy chronicle of the Qonghirat dynasty which was continued after his death by his nephew Āgahi, who carried it up to 1828. In its final version, the manuscript occupies over six hundred leaves, translating into twelve hundred pages of the printed text of the critical edition published in 1988. About half of the text is an annalistic account of the reign of Muhammad Rahim Khan I, during whose reign the chronicle ended, recounting events significant to the court. More significant for our purposes, however, is the image of history which frames the annalistic part of the work, for here the distinctions between dynastic and sacred history begin to dissolve. The work begins with Creation and the short first chapter recounts the Muslim version of the descent of Adam to Earth, his reconciliation with Eve, and the Flood. After the Flood, Noah had three sons, who later propagated the human race. The eldest was Japheth, from whose eight sons sprang all the peoples who inhabited Inner Asia (*Turānzamin*). The eldest of the eight was Turk, the eponymous ancestor of the Turks.[7] The Turks lived peacefully under the sons of Turk, a series of model rulers, until corruption set in during the reign of Alanja Khan. "The children of Japheth had been Muslims from the time of Noah until this time,"[8] but now they fell off from the true path and ceased to be Muslims. Things came to such a pass that if a father heard of Islam, his son murdered him, and if a son understood anything of the faith, his father would kill him."[9] Then was born Oghuz Khan, who could speak at the age of one, and the first word out of whose mouth was "Allah." He rebelled against his father, eventually slaying him, before embarking on a series of conquests that brought Islam to all of "Transoxiana and Turkestan."[10] He ruled for 116 years, before passing away to the afterworld, whereupon his descendants split up. Eventually, one descendent called Jurliq Markan produced Qonghirat, who was the forebear of the Qonghirat tribe that ruled Khiva in the nineteenth century. Jurliq Markan's younger brother Tusbuday sired Qorlās, whose line ultimately produced Chinggis Khan. Qorlās's descendants conquered the children of Qonghirat well before Chinggis Khan appeared, and the children of Qonghirat were active participants in the rulership of Chinggis Khan and his descendants.[11] But during this time, the sons of Qorlās had fallen off the path of Islam again until they were reconverted. This happened when the mystic Sayyid Atā, accompanied by Naghday, a Qonghirat *amir,* went to the court of Özbek Khan, the ruler of the Golden Horde, and brought him into the fold of Islam.[12]

Dynastic history was thus anchored in a highly sacralized mythic account of the origin of the world and its peoples. Until Chinggis Khan, *Firdaws ul-Iqbāl* narrates events in mythic time, without making any attempt at historical verisimilitude. After Chinggis Khan the narrative crosses the horizon into "historical" time and, except for the conversion of Özbek Khan, narrates events more "realistically," although the miraculous and the supernatural continue to be used as explanatory devices. But the myth of origin was crucial: it asserted a number of things that were fundamental to the identity of the dynasty precisely because they appealed to widely held beliefs legitimating rule in Inner Asia. In 1804 Eltüzer Khan had deposed the last Chinggisid puppet ruler and assumed power in his own name. By deriving the Qonghirats from a lineage superior to that of the Qorlās, Munis asserted the legitimacy of the dynasty to rule in place of the Chinggisids.[13] Similarly, in asserting that the Turks had been

Muslims since the time of Japheth, it completely indigenizes Islam; the community is re-Islamized by Oghuz Khan, still in mythical time; and finally by an Inner Asian mystic in the company of a warrior of the house of Qonghirat. This history asserts the Islamic identity of the Turkic peoples, as well as the great antiquity of that identity. It is striking that no mention is made of the Prophet, the rise of Islam in Arabia, or of the Arab conquest of Central Asia. Rather, Islam becomes an integral aspect of the self-definition of the community. The community originates in an eponymous ancestor, who becomes the ancestor, ruler, and Islamizer. The appeal to religious authority and to political legitimacy become completely intertwined. The origins of the community are narrated through assertive religious history rather than descriptive history of religion.[14] Also, the lines between sacred and dynastic history completely disappear.

Once it switches to historical time, *Firdaws ul-Iqbāl* is concerned with narrating the exploits of the dynasts it is meant to glorify. In addition, it also strives to point out lessons from the past, narrate edifying anecdotes (*tanbih*) in the form of long asides, provide admonition (*ibrat*) for future generations of readers, and record the experience of preceding generations.[15] History represented a repository of experience of past generations; it was not a road to progress. The analysis of change over time played an extremely minor role.[16] Although authors did attempt to find the best sources for their information, objectivity and factuality remained secondary concerns. Moreover, the attitude toward the sources was respectful rather than critical. Alternate versions of past events could be cited without undue concern for establishing a single truth. The manuscript tradition did not require rigorous citation of sources, and Munis and Āgahi, like other authors in their tradition, mention only a few. The bulk of their sources remain historical narratives composed before them, although they also make use of oral tradition and verbal communication. Dynastic histories shared these concerns with other forms of history writing. As DeWeese has recently argued, it is a mistake to believe that communities remember events primarily for their historical meaning; rather, the point is to imbue them with religious and political meaning. To use premodern histories primarily as sources of information—or to attempt to prize "kernels of historical truth" out of narratives written for markedly different purposes—is misguided.[17]

Beginnings of Change

The historiographical tradition to which *Firdaws ul-Iqbāl* belonged was rapidly transformed in the half century after its completion. The single most consequential reason for change was, of course, the Russian conquest of

Central Asia in the 1860s and 1870s, and the new kinds of knowledge that Russian rule brought with it. But the sources of this transformation were many, and as we shall see, they interacted in often complex ways.

The impact of Russian rule was modulated by the fact that the khanates of Bukhara and Khiva avoided complete annexation and survived as internally autonomous protectorates. Hence, court patronage continued and allowed the survival of culture in the traditional mold. The first generation after the conquest therefore saw little drastic change in the cultural production of the region. The introduction of printing seemed to have little effect in the beginning other than to make the written word more ubiquitous. The first printed books differed little from their manuscript antecedents. Indeed, lithography simply seemed to replace copying as a means of reproducing texts without any effect on the content.[18] For instance, Muhammad Hakim Yāyfāni's *Khullas ut-tawārikh* [Abridgment of Histories], an anthology of brief accounts of the khans of Kokand and selected other rulers of the past published in 1913, differed little in conception from the dynastic histories described above. It too started with a genealogy of the khans of Kokand, which it traced back, through Babur, Timur, and Chinggis Khan, to Noah and Adam, meticulously listing sixty-six generations. After that, Yāyfāni included brief accounts of various mythical figures from the pre-Islamic Iranian tradition as well as the Sasanid house, the genealogy of the Prophet Muhammad, and short notices on Shi'i *imām*s, and the Samanid and Seljuq dynasties from Central Asia.[19] The mix of real and mythical figures is striking testimony to the continuing hold of the traditional historical imagination. Nevertheless, the brevity of the volume as well as its demotic language were signs that the writing of history now existed in the domain of the market and served a much larger audience (lithographed books were quite cheap) than the court-centered dynastic histories described above.

At the same time, the manuscript tradition continued, at the two surviving courts as well as beyond, largely unaffected by the advent of print. While the Russian conquest did not revolutionize the historical imagination of these authors, it nevertheless gave them reason to ponder the causes of the defeat of the Muslim rulers of Central Asia. The *Ta'rikh-i salātin-i manghitiyya* (1906), a history of the Manghït dynasty of Bukhara by a disaffected (and disgraced) worthy at court is an example of this change, written in the traditional style, yet highly critical of the state of affairs. Instead of courtly panegyric, it contains sharp criticism of those at the helm. For Abdulaziz Sāmī, its author, the failure of Muslim armies to repel the Russians outweighs the fact of the Russian army's victory. He locates the reasons for this in character flaws in the amir and his confidants. Amir Muzaffar was afflicted with arrogance and conceit, which led him to coercion and oppression, reneging on his duty as a Muslim sovereign to provide justice to his subjects. Moral deficiency led to the loss of territory and effective sovereignty.[20] Sami differs from Munis and Āgahi in the critical posture he assumes toward his subject, but little else in his moral universe or his historical method—providentialism, the primacy of moral consideration, and the absence of causal analysis—distinguish him from the traditional mode of historiography.

Searching for a similar authentic native account of the fall of Āqmasjid (Perovsk) in 1853, the Russian orientalist N.I. Veselovskii found himself in possession of the manuscript of a narrative poem, very much in the epic tradition of Central Asia, that a Kazakh poet had written at the insistence of the orientalist's native informant. Veselovskii threw the full force of his textual prowess into this poem and published a text and translation in St. Petersburg.[21] The poem is rather unexceptional in itself, but it represented something of broader significance: it embodied the intrusion of colonial knowledge into indigenous discourse. The poem was produced on demand to satisfy imperial curiosity. In other cases, imperial interests fed back more actively. Almost immediately after the conquest, the Russian orientalist Aleksandr Kun wrote a brief history of Peter I in Persian, which a Samarqand bookseller had printed in St. Petersburg.[22] In 1870, the chancellery of the governor-general in Tashkent began publishing the *Turkistān wilāyātining gazeti* [Turkestan Gazette] in Turkic, which often included short pieces on historical subjects, ranging from the history of the Romanov house, through a brief history of Egypt and a life of Columbus, to numerous articles on the history and antiquities of Central Asia itself. Many of these pieces were written by N.P. Ostroumov, a student of N. Il'minskii, an accomplished orientalist in his own right and a longtime resident of Tashkent, who edited the newspaper from 1883 to 1917. Over the years, he published several of these articles in pamphlet form.

Such activity went further. Although the vast majority of Russian functionaries in Turkestan remained blissfully ignorant of any local languages, a small number of fine orientalists also found employment in imperial service there. In 1895 they organized the Turkestan Circle for the Amateurs of Archeology with a substantial program of publications. The main focus of the circle's attention was the study of Central Asia's antiquities, but its members also paid considerable attention to reconstructing the recent history of the region. Its ranks included some members of the local population, and it occasionally published brief papers in Turkic.

The circle was an offshoot of an empirewide interest in oriental studies. While Russian orientalism had existed in institutionalized form since at least the beginning of the nineteenth century, its activities redoubled in the late imperial period.[23] An Orientalist Society (Obshchestvo vostokovedeniia) was founded in St. Petersburg under the patronage of Grand Duke Mikhail Nikolaevich. A Tashkent branch opened the following year.[24] In addition, orientalists from inner Russia began to travel to Central Asia in search of rare manuscripts or archeological and numismatic information. This activity had a considerable influence on the transformation of the historical imagination of Central Asian elites.

This influence was, however, seldom direct. The Circle of the Amateurs of Archeology included among its members several local inhabitants who occasionally made presentations at its meetings.[25] Others came into contact with Russian orientalism as informants and gatherers of information. But few of them were historians in their own right, and they produced no substantial works of history. Instead, intellectual challenges often came to Central Asia through the medium of Tatar and Ottoman writings.

The modern Tatar historiography flourished toward the end of the nineteenth century. Here the influence of Russian (and through that, European) orientalism was substantial.[26] Newly discovered texts and newly recorded ethnographic and folkloric data were now available to historians, but more crucially, they were being used in new ways. Old manuscripts now served as sources of historical information, which was adjudged in an analytical manner that implied a critical distance between the author and his sources. Texts now bore authority because of their verisimilitude and their openness to corroboration by other sources (numismatic, archeological, and so on), rather than the sacral aura of the past. A similar process transpired in the Ottoman empire in the second half of the nineteenth century.[27] This new Turkic-language historiography began to appear in Central Asia by the turn of the century.

It was nevertheless a transitional period, and many aspects of traditional Muslim historiography remained. This is clearly visible in a general history of the Turkic peoples published by Hasan Ata Gabashi in Ufa in 1911. For all his use of historical materials, the book provides ample evidence of its author's Islamic education. It is framed by the legend of the division of humanity into three races descended from the three sons of Noah. The sons of Japheth were divided between the Aryans and the Turanians, with the latter splitting into various Turkic tribes. Nevertheless, the bulk of Gabashi's work is concerned with tracing the history of each tribe to the author's time. Although Gabashi uses providential explanation, much of his treatment is grounded in historical time, and the explanation is more human-centered.[28] Far more modern was the work of the Bashkir scholar Ahmed Zeki Velidi published in 1914. This *History of the Turko-Tatars* began with an account of the Turkic peoples in antiquity, and continued through their conversion to Islam to the Mongol conquest, ending with the decline of Inner Asian states and their loss of sovereignty. Providentialism and the Qur'anic view of creation are completely abandoned here, and Velidi's voice is that of a modern historian. With the abandonment of the Qur'anic framework, the identity of the community comes to be anchored in a national vision of universal history.[29]

The Beginnings of Modern Central Asian Historiography

The emergence of a modern Central Asian historiography was intimately connected to these intellectual currents. Contacts between Central Asians and other Turkic peoples had been significantly strengthened by the Russian conquest itself. But while intellectual influences were significant, it was the emergence of new contexts for the production and consumption of history that proved decisive in the transformation of history writing in Central Asia. The emergence of Jadidism, a movement for cultural reform in Muslim society, cannot be separated from the topic at hand.

Jadidism took its name from the movement for new-method (*usul-i jadid*) education advocated by the Crimean Tatar activist Ismail Bey Gasprinskii in the 1880s. Beginning with the reform of Muslim elementary education, the proponents of the new method came to advocate a far-reaching transformation of Muslim society and culture. Although Jadid ideas spread to all parts of the Russian empire with a Muslim population, Jadidism as a movement remained loosely organized, showing a wide variety of concerns in different parts of the Russian empire. Among the Tatars of the Volga and Crimea, cultural reformism soon gave way to an increasingly politicized nationalism, in which the new vision of history that assimilated the results of European orientalism and linguistics came to underlie a form of identity: a racially based conception of Turkicness common to the Turkic peoples of the Ottoman, Russian, and Chinese empires (as well as those inhabiting Iran and Afghanistan). In Central Asia, where the first new-method schools appeared in significant numbers only in the first decade of the twentieth century, the movement remained concerned with questions of cultural reform until 1917. It found a base in a small but growing stratum of the urban population that had emerged as a result of the socioeconomic changes experienced by the region in the two generations after the Russian conquest. The group was small. Russian administrative policies in Turkestan encouraged the rise of a group of notables (the administration of the region was bifurcated into Russian and "native" spheres, the latter the domain of notables), who, having made their compromises and—in the case of the newly wealthy merchants—their fortunes under the new regime, saw little reason for the transformation of Central Asian culture. On the other hand, the Jadids, most of whom came from middling backgrounds, saw the need for a thorough reconfiguration of Central Asian culture, if their society was to survive the challenges of modernity.[30] A new historical imagination played a key role in their reformist project.

The Jadid press, which had a fitful existence from 1906 on, often published articles of historical interest embodying a new, historicized vision of history. Similarly, in many of their polemical works aimed at exhorting their society to reform, the Jadids gave evidence of a new historical imagination. But it was the new-method school that led to the publication of the first relatively substantial works in the new mold. The Jadids of Central Asia also centered their activity around the creation of the new-method school, in which they paid considerable attention to history. History was seen as "a science that explains the circumstances of past communities and the reasons for their rise and fall."[31] The Jadids drew the distinction between two kinds of histories, the general (*tarikh-i umumi*) and the particular (*tarikh-i khususi*), the latter discussing the past of a single community.[32] The particular history taught in Jadid schools was the history of Islam, which "discusses the rise of the Prophet (peace be upon him) and the spread of Islam and explains to us the reasons for the rise and fall of the world of Islam. Therefore, its knowledge is required of every Muslim."[33]

While the Jadids saw the study of Islam and Muslim civilization as necessary for the cultivation of good Muslims, the mere fact of such study began the process of historicizing Islam. The rise of Islam was placed on a historical plane, making it the work of human beings and not merely divine intervention in mortal affairs. In writing history, the Jadids went back to early Muslim chronicles in Arabic instead of using the Timurid and post-Timurid chronicles that had been the norm in the nineteenth century. In doing so, they appraised these textual sources with a new eye, going beyond the sacralized deference of traditional historiography.

Religion occupied an important place in the curriculum of new-method schools. The Jadids copied Russian schools in including "sacred history" as a subject. The Jadids sought to create an Islamic equivalent of a modern Russian phenomenon. As Mahmud Khoja Behbudi, the leading Jadid of Turkestan, wrote,

> All nations (*millatlar*), whether Christians or Jews, teach the history of their religion and the lives of the prophets in their schools. Every Christian and Jewish student learns the guidance and formation of his religion and becomes acquainted with historical events. This is the cause of the development of religious and national energy and zeal.
>   . . . Europeans and [students in] in the organized schools of Russia also study other religions [including] the history of Islam. A Christian student knows more about the history of Islam than a Muslim student.[34]

Muslim students should thus know more about their religion, and this knowledge should be structured in the same way as corresponding fields developed by Europeans. In practice, the sacred history of Jadid schools was directly descended from the *qisas ul-anbiyā* genre described above, but it was taught from textbooks written in simple language specifically for schoolchildren, differing markedly in style from the works of Rabghuzi and others. More important, however, was the fact that such sacred history increasingly came to be separated from other history, which accordingly came to be completely historicized. Whereas in traditional historiography the sacred had informed all historical knowledge, in the new-method curriculum, for all the centrality accorded it, sacred history was separated and marginalized.[35]

The concern with "the development of religious and national energy and zeal" invoked by Behbudi was central to the Jadid project. "Development" was signified by the same word as "progress" (*taraqqi*), which came to acquire a central place in Jadid thinking and profoundly altered their historical imagination. Instead of being rooted in the sacral myths of the origins of the community, history now meant the gradual elaboration of communal identities in conjunction—and competition—with other simultaneously existing communities. History was also a record of progress, or of its opposite, backwardness, which were increasingly, though not yet totally, separated from the personal moral qualities of rulers and notables.

While the Jadids published several textbooks for sacred history and the history of Islam, they were less successful in reworking the history of Central Asia. While works on Turkic history published in Tatar or Ottoman were available in Central Asia, none was published locally, although the need for such history was often expressed in the Jadid press.[36] Velidi (Togan) reports that some Jadid activists were concerned with writing such a history before the war, but nothing came of the effort.[37]

By the end of the old regime, then, a new historical vision had begun to take shape among Central Asian intellectuals, but it had not resulted in any significant historiographical production. This new vision was indirectly shaped by European (including Russian) orientalism, as well as intellectual currents emanating form the Tatars and the Turks, and operated in a world of print and an international market for books. Nevertheless, this new historiography remained the province of amateurs, no matter how enthusiastic. Beyond the Russian orientalist organizations mentioned above, there existed in Turkestan no institutions for higher learning that could provide a professional context for this new historiography. The very freedom from court patronage that allowed new directions to be taken also meant that the future of the new historiography was insecure as long as the market did not expand drastically. On the other hand, the courts at Bukhara and Khiva continued to support traditional manuscript production.

A Revolution in Historical Imagination

The February revolution transformed political and intellectual life in Central Asia. The first weeks of the new order saw a rush to political organization, which was also reflected in the renaissance of the vernacular press.[38] By April, the First All-Turkestan Muslim Congress had met in Tashkent to demand political autonomy for the region. Yet very soon the new politics brought the animosities between the Jadids and their conservative opponents out into the open. While the debates were far-reaching and fundamental, for our purposes the most significant result was a drastic secularization of Jadid thought. Up until the revolution, the Jadids had called for the reform of Muslim culture as a prerequisite for the strengthening of the Muslim community. But in the open politics of 1917, the culturally conservative established elites upstaged the Jadids in their quest for leadership by arguing in the name of Islam itself. By the end of the year, Muslim politics in Turkestan had irreparably split into two camps that often spoke mutually incomprehensible languages. Increasingly throughout the year, the Jadids found themselves staking their claim to leadership on a purely nationalist platform. Their opponents' appropriation of Islam as a symbol largely accounted for the change, but the very active participation of Tatars and Azerbaijanis in Turkestani politics was also significant in this regard.

In Bukhara, the situation took a more radical turn. The Jadids led a demonstration demanding radical reform from the emir and were crushed, despite having the sympathies of the all-Russian Muslim movement and the Provisional Government. The emir's brutal reprisals went a long way in transforming the movement for cultural reform into a revolutionary movement. Ultimately, the Young Bukharans (as the Jadids of Bukhara came to be known) succeeded in taking the city in 1920 with the help of the Soviet Army, after which they instituted a short-lived People's Republic. By that time, the Soviet regime was secure in Turkestan as well. After considerable initial hostility and under pressure from Moscow, the Communist Party of Turkestan had welcomed members of the local population into its ranks. Having been disillusioned with the experience of 1917, many Jadids found the revolutionary promise of the Party extremely attractive and threw their support behind the new regime. The next few years marked a period of considerable dislocation and chaos, which nevertheless saw the creation of new institutions for the (re)production of knowledge. One of the casualties was the lithography-based print trade of prerevolutionary Central Asia, whose demise also sounded the death knell for the traditional historiography of Central Asia. In its place emerged a state-controlled publishing system organized quite differently. The new regime also initiated efforts at creating a network of secular schools, which was based on the existing new-method schools of the Jadids.

At the same time, these years saw a sea change in the local intelligentsia's vision of history. The disillusionment with reformism led the Jadids to a thoroughgoing secularization. Over the next few years, they rapidly assimilated Marxist vocabulary to their discourse of revolutionary change in society, without necessarily buying the version of Marxism emanating from Moscow. Concerns with "sacred history" and even the early history of Islam were displaced by concern over the cultural and political decline of Central Asia in more recent times. The demise of traditional historiography also contributed to this transformation in the parameters of Central Asian historiography. Henceforth, two interrelated concerns drove Central Asian historiography: the need, most keenly felt by the Young Bukharans who had overthrown the emir, to seek legitimacy for the new regime by discrediting the pre-Soviet order in Central Asia and the need to (re)define Central Asian identity in the new age. The two aims were interrelated, and both were highly political.

The need to delegitimize the old order brought about a transformation of the historical imagination. The critique of Central Asian society had been an integral part of the Jadids' reformist project since its inception, but now the purview of the critique was extended much farther. The Jadids of Bukhara, for instance, had seldom questioned the right of the emir to rule until 1917 (even the demonstrations of 1917 had sought concessions and reform). Now, a new historiography of Bukhara depicted its rulers as despotic, tyrannical dissolutes, who exploited the people and stood in the way of progress of the land and the people. The invocation of "the people" (*khalq, ahāli*) marked a sharp departure from the past tradition of annalistic accounts of kings' battles. Much of this critique took shape in the press or in pamphlets published by the Young Bukharans in exile (in Tashkent and Moscow), but later formed the basis of the first substantial historiography in the vernacular. In 1923, three years after the revolution in Bukhara, Sadriddin Aini, a prominent Bukharan Jadid and would-be father of modern Tajik literature, published a history of the Mangit dynasty, followed by *Materials for the History of the Bukharan Revolution* three years later.[39] In spite of its name, the volume was based on Aini's personal knowledge of the events and the people involved. In both these volumes, the tone and the concerns are those of radicalized Jadidism with little concern for a Marxist framework. More Marxist was a similar volume (published the same year) by Fayzullah Khojaev, leader of the Young Bukharans and first president of

Uzbekistan.[40] What both authors—and many others—agreed on was the condemnation of the Manghït political order as despotic and backward.[41] Although these volumes dealt with recent events and were based on the personal experiences of their authors, they were arguably the first examples of a truly modern Central Asian historiography.

The debate over Central Asian identity was even more highly charged. The revolution ushered in a period of great flux as Central Asian intellectuals debated various conceptions of group identity. The debate was obviously highly charged politically, since the state was an important actor. The politics of this period are extremely complex and not very well understood, but briefly, the largely territorial conceptions of Turkestan and Bukhara were displaced in this period by ethnic conceptions of nationhood.[42] However, the ethnic boundaries were never self-evident, and there was room for debate about what the new ethnic designations (and the boundaries that went with them) would be. History was invoked on both sides. In 1918 Abdurrauf Fitrat was the moving force behind the creation of the Chighatāy Gurungi (Chaghatay Conversation), a literary circle that brought together many leading activists of the area. Its members were concerned with the reform of the Central Asian Turkic literary language and script, an enterprise intimately connected with rethinking identities. Members of the circle sought to define an identity for the people of Central Asia rooted in ethnicity as well as in history. As Fitrat argued,

> everyone knows that Turks lived in Central Asia since the ancient period. . . . Of course, these people . . . had their own literature. In the course of history, their literature, being influenced by neighboring peoples, attained the high stage of its development and came to be known as Chaghatay literature, corresponding to the rule of the Chaghatayids. Even after the beginning of Uzbek rule, this literature survived until Jadid literature emerged. Therefore it is incorrect . . . to approach our literary history by ignoring the pre-Uzbek period of Central Asian Turkic literature, especially Chaghatay literature.[43]

"Chaghatayism" sought to create a common national identity for Turkic Central Asia. The term *Chaghatay* referred to the name of the Eastern Turkic literary language around which the fifteenth-century florescence of Central Asia had taken place. It also evoked the Chinggisid heritage of the region, although the central role in the Chaghatayid tradition was played by Timur (Tamerlane), the Turkic Muslim conqueror of the fourteenth century. The realm of Chaghatay was also an eastern counterpart to the western Turkic empire of the Ottomans. As such, Chaghatayism was manifestly anti-pan-Turkic, since it asserted the existence of local group boundaries within the Turkic world. At the same time, it had little place for Marxist categories; history remained the domain of national identity rather than of class analysis.

This vision of history was enshrined not in formal historiography but in a number of works of *belles lettres* (historical plays became a significant medium for the articulation of a historical vision after the revolution). As early as 1918 Fitrat wrote a play called *Timur's Mausoleum,* in which the protagonist, "a son of the Turkic people," made the following speech before Timur's tomb in Samarkand: "My sovereign! A son of the oppressed and plundered Turkic ethnic group, badly wounded in the dust, has come to thee to plead for aid! To thee with a complaint came the frontier guard of Turan, whose gardens are destroyed, whose flowers wound round and unintentionally silenced the nightingales. . . . The Uzbek is crushed, the Kazak dead from hunger—rise up, my sovereign!"[44] Other members of the Chighatāy Gurungi wrote under pen names such as Batu, Uyghur, Chinggis, and Temochin. In 1928 Fitrat published the first volume of an anthology of Turkic literature, which was in effect a canon of the newly created Chaghatayist literary tradition.

But the Chighatāy Gurungi was suppressed as early as 1922 for "panTurkism." Chaghatayism flew in the face of policies favored by Moscow. Nor did opposition to Chaghatayism emanate solely from the center: many in Central Asia itself were opposed to this conception of identity, most notably the non-Turkic Tajiks. The national delimitation of 1924 marked the victory of the ethnic conception of identity, although the nature of Uzbek identity, most complex of all, remained a matter of much debate, and Chaghatayist ideas reemerged in Uzbek national garb, since no clear distinction was possible between "Central Asian Turkic" and "Uzbek." Fitrat's Chaghatayist canon was originally commissioned by the Uzbek republican government as part of its attempts to preserve the literary heritage of the new republic. Charges of Chagatayism and pan-Turkism were again leveled at Fitrat and his cohorts in the late 1920s and the 1930s and played a significant role in their eventual arrests and deaths.[45]

The Perils of Professionalization

The fate of Chaghatayism is doubly ironic. The conflation of Chaghatayism and pan-Turkism suited the interests of the regime in Tashkent (as well as in Moscow) but, as pointed out above, bore little connection to the logic of Chaghatayism. Later in the Soviet period, moreover, Uzbek nationalism was to assimilate most features of Chaghatayism, as Uzbekistan came to lay claim to the Turkic heritage of Central Asia. Fitrat's canon of 1928 bears a striking resemblance to the canon enshrined in post-Stalin official literary histories, although some authors included by Fitrat might have been deprecated in Soviet works for not being progressive enough. Since independence in 1991, even Timur (treated very cautiously in the Soviet period) has made a comeback: the former October Revolution Square in Tashkent is now adorned by an equestrian statue of the ruler, the centerpiece of a cult promoted by the state, while other Timurid figures such as Alisher Nawā'i and Mirzā Ulughbek are hallowed members of the new Uzbek pantheon.

The other irony of the suppression of Chaghatayism in the 1930s lies in its intimate connection with the institutionalization of intellectual life in Central Asia. One of the first acts of the Soviet regime in Tashkent was the creation of a "people's university" (*narodnyi universitet*), which soon became the Central Asian State University and came to include a faculty of social studies. Beyond the university, the Central Executive Committee of the USSR sponsored other scholarly organizations and these were replicated at the Central Asian level. Thus, in 1921 the Circle of Amateurs of Archeology was transformed into the Turkomstaris (Turkestanskii komitet po delam muzeev i okhrane pamiatnikov stariny, iskusstva, i prirody) by official decree. In Moscow and Leningrad, too, state-sponsored scholarly organizations began to emerge, such as the State Institute of the Living Languages of the East (Gosudarstvennyi institut zhivykh vostochnykh iazykov) or the Scholarly Association for Orientalism (Nauchnaia assotsiatsiia vostokovedeniia pri TsIK SSSR), which worked closely with regional organizations. After the national delimitation of 1924, the state sponsored a campaign for *kraevedenie* which involved the publication for a popular audience of the results of a new kind of history.[46] Gradually over the 1920s, republican affiliates of the USSR Academy of Sciences were created in each of the new republics, which consolidated these organizations.

These institutions provided, for the first time, a professional base for a Central Asian academe. They were initially staffed by Russian scholars—in fact, the personnel turnover from the tsarist period was not dramatic—but they also provided a material base for many local historians. In time, these institutions also trained local historians in large numbers; many others (including such luminaries as Fitrat) studied in Moscow. Moreover, many organizations possessed their own publishing houses or had access to others newly created (such as the Publishing House of the Peoples of the USSR [Izdatel'stvo narodov SSSR]). The earliest substantial histories published in Central Asia were published and often commissioned by such organizations. In addition, of course, there was the party and state press, which continued to be the site of lively debate until the end of the 1920s.

Yet this very professionalization, so essential to the creation of a professional historiography, also proved to be its greatest liability. The new history was by its very nature intimately enmeshed in the politics of the age, and the professionalization of historical writing made both its content and the lives of its practitioners vulnerable to control by the state in a way that courtly patronage could never do. By the 1930s the state was ever less tolerant of divergent opinions and ever more able and willing to assert its will. The fate of Chaghatayism was a sign of things to come. By 1938 the regime had decimated practically the entire prerevolutionary intelligentsia in Central Asia. Yet the size and institutionalization of academia increased at the same time as the bounds of the acceptable shrunk. The Uzbek *filial* of the USSR Academy of Sciences was upgraded to a republican Academy of Sciences in 1943.[47] Over the next decades, there emerged a Soviet Uzbek intelligentsia whose historical vision was shaped by Soviet Marxism, with its evolutionary vision of history informed both by an increasingly vaguely defined view of class struggle and an increasingly central concern with nationality and ethnicity (*etnos*).[48] The mix has proved enduring: Central Asian historians conducted numerous subterranean polemics with their Russian counterparts through the decades without, however, questioning the basic assumptions.[49] In that sense, post-Soviet scholarship in Central Asia is still largely tied to its Soviet past.

Notes

This article benefited greatly from comments by Jo-Ann Gross, to whom goes my gratitude. The opinions expressed here are, of course, mine alone.

1. R. Stephen Humphreys, *Islamic History: A Framework for Inquiry* (Minneapolis, 1988), 120–27. See also Marilyn R. Waldman, *Toward a Theory of Historical Narrative: A Case Study in Perso-Islamicate Historiography* (Columbus, Ohio, 1980).

2. For a survey of Central Asian historiography of this period, see B.A. Akhmedov, *Istoriko-geograficheskaia literatura Srednei Azii XVI–XVIII vv.: pis'mennye pamiatniki* (Tashkent, 1985).

3. Tarif Khalidi, *Arabic Historical Thought in the Classical Period* (Cambridge, 1994), 68–73.

4. As Nancy Partner, *Serious Entertainments: The Writing of History in Twelfth-Century England* (Chicago, 1978), 3, points out, in Western Europe too the distinction between history and literature began to be made only at the end of the eighteenth century.

5. Yuri Bregel, "Introduction," in Shir Muhammad Mirāb Munis and Muhammad Rizā Mirab Āgahi, *Firdaws al-Iqbāl,* ed. Yuri Bregel (Leiden, 1988), 12–13 (Bregel's translation), 18–19 (text).

6. Bregel, "Introduction," 34.

7. *Firdaws-i Iqbāl,* 50–51.

8. Ibid., 54.

9. Ibid., 57.

10. Ibid., 65.

11. Ibid., 75–81.

12. Ibid., 204–5.

13. Nor was this attempt at seeking legitimacy in (fictive) genealogy unique in Inner Asia. The upstart khans of Kokand asserted descent from Babur, the Timurid emperor of India, whose descent they traced both to Chinggis Khan and to an ancestor of Chinggis Khan. Cf. T.K. Beisembiev, "Legenda o proiskhozhdenii

kokandskikh khanov kak istochnik po istorii ideologii v Srednei Azii," in *Kazakhstan: Sredniaia i Tsentral'naia Aziia v XVI–XVII vv.* (Alma Ata, 1983), 94–105.

14. The foregoing discussion owes a tremendous debt to the remarkable recent book by Devin DeWeese, *Islamization and Native Religion in the Golden Horde: Baba Tükles and Conversion to Islam in Historical and Epic Tradition* (University Park, Penn., 1994).

15. *Firdaws ul-Iqbāl* shared these concerns with much late medieval historiography in the Muslim world; see, for example, T.I. Sultanov, "Vzgliady pozdnesrednevekovykh musul'manskikh avtorov na istoricheskuiu nauku," *Narody Azii i Afriki,* 1988, no. 1: 50–57.

16. On annals as a genre, see also Hayden White, "The Value of Narrativity in the Representation of Reality," *Critical Inquiry* 7 (1980–81): 5–27.

17. DeWeese, *Islamization and Native Religion,* pp. 160ff. For a particularly futile attempt at the "kernel approach," see Julian Baldick, *Imaginary Muslims: The Uwaysi Sufis of Central Asia* (New York, 1993).

18. Adeeb Khalid, "Printing, Publishing, and Reform in Tsarist Central Asia," *International Journal of Middle Eastern Studies* 26 (1994): 187–200.

19. Mahmud Hakim Yāyfāni, *Khullas ut-tawārikh: ta'rikh-i salātin-i Farghāna wa ghayrahum min as-salātin ul-māziya* (Kokand, 1333/1913).

20. Jo-Ann Gross, "Historical Memory, Cultural Identity, and Change: Mirza 'Abd al-'Aziz Sami's Representation of the Russian Conquest of Bukhara," in Daniel R. Brower and Edward J. Lazzerini, eds., *Russia's Orient: Imperial Borderlands and Peoples, 1700–1917* (Bloomington, 1997), 203–26.

21. Mulla Khalibay Mambetov, *Urus leshkerining Türkistanda tarikh 1262–1269 senelarda qilghan futuhlari,* published as N. Veselovskii, ed., *Kirgizskii razskaz o russkikh zavoevaniiakh v Turkestanskom krae* (St. Petersburg, 1894).

22. Iskandar Tūrā [Aleksandr Kun], *Ta'rīkh-i imparātūr-i buzurg, pādishāh-i jamī-i mamlakat-i Ūrūsiya* (Samarkand, 1872).

23. *Istoriia otechestvennogo vostokovedeniia do serediny XIX veka* (Moscow, 1990).

24. B.V. Lunin, *Nauchnye obshchestva Turkestana i ikh progressivnaia deiatel'nost' (konets XIX–nachalo XX v.)* (Tashkent, 1962), 126–41.

25. In 1900, for instance, one Mullā Ālim Abulqāsimov gave two presentations in Uzbek, marked by a highly traditional style (cf. *Protokoly Turkestanskogo kruzhka liubitelei arkheologii* 5 [1899–1900]: 116–18).

26. Dzhamaliutdin Validov, *Ocherk istorii obrazovannosti i literatury Tatar* (Oxford, 1986 [orig. Moscow, 1923]), 150–53; Abdullah Battal-Taymas, *Kazan Türkleri,* 3d ed. (Ankara, 1988 [orig. 1925]), passim.

27. David Kushner, *The Rise of Turkish Nationalism, 1876–1908* (London, 1977).

28. Hasan Ata Mulla Muhammad oghli al-Gabashi, *Mufässil tarikh-i qävm-i Türki* (Ufa, 1909).

29. Ahmed Zeki Velidi, *Türk-Tatar Tarikhi* (Kazan, 1912). Velidi (1890–1970), the son of the imam of a small village on the Bashkir steppe, put himself through a Russian education in Kazan. By 1914 he was an accomplished orientalist. During the Civil War, he headed the Bashkir national movement, before emigrating to Turkey where he again found fame, under the surname Togan, as one of the most eminent Turkologists of this century.

30. On Central Asian Jadidism, see Adeeb Khalid, *The Politics of Muslim Cultural Reform: Jadidism in Tsarist Central Asia* (forthcoming, Berkeley, 1998).

31. Abdurrauf Fitrat, *Mukhtasar ta'rīkh-i Islām* (Samarkand, 1915), i.

32. Ibid.

33. Ibid.

34. Mahmud Khoja Behbudi, *Mukhtasar tarikh-i Islam* (Samarkand, 1909), 2.

35. Indeed, the historicizing impulse reached sacred history in its own stronghold in the world of the *ulama* (religious scholars). In 1913 Abdurrahmān Sayyāh sought to

prove that the Muslim story of Alexander's wall (*sadd-i Sikandari*) was true and that the wall had existed in historical time (*Tarikh-i azālat ul-ghayn an qissa-yi Zi'l Qarnayn* (Tashkent, 1913).

36. See, e.g., Hāji Muin, "Milli tarikh haqqinda," *Āyina,* 28 February 1915, 258–59.

37. A. Zeki Velidî Togan, *Hâtiralar: Türkistan ve Di er Müslüman Do u Türklerinin Millî Varlik ve Kültür Mücadeleleri* (Istanbul, 1969), 108–9.

38. Adeeb Khalid, "Tashkent 1917: Muslim Politics in Revolutionary Turkestan," *Slavic Review* 55 (1996): 270–96.

39. S. Aini, *Ta'rikh-i amirān-i Manghitiyya* (Tashkent, 1923); idem., *Bukhara inqilabi tarikhi uchun materiallar* (Moscow, 1926).

40. This work exists in both a Russian and an Uzbek version with considerable differences between the two: Faizulla Khodzhaev, *K istorii revoliutsii v Bukhare* (Tashkent, 1926); Fajzulla Xoçajïv, *Buxara inqïlabïnïn tarïxïga materjallïr* (Tashkent, 1930).

41. The demonization of Ālimkhān, the last emir, was perhaps most extreme in Fitrat's Tajik-language *Davrai hukmronii amir Olimkhon* (1934 [reprint 1991]), with its gory accounts of the emir's gluttony and sexual depravity; cf. Shawn Lyons, "Traversing the Distance: The Bukhara of Abdurauf Fitrat," paper presented at the AAASS convention in Philadelphia, November 1994. The representation of the emirs, especially the last incumbent Ālimkhān, as dissolute tapped into Muslim traditions of depicting unjust rulers in these terms, but it also contained echoes of European discourse of oriental despotism combined with the vast array of tropes of lasciviousness and sexual depravity of "the Orient" that were commonplaces of the European imagination of the time. Here were the makings of a Soviet postcolonial discourse.

42. For a conventional account of this period that sees Russian imperial machinations as the main cause, see Edward Allworth, *The Modern Uzbeks* (Stanford, 1990), 176–88; a more sensitive account is Ingebourg Baldauf, "Some Thoughts on the Making of the Uzbek Nation," *Cahiers du monde russe et soviétique* 32 (1991): 79–96, as well as the work by Hisao Komatsu cited below.

43. Fitrat, *Ozbek adabiyati namunalari,* vol. 1 (Tashkent, 1928), xi–xii, quoted in Hisao Komatsu, "The Evolution of Group Identity Among Bukharan Intellectuals in 1911–1928: An Overview," *Memoirs of the Research Department of the Toyo Bunko,* no. 47 (1989): 135 (Komatsu's translation).

44. Quoted by Allworth, *Modern Uzbeks,* 174 (his translation).

45. See, e.g., Dzh. Baibulatov, "Uzbekskaia literatura i chagataizm," *Pechat' i revoliutsiia,* 1929, no. 9: 95–103.

46. Ingeborg Baldauf, "*Kraevedenie* and Uzbek National Consciousness," Papers on Inner Asia, no. 20 (Bloomington, 1992); see also T. Saidkulov, *Ocherki istoriografii istorii narodov Srednei Azii* (Tashkent, 1992), 180–87.

47. T.N. Kary-Niiazov, *Ocherki istorii kul'tury sovetskogo Uzbekistana* (Moscow, 1955), 239.

48. Yuri Slezkine, "The USSR as a Communal Apartment, or How a Socialist State Promoted Ethnic Particularism," *Slavic Review* 53 (1994): 414–52; cf. Julian Bromley and Viktor Kozlov, "The Theory of Ethnos and Ethnic Process in Soviet Social Sciences," *Comparative Studies in Science and Society* 31 (1989): 425–38.

49. Some of these exchanges have been laboriously reconstructed recently by Eli Weinerman, "The Polemics Between Moscow and Central Asians on the Decline of Central Asia and Tsarist Russia's Role in the History of the Region," *Slavonic and East European Review* 71 (1993): 428–81.

20

The Development of a Ukrainian National Historiography in Imperial Russia

Zenon E. Kohut

A fully developed modern Ukrainian national historiography emerged at the beginning of the twentieth century.[1] Its appearance was one of the results of the nineteenth-century Ukrainian cultural and national awakening. The stages of development of a Ukrainian national historiography, therefore, parallel and are very much a part of the evolution of a modern Ukrainian identity.

Before there could be a distinct national historiography, Ukrainian historians had to demonstrate that Ukraine had a history with time-honored origins and that this history was continuous and distinct. Establishing time-honored origins meant linking Ukrainian history with Kievan Rus′, the ninth-century state located primarily in central Ukraine but also including Belarus and some parts of Russia. Demonstrating historical continuity required identifying a Ukrainian historical process extending from the ninth century to the nineteenth, despite long periods when parts of Ukraine belonged to the Polish–Lithuanian Commonwealth, Imperial Russia, or the Austro-Hungarian Empire.

The most difficult question to resolve was the degree of distinctiveness of Ukrainian history and of the Ukrainian historical process. At the beginning of the nineteenth century, Ukrainian and Russian history were seen as currents in a single stream, and Ukrainian historians regarded Russian history and culture as their own. In the first quarter of the nineteenth century, Ukrainian historians believed that their studies of Ukraine were also enriching a larger Russian historiography. But the rapid evolution of both Ukrainian and Russian historiography quickly raised questions of origins, as well as similarities and differences between Ukrainians and Russians. For the most part, Ukrainian historiography was a step behind Russian imperial historiography and, accordingly, reactive to it. Ukrainian historiography had either to accommodate or to challenge evolving Russian and Polish historiographies.

**The Denial of a Distinct Ukrainian Historical Experience:
Imperial Russian and Polish Historiography**

Plato's dictum that those who tell stories also hold power is highly applicable to Ukraine. As a stateless people whose culture was suppressed, Ukrainians had relatively few means to tell their "story." For the most part, history writing in Ukraine and the Russian Empire represented or accommodated the views of the state or, as in the case of the Poles, those of a dominant culture. The most pervasive historical scheme in nineteenth-century Russia was the "traditional scheme of Russian history," a grand narrative of the origins and evolution of the Russian Empire. The imperial "grand narrative" combined dynastic, religious, imperial, and Russian national history in order to present a virtually unbroken thousand-year history of "Russia" and the "Russian people."

Although many elements of the Russian "grand narrative" can be traced to dynastic claims to Kiev presented in Muscovite chronicles, it was a seventeenth-century Ukrainian work that first linked Muscovy and Ukraine through dynasty, religion, and even ethnos. The *Sinopsis,* frequently described as the first history of the Eastern Slavs, has been attributed to Innokentii Gizel', the archimandrite of the Kievan Caves Monastery, and first appeared in Kiev between 1670 and 1674.[2] To enlist the protection and assistance of the Muscovite tsar, the author attempted to connect Kiev with Muscovy in several ways: (1) a common dynasty—the house of Rurik—and a common Orthodox faith, (2) an Orthodox "Rossian" people *(pravoslavnyi rossiiskii narod)* inhabiting the territory of the house of Rurik; (3) a common territory called *Rossiia,* which included Muscovy and Ukraine and was the rightful patrimony of the house of Rurik; and (4) the Muscovite tsar as the scion of the house of Rurik (the fact that the tsars were no longer Rurikids was ignored).

The *Sinopsis* went through thirty printings by 1836, twenty-one of them in St. Petersburg. It was so popular because it provided an expanding dynastic empire with a larger historical framework. As Muscovy was transformed into the Russian Empire, the *Sinopsis* was utilized as a springboard for a Russian imperial historiography. The first comprehensive and scholarly outline of the "traditional scheme" of Russian history was written by Nikolai Karamzin. His *Istoriia gosudarstva rossiiskogo* [History of the Russian State, 1816–24] begins in the ninth century in central Ukraine with the "Kievan period," then shifts in the thirteenth century to the Russian Vladimir–Suzdal', then again to fifteenth-century Moscow, and finally culminates in eighteenth-century St. Petersburg. In general, Russian history is identified with the history of the dynasty and the state or a succession of states.[3]

In Karamzin's scheme, "Russian" history begins in Ukraine, then moves to Russia. But what is the status of Ukraine, when it is not linked to a Russian state? Is Ukraine then part of Russian history? This obvious gap in Karamzin's *magnum opus* was filled by Nikolai Ustrialov. In the first officially approved textbook of Russian history, Ustrialov argued that "Rossiia" already existed as a political nation with a common language and a shared belief in autocracy in Kievan times. He challenged the accepted practice of focusing exclusively on Vladimir–Suzdal' and Muscovy after 1157 by claiming that the Grand Duchy of Lithuania was also a "Russian" state. Thus, Russia was divided by the Mongol invasion and the subsequent establishment of Polish rule over Ukraine and Belarus. According to Ustrialov, the major trend of Russian history was the "re-establishment of the Russian land."[4] It was in the context of this "joining together of Russia" that Ustrialov provided, perhaps for the first time in imperial Russian historiography, a detailed account of sixteenth- and seventeenth-century Ukrainian history as part of a general survey of "Russian" history.

In placing the original Russian state in Ukraine, the traditional imperial scheme had difficulty accounting for the existence of Ukrainians. In 1856 Mikhail Pogodin advanced the thesis that ancient Kiev had been inhabited by Russians, but the Mongol invasion resulted in a massive out-migration to territories in Russia. New tribes from the Carpathians settled in Ukraine during the fourteenth and fifteenth centuries, forming the ethnic basis for the Ukrainian people.[5] Although Pogodin's theory enjoyed some popularity, the occurrence of such a population exchange could not be substantiated. Most later Russian historians explained the substantial differences in speech, custom, and outlook between Russians and Ukrainians as a corruption of the basically Russian ethnos by Polish influences. Still, repercussions of Pogodin's theory are to be found in the works of some leading Russian historians of the second half of the nineteenth century and even of the twentieth century.[6]

The imperial grand narrative reached virtual canonicity when it was incorporated into the writings of Russia's two most influential nineteenth-century historians, S.M. Solov'ev and V.O. Kliuchevskii. Sergei Solov'ev's monumental *Istoriia Rossii s drevneishikh vremen* [History of Russia from

Ancient Times], written in the 1850s and 1860s, defined Ukraine as nothing more than the "western Russian" lands that had been Polonized and Catholicized by Poland but had struggled to maintain a "Russian" national identity and were destined to be united with Great Russia.[7] His student and successor in the chair of Russian history at Moscow University, Vasilii Kliuchevskii, also traced the history of the Russian nation back to Kievan Rus'. His *Kurs russkoi istorii* [A Course in Russian History, 5 vols., 1904–12] paid less attention to the role of the state and emphasized instead Russian national and socioeconomic development, particularly territorial expansion by colonization.[8]

To sum up, the imperial "grand narrative" or "traditional scheme" of Russian history viewed the Kievan Rus' state, which emerged in the ninth century primarily in central Ukraine, as the first Russian state and its East Slavic inhabitants as Russians. This state, despite the "Mongol yoke," survived in the Russian areas of the northeast, first as the principality of Vladimir-Suzdal', then under Moscow's rule as the principality of Muscovy, and finally as the Russian Empire with St. Petersburg as its capital. Thus, in a series of territorial shifts, the Russian state developed from Kievan Rus' into the nineteenth-century Russian Empire, although the southwestern parts of "Russia" (Ukraine and Belarus) were lost to foreign powers, first to Lithuania and then to Poland. From this point of view, Ukrainian history could only be a local offshoot of Russian national history; Ukrainians and Belarusians could only be wayward branches of the Russian national family.

Paralleling the Russian traditional scheme was a Polish "grand narrative" that also marginalized any Ukrainian historical experience. For Polish historiography of the nineteenth century, the paramount questions were Poland's loss of statehood, the injustice done to Poland by the partitioning powers, and Poland's glorious past as a major European power. Since parts of Ukraine were included in the Polish–Lithuanian Commonwealth, a great deal of the Ukrainian experience was presented as part of Polish national history. Even the Kievan Rus' period, with its Byzantine Orthodox and Church Slavonic culture, was treated as Polish. The early modern Polish writers viewed the Polish dynastic intermarriages with the Rurikids and the subordination of some Rurikids to the Polish kings, as well as Polish control over Kiev itself, as proof of a Polish claim to the Kievan inheritance.[9] Such prominent nineteenth-century historians as Lelewel and Moraczewski argued that Ukraine–Rus', which entered the Commonwealth first through Lithuania and then through the Union of Lublin, had become part of Poland itself, and that Ukraine would have remained in the Commonwealth were it not for the Cossack revolts of the seventeenth century.[10] For Polish historiography, the era of Jagiellonian rule (1385–1572) represented an ideal period of religious and national tolerance in which all parts of the Commonwealth, including Ukraine, proudly participated.

From the Polish point of view, this ideal situation was destroyed by a series of Cossack uprisings that severed parts of Ukraine from the Commonwealth, a tragedy that weakened the state and ultimately led to the eighteenth-century partitions of Poland. Some Polish historians—Szujski, Bobrzyński and Lewicki—were willing to admit that there were objective reasons which helped spark these revolts (the excesses of the Polish nobility and the Roman Catholic clergy). But they still believed that the Polish presence in Ukraine was justified by the "mission" of bringing these lands within the orbit of Western and Catholic civilization.[11] Other, more conservative Polish historians—Moraczewska, Wróblewski, Bartoszewicz and Rawita-Gawroński—depicted the Cossack revolts as unjustified, violent outbursts by barbarians who could not appreciate true Christianity and culture.[12] Even Aleksander Jabłonowski, a historian known for his sympathy to Ukrainians, echoed such views in modified forms.[13] Thus, while recognizing Ukrainians as somewhat distinct, Polish historiography, particularly in the late nineteenth and early twentieth centuries, presented them as primitives who needed to be civilized by Polish religion and culture. Moreover, in its insistence that Poland be reconstituted within its "historical" boundaries, Polish historiography maintained that at least the Right Bank, if not most of Ukraine, should be part of a future Polish state.

Traditions of Ukrainian History Writing

In dealing with the developing Russian and Polish interpretations, Ukrainians had their own traditions on which to draw. One tradition, exemplified by the *Sinopsis,* attempted to ascribe affinity with Muscovy/Russia in religion, dynasty, high culture, and even ethnos. Another, while not denying these affinities, insisted on Ukraine's distinctiveness in the political and social order. For the most part, the proponents of Ukrainian political and social distinctiveness were the secular political elite, the Cossack officers, and the Cossack administration that de facto ruled an autonomous Ukraine on the basis of the 1654 Pereiaslav agreement with the Russian tsar. This elite produced a new genre of historical writing, the Cossack chronicles. Two of the most influential works in this genre were those of Hryhorii Hrabianka (1710) and Samiilo Velychko (1720).[14]

Unlike the *Sinopsis,* these and other Cossack chronicles did not put forward any general scheme of East European history, nor did they seek to justify tsarist intervention on the basis of dynastic claims, or even to link Ukraine with Russia on the basis of religion or ethnicity. Their authors strove to present the story of Ukraine from the Ukrainian Cossack point of view. For them, the Kievan Rus´ period was the murky past: their primary interest was in Cossack Ukraine under Poland, the great liberator Hetman Bohdan Khmelnyts´kyi, and Ukrainian and Cossack rights and liberties, both under Polish kings and Russian tsars. They attempted to demonstrate that there were two Rus´ entities, Russia and Ukraine or Little Russia (as it was called by the middle of the eighteenth century), and that Little Russia had entered into voluntary agreements first with the Polish king and then with the Muscovite tsar.[15]

The Cossack chronicles and the historical literature of the eighteenth century established a historical justification and lineage for Little Russia as an autonomous region of the Russian Empire. In the last quarter of the eighteenth century Ukrainian autonomy was abolished, sparking another spurt of historical writing. The most important early nineteenth-century work was an anonymous anti-Russian polemic, *Istoriia Rusov* [History of the Rus´]. Its underlying thesis is that Ukrainians have a natural, moral, and historical right to their own political development. Moreover, the Rus´ (Ukrainian) nation has existed as a political entity since Kievan times: "As is well known, once we were what the Muscovites are now: government, seniority, and the very name Rus´ went over to them from us."[16] The Rus´ people were independent under the rule of their princes, until the Tatar threat drove them into contractual relations with Lithuania and Poland "as equal to equal, and free with free."[17] The same contract theory is applied to the Pereiaslav agreement of 1654 with the Russian tsar and the existence of an autonomous Little Russia within the Russian Empire.[18] Thus, Ukraine was never conquered and entered all the unions in its history as a free and equal partner.

The Cossack chronicles, historical writings, and particularly *Istoriia Rusov* had a profound impact on the development of a Ukrainian historiography.[19] In the face of the prevailing denial of a peculiarly Ukrainian historical experience, these premodern historical works present Ukraine as an actor in history, whether affiliated with Poland or Russia. They describe Ukrainians as endowed with specific "rights and liberties." Moreover, *Istoriia Rusov*'s insistence that the Russians had appropriated Ukraine's history and that Ukraine had played an important role as a European power foreshadow Hrushevs´kyi's rejection of the imperial narrative and the development of the state school in Ukrainian historiography. In explaining the difference between Russians and Ukrainians in terms of Russian toleration of slavery as opposed to Ukrainian love of liberty, *Istoriia Rusov* hints at an argument that would be developed by Ukrainian populist historiography of the second half of the nineteenth century.

Expanding the Russian Imperial Narrative:
Bantysh-Kamens´kyi and Markevych

Considering these Ukrainian historical traditions, it is little wonder that the appearance of Karamzin's Russian grand narrative sparked dissatisfaction among the Ukrainian gentry. For the most part, the Ukrainian gentry had accepted the idea of an all-Russian tsar, an all-Russian Orthodox faith and church, and an all-Russian empire. To them, Little Russia as a political entity was long dead. What lingered for some was a nostalgia for the distinctiveness of the past and a desire for Little Russia to have an honored place within the larger all-Russian scheme. But Karamzin's history had barely mentioned Little Russia. In response to the grumblings of the Ukrainian gentry, the Little Russian governor-general Nikolai Repnin encouraged one of his administrators, Dmytro Bantysh-Kamens´kyi (1788–1850), to write a history of Ukraine. The result was the four-volume *Istoriia Maloi Rossii* [History of Little Russia, 1822].

The main value of the work is its systematic character and use of a large variety of sources. It is profoundly loyalist in tone and interpretation: the author dedicated the second edition of his history to Tsar Nicholas I. Bantysh-Kamens´kyi followed Karamzin, borrowing material from him and attempting to write in the same style. Like Karamzin's, his *Istoriia* is based solely on political events and the lives of the rulers. The interpretation reveals no trace of the critique of tsarist centralism found in some of the historical writings of the late eighteenth century or in *Istoriia Rusov*. The work did succeed in placing Ukraine in the evolving imperial framework, thus making knowledge about Ukraine much more readily available. But in the end, Bantysh-Kamens´kyi's history was nothing more than a detailed regional history of one of Russia's numerous provinces.[20]

Ironically, it was the Russian journalist and historian Nikolai Polevoi who most clearly identified these shortcomings of Bantysh-Kamens´kyi's work. A proto-Slavophile and protopopulist, Polevoi was out of sympathy with this "year-by-year recitation of events" that admitted no difference between Ukraine and Russia. To read it, argued Polevoi, one would think that "Little Russia" differed from Moscow province no more than a province like Iaroslav or Vladimir. For him, Little Russians were different both physically, culturally, and spiritually; they were "ours, but not us."[21]

Two decades later, Mykola Markevych (1804–1860) produced a work depicting Ukraine as "ours (that is, part of Imperial Russia), but not us" (that is, not Russian). A friend of Pushkin, Glinka, and Ryleev, he was known to his contemporaries as a poet, musician, composer, ethnographer, and historian. A long-time collector of manuscripts pertaining to the history of Ukraine, he finally published the five-volume *Istoriia Malorossii* [History of Little Russia] in Moscow in 1842–43.

Greatly influenced by the as-yet-unpublished *Istoriia Rusov,* Markevych presents the history of Ukraine as an independent, uninterrupted process from the earliest times to the late eighteenth century. Although Markevych accepted the imperial grand narrative's view of ancient Ukrainian–Russian unity, he posited that the Russians were the younger brothers of the Ukrainians; that Southern Rus' "separated itself from its younger brothers, the population of the North, liberated itself from the Tatar yoke, assumed the name of Little Russia, joined Lithuania and then Poland, but has been ruled by its own appanage princes, the descendants of Rurik, and *voevodas* recognized by Lithuania and the Polish king."[22] He stressed the distinctiveness of the Russians and Ukrainians and their different state traditions, claiming that Ukrainians both feared the Russians and held them in contempt. He characterized the Pereiaslav agreement as a union of "the free with the free and equal with equal" (a phrase borrowed from the 1569 Union of Lublin between Poland and Lithuania).[23] Markevych ignored most all-Russian events that were treated in detail by Bantysh-Kamens'kyi. But he was loyal to the Russian Empire in his interpretation of the eighteenth-century history of Ukraine, particularly the partitions of Poland, which he viewed as positive in uniting Ukrainian lands within the empire.

Markevych's history was the apogee of Ukrainian patriotic gentry historiography. In contrast to Karamzin's unilinear development of Russian history, Markevych insisted on two historical lines, Ukrainian and Russian, with the former being the more ancient. Like Karamzin, Markevych assigned a fundamental role to the Russian monarchy and the Russian state. In essence, Markevych and the other historians of the early nineteenth century wanted Ukraine to have its proper place within the history of this monarchy and state. Markevych's history provided subject matter and ideas for Ukrainian Romantic writers, particularly his friend Taras Shevchenko, and thus contributed to the formation of a modern Ukrainian national identity.[24] In the development of Ukrainian historiography, Markevych served as a bridge between early nineteenth-century gentry historical writing and Ukrainian Romantic populism.

Challenging the Imperial Grand Narrative:
Ukrainian Romantic Populism

Soon after the publication of Markevych's history, there occurred a profound shift in the approach to Ukrainian history. Under the influence of Romanticism, Ukrainian historians began focusing on the history and life of the common people. The very term "populism" *(narodnytstvo)* referred to the "people." The populists' favorite field of study was ethnography, which greatly influenced the development of historiography. For populist historians, it was not the state but the people that was the principal agent of historical development. Thus, populism provided a convenient theoretical position for a critique of the statist "traditional scheme" of Russian history. It also allowed the historian to oppose the (Ukrainian) *people* to the (Russian) absolutist *state,* thus implicitly stressing the separateness of Ukrainian history from Russian. At the same time, the populists were Slavophiles, believing in the fundamental unity of all Slavs and espousing a federalist Imperial Russia.

One of the earliest Romantic populists was Mykhailo Maksymovych (1804–1873), a person of very diverse interests, from botany to history. A friend of Pushkin, Gogol, and Shevchenko, he taught at Moscow and Kiev universities and served as the first rector of the latter. He was widely known as a folklorist and publisher of Ukrainian folk songs. In the field of Ukrainian history, he wrote numerous studies on the history of Kievan Rus', the Cossack–Hetman period, and Cossack historiography. Maksymovych defended the notion of an organic link between the Kievan Rus' and Cossack eras in Ukrainian history. In the article "O mnimom zapustenii Ukrainy v nashestvie Batyia" ["On the Supposed Desolation of Ukraine during Batu's Invasion," 1857] and in his open letters to Pogodin he exposed the faulty basis of Pogodin's theory. He also polemicized with Pogodin on the independent status of the Ukrainian language.[25]

Maksymovych, in turn, supported and had a profound influence on Panteleimon Kulish (1819–1897), particularly during Kulish's early career. A prominent writer, translator, and organizer of Ukrainian cultural life, Kulish wrote his major works of historical synthesis late in life, following a radical change in his political worldview. His *Istoriia vossoedineniia Rusi* [The History of the Reunification of Rus', 3 vols., 1874–77] was condemned by Ukrainian patriots, because it was supportive of the Russian grand narrative. It was mostly in his early writings that Kulish appeared as a Ukrainian Romantic populist. Most characteristic in this respect are his ethnographic studies of the 1840s, his poem *Ukraina* (1843), and his historical novels and scholarly articles of the *Osnova* period.[26] *Ukraina* was an imitation of Slavic epic poetry that traced events to 1648 in the spirit of the Cossack chronicles. Kulish identified the Cossacks with the Ukrainian nation. His *Povest' ob ukrainskom narode* [Tale of the Ukrainian People, 1846], presumably written for schoolchildren, focuses on the unfolding of the "spirit of the people" in the course of their historical struggle for freedom. This book asserted the continuity of Ukrainian history, basing this claim on ethnic and linguistic grounds. *Povest'* contained many bold statements about the unique character of the Ukrainian people and their history. The very notion of *ukrainskii narod* or even *natsiia* was a huge step forward in the development of Ukrainian historical thought. Kulish claimed that Khmelnyts'kyi's initial aim had been "to make Ukraine a free country again, as it was under the Viking Rus' princes."[27] His treatment of Hetman Ivan Mazepa is quite ambivalent. Mainly because of this treatment of Ukrainian history, Kulish was forbidden to write while in exile in Tula in 1847–50.[28]

Among Kulish's other significant contributions to the development of Ukrainian historical thought and national identity were *Zapiski o Iuzhnoi Rusi* [Notes on Southern Rus', 1856–57] and his historical novels on Cossack subjects. *Chorna rada* [The Black Council, 1845–57], in particular, earned him the reputation of a Ukrainian Sir Walter Scott.

It was Kulish's friend and fellow member of the illegal Cyril and Methodius Brotherhood who proved to be the most famous, important, and representative of the Romantic populists. Mykola (Nikolai) Kostomarov (1817–1885) graduated from Kharkiv University and briefly taught at Kiev (1846–47) and St. Petersburg (1859–62) universities, but most of his life was devoted to research and writing. He started to collect folk songs and to write fiction in Ukrainian during his student days in Kharkiv. As a newly appointed professor of Russian history at Kiev University in 1846, he helped established the Cyril and Methodius Brotherhood, dedicated to the promotion of freedom and equality of the people, Slavic brotherhood, and Ukraine. Kostomarov penned the Brotherhood's manifesto, *Knyhy bytiia ukrains'koho narodu* [Books of the Genesis of the Ukrainian People]. Written under the influence of A. Mickiewicz's *Księgi narodu polskiego i pielgrzymstwa polskiego* [Books of the Polish People and Polish Pilgrimage, 1832–33], it surveyed the history of Ukraine from the point of view of republican democracy, Pan-Slavism, and Ukrainian messianism. Every nation, according to the work, ended up under despotic monarchical rule or foreign domination. Only the Ukrainians had established a truly democratic Christian society, the Cossack Host, idealized throughout Kostomarov's treatise, which also envisaged the establishment of a union of autonomous Slavic states under the leadership of the "resurrected" Ukrainian nation.

Arrested, imprisoned, exiled, and deprived of an academic position, Kostomarov nevertheless became a prolific historian. His fundamental views were expressed in two articles published in the 1860s, "Mysli o federativnom nachale v drevnei Rusi" [Thoughts on the Federative Principle in Ancient Rus'] and "Dve russkie narodnosti" [Two Rus' Peoples]. In "Mysli" he developed the idea that the population of ancient Rus' comprised six nationalities—Ukrainian, Siverian, Russian, Belarusian, Pskovian, and Novgorodian. They were united in one "federation," a natural polity for the Eastern Slavs, but this ideal state was destroyed in the thirteenth century by the Mongol invasion and superseded by the rise of an autocratic Muscovy.[29] In "Dve russkiie narodnosti" Kostomarov attempted to differentiate Ukrainians from Russians. According to him, "Ukrainians are characterized by individualism, Great Russians by collectivism. . . . The striving of Ukrainians was toward federation, that of Great Russians toward autocracy and a firm monarchy."[30] Even more important for the formation of a Ukrainian national historiography was Kostomarov's article "Ukraina," which appeared abroad anonymously, and therefore free of tsarist censorship, in 1860 in Herzen's Geneva-based *Kolokol* [The Bell]. The freedom-loving spirit of the Ukrainian people is again presented as the guiding force of Ukrainian history. Seventeenth-century Ukrainian state building failed because the Ukrainian upper classes were intoxicated with "Polish ideas" hostile to this spirit. Kostomarov stressed that "neither the Russians nor the Poles should call their own the land settled by our people" and maintained the necessity of establishing a Ukrainian state as a member of a Slavic Union "on the territory where the people speak Ukrainian."[31]

Kostomarov saw all-Russian history primarily as the struggle of two principles, federative versus autocratic. For the most part, Ukrainian history represented the "best part" of this opposition, federalism, while Muscovite history was largely the embodiment of the autocratic side. Kostomarov devoted himself mostly to the political history of the Cossack period, producing fundamental monographs on the Khmelnyts'kyi period (1648–57), the period of Ruin (1657–87), and the rule of Hetman Mazepa (1687–1709). He also wrote many works on Russian history and was one of the most popular historians of Imperial Russia.[32]

If Kostomarov was to be considered the pinnacle of Ukrainian Romantic populism, then Oleksander Lazarevs'kyi (1834–1902) represented its last stage. Lazarevs'kyi belonged to the next generation of historians and can be considered a transitory figure between the Romantic populism of Kostomarov and the positivist populism just beginning to be developed by Lazarevs'kyi's contemporary, Volodymyr Antonovych. A lawyer by profession, Lazarevs'kyi was long an active member of the Historical Society of Nestor the Chronicler in Kiev and was one of the founders and close collaborators of the journal *Kievskaia starina* [Kievan Antiquity]. This learned Russian-language monthly for Ukrainian studies was published in Kiev (1882–1906) by a circle of patriotic Ukrainian intellectuals. For almost twenty-five years it was the only printed medium of Ukrainian scholarship in the Russian Empire, making an enormous contribution to the formation of national historiography.

Most of Lazarevs'kyi's works were published in *Kievskaia starina,* as well as in *Zapiski Chernigovskogo statisticheskogo komiteta* before the 1880s. He studied mainly the socioeconomic history of Left-Bank Ukraine in the seventeenth and eighteenth centuries, writing about the peasantry, the Cossack officers, the nobility, land tenure and colonization, and the administrative and judicial system of the Hetmanate. In such articles as "Malorossiiskie pospolitye krest′iane, 1648–1783" [Little Russian Common Peasants, 1648–1783] and the three-volume *Opisanie staroi Malorossii* [A Description of Old Little Russia], he emphasized the exploitation of the peasants by the Cossack officers and regarded the Ukrainian Hetman state with disapproval. Such an approach was characteristic of the Ukrainian populist historiography of the 1870s–90s, which opposed the Ukrainian "people" to all state formations, even Ukrainian ones. It was later modified by Mykhailo Hrushevs′kyi, who showed that the Ukrainian Cossack officers were not free agents, that Russian government policy had to share the blame for the plight of the peasant, and that Cossack officers were at times patriots capable of acting in the best interests of their "Little Russia."

While not overturning the Russian grand narrative, the Ukrainian Romantic populists subverted it. They readily agreed that Kievan Rus′ was a political entity common to the Eastern Slavs and that Imperial Russia could be considered its successor state. However, they attributed little importance to state structures. According to them, the "people" of various parts of Rus′ had developed their own peculiar characteristics, and it was the object of historical study to discover these characteristics rather than concentrate on dynasty or state structure. In looking at the Ukrainian people, the Romantic populists saw them as essentially individualistic, democratic, and federalist, while the Russians were communalist, autocratic, and centralist. Moreover, the Romantic populists ascribed to Ukrainians a unique, indeed messianic, role in history—the preservation of the ideas of freedom and democracy.

Despite their emphasis on Ukrainian distinctiveness and their debunking of the imperial state, the Ukrainian Romantic populists were still operating within a meta-Russian mindset. For the most part, they believed that Ukrainians were a nationality within a larger Russian nation. In this belief, they reflected the state of development of Ukrainian identity in mid- to late nineteenth-century Ukraine. The Ukrainian intellectuals sought the recognition of a Little Russian or Ukrainian nationality within a meta-Russian state and nation just as the Welsh, Scottish, and English nations were acknowledged as components of a British state and nation.

Neither Russian historiography nor the imperial government nor the liberal opposition was willing to accept the Ukrainian terms for inclusion in an all-Russian nation. To the Russians, Ukrainians were simply corrupt compatriots, who could and should achieve full "Russianness" by abandoning their "Little Russian" ways. In historiography, the imperial grand narrative continued to prevail. At the same time, the imperial government decided on a policy of suppression of Ukrainian culture and intellectual life, including the prohibition of publications in the Ukrainian language (the Valuev Decree of 1863 and the Ems Ukase of 1876).

Overturning the Polish Myth and Laying the Foundations for a Ukrainian National Historiography: Volodymyr Antonovych and the Documentary School

The Romantic populists' inability to transform or even adjust the Russian grand narrative, coupled with the fear of governmental reprisals, caused the next generation of historians to avoid general syntheses and concentrate on specific topics and documentary research. The basis for this new documentary school of Ukrainian historiography had been provided, inadvertently, by the imperial government. After the Polish uprising of 1830–31, the imperial government was particularly eager to prove on the basis of historical documents that Right-Bank Ukraine had always been authentically Russian. In 1843 the government created a Provisional Commission for the Study of Ancient Documents (Vremennaia komissiia dlia razbora drevnikh aktov) and appointed Mykola Ivanyshev (1811–1874) as the chief editor of its publications.[33] Ivanyshev had been specially prepared for his task by study in Berlin, particularly in the methodology of document collection, editing, and publishing. The commission began a mammoth task of collecting and publishing documents. Many Ukrainian historians, including Maksymovych and Kulish, were able to do research and publish under its umbrella. More importantly, Ivanyshev was able to train and employ a young historian, Volodymyr Antonovych (1834–1908), who in 1864 succeeded Ivanyshev as the commission's chief editor (a position he held until 1880).

Of Polish gentry origins, Antonovych was active in Polish student organizations until the 1860s. Under the influence of populism, he decided to renounce his class—the Polish *szlachta*—and work for "the people" (that is, the Ukrainian peasantry). Antonovych became an ardent Ukrainian patriot and for half a century played a leading role in Ukrainian civic and political life. A professor of Russian history at Kiev University for thirty-one years (1870–1901), he also laid the foundations for a modern Ukrainian national historiography.

A true populist, Antonovych called for a history based on the experience of the people. In his inaugural lecture at Kiev University, he stated: "In the history of the state we see only the ostentatious part [of history]; we see only the actors on the stage without knowing what happens behind the scenes. Thus history should study the life of the people proper, who constitute the nation [*narodnost*'].["34] At the same time, Antonovych adhered to a positivist methodology, with strict rules of evidence and a solid documentary base. In his writings, Antonovych avoided synthetic theories and concentrated on documentary research. He collected, edited, and published introductions to nine volumes of the *Arkhiv Iugo-Zapadnoi Rossii* [Archive of Southwestern Russia], as well as numerous other collections of historical documents, memoirs, chronicles, maps, and historical songs. These voluminous documents and his own writings concentrated on the political history of the Lithuanian–Ruthenian state and the socioeconomic history of Right-Bank Ukraine during the sixteenth to eighteenth centuries.[35]

Under the influence of Kostomarov's vision of the social system of ancient Rus', Antonovych saw the Cossacks as a new form of the old *viche* (assembly) social order. This view is clearly expressed in his introduction to the first volume of the third series of *Arkhiv Iugo-Zapadnoi Rusi* (1863).[36] But it was only in the 1890s that Antonovych attempted to offer a survey course in Ukrainian history, beginning with Cossack times. This was realized in the lectures he delivered to a private circle in 1895–96 and published in 1897 in Chernivtsi (then part of the Austro-Hungarian Empire) under the title *Besidy pro chasy kozats'ki na Ukraini* [Conversations on the Cossack Period in Ukraine]. According to Antonovych, during the Cossack period "the basic idea that expressed the will of the people best manifested itself." The central idea of the Great Russian nation was state power, which the Russian people honored so much that they renounced their personal liberties. Great Russian absolutism made it possible to organize a powerful state and conquer other nations. The Poles, according to Antonovych, embraced the principle of democratic aristocracy. The central idea of the Ukrainian nation, on the contrary, was "the principle of the assembly, the principle of broad democracy and recognition of equal political rights for each individual in society."[37] In his works, especially "Kiev, ego sud'ba i znachenie s XIV po XVI stoletie" [Kiev, Its Fate and Importance from the Fourteenth to the Sixteenth Centuries], Antonovych connects the history of Kievan Rus' with the subsequent history of the Ukrainian lands. Seeking to underscore this link, Antonovych was the first Ukrainian scholar to use the term "Ukraine-Rus'," which later appeared in the title of Hrushevs'kyi's *magnum opus*.[38]

Antonovych's major contribution as a historian was the de facto debunking of the Polish myth. He accomplished this not by any great synthesis but by the publication of documents and monographs on specific questions. For example, Polish nationalist historiography cited the *haidamak* uprisings of the eighteenth century as evidence that Ukrainians were in essence mere brigands. Antonovych published the documentation relating to the *haidamak* movement and a biography of one of its leaders, Ivan Honta.

These works showed that the *haidamak* revolts were the result of social and religious oppression and that some of the leaders had idealistic goals.[39] Thus, Antonovych's life's work on the history of Right-Bank Ukraine demolished Polish claims to the Right Bank brick by brick. In this, he was supported by the imperial government, which through the Provisional Commission sponsored the collection and publication of these documents. After the 1863 Polish insurrection, the imperial authorities were even more adamant than in the 1840s on proving that the Right Bank was not Polish but Russian. Antonovych, however, demonstrated that the Right Bank was associated with a specifically Ukrainian historical process.

Perhaps Antonovych's greatest achievement was the organization of historical scholarship. He was closely linked with four major centers of Ukrainian historical research: Kiev University, the Kiev Archeographic Commission, the Historical Society of Nestor the Chronicler, and the circle that published the journal *Kievskaia starina*. Most importantly, Antonovych trained the next generation of Ukrainian historians, all of whom were his students at Kiev University: D. Bahalii, I. Lynnychenko, M. Dovnar-Zapol's'kyi, M. Dashkevych, P. Holubovs'kyi, V. Liaskorons'kyi, M. Hrushev'skyi, O. Hrushevs'kyi, V. Danylevych, O. Andriiashev, P. Ivanov, N. Molchanovs'kyi, and others.[40]

The Rejection of the Russian Imperial Narrative and the Establishment of a Ukrainian Historical View: Mykhailo Hrushevs'kyi

By the last decade of the nineteenth century, a third generation of professional historians, mostly students of Antonovych, were teaching at universities all over Ukraine. As their regional studies and research intensified, most periods of Ukrainian history and regions of the country were covered by scholarly monographs and articles. Clearly, there was a need for a new synthesis. The official Russian grand narrative had been challenged two generations previously by the Romantic populists and had little to offer Ukrainian historians at the beginning of the twentieth century. Yet there were political and intellectual obstacles to the production of such a synthesis. An open break with the "traditional scheme" of Russian history was dangerous for a professionally employed historian in Russian Ukraine (at the very least, there was the danger of loss of employment). Ukrainian historical thought had gone far in deconstructing various aspects of the imperial scheme, but no one had taken up the intellectual challenge not only of constructing a "national" history, but also of reinterpreting the entire history of the Eastern Slavs.

It was Mykhailo Hrushevs'kyi, a historian born and educated in the Russian Empire but holding a chair in history at Lviv University (in Austria-Hungary), who set himself to these tasks. Without the risk of tsarist reprisals or censorship, he was able to elaborate the first comprehensive theoretical scheme of the history of the Ukrainian people. The most outstanding student of Volodymyr Antonovych, Mykhailo Hrushevs'kyi (1866–1934) graduated from Kiev University in 1890. A professor of Ukrainian history at Lviv University from 1894 to 1913, he was a prominent organizer of Ukrainian scholarly life in both Galicia and Russian-ruled Ukraine. In 1917 he became the chairman of the Central Rada and thus the head of an independent Ukrainian state. With the collapse of Ukrainian independence, Hrushevs'kyi was forced to emigrate. In 1924 he returned to Ukraine, was elected a full member of the Ukrainian and, subsequently, all-Union Academies of Sciences, and until the end of his life remained the central figure in Ukrainian historical scholarship.

Although Hrushevs'kyi published more than two thousand works (books, articles, reviews, and edited collections), including his monumental *Istoriia Ukrainy-Rusy* [The History of Ukraine-Rus', 10 vols., 1898–1937], the clearest and most precise theoretical expression of his new synthesis was formulated in a short article written in Ukrainian for the first volume of *Sbornik statei po slavianovedeniiu* [Collection of Essays in Slavic Studies]. It was entitled "Zvychaina skhema 'rus'koi' istorii i sprava ratsional'noho ukladu istorii skhidnoho slov'ianstva" ["The Traditional Scheme of 'Russian' History and the Problem of a Rational Ordering of the History of the Eastern Slavs"]. The essence of Hrushevs'kyi's conceptual revolution was the deconstruction of the "traditional scheme" of Russian history, the separation of Ukrainian history from Russian, and a new periodization of Ukrainian and East European history. According to Hrushevs'kyi:

> The Kievan period was not succeeded by the Vladimir–Moscow period, but by the Galician–Volhynian period of the thirteenth century and later by the Lithuanian–Polish period of the fourteenth to the sixteenth centuries. . . . The Vladimir–Moscow state was neither the successor nor the inheritor of the Kievan state. It grew out of its own roots, and its relations with the Kievan state can more readily be compared to the relations between Rome and the province of Gaul than described as two successive periods in the political and cultural life of France. The Kievan government transplanted onto Great Russian soil the forms of a sociopolitical system, its laws and culture—all nurtured by Kiev's historical development—but this is no reason to include the Kievan state in the history of the Great Russian nationality. The ethnographic and historical proximity of the Ukrainian nationality to the Great Russian should not lead to any confusion between them. Each lived its own life above and beyond their historical contacts and encounters.[41]

Hrushevs'kyi noted that, because the Kievan period had traditionally been attached to Russian history, the true beginnings of the history of the Russian people remained unexplained. Hrushevs'kyi also opposed the inclusion of the Grand Duchy of Lithuania in the history of "Russia." In his opinion, the two Slavic nationalities in the Grand Duchy were the Ukrainian-Rus' and the Belarusian. In general, he criticized the excessive emphasis on the role of the state in the narration of "Russian history" (in fact, the history of the Eastern Slavs) and called for a shift toward the history of the people and society. His populist understanding of Russian history is clearly reflected in his conclusion: "After all, there can be no 'all-Russian' history, just as there is no 'all-Russian' nationality. There may be a history of all the 'Russian nationalities,' if anyone wishes to call it so, or a history of the Eastern Slavs. . . . It seems to me that the most rational approach is to present the history of each nationality separately according to its genetic development from its beginnings to the present day."[42]

This was the basis of Hrushevs'kyi's own approach to the history of the Ukrainian people. The first volume of his monumental *Istoriia Ukrainy-Rusy*, published in 1898 in Lviv, covered the history of Ukraine from prehistoric times to the early eleventh century. Volume 10, which covered the Cossack period up to the year 1658, was published after Hrushevs'kyi's death in Kiev in 1937. Thus, Hrushevs'kyi was not able to bring his *magnum opus* up to contemporary times, but he did publish several one-volume surveys of Ukrainian history. The first of them was *Ocherk istorii ukrainskogo naroda* [A Survey of the History of the Ukrainian People, 1904], written in Russian, as the publication of scholarly books in Ukrainian was not allowed in the Russian Empire at the time.[43] The book, based on the results of Hrushevs'kyi's previous research, presented Ukrainian history as an uninterrupted process from ancient times to the end of the eighteenth century. Subsequently Hrushevs'kyi was able to publish a Ukrainian-language survey, somewhat more popular, with hundreds of illustrations, covering events up to the beginning of the twentieth century under the title *Iliustrovana istoriia Ukrainy* [Illustrated History of Ukraine, 1911].[44] In 1914 Hrushevs'kyi published another one-volume history in Russian, *Istoriia ukrainskogo naroda* [History of the Ukrainian People, 1914], in which developments in Ukraine were more closely connected with trends in European history, such as the Reformation and the international grain trade.[45]

Although Hrushevs'kyi's historical scheme was adopted by very few Russian historians, it gained immediate acceptance by most Ukrainian historians, even those who rejected his populist views. Such popularity was due to Hrushevs'kyi's ability to resolve the fundamental issue involved in establishing a Ukrainian national historiography. With his scholarly critiques, he challenged the prevailing imperial methodology and raised a new historical structure. Hrushevs´kyi replaced a paradigm in which Ukrainians played virtually no role in history, even on their own territory, with one in which they had an ancient past. He provided the intellectual tools that made possible the ultimate separation of Ukrainian historiography from Russian.

The Revolt Against Populism: The Ukrainian State School

Just prior to World War I, when the question of a future independent Ukraine was only beginning to be raised by several Ukrainian thinkers, there emerged a new school of Ukrainian history, the state school. These historians faulted their populist predecessors for concentrating too much on "the people" and ignoring the state, particularly Ukrainian state structures. The impulse for this second revolution in Ukrainian historical thinking came from outside traditional Ukrainian historiography. It was given by Viacheslav Lypyns´kyi (1882–1931), a Polish nobleman from Right-Bank Ukraine who had been educated primarily as a sociologist in Cracow and Geneva.

As a member of the Polish nobility living in Ukraine, Lypyns´kyi faced the same problem as Antonovych had three decades earlier—that of defining relations between a small upper class of Polish gentry landowners and the mass of Ukrainian peasants. Antonovych's resolution of this sociological and, to him, moral dilemma had been to renounce his class and, at least symbolically, identify himself with and help lead those Ukrainian peasants. Lypyns´kyi's solution was different. He would not abandon his position in the Polish *szlachta* but would attempt to sway his fellow Polish noblemen toward a pro-Ukrainian position. He envisioned a Ukrainian nation that would include individuals of diverse ethnic background, religion, and social position. Thus, the Polish *szlachta* could continue to be an elite in Russian Ukraine, but it would be the elite of a Ukrainian nation, not of a Polish or Russian one. For Lypyns´kyi, such a nation could evolve only in a Ukrainian state. The development of a territorial patriotism binding all social strata was the first step toward nationhood, and Ukrainian statehood was both a vehicle for and the prerequisite of the establishment of full Ukrainian nationhood.

Lypyns´kyi applied these political presuppositions to his approach to history, concentrating on the Khmelnyts´kyi period. In 1912 Lypyns´kyi published a large work, *Z dziejów Ukrainy* [From the History of Ukraine], and in 1920 a monograph, *Ukraina na perelomi 1657–1659* [Ukraine at the Turning Point of 1657–1659].[46] These works completely contradicted the populist view. Where the populists saw merely an uprising of the people primarily against social oppression, Lypyns´kyi saw Ukrainian state building and even nation building. For him, Khmelnyts´kyi was not simply a leader of the masses, but a statesman. Lypyns´kyi demonstrated that the lesser Orthodox—and even some Catholic—nobles actively participated in the organization of Ukrainian state structures during the Khmelnyts'kyi uprising. He was especially interested in the process by which the military (if not seminomadic) organization of the Cossacks was gradually transformed into an essentially governmental territorial structure. He paid considerable attention to monarchist tendencies within the Cossack polity created by Khmelnyts'kyi.

Lypyns'kyi regarded the Pereiaslav agreement as a military alliance between Ukraine and Muscovy. For him, it had not been imposed by unfavorable circumstances but was part of Khmelnyts'kyi's scheme to establish an "independent and sovereign statehood" for Ukraine.[47] As Lypyns'kyi showed in his brilliant study of one of Khmelnyts'kyi's colonels, Mykhailo Krychevs'kyi, the Ukrainian nobility played a prominent role in the Khmelnyts'kyi uprising, especially in diplomacy and administration. After the hetman's death, however, the nobility failed to preserve the Ukrainian state and preferred their own estate interests to the public good.

Lypyns'kyi's historical studies were limited to the Khmelnyts'kyi period. He produced no general outline of Ukrainian history. For the most part, Lypyns'kyi was a political theorist and sociologist rather than a historian. Nevertheless, he sparked a revolution in Ukrainian historiography by introducing, or rather reintroducing, the concept of territoriality and the study of state institutions and elites in Ukrainian history. The populists were primarily interested in ethnicity, the Ukrainian "people." Lypyns'kyi looked favorably on elites, both Ukrainian and non-Ukrainian; the populists despised them.

Like Hrushevs'kyi, Lypyns'kyi was active in Ukrainian politics and community life. He was a diplomat in the service of Hetman Skoropads'kyi's Ukrainian monarchical government (1918) and even stayed to represent the Directory of the Ukrainian People's Republic, when it overthrew the hetman in 1919. Until his death, Lypyns'kyi was a very active publicist and the principal ideologue of Ukrainian monarchical conservatism.

At the same time that Lypyns'kyi was beginning his forays into the history of the Khmelnyts'kyi revolt, the most promising student of Hrushevs'kyi at Lviv University, Stepan Tomashivs'kyi, was becoming increasingly dissatisfied with his mentor's populism. In his articles on the Mazepa period and his book *Prychynky do istorii Mazepynshchyny* [A Contribution to the History of the Period of Mazepa, 1910], Tomashivs'kyi was moving in the direction of portraying Hetman Mazepa as a state leader and the Cossack polity as a Ukrainian Cossack state. By 1919, in *Ukrains'ka istoriia, tom 1: Starynni i seredni viky* [Ukrainian History, vol. 1: Ancient Times and the Middle Ages], Tomashivs'kyi was fully applying the statist approach when describing Kievan Rus'. In this work, he singled out the principality of Galicia–Volhynia, a successor state to Kievan Rus', as the first decidedly Ukrainian state.[48]

By the early 1920s, the state school had covered certain periods of Ukrainian history—Kievan Rus', the principality of Galicia–Volhynia, and the Cossack state—but had not produced a systematic history of Ukraine. It was Dmytro Doroshenko, a descendant of a Cossack hetman family, who attempted to write a full synthetic survey of Ukrainian history from the perspective of Ukrainian statehood, elites, and the Ukrainian national idea. Like other statist historians, Doroshenko was active in politics. He played an important role in the Ukrainian revolution, becoming minister of foreign affairs in the conservative government of Hetman Skoropads'kyi in 1918. Only after the collapse of Ukrainian statehood and in emigration was Doroshenko able to turn to teaching and scholarship.

Doroshenko left a large legacy of scholarly and literary works (approximately one thousand) on historiography, the Cossack period, the Ukrainian revolution of 1917–21, and Ukrainian church history. His two-volume textbook published in Warsaw in 1932–33 was until recently the most authoritative and generally accepted history of Ukraine outside the Soviet Union.[49] This work represents a moderate state-centered position. Doroshenko presents Kievan Rus', the Principality of Galicia and Volhynia, and even Lithuanian Rus' as a continuous line of proto-Ukrainian states. At the same time, he emphasizes ethnography, economy, culture, literature, education, and religion—the basic approach taken by Hrushevs'kyi. Thus, Doroshenko bridges the gap between the fourteenth century and the establishment of a Cossack polity in the seventeenth. Like the populists, Doroshenko and the statist historians needed "the people" in order to present a continuous Ukrainian historical process from the ninth to the twentieth century. But Doroshenko understood the Ukrainian people not as a monolithic peasant class, as envisioned by the populists, but as socially variegated. As a true statist, Doroshenko believed in the creative power of elites and the sometimes destructive influence of the masses. He was particularly favorably disposed to the Cossack officer class, from which he was descended and which, in his view, had provided leadership for Ukraine from the seventeenth to the late eighteenth century.[50]

The state school had a major influence on Ukrainian historical thought from the 1920s until the imposition of political control over scholarship by the Soviets in the early 1930s. It continued in Western Ukraine (under Polish rule) and in the Ukrainian diaspora. Many of its ideas have been taken up by postcommunist historians in contemporary Ukraine.

Summary and Conclusions

By the beginning of the twentieth century, modern Ukrainian scholarship had established a national historiography with its own subject matter and generally accepted historical scheme. This was a remarkable result, considering the negation of Ukraine as a distinct historical entity by the two dominant historiographic traditions in Ukraine, the Imperial Russian and the Polish. A developing Russian imperial grand narrative saw Ukrainians as ethnic Russians and Ukrainian history as provincial Russian history. Many Polish historians viewed Ukrainians as simply rebellious peasants and laid claim to Right-Bank Ukraine on the basis of historical legitimacy.

The path toward the establishment of a national historiography paralleled, and was part of, the process of developing a modern Ukrainian identity. At first, the Ukrainian gentry historians wanted simply to modify the imperial grand narrative, to establish within the Russian traditional scheme a suitable and honorable place for Ukraine and Ukrainian history. The Romantic populists of the 1860s challenged the Russian grand narrative more directly by negating the imperial state and demonstrating the separate development and identity of the Ukrainian people. At the same time, Ukrainian historians were able gradually to demolish the Polish myth.

Despite the increasing emphasis on Ukrainian distinctiveness, Ukrainian historians and other intellectuals were not yet able to sever the Russian connection completely. Their purpose was to develop a distinct Ukrainian nation and historiography within a meta-Russian nationality and state. Only toward the end of the nineteenth century did certain Ukrainian intellectuals begin to posit that Ukraine was different from Russia in all respects: language, literature, culture, history, and politics.

The writing of history played a crucial role in this revolution in Ukrainian national identity. The works of Mykhailo Hrushevs'kyi marked a complete break with the Russian grand narrative, the construction of an alternative scheme of East European history, and, in fact, the formation of a Ukrainian national historiography. Hrushevs'kyi was soon followed by the state school, which focused on instances of past Ukrainian statehood and moved Ukrainian historiography even further from any meta-Russian conception.

In the first quarter of the twentieth century, Ukrainian national historiography, frequently a combination of the Hrushevs'kyi and state school approaches, became dominant in Western Ukraine (under Poland), the Ukrainian diaspora, and Soviet Ukraine. Ukrainian national historiography, suppressed in Soviet Ukraine in the 1930s, was replaced by official Soviet historiography, which followed a modified Russian grand narrative. Thus, official Soviet historiography posited the common origin of Ukrainians and Russians, the unfortunate separation of the two people owing to Mongol, Lithuanian, and Polish "aggression," and their joyous "reunion" in the Russian state. The Soviet interpretation did, however, allow, at least in theory, for the development and even the "flourishing" of a Ukrainian nation and culture. With the demise of the Soviet Union, Ukrainian national historiography was revived in Ukraine. At the same time, the Russian grand narrative, either in modified form or in its original nineteenth-century version, continues to dominate in Russia.

Notes

1. The best available surveys of the development of Ukrainian historiography are Dmytro Doroshenko, *A Survey of Ukrainian Historiography* (published as a special issue of *The Annals of the Ukrainian Academy of Arts and Sciences in the U.S.*, vol. 5–6 [1957]; the volume also contains an article by Olexander Ohloblyn, "Ukrainian Historiography, 1917–1956"); and Stephen Velychenko, *National History as Cultural Process: A Survey of the Interpretations of Ukraine's Past in Polish, Russian, and Ukrainian Historical Writing from the Earliest Times to 1914* (Edmonton: Canadian Institute of Ukrainian Studies Press, 1992).

2. The scholarly literature on the *Sinopsis* is examined in the introduction to Hans Rothe, ed., *Sinopsis, Kiev 1681: Facsimile mit einer Einleitung* (Cologne: Böhlau Verlag, 1983). Of particular note is S.I. Maslov, "K istorii izdanii kievskogo *Sinopsisa*," in *Stat'i po slavianskoi filologii i russkoi slovesnosti: Sobranie statei v chest' akademika A.I. Sobolevskogo* (Leningrad, 1928), pp. 341–48; I.P. Eremin, "K istorii obshchestvennoi mysli na Ukraine vtoroi poloviny XVII v.," *Trudy otdela drevnerusskoi literatury* (hereafter *TODRL*), vol. 10 (1954), pp. 212–22; and S.L. Peshtich, "'Sinopsis' kak istoricheskoe proizvedenie," *TODRL*, vol. 15 (1958), pp. 284–98. An interesting recent addition to the literature is Gianfranco Giraudo, "'Russkoe' nastoiashchee i proshedshee v tvorchestve Innokentiia Gizelia," *Medievalia Ucrainica: Mental'nist' ta istoriia idei* (Kiev: Naukova dumka, 1992), vol. 1, pp. 92–103.

3. N.M. Karamzin, *Istoriia gosudarstva rossiiskogo*, 5th ed., 12 vols. (St. Petersburg, 1842–43). On Karamzin, see J.L. Black, *Nicholas Karamzin and Russian Society in the Nineteenth Century: A Study in Russian Political and Historical Thought* (Toronto: University of Toronto Press, 1975).

4. N.G. Ustrialov, *Russkaia istoriia*, vol. 1 (St. Petersburg, 1839), p. 16.

5. On Pogodin's views, see vol. 7 of his work, *Issledovaniia, zamechaniia i lektsii o russkoi istorii* (Moscow, 1856), especially pp. 425–28.

6. See Lubomyr R. Wynar, *Mykhailo Hrushevsky: Ukrainian–Russian Confrontation in Historiography* (Toronto: Ukrainian Historical Association, 1988), 14 (n. 31).

7. S.M. Solov'ev, *Istoriia Rossii s drevneishikh vremen*, 15 vols. (Moscow, 1959–66). On Solov'ev's view of the history of the empire's non-Russian nationalities, see Carl W. Reddel, "S.M. Solov'ev and Multi-National History," *Russian History/Histoire Russe* 13, no. 4 (Winter 1986): 355–66.

8. V.O. Kliuchevskii, *Sochineniia*, 8 vols. (Moscow: Gospolitizdat, 1956–59). A helpful survey of Kliuchevskii's views is Robert Byrnes, "Kliuchevskii on the Multi-National Russian State," *Russian History/Histoire Russe* 13, no. 4 (Winter 1986): 313–30.

9. For a thorough study of the Polish treatment of eleven topics in Ukrainian history, see Velychenko, *National History as Cultural Process*, pp. 4–75.

10. Joachim Lelewel, *Polska: Dzieje i rzeczy jej*, 20 vols. (Poznań, 1858–68). See, for example, 3: 255, 364–69. Jędrzej Moraczewski, *Dzieje Rzeczypospolitej Polskiej*, 9 vols. (Poznań, 1843–48).

11. Michał Bobrzyński, *Dzieje Polski w zarysie*, 2d ed. (Warsaw, 1880–1); Anatol Lewicki, *Zarys historii Polski i krajów ruskich z nią połączonych*, 2d ed. (Cracow,

1887); Józef Szujski, *Dzieje Polski* in his *Dzieła,* series 2 (Cracow, 1885–96), especially vols. 1–3.

12. Bibiana Moraczewska, *Co się działo w Polsce* . . . *do pierwszego rozbioru kraju* (Poznań, 1852); Julian Bartoszewicz, *Szkice dziejów kościoła ruskiego w Polsce* (Cracow, 1880); Franciszek Rawita-Gawroński, *Historia ruchów hajdamackich,* 2 vols. (Lviv, 1899); Walerian Wróblewski [as W. Koronowicz], *Słowo dziejów polskich,* 2 vols. (Lipsk, 1858).

13. A. Jabłonowski, *Pisma,* 7 vols. (Warsaw, 1910–11), esp. his "Kresy Ukrainne," in *Pisma* 2: 102–4.

14. Hrabianka's work was published under the title *Deistviia prezel′noi i ot nachala poliakov krvavshoi nebuvaloi brani Bogdana Khmelnitskogo* . . . *Roku 1710* (Kiev, 1854); and Velychko's under the title *Letopis′ sobytii v Iugo-Zapadnoi Rossii v XVII veke: Sostavil Samoil Velichko byvshii kantseliarist Voiska Zaporozhskogo, 1720* (Kiev), vol. 1 (1848), vol. 2 (1851), vol. 3 (1885), vol. 4 (1864). My references are to the facsimile edition of Hrabianka in Hryhorii Hrabianka's *The Great War of Bohdan Xmel′nyc′kyj* (The Harvard Library of Early Ukrainian Literature, Texts, vol. 9) (Harvard: Harvard Ukrainian Research Institute, 1990) and Valerii Shevchuk's translation of Velychko in Samiilo Velychko, *Litopys,* 2 vols. (Kiev: Dnipro, 1991).

15. According to Velychko's account, in 1654 the tsarist envoys at Pereiaslav swore in the name of the tsar that all Ukrainian rights would be respected in perpetuity. See Velychko, *Litopys,* vol. 1, p. 137. In fact, the tsarist envoys refused to take such an oath.

16. *Istoriia Rusov ili Maloi Rossii* (Moscow, 1846), p. 204. *Istoriia Rusov* identifies Archbishop Georgii Konisskii (Heorhii Konys′kyi) as its author. Later scholars proved that he did not write this work.

17. Ibid., pp. 6–7, 209.

18. Ibid., pp. 209, 229.

19. See Frank E. Sysyn, "Concepts of Nationhood in Ukrainian History Writing, 1620–1690," *Harvard Ukrainian Studies* 10, no. 3/4 (December 1986): 393–423; idem, "The Cossack Chronicles and the Development of Modern Ukrainian Culture and National Identity," *Harvard Ukrainian Studies* 14, no. 3/4 (December 1990): 593–607.

20. D.N. Bantysh-Kamenskii [Bantysh-Kamens′kyi], *Istoriia Maloi Rossii ot vodvoreniia slavian v sei strane do unichtozheniia getmanstva,* 3 vols., 4th ed. (St. Petersburg, 1903). There is no monographic study of Bantysh-Kamens′kyi's views. The most recent scholarly article about him is V.V. Kravchenko, "D.M. Bantysh-Kamens′kyi," *Ukrains′kyi istorychnyi zhurnal,* no. 4 (1990): 88–94; no. 5: 72–80.

21. Quoted in David B. Saunders, *The Ukrainian Impact on Russian Culture, 1750–1850* (Edmonton: Canadian Institute of Ukrainian Studies Press, 1985), pp. 186–87.

22. N. Markevich [Markevych], *Istoriia Malorossii,* vol. 1 (Moscow, 1842), p. 4.

23. Ibid., pp. 227–28, 256–59. See also Velychenko, *National History as Cultural Process,* p. 166.

24. For Markevych's friendship with and influence on Shevchenko, see E.M. Kosachevskaia, *N.A. Markevich, 1804–1860* (Leningrad: Izdatel′stvo Leningradskogo gosudarstvennogo universiteta, 1987), ch. 9. Written by a Soviet Russian scholar, this book does not pay sufficient attention to the development of the Ukrainian national movement.

25. Most of Maksymovych's scholarly texts were written in the form of letters, reviews, and replies. They are published in his *Sobranie sochinenii,* 3 vols. (Kiev, 1876–80).

26. The Ukrainian monthly journal *Osnova* was published in St. Petersburg in 1861–62.

27. P. Kulish, *Povest′ ob ukrainskom narode* (St. Petersburg, 1846), pp. 13, 27, 33, 51, as quoted by Velychenko, *National History as Cultural Process,* p. 169.

28. See G.S.N. Luckyj, "Kulish, Panteleimon," *Encyclopedia of Ukraine* (Toronto: University of Toronto Press, 1988), 2: 709. Kulish, however, wrote a great deal in Tula. See George S.N. Luckyj, *Panteleimon Kulish: A Sketch of His Life and Times* (Boulder: East European Monographs, 1983), pp. 45–72.

29. N.I. Kostomarov, "Mysli o federativnom nachale v drevnei Rusi," *Osnova*, no. 1 (1861): 12–58.

30. N.I. Kostomarov, "Dve russkie narodnosti," *Osnova*, no. 3 (1861): 33–80 (as quoted in Doroshenko, *Survey*, p. 137).

31. This article was first published as an anonymous letter to the editors under the title "Ukraina" in *Kolokol*, 1861, no. 61. It was published in Ukrainian as M. Kostomarov, *Pys'mo do vydavtsiv "Kolokola"* [with an Introduction by M. Drahomanov] (Lviv, 1902).

32. Two major recent monographs on Kostomarov are Iu.A. Pinchuk, *Mykola Ivanovych Kostomarov, 1817–1885* (Kyiv: Naukova dumka, 1992) and Thomas M. Prymak, *Mykola Kostomarov: A Biography* (Toronto: University of Toronto Press, 1996).

33. See O.I. Zhurba, *Kyivs'ka arkheohrafichna komisiia 1843–1921: Narys istorii i diial'nosti* (Kyiv: Naukova dumka, 1993).

34. "Kafedral'ne 'Viruiu' Volodymyra Antonovycha: Z neopublikovanoi spadshchyny," *Kyivs'ka starovyna*, no. 3 (1992): 68.

35. On Antonovych as a historian, see V.M. Rychka and V.A. Smolii, "V.B. Antonovych iak istoryk ukrains'koho kozatstva," *Ukrains'kyi istorychnyi zhurnal*, no. 9 (1990): 109–15. The most representative one-volume collection of Antonovych's major articles is the recently published *Moia spovid': Vybrani istorychni ta publitsystychni tvory* (Kyiv: Lybid', 1996).

36. V. Antonovich [Antonovych], "Soderzhanie aktov o kozakakh (1500–1648)," in *Arkhiv Iugo-Zapadnoi Rossii,* series 3, vol. 1 (Kiev, 1863), pp. i–cxx, here cxvii.

37. V. Antonovych, *Besidy pro chasy kozats'ki na Ukraini* (Chernivtsi, 1897), pp. 6–7.

38. O.I. Kyian, "Zhyttievyi i tvorchyi shliakh V.B. Antonovycha," *Ukrains'kyi istorychnyi zhurnal*, no. 2 (1991): 74–75.

39. See his *Issledovanie o gaidamachestve po aktam 1700–1768 gg.* (Kiev, 1876) and *Umanskii sotnik Ivan Gonta*, in *Moia spovid'*, pp. 197–218.

40. Lubomyr R. Wynar, *Mykhailo Hrushevsky*, pp. 6–7. On the scholarly activities of Antonovych and his students, see Doroshenko, *A Survey of Ukrainian Historiography*, pp. 116–205.

41. Mykhailo Hrushevs'kyi, "Zvychaina skhema 'russkoi' istorii i sprava ratsional'noho ukladu istorii skhidnoho slov'ianstva," in Liubomyr Vynar [Wynar], *Naivydatnishyi istoryk Ukrainy Mykhailo Hrushevs'kyi (1866–1934)* (n.p., 1985), pp. 102–3.

42. Hrushevs'kyi, "Zvychaina skhema," pp. 41, 42.

43. M. Grushevskii [Hrushevs'kyi], *Ocherk istorii ukrainskogo naroda* (St. Petersburg, 1904).

44. M. Hrushevs'kyi, *Iliustrovana istoriia Ukrainy* (Kiev, 1911).

45. M. Grushevskii [Hrushevs'kyi], *Istoriia ukrainskogo naroda*. In F. Volkov, ed., *Ukrainskii narod v ego proshlom i nastoiashchem*, vol. 1 (St. Petersburg, 1914).

46. W. Lipiński [Lypyns'kyi], ed., *Z dziejów Ukrainy* (Cracow, 1912); Viacheslav Lypyns'kyi, *Ukraina na perelomi, 1657–59: Zamitky do istorii ukrains'koho derzhavnoho budivnytstva* (Vienna, 1920).

47. W. Lipiński [Lypyns'kyi], "Stanisław Michał Kryczewski," in *Z dziejów Ukrainy* (Cracow, 1912), pp. 394, 546.

48. Stepan Tomashivs'kyi, *Prychynky do istorii Mazepynshchyny* (Lviv, 1910) and *Ukrains'ka istoriia,* vol. 1: *Starynni i seredni viky* (Munich, 1948). Unfortunately, there is no study on how Tomashivs'kyi and Lypyns'kyi may have influenced each other.

49. D. Doroshenko, *Narys istorii Ukrainy* [A Survey of Ukrainian History, 2 vols., Warsaw, 1932–33], translated into English as *History of the Ukraine* (Edmonton: Institute Press, 1939) and later as *A Survey of Ukrainian History* (Winnipeg: Humeniuk Publication Foundation, 1975).

50. Oleh W. Gerus, "Dmytro Doroshenko (1882–1951): A Biographical Sketch," in Doroshenko, *A Survey of Ukrainian History,* pp. 11–12b.

IV

Concluding Essays

21

Toward a New Paradigm?

Marc Raeff

Can historical studies be fitted into a paradigm? In my opinion this broader question should precede the one I was asked to consider here. The notion of paradigm in the sense popularized by Thomas Kuhn in his ground-breaking work *The Structure of Scientific Revolutions* implies that, given the proper procedures and conceptual framework, we can formulate laws or regularities about natural phenomena. But are there any laws and regularities (*zakonomernosti* in Russian) in history, and can one formulate relatively accurate explanatory schemes of historical development? Alongside Western positivist scholars, Russian professional historians, whose rise and circumstances are so well described in the present volume, firmly believed that a positive answer was possible. And since the presence of a seemingly overweening institution—the imperial centralized government—shaped their personal as well as professional existence, it is not surprising that the origins, character, and evolution of the imperial polity provided the basic framework for their research and interpretations of Russia's history. One may even add that to the extent that the monarch symbolized the Russian empire the "pragmatic" historians (that is, those who wrote history that offered political and moral lessons) and dynastic historians of the eighteenth century, whose work culminated in the literary and public triumph of N.M. Karamzin, partook of a similar intellectual inspiration. At the end of the nineteenth century the "scientific" aspiration of Marxism only served to reinforce this philosophic orientation. In short, Russian historiography claimed to be a "science" to which Kuhn's notion of paradigm could be applied.

Let us look briefly at some implications or consequences of this state of affairs. To begin with, in the minds of most historians considered here there was an imputation that historical evolution would have a positive—by whatever criteria—goal. In the cases we are concerned with this meant a unitary, more or less centralized national state, dedicated to international recognition, the attainment of social–economic prosperity, and a high cultural level of a European type. I would be so bold as to suggest that the discourse of even those who at first glance seemed to advocate a spiritual and traditional religious culture (the Slavophiles) and those who argued for an "Asiatic" component (the Eurasianists) in fact accepted the same assumptions. This was true as well of the non-Russian, "nationalist" historians whose work promoted a similar goal, except that the national state or confederative unit in the empire would be based on the primacy of their own nationality or ethnicity. And as the existing imperial regime was or seemed repressive of the individual and of the freedom of expression, historians unanimously stood for "liberalization" and reform, if not revolution, and thus found themselves to some degree in opposition to the imperial sociopolitical system.

It is surely a curious paradox—given these basic presuppositions—that Russian historians paid so little attention to the international context in which the imperial state arose and developed. This circumstance did not preclude some documentary publications and a few monographs on individual diplomatic events and their main actors. There is an odd neglect, if not outright ignoring, of diplomatic and military history in their broadest context. Again the message conveyed is that Russia was "right" in achieving great-power status, extending its borders, and developing a sociopolitical system in the service of this result. A concomitant aspect was a well-nigh total ignorance of the multiethnic and multicultural features of the empire. Yet by 1900, the ethnic Russians constituted a minority—sizable, it is true—of the empire's total population and the various individual ethnic cultures had to be taken into account as factors that were in the position of furthering or handicapping the evolution toward a unitary—that is, Russian and West European—culture. In Soviet times, too, in spite of numerous histories of constituent republics and regions, the underlying belief in the historical process (a much abused but significant term) leading to a unitary, universal culture was forever present.

Another consequence of the "centralistic" and teleological perspectives—as in the case of the major contemporary West European historiographies—was the neglect of local and regional historical studies. Since the seventeenth-century *Sinopsis,* Russian histories dealt almost exclusively with the emergence of the ruler of Moscow as sole sovereign, without bothering to pay more than a minimum of attention to the particularities of the histories of principalities that also competed for supremacy in Central European Russia. The observation may be qualified, although only to a degree, for the

Lithuanian–Polish Commonwealth and the Tatar succession states of the Golden Horde. No wonder that N. Kostomarov's attempt at viewing Russian history from a "federal" perspective fell on deaf ears. It is also the case that toward the end of tsarist Russia we witness the emergence of several regional historiographies—for example in Siberia, Tver' and Novgorod. But they had little impact either on general histories or on most prominent historians. True, signs of change had begun to appear on the eve of World War I—for example, the original work of A. Presniakov, especially his innovative and magisterial study of the *Formation of the Muscovite State,* and to a lesser degree the monographs from the pen of M. Liubavskii. The situation did not improve under the Soviets, in spite of some factually rich monographs on some towns or districts. Only now does one observe a renewed effort at serious local history and at incorporating it into the broader scheme of all-Russian and imperial historiography. Western historians, it might be added, have played and continue to play a notable role in a federalist reinterpretation as pioneered by Kostomarov (A. Kappeler, G. von Rauch, D. von Mohrenschildt).

Not surprisingly, the positivist and state historians—secular and Western in their inspiration—paid inadequate attention to such a major aspect of Russia's history as Church and religion. And this even though not a few historians came from clerical families and had some ecclesiastic schooling themselves (S. Solov'ev, V. Kliuchevskii, to mention but the most outstanding). Only when Church and religion could not be avoided altogether (for example, the spread of Christianity, the heretical movements and princely politics, Old Belief and its immediate consequences, Peter I's abolition of the patriarchate, Catherine II's secularization of church lands) do we find a superficial, and on the whole anticlerical, treatment. This despite the fact that in the course of the nineteenth century there appeared a very substantial body of studies on a high professional level on a number of topics in church history and practices carried out by faculty members of ecclesiastic academies (*dukhovnye akademii*). Only in emigration did innovative, seminal works on the Church make their appearance. They in turn inspired the research of younger Western historians; it is only now that their studies begin to be used by general historians as well.

As noted earlier, a secularist and westernizing preference led most historians to be sympathetic to the opposition-minded intelligentsia. This largely accounts for the negative attitude shown by them toward "medieval" and popular traditional culture and their giving exclusive attention and praise to post-Petrine, modern (i.e., strongly Europeanized) Russian literature and arts. Yet at the same time, whenever censorship rules permitted it, historians showed and stressed the abysmal material and social circumstances of the common people and extolled the intelligentsia's selfless devotion and sacrifices in bringing about reforms. The aim of the few influential social historians, therefore, was to demonstrate and illustrate the exploitation and oppression of the peasantry with little or no attention paid to other classes or aspects of Russia's socioeconomic development. These monographic findings of social historians were readily incorporated in the general histories of Russia, but they did not lead to a displacement of focus on the determining role of the state in shaping the empire's destinies, despite an awareness of the cultural gap between the elites and the people that had appeared in the early eighteenth century and had deepened perhaps because of Russia's success in assimilating European cultural and political values. Soviet historians for their part quite naturally increased in geometric proportion the evidence to support the same conclusions, albeit in a Marxist vocabulary. In a similar vein, the history of the intelligentsia, to the extent that it could be and was dealt with in tsarist times, served to bolster the critique and opposition to government practices in terms of Western political precepts, without much thought as to their applicability to Russian circumstances or the population's receptivity. Under the Soviets the situation in this respect was similar to that regarding the peasantry—that is, an increase in factual information alongside a strict adherence to the Herzian mythology and Lenin's Marxist vocabulary. Neither émigrés nor Western historians brought an appreciable change to this basic picture.

Belief in and explicatory reliance on the theoretical assumptions of positivism and the working out of "vast impersonal forces" were conducive to the slighting of the role of individuals and the vagaries of human behavior. In contradistinction to their pragmatic and dynastic predecessors in the eighteenth century, there is, therefore, in the nineteenth century a dearth of biographical information on the main actors in modern Russian history. In striking contrast to the abundant biographical information in English, French, or German historiography, we have been until rather recently quite ignorant of the lives, careers, and motives of Russia's public figures. Only Emperor Alexander I and members of his immediate family, as well as some military leaders (Suvorov, Rumiantsev, Kutuzov), received adequate biographical treatment, either in pre-revolutionary or Soviet historiography. To my knowledge only two influential historians have paid attention to and given a portrait of historical personages: Karamzin and Kliuchevskii; this may have been a factor in their wide popularity. But even in their case the portraits constitute picturesque additions to what are in fact impersonal treatments of broad historical forces and trends. Another portraitist historian, A. Kizevetter, turned to the biographical genre after completing his major research monographs and in emigration, far from access to archives.

Last but not least, a positivistic approach and teleological perspective surely led to historical determinism. As a matter of fact, it is the often-unspoken aim of such historiography to discover or define those forces that will help formulate inexorable laws of history. Besides the difficulty—nay, impossibility—of formulating such laws or discovering regularities, the approach rejects the probability or even possibility of chance or alternative developments. It is, of course, perfectly true that the historian knows only the outcome of past events—not the turns that have not been taken. Essentially, therefore, he should discover the background, as well as know the future consequences of the events or developments he is studying. Reinhard Kosellek, therefore, is quite right when he speaks of a *Vergangene Zukunft,* for the historian thinks and interprets with the benefit of his knowledge of what the past has led to, and he does so in terms of his own contemporary concerns, values, and conceptual schemes. Yet as long as he believes in human freedom and the unpredictable or chance concatenation of circumstances, if he aims at understanding the causes and characteristic traits of the past, he should not disregard the possibility of events happening differently (maybe not happening at all) or of individuals making other decisions. In short, to speculate about alternative developments that did not happen often helps to understand better what in fact did occur. As Alexander Demandt has provocatively and suggestively shown in his book *Ungeschehene Geschichte,* when properly approached, what did not happen may be part of a comprehensive historiography.

This brings me to a final comment. I have argued that the dominant historiographic tradition in Russia—ably and convincingly illustrated in the present volume—involves a deterministic and quite selective approach to Russia's past. In my opinion the task confronting today's historians in Russia and abroad is not so much to discover and develop a new paradigm—which I consider to be undesirable. Rather it is to view the past from a variety of perspectives and include all social groups, as well as cultural manifestations, all the while keeping firmly in view the accidental, fortuitous, and unpredictable features that make for the appeal, variety, and suspensefulness of the irretrievable past experience. This would require the incorporation of the many concepts, methods, and types of evidence that have served historians of the West and from which the Russians have largely been cut off since 1914. For as we know, during the decades of Russia's relative isolation from the outside world, many innovative methods and objects of historical research have come into the practice of scholars in Western Europe and the United States. We need only to mention Weberian historical sociology, E. Panofsky's and E.P. Schramm's iconology and sociopolitical symbols, the French Annales school, American anthropological and feminist concerns, and psychoanalytically informed individual and social psychology. Some of these innovations have been taken up and applied to Russian history in the West as well. It is a direction of research that should be followed critically and broadened by historians in Russia, too. It will surely set to rest a number of myths and prejudiced interpretations, while at the same time intellectually liberating Russian national consciousness and self-image from the narrowness, if not bigotry, of its image of Russia's past.

22

Russian History at a Turning Point

Notes from a Benevolent Distance

Manfred Hildermeier

Russian and East European historical research has come under pressure from both internal and external events. The external events are well known. The collapse of the communist regimes, first in Eastern Europe and then in the Soviet Union, has shaken disciplines specializing in the current events of that region to their foundations and has sunk them in self-doubt. Of course, history can point with justification to the fact that it is not in the futures business and flee to the protection of the past. Still, the past remains mute without a picture of the present and the future, so the historical discipline is feeling the tremors of this political earthquake, too.

Another factor that has to be taken into account in considering the impact of the massive political changes on historical research is the fact that, in recent decades, historical writing on Russia and Eastern Europe has not been satisfied with the mere narration of historical stories. In the seemingly endless oscillation between explanation and description as the dominant mode of historical writing, the former stepped to the front, and the role of argumentation and interpretive ideas in historical writing increased. To the degree that historiography became "theoretical" and oriented toward explanation over narration, the oft-cited connection between current events and historians' interpretations and ideas became more evident. As a result, the correlation between contemporary sociopolitical developments and historians' worldviews and visions of the future became more visible in historical writings on Eastern Europe. Of course, facts don't speak for themselves. Selection and points of view—no matter how implicit or explicit they may be—will always be necessary. This is an inherent aspect of historical epistemology. Because of this and the greater prominence of interpretation, Russian/Soviet and East European historical research cannot escape the imperative of radical self-examination that the end of Europe's cold war division placed on the political and cultural agenda.

At the same time, developments internal to our discipline put historiographical changes in motion, too. New methods from other fields of history lapped over into Russian and Soviet historical research. The young generation did what it should: it discovered new fields of research and tried out new methods. In particular, the cultural reinterpretation of the past, accompanied to a degree by so-called "microhistorical" approaches, took hold in East European historiography as well. It was not accidental that major developments in Eastern Europe and historiographical innovations occurred simultaneously. The new questions for the most part could only be answered after the archives began to open up under Gorbachev's perestroika and glasnost. All the stronger, then, was the impulse to weld together the new ideas and possibilities into an identifiable historical "school."

This is precisely what occurred toward the end of the 1980s, and it has thrived ever since. This raised the possibility of a new understanding of historical reality. This possibility arose, on the one hand, owing to altered research goals whose result hopefully would be the elimination of the well-known "blank spots" in Soviet and East European history. On the other hand, the new methods brought up the old issue connected with other "paradigm shifts"; that is, the status of the new procedures and how fundamentally they have changed the study of the past. This is the famous question as to whether new strategies only discover previously neglected areas of history or whether they produce new interpretations of use ultimately in all fields of history. Judging from our experiences since the late 1980s and on the basis of general reflection, it seems clear that the question needs to be addressed. In sum, do they merely complement "old" strategies while extending them into new fields of research, or do they have the potential to provide entirely new answers?[1]

Looking at nineteenth- and twentieth-century Russian and Soviet history, two new research areas and methodological orientations are especially evident. First of all, women's history (less gender studies in the strict sense) has come to the fore. There are two obvious reasons for this. For one thing, there was no doubt a pent-up demand. Well into the 1980s relevant topics had been only sporadically examined. The exception proves the rule, and in women's history the exceptions involved the most conspicuous deficiencies in research that categorically demanded attention. Thus, for example, even a superficial survey of revolutionaries during the late imperial period showed that the feminist movement was closely connected to political protest movements against the autocracy and its social order. Alexandra Kollontai and Inessa Armand represented this symbiosis, as did Anna Miliukova in the liberal camp. This innate affinity (*Wahlverwandtschaft*) was, by the way, not a Russian peculiarity, but was rooted, as were most opposition ideas, in the broad West European political and nonpolitical emancipation movement. Given this, and the fact that in Russia the political opposition's center of gravity was shifted to the revolutionary left, the subject has been treated so extensively and so well that no one dares touch it again.[2] Similarly, the "contradictory" position of women in the Soviet Union was detected early. Marxist ideology loudly proclaimed that the "other gender" should have not only the same rights as males but also the same position in society. This included social status as well as equal opportunities at work, and the old demand of "equal pay for equal work" was declared to have been achieved. But, as pioneering research of the 1960s and 1970s soon made clear, these claims were pure ideology. Here, too, economic and historical studies were published that have not been surpassed.[3]

But all other areas of historical research in Russian and Soviet women's history have only recently been discovered. Broadly speaking, two approaches can be distinguished. Most of the research involved turning attention to the woman's role within historical reality as it was already known and understood. This research spanned the spectrum of topics from examination of feminist political engagement and the legal status of women to consideration of the unique position of working-class and peasant women.[4] What was thus researched and described for the first time broadened the horizon of our knowledge significantly. At the same time, on the whole it did not open up new perspectives. While new light fell, so to speak, on uninvestigated areas of known historical reality, it did not illuminate new, hitherto hidden dimensions. Moreover, the results proved what one would already expect on the basis of existing research. Most studies found that women were worse off than men no matter what the social circumstances. Whether in the villages where social roles were very strict or in the factories, whether in the *otkhod* or in the cities, whether concerning their general rights or in public life—Russia and the Soviet Union were patriarchal societies, which held on to their traditions with special tenacity. To be sure, some new findings have differed from what was thought previously.[5] The medieval practice of divorce, for instance, took great pains to save women from material as well as social decline. In fact, a woman's authority in the house often surpassed her official rights. Before the death of the *pater familias,* she was in charge of an important part of the household. She was also responsible for the daughters-in-law and, where present, the maids. When the man of the house died, she became (as in the often-mentioned instance of merchants' widows in the cities) master of the house. In general, though, women's history did not envision new approaches to history. New approaches emerged only if the subject of research itself generated them—as, for example, the correlation of peasant wives' roles with peasant family circumstances and the structure of peasant households, owing to the inseparable nature of these elements in peasant life. But the new methods were more a by-product than an intended goal, and only "blank spots," not previously unknown regions, were filled in by these studies.

Although other studies of the same subject do not claim to be wiser, their aim is different. In some ways, they represent a later phase, inspired by impulses emanating from "general history" and a methodological reorientation that paid great attention to culture in the broad sense of collective values and "mentalities." As was true in other disciplines, there was visible in this methodology the ontological influence of linguistic philosophy and semiotics, as well as "postmodern" ideas, which view any hint of a universal idea and especially any evolutionary concepts with radical skepticism. It is precisely the tendency to describe trans-subjective (*not* objective) phenomena and actions in their communicative context and construction that has led to the global recognition of some of the research results of this *linguistic turn.* It is understood that these methodological explorations transcend women's studies and represent a new "sector" of research where new roads will be opened. Of course, this raises a question. Do these studies serve as a complement to existing studies, or do they offer a perspective that will serve as a new integrating point of view? It is exactly this question that an evaluation of new research methods and fields of study has to answer.

One can argue what the terms ought to be for judging these results. Surely, aside from the intellectual level and the empirical density of new works, the extent to which they correspond to our spoken and unspoken expectations and the new insights they provide will be important. The scientific model, according to which paradigm shifts occur as a means of better explaining experiments and results that were previously only partially understood,[6] certainly is not applicable to history and other "cultural sciences."[7] Rather, what exists is something like a widely felt need for new methods and new perspectives, which as a rule would lead to the discovery of new fields of research. Uneasiness about one-sidedness or interpretive bias and about "blind" corners may be an equally valid motive behind the indispensable compulsion for new discoveries and interpretations. W.J. Mommsen's assertion in connection with the debate on the "historical social sciences"—that new approaches and research strategies display their effectiveness particularly well when they take up key, unsolved questions and give fresh answers that are perceived by others as superior.[8] On the other hand, when they are not able to establish linkages with existing questions, innovations run the risk of causing the foundation of new, specialized disciplines and of leading separate lives. In part, such a separation is unavoidable. Economic history in the professional sense or demography, for instance, demand special qualifications, which the general historian does not have, so that some of their publications are hardly understandable to the less informed reader. On the other hand, such a rationale is often missing, and innovations occur as part of a series of differentiations that create confusion even as they expand historical knowledge.

Questions about the workings of common values and goals within delimited social, institutional, or public spheres, about their "discursive" or "interactive" genesis and their effects on the identity of their members probably should be left to those who are in a position to effect change in these areas. However, it is still necessary consciously to reflect on and integrate these themes. Not all social subsets become more interesting or stronger when we give them a new label. But when a "nerve" is hit, the likelihood of new insights is high. Thus, it appears that an exploration of the change in Russia toward a Western middle-class pattern within the context of liberalism is destined to hit the mark from a new perspective. It lies at the intersection point of political and cultural developments, on the one hand, and the still-unsolved main question of the nineteenth century over the relationship of Russia and the West, on the other.[9] Looked at more closely, it turns out that this takes up the problem that the old developmental theory—stripped of the misleading mechanism with which A. Gerschenkron set back this venerable historical-philosophical device[10]—once asked: to view Russia's relationship with the (changing and "wandering") "West" not only from the point of view of its economic growth ratios and sociopolitical institutions but also from a cultural perspective. But the description of the spiritual breakup of Russia and the uncovering of the multiple compartmentalizations separating the known and unknown has been left up to cultural semiotics and literary studies, insofar as these fields study such issues.[11] And analogous studies for periods after the eighteenth century are lacking completely. All the greater, then, is the promise of a study that is to date the only one to claim that "the time of pure political revolutions" is over.[12] Instead, the valid question concerns cultural change or, in the extreme, cultural *revolution*. Inevitably, the question of the origin of the cultural models and of obstacles to their transmission comes into the picture. This, however, is the question of their postponement and of possibly inherent contradictions to the ever-changing model.

The assumption that answers are to be found where they are now being sought assumes a number of premises, premises that even observers who are skeptical of the shift in orientation in our field accept. It is clear, for example, that the sociohistorical paradigm of the late 1960s to early 1980s neglected the cultural realm. Moreover, no one would want to argue that historical change is imaginable without values. Thus, "instrumental" reason alone demands that socioeconomic and political studies be augmented by cultural ones. People of the revolutionary era knew that. The antibourgeois and antipatriarchal "dreams" (which all took root prior to the revolutionary era) bear witness to this, as do penetrating Soviet-era analyses. Lenin's frequent refrain concerning the necessity of a "cultural revolution" and Trotsky's ideas of a change of the everyday point to the fact that they understood the problem: whoever wanted to build a new society—regardless of their materialistic worldview—could not stop with the transformation of socioeconomic relations. To put it pointedly, the true insight that the revolution could only be completed through the control of minds refuted its own basic ideological assumptions. Cultural history recognizes this same truism and corrects the inclination to shorten historical reality, a direction to which political and socioeconomic historical views tend. However, one should take into account, prior to resorting to the categories of philosophical social criticism, that the ontologized mixing of language and power in the end evades historical analysis. Change as *the* basic definition of everything historical in the end turns into a mere exchange of ideologically constructed realities.

To me, this is where the border runs between a considerable and obvious gain in knowledge resulting from the new research direction and a bare reformulation of more or less traditional strategies framed in new terminology. New words do not in every instance convey new insights. Something else must be added, which can be measured by the standards of conventional historical science. Different categories must be condensed into a concept that could not be arrived at any other way and that is superior when compared to existing studies. Following such criteria, there is still an advantage to studying new subjects. Whoever treats the phenomenon of rowdyism—as *khuliganstvo* probably is best translated—achieves *eo ipso* both: this researcher dedicates himself to a problem that does not appear in conventional social history (not to mention political history and traditional cultural history), and he needs a new method. *Khuliganstvo* was first and foremost a product of class-specific perception and only secondarily a real occurrence, that became part of the criminal statistical records. Thus, it is certainly correct to interpret it as a "cultural conflict"[13] and to subject it to historical questioning. Through this process of investigation, the historian explores central questions pertaining to its causes, to the particularities of place and time in which it appeared, to discrepancies between how it was perceived and the real threat it constituted, to the effect of specific events on it (for example, the revolution of 1905–6), and to its relationship to long-term political and socioeconomic changes. Projections of class-based anxieties and values come to light, which certainly warrant separate consideration and which express more about collective social perceptions than about the deplored phenomenon of "rowdyism" itself. In this sense, mentalities become visible that remain bound to the total political and social situation. The conflict of values and behaviors remains incomprehensible without taking into account the influx of peasants resulting from industrialization and the turbulences affecting the entire imperial social order. Political, social, and "perceptional" history complement each other in an ideal manner, and no one would deny that in this expansion of analysis there lie significant discoveries. Indeed, socioeconomic and cultural dividing lines are not congruent, and the latter are not deducible from the former. In this sense, cultural categories are autonomous and must be taken seriously in terms of their own value and in terms of their own internal code. Though such a cultural history thus cannot be a derivative of social history, it remains connected to it and to other realms of historical reality. Only by means of this interpretive symbiosis is explanatory power created. And even if it turns out that cultural perception merely confirms the political "polarization" between "educated society" and the underclass,[14] one will still have been forced to think twice about the causes of the violence and the extent of the revolution resulting from it.

A still greater challenge is posed by those studies that take the linguistic concept of "postmodern" philosophy so seriously that they aim not for complementary interpretations but for different ones. Since only a few have been published to date, it is too early for any classification or specific judgment. It will suffice to describe the theoretical–methodological boundary lines that result, in my opinion, from a historical view of the situation. The question is how powerful discourse and discourse analysis are. No one will doubt that collective views, among other things, can be considered as a "communicative condensation" of shared dispositions and values. Similarly, it is evident that they affect and change the interpreted object. The idea of a reality—so to speak—existing *prior* to all perception belongs to a naive positivism, which even in the nineteenth century was exposed as a caricature by its hermeneutic opponent.[15] But discourse-centric interpretations far surpass the assumption of an exchange existing between impulses of reality and their collective mental reception. On closer inspection, they assert a *constitutive* meaning to the process of "synthesis" of the perceptions taking place in ourselves and in others that occurs through the use of terms in the discursive process. As a result, the *language of class*[16] does not take its place beside differently established social identities and interests, but actually *takes their place.* The fact that socioeconomic position does not directly translate into consciousness and political action has been a commonplace since E.P. Thompson's magisterial work appeared.[17] But the next step runs the risk of inverting the crude materialist credo, replacing it with one according to which being is determined by consciousness in an equally crude manner.

If radical social critique and revolutionary attitude exhaust themselves in an identity based solely on perception and ideas, the question arises whether a large part of previous historical research has dealt with imaginary or, in the best case, misunderstood phenomena. In addition, from a methodological perspective, the problem emerges of why the described discourse took place in a certain context. A fundamental theoretical inconsistency of this approach has been pointed out with good reason: It fails to include at its very center the *conditions* of the possibility of a "common language"[18] (an accidental recognition is not enough). In closing this obvious gap, this approach would necessarily make allowance for the total *historical* context, which other historiographical approaches are right not to ignore. Nobody would want to declare revolutions to have been purely rhetoric. But there are consequences to not doing so. In that case, the idea behind revolution has to become a *constitutive* part of a research strategy that asks the questions why, when, and which themes were assimilated into which concept. Some time ago, a Russian civil rights activist answered a question about why the collapse of the Soviet Union was not done in a revolutionary manner with the response that the opposition movement did not *want* a revolution. This brings up the interesting idea that the tsarist regime and later the February government went down because their opponents were thinking in terms of a revolution and strove for one. They could, after all, have come to a different understanding of other concepts and goals. Nevertheless, the fact remains that the context at least allowed for one or another kind of discourse and orientation, if it did not force them to occur.

The threat of "reverse" one-sidedness is evaded by a cultural-historical approach, which, both because of its novelty and because of its far-reaching historical claims, has earned much respect.[19] In this case, too, the idea suggests itself that it is precisely the combination of a relatively conventional historical approach with the discovery of a completely neglected subject (connected naturally with high professionalism) that has to a large extent contributed to this attention. For the question itself is not new. The "myth of the tsar" has been dealt with more than once. However, the answer was usually sought by examining the peasant mentality. While there are many good reasons for this, there are few to explain why a complementary perspective never gained ground. The main idea was not far away, though located mainly outside the historical sciences. It seems, then, that the concept of symbolic power was transferred to Russia as an ideal instance of borrowing from neighboring disciplines. The point of this research, as was most effectively demonstrated from "macrohistorical" and sociological perspectives by the cultural sociologist N. Elias,[20] is that ceremonies and rites are not simply noise and smoke, but release a real force. If power (as opposed to an amorphous force, according to the classic definition by M. Weber) means the real chance to find obedience within a certain group,[21] then the representation of the court formed an indispensable link to the functional context of power, especially *before* the era of mass media's intrusion into every home. Pomp and glory did not arise—if such an ahistorical thought is permitted at all—from subjective decisions, but instead belonged to the inseparable attributes that the subjugated (or ruled) attributed to the rulers. To renounce them would have been equivalent to capitulation. In that respect the self-representation was subjected to a core of imperatives, which had to be obeyed. On the other hand, these were not invariable. The study of monarchical–imperial self-representation over the centuries discloses to the contrary an extensive change in style. Both the chosen models—in this respect, too, they were imported whole cloth from Western Europe—and the expectations of the population changed. How continuity and innovation related to each other, why claims and "attributions" (perhaps as a result of a certain rationalization of rule) changed their character: all this belongs to the most exciting problems of a cultural history understood as the history of collective mentalities within the context of social history in a broad sense. Cultural history thus becomes part of the history of governance, related to specific historical settings. It illuminates a new dimension of governance, which has not been captured by "classical" definitions. It not only expands the "territory" of the known but makes some supposedly known fields truly understandable.

New studies of political culture of the 1920s and 1930s aim at a similar goal. What they try to elucidate is in essence the same: the means and forms of a primarily *affective* bond between the people and the regime. However, here the effort not only involved a different political and social context, but also implied an additional new dimension.

If the autocracy could reach back to a traditional legitimacy without any limitations, the new revolutionary state *by definition* could not and would first have to cultivate new ties. Beyond a doubt, the cultural-historical perspective has sharpened our consciousness of the fact that pure pressure is not enough to stabilize a regime in the long run. It indicated those collective dispositions and mentalities that created emotional integration and described the mechanisms with which the authorities addressed them. Certainly for some time there will continue to be discussion over the question to what extent traditional orthodox religiosity was exploited to this end (as up to now has been maintained), even though the opposing thesis involving a modern "political mythos" can claim superior archival evidence.[22] The question of the relationship between old and new appears to be even more wide open in the broader realm of political culture. The regime was able by its own force to create a "cult," even if it was well advised to take into consideration the mental horizon and the forms of perception of the recipients. But the oft-mentioned "new man," of whom Lenin and his compatriots dreamed, had to develop as a mass phenomenon from the everyday, and this presupposed a fundamental change of the traditional lifestyle. Thus, the "political culture" became a trial arena for revolutionary concepts to no less an extent than the economy and society. If one takes seriously the revolutionaries' claim to create a new social order (in the broad sense of the term) and to bring the history of mankind closer to completion, then there is enough reason to assert that the cultural anthropological claim was the highest of all goals and a model for changes in other areas. In any case—and this is significant in our context—the multiplicity of such interpretations testifies to the fact that, compared to the scholarly interest in issues such as the organs of government and the winners and losers of 1917, important links between the rulers and the ruled have been overlooked in previous scholarly research.[23]

Certainly, it is compelling to attempt to utilize this perspective also to test the "acceptance" of the new order among the population and its relative stability. Such a focus brings research down to the level of the everyday and to the experience of the average citizen. The first such study, no doubt pioneering, sets as its object of inquiry the desires, motives, and hopes of "simple people" at the work sites of Magnitogorsk, *the* prestigious and symbolic project of the early Stalin era. The focus is on the perceptions of concrete subjects, not in abstract orders and impersonal collectives, such as class or social strata. Simultaneously ideology comes back into the circle of favorite research subjects. The search is directed at the *social identity* of lower and small-scale social formations, not as a product of any attributes imposed on them from outside or connected with any statistically quantifiable factors, but rather as the result first and foremost of self-realization and self-definition. It is precisely here that a danger lies, a danger that this study of Magnitogorsk brings to light. While the thoughts and feelings reconstructed mirror the perception of the historical actors, one should be careful about seeing the totality of historical reality in their perceptions. The history of experience represents only a part of reality—the subjectively experienced and perceived. Even if the experience of an entire collective can be uncovered, the outsider's view is still missing. Thus, one may be warranted in leveling the reproach that previous research underestimated the enthusiasm of the "affected" and did not really reflect the fact that "Stalinism as civilization"[24] in particular meant a belief in progress and in socialism. But apart from the counterargument that many of the builders of *magnitostroi* were not working there voluntarily, the question arises whether in this research the clouding of minds has not been confused with reality. This no doubt pertains both to the author's interpretation and to the methodology in general. It is an inherent danger of the approach: he who tries to reconstruct reality from perception tends to take perception for reality. He lacks any corrective, unless he reaches out to perspectives and themes he has explicitly rejected.

Last but not least, a research strategy of relevance here is that concerned with a history of *consciousness* rather than with a history of the everyday. Such a history has as its goal to describe reality—in this instance the reality of life under Stalin before World War II—from the *inside* rather than from below. Here too, the mental reflection of everyday experience becomes central. The "sum" of impressions and reflections in the background of an individual biography is examined for its value as an indicator of the integrative capacity of the whole system. This approach normally rejects assumptions both of a helpless deliverance of the individual to the totalitarian apparatus and of rational, purposeful strategies of individual action of a social historical type. Stalinist rule, as was stated earlier, was not based on force and terror alone, but also on compromises, regardless of the reservations and the reasons involved. Behind this approach, there lurks, on the one hand, the concept of the well-known dialectic between ruler and ruled; on the other hand, however, there is uneasiness over the dominant view—that an entire system that endures for some time had to have rested on opportunistic adaptation. The search for personal advantage as a central motive for participation and tolerance does not suffice. In contrast, a multiplicity of motives is asserted, which are reflected in particular learning processes.[25]

To draw a conclusion from so many different approaches is only possible in a very general way. He who takes seriously the beautiful sentence of Max Weber—that it is not just our fate but our purpose to be surpassed[26]—will remain open-minded. There can be no doubt that the new attention to mentalities, experience, consciousness, and the collective mental reflection of experience and reality has opened up new dimensions of historical reality. If it is not the case that things completely unknown were pulled into the light, it is true that new references and interpretive contexts were created. It makes a qualitative difference whether the same objects (for example, mass spectacles, art, and propaganda in the early 1920s) are viewed by a contemporary outsider or at the end of intensive sociohistorical research. It is hardly an overstatement to say that the entire complex mediation between stimuli of reality and actions has been newly discovered. The attempt to answer the question of how class consciousness was formed created a new combination of "hard," tangible data with material derived from the study of the way that this quantifiable "reality" was processed in the spiritual-cultural realm.[27] From similar problems (such as the usually accepted belief in the socioeconomic causes of the French Revolution),[28] more questions arose and "peeled" away the surface of the socio-economic reality by uncovering new ones beneath. Whether one calls these "deeper layers" different realities or different views shaped by the actors is irrelevant. In sum, great conceptual differentiations and the development of new fields of insight result. Instead of the *one* "layered" reality, *many* have been detected, which can be understood as a "bulge" of such a layer or line. The well-known contrast between "widening" and "deepening" is close at hand, as is the comparison with a powerful, complex lens system that can focus on and enlarge specific items the way a magnifying glass does and can also—like a wide-angle lens—provide a picture of larger entities.

This comparison, in particular, also throws light on the disadvantages of the new perspective. Most serious probably is the objection that the price of detailed insight is high or even too high, because the proximity has to be "bought" by a loss of general survey and criteria for a general interpretation. What is won in precision, is lost in structured, "strategic" insight. This counterargument includes the premise that from an exemplary study of a more or less limited section, no perspective for contextual analysis can be gained. The "description" may be as "dense" as possible—it is about as likely that standards that could help to measure them can be generated from the sources as it was for Baron Munchhausen to pull himself out of a swamp by his own hair.[29] If the "enlargement" remains "meaningless" by itself, however, it turns out that the total perspective cannot be left out. To be sure, this danger will only materialize in one-sided, unbalanced versions of the cultural-historical approach. The importance of an analysis of collective mentalities, of the description of tsarist self-representation, "of revolutionary dreams" or manifold forms of forced secularization, remains unaffected. Nonetheless, the reproach has a target, which in the wider sense can be seen in the linguistic and discursive analytical construction of collective levels of consciousness and identities. Here, indeed, the claim is raised to reconstruct not just an "additional" reality, but the "real" one. With this, the process nears the point of dissolution and of negation of the trans-subjective reality. Inasmuch as this consequence is implied, a clear border will have to be drawn. That the revolution was only or even mostly a mental fact is unlikely. Instead, all evidence supports the assumption to presuppose several "layers" of reality and to combine various methodological approaches. To replace "society" with "culture" is senseless. In this way one supports merely the inflated and blunt use of culture as a handy barometer of the spirit of the time.[30] Much more important would be to complement the unquestionably simplistically viewed "structural" reality with the dimension of experience and processing (emotional as well as intellectual). Both approaches are not mutually exclusive but rather should be combined, as the metaphor of the differing enlargements based on differing purposes of realization suggests. This is what is meant by the notion "social history in its expansion," which does not necessitate a devaluation of cultural history in the sense of an addition. Only the "objective" and the "subjective" reality *together* form the "whole" reality.

Notes

Translated by Clementine Creuziger, Manfred Hildermeier, and Thomas Sanders.

1. Compare the similar discussion about the status of "social history" summed up in J. Kocka, *Social history: Meaning—development—problems,* 2d ed. (Göttingen, 1986), p. 82.
2. See R. Stites, *The Women's Liberation Movement in Russia: Feminism, Nihilism, and Bolshevism, 1860–1930* (Princeton, 1978).
3. See G.W. Lapidus, *Women in Soviet Society: Equality, Development, and Social Change* (Berkeley, 1978). D. Atkinson, A. Dallin, and G.W. Lapidus, eds., *Women in Russia* (Stanford, CA, 1977); N.T. Dodge, *Women in the Soviet Economy: Their Role in Economic, Scientific, and Technical Development* (Baltimore, 1966).
4. See among others, R.L. Glickman, *Russian Factory Women: Workplace and Society, 1880–1914* (Berkeley, 1984); B.E. Clements, B.A. Engel, C.D. Worobec, eds., *Russia's Women: Accommodation, Resistance, Transformation* (Berkeley, 1991); B.A. Engel, *Women of the Intelligentsia in Nineteenth-Century Russia* (Cambridge, 1983); B.A. Engel, *Between the Fields and the City: Women, Work, and Family in Russia, 1861–1914* (Cambridge, 1994); L. Edmonson, ed., *Feminism in Russia, 1900–1917* (Stanford, 1984); O. Crisp and L. Edmonson, eds., *Civil Rights in Imperial Russia* (Oxford, 1989); L. Edmonson, ed., *Women and Society in Russia and the Soviet Union* (Cambridge, 1992); E. Waters, *From the Old Family to the New: Work, Marriage, and Motherhood in Urban Soviet Russia, 1917–1931* (Birmingham, 1985); W.Z. Goldman, *Women, the State, and Revolution: Soviet Family Policy and Social Life, 1917–1936* (Cambridge, 1993); L. Engelstein, *The Keys to Happiness: Sex and the Search for Modernity in Fin-de-Siècle Russia* (Ithaca, 1992); L. Engelstein, *Women and Society in Russia and the Soviet Union* (Cambridge, 1991).
5. N.L. Pushareva, *Zhenshchiny drevnei Rusi* (Moscow, 1989), p. 211; idem, "Women in the Medieval Russian Family of the Tenth Through Fifteenth Centuries," in Clements, Engel, Worobec, eds., *Russia's Women,* pp. 29–43; idem, *Chastnaia zhizn'*

russkoi zhenshchiny v X–nachale XIX veka: Nevesta, zhena, mat', khoziaika, liubovnitsa (Moscow, 1997), p. 251; idem, *Women in Russian History: From the Tenth to the Twentieth Century* (Armonk, NY, 1997); C.D. Worobec, *Peasant Russia: Family and Community in the Post-Emancipation Period* (Princeton, 1991).

6. See Thomas S. Kuhn, *The Structure of Scientific Revolutions* (Chicago, 1962).

7. As a plea for this notion see O.G. Oexle, "Geschichte als Kulturwissenschaft," in W. Hardtwig, H.-U. Wehler (Hg.), *Kulturgeschichte heute* (Göttingen, 1996).

8. See W.J. Mommsen, *Geschichtswissenschaft jenseits des Historismus* (Düsseldorf, 1973).

9. Of course, I have in mind Engelstein, *The Keys to Happiness*.

10. See M. Hildermeier, "Das Privileg der Rückständigkeit: Anmerkungen zum Wandel einer Interpretationsfigur der neueren russischen Geschichte," in *Historische Zeitschrift*, 244 (1987), p. 557–603.

11. See Ju.M. Lotman and B.A. Uspenskii, *The Semiotics of Russian Culture* (Ann Arbor, 1984); Iu. Lotman, *Besedy o russkoi kul'ture: Byt i traditsii russkogo dvorianstva XVII–nachalo XIX veka* (St. Peterburg, 1994); B.A. Uspenkii, *Semiotik der Geschichte* (Vienna, 1991); Yu.M. Lotman, *Universe of the Mind: A Semiotic Theory of Culture* (Bloomington, 1990).

12. See Engelstein, *Keys to Happiness*, p. 7.

13. See J. Neuberger, *Hooliganism: Crime, Culture, and Power in St. Petersburg, 1900–1914* (Berkeley, 1993), p. 12; see also H.F. Jahn, *Patriotic Culture in Russia During World War I* (Ithaca, 1995).

14. See Neuberger, *Hooliganism*, p. 277, as well as M. Stadelmann, *Das revolutionäre Rußland in der Neuen Kulturgeschichte: Diskursive Formationen und soziale Indentitäten* (Jena, 1997), p. 76.

15. See O.G. Oexle, " 'Historismus': Überlegungen zur Geschichte des Phänomens und des Begriffs," in *Jahrbuch der Braunschweigischen Wissenschaftlichen Gesellschaft* (1986), pp. 119–55; O.G. Oexle, J. Rüsen (Hg), *Historismus in den Kulturwissenschaften: Geschichtskonzepte, historische Einschätzungen, Grundlagenprobleme* (Cologne, 1996).

16. See M.D. Steinberg, *Moral Communities: The Culture of Class Relations in the Russian Printing Industry, 1867–1917* (Berkeley, 1992), p. 211–12, citation p. 212.

17. See note 27.

18. See W. Hardtwig and H.U. Wehler (Hg), *Kulturgeschichte heute* (Göttingen, 1996), p. 9.

19. See R.S. Wortman, *Scenarios of Power: Myth and Ceremony in Russian Monarchy*, vol 1: *From Peter the Great to the Death of Nicholas I* (Princeton, 1995).

20. See N. Elias, *Die höfische Gesellschaft: Untersuchungen zur Soziologie des Königtums und der höfischen Aristokratie* (Frankfurt am Main, 1969); S. Wilentz (Hg), *Rites of Power: Symbolism, Ritual, and Politics Since the Middle Ages* (Philadelphia, 1985). See also the works cited by Wortman.

21. See M. Weber, *Wirtschaft und Gesellschaft: Grundriß der verstehenden Soziologie*, 5th rev. ed. (Tübingen, 1972), p. 28.

22. See B. Ennker, *Die Anfänge des Leninkults in der Sowjetunion: Ursachen und Entwicklung in der Sowjetunion in den zwanziger Jahren* (Cologne, Weimar, Vienna, 1997); idem, *Führerdiktatur-Sozialdynamik und Ideologie: Stalinistische Herrschaft in vergleichender Perspektive: Strukturelemente der nationalsozialistischen und stalinistischen Herrschaft* (Opladen, 1996), pp. 85–117, contra. N. Tumarkin, *Lenin Lives! The Lenin Cult in Soviet Russia* (Cambridge, MA, 1983).

23. See S. Plaggenborg, *Revolutionskultur: Menschenbilder und kulturelle Praxis in Sowjetrussland zwischen Oktoberrevolution und Stalinismus* (Cologne, 1996); R. Stites,

Revolutionary Dreams: Utopian Vision and Experimental Life in the Russian Revolution (New York, 1989); R. Fülöp-Miller, *Geist und Gesicht des Bolschewismus: Darstellung und Kritik des kulturellen Lebens in Sowjetrußland* (Zurich, 1926). For more literature, see M. Hildermeier, "Revolution und Kultur: Der 'neue Mensch' in der frühen Sowjetunion," in *Jahrbuch des Historischen Kollegs* (Munich, 1996), pp. 51–68.

24. See S. Kotkin, *Magnetic Mountain: Stalinism as a Civilization* (Berkeley, 1995), p. 355ff; I. Halfin and J. Hellbeck, "Rethinking the Stalinist Subject: Stephen Kotkin's 'Magnetic Mountain' and the State of Soviet Historical Studies," in *Jahrbücher für Geschichte Osteuropas* 44 (1996), pp. 456–63.

25. See J.A. Hellbeck, "Fashioning the Stalinist Soul: The Diary of Stepan Podlubnyi (1931–1939)," in *Jahrbücher für Geschichte Osteuropas* 44 (1996), pp. 344–73; idem, "Self-Realization in the Stalinist System: Two Soviet Diaries of the 1930s," to appear in M. Hildermeier and E. Mueller-Luckner (Hg), *Stalinismus vor dem Zweiten Weltkrieg: Neue Wege der Forschung/Stalinism Before the Second World War: New Avenues of Research* (Munich, 1998); idem, *Tagebuch aus Moskau, 1931–1939* (Munich, 1996); V. Garros, N. Korenevskaya, and T. Lahusen (Hg), *Intimacy and Terror: Soviet Diaries of the 1930s* (New York, 1995).

26. See M. Weber, "Wissenschaft als Beruf," in *Max Weber Studienausgabe*, vol. I/17 (Tübingen, 1994), p. 8.

27. Not least here is E.P. Thompson, the "founding father" of the experiential historical revision of "classical" social history. See E.P. Thompson, *The Making of the English Working Class* (Harmondsworth, 1968). See also his frequently reprinted essay: "The Moral Economy of the Crowd in the Eighteenth Century," in *Past and Present* (1971), pp. 76–136.

28. See L. Hunt, *Politics, Culture, and Class in the French Revolution* (Berkeley, 1984); F. Furet, *Zur Historiographie der Französischen Revolution heute* (Munich, 1989).

29. For the pros and cons, see W. Schulze (Hg), *Sozialgeschichte, Alltagsgeschichte, Mikro-Historie* (Göttingen, 1994). An influential source is C. Geertz, *Dichte Beschreibung: Beiträge zum Verstehen kultureller System,* 4th ed. (Frankfurt am Main, 1995).

30. See W. Kaschuba, "Kulturalismus: Kultur statt Gesellschaft?" in *Geschichte und Gesellschaft* 21 (1995), pp. 80–95.

Index